INDUCTIVE APPROACH

The text employs an inductive approach to teaching grammar and usage. Examples are presented first and rules follow to explain the example. This enables students to increase their knowledge of grammar by intuitively understanding concepts, rather than memorizing rules. The inductive approach also encourages students to think critically and helps them to remember what they have learned.

13a Placing modifiers near the word modified

The following sentences illustrate the problem known as the misplaced modifier.

13a
mm

1. The police officer told Eileen ~~carefully~~ to drive *carefully* across the bridge.

The problem here is with the adverb *carefully*. Did the police officer speak carefully, or did he tell Eileen that she should drive carefully? The meaning is not clear because the adverb *carefully* is placed in between *told* and *to drive* in such a way that it could be modifying either one. Moving *carefully* to a position after the words *to drive* eliminates the confusion.

2. *In my rearview mirror,* I saw a man pushing a baby carriage ~~in my rearview mirror~~.

This time the confusion is caused by the placement of the prepositional phrase *in my rearview mirror*. Because of its placement, the sentence seems to say that the man and his baby carriage were *in the mirror*. It is unlikely that this is what the writer intended, so the original sentence sounds a little funny. When the writer corrects the problem by placing the phrase so that it clearly modifies the verb *saw*, the sentence sounds fine.

3. ~~Hanging over the fireplace,~~ Jackie saw a portrait of her grandmother *hanging over the fireplace*.

This sentence sounds funny because of the placement of the participial phrase *hanging over the fireplace*. Participial clauses at the beginning of a sentence always modify the first noun or pronoun after the phrase—in this case, *Jackie*. However, common sense tells us that Jackie wasn't hanging over the fireplace; the portrait of her grandmother was. When the writer moves the participial phrase to the end of the sentence, it becomes clear what was hanging over the fireplace, and the oddness of the sentence disappears.

ESL COVERAGE

ESL instructor Amy Tickle integrates ESL sections throughout the grammar and usage chapters. Special attention is paid to the top twenty-five problem areas for non-native speakers—as identified by extensive research. ESL sections are highlighted in a non-intrusive way with a globe symbol and a rule in the margin, and the letters ESL below the tab.

29b   Determiners

Whereas most native speakers of English have little trouble with articles, writers for whom English is a second language often find articles one of the most difficult aspects of English to master. The rules for determining when not to use an article, when to use *the*, and when to use *a* or *an* are surprisingly complex and subtle. To make the matter even more problematic, many languages, such as Chinese, Japanese, Korean, most Slavic languages, and most African languages, do not use articles at all. And those that do, such as French, Spanish, Persian, and most Semitic languages, use articles in ways that are quite different from the way English uses them.

Determiners are a category of words that precede nouns and modify their meaning. Only one determiner can be used for each noun. Articles are in this group; so are a number of other words, as shown in the chart.

29b
art

ESL

DETERMINERS IN ENGLISH

Articles	Other Words			
a	any	this	my	possessive nouns
an	each	that	his	
the	every	these	her	
	much	those	its	
	many		your	
	some		our	
			their	

The rules concerning article use will help you determine when to use an article in front of a noun. But you also need to remember that each noun can have no more than one determiner. This means that if you use one of the other determiners, you should *not* also use an article.

To select the correct article (or the option of using no article), you must make four distinctions about the noun that the article modifies:

2d   Prewriting on a computer

2d
plan

In this chapter we have discussed many techniques to help you plan your writing and to generate ideas to support your thesis. Most of these techniques work even better if you are writing on a computer.

In the discussion of freewriting, we pointed out that if you find yourself unable to resist the temptation to stop writing and make changes in what you've already written, you might try turning the screen of your computer off so that you can't see what you've written and therefore can't edit it. Another advantage to freewriting on the computer is that when you're finished, you can return to what you've written and cut and paste the sections that you actually want to use in your first draft.

When you are brainstorming, an even more useful technique is available. Using the cut-and-paste function, you can move the various items on your list around, grouping those that are related and eliminating those that don't seem useful. You end up with an organized list that is much like an informal outline.

Keeping a journal is also enhanced on a computer, but only if you have easy access to a computer in your room or at your home. If the only computer you can use is at school or at work

INTEGRATED COMPUTER COVERAGE

Special sections highlight the increasingly important role computers play in composition. The text provides useful tips for writing on a computer at every stage of the writing process. These sections are indicated by a computer symbol.

CRITICAL THINKING

Critical thinking is treated as an integral part of the writing process to help students develop new insights and convincing arguments for all types of writing.

3b   Distinguishing between generalizations and evidence

3b
crit

Generalizations

At one time or another, you've probably heard someone say, "Never generalize." Perhaps someone has even said it to you. Actually, this piece of homespun philosophy is wrong. We all generalize all the time. If you didn't generalize, you would have to stick your hand in every fire to see whether it was hot. If you got off a plane in Peru, you would have to try out languages randomly until you found one that people understood. You wouldn't be allowed to assume that most people in Peru speak Spanish. Generalizing is how we make sense of the world.

So why does the caution never to generalize exist? Probably because generalizing is a powerful and therefore dangerous

12b Using parallelism with coordinate conjunctions

The following sentences illustrate one situation in which items must be parallel.

         swimming
1. Jogging and ~~swim~~ are two good forms of exercise.

                lit
2. We placed flowers on the table and candles ~~burning~~ nearby.

    Note that in each of these sentences, two items joined by a coordinate conjunction (see 19g) must be parallel.

12c Using parallelism with items in a series

The following examples illustrate a second situation in which items must be parallel.

1. I bought a loaf of bread, a jar of peanut butter, and ~~I bought a~~ Diet Coke.

        having
2. Walking your dog, picnics, and playing baseball are forbidden in this park.

As you can see from these examples, items in a series must be parallel.

Hand-corrected examples simulate the corrections students make on their own edited papers. This feature helps students anticipate the kinds of comments professors make and encourages students to revise and proofread their own writing.

BOXED MATERIAL

Key information, tips on writing, activity flow-charts, and lists of examples are boxed off from the rest of the text for quick reference.

TECHNIQUES FOR OPENING PARAGRAPHS

Technique	Example
Opening with a question	Do you know how much of each dollar that you donate to charity pays the salaries of administrators?
Opening with a quotation	"No new taxes," promised George Bush.
Opening with a provocative statement	The new law requiring motorcyclists to wear helmets violates the basic principles of democracy.
Opening with a striking image or description	A shiny bright green frog stared up at me from the bathroom floor.
Opening with humor	It occurred to me . . . in the course of watching first . . .

TABLE OF CONTENTS

The table of contents includes sample words and sentences that illustrate grammatical rules and problems. This makes it easier for students to locate the section they need to solve a particular kind of problem.

25. FINDING AND REVISING ERRORS WITH VERB FORM

a. Regular verb forms

   jump, jumped, jumping

b. Irregular verb forms

   go, went, gone, going

c. Phrasal verbs

   look up, put down, or *call on*

d. *Lie* and *lay*

   lies
   My father often ~~lays~~ down after dinner for a nap.

EXERCISE 12-4 (12a-f) Revise the following passage to eliminate faulty parallelism.

International efforts to protect giant pandas and Asian tigers proved less successful than those to some other species. Wildlife biologist George Schaller, who has written books on lions and gorillas and he lived among pandas in China for nearly a decade, argues that the conservation measures of the Chinese government, like many other nations, function more as a front for the exploitation of high-profile endangered species instead of a program for the protection of key natural habitats. For example, while less than a thousand giant pandas exist in the wild, China continues to trap, confine, and to relocate these animals as loans to zoos that are willing to pay approximately a million dollars per year for a mating pair. Similarly, the state-owned Chinese National Native Produce Corporation encourages the trapping and shooting of most wildlife species commanding an international market, including the Asian tiger. Some reports indicate that these great cats no longer exist in the wild, but thriving on commercial breeding farms. The species' survival now depends upon a strong market for tiger by-products and the possibility of successfully reintroducing large numbers of the tigers to their former habitat.

Extinction through sanctioned exploitation once threatened the American bison, alligator, and the puma in the United States, but pressure by domestic and international environmental groups forced the government to enact tougher conserv...

EXERCISES IN HARDCOVER EDITION

For maximum flexibility, *The HarperCollins Concise Handbook for Writers* is available in two formats: hardbound with exercises in the back of the text and paperbound for portability and cost savings. Exercises are all connected discourse on interesting and informative topics.

The HarperCollins Concise Handbook for Writers

Peter Dow Adams
Essex Community College

ESL sections by Amy Tickle
Michigan State University

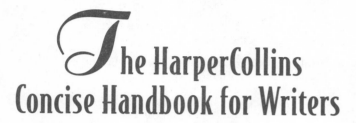 HarperCollins*CollegePublishers*

Senior Acquisitions Editor: Jane Kinney
Senior Developmental Editor: Carla Kay Samodulski
Design Supervisor: Jill Yutkowitz
Text Design: Dorothy Bungert
Cover Design: Jill Yutkowitz
Production Administrator: Valerie A. Sawyer/Joe Campanella
Compositor: BookMasters, Inc.
Printer and Binder: R. R. Donnelley & Sons Company
Cover Printer: Coral Graphics

Cover Illustration: *Orfeo* by Orlando Agudelo-Botero, 1989. Multi-media painting on Papier d'Arches. 29″ × 41″. Courtesy of Engman International, Laguna Beach, CA.

The HarperCollins Concise Handbook for Writers

Library of Congress Cataloging-in-Publication Data

Adams, Peter Dow.
    The HarperCollins concise handbook for writers / Peter Dow Adams ; ESL sections by Amy Tickle.
        p.   cm.
    Includes index.
    ISBN 0-06-040168-0 (hardcover with exercises). — ISBN 0-06-501994-6 (pbk.)
        1. English language—Rhetoric—Handbooks, manuals, etc.
    2. English language—Grammar—Handbooks, manuals, etc.   I. Tickle, Amy.   II. Title.
    PE1408.A3175   1994   93-50599
    808′.042—dc20   CIP

ISBN 0-06-360215-6 (instructor's edition)

94 95 96 97 9 8 7 6 5 4 3 2 1

Contents

The sections marked with 🌐 *contain extended discussions of issues of special interest to students for whom English is a second language. Native speakers may also find useful material in these sections, and ESL students will find much that is helpful elsewhere too.*

Sections marked with 💾 *discuss the use of computers in writing.*

PART I   DRAFTING AND REVISING THE WHOLE PAPER 1

Chapter 1   Writing Processes 2

Chapter 2   Planning 13

iii

       writes
My sister ~~write~~ me every week.

       costs
The concert ~~cost~~ too much.

Chapter 22   Finding and Revising Pronoun Reference Errors 241

Preface

When I started working on *The HarperCollins Concise Handbook for Writers,* I knew that if I wanted to write a handbook for the reality of today's classroom, it would have to recognize the diverse backgrounds, abilities, and experiences of the students who would be using it. Amy Tickle and I believe that with the help of our editors and reviewers we have done just that. *The Harper-Collins Concise Handbook* will be useful to today's students for the following reasons:

1. **The explanations in *The HarperCollins Concise Handbook* are clear, complete, and understandable.**

During fifteen years of teaching writing, I have been puzzled by two phenomena: the large number of writing instructors who complain that students do not find handbooks very helpful and the large number of instructors who continue to require handbooks. We recognize the need for a reference book to help the student writer, but we also recognize that many students are either unable to find the information they need in handbooks or, once they do find it, are unable to understand it. Therefore, we wanted to make the explanations in this handbook so clear, so comprehensive, and so well supported with examples that even students with the weakest grasp of grammatical terminology would find the book useful.

2. **Concepts in the *HarperCollins Concise Handbook* are presented inductively.**

Students are first given examples to consider and then are provided the rules or explanations. In this way, students discover rules themselves, thereby learning them more thoroughly. This

inductive approach encourages critical thinking rather than memorization.

3. ***The HarperCollins Concise Handbook* is designed for the diverse needs of the students who populate today's writing classrooms.**
   - Teachers and students will find everything in this handbook that traditional handbooks include.
   - Underprepared writers—those who too often find traditional handbooks incomprehensible—will find that *The HarperCollins Concise Handbook* explains concepts in a way they can understand.
   - ESL students will find that this text includes more material addressing their needs than any other text on the market. The material on ESL problems is not relegated to a single section of the text: we have integrated ESL material into every chapter where it is appropriate and have marked it with a special icon to make it easy to find.
   - Students who learn better from visual presentations than written ones will find this text particularly helpful, since it is full of charts and diagrams representing everything from the writing process to punctuation rules.
   - Students writing on computers will benefit from the accessibility of the material on computers, which is integrated into the text.

4. ***The HarperCollins Concise Handbook* is designed to be accessible to the student.**
   - The table of contents includes examples following many entries to help students find the information they need.
   - A brief list of contents inside the back cover and labeled tabs within the text will be the quickest way into the text for some students.
   - Frequent summary boxes allow for quick access to the main points of a section.
   - The detailed index includes not only every important term in the text, but also symbols such as hyphens and colons.

- Icons within the text identify sections of special interest to ESL students 🌐 and sections for students writing on computers 💾.

    In addition, a separate *Quick Reference Summary and Documentation Guide*—a compact listing of virtually every rule in the text with examples—is available. It serves as an extended list of contents to help students locate the information they need.

A number of additional features make this handbook a valuable reference tool for writers.

- *The HarperCollins Concise Handbook* is written to support the concept of writing as a process. Specific chapters on the writing process (such as Chapters 1, 2, 4, and 5), as well as the overall organization of the book, encourage students to see writing as recursive, involving repeated cycles of planning, drafting, and revising. In addition, the chapters on grammar and punctuation emphasize the elimination of error as a final stage in the writing process.
- Hand-corrected examples are used throughout to encourage students to see the need for editing and to view grammar as a tool for eliminating error and not as an end in itself.
- Critical thinking is emphasized throughout, especially in Chapter 3. Students are encouraged to view the quality of the thought behind a paper as a major component of that paper's effectiveness, and they are provided with techniques for thinking more creatively about their writing.
- The text is available in hard- or soft-cover formats. For instructors who prefer a text with exercises, the hardcover version includes exercises on the writing process, grammar, and mechanics following the text, keyed to sections within each chapter.
- A complete package of ancillaries is available, including the following:
    —The *Instructor's Annotated Edition*, which provides teaching tips, classroom activities, and lists of suggested readings.
    —*The 53rd Street Writer*, a writing program created by the Daedalus Group, which includes an easy-to-learn word-

processing program, an on-line handbook keyed to *The HarperCollins Concise Handbook,* drafting and revision programs, and a documentation component that helps students put their citations in MLA or APA format. In addition, a new feature breaks paragraphs into separate sentences for easy editing.

—*SuperShell,* a self-paced grammar and usage tutorial program keyed to *The HarperCollins Concise Handbook.*

—*Answer Key to Accompany the HarperCollins Concise Handbook for Writers,* which contains answers to all text exercises.

—*Transparency Masters to Accompany the HarperCollins Concise Handbook for Writers,* containing approximately 100 reproductions of charts, boxes, and lists from the text to enhance classroom presentations.

—The *Quick Reference Summary and Documentation Guide to Accompany the HarperCollins Concise Handbook for Writers,* a compact listing of virtually every rule in the text, with examples.

—*The HarperCollins Concise Workbook,* which provides exercises keyed to the chapters in the text.

—*The Writing Process: A Guide for ESL Students,* written by Amy Tickle, which provides exercises keyed to the text and emphasizes areas that are usually difficult for ESL students.

HarperCollins Resources for Writers/Instructors is a comprehensive ancillary package available free to adopters. This program includes texts on teaching composition for beginning and experienced instructors, testing packages, videos, additional readings, and practice exercises. For more information contact your local HarperCollins sales representative.

In writing this book, I have been especially fortunate to have worked with an exceptionally fine group of professionals. At my own school, my colleagues Jan Allen, Connie Coyle, Nancy Hume, Neil Kenny, Rae Rosenthal, Lynda Salamon, George

Scheper, Al Starr, Ralph Stephens, and Linda Weinhouse, most of whom have worked with me on our composition committee, have provided support, advice, and most important, patience, as I worked my way through the writing of this book. The advice of fellow composition professionals—Pamela Gay, SUNY–Binghamton; Kay Halasek, Ohio State University; Muriel Harris, Purdue University; Fred Kemp, Texas Tech University; Bill Leyden, Jacksonville University; Bob Schwegler, University of Rhode Island; and Karen Scriven, East Carolina University— who participated in a focus group just as we were formulating the plan for this text, was invaluable. My collaborator, Amy Tickle of Michigan State University, who signed on as an ESL expert but whose contributions can be found in every section of the text, was a delight and an inspiration to work with. Jeff Schiff of Columbia College contributed Part IX of the text with skill and efficiency. Arthur Richard Watson, Charlotte Smith, and Jeff Mann prepared the exercises for the hardcover edition.

I want to thank the outstanding team of reviewers, who managed to point out weaknesses in the manuscript and suggest improvements with unfailing grace, diplomacy, and sensitivity: Victoria Aarons, Trinity University; James E. Barcus, Baylor University; Larry Beason, Eastern Washington University; Ellen Bitterman, SUNY–College at New Paltz; Peggy F. Broder, Cleveland State University; Ron Bronson, North Iowa Area Community College; John Burdick, SUNY–College at New Paltz; Janet H. Carr, Northeastern University; Donna R. Cheney, Weber State University; Elizabeth J. Cooper, Virginia Commonwealth University; Charles Croghan, Indian River Community College; Meg Files, Pima Community College; Jacqueline George, Seattle Central Community College; Alfred Guy, New York University; David K. Himber, St. Petersburg Junior College; David E. Hoffman, Averett College; Christine Jensen, University of Kansas; Peter Johnston, Tallahassee Community College; Judy L. Martin, Southwest Missouri State University; Mary McGann, University of Indianapolis; Joan Mellard, Our Lady of the Lake University; Lyle W. Morgan II, Pittsburgh State University; Marie Nigro, Lincoln University;

Faye G. O'Neal, Del Mar College; Penny Partch, Monterey Institute of International Studies; Kirk G. Rasmussen, Utah Valley Community College; Nancy Rosen, Broward Community College; Mary Sauer, Indiana University; Melanie L. Schneider, Beloit College; Charles Schuster, University of Wisconsin at Milwaukee; Alice Sink, Indiana University–Purdue University at Indianapolis; Meritt W. Stark, Jr., Henderson State University; John Taylor, South Dakota State University; Mara Thorson, University of Arizona; Linda Tixier, Miami-Dade Community College–North Campus; Andrea Van Vorhis, Bowling Green State University; Cheryl L. Ware, McNeese State University; Wendy Warren, Edinboro University; Thomas Whissen, Wright State University; and Lisa Yoder, Ohio State University. In addition, I would like to thank Debora A. Person for her helpful comment on the library research sections.

I would also like to thank the following ESL specialists and composition instructors, who responded to surveys we conducted to determine the most common errors made by ESL students in freshman composition classes: Diane Belcher, Ohio State University; Gwen Bindas, Northeastern University; Ellen Bitterman, SUNY–College at New Paltz; William Blades, Essex County College; Ron Bronson, North Iowa Area Community College; John Burdick, SUNY–College at New Paltz; Cherry Campbell, Monterey Institute of International Studies; Jo Cone, Rochester Institute of Technology; H. Gary Cook, Michigan State University; Linda G. Corrin, Essex County College; Charles Croghan, Indian River Community College; Lisa M. Cullen, Monterey Institute of International Studies; Sarah Cummings, St. Michael's College; Meg Files, Pima Community College; Jacqueline George, Seattle Central Community College; Nancy Hayward, Indiana University of Pennsylvania; Christine Jensen, University of Kansas; Peter Johnston, Tallahassee Community College; Anne King, Prince George's Community College; Melinda Knight, University of San Francisco; Carl Luster, San Diego State University; W. H. Macpherson, Essex Community College; Alan Meyers, Harry S Truman College; Faye G. O'Neal, Del Mar College; Penny Partch, Monterey Institute of

International Studies; Charlene Polio, Michigan State University; Mary Prindiville, University of Wisconsin at Green Bay; Kirk G. Rasmussen, Utah Valley Community College; K. Ronstedt, Ohio State University; Nancy Rosen, Broward Community College; Melanie L. Schneider, Beloit College; Alice Sink, Indiana University–Purdue University at Indianapolis; Charlotte Smith, Virginia Polytechnic Institute; Meritt W. Stark, Jr., Henderson State University; Fredricka Stoller, Northern Arizona University; John Taylor, South Dakota State University; Mara Thorson, University of Arizona; Linda Tixier, Miami-Dade Community College–North Campus; Wendy Warren, Edinboro University; Linda Watkins-Goffman, Hostos Community College; Lisa Yoder, Ohio State University.

The professionals at HarperCollins have contributed greatly to the success of this project. My acquisitions editor, Jane Kinney, was talented enough to focus my discontent with existing texts into a positive plan for this one. My developmental editor, Carla Samodulski, has guided my writing and revision with unusual tact and intelligence. Marketing manager Ann Stypuloski has developed a marketing plan that sensitively reflects the pedagogical concepts of the book. In addition, I would like to thank Anne Smith and Patricia Rossi, who helped with the initial stages of conceptualizing the book.

I would also like to thank my daughters, Melia Ann Adams and Emily Dow Adams, of whom I am even prouder than I am of this book.

Finally, I'd like to hear from you. As you work with this text, you will undoubtedly come up with suggestions that would improve it. We are always interested in such suggestions, and I would appreciate your taking the time to send me a note with your comments. Correspondence should be sent to me c/o Jane Kinney, Senior Acquisitions Editor, HarperCollins College Publishers, 10 East 53rd Street, New York, New York 10022-5299.

PETER DOW ADAMS

To the Student

Writing is important. It can make a difference in your grade in almost every course you take, it can make a difference in your getting a job, and it can be an important factor in when and how you are promoted in your career. In nearly every profession, even highly technical ones, people who move into managerial ranks must be able to write. Writing can also make a difference in your personal life. Being able to write about ideas is one way of making sense of those ideas; writing is a form of thinking. If you feel comfortable with writing, you will have one more way to grapple with the complexities that life presents to all of us.

Writing is important, but it is also hard work. It's easy for writers to become discouraged and frustrated. It happens to all of us. Sometimes the hard part is getting started; sometimes we run out of steam while revising a draft; sometimes we are disappointed when a teacher or a supervisor doesn't think that what we've written is any good. While this book can't make that discouragement or frustration go away, we do want to assure you that these feelings are a normal part of being a writer. If you find yourself feeling discouraged or even frustrated, don't give up. Remember that all of us experience these same emotions when trying to write.

Even though this book can't make writing easy, it can serve as a tool to help you be a better writer. In it you will find the answers to almost any writing question you might ask. You will find advice on choosing something to write about; strategies for coming up with something interesting to say; help with revising good writing to make it better; answers to most of your questions about grammar and punctuation; and even help with special writing

situations, like the research paper or business writing. *The HarperCollins Concise Handbook for Writers* won't solve all of your writing problems, but if you keep it nearby and refer to it when you have questions, it will help you answer many of them.

Part I of the book describes the writing process—the way writers go about writing. We don't spell out a rigid procedure you have to follow, but we do discuss the various activities that go into the process of writing and suggest strategies that will help with each of them. Part II looks at problems that may arise in the paragraphs you write—problems of organization, development, and consistency. Part III focuses on sentences—not questions of grammar, but how to write sentences that are graceful, clear, and sprightly. In Part IV we look at choosing words—using just the right word to express the meaning you intend as powerfully as possible. Parts V, VI, VII, and VIII offer detailed discussions of all those questions about correctness—grammar, punctuation, and mechanics (capitalization, spelling, format, and the like)— that may be the most common reason writers consult handbooks. Finally, Part IX considers special writing situations, particularly research papers, writing about literature, and business writing.

We've tried to make this book as easy for you to use as possible. The conventional way to find information in it is to use the index in the back. But if your instructor has marked your paper with any of the abbreviations listed on the overleaf of the front endpaper, you can use that list to find the chapter and section where that topic is discussed. Or perhaps you will find that the easiest way to locate a topic is to look through the contents at the front of the book or the brief list of contents on the inside back cover. You also will want to be aware of the tabs on each page, which contain abbreviations keyed to the brief list of contents. Finally, we suggest that you acquaint yourself with the separate *Quick Reference Summary and Documentation Guide*. Virtually every rule in the handbook is listed in the booklet, along with an example. Sometimes this listing alone will answer your question, so you may want to carry it with you when you go to the library, to the writing center, or to a friend's house to work on a paper. If you need more information than the *Quick Reference Summary*

provides, each entry also includes a reference to a chapter and section in the text where that topic is discussed in detail.

If English is not your native language, you may want to look for discussions of topics of special interest to ESL writers. These are indicated by a globe symbol ● at the beginning of the discussion and a vertical rule down the left margin. Native speakers of English may also find some of these ESL sections useful. For example, many native speakers might want to consult the section on choosing the most effective preposition (see 19f).

If you do most of your writing on a computer, you may want to read the discussions of computer techniques that are marked with a small picture of a computer disk ▥ .

We hope that you'll find this book helpful as you work to improve your writing skills in college, and we hope that it will continue to serve as a useful reference in the future.

PETER DOW ADAMS

DRAFTING AND REVISING THE WHOLE PAPER

This chapter introduces writing as a process that everyone who writes must share. Remind students that planning, composing, and revising are activities necessary to all kinds of written communication, not just to essays assigned in your course. Stress, however, that the ways in which individual writers approach those activities may vary widely. This chapter is not just about conforming to a single inevitable process, but rather about the opportunities for self-expression that writing affords.

RESOURCES
How Writers Write

Emig, Janet. "Writing as a Mode of Learning." *College Composition and Communication* 28 (1977): 122–28.

Flower, Linda, and John R. Hayes. "A Cognitive Process Theory of Writing." *College Composition and Communication* 32 (1981): 365–87.

Hairston, Maxine. "Different Products, Different Processes: A Theory about Writing." *College Composition and Communication* 37 (1986): 442–52.

Perl, Sondra. "Understanding Composing." *College Composition and Communication* 36 (1980): 363–69.

Selzer, Jack. "Exploring Options in Composing." *College Com-*

1 WRITING PROCESSES

In this chapter we're going to discuss, not what "good writing" looks like, but what the processes of producing good writing look like. Notice that we are talking about "processes" in the plural— that's because there are many successful writing processes. Good writers do not all use the same process; in fact, many good writers follow different writing processes when they are involved in different writing tasks. The best way to go about a particular writing task depends on both the task and the writer. Don't worry that we are going to try to convince you to follow a rigid procedure for writing; on the contrary, we're going to talk about the flexibility that is necessary in the process of writing.

Even though we encourage you to be flexible in how you go about writing, that does not mean that any process you use will be as effective as any other or that you can't improve the process you use. In this chapter we will discuss what recent research reveals about how effective writers go about their craft. We encourage you to think about the ways you go about writing and to consider whether some changes in the processes you use might make them more effective.

1a How writers write

Researchers studying how people write have identified three activities that make up the writing process: planning (see 2), drafting (see 4), and revising (see 5). Initially, experts thought that good writers did these activities in three distinct stages, as represented by the following diagram:

However, when researchers studied the processes writers actually use, the results did not support this model. Few writers did all their planning, then all their drafting, and finally all their revising in three distinct and mutually exclusive stages. The way people go about writing—whether they are professional writers or hesitant amateurs—is better illustrated by the following dramatization of the thoughts of a woman as she writes. The italicized sentences represent what she actually wrote in her paper.

position and Communication 35 (1984): 276–84.

Tarvers, Josephine Koster, ed. *HarperCollins Resources for Writers: Teaching Writing, Theories and Practice*. 2nd ed. New York: HarperCollins, 1991.

Planning	Okay. What does he want us to write about? "Tell about a time when an event you participated in turned out differently from what you expected." What do you suppose counts as an event? Well, knowing Professor Wolfe, I'll bet he expects us to write about something political. How about the time I challenged my boss about the way the restaurant distributed the tips among all the people who worked there? No. That won't work because I was sort of a jerk about it, and my boss was probably right. How about the time I volunteered to work with disadvantaged
Drafting	kids? He might like that. *At seven o'clock on Saturday morning my alarm went off. I couldn't believe I had really volunteered to work with disadvantaged kids on Saturday. All I wanted to do was stay in bed for about four more hours. I had been out with Greg the night before, and we had had*
Revising	*a great time.* Wait a minute. I don't need to tell Professor Wolfe about Greg; that's getting way off my main point,
Drafting	so I'll scratch that. *But I dragged myself out of bed, and a half hour later I was tutoring nine-year-olds at the community*
Planning	*center.* Now how did that experience turn out differently from what I expected? What did I actually expect? I guess I thought I would know a lot of math and the kids would know nothing. But I didn't say I was tutoring in
Revising	math, so I should change it to *a half hour later I was tutoring nine-year-olds in math at the community center.*

This brief sample is typical of what the writing process is like for most writers. It is not a neat sequence that follows a particular pattern. It certainly doesn't conform to our diagram. If you

FOR DISCUSSION

Ask students to discuss kinds of personal writing they have done in the past, giving special attention to what they might still be doing (e.g., letters, notes, postcards, diaries, etc.). Encourage those who have found particular kinds of writing enjoyable to explain why. You might also invite those who have found writing painful or difficult to air their grievances. Conclude by asking students to consider the kinds of writing they anticipate doing in college and in their future careers.

had to draw a diagram to represent what the process is like for most writers, it would look something like this:

Writers do engage in three different activities, but *not* in three discrete steps. Instead, they weave back and forth among the three activities in a fairly unpredictable order, doing whatever needs to be done at a particular point. At first glance, it would seem that the processes by which writers write are so irregular that there is nothing to be taught to beginning writers. But further research in recent years has revealed some interesting patterns. When researchers compared the processes of successful writers with those of beginning writers, they found three interesting differences.

First, they discovered that different writers devote different percentages of time to planning, drafting, and revising. When researchers added up the *total* amount of time spent in each of the three activities, they found significant differences between expert and novice writers. *Expert writers spent more time in planning and considerably more time in revising than beginners did.* Beginners spent almost all their time drafting.

If you want to become more expert as a writer, it would seem that all you need do is spend more time planning and revising. It's not that simple, however. Spending more time will not help unless you know how to use planning and revising to improve your writing. These two skills are so important that we have devoted Chapter 2 to planning and Chapter 5 to revising. We do

recommend that you spend more time on these two activities, but we also want to ensure that the time you do spend is fruitful.

A second distinction researchers found between expert writers and beginners is that *experts do very little editing of grammar, punctuation, and spelling until they are almost finished writing.* Instead, while they are drafting and making initial revisions, they work on sharpening their focus, improving their organization, addressing their audience, and mustering support for their argument. They generally postpone any concern with correctness until these larger issues have been taken care of.

We recommend a similar process for you. If you worry about surface errors like grammar, punctuation, and spelling at the same time you are attempting to generate, organize, and express your ideas, you will probably not do a good job of either activity. In addition, postponing editing will save you time. As you draft and revise, you will probably delete some material and add some as you narrow your thesis and focus on your audience and purpose. Imagine how frustrated you would be if you spent several hours correcting errors in a section of your paper and then later decided to remove that section because the content no longer fit with your thesis.

Finally, the activities writers perform while revising are different for experts than for beginning writers. *Beginners tend to limit their revising to editing for errors in grammar, punctuation, and spelling; experts do much more.* They revise by changing the tone of their writing, by tightening the focus, by clarifying the organization, and by adding support for their arguments. We will discuss this kind of revising in greater detail in Chapter 5.

1b Collaboration (talking to other people) in the writing process

In the world of work, most important writing is read by many people before it is sent to its intended audience. An author often passes his or her memo, report, or proposal around to several coworkers and asks their suggestions for improvement. In many work environments, a piece of correspondence is routed to a series of staff members, who are asked formally to "sign off" on

COLLABORATIVE ACTIVITY

Though writing always remains in some measure a private activity, collaborative discussion of drafts or questions associated with the development of a writing project can widen the dimensions of a writing course. Students can benefit from suggestions made by their peers and may gain confidence through mutual support. Having small groups meet in class to consider each other's works-in-progress is now a regular feature of many freshman composition courses, though some instructors favor a less interactive approach. If you do choose to make extensive use of collaborative learning in your course, you might consider applying some of our "Collaborative Activity" suggestions offered at many points throughout the Instructor's Annotated Edition.

the correspondence to indicate that it is acceptable from their point of view.

Because this practice is so widespread, many writing teachers have adopted it in their classrooms. They ask students to share their drafts with classmates and to listen to their comments before revising. Besides producing improved writing, this practice helps writers develop a better sense of how readers respond to their work. Writers also get a chance to see the many ways in which different students respond to a single assignment. Seeing these different approaches encourages students to be more flexible in the approaches they take to future assignments.

If your class provides an opportunity for peer collaboration or peer response groups, the two most common terms for this practice, we have some advice on how to participate in them most fruitfully. But if your class doesn't provide a formal opportunity for such activity, you can still do it informally by asking your friends, family, or classmates to read and respond to your paper.

Sometimes students ask, "Why should I listen to the comments of my classmates? They don't know any more about writing than I do." That may be so, but your classmates do have one advantage over you in reading your writing: *they didn't write it.* They don't know what you are trying to say. They can respond only to what you *did* say, not to what you *meant* to say. Therefore, they can give you insights into your writing that you may not be able to provide yourself. So you are right if you reject the notion of your classmates (or your teacher, for that matter) as experts whose advice is always right. But you are dead wrong if you think that you will find none of their comments useful.

A word of caution is in order, however. In the past, teachers generally insisted that the work on a paper be completely the writer's own. In many cases, the kind of collaboration that is frequently encouraged today would have been seen as cheating. Though most teachers today view collaboration as a legitimate part of the writing process, some would still prefer that you work alone. If there is any question in your mind about your professor's attitude toward such collaboration, ask. If your instructor would prefer that you not seek other people's opinions about

your papers before you turn them in, you should of course respect that preference.

If, however, your professor encourages or at least allows collaboration, then the following advice may help you participate in this writing activity more productively.

When you ask others for their response to your writing,

- Assure your reviewers that you want helpful criticism; you don't want merely to be told that the paper is "fine."
- Be specific about the kind of response you want. For example, you might tell reviewers to ignore errors in grammar and punctuation; you aren't ready to work on that yet. Maybe you would like to know any places where they find the argument hard to follow or unconvincing. Or perhaps you merely want them to tell you what they think your thesis is. Such specific requests will elicit responses that are really useful. Just asking readers to "respond generally" to the paper is likely to produce broad, nonspecific comments that are not helpful.
- Try to listen attentively without becoming defensive. Remember that you don't have to take your reviewers' advice, so when someone makes a criticism that you don't agree with, it is probably better simply to listen than to try to convince the person that he or she is wrong.
- As you listen, try to think more like a reader and less like the writer of the essay. Being able to put yourself in the place of the reader will improve your ability to revise your writing.
- Remember that *you* are ultimately responsible for your writing. You should listen carefully to everything your reviewers tell you, but *you* must decide which advice to follow and which to ignore. The final form of the paper is your responsibility, not theirs.

When you review someone else's writing,

- Read the paper carefully, giving it your full attention.
- Try to express your comments as suggestions for revision. In most cases that is what the writer wants; he or she is not showing you a final draft but a work in progress that he or she expects to revise. Suggestions for revision are usually much more helpful than judgments by a critic.

1c
writ

- It's always easier to point out mistakes than to comment on strengths. Try to resist this natural tendency by pointing out things you like about the paper. But don't be dishonest. Praise that you don't really mean will probably not be believed and, if it is, will be harmful to the writer, who really wants to know how to improve the paper.
- Unless the writer is ready to talk about grammar and punctuation, ignore mistakes in this area. These are the easiest to talk about, but there is no real purpose in doing so until the bigger issues have been taken care of.

RESOURCES
Audience, Purpose, Assignment, and Subject

Ede, Lisa, and Andrea Lunsford. "Audience Addressed/Audience Invoked: The Role of Audience in Composition Theory and Pedagogy." *College Composition and Communication* 35 (1984): 155–71.

Elbow, Peter. "Closing My Eyes As I Speak: An Argument for Ignoring Audience." *College English* 49 (1987): 50–69.

Kinneavy, James L. *A Theory of Discourse.* New York: Norton, 1980.

Ong, Walter J. "The Writer's Audience Is Always a Fiction." *PMLA* 90 (1975): 9–21.

There are many pedagogical theories concerning "audience," an issue that in turn affects purpose, assignment, and subject. See Ede's article and Kinneavy's book for analyses of how audience relates to purpose and subject matter. Ong's famous article argues that a writer's audience is a

1c **Audience, purpose, assignment, and subject: contexts in which writers write**

One of the reasons that writing processes change is that the context—the situation in which writing takes place—is never the same twice. Several components combine to make up the writing context.

Audience

One of the most important features of the writer's context is the **audience.** Before you begin writing, it is a good idea to give some thought to who the audience for a particular piece of writing will be. It is quite likely that the letter you write to a friend in another city describing where you live will sound different from an essay for your English teacher on the same subject.

The answer to the question "Who is my audience?" is often not as simple as it seems. You may be able to say fairly quickly that the audience is your psychology teacher or readers of the school paper or your employer at the department store, but that really doesn't give you much to go on. *Who* is your psychology teacher? What does he know about your subject? What are likely to be his attitudes toward and expectations for this piece of writing? If he disagrees with the point you are making, what reasons might he give for disagreeing? How much time will he have to read this? What will impress him? This same series of questions could be applied to readers of the school paper or your employer. The

point is that you must think about the audience in some detail and then tailor the content and the style of the paper to that audience.

The matter of audience can sometimes be even more complicated because you are writing to more than one audience. For example, you may be writing a report of a shoplifting incident that will go to your employer and also to the chief of security. You may be writing a set of instructions for new student workers at the college gymnasium, but you know that the instructions will first be read by the woman who supervises the students. In these cases it is even more important that you analyze your audience carefully and decide on an approach that is likely to be effective with everyone who will read your writing.

In college, most of your writing will be for your instructor. Even this situation is more complicated than it seems at first, however. Your instructor may expect you to write for a nontechnical audience even though he or she is technically qualified. For example, sometimes, to give you practice in writing for other audiences, your instructor will tell you to imagine that your audience is new students arriving at your school or the manager of your local department store. These assignments are especially difficult because they require an act of imagination on your part; you have to pretend you're writing to new students even though you know that your paper will really be read *and graded* by your instructor. Despite the difficulty, it is important that you choose an approach to the writing assignment that is appropriate for the specified audience.

Purpose

A second aspect of the context in which you write is the **purpose** of your writing. Traditionally, the purposes for writing have been defined as four: to explain, to persuade, to entertain, or to express yourself. In reality, however, almost every piece of writing is a combination of these.

Writing to explain, sometimes called **expository writing,** focuses on the subject being written about; it is primarily concerned with conveying information. *Writing to persuade,* sometimes called **argument,** is focused on the reader; it tries to

"fiction" in the sense that writers are addressing ideal readers, not real ones. Elbow's article suggests that one way of coping with the "audience" problem is to ignore it. As a practical matter, the question of audience may strike students as being simply a question of what you, as their instructor, expect from them. You might assure them that you are not the only audience they need to address.

COLLABORATIVE ACTIVITY

Have groups list examples of writing whose purposes are mainly expository, persuasive, or self-expressive. Alternatively, list several writing forms on the board and have students classify them according to purpose. The list might include the following: dictionary, political speech, technical manual, thankyou note, car advertisement, bank statement, and college research report.

convince him or her to agree with the writer's main point. *Writing to entertain* is also focused on the reader but is primarily intended to provide an amusing or enjoyable experience. Novels, poetry, drama, and humorous writing are examples of writing to entertain. *Writing to express yourself* is focused on you, the writer; it may take the form of a diary, a journal, or even poetry, but it is not intended for an outside audience.

However, seldom is the purpose of a particular piece of writing purely one of these four to the exclusion of the others. If you are *explaining* how to change the oil in a car, you are also attempting to *persuade* your readers that they can accomplish this task. If you are writing an argument that the company should buy a new copier, you also probably are attempting to *explain* what's wrong with the present copier. And in almost all writing, the writer has to have some concern for entertaining the reader, or no one will read what he or she writes. Further, all writing contains a certain amount of self-expression, no matter how impersonal it is. In fact, it is often impossible to say with certainty which of these four is the primary purpose of a particular piece of writing.

We suggest that you examine the purpose of each piece of writing you do more deeply than is indicated by the four traditional purposes. You need to think about *what you want to happen* as a result of the writing. For example, if you write a letter to the manager of the small appliance department at a department store, are you trying to get your money back for a defective toaster? Are you trying to get the clerk who refused to refund your money fired? Are you establishing the legal groundwork for taking the store to court? Are you just trying to make yourself feel better by blowing off steam? Each of these purposes would result in a letter with different content and a different tone, and indecision on your part about your purpose could result in a confusing and ineffective letter.

Assignment

Another part of the context in which you write is the *assignment*. You are undoubtedly used to receiving assignments for

writing in school. Sometimes the assignment is given in writing and sometimes orally. However it is given, pay close attention to it. Many student papers receive lower grades simply because they don't do what the assignment asked them to do. If you have questions about the assignment, be sure to ask them—either in class or afterward—so that you don't misunderstand what is expected. If you visit your instructor outside of class time, however, try to make that visit during his or her office hours. In some cultures, it is unusual to visit with professors to seek more information; in American schools, however, the practice is common, and you should not hesitate to do so.

Often the assignment will include words like *compare, explain, trace, analyze, describe,* or *define.* Pay attention to these words; they are important clues to what the person who made the assignment expects from you. If the assignment asks you to describe a spider and instead you define one, you will not do well on the assignment. Make sure you understand what kind of writing the assignment calls for.

The same advice applies to much writing done in the workplace. If your boss walks by your desk and asks for a report on losses of equipment over the past twelve months, you may need to ask some questions before you start writing. Does she mean losses from all sources or only from damage? How about losses from theft? From normal aging of equipment? And does she want just the facts or a recommendation about those losses as well? Making sure you understand the assignment is just as important in business writing as it is in college writing.

Subject

One last part of the context for writing is the **subject** you are going to write about. Again, the subject will influence both the content of your writing and the style or tone with which you write. You should think about the style that would be most appropriate to your subject before you start writing, during drafting, and while revising. We will discuss how to arrive at a subject to write about in 2b.

RESOURCES
Computer-Assisted
Instruction

Not all students own computers. If your campus makes computer labs available to students, make sure your class is aware of the location and hours. Though many schools have software systems already in place, students may wish to investigate some of the newer programs designed for special tasks. Programs that assist in essay planning, for example, include Writer's Helper from CONDUIT and MindWriter from Daedalus. Instructors' opinions vary as to how extensively software ought to be applied in composition courses. You might specify at the outset whether you encourage the use of computerized spelling or style checkers, or other components, and under which circumstances, if any, you advise restricting their use.

1d **Writing processes on computers**

Just as there is no single correct writing process, there is also no single correct way to write on a computer. Writers just learning the computer frequently do most of their writing with pencil and paper and then use the computer merely as a versatile typewriter into which they type their final draft so they can print it. Writers who are more comfortable with the computer tend to carry out more and more of their writing processes on the computer, but not always. Some writers, even after years of working on a computer, still prefer to do much of their planning, drafting, and revising with pencil and paper. We encourage you, if you have access to a computer, to experiment with various combinations until you discover which parts of the writing process work best for you on the computer and which on paper.

The major advantage of the computer over writing with pencil and paper is fluidity: the ease with which one can make changes on a computer without creating a mess or having to retype the entire paper makes the whole process of writing more flexible. You can experiment with and even be playful about your writing, trying out different ways of expressing the same idea and deleting those that don't work with a keystroke or two or moving text into different places to see how it looks there, or writing three different introductions to see which seems most effective.

How this fluidity will best affect your writing process is something you will have to work out. Our best advice is that you experiment—try using the computer at different points in your writing process and see how it works. But don't assume that the computer will be useful only during revising; the computer can improve your writing process during planning (see 2d), drafting (see 4d), editing for word choice (see 16j), editing for grammar (see 30), checking for spelling (see 44h), doing research (see 45c), and taking notes (see 45g), as well as during revision (see 5d). Try it out during all these stages of your writing process and see whether it improves your effectiveness.

2 PLANNING

In Chapter 1 we discussed the complex process of writing—how writers blend planning, drafting, and revising to produce an effective piece of writing. We also pointed out that successful writers spend more time planning their writing than beginning writers do. In this chapter we will discuss techniques that will help you become more effective at planning your writing so that when you spend more time planning, that effort results in improved writing.

Most of us who attended American high schools learned a technique for planning our writing: the formal outline, with its Roman numerals and capital letters, its staggered indentions, and its rules like "If you have an 'a,' you must have a 'b.'" (If you haven't been introduced to formal outlining, you may want to take a look at 2c, where it is discussed and illustrated.) Most of us dutifully turned in our formal outlines when they were due, but most of us have also never used a formal outline since. And that may be for the better. If formal outlining does not seem helpful to you, you probably shouldn't use it unless your instructor requires it. However, the problem is that when we rejected formal outlining, we didn't substitute anything else. We just jumped immediately into drafting with no effort to organize and focus our thoughts first. And that was probably a mistake. Although you may not use formal outlining for every writing task, you should spend some time planning your writing in less formal ways. In this chapter we will discuss some of the types of planning you might do.

2a Thinking about the writing context: audience and purpose

Planning does not necessarily involve writing anything down. In fact, our first recommendation for planning involves *thinking* rather than writing. We urge you to spend some time before you launch into any writing project thinking about the context. We discussed this context in 1c; it involves the audience, the purpose, the assignment, and the subject.

Students who are new to college writing may find themselves wondering where and how to begin. This chapter reviews useful techniques for planning an essay and stresses the importance of focusing on a manageable topic.

2a
plan

RESOURCES
Planning

Berthoff, Ann E., and James Stephens. *Forming/Thinking/Writing: The Composing Imagination.* 2nd ed. Portsmouth: Boynton/Cook, 1988.

Elbow, Peter. *Writing without Teachers.* New York: Oxford UP, 1973.

Larson, Richard L. "Discovery through Questioning: A Plan for Teaching Rhetorical Invention." *College English* 30 (1968): 126–34.

Lauer, Janice. "Heuristics and Composition." *College Composition and Communication* 21 (1970): 396–404.

Murray, Donald. "Write before Writing." *College Composition and Communication* 29 (1978): 375–81.

Before you begin writing, you must be clear about the audience—the people who will read your writing. Who are they? How familiar are they with any technical language you might use? What knowledge do they have about your subject? What attitudes do they have about it? How much time do they have to read your writing? If they disagree with you, what reasons are they likely to have for that disagreement?

It is equally important to make sure that you understand the assignment—what is expected of you in this piece of writing. To write less or more than was asked for is usually to produce unsuccessful writing. Whether it comes from a teacher or a boss, read or listen to the assignment carefully, and ask questions about points that are not clear.

It is also important to understand what you want the writing to accomplish—what its purpose is and what you want or expect to happen as a result. To close a cover letter for your résumé with the sentence "I hope that after reviewing the attached résumé, you can offer me a position in your company" is to misunderstand the purpose of a cover letter and résumé. Seldom do American companies hire on the basis of such documents, but they do use them to make decisions on whom to interview. So a closing sentence based on a realistic sense of purpose might read, "I hope that after you have reviewed the attached résumé, we will be able to talk directly about my qualifications for your position."

Finally, even at the earliest stages of writing, you often have some idea of what your subject will be. Of course, you may revise your subject, or for that matter your audience or purpose or even your conception of the assignment, at any time as you are working on the writing. The point here is that you should start out with as clear an idea as possible of the context in which you are doing the writing.

Stress the importance of understanding the assignment by pointing out the practical need to follow directions in college test situations or on the job. Encourage students to meet with you for individual conferences if they are in doubt as to the objectives of an assignment you have given them.

2b Focusing: subject and thesis

Finding a subject

Often the choice of a topic is left completely up to you: "By October 30, submit a ten-page paper in which you discuss the

2b
focus

causes of one ecological problem and possible solutions to it" or "In the next two hours, compare two characters from one of the novels you have read in this course" or "Write an essay in which you describe a person whom you admire."

In such a case, the process of arriving at a subject is usually gradual. You consider several alternatives. You may write a little about one or two of them to see which seems to produce the best writing. As you work on the paper, you may narrow the subject down a little or even change it. But during all this process, you are trying to arrive at a subject that has the following characteristics:

- It satisfies the assignment.
- It is something you find interesting to write about.
- It is something you know enough about or can find out enough about to write a paper of the required length.
- It is not too broad for the length specified.
- It is not too narrow to write a significant paper about.
- It is not a subject that has been discussed so many times that you will be unlikely to say anything that your audience hasn't heard before.

Sometimes the subject for a piece of writing is given to you by someone else. On a final exam, your history professor asks you to discuss the causes of the Civil War, or your boss asks you to recommend a new procedure for cutting overhead costs. But even when someone gives you a subject, it is usually too general for you to write about; you still need to narrow it down, to focus it, until it is appropriate for the length of writing expected.

A number of techniques may help you arrive at a subject with the appropriate characteristics. Try some of these. You will probably find that some of them work better for you than others and that you prefer some for certain kinds of writing.

Brainstorming. Let your mind just spew out ideas like a volcano. Write them down in any form that makes sense—a list is probably the easiest form. Your dual objective is quantity and creativity. Don't censor. Don't worry about whether you spell

As the instructor, you will be deciding how specific to make the writing assignments in your course. Some teachers favor allowing collaborative activity groups to come up with their own subjects and thesis ideas, while others prefer to issue detailed instructions, as for essay exam questions. A middle-of-the-road approach is to assign a generic category of writing—such as a personal narrative, a comparison/contrast exercise, or a persuasion essay—but to leave students free to arrive at their own specific subjects and viewpoints within the prescribed category.

Encourage students to review this list often during the early stages of writing. By doing so they can test the acceptability of their plans and make adjustments as needed.

COLLABORATIVE ACTIVITY

After students have read the following section, have them practice brainstorming in groups. Offer them a general subject of your choice and allow at least fifteen minutes for nonstop listing of ideas. Then have students compare lists to see how they responded. This activity can reveal the variety of possible responses to a subject, as well as help prepare students for future collaborative activities.

anything wrong. Just get those ideas down as fast as possible. When you run out of ideas, don't stop. Force yourself to think harder. Sometimes the best ideas are the ones that come after you've listed all the obvious ones. (Of course, sometimes the best ideas are the first ones.) Here is one student's brainstormed list on the topic of being surprised by someone's behavior:

> when the Blue Jays won the American League pennant
>
> the woman who gave me a ride to town last Saturday
>
> the time I couldn't stop crying in the movie *Out of Africa*
>
> the man who returned my wallet
>
> Nazi Germany
>
> the teacher who flunked half my high school class in history
>
> how I cried at my high school graduation
>
> how flustered my father used to get when my mother would cry (which she did often)
>
> how my mother didn't cry at my father's funeral
>
> Michael Jordan
>
> how I discovered that my boss could be trusted

Once you've generated as many different ideas for a subject as you can, read the list over. As you read, you may get new ideas; add them to the list. Finally, narrow the list down until you've identified one idea or a cluster of ideas to write about.

The student whose list was just presented reread the assignment and discovered that it asked him to write about "a time when the behavior of someone you know surprised you." So he eliminated from his list everyone he did not know personally:

> ~~when the Blue Jays won the American League pennant~~
>
> the woman who gave me a ride to town last Saturday
>
> the time I couldn't stop crying in the movie *Out of Africa*
>
> the man who returned my wallet
>
> ~~Nazi Germany~~
>
> the teacher who flunked half my high school class in history
>
> how I cried at my high school graduation

how flustered my father used to get when my mother would cry (which she did often)

how my mother didn't cry at my father's funeral

~~Michael Jordan~~

how I discovered that my boss could be trusted

Next he decided that three of his topics seemed naively optimistic and would produce predictable writing about people being basically "good at heart." He wasn't sure if he believed this about people, but he was sure that any paper he would write about it would sound like one big cliché.

~~the woman who gave me a ride to town last Saturday~~

the time I couldn't stop crying in the movie *Out of Africa*

~~the man who returned my wallet~~

the teacher who flunked half my high school class in history

how I cried at my high school graduation

how flustered my father used to get when my mother would cry (which she did often)

how my mother didn't cry at my father's funeral

~~how I discovered that my boss could be trusted~~

Reviewing the remaining topics, he discovered a cluster of them about the subject of crying; obviously that was something he was interested in. He also noticed that what was interesting in the list was when people behaved in ways that were unexpected: when men cried or women didn't.

the time I couldn't stop crying in the movie *Out of Africa*

~~the teacher who flunked half my high school class in history~~

how I cried at my high school graduation

how flustered my father used to get when my mother would cry (which she did often)

how my mother didn't cry at my father's funeral

He decided to write a paper about stereotyped attitudes toward crying and how his crying violated the stereotype. Now he was worried that the assignment had said to write about "a time

when the behavior of someone you know surprised you." Would his professor object to his writing about himself? He wasn't sure, so the next day in class, he asked and learned that it would be fine to write about himself.

Of course, this doesn't mean that "the time I cried at graduation" will necessarily remain the subject of his paper. As he starts drafting and revising, he may discover a different aspect of crying or a different event that will work better for him (perhaps the time he cried in the movie). But at least brainstorming has produced a tentative subject for him to start writing about.

ACTIVITY

Have students set aside a special notebook or computer file for their freewriting activities. Assure the class that you won't be grading their freewriting, though you might give them class participation credit for doing it. The aim of freewriting is to reduce anxiety and get students to express themselves quickly and freely.

Freewriting. What a delightful name for a writing technique! So much of writing seems to be a matter of organizational patterns and grammatical rules that the idea of writing freely seems very attractive, and it is. Freewriting is writing without rules, without constraints, without even a goal. It's just turning your mind loose and letting whatever streams out appear on the page or screen. Of course, you don't worry about spelling or punctuation or even making sense. You just write whatever occurs to you. The only restraint is that you write freely without stopping and without correcting, just writing whatever comes to mind. Some people find that it helps to establish a time limit— say, five or ten minutes—during which they keep writing without pause. Some writers even set an alarm—a kitchen timer works well. But use this technique only if it frees you up, not if it adds pressure.

If you are freewriting on the computer, you might want to try a trick. Get everything ready to begin freewriting, with the cursor right where you want it. Then turn the *screen* (not the computer) off and start typing. You won't be able to edit your writing because you won't be able to see it. Then, after the five or ten minutes is up, turn your screen back on, and edit what you have written.

Like brainstorming, freewriting produces lots of material, much of which will not be useful. But the freedom that comes from letting your mind explore without restraint can produce just

the right idea for the paper you want to write. So write freely and then edit vigorously. What you are left with may be exactly the idea you need to get started on a great paper.

A variation of freewriting is "focused freewriting." You start with a general idea you want to write about or have been assigned, and you write about it for a set period of time. You still write freely and without worrying about correctness or even the quality of the ideas, but you attempt to keep all your writing focused on the general idea you started with.

Keeping a journal. A journal is different from a diary in that a diary is a record of what happened to you over a period of time, whereas a journal is a record of your thoughts. Many people who have to write regularly keep a journal of good ideas that occur to them as they read, as they go to sleep at night, as they talk with others, as they listen to the news on television, or at any other time when they are likely to come up with interesting ideas. When they get ready to write a paper, they read over their journals, looking for possible ideas to write about. If they've been conscientious about recording their ideas, their chances of finding a good topic to write about are excellent.

Finding the ideas is the easy part; writing regularly in the journal is not so easy. We recommend two practices. First, keep your journal near you at times when you are likely to have ideas. If you read the paper every morning and frequently get good ideas while doing so, you are unlikely to write them down if your journal is all the way upstairs in your bedroom. Keep it handy. Second, set aside some time daily—at least fifteen minutes—during which you write down your ideas. Using both of these techniques is best; using either one will help.

Reading. If you don't have any idea what to write about, make a trip to the library. A half hour of browsing in magazines, journals, or a particular section of the stacks that interests you is likely to suggest a topic that you will find interesting to write about. It will also provide you with some facts with which to back up your argument.

ACTIVITY

Encourage students to keep a journal throughout the course and offer them class-participation credit for the activity. As with brainstorming and freewriting, journal notes should not be subject to a teacher's editorial corrections unless a student raises questions about the composition of a passage. Like other prewriting activities, keeping a journal should give writers a chance to work without fear of being judged.

ACTIVITY

The importance of reading as a basis for a writer's development cannot be overemphasized. Encourage students to set aside at least one hour a week as library time even if they are not presently engaged in a research project. If you have spent many hours in libraries yourself, you may want to reminisce a bit about the atmosphere of "the stacks." Invite students to comment on books or articles they may have come across while browsing.

The following segment distinguishes between the *subject* as a noun phrase and the *thesis* as a complete sentence about that noun phrase. You might encourage students to read this discussion in the light of prewriting activities they have already practiced. Have students review their brainstorming lists and freewriting for possible thesis statements

Identifying a thesis

Brainstorming, freewriting, keeping a journal, and reading will help you come up with a subject, but in most cases these techniques will not guarantee that you write a well-focused paper. A paper that discusses Washington, D.C., for example, has a subject but may still be organizationally out of focus. For example, a paper on Washington that included paragraphs on the following topics would have a problem:

monuments	statehood
the climate	museums
crime	the Capitol
politicians	the ratio of women to men
the White House	the Metro

A reader might ask, "What's the point? What does this prove?" The paper doesn't really add up to anything. It just rambles around topics that are unrelated except that they involve Washington. A well-focused paper has to have more than just a subject. The reader must be able to see what the point was, what the writer was getting at.

A paper about Washington with a better focus might set out to prove that "Washington is an attractive city to visit" and might include the following topics:

monuments	the White House
the climate	the Capitol
museums	the Metro

Each of these topics is about some aspect of Washington, but more than that, each of them helps prove a specific assertion about Washington: it is an attractive place to visit. A person who finishes reading a paper that discusses these topics will not have to wonder what the point of the paper is. The point will be quite clear, and that is the advantage of a paper focused around a **thesis** rather than just a subject. A thesis, then, is an assertion about the subject that is the main idea of an essay. In other words, a subject is merely a topic that the paper focuses on; a thesis is a subject and some point about that subject.

SUBJECTS AND THESES

Characteristics of a Good Subject:
- It satisfies the assignment.
- It is something you find interesting to write about.
- It is something you know enough about or can find out enough about to write a paper of the required length.
- It is not too broad for the length specified.
- It is not too narrow to write a significant paper about.
- It is not a subject that will lead you into rehashing obvious arguments.

Techniques for Generating a Subject:
- Brainstorming
- Freewriting
- Keeping a journal
- Reading

Characteristics of a Good Thesis:
- It includes both a subject and some point about that subject.
- It is not too broad.
- It is not too narrow and factual.
- It is not a question.

COLLABORATIVE ACTIVITY

2b
focus

This checklist can serve as a basis for group work. Students who are devising thesis statements for a writing assignment can meet and evaluate one another's prospective thesis statements in the light of the points covered here.

SUBJECTS	THESES
Washington	Washington is an attractive place to visit.
credit cards	Credit cards charge too much interest.
libraries	Libraries can be intimidating.
motorcycles	Motorcycles are too dangerous.
jogging	Jogging does your body more harm than good.

Notice that each thesis includes both a subject and a point to be made about that subject. Here are some other guidelines for effective theses:

1. *A thesis must not be too broad.* A five-hundred-word essay that tries to prove that "the Supreme Court has a long record of protecting individual rights" is probably not going to succeed because the thesis is too broad for so short a piece of writing.

2c
thesis

2. *A thesis must not be too narrow and factual.* A thesis that merely states a fact will not provide an opportunity for you to write an essay of any length at all. For example, after you've stated a thesis like "Lagos is the capital of Nigeria," there is nothing left for you to prove. If you start adding information about Lagos— the climate, living conditions, the school system, and the like— you will not be supporting the thesis; those facts about Lagos may describe the city, but they don't help prove that it is the capital of Nigeria. In fact, once you've stated such a thesis, there's hardly anything left to be said about it, and that is why it is too narrow.

3. *A thesis cannot be a question.* A thesis has to make an assertion that you are going to prove in your paper; a question is not an assertion.

This section reviews planning techniques as methods for generating essay content. Whether students use brainstorming, freewriting, journal writing, mapping, or outlining, have them keep their sketch material handy as a record of their progress in developing an assignment. Often problems or "blocks" can be analyzed more easily in the generative stages than by a retrospective analysis of the final draft.

2c **Generating content: what to say about the thesis**

Now you've thought about the writing context, you've made sure you understand the assignment, and you've even come up with a tentative thesis, but you still haven't got any content, any of the ideas that will fill up the body of the essay. At this point, some people like simply to start writing and discover their content as they go. If this technique works for you, use it. But many writers find that a little more planning at this stage makes their actual drafting easier and the writing that they do much better.

Once again, a range of activities can help you generate ideas before you begin writing. What these techniques have in common is that they produce a large quantity of raw ideas that can then be sifted through, organized into groups, and written about in the first draft of the paper.

Brainstorming. The brainstorming technique you learned earlier in this chapter for coming up with a subject for your writing can also be used for generating content. When used this way, it is sometimes called *focused brainstorming* because you try to keep your mind focused on the thesis you have tentatively decided on as you write down, without censoring, every idea that

pops into your head. You will end up with a list of ideas that can then be pruned, grouped, and used as a rough outline for your first draft. Often during this process, you will discover a revised or even a totally new thesis that seems to produce better ideas than your original one. That's fine. Remember that the entire planning process is meant to be fluid and flexible; *everything* can be revised as you go along.

Freewriting. Freewriting, which we discussed earlier in this chapter as a way to find a subject to write about, is also an excellent method of generating ideas for the body of your paper. When used for this purpose, the technique is sometimes called *focused freewriting* because, as with brainstorming, you try to keep your freewriting focused on the subject you have tentatively decided to write about. You merely let your mind generate as many thoughts about that subject as you can and try to write them down as fast as you think of them. Of course, you don't do any editing at this stage; you're just trying to get as many ideas as you can down in writing. Later you will go back and pick through the pages of freewriting, pulling out the best ideas to use in the essay itself and discarding the rest.

Keeping a journal. Keeping a journal, another technique discussed earlier, also can be used as a source of content for your paper. Keeping a journal of ideas is especially useful for college writing. As you sit in class and as you read your texts, jotting down ideas that occur to you in a journal can make the job of writing a paper much easier. All you do is read through the journal, noting ideas relevant to a paper about the subject you have chosen.

Mapping. Sometimes called *clustering,* **mapping** is a highly visual technique that leads you to think about many different aspects of a topic. To start mapping, write your subject in the center of a blank piece of paper and draw a circle around it. Then think of the main subideas that make up or support your subject. Write those around the subject, draw circles around them, and draw lines connecting them to the subject. Continue in this fashion until you have a rich diagram of the topic you in-

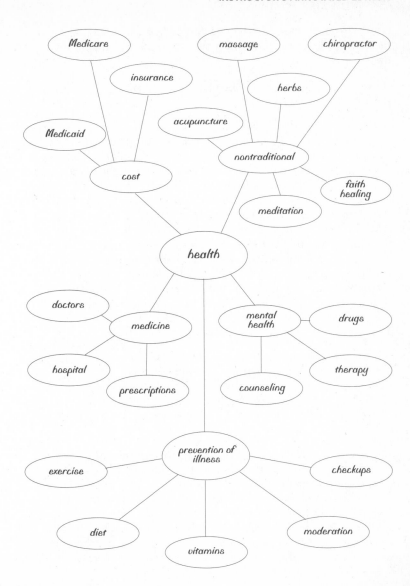

tend to write about. A simple mapping diagram like the one on the facing page can help you remember all the topics you planned to discuss and suggest the order in which you might discuss them.

Formal outlining. Making a formal outline is a technique you were probably taught in high school. Many writers have never used outlining since then because it seems too formal, confining, and time-consuming. However, many people actually find a formal outline to be quite helpful. We recommend that you consider using a formal outline in two situations: when you are required to do so by your instructor and when you are writing a long and complex paper. The following guidelines will be helpful.

1. Write the thesis at the beginning of the outline.
2. Decide whether to use a topic or a sentence outline. In a topic outline, each entry is a word or phrase; in a sentence outline, each entry is a sentence. Topic outlines are faster and less demanding. Sentence outlines get you further toward a first draft; they require that you write actual sentences, some of which will later be incorporated into your paper. Some instructors object to mixing the two types.
3. Place ideas of equal generality at corresponding levels of the outline. In the sentence outline in the box on page 27, for example, the four main ideas of the paper are listed at the first level, the level indicated by Roman numerals.
4. Use the standard system for numbering levels:

I. _____
  A. _____
  B. _____
    1. _____
    2. _____
      a. _____
      b. _____
        (1) _____
        (2) _____
          (a) _____
          (b) _____
II. _____

2c
thesis

> **TOPIC OUTLINE**
>
> THESIS: Art has played many roles in society.
> I. Art as decoration
>   A. Painting as beauty
>   1. Monet's landscapes
>   2. Matisse's comments on beauty
>   B. Sculpture as beauty
> II. Art for utility
>   A. Useful items as works of art
>   1. Eames chairs
>   2. The Movado watch
>   B. African art for utility
>   1. Masks
>   a. Dances and festivals
>   b. Reminders of heritage
>   c. Religious significance
>   2. Musical instruments, chairs, and pots
> III. Art with a message
>   A. The artist's political statement
>   1. Picasso's *Guernica*
>   2. Mapplethorpe's photographs
>   3. Judy Chicago's *Dinner Party*
>   B. An institution's statement
>   1. Cathedrals as religious teaching
>   2. Socialist art
>   3. Corporate art
> IV. Art as status symbol
>   A. Art as demonstration of power
>   B. Art as symbol of wealth

5. Make items at the same level parallel (see 12).
6. If you use subdivisions under a heading, there must be at least two.
7. Move from the very general at the first level to the more specific as you progress down the levels. For example, in the accompanying sentence and topic outlines, the first level (indicated by Roman numerals) presents four broad roles for art. The third

SENTENCE OUTLINE

THESIS: Art has played many roles in society.

I. Art is often decorative.
   A. Paintings can be beautiful to look at.
      1. Monet's landscapes are beautiful.
      2. Matisse wrote that his works were intended primarily to create beauty.
   B. Sculpture can add beauty to a building.
II. Art can be utilitarian.
   A. Works of art can be useful household items.
      1. Eames chairs are beautiful but also useful items of furniture.
      2. The Movado watch is a functional timepiece but is also in the Museum of Modern Art in New York.
   B. African art often emphasizes the usefulness of the object rather than its aesthetics.
      1. Masks play a role in society.
         a. They are used in dances and festivals.
         b. They remind tribal members of their heritage.
         c. They have religious significance.
      2. Musical instruments, chairs, and pots that can be seen in American museums are used in daily life in Africa.
III. Art can communicate a message.
   A. The artist can make a political statement through his or her art.
      1. Picasso's *Guernica* expresses his outrage at war.
      2. Mapplethorpe's photographs make a statement about gay life.
      3. Judy Chicago's *Dinner Party* expresses her pride in women's accomplishments.
   B. An institution can make a statement by commissioning a work of art.
      1. The Catholic church represented biblical events through statues, murals, and stained-glass windows in its cathedrals.
      2. The Soviet Union represented its views of heroism and dedication to the state through large statues and paintings.
      3. American corporations try to win customers through the development of logos.
IV. Art can be a status symbol.
   A. In the past, rulers attempted to demonstrate their power by commissioning magnificent works of art.
   B. Wealthy people today frequently collect art as a symbol of their wealth.

level (indicated by Arabic numbers) gives specific examples of paintings and other works of art.

An outline forces you to think; writing one makes you keep saying to yourself, "What's another reason or another example that will support this point?" That kind of thinking is important; it's how you come up with content that will make your paper convincing.

Further, an outline provides an early opportunity for revision. In an outline, you lay out the general shape of your paper so that you can study, evaluate, and change it. You should take this opportunity to rearrange the order of your points and to look for places where you need to add more evidence.

Informal outlining. If a formal outline seems like more work than it's worth, you may find that an informal or "scratch" outline is all you need. An informal outline is usually no more than a thesis statement and a listing of your main points in the order you will discuss them. The informal outline below is on the same topic as the formal outlines. With a minimum of time and effort, this kind of outline allows you to sketch out the main ideas of your paper so that you have some idea where you are going before you start drafting.

INFORMAL OUTLINE

THESIS: Art has played many roles in society.
- Art as decoration
- Art for utility
- Art with a message
- Art as status symbol

Arguing. Starting an argument with a friend can be a great way to force yourself to think hard about a topic and generate

some good ideas. It also guarantees that you have considered other points of view and have an awareness of your audience. All you need do is find a friend and perhaps offer him or her a cup of coffee or a glass of wine. Then bring up the subject you're going to write about. By listening to your friend's arguments and forcing yourself to respond to them, you will guarantee that your paper is convincing. Just keep the argument going until you have enough material for your paper; then announce that you've got to get to work on an essay for your English class. Of course, this technique can be a little hard on friendships, but it can produce great ideas for your writing.

Using rhetorical patterns. Rhetorical patterns, discussed in detail in 7e, can be useful in generating content. Because these patterns require that you organize information in a certain way, they remind you of the kind of information you might include.

2d Prewriting on a computer

In this chapter we have discussed many techniques to help you plan your writing and to generate ideas to support your thesis. Most of these techniques work even better if you are writing on a computer.

In the discussion of freewriting, we pointed out that if you find yourself unable to resist the temptation to stop writing and make changes in what you've already written, you might try turning the screen of your computer off so that you can't see what you've written and therefore can't edit it. Another advantage to freewriting on the computer is that when you're finished, you can return to what you've written and cut and paste the sections that you actually want to use in your first draft.

When you are brainstorming, an even more useful technique is available. Using the cut-and-paste function, you can move the various items on your list around, grouping those that are related and eliminating those that don't seem use-

---

COLLABORATIVE ACTIVITY

2d
plan

Friendly arguments can also be conducted in groups. Remind students that the aim of the argument is not to "win," but only to help develop ideas that individual writers can pursue further in their papers.

As traditional organizing techniques, rhetorical patterns such as narration, definition, and division predispose an essay to certain kinds of content. Many instructors make rhetorical patterns the basis for general writing assignments. Refer students to 7e for further discussion of the patterns.

RESOURCES
Computer-Assisted
Instruction

A number of recent programs have been developed to help students cope with the planning stages of essay writing. Some that work by posing questions are Writer's Helper by CONDUIT, Mind-Writer from Daedalus, and SEEN from CONDUIT. Outlining programs include Acta Advantage from Symmetry Corporation and More from Symantec. There are also notetaking programs such as StorySpace from Eastgate Systems, Inc. Mapping programs include Inspiration from Ceres and Calliope Plus from Innovision.

ful. You end up with an organized list that is much like an informal outline.

Keeping a journal is also enhanced on a computer, but only if you have easy access to a computer in your room or at your home. If the only computer you can use is at school or at work, it is probably better to keep your journal on paper. You will have too many ideas that will get away from you before you have a chance to type them in if you must wait until you're at school or at work. But if you do have easy access to a computer, think about keeping your journal on it. Just open a document titled "Journal" or something like that and write in it every day. A computerized journal will allow you to cut and paste sections you want to use in various papers without retyping them. Further, sometimes finding a particular entry in a journal can be a little difficult, especially if you've written a lot. This task can be much easier if you use the search or find function on a computer. Just think of a word you are likely to have used in the section you want to find, and ask the computer to find that word.

Informal, topic, or sentence outlines are also easier to make on the computer. Setting tabs allows you to make all the indentions fairly easily, and the cut-and-paste function allows you to move sections around as you discover more effective ways to organize your writing. It's also easy to add material at any point. If you move material around or add material at various points, many computers can renumber your entries automatically. If your computer can do this, tell it to renumber "by example." This means that the computer will renumber your entries following the numbering scheme you have established.

When you have finished a paper outline, it becomes something you place to one side and look at periodically as you draft your paper. If you outline on a computer, you can print out the outline and use it the same way, but there is another technique many writers find even more helpful. You can bring the outline up on the word processor, change its name to "Paper 1," "Draft 1," or something like that, and start writing the paper within the outline. This means that you can incorporate what you've al-

ready typed right into your draft, and it makes following the out-line much easier; it's right on the screen as you write.

Besides word processing, other programs have been devel-oped to assist in planning:

- A number of programs can help you generate ideas by asking you questions. You tell the computer what your subject is and perhaps what kind of paper you want to write, and it asks you a series of questions designed to encourage you to think about the topic in creative ways.
- Formal outlining programs automate much of the process of outlining. These programs do all the indenting and numbering for you and renumber whenever you change things.
- Note-making programs are now available that allow you to cre-ate note cards, which can be nested inside each other to create a detailed outline (see 45g).
- Recently, programs that allow you to do the kind of mapping we talked about earlier in this chapter have come on the market.

If you don't have any of these programs, ask at the computer fa-cility at your school. If the people there don't have them, they may be able to acquire them for you. If you would like a demon-stration, your local computer store probably has many of them.

3   USING CRITICAL THINKING TO DEVELOP YOUR IDEAS

We're going to begin this chapter on thinking with a story about one English teacher's first semester teaching freshman composi-tion. Things didn't go badly. No one complained to the dean about him. The students wrote eight papers, and he returned them all with grades on them. At the end of the semester, he turned in his grades just as the registrar instructed him to. Noth-ing disastrous happened.

Early in the next semester, this young teacher bumped into Joyce, a student from the previous semester who had gotten an

Even when you assign essays whose purpose is more explanatory than argumentative, students should be concerned about the underlying logic of their writing. This chapter is about how to reason effectively and from an original viewpoint. It also reviews key types of fallacies.

RESOURCES
Critical Thinking

Aarons, Victoria. "Ethical Issues: A Rhetorical Methodology." *The Writing Instructor* 4 (1985): 83–85.

Browne, Neil M., and Stuart M. Keeley. *Asking the Right Questions: A Guide to Critical Thinking.* 3rd ed. Englewood Cliffs: Prentice-Hall, 1990.

Chaffee, John, ed. *Thinking Critically.* 2nd ed. New York: HarperCollins, 1988.

Christenbury, Lelia, and Patricia Kelly. *Questioning: A Path to Critical Thinking.* Urbana: NCTE, 1983.

Golub, Jeff, ed. *Activities to Promote Critical Thinking.* Urbana: NCTE, 1986.

Hahn, Stephen. "Counter-Statement: Using Written Dialogue to Develop Critical Thinking and Writing." *College Composition and Communication* 38 (1987): 97–100.

Levin, Gerald. "On Freshman Composition and Logical Thinking." *College Communication and Composition* 28 (1977): 359–64.

McCleod, Susan H. "Cultural Literacy, Curricular Reform, and Freshman Composition." *Rhetoric Review* 8 (1990): 270–78.

McCormack, Kathleen. "Teaching

A. When he asked her what she thought of the course, she replied that it had been great. She added, "I caught on right away to what the trick was, so I got A's on all my papers."

This novice teacher was a little upset to hear this business about her catching on to "the trick." Most upsetting was the fact that he had no idea what she was talking about. He didn't know what "the trick" was, but if she knew, he was worried that other students might have found out too. When he asked her what she thought this "trick" was, she replied, "Oh, you just had to make sure you had something interesting to say, and you could get an A every time."

"What if all my students were to find out about 'the trick,' " the young teacher fretted. After some time, though, he began to relax; it gradually occurred to him that Joyce was right. Thinking of something interesting to say is a big part of writing well. If all his students found out about this trick, they would all become better writers. And, of course, that's the whole point of being a writing teacher—to help people become better writers.

Now he announces "the trick" to all his students on the first day of class, and here he is giving it away in this book. It really does work. Having something interesting, thoughtful, witty, perceptive, or convincing to say will go a long way toward producing successful writing.

Of course, *knowing* the trick and *doing* it are two different things. So in the rest of this chapter we will talk about ways to help you pull off the trick, ways to help you think harder, deeper, more perceptively about the topics of your papers.

3a Thinking

We start out, then, with one assumption: you should strive to make your writing interesting, thoughtful, clever, perceptive, analytical, surprising, profound, creative, entertaining, convincing, or some combination of these. Of course, your teacher in a basic writing course, a freshman composition course, or any under-

graduate course for that matter, is not expecting writing that will win a Pulitzer Prize; we are not unrealistic, but we do expect you to think.

Too often, however, students assume that the only thing teachers expect is writing that is correct, that doesn't have errors in it. They assume that what they have to say doesn't really matter as long as it's said correctly. Or they assume that all they are expected to do is demonstrate that they have listened to the lectures and read the assignments by giving back to the instructor facts from lectures or reading assignments. But good writing requires more than merely spouting back facts; it requires that you actively think about those facts and come up with something interesting and thoughtful to say about them.

It may seem that this idea about having something interesting to say is just making your task that much harder, but in some ways it's actually making it easier. Thinking until you come up with something perceptive to say will actually make writing a successful paper easier because it's usually less work to write about something interesting than something boring. So making this effort to be thoughtful will, in the long run, make your job of writing less of a chore.

It is certainly possible to write *acceptable* papers in most classes without really being interesting, perceptive, or provocative—but what we're talking about here is the difference between a passable C or D paper and an excellent A or B paper. Quite often that difference is the amount of thought that went into the writing—the degree to which the paper is interesting.

The basic principle is to avoid writing a paper that merely proves something that everyone already agrees with. When you think you've arrived at a thesis for a paper, picture yourself standing up in front of your class, reading your thesis out loud, and then asking, "How many of you disagree with my thesis?" If you can imagine only one or two hands going up, your thesis is probably too obvious; if nearly everyone already agrees with your point, why write a paper to convince them? You'll just belabor

Critical Thinking and Writing." *The Writing Instructor* 2 (1983): 137–44.

Ruggiero, Vincent Ryan. *The Art of Thinking: A Guide to Critical and Creative Thought*. 3rd ed. New York: HarperCollins, 1991.

Zeller, Robert. "Developing the Inferential Reasoning of Basic Writers." *College Composition and Communication* 38 (1987): 343–46.

FOR DISCUSSION

If you are using a college reader in your course, assign an essay by a popular author who argues in favor of a social position that many would mistrust. Have students discuss what they may have found interesting about the essay even if they did not find the author's argument convincing.

the obvious. To give some fairly extreme examples, consider the following theses, which are too obvious:

- Drunk driving is terrible.
- Parents should act responsibly toward their children.
- Kids shouldn't get married too early.
- Corruption should not be allowed in government.
- People shouldn't pollute the environment.

Most people would agree with each of these, and that is precisely the problem with them. Everyone would already agree. No one is going to find a paper very interesting if it merely states something the reader already knows. It will be much easier to write a successful paper if you start with an idea that everyone doesn't already agree with.

A slightly different problem is illustrated by the following theses:

- Capital punishment should be abolished.
- Every woman has the right to abortion.
- Handguns should be outlawed.
- Sex and violence should not be shown on television.
- Welfare should be eliminated.

Surely everyone would *not* agree with these ideas, yet they are no more likely than the first group to produce interesting, thoughtful writing. The problem is not that everyone agrees but that everyone knows the arguments on both sides of these controversial issues so well that a paper rehashing them is unlikely to succeed. Of course, if you have an argument on one of these topics that is not predictable, you may be able to write an excellent paper.

One other way to see the difference between theses that are interesting and those that are predictable is to look at a collection of theses and analyze the differences between the successful ones and those that are not so successful. One September, a group of freshman composition students were asked to write a paper that told their instructor *one* thing about the kind of person they were. The following is a list of the theses from this first set of papers; these are what twenty-two students chose to write about. Which

3a
crit

of these seem most promising to you? Which are likely to produce the most interesting writing? Identify the five you find most
interesting.

1. I am a good friend.
2. I am a caring person.
3. I am very outgoing because I am really afraid to be alone.
4. I am an outgoing person.
5. My desire to help other people is really selfish at heart.
6. I want to improve myself.
7. Over the years, I have been known as a quiet person.
8. One of the major components in my personality is my ability to
   work hard.
9. I'm a shy person.
10. One thing about the kind of person I am is that I work hard.
11. I enjoy meeting new people.
12. I am something of a chameleon.
13. Most of the time I am angry.
14. I am a compassionate person.
15. I'm a hard worker.
16. I am a procrastinator.
17. I am not an outgoing person.
18. Responsibility is a major factor in the kind of person I am.
19. I would like to consider myself a somewhat outgoing person.
20. I am easygoing.
21. I actually think I am better than most people I meet.
22. Music is important to me.

The five that most people identify as most promising are these:

3. I am very outgoing because I am really afraid to be alone.
5. My desire to help other people is really selfish at heart.
12. I am something of a chameleon.
13. Most of the time I am angry.
21. I actually think I am better than most people I meet.

The first two theses would seem to be more interesting because
they are more thoughtful. Most of the twenty-two ideas on the
list just tell the reader about some quality the writer thinks of as
a major characteristic: the writer claims to be shy or outgoing or
hardworking or kind or caring or responsible. The reason these
are unlikely to result in interesting writing is that they are pre-

COLLABORATIVE ACTIVITY

Groups can use the brainstorming
technique discussed in 2c to generate a list of thesis statements for
an essay you have assigned. Have
students discuss which statements
seem most promising for further
development.

dictable and not thoughtful. Theses 3 and 5, on the other hand, don't just tell us a characteristic about the writers; the writers have actually *thought* about that characteristic. In thesis 3, the writer doesn't merely tell us he or she is "outgoing"; this writer has actually come up with an interesting analysis of the psychological motivation behind that outgoing nature. A number of these writers said they were kind or caring, but the writer of thesis 5 did more. By thinking about why he or she is always helping other people, this writer came up with a reason that makes us want to read the paper.

The other three successful theses are interesting for a different reason. The writers of these theses didn't decide to write about something everyone else would be writing about. Instead they came up with qualities about themselves that are interesting, unusual, and perceptive: "I am a chameleon," "I am angry," "I am better than everyone else." These are not predictable theses; in fact, the main thing that makes them interesting is that we can't predict what the papers will say. We want to read the papers to find out in what way the first writer is a chameleon, why the second writer is angry, what makes the final writer think he or she is so good.

So now you know what we mean when we say that you should write about something interesting, but so far we haven't made any suggestions about how to do it—how to find something interesting to write about.

If you think you want to write about a particular subject but you know your thesis is too obvious, one piece of advice is to think harder. If you are using brainstorming to come up with a topic to write about, brainstorm some more. Try to get your mind to generate some ideas that are not so easy and so conventional.

Instead of thinking harder, surprisingly, sometimes the best advice is just the opposite: don't try so hard—lighten up, relax, and let it come to you. This situation is a little like those puzzles in the shape of a straw tube. You put a finger in each end of the tube and then try to pull your fingers out. The harder you pull, the more the tube tightens on your fingers. If you relax and take the tension off the tube, it will loosen up and allow you to slip

your fingers out. Sometimes thinking of something to write about is like that straw tube: the more you strain, the less you come up with.

"Think harder" and "Relax and let it come to you" are both good advice (even though they seem contradictory), but they are not very concrete. Here is a suggestion that is.

When you feel that the topic you are thinking about is too obvious, *try saying the opposite*. For example, if you were thinking about writing a paper proving that communication is important to a good relationship, you are about to belabor the obvious. Everyone already knows that communication is important; it's the first piece of advice everyone gets when a relationship sours. So try the opposite. Of course, the literal opposite—"communication is *not* important to a good relationship"—would be fairly hard to prove, but how about some other forms of the opposite, some "sort of" opposites? How about a paper that argues that there is such a thing as too much communication in a relationship? Now there's a thesis that is more thoughtful, more interesting, and more promising. Thinking about the opposite of an obvious thesis has two advantages: first, it can produce a more thoughtful thesis, and second, it still allows you to write about a subject you are interested in.

In addition to this technique, we suggest that you use all the planning activities discussed in 2c: brainstorming, freewriting, mapping, keeping a journal, outlining, reading, arguing with a friend, and using organizational patterns. As you use these techniques, keep in mind that your goal is to produce an idea to write about that will allow you to be interesting, thoughtful, clever, perceptive, analytical, surprising, profound, creative, entertaining, or some combination of these.

3b   Distinguishing between generalizations and evidence

Generalizations

At one time or another, you've probably heard someone say, "Never generalize." Perhaps someone has even said it to you. Ac-

Remind students that generalizations are a necessary part of formal reasoning, especially in the case of deductive arguments. Refer them also to 3d below for more about the role of generalizations in such arguments.

tually, this piece of homespun philosophy is wrong. We all generalize all the time. If you didn't generalize, you would have to stick your hand in every fire to see whether it was hot. If you got off a plane in Peru, you would have to try out languages randomly until you found one that people understood. You wouldn't be allowed to assume that most people in Peru speak Spanish. Generalizing is how we make sense of the world.

So why does the caution never to generalize exist? Probably because generalizing is a powerful and therefore dangerous act, especially when applied to human beings (see 3f). Because generalizations are powerful, we need to use them; because they are dangerous, we must use them carefully.

To understand generalizations better, read the following statements, which are based on a Sears, Roebuck catalog for 1908. Sears was a popular American mail-order department store even back in 1908. The student making the list was asked to study the catalog and to determine in as many ways as she could how life in America was different in 1908 from the way it is today. Some of the statements have been underlined. Study all the statements and determine how the ones that are underlined are different from those that are not.

The 1908 catalog had a lot more writing in it than today's catalog has.

In 1908 people were more used to reading than they are today.

In 1908 you could buy an entire house for $1,800.

The 1908 cream separator was designed so that a young boy could help his parents operate it.

The country was more rural in 1908 than it is today.

There is a picture of a family sitting around reading together in the 1908 catalog.

You could buy little things like combs and kitchen utensils from the 1908 catalog.

You could buy eyeglasses from the 1908 catalog.

A telephone could be bought in 1908 for $10.

The 1908 catalog listed a lot more farm implements—plows, harrows, balers—than today's does.

You could buy a carriage in 1908.

The print in the 1908 catalog was much smaller than it is today.

Things cost much less money in 1908 than they do today.

There is a picture in the 1908 catalog of a family sitting in the living room looking at a stereopticon together.

Families spent more time together in 1908 than they do today.

You could buy seed in the 1908 catalog.

The 1908 washing machine ran by hand cranking and was designed so that a young girl could assist her mother in operating it.

The statements that are not underlined in the list above are *facts* that the student ascertained directly by looking at the 1908 catalog. The underlined statements, on the other hand, are *conclusions* that the student reached by thinking about the facts; in other words, they are generalizations. If we rearranged the list and placed the various facts under the generalizations that are based on them, we would have something like an outline of a paper:

The country was more rural in 1908 than it is today.
  The 1908 catalog listed a lot more farm implements—plows, harrows, balers—than today's does.
  You could buy a carriage in 1908.
  You could buy little things like combs and kitchen utensils from the 1908 catalog.
  You could buy eyeglasses from the 1908 catalog.
  You could buy seed in the 1908 catalog.
In 1908 people were more used to reading than they are today.
  The 1908 catalog had a lot more writing than today's catalog has.
  There is a picture of a family sitting around reading together in the 1908 catalog.
  The print in the 1908 catalog was much smaller than it is today.
Things cost much less money in 1908 than they do today.
  In 1908 you could buy an entire house for $1,800.

A telephone could be bought in 1908 for $10.
Families spent more time together in 1908 than they do today.
> The 1908 cream separator was designed so that a young boy could help his parents operate it.
>
> The 1908 washing machine ran by hand cranking and was designed so that a young girl could assist her mother in operating it.
>
> There is a picture in the 1908 catalog of a family sitting in the living room looking at a stereopticon together.

This outline shows clearly the difference between generalizations and facts, but it also shows how generalizations and facts work together to make up a coherent argument. One very effective way to structure an argument is to make a generalization and then follow it with a series of facts that back it up. Then make another generalization, followed by another group of supporting facts. Continue this sequence until you have made and supported enough generalizations to convince the intended audience of the thesis, which is itself just a broader generalization.

Evidence

Suppose that the student who examined the 1908 Sears catalog became intrigued by two items on her list:

- The 1908 cream separator was designed so that a young boy could help his parents operate it.
- The 1908 washing machine ran by hand cranking and was designed so that a young girl could assist her mother in operating it.

Instead of concluding that families spent more time together in 1908, the student might wonder if children were expected to do harder manual labor in 1908 than they are today, a generalization that becomes the writer's working thesis. By themselves, the two facts from the catalog are not enough evidence to support this generalization. To explore this topic further and develop and refine the thesis, the student would have to uncover more evidence about the kinds of work children did during the first decade of the twentieth century, as well as evidence about the work children do today.

Although it is important to gather enough evidence to support your thesis, it is also important to judge the quality of that

Remind students that not all evidence is conclusive. The value of evidence will depend on the reliability of one's sources. Warn students to avoid relying on only one or two for evidence. Advise them to search for several corroborating sources on subjects they choose to investigate.

evidence. Writers of diaries and letters can be selective in their recollections, or they can embellish the truth. People who were children in 1908 are now in their eighties and nineties and may not remember their childhoods accurately. For more on judging the quality of evidence, see 3c and 45.

For some papers, your own experience may provide enough evidence for you to make your argument successfully. For example, if you were writing a paper on Korean culture and you grew up in Korea, your experience would provide strong support for your thesis. However, whenever you use facts or other evidence that is not commonly known or is from a source outside of your own experience, you must document that evidence. Such documentation lends credibility to your argument; it makes it possible for readers, if they want more information, to look up the sources of your information themselves. For more on documenting sources, see 46.

3c Using an inductive argument to support your thesis

As she explores the topic of child labor in 1908 and today, gathers evidence, and refines her thesis, the student discussed in 3b might consider using inductive reasoning to learn more about her subject and present her conclusions. In the following example, two scientists use inductive reasoning to learn the truth about a disturbing phenomenon.

In the fall of 1987, biologists Lucy Bunkley-Williams and Ernest H. Williams, Jr., learned of a number of instances of bleaching in the coral reefs off the coast of Puerto Rico. Algae that normally live within the reefs were being expelled, weakening the coral and causing it to turn white. The two biologists first investigated the bleaching themselves; then they called biologists and divers on other islands in the Caribbean, who reported similar bleaching. Satisfied that the bleaching was more than a local phenomenon, they took their next step.

We quickly sent a letter to *Science* magazine to alert others to the widespread nature of the bleaching, and we spoke

COLLABORATIVE ACTIVITY

If you are using a college reader in your course, have students read an article that deals with science or history, preferably one with footnotes or other documentation. Have groups analyze the essay to detect which primary sources the author may have used. Then have them review the essay again for evidence based on secondary sources. Discuss findings with the class as a whole.

ACTIVITY

Convince students of the importance of inductive reasoning by exposing them to scientific discourse. You might circulate current issues of periodicals such as *Scientific American* or *The New England Journal of Medicine* as examples. Also, encourage students to examine scientific journals at the campus library.

at several international meetings of marine biologists in Puerto Rico. We also sent out questionnaires to gather the specific information we would need to document the problem and possibly determine a cause.*

The responses to their questionnaire indicated that the bleaching was a worldwide phenomenon and that a similar event had occurred earlier in the decade.

Although we recognized the cyclic nature of coral reef bleaching, we still needed to determine a cause. As the number of questionnaires returned to us grew, we hoped that the responses to the many questions about the nature of the bleachings, and the conditions that prevailed when they occurred, might point to a single factor capable of affecting the reefs on a global scale. Eventually, we received hundreds of reports, but the character of bleaching in each area differed somewhat, making the search for a common factor seem hopeless.*

Eventually, the two scientists were able to rule out disease and an overdose of ultraviolet light as causes. Although the data were contradictory and difficult to analyze, researchers *had* detected a significant rise in the temperature of the water off the Caribbean.

We believe that the increasing severity of recent global cycles of bleaching was apparently caused by the general global warming trends in the 1980s, which led to some of the hottest years on record (see "Where's the Heat?" *Natural History,* March 1990). During the seasons when the reefs normally experience their highest temperatures, this warming was sufficient to force water temperatures above the limit that corals could tolerate, and bleaching resulted. Overall seawater temperature increases, as well as those limited to areas near shore, were responsible. Most bouts of major

---

*Lucy Bunkley-Williams and Ernest H. Williams, Jr., "Global Assault on Coral Reefs."

bleaching and many of the minor ones happened either during elevated temperatures or during the normal warmest
water period of the year.*

As they investigated the problem of bleaching and formu-
lated their hypothesis, or theory, as to its cause, Bunkley-
Williams and Williams were following the methods of **inductive**
(or *scientific*) **reasoning:** they gathered a large amount of data
and then reached a conclusion that accounted for those data.
The two researchers first sought to learn more about the phenomenon by interviewing local scientists and divers and distrib-
uting a detailed questionnaire. As they gathered their evidence,
they ruled out other possible explanations (disease, ultraviolet
light) and settled on the conclusion that was most consistent with
their data. Their evidence is credible because it was gathered
from experts (scientists) and from a large number of sources
throughout the world ("Eventually, we received hundreds of
reports").

Finally, although Bunkley-Williams and Williams built a
strong case for their explanation, there is always the possibility
that new evidence could change their conclusion. Notice that
they recognize this possibility and carefully qualify their hypothesis. In the excerpt below, the words that qualify the hypothesis
are highlighted.

> We believe that the increasing severity of recent global cycles of
> bleaching was apparently caused by the general global warming
> trend in the 1980s, which led to some of the hottest years on
> record.

Because they recognize and acknowledge that their conclusion
is tentative, the two scientists lend further credibility to their
argument.

Although most students don't have the resources to conduct
the kind of research that the two marine biologists did, inductive
reasoning is still a useful method for investigating your topic and

*Ibid.

testing your generalizations. The student studying child labor could probably find statistical information on that subject, gathered and published by the U.S. Department of Labor, in her college library, along with magazines and newspapers from that period and books on the subject (for more information on conducting library research, see 45c). A student who wanted to investigate attitudes toward college athletics could conduct a survey of a representative number of students on campus, look up the results of other surveys in the library, and interview athletes and other students. The inductive method itself—gathering relevant facts, formulating a hypothesis, and testing that hypothesis—remains the same.

CHARACTERISTICS OF STRONG INDUCTIVE ARGUMENTS

- They are based on an *adequate* amount of evidence.
- The sample that the conclusion is based on is *representative* of the entire population.
- The evidence is *relevant*.
- Although a conclusion based on credible evidence may have a high degree of probability, it can never be proved absolutely because it is based on a sample.

3d Using a deductive argument to support your thesis

While a hypothesis that you arrive at through inductive reasoning can never be proved with absolute certainty, the truth of a deductive argument depends on the accuracy of the assumptions, known as *premises,* on which it is based. In the following example, geologist Terry Jordan uses **deductive reasoning** to argue that Europe is not a continent.

Defining Europe is by no means so simple as might be imagined. The most commonly encountered definition, and the one that first comes to mind, is "a continent." Many may recall from elementary school days being asked to recite the names of the family of continents, in which Europe held a

place of full membership. Impressive support for the continental status of Europe can be found in various dictionaries and in the writings of numerous twentieth-century geographers. . . . In this view, then, Europe is a distinct physical entity, because a continent is understood by geographers to be a sizable landmass that stands more or less separate from other landmasses. North and South America, connected by the narrow Isthmus of Panama, are continents, as are Africa, linked to Asia only by the severed land bridge at Suez, and Australia, which is isolated from other landmasses by surrounding seas.

Close inspection reveals, however, that Europe cannot satisfy the definition of continentality, for it is not a separate landmass. To be sure, there is a clear separation from Africa to the south in the form of the Mediterranean Sea, and the western and northern limits are well defined by the Atlantic and Arctic oceans. It is in the east that the idea of continentality founders. Only the beginning of a water separation is found in the southeastern fringe, where the sea reaches northward from the Mediterranean, through the Aegean, Dardanelles, and Bosporos to the Black Sea, and still beyond to the Sea of Azov. There the division ends, and to the north of Azov stretch the vast expanses of Russia. Instead of a narrow isthmus similar to Panama or Suez, the map reveals a wedge of land broadening steadily to the east, welding Europe and Asia into one large continent called Eurasia. Europe lacks the clear-cut physical border, and as a result is not a continent.

—Terry Jordan, *The European Culture Area*

The accuracy of Jordan's conclusion, that Europe is not a continent, depends on the truth of an assertion he makes near the end of the first paragraph: "a continent is understood by geographers to be a sizable landmass that stands more or less separate from other landmasses." Jordan's argument, then, can be broken down into three parts:

1. A continent is a sizable landmass that is separate, or nearly separate, from other landmasses.

RESOURCES
Deductive Argument

Conners, Robert J., ed. *Essays on Classical Rhetoric and Modern Discourse*. Carbondale: Southern Illinois UP, 1984.

Gage, John. "Teaching the Enthymeme: Invention and Arrangement." *Rhetoric Review* 2 (1983): 38–50.

Fahnestock, Jeanne, and Marie Secor. "Teaching Argument: A Theory of Types." *College Composition and Communication* 34 (1983): 20–30.

The traditional way of teaching deduction is by means of the enthymeme, or categorical syllogism, derived from classical reasoning. Our text follows that procedure. Some instructors take a slightly different approach, emphasizing a "claims and warrants" analysis based on the theories of Stephen Toulmin. See Fahnestock's article for more about Toulmin's alternative.

3d
arg

Make sure students understand that an untrue conclusion can be reached by means of a correctly deduced syllogism (e.g., "All planets are made of cheese" / "Mars is a planet" / "Therefore Mars is made of cheese"), and that a truthful conclusion can be reached by means of a faulty syllogism whose premises do not coincide (e.g., "All planets are made of cheese" / "Mars is made of cheese" / "Therefore Mars is a planet"). The point is that one can reason correctly and still be wrong, or reason fallaciously and still be right. Validating the premises upon which arguments are based is therefore extremely important. Because inductive evidence is usually needed to validate deductive premises, both types of reasoning must work together in a successful argument.

2. Europe is not separate or nearly separate from Asia.
3. Europe is not a continent.

The first two statements are the *premises*, and the final statement is the *conclusion*. The entire three-part argument is known as a *syllogism*.

In order for a deductive argument to be sound, the two premises must be true. In our example, the accuracy of Jordan's conclusion depends on the truth of *both* of his premises and on the conclusion following logically from them. If continents are not understood to be large, separate landmasses or if someone could demonstrate that Europe is indeed separate from Asia, one or both of the premises would not be true. The argument would not be sound, and Europe would be a continent after all.

Further, for a deductive argument to be sound, the conclusion must also follow logically from the two premises. Consider the following faulty argument.

Faulty argument

1. A continent is a sizable landmass that is separate, or nearly separate, from other landmasses.
2. The United Kingdom and Ireland are separate from the European mainland and from each other.
3. The United Kingdom and Ireland are continents.

Although both premises are true, the conclusion does not follow logically from them. A geographer would probably argue that the United Kingdom and Ireland are not sizable landmasses—they are not comparable in size to Africa or North or South America. The argument is not sound because the conclusion does not follow from the two premises.

Often writers who are making deductive arguments will leave one of their premises unstated. Cautious readers must look for such unstated assumptions and judge whether they are true. For example, suppose that a writer were to argue that women should not be allowed to serve in combat units because their presence would lower the effectiveness of these units. The unstated premise in this argument is that the presence of women automatically decreases a unit's effectiveness.

An important part of learning to read critically (see 6) is de-

veloping the ability to spot unstated assumptions, determine their accuracy, and question arguments that depend on faulty premises. It's also important to check your own writing for faulty assumptions and conclusions that don't necessarily follow. Stating both your premises has the merit of making the basis of your argument clearer. On the other hand, leaving one of your premises unstated involves your reader more actively in the argument by requiring that he or she participate in the thinking.

CHARACTERISTICS OF STRONG DEDUCTIVE ARGUMENTS

- A deductive argument depends on the truth of the two premises on which it is based.
- In a strong deductive argument, the conclusion the writer draws must follow logically from the two premises.
- In some deductive arguments, one of the premises is left unstated. Readers must develop the ability to detect unstated premises and determine their accuracy.

COLLABORATIVE ACTIVITY

As students develop essays involving deductive logic, have them work with this checklist as a means of evaluating the persuasiveness of their classmates' arguments. Remind them that it is not always necessary to convince the reader in order to reason successfully.

Because deductive arguments depend on established principles or premises that the writer proves with evidence, they can be very persuasive. On any given day, the editorial page of your local newspaper will probably feature editorials that rely on deductive logic. Suppose that the student who chose child labor as her topic decided to argue that the hard labor children performed at the turn of the century was beneficial to them and that children today should be required to perform manual labor. Depending on the quality of her evidence, she could make a strong case by arguing her point deductively.

3e Anticipating objections

Part of thinking critically about a piece of writing is thinking about why the reader of your writing might disagree with it. This process—thinking about objections the reader might have—is called *anticipating objections*. In the example in 3d, Terry Jordan presents arguments that Europe *is* a continent in his first para-

3f
logic

ACTIVITY

Taking opposing views into account is a skill common to both academic writing and forensic debate. Besides having students study how authors of assigned readings anticipate objections, you might arrange with your school's forensics team to have your class observe a debate on campus. Students might benefit from learning how debaters meet each other's objections in order to score points.

graph, thus anticipating objections that his readers might raise to his assertion that Europe is not a continent.

If you were writing a memo to your boss proposing that the office switch from IBM to Macintosh computers, you would first include all the reasons for making the switch that you could think of as well as all the supporting facts that your research could produce. Then you should imagine your boss saying no to your proposal. What reasons would he or she give for saying no? What responses could you give to those reasons? Put those responses in your memo so that you anticipate the objections before they are made.

Similarly, in an essay in which you argue that grades should be abolished in colleges and universities, you would first give all the reasons for abolishing grades that you can think of and all the support that your research can produce. But then, to strengthen your argument, you should try to imagine someone who completely disagrees with your position. What reasons would that person give for objecting? What would your answers to those objections be? Put the objections and, most important, your answers to them into your paper.

Let us be clear about what we are suggesting here. You are not trying to present both sides of an argument equally. You are trying to convince your audience to agree with your position. If there are fairly obvious arguments in opposition to your position, your paper will be stronger if you include those objections together with strong responses to them. Anticipating objections is part of making an argument as strong as possible.

3f Avoiding logical fallacies

Strong, persuasive arguments are well reasoned and backed by credible evidence (see 3b, 3c, and 45). The writer treats the reader fairly by presenting the evidence clearly, documenting it when it comes from sources outside of the writer's experience, carefully qualifying his or her conclusions, and anticipating and dealing with the reader's objections. If arguing deductively, the writer makes sure that the premises on which the argument is

based, whether stated or unstated, are true and that the conclusion follows logically from the premises.

One way to strengthen your argument is to check your writing carefully for logical fallacies. *Logical fallacies* are common mistakes in reasoning—false premises, conclusions that do not follow, arguments that appeal to readers' emotions unfairly. Some of them are also known as *propaganda techniques,* and you'll often find them in advertising and political debate.

Hasty generalizations

Although it's true that we must generalize in order to make sense of the world, writers who want to be fair resist the temptation to make sweeping statements based on insufficient evidence. In a paper on bias in the mass media, for example, the following statement would be a hasty generalization.

Hasty generalization

It is a well-known fact that television reporters are all liberal Democrats.

"Oh really?" the alert reader asks. "And how do we know this?" Even if the writer can present evidence that many television reporters are liberals, it is impossible to prove that all of them are. The following statement takes this uncertainty into account and is far more credible.

Fairer generalization

Several surveys of television reporters indicate that a large number of them hold liberal views.

The writer would then have to cite these surveys so that readers could examine the evidence for themselves.

Stereotypes are notorious examples of hasty generalizations. We've all heard ugly stereotypes of different groups of people—"Women are too emotional," "African-Americans are good dancers," "Asians work too hard." These generalizations are dangerous because they are inaccurate and because they and others like them have done much harm over the centuries to individuals from various groups. Such generalizations are haz-

COLLABORATIVE ACTIVITY

3f
logic

If students meet in groups to read one another's papers, have them look for the fallacy types defined in the following pages. Remind students that even professional arguments will remain open to at least a few fallacy charges, no matter how careful the reasoning may be. Even the best boxer must sometimes take a punch. The aim is to minimize, not totally eliminate, one's vulnerability to attack.

3f
logic

ardous because they are often untrue. They are based on erroneous information and are usually a result of bias. But even when they are true *in general,* they are dangerous because they lead us to ignore the fact that many individuals in a particular group will differ from the generalization.

Non sequitur

Non sequitur means "does not follow" in Latin. Here is an example of a non sequitur.

Non sequitur

Darlene wore a fur coat to the party, so she must not care about animals.

A person's opinion of animals, favorable or unfavorable, cannot be inferred from the fact that she wore a fur coat. A non sequitur, then, is a faulty conclusion—it "does not follow" logically from the statement that precedes it (see 3d).

Careless statements about cause and effect

Just because one event follows another in time, you cannot conclude that the first event caused the second. Such relationships are difficult to prove, and the following statement would have to be backed up by a good deal of evidence (see 3c).

Careless statement about cause and effect

The introduction of rock 'n' roll in the 1950s led to the decline in the quality and popularity of Broadway show music.

Either-or fallacy

Many things in this world come in pairs—there are two sexes, two hemispheres, two houses of Congress. Therefore, it seems natural to think that there are only two solutions to every problem or two answers to every question, as in the following example.

Either-or fallacy

If you don't learn to drive a car, you'll have to depend on friends and relatives for your transportation.

3f
logic

This statement assumes that depending on friends and relatives is the only alternative to learning to drive. It ignores the possibility of using public transportation, walking, or riding a bicycle.

False analogy

Analogies are comparisons, such as that found in Shakespeare's famous question, "Shall I compare thee to a summer's day?" Analogies add interest to writing, and skillful writers use them to help make their points vividly. Just because two things can be compared, however, does not mean they are alike in every way. Shakespeare's love really isn't a summer's day, though in certain ways she resembles one. The following statement is a false analogy.

> **False analogy**
>
> It's to be expected that some people are starving; after all, in nature only the strong survive!

It may be true that only the fittest animals survive in the wild, but human society is a different situation.

Circular reasoning

This fallacy, also known as *begging the question,* is a favorite technique of people seeking to avoid giving a direct answer. A writer or speaker guilty of circular reasoning simply restates his or her assertion in another way, without offering evidence or drawing a conclusion.

> **Circular reasoning**
>
> There is a great deal of crime in inner-city neighborhoods because the crime rate in most urban areas is very high.

Red herring

In mystery novels, a *red herring* is a clue that distracts readers from the real culprit; the phrase comes from the practice of misleading hunting dogs by drawing a fish across their trail. A writer using a red herring seeks to distract readers by bringing up an irrelevant issue.

Red herring

With so much hunger in the world, why should we worry about saving endangered species?

Appealing to your readers' emotions unfairly

It's not necessarily wrong to appeal to your readers' emotions. Sometimes a compelling example can add power to your argument. An account of a camping trip in a national park, for example, could bring a welcome personal note to an argument against cutting down trees on park lands and make the essay more persuasive. Stories that appeal to your readers' emotions are usually not enough to make a convincing case, however. And the following tactics, all of which appeal to a reader's emotions unfairly, will weaken your argument.

Ad hominem attack. *Ad hominem* means "to the man" in Latin. If you attack your opponent personally instead of challenging his or her argument, you are indulging in an ad hominem attack.

Ad hominem attack

Ms. Tenaka has no business talking about women's rights—after all, she used to be a fashion model.

Bandwagon appeal. This appeal depends on the pressure that people often feel to conform to the views of the majority. Writers who use a bandwagon technique claim that you should support a position because "most people" do.

Bandwagon appeal

Most people in this city want a new highway, so you should vote for the bond issue that will provide the funds to build it.

Transfer. A favorite technique of advertising copywriters, *transfer* involves equating an argument or a product with an image that readers probably find desirable.

Transfer

Discriminating drivers prefer Cadillacs.

3g Defining terms

Sometimes arguments are ineffective because the writer uses terms in a way that is not clear to the reader. He or she may use a term in several different ways in the same paper. Or he or she may use a term in such a vague way that its meaning is never precise. Such problems can be the result of careless thinking. Careful thinking will probably lead you to clarify the meaning of any confusing terms early in the paper or at least at the first point you use them. (For a discussion of definition in writing, see 7e.)

4 DRAFTING

4a Letting your writing flow

We've deliberately chosen the word *drafting* rather than *writing* as the title of this chapter because *drafting* has a more tentative and less final sound to it. Drafting implies that later you will go back and revise what you have drafted. It is this idea that what you are doing is "just getting your thoughts down on paper" that we want you to keep in mind while drafting.

4b Keeping the plan in mind

It is important while drafting to remind yourself occasionally of the writing context: the audience, the purpose, the assignment, the subject, and, if you have settled on one, the thesis. If you periodically think back over this context as you write, you are less likely to wander into areas outside those defined by the context. You might even go so far as to write these basic parameters of the context on an index card and post them on the wall above your desk so that you can glance up at them occasionally. Even if you don't need to go that far, you can still mentally look up and remind yourself whom you are writing for, what you intend to

RESOURCES
Defining Terms

Morris, William, and Mary Morris. *Morris Dictionary of Word and Phrase Origins.* New York: HarperCollins, 1988.

Hayakawa, S.I. *Language in Thought and Action.* 3rd ed. New York: Harcourt, 1972.

Investigating the history of words is one way for students to become more precise in their use of language. They should also be aware of how meanings are affected by context, as Hayakawa's book explains.

4b
draft

This chapter covers the all-important stage of drafting an essay. Crucial as it is to the outcome of a writing project, drafting is also a personal activity that varies among individuals according to their habits. You might begin by asking students to discuss their prior experiences in drafting high school or college essays, giving special attention to such issues as procrastination and finding time to write. Encourage students who have trouble beginning or finishing an essay to study the advice given in this chapter.

4c
draft

RESOURCES

Rose, Mike. *Writer's Block: The Cognitive Dimension.* Carbondale: Southern Illinois UP, 1984.

Zinsser, William. *On Writing Well.* 4th ed. New York: Harper-Collins, 1990.

Stress that changing one's mind while drafting is not a sign of weakness or confusion, but rather a natural aspect of writing. Drafting means bringing ideas into conscious focus, and few successful writers expect first drafts to be final. To cite an extreme example, the great novelist Balzac made so many changes on his printer's proofs that his books often cost him more to publish than he made from their sales.

ACTIVITY

Students who worry that they must polish every sentence before writing the next are often good students, yet they may be missing the forest for the trees. Encourage them to try writing more often in circumstances where grading or peer criticism is not a factor. Freewriting and journal keeping activities as described in Chapter 2 may be especially helpful.

accomplish, what assignment you have been given, and what subject and thesis you are writing about.

On the other hand, you may find as you draft that you change your mind about some elements of the context. You might change the thesis or the audience or the purpose of the writing. It is unlikely that you will have the latitude to change the assignment, but if you have been given several options to write about, you might find yourself switching from one to another. Changing your mind about any of this is fine; in fact, that's the kind of flexibility and fluidity that produce good writing. But you should make these changes deliberately and not accidentally; otherwise, the results may be confusing to your reader.

In addition, if you have completed some of the planning techniques suggested in Chapter 2 before you started drafting, make use of that plan, whether it is an outline, a mapping diagram, a brainstormed list, some freewriting, or a particular organizational mode, to guide your drafting. But *guide* is the important word here: you should not feel obligated to stick with your original plan; in fact, you will undoubtedly modify it as you write. Keeping it nearby to *guide* you as you write your first draft is a good idea, however.

4c Postponing editing

Have you ever tried to pat your stomach and rub your head at the same time? Either of these actions is fairly easy by itself, but most people have difficulty doing both at once. The human mind seems to do a better job if it can focus on one task at a time. This is just as true of writing as it is of patting and rubbing.

When drafting, you are trying to get ideas into words and down on paper in a coherent order; that's a lot. If on top of that you attempt also to worry about the thousands of intricacies of English grammar, punctuation, and spelling, you are unlikely to do either task well. For this reason, you will produce better writing if you postpone concern about errors until you've gotten at least a first draft down on paper. Errors in grammar, punctuation, and spelling are important, of course, but you will do a bet-

ter job of eliminating them if you work on them after you've gotten your ideas down on paper. In addition, time spent in correcting surface errors at the early stages of drafting may be wasted because you may rewrite completely as you revise.

4d   Drafting on the computer

One of the major reasons we recommend that you try to do your writing on a computer is that the fluidity of the computer environment—the ease with which things can be changed—encourages the attitude toward drafting that we have been discussing in this chapter. If you know that you can later make changes easily, you are probably going to be much more willing to write paragraphs with the kind of openness and sense of experimentation that lead to creativity. If you can change the wording of a sentence just by typing over it, you are going to be more experimental in the wording you try out as you write.

Some writers even find themselves trying out several ways of saying the same thing when they write on a computer. Then they can look at the different versions and eliminate all but the most effective.

4e   Sample student paper

In this section we are going to follow a student writer as he takes a paper through several drafts. Steve Shaver wrote this paper, "Hidden Bitterness," after reading an essay titled "The Dying Girl That No One Helped" by Loudon Wainwright. As Steve described it, the essay told about "a gut-wrenching event involving a young lady [Kitty Genovese] who was brutally stabbed to death in the middle of the street practically on her own doorstep while walking home to her apartment one night in New York City." The worst part of the story, according to Steve, was that there were

> thirty-eight witnesses who admitted seeing the crime without doing a damned thing about it. In her last breaths on earth, [Ms. Genovese] even went as far as singling out one

person, a neighbor, and calling him by name in a cry for help, but instead of helping he quietly shut the blinds and went to bed, not wanting to become involved.

In response to the story, everyone in Steve's class was asked to freewrite for a few minutes (for a discussion of freewriting, see 2b). Steve found the story of Kitty Genovese hard to believe. Having grown up in the country, Steve had trouble accepting the idea that people wouldn't do anything to help a woman being assaulted, much less murdered. The following is what Steve produced during the freewriting.

I think the helpful attitude toward other people still exists out in the country where people aren't exposed to crime as much as city people they see it on the news and in the news papers but it doesn't happen in front of their house or even in their neighborhoods (if thats what you want to call them) like people in cities. About the most violence they see in the country is a big pig rooting the smaller pigs away from the feed bin but people are constantly seeing or hearing about crime and violence because it happens so frequently around them they can't stay away from it and maybe thats why a lot more

violence happens in the City as well as the fact that many cities may be overpopulated and the people feel other people are invading their space so they deal with it in ways that sometimes are very harsh and many times irreversible to correct.

After a few minutes of freewriting, Steve's class discussed what they had written. He was surprised to learn that a majority of his classmates, most of whom had lived all their lives in the city, said they would have reacted the same way as the people in New York. They wouldn't have gotten involved.

Steve's first draft of his paper follows. In it he tried to present both sides of the issue: the arguments he had heard his classmates give for not getting involved as well as his own feeling that no one should be able to stand by and let such a thing happen.

FIRST DRAFT

                    Hidden Bitterness

     Being raised in the country I can see a big contrast

in the way city dwellers and country folk react when it

comes time to help another human being who is in need of

help. Country folk are more willing to at least try to

help someone in need for the main reason that they seem

closer to their neighbors because of the fact that they

know them or try to get to know them. They dont feel

4e
draft

COLLABORATIVE ACTIVITY

Some instructors prefer to have students read one another's drafts in groups and respond with suggestions, either in writing or orally. Use this paper as a model for practicing that kind of group critique, asking each student to write a brief commentary that notes positive aspects of the draft as well as problems. Students may discover that they disagree about strong points and weaknesses; this will not be uncommon when students review one another's work in their own groups.

strict limitations of valuable space that the city people feel even though country folks are exposed to the same amount of violence due to media coverage. The stone etched impression of seeing it first hand is not there in many cases which in my opinion is why many people are afraid to help someone else for fear of ending up being hurt or in trouble themselves, and another reason is city life style and general pace is so much faster compared to the slow day by day attitude of the country it is understandable when a person has to spend 45 minutes getting out of downtown of big city U.S.A. Why he would not want to stop and help someone off the highway with a flat tire because they're more than likely got dinner and theater reservations for the evening or something planned but on the other hand the country folk are pretty much on the same schedule all the time so if they stop to help someone the only inconvenience it would cause might be a short delay in starting to milk or something to that effect but it wouldn't hurt their schedule all that much.

Steve later revised this paper several times. Some of those revisions and the thinking behind them are reproduced in 5e.

Students should find revision less daunting if they can learn to distinguish between large- and small-scale revision. This chapter describes the major kinds of change that a writing project undergoes on its way to a final draft.

5 REVISING

Sometimes beginning writers think of revising as nothing more than reading a paper over and correcting any errors they find. We're using the term to describe a much more complex activity,

however, one that usually involves reading a paper over several times, looking for a different set of problems with each reading. The process will vary from paper to paper. Sometimes you will have the time to spend hours, perhaps even days, polishing a piece of writing; sometimes, such as when writing an in-class essay exam, you will have only a few minutes for revision. But regardless of the variables, you should not attempt to revise every aspect of a paper at once. You should instead read the paper several times, each time looking for just one type of problem.

Revision can be divided into two types of activities. During large-scale revision, you worry about the big picture—the overall organization, focus, and development of your argument. During small-scale revision, you zero in on the details to improve the wording and the correctness of the paper.

5a Large-scale revision

When you revise any piece of writing, you should begin with large-scale changes and should move to small-scale corrections only after the large-scale changes have been made. Depending on the length and complexity of the writing and the amount of time available, you might make large-scale revisions in one reading or in two or three separate readings.

Some of the items you need to check as you make large-scale revisions are listed in the box below.

MAKING LARGE-SCALE REVISIONS

Content:
- Is the content interesting? Thoughtful? Or have you merely repeated arguments everyone is familiar with?

Purpose:
- Will the paper accomplish the purpose you intend?
- Have you changed your mind about the purpose since you began drafting? If so, has that change caused any inconsistencies in the paper?
- Is the purpose clear to the reader? Is it clear what the reader should do or think, if convinced, after reading the paper?

(continued)

RESOURCES
Revising

Beach, Richard. "Self-Evaluation Strategies of Extensive Revisers and Non-Revisers." *College Composition and Communication* 27 (1976): 160–64.

Faigley, Lester, and Stephen Witte. "Analyzing Revision." *College Composition and Communication* 32 (1981): 400–14.

Flower, Linda, John R. Hayes, et al. "Detection, Diagnosis, and the Strategies of Revision." *College Composition and Communication* 37 (1986): 16–55.

Sommers, Nancy. "Revision Strategies of Student Writers and Experienced Adult Writers." *College Composition and Communication* 31 (1980): 378–88.

5a
revise

5b
revise

COLLABORATIVE ACTIVITY

The checklist of points in 5a might prove a useful basis for group discussion as students suggest changes in one another's drafts. This section also offers a convenient summary of advice given in the first four chapters.

FOR DISCUSSION

Small-scale revision addresses diction, grammar, punctuation, and other aspects of sentence-level style. If students are in doubt as to how much those factors weigh in your grading of their papers, now might be a good time to remind them.

MAKING LARGE-SCALE REVISIONS (continued)

Audience (see 1c):
- Is the paper appropriate for the audience that will read it? Is the voice too formal and stuffy? Is it too informal and personal? Is it too committed and narrow-minded? Is it too unsure and tentative? Is the voice too brief and businesslike? Is the paper too rambling and conversational?
- How about the technical aspects of the paper? Have you used terminology that your audience won't understand? Have you explained any concepts that your readers may not be familiar with? Have you explained too much? Have you forgotten how knowledgeable your audience is about this subject?

Thesis and Unity (see 2b):
- Does the paper have a single clear thesis? Is the thesis consistent throughout, or does it change from the beginning to the end of the paper? Will the reader experience any confusion about the thesis?
- Does everything in the paper support the thesis? It is not enough that everything be about the *subject*; everything also should support the *thesis*. This means that each detail in the paper should help support whatever point you are making about the subject.

Organization:
- What are the main points in your essay? Are they presented in a logical order? Would a different order be more effective? Is the amount of attention you devote to each point proportional to its importance in the paper?

Development of Ideas:
- Does each point in the essay have sufficient support to convince the intended audience? Are there places where additional concrete details or specific examples would make the paper more convincing or clearer? If someone were to disagree with your thesis, what reasons might that person give? Have you provided responses to those arguments? Could you?

5b **Small-scale revision**

Once the large-scale revision is complete, it is time to focus on small-scale issues. Again, depending on the length and complexity of the paper and the amount of time available, small-scale revision might be accomplished in one reading or in several.

During small-scale revision, you should review the following aspects of the paper and, where necessary, make changes.

MAKING SMALL-SCALE REVISIONS

- Review your choice of words. Are there places where the language is awkward? Unclear? Wordy? Redundant? Vague? Unnecessarily abstract? Incorrect? (A detailed discussion of expression problems can be found in Part IV.)
- Review your paper, looking for errors in grammar, punctuation, and mechanics. You may be aware of certain types of errors to which you are particularly prone. If so, you may want to read the paper once again looking just for these. (A detailed discussion of editing for grammar errors can be found in Part VI; punctuation is discussed in Part VII; and mechanics, including spelling, is discussed in Part VIII.)

5c **Correctness versus appropriateness**

Most of us are capable of speaking several forms of English. People interviewing for jobs or speaking in class may sound formal and thoughtful. People in a hurry may speak in brief, incomplete sentences. People talking to small children simplify their vocabulary and syntax. People delivering political speeches or commencement addresses tend to use highly rhetorical language. Those telling stories are often folksy and colloquial. Angry people may resort to profanity, but they would avoid that part of their vocabulary when talking to a member of the clergy.

Similarly, many styles of writing are possible. Take contractions like *isn't,* or *don't,* for example. In most writing, these words are perfectly acceptable, but in very formal prose they should be avoided.

Then there is the matter of dialect. Groups of English speakers in different parts of the world or even in different parts of the United States frequently speak versions of English that are significantly different from one another. For example, in England people might drive their lorry round the roundabout, park near a theatre, and carry their belongings into the lift. In

ESL ADVICE

Non-native speakers in your class may find small-scale revision especially difficult. Those who have serious problems with diction, spelling, and verbs can benefit from ESL tutoring, assuming that your campus provides this service. Encourage students with language difficulties to ask you about issues of concern to them. Have them keep a record of mistakes that occur in their usage or grammar. Also encourage your ESL students to examine those sections in Parts IV, V, and VI that deal with verbs and diction.

England, a truck is a lorry, a traffic circle is a roundabout, *theater* is spelled *theatre,* and an elevator is a lift. And the differences are not just in vocabulary and spelling. Whereas an American might be in school, he or she would be in *the* hospital; an English person would be in school, too, but also in hospital (no article).

Here in the United States, there are dialect differences too. In the South, one might tote a case of soda (in the Midwest, it would be pop; in New York City, it would be a soft drink) into the kitchen or place one's lunch in a poke (a bag or sack). In Baltimore, people on vacation often go *down the ocean* unless their car *goes up* and they have to have it repaired. In some versions of black dialect, if a movie or a song is really *bad,* that means it's great, and someone who's *fixin' to buy some new kicks* is about to visit a shoe store.

Sometimes these different dialects sound "funny" or even "wrong" to people who don't speak them. But in fact they are not wrong or funny. Each of them is correct and even has its own set of rules. Most of us have heard someone try to speak an unfamiliar dialect—a parent trying to sound like a teenager, for example, or a white person trying to sound like an African American. Most of the time it doesn't work because the person unfamiliar with the dialect just doesn't understand how it works or doesn't understand the rules. So there are rules; they're just different rules from those of other dialects.

If dialects are logical and follow a set of rules, what's wrong with them? The answer is complex. In the first place, it is inaccurate to say that anything is "wrong" with them. It's not a matter of right or wrong. The issue is appropriateness. Precisely because people speak different dialects, we have agreed on one particular dialect that we use for formal communication, particularly in writing. This form of English is commonly known as Standard Written English. It is the version of English you read in business correspondence, textbooks, and newspapers, and it is the version you should use for most college writing. We use it not because it is better or more correct or more accurate or more col-

Distinguishing between correctness and appropriateness is important for students who are confused about which level of diction they should aim for in college writing. You may find that some tend to vacillate between a slangy informality and a stilted effort to mimic jargon. Whereas both slang and jargon do have their places in literature, you might remind students that a basic test of Standard Written English is its clarity across disciplines, geography, and time.

orful or more logical—we use it because it is the one version we have agreed to use for formal communication. It is what people expect in letters of application, in biology papers, in magazine articles, in business reports. It is the version of English described in this book.

It is important that you learn to be fluent in Standard Written English because it is used so often in important communication, but it is also important that you understand that whatever dialects you might use in other circumstances are not inferior, illogical, or wrong; they are just not appropriate for formal writing.

5d Revision on the computer

The greatest benefit of computers in revising is that they make it much easier to change, insert, delete, or move text. If you find a place that needs more concrete details, you just move the cursor to that spot and type in what you've decided to add. If you decide that the fifth paragraph would work better as the second paragraph, you just move it up there. If you decide that the thesis in the opening paragraph isn't clear, you just revise it until it is.

But there are other, less obvious uses for the computer. If you're not sure the organization of a paper—especially a long paper—is as effective as it might be, there is a computer technique that may be helpful. All you do is find the sentence in each paragraph that expresses the main idea of that paragraph. (These sentences, called *topic sentences,* are discussed in 7.) Use the copy function of your computer to copy each of these sentences, in order, at the end of your paper. When you've finished, you'll have a list of the main ideas of your paper. Reviewing this list will often reveal weaknesses in the organization of the paper: paragraphs that don't support the thesis, paragraphs in the wrong order, missing parts of your argument, and the like.

Suppose that you aren't happy with your conclusion—it's not bad, but you think you could do better. Another computer

Again, not all of your students may have access to computers. You might assure those who don't that you are not teaching a course in computer science and that they are not being graded for computer literacy. It might also bolster the spirits of the technologically disadvantaged if you point out that major authors have been revising their drafts by hand for more than twenty-five centuries. But if the same students say they're thinking of enrolling in a basic computer course next term, don't discourage them.

technique can help with this kind of revision. Use your computer's copy function to make a copy of the paragraph in question just below the original. Now you can experiment with the copy to see if you can improve it, but if you decide that the original was better than the revision, just delete the revised paragraph, and the original is still there.

The computer also makes it much easier to get peer comments on your drafts (see 1b for a discussion of peer commenting). The most obvious advantage is that you can print out copies (double- or triple-spaced, if you like) for each person who will be reviewing your paper. Another technique is to save a copy of your paper on a disk or several disks and ask your peers to enter their comments right on the computer—perhaps in all capital letters or in brackets or underlined to make it easier for you to distinguish the comments from your own writing. When they've finished commenting, they save your paper back onto the disk as a new file with their initials after the name of the file so that you can identify which version was by which classmate.

For more sophisticated commenting, commercial software packages are available that make commenting easier and even allow the commentor to draw arrows, circles, squiggly lines, and other graphics, just as on paper.

The main advantage of writing on a computer is the ease of making changes, however. If you have the opportunity to write on a computer, you will probably produce improved writing, but not until you become comfortable with using the computer. Don't try to learn how to use a word processing program on the night before a ten-page paper is due. The computer will only make your job harder until you become comfortable with it.

But once you are comfortable with the computer, you can begin to make use of the flexibility it gives you. Let your writing process become looser, more playful, more creative. Try out ways of expressing yourself that you would not have tried in the confining world of typewriters and correction fluid. When you are comfortable with the computer, you can also become more comfortable with the fluidity of the writing process.

5e   Sample student paper

In this section we return to the sample paper by student Steve Shaver that was shown in an early draft in 4e. Steve wrote the paper in class after reading an article about the murder in New York City of Kitty Genovese, which was witnessed by dozens of people who did nothing to help. Steve, who grew up in rural Ohio, was outraged by the story and thought it illustrated the difference between country and city dwellers. After some class discussion, during which most of his classmates admitted that they probably wouldn't have gotten involved either, Steve wrote his first draft.

Steve read over his first draft and decided that it seemed unfocused and unconvincing because he had tried to express both sides of the debate. He revised it to express only his view on "getting involved." Next he looked for places to add concrete examples and details to make the paper clearer and more convincing. (For a discussion about providing concrete details to support your position, see 3b and 7d.) Steve inserted these details in a third draft. Then he read the paper again, looking for places where he could improve the expression—the wording.

REVISION

Hidden Bitterness

                                                 but

I was born and raised in the country ~~and~~ I am presently living in Akron while attending college and it is sometimes difficult adjusting from cornfields and dirt roads to towering skyscrapers and four lane roads through town but the hardest thing I have found trouble adjusting to so far is the hidden bitterness in many of the people ~~you see~~ walking around. I think the media has a lot to do with why people are sometimes afraid of their fellow human beings because all they like to talk about on the

COLLABORATIVE ACTIVITY

5e revise

In order to practice peer editing, have groups meet to consider the sample student drafts in 5e as well as the earlier draft of the same paper in 4e. Have them take special note of the large-scale revisions that mark the difference between the earliest and latest drafts. Then urge them to make a list of the kinds of small-scale revisions that take place in later drafts. Remind students that they may be called upon to suggest similar kinds of revision in one another's papers.

news anymore are all the bad things people are doing

which is bound to make people leery of there fellow human

beings. But what ~~makes a guy even more skeptical is~~ *what really left an indelible impression with me*

~~seeing such a crime first hand which in turn leaves an~~ *was seeing such an act of violence in person with my own two eyes.*

~~indelible impression.~~

My roommate and I were downtown in the cascade

plaza. *on a gloomy, dreary day in early fall.* After paying our gas bill we were walking around

in the courtyard minding our own business. Just as we

were heading to our car which was parked on Main Street *our attention was drawn to*

~~we saw~~ a boy who looked to be in his teens, wearing a *. The boy was*

tattered leather coat that looked to be about three sizes

too big, a pair of worn out Nike high topps, and a holey

pair of Levi's. He was riding a red moto-cross bicycle *skillfully*

on the crowded lunch hour street ~~when~~ he approached an *as*

elderly woman. She appeared to be no more than a bag

lady who was wearing very worn-out red tennis shoes, a *old*

coat that looked like an army jacket that had been

through a war, and a knit hat which was pulled down over

her ears only ~~showing~~ her dirty face. She was pulling a *revealing*

little cart which was full of groceries that could very

well have been all she owned. The boy followed the lady

for a couple of minutes suddenly he produced a cunning

grin and look of determination on his face he picked up *gradually*

speed, gracefully dodging people as he approached the

lady, kicking the cart with his left foot knocking it and

the lady over with a thud as this poor old lady's

groceries rolled everywhere that little bastard rode away

laughing yelling back at her to ask if it was her first

day on new legs. As if that wasn't bad enough there were

as she lay helpless on the ground, but

people practically tripping over this poor old woman due

would

~~to the fact that~~ no one ~~wanted~~ to stop and help. By the

struggling

time we got over to her she was ~~trying~~ to get up looking

like a new born fawn, trying to get to her feet on wobbly

legs. I put my hand under her shoulder to help her to

her feet and she went into a panic stricken rage because

she was afraid that I was going to rob her. While

assuring her that all we wanted to do was help, I got her

to sit on a bench and relax a little bit as my roommate

was picking up groceries that people had kicked all over

the place I can still see the Campbell's soup can rolling

New Paragraph

down the street. That day was a first for myself and

Jean, the old lady. It was a first for Jean because she

said it was the first time in many years that she can

remember someone other than a family member wanting to

help her without wanting something in return. It was a

first for me because I had never been in downtown Akron

before and to be honest I was not impressed.

Adding or eliminating paragraph breaks can sometimes greatly improve the coherence of a draft. For more about paragraph unity, refer students to 7.

You might call attention to the student's rewording of sentences to improve emphasis and clarity. Much of small-scale revision has to do with just such minor adjustments in language.

Finally, having gotten the paper to say what he wanted with plenty of concrete details and with language that was clear and powerful, Steve was ready to turn his attention to grammar and punctuation. The draft shown on pages 68–70 incorporates the changes Steve made in wording. The handwritten changes are Steve's corrections of errors in grammar, punctuation, and

5e
revise

spelling. Steve would retype or—if he were working on a computer—reprint the paper with these changes made before he turned it in.

FURTHER REVISIONS

Hidden Bitterness

I was born and raised in the country, but I am presently living in Akron while attending college. It is sometimes difficult adjusting from cornfields and dirt roads to towering skyscrapers and four-lane roads through town, but the hardest thing I have found trouble adjusting to so far is the hidden bitterness in many of the people I see walking around. I think the media has *ve* a lot to do with why people are sometimes afraid of their fellow human beings because all they like to talk about on the news anymore are *is* all the bad things people are doing, which is bound to make people leery of there *their* fellow human beings. But what really left an indelible impression with *on* me was seeing such an act of violence in person with my own two eyes.

My roommate and I were downtown in the Cascade Plaza on a gloomy, dreary day in early Fall. After paying our gas bill, we were walking around in the courtyard minding our own business. Just as we were heading to our car, which was parked on Main Street, our attention was drawn to a boy who looked to be in his teens. The boy was wearing a tattered leather coat that looked to be about

Capitalization is another factor to consider in small-scale revision. If students are in doubt as to why the writer has changed several lower-case letters to capitals on this page, refer them to the list of capitalization rules in 38.

three sizes too big, a pair of worn-out Nike high topps, and a holey pair of Levi's. He was skillfully riding a red moto-cross bicycle on the crowded lunch-hour street as he approached an elderly woman. She appeared to be no more than a bag lady who was wearing very old worn-out red tennis shoes, a coat that looked like an army jacket that had been through a war, and a knit hat that [which] was pulled down over her ears, (only) revealing her dirty face. She was pulling a little cart which was full of groceries that could very well have been all she owned. The boy followed the lady for a couple of minutes. Suddenly he produced a cunning grin and a look of determination on his face. He gradually picked up speed, gracefully dodging people as he approached the lady, kicking the cart with his left foot and knocking it and the lady over with a thud. As this poor old lady's groceries rolled everywhere, that little bastard rode away laughing, yelling back at her to ask if it was her first day on new legs. As if that wasn't bad enough, there were people practically tripping over this poor old woman as she lay helpless on the ground, but no one would stop and help her. By the time we got over to her, she was struggling to get up, looking like a new born fawn, trying to get to her feet on wobbly legs. I put my hand under her shoulder to help her to her feet, and she went into a panic-stricken rage because she was afraid that I was going rob her. While assuring her that all we wanted to do was help, I got her to sit

For many students, comma placement is among the most confusing aspects of the editing process. Have them take note of the comma corrections on this page of the student's draft. If they are in doubt about the reasons for the changes, refer them to 33 and 34.

5e
revise

```
on a bench and relax a little bit as my roommate was
picking up groceries that people had kicked all over the
place.  I can still see the Campbell's soup can rolling
down the street.

     That day was a first for myself and Jean, the old
lady.  It was a first for Jean because she said it was
                                        could
the first time in many years that she can remember
someone other than a family member wanting to help her
without wanting something in return.  It was a first for
me because I had never been in downtown Akron before, and
to be honest, I was not impressed.
```

The importance of reading to the education of any writer is fundamental. This chapter serves to remind students that the most lasting influences on their development as writers will not be abstract rules but their experiences as readers. There is truth in the view that writing is to reading as speech is to listening. As you discuss this chapter, encourage students to talk about the kinds of reading they have done, the kinds they have enjoyed, and the kinds they believe will be necessary to their future careers.

6 READING AND WRITING

You may be wondering what a chapter on reading is doing in a handbook for writers. The fact is that writing and reading are so closely related, even intertwined, that it is impossible to talk about one without discussing the other. In fact, we believe that there is a direct correlation between the ability to read and the ability to write.

Reading and writing are human processes that are intimately connected. In one sense, the two processes are mirror images: writers translate thoughts in their minds into written language on the page; readers look at written language on the page and construct thoughts in their minds. But reading and writing are connected in other ways as well. Much of a writer's time is spent reading what he or she has written in order to revise it. Sometimes writers even read what they've written out loud to hear how it sounds. And serious readers frequently take notes as they read—writing down thoughts in the margin of the book, in a journal, in a notebook, or just on sheets of paper. Reading is

often done to prepare for writing; a writer reads other people's writing on a subject in order to clarify his or her own thoughts before writing.

Reading and writing are intertwined in another sense: both are processes through which we attempt to make meaning. Reading is much more than a mere translation of marks on a page into ideas; there is a great deal of thinking involved as well. We *construct* the meaning a text has for us, and each of us constructs a meaning that is influenced by our own ideas, biases, interests, experiences, and knowledge. We've all had the experience of reading something and then sitting back and asking ourselves, "Now what did that *mean*?" We have to think actively to construct a meaning from those marks on the page; we don't merely discover a meaning that lies there passively.

Writing is also a process of constructing meaning. Sometimes we start out in advance knowing what we want to say, but more often in the process of writing our ideas down, we discover what those ideas are. Sometimes, when writing is really productive, the process itself generates new ideas.

Researchers have discovered another connection between reading and writing: people who read more are better writers. So we urge you to read as you work on improving your writing skills because as you read, your mind will be trying on different writing styles and learning how flexible language can be.

And we urge you to work on becoming a better reader because that will also make you a better writer. It will help you respond sensitively and perceptively to other people's writing, but it will also help as you become a better reader of your own writing—as you work on evaluating and revising what you have written. If you put yourself in the position of an alert reader, you will be better able to see where the gaps and the excesses in your writing occur. Reading your own writing more perceptively will make you a better writer.

Reading contexts

The same contexts that we have urged you to think about as a writer are also issues for you as a reader. As you approach a

RESOURCES
Reading

6
read

Nell, Victor. *Lost in a Book: The Psychology of Reading for Pleasure.* New Haven: Yale UP, 1988.

Olson-Fallon, Judith. *Reading Critically.* New York: HarperCollins, 1993.

Peters, John. *The Elements of Critical Reading.* New York: Macmillan, 1991.

Smith, Frank. *Understanding Reading: A Psycholinguistic Analysis of Reading and Learning to Read.* 3rd ed. New York: Holt, 1982.

ACTIVITY

Encourage students to use their journals for recording personal responses to what they read. They might also use their journals for recording quotations that they may someday cite in term papers or other kinds of writing. Advise students to record the page numbers of any quoted passages, as well as bibliographical information that might be needed in formal citations. Refer them also to 45f for guidelines on taking notes.

text, you need to think about the audience: if you as an undergraduate are reading a highly technical journal article on superconductivity, you should expect to find both vocabulary and concepts with which you are unfamiliar. You also need to think about purpose: What is the author of this text trying to accomplish? Content is another consideration: What is the point here? What is the author trying to prove? Being aware of these issues as you read will help you recognize what is important in a piece of writing and what is not. It will help you respond perceptively to the writing, either positively or negatively. It will make you a better reader.

Reading and memory

When reading texts that are long and complex, readers are sometimes concerned about the fact that they cannot remember everything they have read. Don't worry. The point of reading is not to memorize the writer's words or ideas. The point is to end up with something that *you* make as a reader: a meaning for the text—a complexly woven structure of what seem *to you* to be the most important ideas and the most vivid images. You can almost always go back to a text to review sections when your memory can't reconstruct them. This task—reviewing the text after you've read it once to polish up the meaning you've constructed—will be easier if you've marked the text up as you read it. Checks in the margins, underlined passages, and notes at important points will all help you bring the entire text into focus as you review it. So don't hesitate to make a text yours by marking it up.

Reading and vocabulary

As you read, you will undoubtedly come to words and phrases with which you are not familiar. Often it is possible to figure out the meaning, or an approximation of the meaning, from the context in which the expression appears. At other times you will have no idea what a particular word or phrase means. To handle these cases, you'll need to develop some discretion. If you stop to look up the meaning of every word you don't know, you

6
read

may read so slowly that you begin to lose the big picture. But if you just keep reading and ignore every unfamiliar word or phrase, you may miss or misunderstand the gist of the argument. What you need is the sensitivity to distinguish between expressions that are critical to the argument and should be looked up and those that are less important and can be skipped over. The ability to make this distinction is a skill that is developed through reading and practice.

Reading styles

Just as there are different styles of writing, there are also different styles of reading. Sometimes you can just allow your mind to skim over the surface of what you're reading, letting it flow along without much intensity on your part. At other times you need to slow down and let your mind wrap around the words you're reading, savoring their sound and their sense. Often when you study, reading is more like wrestling; your mind has to struggle with the language to get at complex and subtle ideas that require great attention from you. And then there is the kind of reading you must do of your own writing when you are getting ready to revise it: reading in which you are paying close attention to the effectiveness of your own language, the power and the clarity of what you have written.

Each of these different styles of reading works well when it is appropriate, but using the wrong style for a particular situation can lead to misreading or shallow reading.

Practicing different styles of reading is as important as practicing different styles of writing, and luckily, most reading is a lot of fun. That's why people read for pleasure. So get yourself a good book and experience some of that pleasure!

COLLABORATIVE ACTIVITY

If you are using an anthology in the course, assign an essay to be read critically according to principles discussed in 4. Also ask students to comment on the essay in terms of its emotional appeal, social viewpoint, and ethical standards. You might also have students discuss the style and tone of the essay.

DRAFTING AND REVISING: PARAGRAPHS THAT WORK

Paragraphing is a complex issue in which rules have only a limited role to play. This chapter stresses the need for internal coherence within paragraphs and defines several patterns of rhetorical development. As you review this chapter, remind students that paragraphs always exist in relation to the larger composition and in that sense remain subject to the same considerations of form and development discussed in 1–6.

7a
¶ foc

RESOURCES
The Paragraph

Popken, Randall L. "A Study of Topic Sentence Use in Academic Writing." *Written Communication* 4 (1987): 209–28.

Rodgers, Paul C., Jr. "A Discourse-Centered Rhetoric of the Paragraph." *College Composition and Communication* 17 (1966): 2–11.

Stern, Arthur A. "When Is a Paragraph?" *College Composition and Communication* 27 (1976): 253–57.

7 THE PARAGRAPH AS A UNIT OF THOUGHT

In this chapter you will learn how to construct tightly organized paragraphs, the building blocks of the essay. Paragraphs are an important way the writer can help readers see the structure of a piece of writing. When readers come to a paragraph break, they know that one section of the discussion is ended and a new section is beginning. These paragraph boundaries make the discussion easier to follow.

Formatting paragraphs

There are two ways to indicate when you are starting a new paragraph. The more common way, and the one you will use for most personal and college writing, is to indent the first word of a new paragraph five spaces if you are typing or one inch if you are writing by hand. The alternate method, more appropriate for business correspondence, is not to indent but to double-space between paragraphs.

For longer pieces such as master's theses, monographs, and business reports, you may want to use headings to indicate the content of various sections of the writing. The phrase *Formatting paragraphs* above is such a heading. In most academic writing, especially writing that is less than ten pages long, such headings are inappropriate. In no circumstance would it be correct to use such headings as a substitute for the topic sentences of paragraphs.

7a Focusing on one point

The first principle in writing effective paragraphs is that each paragraph must focus on *one* point or main idea. Look at the following two paragraphs and decide which one is more effective. Which one is easier to understand?

VCRs have made a great improvement in the way Americans spend their leisure time. VCRs have made a wide range of movies

available, from classic films of the 1940s and 1950s to movies that were showing in theaters just a few months ago. If we own a VCR, we can watch a movie whenever we are ready and not have to wait until a theater is showing it. Further, VCRs in our homes save us money. Renting a video is much cheaper than buying a ticket to a movie, and we don't have to get a baby sitter for our children or pay for parking when we watch a video.

Watching movies on VCRs has transformed entertainment in America. Many people now stay home and enjoy the movie they want to see at the time they want to see it and for a very reasonable price. Home video games like Nintendo have also made a big difference in our lives. On the other hand, many people are enjoying camping and other outdoor recreation too these days. The number of people using our national parks is at an all-time high.

The first paragraph is more effective because it focused on a single point: *VCRs have made a great improvement in the way Americans spend their leisure time.* When you finished reading it, you probably had no doubt about what the point was. You knew what this writer was trying to prove as you read the paragraph. In general, well-focused paragraphs make a single point, and the reader has no doubt what that point is. Such a paragraph has **unity.**

The second paragraph does not exhibit such unity. It begins with a topic sentence about VCRs, but by the third sentence its focus has shifted to video games. In the fourth and fifth sentences the focus shifts even more dramatically to camping and outdoor recreation, leaving the reader puzzled about the point of the paragraph. This paragraph lacks unity.

Topic sentences

One way to achieve this unity and focus is to provide your paragraphs with topic sentences. The **topic sentence** is simply the sentence that states the main point of the paragraph. In the first of our two paragraphs, the first sentence, *VCRs have made a great improvement in the way Americans spend their leisure time,* is the topic sentence. In the second paragraph, there is no single, clear topic sentence. At first, it seems that the first sentence,

RESOURCES
Focus

Braddock, Richard. "The Frequency and Placement of Topic Sentences in Expository Prose." *Research in the Teaching of English* 8 (1974): 287–302.

Christensen, Francis. "A Generative Rhetoric of the Paragraph." *College Composition and Communication* 16 (1965): 144–56.

7a
¶ foc

The article by Braddock challenges the assumption that all paragraphs must have topic sentences. Christensen offers an interesting comparison between paragraph structure and sentence structure. He argues that paragraphs develop much as sentences do, with the topic sentence acting as a main clause.

ACTIVITY

Students may have been taught to assume that topic sentences are always found at the openings of paragraphs. In fact, as the following discussion demonstrates, topic sentences can appear at any of several locations and in some cases are absent altogether. If you are using a college reader, let students hunt for topic sentences in several paragraphs from an assigned reading. Have them call attention to paragraphs where topic sentences appear in the middle, at the end, or nowhere at all.

7a
¶ foc

about VCRs, is the topic sentence. But shortly thereafter, a sentence about Nintendo seems as if it might be the topic sentence, and at the end the sentence about outdoor recreation seems to be the topic sentence. The paragraph is flawed because it lacks a single, clear topic sentence.

A topic sentence can be divided into two parts: the subject of the paragraph and a point that is being made about the subject. In the first of our paragraphs, the subject of the paragraph is VCRs, and the point being made about the subject is that they have greatly improved the way Americans spend their leisure time.

In 2b we discussed the thesis of an essay. The topic sentence performs the same function for a paragraph that the thesis does for an essay: it provides a focus.

The topic sentence does not have to be the first sentence in the paragraph. However, placing it first ensures that the reader is aware of the point of the paragraph from the beginning. This is the most straightforward and clear way to organize a paragraph. In the paragraphs that follow, the topic sentences have been highlighted.

For the first time in the history of the world, every human being is now subjected to contact with dangerous chemicals, from the moment of conception until death. In the less than two decades of their use, the synthetic pesticides have been so thoroughly distributed throughout the animate and inanimate world that they occur virtually everywhere. They have been recovered from most of the major river systems and even from streams of groundwater flowing unseen through the earth. Residues of these chemicals linger in soil to which they may have been applied a dozen years before. They have entered and lodged in the bodies of fish, birds, reptiles, and domestic and wild animals so universally that scientists carrying on animal experiments find it almost impossible to locate subjects free from such contamination. They have been found in fish in remote mountain lakes, in earthworms burrowing in soil, in the eggs of birds—and in man himself. For these chemicals are now stored in the bodies of the vast majority of human beings, regardless of age. They occur in the mother's milk, and probably in the tissues of the unborn child.

—Rachel Carson, *Silent Spring*

Note that Carson begins by telling us the main point of the paragraph, that we all live in daily contact with dangerous chemicals, and then follows with a more concrete discussion of various ways that these chemicals are present in our environment, concluding with her most powerful example, chemicals in the mother's milk.

A variation on this first approach is to place the topic sentence at the beginning of the paragraph and then to repeat it in different words at the end.

> Many African sculptures serve more than a single purpose, yet generally they may be described as protective. The focus of the sculpture may be the family or the group; it may specialize in protection against witchcraft or the effects of witchcraft, such as disease or infertility, and yet appear at funerals or other rites or festivals. Whatever the complex of uses to which the sculpture may be put, it most often serves to reinforce belief in the acts that make the world a more secure and pleasant place in which to live.
>
> —Roy Sieber and Roslyn Adele Walker,
> *African Art in the Cycle of Life*

Another approach is to place the topic sentence at the end of the paragraph. This variation is especially helpful when the topic sentence is controversial and the presentation of some evidence first may prepare the reader to be more accepting of the thesis. Starting the paragraph with a highly controversial topic sentence might alienate the reader. Withholding the topic sentence until the end of the paragraph can also build a little suspense, and hence interest, and can provide variety in your paragraphs so that they are not all organized in a single pattern. In the following paragraph, Shelby Steele writes about the paradox of being black and middle-class.

> I started the sixties in high school feeling that my class-conditioning was the surest way to overcome racial barriers. My racial identity was pretty much taken for granted. After all, it was obvious to the world that I was black. Yet I ended the sixties in graduate school a little embarrassed by my class background and with an almost desperate need to be "black." The tables had turned. I knew very clearly (though I struggled to repress it) that my aspirations and my sense of how to operate in the world came from my class background, yet "being black" required certain attitudes and

From reading magazine articles and assigned professional essays, students may discover that paragraphs that conclude with topic sentences are often found at the very beginning of the essay. A strong topic sentence at the end of the first paragraph can double as a thesis statement that forecasts the content or argument of an essay. Have students be on the lookout for examples from their outside reading.

stances that made me feel secretly a little duplicitous. The inner compatibility of class and race I had known in 1960 was gone.

—Shelby Steele, "On Being Black and Middle-Class"

Steele creates suspense and avoids alienating the reader in this passage by withholding his topic sentence until the end of the paragraph.

A fourth approach is to place the topic sentence in the middle of the paragraph. This compromise between the first and third approaches can have some of the advantages of each.

The following paragraph is from a discussion of West African women's art by Maya Angelou. She is discussing the women's use of clay and various paints to create designs on the outside of their houses. The word *plastic* in the first sentence does not refer to the material we call plastic in Western society; instead, it refers to the quality of being flexible in shape, so *plastic designs* are designs that can be varied as they are applied to differently shaped surfaces.

These simple materials are forged into plastic designs which will be as temporary as the length of time between rainfalls, and with no lasting staying power against the insistent sun. These artists, however, do not seem to need promises of longevity, nor do they exhibit a craving for notice out of the ordinary. In fact, one of the most notable characteristics of house painting among West African women is the camaraderie found among the women sharing the creation of design. Family members and those attached by friendship often join together in the industry of decoration. When they do, it is agreed that the principal owner will contribute the major design, but it is also expected that every woman will bring something of her own soul to add to the overall effect.

—Maya Angelou, foreword to *African Canvas*
by Margaret Courtney-Clarke

Quite often writers place the topic sentence just after one or two transitional sentences that link the paragraph to what has gone before. Transitional sentences are discussed in detail in 8a.

In discussing the Chinese phrase *wu li*, Gary Zukav first explains that pronunciation and inflection in English are not essential to meaning—whether we pronounce *tomato* "to-may-to"

or "to-mah-to" will make little difference in how well we communicate. His next paragraph, reprinted here, illustrates the technique of opening with two transitional sentences and then immediately following with a topic sentence.

> This is not so in Chinese. Most Chinese syllables can be pronounced several different ways. Each different pronunciation is a different word which is written differently and which has a meaning of its own. Therefore, the same syllable, pronounced with different inflections, which unaccustomed western listeners scarcely can distinguish, constitutes distinctly separate words, each with its own ideogram and meaning, to a Chinese listener. In English, which is an atonal language, these different ideograms are all written and pronounced the same way.
>
> —Gary Zukav, *The Dancing Wu Li Masters*

It is also possible to write a well-focused paragraph without a sentence that can be identified as the topic sentence. This does not mean the paragraph is unfocused; it simply means that the topic sentence is implied rather than stated. The evidence is so powerful and convincing that it is unnecessary to state the topic sentence because it would be impossible for a reader not to understand it from the evidence. There are even a few situations in which effective paragraphs actually have no topic sentences, present or implied. Introductions, conclusions, and transitional paragraphs (see 10a, 10b, and 10c), often do not have topic sentences.

Occasionally, experienced writers will write a topic sentence that governs the next several paragraphs, each of which adds to the evidence that supports the topic sentence. This technique of chaining several paragraphs together under one topic sentence requires considerable expertise on the part of the writer and is probably best avoided by inexperienced writers.

7b Sticking to the point (unity)

In 7a you learned that a well-constructed paragraph focuses on a single point, usually expressed in a topic sentence. Here you

7b
¶ un

FOR DISCUSSION

Ask students to discuss past difficulties with paragraphing. Chances
are that some have found it hard to
stick to the point after two or three
sentences. As Mandela's paragraph
(the first) demonstrates, strong
paragraph unity depends on how
clearly supporting sentences relate
to the topic. Encourage students to
look for other examples in their
reading.

7b
¶ un

will learn how to make sure that everything in each paragraph
supports that main point.

Look at the following two paragraphs, and decide which one
is more effective.

> South Africa is now [1962] a land ruled by the gun. The
> Government is increasing the size of its army, of the navy, of its
> air force, and the police. . . . Pill-boxes and road blocks are being
> built up all over the country. Armament factories are being set up
> 5 in Johannesburg and other cities. Officers of the South African
> army have visited Algeria and Angola where they were briefed ex-
> clusively on methods of suppressing popular struggles. All oppor-
> tunities for peaceful agitation and struggle have been closed.
> Africans no longer have the freedom even to stay peacefully in
> 10 their houses in protest against the oppressive policies of the
> government. During the strike in May of last year, the police
> went from house to house, beating up Africans and driving them
> to work.
>
> —Nelson Mandela, *No Easy Walk to Freedom*

> South Africa is now a land ruled by the gun. The Govern-
> ment is increasing the size of its army, of the navy, of its air force,
> and the police. . . . Pill-boxes and road blocks are being built up
> all over the country. Armament factories are being set up in Jo-
> 5 hannesburg and other cities. Johannesburg is a modern city of
> more than three million people. Officers of the South African
> army have visited Algeria and Angola where they were briefed ex-
> clusively on methods of suppressing popular struggles. The officer
> corps in South Africa is almost completely comprised of whites.
> 10 Because of the system of apartheid, there is little opportunity for
> black South Africans to gain a position of authority in the military
> or in business or industry, for that matter. The education provided
> for blacks is another source of discrimination; blacks must attend
> separate schools, which are far inferior to those for whites.

Most readers find the first paragraph more effective. The
trouble in the second paragraph begins in line 5, where the writer
forgets that the topic sentence is *South Africa is now a land ruled
by the gun.* Instead the writer wanders off into a sentence about
Johannesburg, which doesn't belong in this paragraph at all. The
next sentence is fine, but then the writer wanders away from the

topic sentence a second and more serious time. The remainder of the paragraph has nothing to do with the topic sentence; it has switched over to a discussion of the evils of apartheid, perhaps because of the intensity of the writer's abhorrence of that system. This is not effective writing because it results in a paragraph that is disjointed—that has no unity.

A well-written paragraph, then, has a single point to make and sticks to that point throughout the paragraph.

7c | **Deciding how long a paragraph should be**

How long should a paragraph be? Clearly, a paragraph needs to be long enough to prove its point or accomplish its purpose, but that really doesn't answer the question.

Actually, the length of a paragraph may vary considerably. Whereas transitional paragraphs are often quite short, body paragraphs, which usually include a topic sentence and a number of supporting sentences, tend to be longer, usually over one hundred words and at least five sentences.

Because the range for acceptable paragraph length is so great, the following guidelines may help you.

WHEN TO START A NEW PARAGRAPH

- To signal that you are starting a new point
- In narration (see 7e), to indicate a major shift in time
- In description, to indicate that you are focusing on a new section or portion of what you are describing
- To emphasize a major point by giving it a paragraph of its own
- To break up an overly long block of text

When you are ready to revise a first draft of your writing, you should check closely all paragraphs that are unusually long or unusually short. The short ones may need more development (see 7d). The long ones may be easier to read if they are broken into two or more shorter paragraphs.

ACTIVITY

Paragraph lengths vary, depending not only on expository purpose but also on the generic form of the writing being done. If students are in doubt about this point, you might ask them to examine the average paragraph lengths of the following: a classified ad, a front page story in a local newspaper, a feature article in a popular magazine, a biographical entry in the *Encyclopaedia Britannica*, and an article in a scholarly research journal. Point out that scholarly writing often has longer paragraphs because of the inclusion of research evidence to support a topic sentence or thesis.

7c
¶ lgth

Stress that although aimlessness or digression is to be expected in freewriting exercises, developed essays should exhibit well-unified paragraphs. Encourage students to study the paragraphs in this section as models of strong expository development.

7d
¶ dev

RESOURCES

Becker, Alton L. "A Tagmemic Approach to Paragraph Analysis." *College Composition and Communication* 16 (1965): 237–42.

This article examines the widespread use of two development patterns in academic paragraphing: (1) topic-restriction-illustration, and (2) problem-solution. Note that the developing drafts in 7d illustrate a working out of the second pattern.

7d Developing the point

In 7c we pointed out that short paragraphs may need to be filled out with more support. A string of short paragraphs is often a sign that you are making a series of assertions without providing much evidence or enough examples to support them. Look at the following selection.

DRAFT 1

Converting our company to desktop publishing would save us a considerable amount of money. In addition, it would allow us to do a better job of meeting deadlines. Further, it would allow us to produce publications of much higher quality. Finally, it would benefit the employees by allowing them to acquire a new skill.

For all these reasons, I hope you will agree with me that this company should move quickly to convert to desktop publishing.

The first paragraph is not likely to be very effective because it does not include convincing evidence to support the four good points it makes. For example, the writer asserts that converting to desktop publishing will save the company money, but once the assertion is made, rather than provide any evidence to back it up, she just makes a second assertion: desktop publishing will help us meet deadlines. This second (and the third and fourth) assertions also need more development.

In the second draft, the writer has expanded the text considerably, but the result is still not very convincing.

DRAFT 2

Converting our company to desktop publishing would save us a considerable amount of money. We could save thousands of dollars each year by doing our own typesetting on Macintosh computers. The savings would be considerable.

In addition it would allow us to do a better job of meeting deadlines. With the computers in our own offices, we could produce copy in time to meet our deadlines. This would be especially helpful when we are running behind schedule. We would be more likely to produce copy on time if we converted to desktop publishing.

Further, it would allow us to produce publications of much higher quality. The results would be more creative and would contain fewer errors. We would improve the quality of our publications considerably if we converted to desktop publishing.

Finally, it would benefit the employees by allowing them to acquire a new skill. They would learn to use desktop publishing and would acquire a new skill, which would benefit them greatly.

For all these reasons, I hope you will agree with me that this company should move quickly to convert to desktop publishing.

To see why the second draft still needs more development, look at the first paragraph. The first sentence is an assertion: converting to desktop publishing *would save us a considerable amount of money.* To support this assertion, the next sentence should give some concrete evidence that helps prove that the conversion would result in this savings. Instead of concrete evidence, the next sentence just restates the assertion in different words: *We could save thousands of dollars each year. . . .* And the third sentence simply makes the same assertion in a third way: *The savings would be considerable.*

The other paragraphs are equally lacking in concrete evidence.

Even though the writer has added several sentences following each assertion, she has not added any real evidence; she has merely repeated the assertion in different words.

Now take a look at the first paragraph of the third draft, in which the writer has added concrete evidence to support her point.

Draft 3

Converting our company to desktop publishing would save us a considerable amount of money. By using Macintosh computers and LaserWriter printers, we will be able to produce camera-ready copy in the office without resorting to professional typesetting. If we make this change, the company will recoup its initial outlay of funds within eighteen months and, after that time, will save approximately $10,000 per year. We will need to purchase four Macintosh computers at about $3,000 each and a LaserWriter printer for $4,000—a total of $16,000. In addition, we will expend about

$100 a month on paper and printer cartridges. We are currently spending approximately $1,000 a month for typesetting. After we convert to desktop publishing, we will save $900 per month. In eighteen months, we will have saved $16,200, more than our initial investment in equipment. Further, every month after that, we will save another $900, resulting in a savings of $10,800 per year.

Instead of merely asserting that desktop publishing will save the company money, the writer now gives some concrete examples of the savings. This is what we mean by development: the use of concrete evidence—facts, examples, description, data, figures, or expert testimony—to support the assertions in your writing.

ACTIVITY

If you are assigning essays in a college reader, have students locate other examples of the rhetorical patterns discussed in 7e.

7e Using rhetorical patterns to develop the point

Rhetorical patterns are organizational schemes that have been used by many writers to structure their paragraphs. Not every paragraph must follow one of these patterns, but they are often useful for structuring your thoughts. The following patterns can frequently be identified in the paragraphs of well-organized essays.

Narration is the organizational form used to tell about something that happened—to tell a story or report an event. An essay about the first time you learned that your parents were not perfect would be an example of narration. The events are normally organized in chronological order (the order in which they happened), although there may be flashbacks or leaps over sections of time. When using narration as the organizational mode for a paragraph or for an entire paper, it is important to provide enough information and transitional phrases to make sure that the reader can follow the course of events.

My father was a court stenographer. At his less than princely salary, we watched Yankee games from the bleachers or high in the third deck. But one of the judges had season tickets, so we occasionally sat in the lower boxes when hizzoner couldn't attend. One afternoon, while DiMaggio was going 0 for 4 against, of all people, the lowly St. Louis Browns, the great man fouled one in

our direction. "Catch it, Dad," I screamed. "You never get them," he replied, but stuck up his hand like the Statue of Liberty—and the ball fell right in. I mailed it to DiMaggio, and, bless him, he actually sent the ball back, signed and in a box marked "insured." Insured, that is, to make me the envy of the neighborhood, and DiMaggio the model and hero of my life.

—Stephen Jay Gould, *Bully for Brontosaurus*

7e
¶ dev

Process is much like narration in that events are organized in chronological order. However, this organizational mode is used to describe an actual process—how to do something or how something was done. When explaining a process, remember that your audience may not know much about the process you are explaining; provide enough detail so that anyone could follow your explanation.

The following paragraph on how to make musical bottles is an example of a process paragraph.

The easiest way to make this instrument is to begin with a limited number of bottles, eight, for example. The left-hand bottle is almost filled with water. Play middle C on a piano or electric organ, strike the bottle and compare the pitch. Add or remove a little water until the bottle is "tuned." Repeat this operation for the other seven bottles, tuning them respectively to D, E, F, G, A, B, and again C. Tuning whistles or forks can also be used, of course.

—Afke den Boer and Margot de Zeeuw, trans. Anthony Burrett, *Making and Playing Musical Instruments*

Description is used to sketch a picture of a person, a thing, or a place. A paragraph describing the inside of a prison cell would be an example of description. The details are organized in a logical spatial order such as near to far. When writing description, it is important to provide concrete sensory details to describe the object dramatically. The following paragraph, with its clutter of concrete objects, captures the look and the feel of this southern dining room.

The table was in the middle of the large room. . . . But besides the walnut-and-cane chairs (Great-Grandfather made them)

7e

¶ **dev**

there were easy chairs covered with cotton in a faded peony pattern, and rockers for the two great-aunts, sewing stands and fire shields beside them, all near the watery-green tile hearth. A spready fern stood in front of the grate in summertime, with a cricket in it now, that nobody could do anything about. Along the wall the china closets reflected the windows, except for one visible shelf where some shell-pattern candlesticks shone, and the Port Gibson epergne, a fan of Apostle spoons, and the silver sugar basket with the pierce-work in it and its old cracked purplish glass lining. At the other end of the room the Victrola stood like a big morning-glory and there, laid with somebody's game, was the card table Great-Grandfather also made out of his walnut trees when he cut his way in to the Yazoo wilderness.

—Eudora Welty, *Delta Wedding*

Cause and effect is an organizational pattern used to discuss the causes of a particular event or the results of an event. A discussion of the causes of teenage pregnancy or of the results of drug use would each be an example of cause and effect. The discussion of causes or effects could be organized in chronological order (the order in which they occur) or in order of importance. In asserting that one thing caused a certain effect, be careful to present actual evidence (see 3b). If you report that a new testing procedure took effect at your college last year and that now enrollments have declined ten percent, you have not presented actual evidence that the testing *caused* the drop in enrollment. Because one event follows another does not necessarily mean that the first event *caused* the second.

The following cause-and-effect paragraph reports on the causes of adult-onset diabetes.

But diabetes also depends upon environmental factors. Even if you are genetically predisposed to diabetes, you won't necessarily get the disease, as would be the case if you carried a pair of genes for muscular dystrophy or Tay-Sachs disease. And the risk of developing diabetes does increase with age, and with having diabetic first-degree relatives, and with being born of a diabetic mother, which we can't do anything about. But other risk factors

that predict diabetes are under our control, including being over-weight, how much we eat, and what we eat. Most diabetics (I emphasize again, most adult-onset diabetics) can reverse their symptoms by minimizing those risk factors—especially by reducing their consumption of concentrated sugar and fat and total calories, and thereby losing weight.

—Jared Diamond, "Sweet Death"

7e
¶ dev

Comparison and contrast are used to discuss two subjects by comparing their similarities or contrasting their differences or, most commonly, by doing both. A discussion of how Japan and Korea are similar and how they are different would be a comparison-*and*-contrast essay. Organization is important when following this pattern because you are discussing *two* subjects.

One common pattern is to discuss one subject first and then discuss the second, covering the same points in the same order. The following paragraph is organized in this subject-by-subject order.

Often boys will use phrases like "Gimme that" or "Go away," whereas little girls, according to studies, will say, "Please give that to me," or "Please stop bothering me." Perhaps little boys are conditioned to give commands early on in life because they have been raised this way. On the other hand, little girls' speech and language patterns differ from boys' because they too have been raised differently. In fact, little girls have been found to incorporate many "female" traits in their speech communication patterns as early as four years of age, which may be learned from their mothers or female educators. A recent linguist's observation of 35 nursery school students found the emergence of "female" speech patterns on a consistent basis. The little girls were found to use "tag endings" (i.e., "She has a pretty dress, doesn't she?"). These little girls were also found to use more "terms of endearment" when playing with their dolls.

—Lillian Glass, *He Says; She Says*

Notice that this paragraph first discusses little boys' verbal habits and then discusses those of little girls.

7e
¶ dev

The next paragraph compares and contrasts two types of stew, but it does so point by point, moving back and forth between the two subjects.

> An Irish stew conventionally is a lamb stew. Goatwater obviously is a goat stew. Both dishes contain onions. Irish stew has potatoes while goatwater gets its starch thickening from a slurry of raw flour added toward the end of cooking.
>
> —Raymond Sokolov, "History in a Stewpot"

Definition is used to clarify the meaning you intend for a particular word or phrase *in the particular piece of writing*. Usually you are not claiming that your definition is the only correct one for the term. For example, in a paper contending that Americans work too hard, you might, early on, define *work* as any activity requiring physical or mental exertion that is undertaken for a particular result and not for the pleasure of the activity itself. In another context, you might use a different definition, perhaps specifying that work is activity undertaken *for pay*. Occasionally an entire essay can be devoted to defining a complicated term, but more commonly definitions are short—paragraph or even sentence length. A good definition usually does two things: it places the term being defined in a group or class and then explains how it is different from other members of the group.

> Jazz [is] a form of American music that grew out of black people's musical traditions at the beginning of the twentieth century. Jazz is generally considered a major contribution of the United States to the world of music. It quickly became a form of dance music, incorporating a "big beat" and solos by individual musicians. For many years, all jazz was improvised and taught orally, and even today jazz solos are often improvised. Over the years, the small groups of the original jazz players evolved into the "Big Bands" (led, for example, by Duke Ellington, Count Basie, and Glenn Miller), and finally into concert ensembles. Other famous jazz musicians include Louis Armstrong, Benny Goodman, and Ella Fitzgerald.
>
> —E. D. Hirsch, Jr., Joseph F. Kett, and James Trefil,
> *The Dictionary of Cultural Literacy*

This definition paragraph first puts *jazz* into the class *American music* and then tells the characteristics—big beat, individual solos, improvisation—that distinguish it from other music in this group.

Classification takes a group of items and groups them according to some principle. The following paragraph classifies the ruling class in Aztec society into several subgroups.

> The ruling class, the top level of the social stratification, was itself divided into several categories according to function, importance and standing. Thus a high-priest was the equal of a general, but both would look down upon a poor "parish priest" or a village tax-gatherer. Yet all of them stood apart from what Spaniards called the plebeians, the *maceualtin* (*maceualli* in the singular), who had neither authority nor office.
>
> —Jacques Soustelle, trans. Patrick O'Brien,
> *Daily Life of the Aztecs on the Eve of the Spanish Conquest*

Division is similar to classification except that it takes a single item and analyzes it into constituent parts. A paper analyzing the human body as made up of several systems—digestive, nervous, reproductive, cardiovascular, and so on—would use the organizational principle of division. The following paragraph divides computers into two components: hardware and software.

> Regardless of the type of personal computer you use, the two basic components of the system will be the same, the hardware and the software. The hardware consists of the central processing unit, monitor, keyboard, disk drives and printer. Software is a general term representing the different types of programs that tell the computer what to do.
>
> —Mark Mathosian, *Up and Running with Your Personal Computer*

Problem and solution is an organizational pattern common to business and technical writing but also useful elsewhere. In this pattern, you first describe a problem and then propose one or more solutions; if you propose more than one solution, you may or may not recommend a particular one. A report pointing

7e
¶ dev

out that missing deadlines for filing bids has become a problem for a firm and then suggesting that a new software program would solve the problem would be a problem-and-solution paper. The following paragraph is another example.

> There are some basic reasonable and sensible adjustments that seemingly must be made if the world wants to ensure that tens of thousands of babies won't die each day from diseases exacerbated by malnutrition. Improved agricultural techniques have already increased crop production radically in many areas of the world that once could not support themselves without importing basic foods. Simply upgrading tools from the Stone Age implements still used in Africa would help increase crop yields. Appropriate irrigation and use of fertilizers, the planting of the right crops, and reforesting to lessen the effects of drought and desertification are all simple and relatively inexpensive responses.
>
> —Kenneth C. Davis, *Don't Know Much about Geography*

Note that this paragraph begins by stating a problem—tens of thousands of babies could die of diseases exacerbated by malnutrition—and then suggests a series of solutions to that problem.

Coherence in paragraphing often depends on our sensing an essay's overall direction and means of development. Working out that coherence often takes place during revision of the second or third draft of the essay, at which point the interrelation of paragraphs within the essay can be enhanced through editing. This chapter stresses the value of transitions, repetitions, and other means of fulfilling expectations.

 # 8 COHERENT PARAGRAPHS

Coherence is the quality that allows writing to stick together and to flow smoothly. Problems in coherence can make a piece of writing difficult for the reader to follow. The organization and development of a well-unified paragraph (see 7) contribute to the coherence of a piece of writing. This chapter discusses additional ways to make your paragraphs more coherent.

8a Providing transitions

Look at the following paragraphs and decide which is more effective.

PARAGRAPH 1

The current debate over requiring motorcyclists to wear helmets illustrates how complex our society has become. Basically, our country was established on the principle that government should interfere in the private concerns of an individual only when that person's behavior could affect others. Whether a motorcyclist does or does not wear a helmet involves only the individual motorcyclist. It may be stupid to ride without a helmet, but the only person the bare-headed motorcyclist endangers is himself or herself. This appears to be a case where government has no business interfering. In today's complex society, the case is not so simple. If that motorcyclist is in an accident and requires expensive medical care, it will likely cost an insurance company tens of thousands of dollars, a cost that will be passed on to the other policyholders. If the motorcyclist is uninsured, the taxpayers will probably pick up the tab. The decision to wear or not to wear a helmet turns out to affect more people than just the motorcyclist. It is a proper matter for government to become involved in.

PARAGRAPH 2

The current debate over requiring motorcyclists to wear helmets illustrates how complex our society has become. Basically, our country was established on the principle that government should interfere in the private concerns of an individual only when that person's behavior could affect others. It would seem that whether a motorcyclist does or does not wear a helmet involves only the individual motorcyclist. It may be stupid to ride without a helmet, but the only person the bare-headed motorcyclist endangers is himself or herself. Therefore, this appears to be a case where government has no business interfering. However, in today's complex society, the case is not so simple. If that motorcyclist is in an accident and requires expensive medical care, it will likely cost an insurance company tens of thousands of dollars, a cost that will be passed on to the other policyholders. If the motorcyclist is uninsured, the taxpayers will probably pick up the tab. As a result, the decision to wear or not to wear a helmet turns out to affect more people than just the motorcyclist. Therefore, it is a proper matter for government to become involved in.

Most readers find the second paragraph much easier to follow. If you take a close look, you will see why: a number of short ex-

RESOURCES

Christensen, Francis. "A Generative Rhetoric of the Paragraph." *College Composition and Communication* 16 (1965): 144–56.

Coe, Rich M. *Toward a Grammar of Passages.* Carbondale: Southern Illinois UP, 1988.

Markels, Robin B. *A New Perspective on Cohesion in Expository Paragraphs.* Carbondale: Southern Illinois UP, 1984.

8a
trans

ACTIVITY

Using paragraph 2 as a model, have students freewrite paragraphs of their own. The paragraphs can be on any subject but must incorporate most or all of the transitional phrases found in the model paragraph. Have volunteers read their experiments aloud to the class.

8b
¶ coh

pressions at the beginnings of sentences in the second version did not appear in the first—expressions like *therefore, however,* and *as a result.* These words and phrases are called **transitional expressions** because they make the relationships between individual sentences clearer.

TRANSITIONAL EXPRESSIONS

To Give Examples:

for example	in fact	specifically	to illustrate
for instance			

To Indicate That You Are Going to Give Additional Information:

and	besides	furthermore	moreover
also	further	in addition	too

To Indicate Where Information Fits in a Sequence:

and then	in the first place	last	third
again	in the second	next	
finally	place	second	
first			

To Indicate How Ideas Are Related in Time:

after	earlier	later	soon
after a while	finally	meanwhile	then
afterwards	formerly	next	thereafter
at last	immediately	now	until
at length	in the meantime	presently	when
at that time	in the past	shortly	while
before	lately	simultaneously	

To Indicate That One Idea Is Similar to Another (Comparison):

also	in the same way	likewise	similarly
in the same		
manner		

To Indicate That One Idea Conflicts with or Contradicts Another (Contrast):

but	in contrast	on the con-	regardless
even so	instead	trary	still
for all that	nevertheless	on the other	yet
however	nonetheless	hand	

(continued)

TRANSITIONAL EXPRESSIONS *(continued)*

To Indicate That You Are Summarizing or Concluding:

all in all	in short	to conclude	to sum up
in brief	in summary	to summarize	therefore
in conclusion			

To Indicate How Things Are Related Physically in Space:

above	farther on	there	to the right
below	here	to the east	to the south
beyond	nearby	to the left	to the west
elsewhere	opposite	to the north	

To Indicate That One Idea or Event Is Caused by Another:

accordingly	consequently	so	to this end
as a result	hence	therefore	

8b
¶ coh

A word of caution is in order. Once you get accustomed to using transitional expressions, you may experience a common reaction: overuse. You may find yourself starting nearly every sentence with a transitional expression, to the point that your writing becomes so clogged with these expressions that they hinder reading instead of helping it. Use transitional expressions when they are needed to indicate relations between ideas, events, or objects in your writing, *but do not overuse them.* For a discussion of another way to indicate relationships between ideas, see 11 on subordination and coordination.

8b   Repeating key words and phrases

Another way to achieve coherence in a paragraph is through the repetition of key words and phrases. Notice how the italicized words in the following paragraph serve to repeat the main subject of the paragraph and remind the reader of it.

> My Lands' End *briefcase* is a marvelously well designed contraption. It is first of all a *satchel* for carrying primarily papers but also books, clipboards, tablets, and the like. In addition, this *briefcase* includes numerous pockets just right for other items. I keep

Advise students that repetition can be either effective or awkward, depending on whether it is rhythmically reinforcing or merely wordy. Repetitious use of words such as *very* and *I* might cause readers to blink. Nevertheless, skillful handling of repeated phrases often occurs in great poetry and prose. Among the most famous examples is Lincoln's "Of the people, by the people, for the people." Invite students to recall other examples.

8c
¶ coh

my computer disks in the outer pocket of the *bag,* sealed shut by Velcro. Inside, three pockets carry my eyeglasses, my business cards, and my appointment book. And the *briefcase* also includes a series of tubelike pockets where I keep my supply of pens and pencils. There is even a strap with a clip on the end to which I attach my Swiss army knife. A Lands' End *briefcase* is perfectly designed for today's student.

Notice that the key word *briefcase* is repeated several times—but not so often as to seem repetitious. Occasionally, other words such as *satchel* and *bag* stand in for *briefcase* to prevent overuse.

COLLABORATIVE ACTIVITY

If you have students meet in peer editing groups, have them comment on the "fulfillment of expectations" factor in one another's drafts. Besides discussing effective transitions and repetitions, they might suggest ways of overcoming apparent inconsistencies in their essays' overall development.

8c Fulfilling expectations

Sometimes without even knowing it, writers create expectations in their readers. For example, a writer might say that there are three reasons why tuition should not be raised. Such a statement creates the expectation that what will come next is three reasons. If, through oversight, the writer gives two reasons and then moves on to another point, the reader will feel frustrated and confused.

Sometimes the expectation created is more subtle than saying there are three reasons. Look at the following paragraph.

There are good arguments on both sides of the controversy surrounding capital punishment. Today a number of states have reinstated capital punishment for certain offenses. In these states, the number of persons being executed increases each year.

Notice that the first sentence subtly creates an expectation. When the writer says that good arguments exist on both sides, the reader expects a summary of those arguments. Instead, this writer goes on to discuss states that have reinstated capital punishment, thus failing to fulfill the expectation created in the first sentence.

Failing to meet expectations that you have created in your writing leaves the reader feeling confused—as if he or she has missed something or has skipped a section. This confusion on the part of the reader is, of course, something you want to avoid, so make sure that whenever you create an expectation, you fulfill it.

9   AVOIDING UNNECESSARY SHIFTS

Readers expect consistency. If you start writing in one way and shift to another without any apparent reason, your reader may be confused. In this chapter we will discuss five kinds of shifts that can cause trouble in your writing.

9a   Avoiding shifts in tense

In the original version of the following paragraph, verb tense was used inconsistently.

> When I entered the classroom, I noticed immediately that something was wrong. One student is standing in the front of the room looking very disturbed, and everyone else is crowded against the back wall. Several chairs are turned over, and no one is saying anything. Then I notice that the student in the front of the room is pointing a large, shiny pistol at everyone else. As I walk in, he runs past me, out of the room, and down the hall. Everyone breathed deeply and started talking at once. I finally figured out that the student with the gun had robbed everyone else and then fled.

The problem with the original paragraph was that the tenses were not used consistently. It is, of course, correct to use the past tense to tell about events that occurred in the past, as this paragraph did in the first sentence (*entered, noticed*). It is also correct to use the present tense to tell about events that happened in the past, as this writer does in the second, third, fourth, and fifth sentences (*is standing, is crowded, are turned, is saying, notice, is pointing, walk, runs*). This use of the present tense is a little less common but is correct and is especially effective when the writer wants to give a sense of immediacy to his or her writing, as is the

The problem of unnecessary shifts at the paragraph level is closely related to the problem of parallelism in sentences. Because students sometimes lack the knowledge of syntax terms needed to discuss parallelism, you might consider assigning 19 and 20 as concurrent background reading for this chapter.

RESOURCES
Unnecessary Shifts

Walker, Robert L. "The Common Writer: A Case for Parallel Structure." *College Composition and Communication* 21 (1970): 373–79.

ACTIVITY

Distribute a copy of a paragraph from a professional writer's essay that exhibits well-coordinated structure. Have students focus on its construction, noting consistencies in tense, person, and number where appropriate. Essays by Joan Didion, John McPhee, and E. B. White usually offer excellent paragraph models, though examples could come from anywhere. As an alternative, have students look for good examples of parallelism in any assigned essay from a college reader.

9a
shift

case in this paragraph. However, notice that in the final two sentences, the writer once again shifted back into the past tense (*breathed, started, figured, had robbed*). Either tense would be fine in this paragraph, but it is problematic that the writer shifted from past to present and back to past *for no reason*. The writer revised the paragraph so that it is entirely in the present tense.

Occasionally, there is a reason for shifting tenses within a sentence, and in these cases it is perfectly correct.

> When I was young, I was afraid of the ocean, but now I love to swim in the waves.

Note in this sentence that the verb tense changes from the past tense (*was*) to present tense (*love*), but it changes for a good reason: to indicate that the first part of the sentence discusses the writer's childhood and the second part talks about the present. This kind of deliberate shift to indicate a shift in the time being discussed by the writer is not only correct but also effective.

9b   Avoiding shifts in person and number

The following paragraph has coherence problems that stem from inconsistencies in person and number. Read the paragraph, and see if you can identify the problems.

Version 1

> If someone takes yoga classes, they do not have to do any meditation. They can just do the various positions, which are good for your posture and for reducing tension. If one practices the various positions about three times a week, you will experience considerable progress within six months. One will get out of yoga as much as he puts in.

The following version of the same paragraph has had all the shifts in person and number corrected. Compare it with the preceding example so that you understand this type of problem with coherence.

Version 2

> If you take yoga classes, you do not have to do any meditation. You can just do the various positions, which are good for your

posture and for reducing tension. If you practice the various positions about three times a week, you will experience considerable
progress within six months. You will get out of yoga as much as
you put in.

A different version of the paragraph, just as correct, appears
next. Notice the difference in the pronouns used throughout.

VERSION 3

If people take yoga classes, they do not have to do any medi-
tation. They can just do the various positions, which are good for
their posture and for reducing their tension. If they practice the
various positions about three times a week, they will experience
considerable progress within six months. They will get out of yoga
as much as they put in.

You can see from these three versions of the same paragraph
that number and person have to do with pronouns. In English we
have three different *persons* (first, second, and third) and two
numbers (singular and plural) expressed through pronouns, as
the chart demonstrates (see also 19b).

Version 1 of the paragraph is incoherent because the writer
couldn't make up his or her mind about which person or number to use. The paragraph starts with third-person singular
(*someone*), then shifts to third-person plural (*they*), and then

9b
shift

NUMBER AND PERSON OF PERSONAL PRONOUNS

Person	Number	
	Singular	Plural
First person (the person or persons speaking)	*I, me, my, mine*	*we, us, our ours*
Second person (the person or persons spoken to)	*you, your, yours*	*you, your, yours*
Third person (the person or persons spoken about)	*he, she, it, one* *him, her* *his, her, hers, its*	*they* *them* *their or theirs*

shifts to second person (*you*). Next the third-person singular appears again (*one*), followed by second person (*you*). Finally, in the last sentence, the writer switches back to third-person singular (*one* and *he*).

Inconsistency in person or number makes writing confusing to the reader. In fact, the writer could have used just about any *one* of the persons and numbers, as long as he or she used it consistently.

Notice that version 2, a perfectly fine paragraph, is written consistently in second person. The pronoun *you* is used throughout. You may have been cautioned in the past never to use the pronoun *you* in your writing. Teachers sometimes give this advice because using the pronoun *you* is less formal (more familiar) than using third person; however, the very fact that *you* is more personal can make it the most powerful person to use.

A second reason some teachers warn against the use of *you* may be that it is the most frequent source of inconsistency of person and number. It seems almost natural to start with "If a student wants to get an A in biology," and then to continue, "you must be prepared to memorize a lot of terms." Because this shift occurs so easily, you must guard against it. Whenever you use the pronoun *you,* always make sure that you have not switched from some other person into the second.

Version 3, which is also a well-written paragraph, makes use of the third-person plural point of view (*people, they,* and *their*). Whichever point of view seems most effective in a given writing situation is fine, as long as you are consistent in your use of it.

Even the principle of consistency has some room for flexibility. The following sentence is perfectly correct, even though it shifts its point of view.

> Although many students put off their English courses as long as they can, you should probably take an English course in your first semester.

This sentence begins in the third-person plural (*students, they*). In the second half, however, it shifts to second person (*you*). In

this case, the shift is not a mistake because it represents a genuine shift in whom the writer is speaking about. In the first half of the sentence, the writer is speaking about students in general and so uses the third person; in the second half, the writer addresses the reader directly and so, correctly, shifts to the second-person pronoun, *you*. (For further discussion, see 23a.)

9c Avoiding shifts in mood

Three moods are possible for verbs in English (see 26i):

1. The **indicative mood**—the most common—is used to express facts and opinions.
2. The **imperative mood** is used to express commands or advice.
3. The **subjunctive mood**—fairly rare—is used to express wishes, proposals, or conditions that do not exist.

Notice the mood shift in the following example.

1. Use plenty of concrete examples in your writing, and ~~you should~~ focus on one subject.

   The first half of this sentence is in the imperative mood—it gives a command—and the second half was in the indicative. Either mood would work in this sentence, but shifting from one to the other is confusing for the reader. The correction makes the mood consistent.

In sentence 2, the shift is from subjunctive to indicative.

2. I wish that my job were less stressful and that I <u>were</u> ~~was~~ promoted to manager.

   The first part of sentence 2 is in the subjunctive mood because it expresses a wish. The second half of the sentence, which adds a second wish, was erroneously written in the indicative mood.

Once you start with one mood, do not shift to a different mood for no apparent reason.

9d **Avoiding shifts in voice**

Two voices are possible for verbs in English (see 26g):

1. In the **active voice,** the subject is the person or thing performing the action.
2. In the **passive voice,** the subject is the person or thing receiving the action.

In the following example, the writer shifts from active to passive voice.

My college roommate called me, and ~~I was asked~~ *she asked me* for a donation to the alumni fund.

This sentence begins with a clause in active voice—the subject *roommate* performs the action of calling—but the second half is a clause in passive voice—the subject *I* does not do the asking but is the receiver of the action of asking.

Passive voice is generally seen as less direct and less clear than active voice; it is especially weak when it is the result of a shift like the one in the sample sentence. If you begin a sentence in one voice, do not shift into the other.

9e **Avoiding shifts between direct and indirect quotation**

In English, there are two ways to report someone's words:

Direct quotation: Juanita said, "I am going back to college."

Indirect quotation: Juanita said that she is going back to college.

In direct quotation, the writer reports the exact words of the speaker and places them in quotation marks. In indirect quotation, the writer accurately reports what a person says but not in the exact words the person used.

1. **INCORRECT:** Mr. Hernandez said that `he is firing Jackie` *(Indirect quotation)*

because she did not come to work yesterday

and `she did not call to tell me she was sick.` *(Direct quotation)*

Indirect quotation

2. **CORRECT:**   Mr. Hernandez said that he is firing Jackie

because she did not come to work yesterday

and she did not call to tell him she was sick.

Direct quotation

3. **CORRECT:**   Mr. Hernandez said, "I am firing Jackie

because she did not come to work yesterday

and she did not call to tell me she was sick."

In sentence 1, the writer mixes indirect quotation with direct quotation, and the result is a confusing sentence. In sentence 2, the writer has corrected the problem by making both parts of the sentence indirect quotations. In sentence 3, he or she has corrected the problem by making both parts direct quotations.

Shifting arbitrarily between direct and indirect quotation produces confusing sentences.

10 SPECIAL PARAGRAPHS

Normal body paragraphs, the most common paragraphs in most writing, are discussed in 7 and 8. In this chapter we consider several less common but important types of paragraphs: opening paragraphs, closing paragraphs, transitional paragraphs, and paragraphs used in dialogue.

This chapter explores strategies for writing paragraphs that occupy key positions within essays. Encourage your students to learn how opening, closing, and transitional paragraphs can acquire more than routine formal importance.

10a Opening paragraphs

First impressions count. Opening paragraphs are where you make your first impression in writing, so they count a lot. They are worth some extra time and attention.

First, a word or two about writing an opening paragraph.

RESOURCES
Special Paragraphs

Coe, Rich M. *Toward a Grammar of Passages.* Carbondale: Southern Illinois UP, 1988.

Crew, Louie. "Rhetorical Beginnings: Professional and Amateur." *College Composition and Communication* 38 (1987): 346–50.

Markels, Robin E. *A New Perspective on Cohesion in Expository Paragraphs.* Carbondale: Southern Illinois UP, 1984.

10a
¶

Many writers find opening paragraphs the hardest part of writing. If you are in this group, you might consider one of two strategies:

- *Postpone writing the opening.* Get started on the body of the essay, and wait to write the introduction later, perhaps after you've completed the entire first draft. The problem with this strategy is that sometimes it is difficult to write anything else until you have set the tone and defined the topic in the introduction. The benefit, however, is that this strategy allows you to write more freely and to discover your thesis as you write.
- *Write an extremely tentative opening paragraph.* Get something down, but don't labor over it. Assume that whatever you write will be revised heavily, perhaps even discarded, later on. This attitude may allow you to get something on the page without slowing you down for hours while you struggle for the perfect opening.

An effective opening paragraph accomplishes one or more of the following three goals:

- Getting the reader's attention
- Letting the reader know the point of the writing
- Providing background information or context to help the reader get into the essay itself

Sometimes one of these goals is more important; sometimes, another is. If your reader has no particular reason for wanting to read what you have written, it will be important to capture his or her attention. For example, a letter to potential customers asking them to sign up for the lawn care service you are starting will first need to capture their attention—to get them interested enough to read the rest of the letter. In cases like this, you will need to make your opening paragraph as interesting as possible.

If, on the other hand, the reader is already motivated to read what you've written, that goal becomes less important. Perhaps straightforwardness and clarity will become more important than interest. For example, if you are writing to someone who has applied for a job at your business and you want him or her to come in for an interview, you probably don't need to capture his or her attention. You can assume that the reader is already motivated to read the letter.

The most common pattern for opening paragraphs is to start with the general and move to a specific thesis:

> Traditionally in India sacred knowledge is passed on by a spiritual leader who is a teacher, guide, and example. This is the Guru, meaning one who removes the darkness of ignorance, replacing it with the light of intelligence. The Guru guides the student on the spiritual path. He has wisdom, benevolence, tolerance, and the energy and ability to help others. His knowledge is authoritative. In this century such a teacher is found in Yogacharya B. K. S. Iyengar. He is the world's foremost exponent of Yoga.
>
> —Mira Silva and Shyam Mehta, *Yoga the Iyengar Way*

Notice that the paragraph starts with a general statement about sacred knowledge in India, moves through a discussion of the guru, and ends with the thesis that B. K. S. Iyengar is the world's foremost exponent of yoga. This paragraph focuses on two of the three goals listed: it gives background information about the role of the guru in Indian society, and it announces the thesis of this piece of writing—that Iyengar is the foremost guru of yoga in the world today.

Perhaps because this pattern is the most common for opening paragraphs, it is also the most predictable and the least creative. Other patterns allow you to capture the reader's attention more effectively. If this is a more important goal, you might try one of the techniques in the chart on page 106. Whatever technique you use for writing an opening paragraph, consider your audience and purpose, and try to achieve the most effective balance between being interesting and stating the point clearly.

ACTIVITY

If you are using a college reader in your course, have students examine three or four opening paragraphs of essays and discuss their effectiveness. Ask them to identify whatever clues those openings provide about the essays' topics or overall purposes. The same paragraphs might also serve as strategy models for students as they experiment with leads for a forthcoming essay assignment.

10a
¶

10a
¶

TECHNIQUES FOR OPENING PARAGRAPHS

Technique	Example
Opening with a question	Do you know how much of each dollar that you donate to charity pays the salaries of administrators?
Opening with a quotation	"No new taxes," promised George Bush.
Opening with a provocative statement	The new law requiring motor-cyclists to wear helmets violates the basic principles of democracy.
Opening with a striking image or description	A shiny bright green frog stared up at me from the bathroom floor.
Opening with humor	It occurred to me . . . in the course of watching first the California primary and then the Democratic and Republican national conventions, that it had not been by accident that the people with whom I had preferred to spend time in high school had, on the whole, hung out in gas stations. [Joan Didion, "Insider Baseball"]
Opening with a startling fact	At least 60 million female adults and children in Asia are missing and feared dead. [Jonathan Power]

Some techniques for opening paragraphs are best avoided. Among common mistakes are those listed in the following chart.

THINGS TO AVOID IN OPENING PARAGRAPHS

- Avoid a discussion that is so general and abstract that it appears to be wasting time.
- Avoid saying, "The purpose of this paper is . . ."

(continued)

THINGS TO AVOID IN OPENING PARAGRAPHS (*continued*)

- Avoid saying, "In this paper I will prove . . ."
- Avoid saying, "———— means different things to different people . . ."
- Avoid saying, "Everyone is entitled to an opinion, but . . ."
- Avoid saying, "In this modern world of today . . ."
- Avoid saying, "According to Webster, . . ."
- Avoid apologizing with phrases such as "I really don't know much about this topic" or "I'm not an expert, but . . ."
- Avoid repeating the topic or question you may have been given by your instructor.
- Avoid restating your title, if you have one.

10b
¶

10b Closing paragraphs

The point of a concluding paragraph is to let the reader know that the paper is ending and to do so with a little flair. To restate the thesis is one effective but somewhat unimaginative technique. If you use this technique, avoid using the same wording you used in the opening paragraph.

Other, more creative closing techniques include emphasizing the action you want the reader to take if he or she agrees with your thesis, referring to an image or event that was mentioned at the beginning of the paper, and using a question or quotation.

Here is an example of emphasizing the action you want the reader to take:

> Since I possess both the experience you are looking for and the necessary educational background for the position you have

TECHNIQUES FOR CLOSING PARAGRAPHS

- Restate the thesis of the paper.
- Emphasize the action you want the reader to take.
- Refer to an image or event from the opening of the writing.
- Use a question or quotation.

ACTIVITY

If you use a college reader, have the class examine the closing paragraphs of several anthologized essays. Ask students to discuss the functional strategies of the closings they have read.

10c
¶

advertised, I hope it will be possible for me to come in for an interview in the next few weeks.

Referring to an image or event from the opening can also be effective. For example, in the opening paragraph of an essay on population congestion, Tim Baker describes the beauty of flying over the San Bernardino Mountains and approaching Los Angeles. His description continues as the plane dips into the clouds and descends to the airport. The thick smog at ground level completely obscures his view of the mountains, which rise to nine thousand feet just fifteen miles away. His essay includes much detail about congestion and pollution in Los Angeles. Then he examines the situation in Baltimore, where his column appears. Route 95 is the major interstate highway passing through Baltimore and leading to Washington but not, at least in any literal sense, to Los Angeles. His essay concludes by tying his conclusion back to his original description of Los Angeles.

But the Baltimore-Washington corridor is filling up. Washington and its Maryland suburbs already have the third-worst traffic congestion in the country. If you don't believe me, drive down Route 95 one morning. It's headed straight toward Los Angeles.

A nice sense of completion can be achieved by ending with a question or a quotation. In an essay on the pleasures of visiting

---

THINGS TO AVOID IN CLOSING PARAGRAPHS

- Avoid going on too long. One sentence is sometimes just right for a concluding paragraph.
- Avoid introducing ideas that were not discussed earlier, even if they support your thesis. The conclusion is not the place to bring up new ideas.
- Avoid apologizing. Don't say, "Although I am no expert" or "This may not be convincing, but . . ."
- Avoid overstating your case.
- Avoid using *In conclusion* or *In summary.* These are a little too obvious and heavy-handed. It should be clear from what you say that you are concluding or summarizing.

off-the-beaten-track sights for tourists (such as a forty-foot fiber-
glass pheasant in South Dakota, the Cardiff Giant in New York,
and the Jimmie Rodgers Museum in Mississippi), Mary Hood
explains the tourist's pleasure at stopping to see things and closes
her essay with a question and answer that she borrows from the
jazz musician Louis Armstrong, also known as Satchmo.

10c
¶

> Why stop? As Satchmo answered, when asked to define jazz,
> if you've gotta ask, you're never gonna know.
>
> —Mary Hood, "Why Stop?"

10c Transitional paragraphs

At the end of one major section of your writing, before you start
the next section, you may want to use a short transitional paragraph to alert the reader to the shift that is about to occur and
to make sure that he or she has no trouble following where you
are going.

In *Silent Spring,* Rachel Carson discusses the increasing use
of pesticides in the United States.

> Yet new and more deadly chemicals are added to the list each
> year and new uses are devised so that contact with these materials
> has become practically worldwide. The production of synthetic
> pesticides in the United States soared from 124,259,000 pounds
> in 1947 to 637,666,000 in 1960—more than a fivefold increase.
> The wholesale value of these products was well over a quarter of a
> billion dollars. But in the plans and hopes of the industry this
> enormous production is only a beginning.
>
> A Who's Who of pesticides is therefore of concern to us all.
> If we are going to live so intimately with these chemicals—eating
> and drinking them, taking them into the very marrow of our
> bones—we had better know something about their nature and
> their power.
>
> —Rachel Carson, *Silent Spring*

The second paragraph is a short transition signaling that Carson
has finished discussing the increasing quantity of pesticides in
use and that she is now going to introduce some specific chemicals that are harmful.

One warning about transitional paragraphs: they should be used sparingly—only when such an obvious signal to the reader seems really necessary.

10d You might point out that dialogue paragraphing works much like camera angles in motion pictures, where close shots alternate between faces as the actors speak. Just as it is rare to see two talking heads in a closeup, so it is rare in print to find two voices quoted within the same paragraph.

COLLABORATIVE ACTIVITY

Have pairs of students read each other's drafts, commenting on the effectiveness of openings, closings, and transitions.

10d **Paragraphs that indicate dialogue**

Although dialogue is used most frequently in fiction, it can also add life to many kinds of nonfiction writing, including college essays. When representing dialogue or conversation among two or more people, merely start a new paragraph each time a new speaker speaks, as in the following excerpt from Ralph Ellison's novel *Invisible Man*.

> "Who you looking for down here?"
> "I'm looking for the man in charge," I called, straining to locate the voice.
> "You talkin' to him. What you want?"
> The man who moved out of the shadow and looked at me was small, wiry and very natty in his dirty overalls.

Note that Ellison starts a new paragraph each time there is a new speaker. In addition, he starts a new paragraph after the final line of dialogue when the voice of the novel's narrator begins again.

DRAFTING AND REVISING: EFFECTIVE SENTENCES

11

Some students may be better prepared than others to deal with the formal analysis of sentence structure. Even those who have a good high school background in grammar may wonder why knowing about such principles as subordination and coordination is important to them. You might begin by pointing out that while formal grammar is often unconsciously applied in composition, understanding the fundamental terms of grammar is an indispensable part of editing and proofreading one's own work. Effective prose style and accurate punctuation also depend on a strong fundamental grasp of sentence-level grammar. Therefore, knowing the principles discussed in Part III of this book can help students gain confidence in their own editing skills and become more accomplished writers.

RESOURCES
Subordination and Coordination

Daiker, Donald A., et al. "Sentence-Combining and Syntactic Maturity in Freshman English." *College Composition and Communication* 29 (1978): 36–41.

Faigley, Lester. "Names in Search of a Concept: Maturity, Fluency, Complexity, and Growth in Written Syntax." *College Composition and Communication* 31 (1980): 291–300.

11 USING SUBORDINATION AND COORDINATION

In this chapter we will consider two important ways to relate ideas: coordination and subordination. These techniques are often used to write sentences of greater complexity than simple sentences, sentences that communicate subtle relationships between ideas.

A detailed discussion of punctuation with coordination and subordination can be found in 32 and 33.

Coordination is used to link ideas that are of *equal importance*. These ideas may be independent clauses, phrases, or just single nouns.

Independent clause	Independent clause

1. My father lives in Tampa, and my mother has a condo in Miami.

Noun phrase	Noun phrase

2. The car with red flames on the hood and the blue station wagon with a baby seat in the back are both owned by the same man.

Noun	Noun

3. Lynn or Susan will give me a ride to work.

Subordination is used to link ideas that are of *unequal importance*. The less important idea is subordinated to the main idea.

Main idea	Subordinate idea

4. Give your form to the woman who is sitting at the information desk.

Main idea	Subordinate idea

5. My knees always ache when it rains.

Subordinate idea	Main idea

6. Thumbing through the book, Mr. Song found a five-dollar bill.

A simple sentence contains one independent clause.

Independent clause

7. I like fishing.

When coordination is used to join two *independent clauses,* the result is a **compound sentence.**

Independent clause   Independent clause

8. I like fishing, but I hate hunting.

When subordination is used to join an *independent clause* and a *dependent clause,* the result is a **complex sentence.**

Independent clause   Dependent clause

9. I like fishing when the weather is good.

Noguchi, Rei R. *Grammar and the Teaching of Writing: Limits and Possibilities.* Urbana: NCTE, 1991.

O'Hare, Frank. *Sentence-Combining: Improving Student Writing Without Formal Grammar Instruction.* Urbana: NCTE, 1973.

11a
coord

11a Coordinating equal ideas

When and how to coordinate

A string of short simple sentences is usually not very effective writing:

> Computers make writing easier. They are more expensive than typewriters. They help most people write better. They allow writers to experiment with their writing in a playful way. They make revision much easier.

The first problem with this passage is that it seems choppy and immature. A second problem is that the relationship between sentences is not clear. For example, the relationship between the first sentence and the second one is puzzling. Notice that both of these problems are cleared up in the following revised version, in which some of the simple sentences have been combined using coordination.

> Computers make writing easier, but they are more expensive than typewriters. They help most people write better because they allow them to experiment with their writing in a playful way and to revise more easily.

ACTIVITY

Have students locate examples of coordination in an assigned essay from a college reader. Alternatively, put on the board quoted passages from various authors to illustrate the concept. Hemingway and Gertrude Stein offer influential models of rhythmic coordination, as does the King James Bible (e.g., "One generation passeth away, and another generation cometh: but the earth abideth for ever"—Ecclesiastes 1.4). Authors known for complex uses of subordination include William Faulkner, Annie Dillard, and Henry David Thoreau (e.g., "I went to the woods because I wished to live deliberately, to front only the essential facts of life, and see if I could learn what it had to teach, and not, when I came to die, discover that I had not lived"—*Walden* [1854]).

The immature style of the first version is much improved, and the relationship between the separate sentences makes the passage easier to understand. Notice that the word *but* that was used to join the first and second sentences makes it clear that the second thought is contradictory in some way to the first one.

There are three rules to keep in mind regarding coordination:

1. Coordinate only ideas that are logically equivalent.
2. Use conjunctions that reflect the logical relationship between the ideas.
3. Avoid excessive coordination.

Logical equivalence. Notice that there is something odd about the following sentences.

1. The movie we saw was offensive, and it was filmed in California.

   Here the two ideas—that the movie was offensive and that it was filmed in California—are represented by independent clauses, but the statements are from very different logical categories: that the movie was offensive is a judgment about its content; that it was filmed in California is a fact about its production. These two categories are logically so different that coordination is problematic.

2. The movie we saw was offensive, and it contained crude language.

   The problem in sentence 2 is a little different. Both ideas are judgments about the content of the movie, but the first is a much broader idea than the second. In fact, the second idea is closer to an illustration of the first and is, therefore, not logically equivalent.

Revise sentences like 1 and 2 so that the idea you want to emphasize becomes clear and the other idea is either eliminated or expressed in a separate sentence.

Using conjunctions that indicate the relationship. The following sentences indicate another problem that can arise in coordination.

3. Maxine hasn't read the book, ^but^ and she saw the movie.

   The problem here is that the conjunction *and* is normally used to join two ideas that are equal *and have compatible meanings*. In this

FOR DISCUSSION

Another way of explaining this point is to say that coordinated ideas should be of the same weight, focus, or category. Draw attention to additional examples in an assigned essay from a college reader or from a student paper.

Advise students to consult 33 for details about how punctuation is used with conjunctions.

case, the meanings are not compatible because they make opposite assertions: she has *not* read the book; she *has* seen the movie. Because one assertion is positive and the other is negative, the two are not compatible and should not be joined by *and*. When *and* is replaced by *but*, the problem is eliminated because *but* is used to join ideas that are being contrasted.

4. It was raining this morning, ~~but~~ ^{so} we canceled the softball game.

This time the writer has used the conjunction *but*, which expresses contrast, to join two ideas that are not really being contrasted. The more logical relationship between the rain and the cancellation of the softball game is cause and effect. When *but* is replaced by *so*, the conjunction that indicates cause and effect, the sentence sounds fine.

The chart summarizes the logical relationship indicated by each of the coordinate conjunctions.

11a
coord

RELATIONSHIP INDICATED BY COORDINATE CONJUNCTIONS	
Conjunction	**Relationship**
and	Two ideas are equivalent and compatible.
but	Two ideas are contrasted; they disagree with or contradict each other.
or	Two ideas are alternatives.
for	The second idea causes the first.
so	The second idea is a result of the first.
yet	Two ideas are contrasted; they disagree with or contradict each other.
nor	Two ideas are negative.

Avoid excessive coordination. The following paragraph illustrates another possible problem with coordination.

> Marcy intended to graduate in four years, but she soon discovered that this was not going to be possible. In her first semester she had to drop one course, and she took an incomplete in another, and the next year she registered for only three courses,

11b
sub

and she worked thirty hours per week, and then she learned that the anatomy course she needed would not be offered in the spring, and she had to take another incomplete in statistics, and now she will be lucky if she graduates in six years.

Even though the coordination in this paragraph always involves ideas that are logically equivalent and the conjunctions used are consistently logical, there is still something wrong: there is just too much coordination. The human mind seems to have trouble processing this many coordinated ideas in a short piece of writing. The following revision eliminates some of the coordination and thereby makes the passage more readable and effective.

Although
Marcy intended to graduate in four years, ~~but~~ she soon discovered that this was not going to be possible. In her first
take
semester she had to drop one course, and she took an incomplete in another, ~~and~~ the next year she registered for only three courses, and she worked thirty hours per week, ~~and~~ then she learned that the anatomy course she needed would not be offered in the spring, and she had to take another incomplete in statistics, ~~and~~ now she will be lucky if she graduates in six years.

Regardless of how well it's handled, too much coordination makes a passage difficult to read and therefore less effective.

Punctuation with compound sentences is discussed in 33.

Two serious grammatical problems sometimes occur when writers form compound sentences: comma splices and run-on sentences. See 32 for further discussion of these problems.

11b **Subordinating less important ideas**

If you are not familiar with the term *subordinate clause,* you may want to refer to 20k, where it is defined and discussed.

When and how to subordinate

There are four rules to remember about subordination:

1. Use subordination to emphasize the main idea.
2. Never subordinate the main idea.
3. Use conjunctions that express your intended meaning.
4. Avoid excessive subordination.

Emphasize the main idea. Look at the following examples.

, *who is bald,*
1. Tom is selfish. and bald.

   The main idea this writer wanted to express was that Tom is selfish, so she revised the sentence to place that idea in the main clause and to place the fact that he is bald in a subordinate clause.

Because
2. Michael was cheating, and we dropped him from the team.

   This writer wanted to emphasize the team's response, its dropping of Michael from the team, so he left that idea as the main clause and placed the less important idea, that Michael cheated, in a subordinate clause.

Subordination is useful, then, because it allows the writer to avoid a series of short simple sentences, to indicate which are main ideas and which are subordinate, and, as we shall see in a moment, to indicate the relationship between main ideas and subordinate ones.

Avoid subordinating main ideas. Something about the following sentence seems a little odd.

3. **INCORRECT:** My dog, which was hit by a car last night, was a dachshund.

   It seems likely that the writer intended the main idea to be that the dog was hit by a car, but this idea is buried in a subordinate clause. When revised, the oddness disappears:

4. **CORRECT:** My dog, which was a dachshund, was hit by a car last night.

ACTIVITY

Students can practice making different parts of a sentence "the most important" by rearranging word order. Put on the board the sentence "My car was stolen by somebody on Friday" and rearrange it in at least three ways to emphasize the time, the act, and the car. Remind students that determining which idea is most important often depends on the context in which the sentence is used.

11b
sub

11b
sub

Use conjunctions that express your meaning. The following sentences required revision because of another form of faulty subordination.

When
5. ~~Because~~ Mark took his eyes off the road, a young child ran in front of him.
Because
6. ~~Although~~ Betsy missed eighteen questions out of twenty on the quiz, she got an F.

In each sentence, the wrong subordinating conjunction made the meaning of the sentence confusing. A large number of subordinating conjunctions exist in English, each with a slightly different meaning from the others. It is important to select the subordinating conjunction that expresses exactly the meaning you intend. The chart presents common subordinating conjunctions and their meanings.

Students needn't memorize this list if they are taught to recognize subordinating conjunctions by function. Help them to do that by pointing out that these conjunctions answer adverbial questions ("When?" "How?" and "Why?") about actions in the main clause. For example, in the sentence "Because we left at intermission, we missed the third act," the conjunction *Because* conveys *why* the act was missed.

SUBORDINATING CONJUNCTIONS

Conjunction	Meaning
after	Following in place or time
although	Regardless of the fact that
as	Because, for the reason that
as if	In the same way that it would be if
as long as	For the period of time during which
as soon as	At the time when
as though	In the manner as if
because	For the reason that, as a result of the fact that
before	In advance of the time when
even if	Regardless of the possibility that
even though	Regardless of the fact that
how	By what means, in what manner
if	In the event that
if only	Only in the event that

(continued)

SUBORDINATING CONJUNCTIONS *(continued)*

Conjunction	Meaning
in case	Because of the unlikely event that
in order that	To make possible that
insofar as	To the extent that
in that	Inasmuch as
lest	So as to prevent the possibility that
no matter how	Regardless of the manner in which
now that	At this time in consequence of the fact that
once	As soon as
provided (that)	On the condition that
since	From the time when, as a result of the fact that
so that	In order that
supposing (that)	In the unlikely case that
than	When compared to
that	(Used to introduce a subordinate clause that states a fact, wish, consequence, or reason)
though	Despite the fact that, conceding the fact that
till	Up to the time that
unless	Except under the conditions that
until	Up to the time that
when	At the time(s) that
whenever	At whatever time that
where	At or in the place that
whereas	It being the fact that
wherever	In or to whatever place
whether	Should it be the case that
while	As long as, during the time that
why	For what purpose, for what reason

11b
sub

Note: Many of these words can also be used as prepositions, sometimes with slightly different meanings.

The phrase *in which* is one of the most frequent sources of errors in subordination. Writers frequently use *in which* when some other construction is called for.

7. This is a trail in *by* which you can get to the campsite.

A trail is not something *in which* you can get somewhere.

8. I solved the problem in~~in~~ *with* which our company had struggled with for

   six months.

   A problem is not something *in which* a company can struggle.

Don't use *in which* unless the noun it modifies is really something that logically one can be *in*. In sentence 9, *in which* works fine. Compare it with sentences 7 and 8.

9. The box in which we placed the puppies was not very large.

   A box is something *in which* you *can* place puppies.

One other type of error involving *in which* is illustrated in sentence 10.

10. We must accept the society in which we live ~~in~~.

    The second *in* is redundant.

Avoid excessive subordination. Subordination can be overused, as the following example illustrates.

INCORRECT: My cat, whose name is Jimmy and who was sleeping on the front porch, was dive-bombed by a mockingbird that had a nest in a large holly tree that was planted by my ex-husband when he first came back from the army.

Although there is no official limit to how much subordination is acceptable in a sentence, when the layers of subordination make it difficult for a reader to process the information, the sentence should be revised. The following revision gets rid of the excessive subordination.

CORRECT: Sleeping on the front porch, my cat, Jimmy, was dive-bombed by a mockingbird whose nest was in a large holly tree. My ex-husband planted that tree when he first came back from the army.

Forming complex sentences

There are three types of subordinate clauses. These clauses are highlighted in the following examples.

11. The coach who is crying is from the losing team.

> In sentence 11, the subordinate clause is an adjective (or adjectival or relative) clause. An adjective clause modifies or describes a noun. In this case, the clause describes the noun *coach*. An extended discussion of adjective clauses is in 20k; punctuation with adjective clauses is discussed in 34c.

12. When she quit smoking, Maureen gained twenty pounds.

> The subordinate clause in sentence 12 is an adverb clause. Adverb clauses modify the verb, an adjective, or an adverb in a sentence. Like adverbs, they often answer the questions *why? when?* or *in what manner?* In this sentence, the adverb clause modifies the verb *gained*; it answers the question *when?* You'll find a fuller discussion of adverb clauses in 20k; punctuation with adverb clauses in discussed in 34a.

13. Whoever stole my disk is going to be surprised.

> The subordinate clause in sentence 13 is a noun clause (see 20k); it functions as a noun (see 19a) in the sentence, in this case serving as the subject (see 20b).

11c | **Forming adjective clauses**

Relative pronouns (*who, which,* and *that*)

The relative pronouns *who, whom, whose, which,* and *that* are used to begin adjective clauses. (For more discussion of relative pronouns, see 19b; for a definition of adjective clauses, see 20k.) In each of the following sentences, two independent clauses are combined to form a single sentence. One clause remains an independent clause while the other is changed into an adjective clause. If your writing has too many short, choppy sentences, you may want to try combining some of them in this way.

To combine

Independent clause		Independent clause
The woman is my daughter.	**+**	The woman is wearing a purple dress.

first convert one independent clause to an adjective clause:

11c
sub

ESL

Point out that adjective clauses, like ordinary adjectives, answer questions such as "What kind of?" or "Which one?" about a noun in the main clause.

11c
sub

ESL

Then insert it into the remaining independent clause so that it follows the noun that the relative pronoun (in this case *who*) stands for:

In adjective clauses, the relative pronoun can serve one of four different functions: subject, direct object, object of a preposition, or possessive.

Relative pronouns as subjects

1. The man is the detective. **+** The man smokes a cigar. **=**
The man who smokes a cigar is the detective.

In example 1, the relative pronoun *who* functions as the subject of the adjective clause when the two sentences are combined. In this case, the subjects of the two sentences that are being combined are the same: *man*. (For a discussion of when to use *who* and *whom*, see 24g.)

The following example illustrates a different situation.

2. Christopher went to Columbia University. **+**
Columbia University is in New York. **=**
Christopher went to Columbia University, which is in New York.

Although in this case the subjects of the two independent clauses, *Christopher* and *Columbia University,* are different, you can use a relative pronoun to introduce the adjective clause when the relative pronoun immediately follows the noun it is standing for.

Relative pronouns as direct objects

Example 3 illustrates how a relative pronoun can be used as the direct object (see 20d) in an adjective clause.

3. The butterfly pin is pretty. **+**
Margot will wear the pin to the barbecue. **=**
The butterfly pin that Margot will wear to the barbecue is pretty.

In example 3, the relative pronoun (*that*) replaces the direct object (*pin*) in the sentence *Margot will wear the pin to the barbecue*. In this case, the relative pronoun is functioning as an object pronoun.

Relative pronouns as objects of prepositions

Example 4 illustrates the use of a relative pronoun as the object of the preposition in an adjective clause.

4. Paco was my host in Spain. **+** I received a letter from Paco. **=**
Paco, from whom I received a letter, was my host in Spain.

The relative pronoun *whom* is the object of the preposition *from*.

Relative pronouns used as possessives

Example 5 illustrates how the relative pronoun *whose* can be used as a possessive in an adjective clause.

5. The woman is taking me to court. **+** I hit the woman's car. **=**
The woman whose car I hit is taking me to court.

The relative pronoun *whose* replaces *the woman's* when the sentences are combined.

The chart below summarizes the functions of relative pronouns.

RELATIVE PRONOUNS		
Function	**Human Being**	**Thing**
Subject	*who* *that*	*which* *that*
Direct object	*whom* *that*	*which* *that*
Object of preposition	*whom*	*which*
Possessive	*whose*	*whose* *of which*

Students are sometimes confused by special situations in which the subjective pronoun *whoever* does appear legitimately after a preposition. That happens, you might point out, when an entire noun clause is acting as the object of the prepositional phrase (e.g., "Give the pencils to *whoever* needs them).

11c
sub

ESL

Omitting the relative pronoun and the verb *be* in adjective clauses

Often, omitting relative pronouns or relative pronouns and verbs in adjective clauses will make your writing more concise and idiomatic. The rules for when one can and cannot omit a relative pronoun depend on the distinction between restrictive and nonrestrictive adjective clauses. That distinction is explained in detail in 34c, but briefly put, a *restrictive clause* restricts the word it is modifying to a specific meaning and is essential to the sentence, while a *nonrestrictive clause* is not essential. While it is sometimes permissible to omit the relative pronoun and the verb *be* in restrictive adjective clauses, you can never omit a relative pronoun in a nonrestrictive clause.

If the verb in the adjective clause is followed by a participle and the clause is restrictive, the relative pronoun and the verb can be deleted, as sentences 6 and 7 demonstrate.

6. **Correct:**   The woman who is wearing a blue hat is angry.
7. **Correct:**   The woman wearing a blue hat is angry.

Note that the adjective clause *who is wearing a blue hat* is *restrictive;* it tells us which woman we are discussing.

8. **Correct:**   Stefan Martin, who is wearing a blue hat, is angry.
9. **Incorrect:**   Stefan Martin, wearing a blue hat, is angry.

The adjective clause in sentence 8, *who is wearing a blue hat,* is *nonrestrictive.* The name *Stefan Martin* has already narrowed our focus to one particular man, so the clause cannot restrict the noun any further. The relative pronoun and verb cannot be omitted in this case. They can be omitted only in *restrictive* adjective clauses.

10. **Correct:**   The woman who is in the pool is a champion swimmer.
11. **Correct:**   The woman in the pool is a champion swimmer.

When the verb in a restrictive adjective clause is followed by a prepositional phrase, you can omit the relative pronoun and verb as sentences 10 and 11 demonstrate.

You cannot *always* omit relative pronouns in restrictive adjective clauses, however, as the following sentences illustrate.

12. **CORRECT:**   The woman who bought a blue hat is angry.
13. **INCORRECT:**   The woman a blue hat is angry.

The relative pronoun and verb cannot be omitted even from a restrictive adjective clause if the verb—in this case, *bought*—does not include a form of the verb *be* in front of the action verb.

14. **CORRECT:**   The cat that was under the porch is gone now.
15. **INCORRECT:**   The cat under the porch is gone now.

Omitting the relative pronoun and verb is not permissible if the verb is *be* in the past tense.

16. **CORRECT:**   The women who are wearing campaign buttons are angry.
17. **CORRECT:**   The women wearing campaign buttons are angry.

If the verb *be* is in the present tense, however, the relative pronoun and the verb *can* be omitted.

18. **CORRECT:**   The woman who is angry is my sister.
19. **INCORRECT:**   The woman angry is my sister.

Sentences 18 and 19 show that you may not omit the relative pronoun and verb if the verb is followed by an adjective (in this case, *angry*).

20. **CORRECT:**   The woman whom I am writing to is my sister.
21. **INCORRECT:**   The woman I writing to is my sister.

Sentence 21 is incorrect because you can omit the relative pronoun and the *be* verb *only when the relative pronoun is the subject* of the adjective clause. In sentence 20 the relative pronoun *whom* is the object of the preposition *to,* not the subject.

RULES FOR OMITTING RELATIVE PRONOUNS AND VERBS IN ADJECTIVE CLAUSES

The relative pronoun and the verb *be* in an adjective clause may be omitted if the following conditions are met:
- The adjective clause is restrictive.
- The verb *be* is followed by a participle or a prepositional phrase.
- The verb *be* is in the present tense.
- The relative pronoun is the subject of the adjective clause.

11c
sub

ESL

11c
sub

ESL

Omitting the relative pronoun in adjective clauses

In the preceding section, we learned about omitting both the relative pronoun and the verb *be* in certain adjective clauses. In this section, we will discuss another option: omitting just the relative pronoun when it is not the subject of a restrictive adjective clause. The following sentences reveal the basic principle behind this option.

22. **CORRECT:** A woman whom I respect was elected president.
23. **CORRECT:** A woman I respect was elected president.

In sentence 22, the adjective clause is restrictive and the relative pronoun *whom* is the direct object in the adjective clause. In general, it is more concise and somewhat less formal to omit the relative pronoun, as in sentence 23. When the relative pronoun is *whom*, it is considerably less formal to omit it. We recommend that you do so in all but the most formal writing.

The option of omitting the relative pronoun is not always possible, however, as the following examples demonstrate.

24. **CORRECT:** Joyce Magnatto, whom I respect, was elected president.
25. **INCORRECT:** Joyce Magnatto, I respect, was elected president.

The adjective clause in sentence 24, *whom I respect,* is nonrestrictive. Sentence 25 is incorrect because the relative pronoun should be included in *nonrestrictive* adjective clauses.

26. **CORRECT:** The woman who called me was angry.
27. **INCORRECT:** The woman called me was angry.

When the relative pronoun is the *subject* of the adjective clause, you should *not* omit it. Sentence 27, then, is incorrect.

When the relative pronoun appears in the prepositional phrase, whether or not you can omit it depends on the position of the preposition in the sentence.

28. **CORRECT:** Here is a bowl in which you can put those beans.
29. **INFORMAL:** Here is a bowl which you can put those beans in.

Sentences 28 and 29 illustrate two different ways to form adjective clauses with relative pronouns in prepositional phrases. In sentence 28, the preposition and the relative pronoun appear at the beginning of the clause; in sentence 29, the relative pronoun appears at the

beginning of the clause, but the preposition *in* is located at the end. Both sentences are correct, although many writers object to ending a sentence with a preposition in formal writing. We recommend that you use the form shown in sentence 28.

30. **INFORMAL:**   Here is a bowl you can put those beans in.
31. **CORRECT:**   Here is a bowl in which you can put those beans.
32. **INCORRECT:**   Here is a bowl in you can put those beans.

When the preposition appears at the end of the sentence, as in sentence 30, you can omit the relative pronoun. You should *not* omit the relative pronoun when it is used in a prepositional phrase and both the preposition and the relative pronoun appear at the beginning of the adjective clause, as sentences 31 and 32 demonstrate.

33. **INFORMAL:**   The library is a place that you can do your homework in.
34. **INCORRECT:**   The library is a place in that you can do your homework.

Sentence 34 is incorrect because you may not use the relative pronoun *that* with a preposition at the beginning of the adjective clause. Either change the pronoun to *which,* or, if you are writing in an informal situation, move the preposition to the end of the clause.

When a relative pronoun is used as a possessive in an adjective clause, as in sentence 35, it cannot be omitted.

35. **CORRECT:**   When I moved to Lansing, I met the Bordens, whose dog is a German shepherd.
36. **INCORRECT:**   When I moved to Lansing, I met the Bordens, dog is a German shepherd.

11c
sub

ESL

RULES FOR OMITTING RELATIVE PRONOUNS IN ADJECTIVE CLAUSES

The relative pronoun at the beginning of an adjective clause may be omitted when the following conditions are met:

- The adjective clause is restrictive.
- The relative pronoun is not the subject of the adjective clause.
- The relative pronoun is in a prepositional phrase in the adjective clause and the preposition is located at the end of the clause (only an option in informal writing).
- The relative pronoun is not a possessive.

Remind students that adverb clauses begin with subordinating conjunctions (see 11c). Such clauses usually answer questions such as "Why?" "When?" or "How?" about action in the main clause.

11e
sub

ESL

Because noun clauses sometimes begin with the same words that introduce adjective clauses (*who, whom, that,* etc.), students are sometimes confused in trying to distinguish between the two types of clauses. Remind them that adjective clauses answer the questions "What kind of?" or "Which one?" about a noun, whereas noun clauses answer the question "What?" about the action of a verb. For example, in the sentence "I know who she is," the noun clause *who she is* answers the question "What?" about the verb *know*.

11d Using adverb clauses

Adverb clauses can precede or follow independent clauses.

Adverb clause	Independent clause

1. Because his dog had just died, Larry did not enjoy the party.

Independent clause	Adverb clause

2. Larry did not enjoy the party because his dog had just died.

In sentence 1, the adverb clause precedes the independent clause and emphasizes the fact that Larry's dog had just died. Notice that a comma must be used after the clause (see 34a). In sentence 2, the adverb clause follows the independent clause, emphasizing the idea that Larry didn't enjoy the party. No comma is needed when the adverb clause follows the main clause.

11e Forming noun clauses

Noun clauses can be formed in three ways. In the following sentences, the noun clauses are highlighted.

1. Why she ever dated Jim is a mystery to me.
2. I do not know where the emergency exits are.

The noun clauses in sentences 1 and 2 are derived from questions that ask for information. For example, in sentence 1, the noun clause is derived from the question *Why did she date Jim?* This kind of noun clause—one that is derived from a question that asks for information—can be introduced by one of the following words:

what	where	who
whatever	wherever	whom
when	which	whose
whenever	whichever	why

The following two sentences show a second kind of noun clause.

3. My daughter asked if she could go to the movies.
4. I wonder whether the presidential candidates will debate in my hometown.

The noun clauses in sentences 3 and 4 are derived from questions that can be answered *yes* or *no*. For example, in sentence 3, the noun clause is derived from the question *Can she go to the movies?* This kind of noun clause is introduced by the word *if* or *whether.*

    The next two sentences show a third way you can form noun clauses.

  5. That she was embarrassed was clear by the color of her face.
  6. We decided that Leonie will go to Eastern Europe.

Noun clauses of this type are usually introduced by *that.* The relative pronoun *that* can be omitted under certain conditions, however.

  7. **CORRECT:** I am happy that you are coming to dinner.
  8. **CORRECT:** I am happy you are coming to dinner.

When noun clauses begin with *that* and are used as direct objects, you can always omit *that.*

  9. **CORRECT:**   That you are coming to dinner is a great surprise.
 10. **INCORRECT:** You are coming to dinner is a great surprise.

When a noun clause beginning with *that* is the subject of a sentence, however, *that* cannot be omitted.

12a
//

12 USING PARALLEL STRUCTURES FOR PARALLEL IDEAS

In this chapter we will consider the concept of parallelism and learn several techniques for using it effectively.

12a Using parallelism to emphasize points that are parallel

The following examples illustrate the grammatical concept of parallelism.

While parallelism is often a stylistic rather than a purely grammatical issue, understanding its principal features can help writers achieve balance, rhythm, conciseness, and fluency. Many great prose styles reflect awareness of those virtues. As students study this chapter, stress the practical benefits that parallelism brings to writing.

RESOURCES

Walker, Robert L. "The Common Writer: A Case for Parallel Structure." *College Composition and Communication* 21 (1970): 373–79.

Williams, Joseph M. *Style: Ten Lessons in Clarity and Grace.* 3rd ed. New York: Harper-Collins, 1989.

12b
//

ACTIVITY

You might stress the difference between "equivalent" and "identical" by offering board demonstrations of various lists of items such as groceries or sports activities. Invite individuals to suggest items for inclusion. As they rearrange the items to create parallel structures, remind students that grammatical equivalence reflects the balance of syntactic units (e.g., noun phrases, prepositional phrases, etc.), not phrase lengths as such.

1. **Not Parallel:** Our salads were made of lettuce, tomatoes, and included some bean sprouts.
2. **Parallel:** Our salads were made of lettuce, tomatoes, and bean sprouts.

In the parallel version, notice that the three items are equivalent; they are all nouns (see 19a). In the nonparallel version, the first two items are nouns, but the third is a verb phrase (see 19c), *included some bean sprouts.*

3. **Not Parallel:** Carlos looked under the couch, the refrigerator, and in the closet, but he could not find his keys.
4. **Parallel:** Carlos looked under the couch, behind the refrigerator, and in the closet, but he could not find his keys.

In the parallel version, all three items are prepositional phrases (see 20f); in the nonparallel version, the first and last items are prepositional phrases, but the middle term, *the refrigerator,* is a noun phrase.

5. **Not Parallel:** James Baldwin lived for many years in Paris and who wrote many novels.
6. **Parallel:** James Baldwin, who lived for many years in Paris and who wrote many novels, is one of my favorite writers.
7. **Parallel:** James Baldwin lived for many years in Paris and wrote many novels.

The nonparallel version, example 5, has two items, one a verb phrase *(lived for many years in Paris)* and the other an adjective clause *(who wrote many novels)*. Example 6 is parallel because both items are adjective clauses. Example 7 is parallel because both are verb clauses.

Parallelism requires items that are equivalent, *not necessarily identical*, in structure. In example 1, for example, the first two items consist of one word each—*lettuce and tomatoes*. The third item has two words—*bean sprouts*. Despite this difference, these items are parallel because they are all noun phrases. When the items are of different lengths, the longest should come last.

12b **Using parallelism with coordinate conjunctions**

The following sentence illustrates one situation in which items must be parallel.

swimming
Jogging and ~~to swim~~ are two good forms of exercise.

Note that two items joined by a coordinate conjunction (see 19g) must be parallel.

12c Using parallelism with items in a series

The following example illustrates a second situation in which items must be parallel.

I bought a loaf of bread, a jar of peanut butter, and ~~I bought~~ a Diet Coke.

As you can see from this example, items in a series must be parallel.

12d Using parallelism with comparisons

The following sentence illustrates yet another situation in which items must be parallel.

give
Jamie would rather take a test than ∧ an oral report.

Items compared with *than* or *as* must be parallel.

12e Using parallelism in outlines and lists

The following outline shows another instance in which items must be parallel.

I. Types of African art

   A. Figure sculpture

   B. Masks

   C. Bronze plaques

   Bronze
   D. ~~Casting~~ figures ~~in bronze~~

Items in outlines must be parallel.

The following excerpt from an office memo demonstrates that items in a list must also be parallel.

Placing the longest item last not only gives a rhythmic fall to the sentence, but also avoids possible ambiguity. For example, in the list "hot peppers, chili, and cheese," it's not clear whether the word "hot" modifies all items in the list or merely "peppers." To write "chili, cheese, and hot peppers" clarifies the meaning.

12e
//

Students may ask whether the comma is always required before the "and" in a series of three or more items where only the last two are joined by the conjunction. The simplest answer is that academic usage favors the comma, whereas commercial journalism often does not. Refer students to 34b for further discussion of this point.

In response to the company's recent losses in the small appliance division, the following changes will take place:

- Offices will not fill vacant positions.

- Employees will not travel out of state at the company's expense.
  The company will not purchase equipment costing over $2,000.
- ~~No equipment purchases over $2,000.~~

12f **Repeating key words in parallel structures**

Notice the effect of the words added in the following sentence.

1. My parents decided to request a meeting with the lawyer who had drawn up my grandmother's will, *to* hire an investigator to look into the circumstances of my grandmother's death, and *to* talk to the director of the nursing home where she died.

   The added words—that is, the repetition of the word *to*—make the sentence easier to read because they clearly mark the beginning of each item in the series.

2. My parents decided to sell their house, ~~to~~ retire from their jobs, and ~~to~~ move to Florida.

   This sentence is clearer with the *to*'s removed because the items in the series are relatively short and simple. The repetition of *to* only clutters a perfectly clear sentence. By contrast, in sentence 1, the items in the series are quite long and complex, and so the repetition of *to* is justified to make the structure of the series clearer.

13 **AVOIDING MISPLACED MODIFIERS**

A **modifier** is a word, phrase, or clause that describes or provides extra information about another word or phrase. Adjectives and adverbs are the simplest modifiers, but prepositional phrases, infinitive phrases, participial phrases, appositive phrases, adjective

---

13a
mm

Assign an essay from a college reader or other source for the class to study in groups. Ask students to locate instances of parallelism that might serve as models. Have representatives from each group read discoveries aloud to the class. Then have students review each other's latest drafts for evidence of effective parallelism.

Misplaced or dangling modifiers can lead to awkward problems in sentence-level coherence. This chapter reviews circumstances in which those problems are most likely to occur. Encourage students to give modifier placement close attention during the editing process.

clauses, and adverb clauses are other types of common modifiers. Examples of each are given below. It is not so important that you be able to distinguish among these different types as it is that you recognize *that they are modifiers*. The arrows indicate what the modifiers are modifying or describing. Look these over to make sure you understand what a modifier does in a sentence.

Adjective:	We had our company picnic under a beautiful dogwood tree.
Adverb:	Leslie danced effortlessly even though her toe was injured.
Prepositional phrase:	The little boy in the sandbox is my son Kent.
Infinitive phrase:	Mollie's wedding was an event to remember the rest of our lives.
Participial phrase:	The man wearing sunglasses is my economics professor.
Appositive phrase:	Austin Brightman, my college roommate, is getting married next week.
Adjective clause:	*The Scarlet Letter*, which is set in Salem, Massachusetts, is a novel about adultery.
Adverb clause:	Before I can go anywhere, I have to finish writing my English paper.

13a Placing modifiers near the word modified

The following sentences illustrate the problem known as the misplaced modifier.

1. I saw a man pushing a baby carriage in my rearview mirror.

RESOURCES

Chaika, Elaine. "Grammars and Teaching." *College English* 39 (1978): 770–83.

Connors, Robert J., and Andrea A. Lunsford. "Frequency of Formal Errors in Current College Writing." *College Composition and Communication* 39 (1988): 395–409.

Pixton, William H. "The Dangling Gerund: A Working Definition." *College Composition and Communication* 24 (1973): 193–99.

13a
mm

Because many misplaced modifiers are phrases rather than single words, you might suggest that students review the various types of phrases defined in 20f–i.

The confusion here is caused by the placement of the prepositional phrase *in my rearview mirror*. Because of its placement, the sentence seemed to say that the man and his baby carriage were in the mirror. It is unlikely that this is what the writer intended, so the original sentence sounded a little funny. When the writer corrects the problem by placing the phrase so that it clearly modifies the verb *saw*, the sentence sounds fine.

2. Hanging over the fireplace, Jackie saw a portrait of her grandmother.

This sentence sounded funny because of the placement of the participial phrase *hanging over the fireplace*. Participial clauses at the beginning of a sentence always modify the first noun or pronoun after the phrase—in this case, *Jackie*. However, common sense tells us that Jackie wasn't hanging over the fireplace; the portrait of her grandmother was. When the writer moves the participial phrase to the end of the sentence, the meaning becomes clear .

In summary, a **misplaced modifier** is any modifier placed so that it could be interpreted as modifying more than one word. Misplaced modifiers make sentences unclear and should be avoided.

13b Locating limiting modifiers

The following examples illustrate problems with a special type of modifier.

1. The baby almost cried for two hours.

In its original version, this sentence seemed to say that the baby did something referred to as *almost crying* and did it for two hours. It is unlikely that that is what was intended, however. If the writer intended to say that the baby cried and did so for *almost two hours*, then *almost* needs to be moved to a position directly in front of *two*, the word it is modifying.

2. The cat almost fell off the top of the bookcase.

Notice that *almost* is directly in front of the verb and that it is correct in this position because, in this case, the writer *does* mean to say that the cat *almost fell*.

These examples illustrate that certain modifiers should be placed in front of the verb only when they actually modify the

verb. If they modify some other word in the sentence, you must place them in front of that word. Modifiers of this type are sometimes known as **limiting modifiers** because they limit the meaning of the word following them. They include *almost, even, exactly, hardly, just, merely, nearly, only, scarcely,* and *simply. Almost* and *only* are the ones that are misused most often.

13c Avoiding dangling modifiers

The following examples illustrate what dangling modifiers are and how to correct them if they occur in your writing.

Dangling modifier
1. Running after the bus, my nose got cold.

> Note that the modifier (in this case, the participial phrase) *running after the bus* seems to be modifying *my nose*. But that doesn't make any sense; a nose can't run after a bus. However, syntactically that is just what this sentence suggests because modifying phrases at the beginning of the sentence always modify the noun or pronoun immediately following the phrase, in this case, *my nose*. This contradiction between the syntactic meaning of the sentence and the meaning that common sense tells us the writer intends is disconcerting for the reader.

Another way of understanding this problem is to think of the participle *running* as having a subject—the "doer" of the running. In sentence 1, the subject doing the running would be *I*, the person speaking. The subject of the main clause, however, is *nose*. The fact that the subject of the participle and the subject of the main clause are not the same is a mistake.

Mistakes like this are called **dangling modifiers** because the modifier is not connected to any word in the sentence; it dangles all by itself, usually at the beginning of the sentence.

Dangling modifiers can be corrected in either of two ways:

I got a cold nose
2. Running after the bus, ~~my nose got cold~~.

> One way to correct a dangling modifier is to revise the sentence so that the noun or pronoun immediately following the introductory modifier is the noun or pronoun that the phrase modifies.

13c
dm

Students may wonder about the difference between the terms "dangling" and "misplaced" with respect to modifiers. In general, a modifier is considered *dangling* if the term it is intended to modify is not present within the sentence. A modifier is *misplaced* if the term it is intended to modify is present but not clearly positioned with respect to the modifier. Point out that dangling modifiers, unlike those which are merely misplaced, require the writer to reconstruct the sentence in order to introduce the modified term.

While I was

3. ∧Running after the bus, my nose got cold.

A second way to correct a dangling modifier is to rewrite the modifying phrase so that it is a clause with its own subject. After this revision, there is no question who was doing the running.

13e
mm

If students think squinting modifiers are of minor importance, you might introduce the following example: Suppose an executive assistant receives a memo stating this: "Mr. Wilcox and I agreed Friday to have lunch. Please make arrangements." Does this mean the assistant should make arrangements for the coming Friday? Or does it mean that the decision was made last Friday and that the lunch can take place any day? Obviously, the position of "Friday" in the first sentence could lead to a serious misunderstanding. Moving that word closer to the verb it is intended to modify will solve the problem. "Friday, Mr. Wilcox and I agreed . . ." says the decision took place on Friday. "We agreed to meet on Friday" unmistakably names the day of the appointment.

13d Avoiding squinting modifiers

Squinting modifiers may win the prize for the most imaginative name of a grammar problem in English. To see what a squinting modifier is, take a look at the following sentence.

Squinting modifier

1. The coach told Jimmie carefully to raise himself onto the parallel bars.

The problem is that *carefully* is "squinting"; it's looking in two directions at once. *Carefully* may describe how the coach spoke to Jimmie, or it may describe how Jimmie was to raise himself onto the bars. We can't tell which meaning is intended, so the sentence is ineffective. Squinting modifiers can be corrected by placing them unambiguously near the word they modify, as the following revisions illustrate.

2. The coach told Jimmie carefully to raise himself onto the parallel bars.

3. The coach told Jimmie carefully to raise himself onto the parallel bars.

Squinting modifiers are words or phrases that could be modifying either of two different words. You can correct them by moving them to a position where there is no ambiguity about what they modify.

13e Avoiding split infinitives

The following sentence illustrates a problem known as the split infinitive.

1. Uche decided to ~~daily~~ jog several miles.

    The infinitive is said to be "split" because a modifier, in this case, *daily,* has been placed in between the two parts of the infinitive, *to* and the verb itself, *jog.* When splitting an infinitive causes the kind of awkwardness illustrated by sentence 1, you should definitely correct the problem by moving the adverb.

    However, sometimes a split infinitive is not particularly awkward:

2. My parents decided to legally dissolve their marriage.

    Here the infinitive is split, but no awkwardness results. People disagree about whether there is any problem with a split infinitive like this. Perhaps they disagree because the usual ways of revising a split infinitive, in this case, make the sentence worse:

3. My parents legally decided to dissolve their marriage.

    This revision makes the sentence say that they *legally decided* rather than decided to *dissolve legally* and so distorts the intended meaning.

4. My parents decided to dissolve legally their marriage.

    This revision is incorrect because the direct object must follow the verb without any intervening words.

5. My parents decided to dissolve their marriage legally.

    This revision also changes the meaning somewhat. It sounds like the parents were considering some kind of *illegal* divorce but finally decided instead to do it *legally.*

One solution to this dilemma is to leave the sentence in its original form (sentence 2). Because a split infinitive is offensive to some readers, however, a writer might want to recast the sentence completely and thereby avoid the problem:

6. My parents have decided to file for divorce.

In summary, a **split infinitive** occurs when a modifier appears in between the word *to* and the verb that follows it in an infinitive. Split infinitives that cause awkwardness should always be

13e
mm

COLLABORATIVE ACTIVITY

Have students meet in editing groups to search one another's drafts for the kinds of modifier problems discussed in this chapter. Remind the class that clarity is the basic test for determining whether or not a modifier has been well placed. Clarity may also govern decisions about split infinitives.

revised. Those that are not awkward should also be revised if there is any chance that your audience will find them problematic.

In composition, as in life, variety is a spice. Accomplished writers vary syntax and sentence length much as chefs use herbs, and both skills benefit from experience and good taste. Students should be encouraged to read widely to enhance their appreciation of various prose styles. Meanwhile, this chapter introduces fundamental techniques they may encounter in the works of other writers as well as in their own.

RESOURCES

Read, Herbert. *English Prose Style.* 2nd ed. New York: Pantheon, 1952.

Walpole, Jane R. "The Vigorous Pursuit of Grace and Style." *The Writing Instructor* 1 (1982): 163–69.

Read's classic study of English prose explores sentence variety historically, offering many examples from major works of British literature. Walpole's article discusses methods of varying expression to achieve desired effects.

14 ACHIEVING SENTENCE VARIETY

In much of this book, you learn about avoiding or correcting errors in your writing. This chapter is not about correctness; it is about stylistic choices that will make your writing more varied, more lively, and more interesting.

14a Varying sentence length

The following paragraph illustrates one kind of problem a writer can have with sentence length. This paragraph, adapted from a book on contemporary American folk legends, relates a bizarre tale that is told in many parts of the country.

> A man was camping out in the wilds. He was in his pickup camper. He parked at the edge of a clearing. He ran across a wounded coyote. He hated coyotes anyway. He decided he'd create a little excitement. He had some dynamite in his truck. It was left over from blowing stumps on his farm. He tied a stick of dynamite to the coyote. He lit the fuse. He ran over behind some trees to watch the results. The man was horrified. The man watched the coyote summon his last bit of strength. The coyote dragged himself over to the camper. There was nothing the man could do. The coyote pulled himself under the camper. The coyote blew himself and much of the camper to bits.

This paragraph is unsuccessful for two reasons: it lacks variety both in the lengths of the sentences—they are all fairly short—and in sentence structure—they are all simple declarative sentences with a single subject and verb.

The original version of the paragraph demonstrates how variety in sentence length and sentence structure serves to make the writing more interesting and—by indicating which information is important and which less important—more effective.

A man was camping out in the wilds with his pickup camper. At the edge of the clearing where he was camped, he ran across a wounded coyote. Hating coyotes anyway, he decided he'd create a little excitement. He had some dynamite in his truck, left over from blowing stumps on his farm. So he tied a stick of dynamite to the coyote, lit the fuse, and ran over behind some trees to watch the results. To his horror, the man watched the coyote summon his last bit of strength and drag himself over to the camper. There was nothing he could do as the coyote pulled himself under the camper and blew himself and much of the camper to bits.

—Jan Harold Brunvand,
The Choking Doberman and Other "New" Urban Legends

Sometimes students are tempted to write in a style like the first version of this paragraph because they are worried about making errors. They fear that if they write more complex sentences, they will make mistakes in grammar or punctuation. This fear is understandable. It is more difficult to avoid making errors in complex sentences, but the first paragraph shows that if you try to avoid errors by adopting an overly simplistic style, you will not produce effective writing.

Another word about variety in sentence length is in order. Most modern writers produce sentences that range between ten and forty words. Most of your sentences should be in this general range. Occasionally, however, a very short sentence can be effective. After a string of longer sentences, a short one will stand out, so use a short sentence once in a while to call attention to an important point.

In summary, when revising your writing, watch for a lack of variety in sentence length. In particular, avoid a long sequence of short sentences. When revising, however, do not merely replace a sequence of short sentences with a sequence of compound sen-

COLLABORATIVE ACTIVITY

From a college reader or other source, supply students with a model paragraph that contains interesting sentence variety. Have them write paragraphs of their own imitating the syntax (but not the subject matter) of the model. Then have them exchange papers and comment on one another's experiments. Ask for volunteers to read modeled paragraphs aloud to the class.

14a
var

14b
var

tences. Combine them into more complex sentences that indicate the relative importance of ideas. (For advice on subordinating ideas, see 11b). In a paragraph of medium to long sentences, it can be quite effective to place an important idea in a particularly short sentence.

14b Varying sentence openings

Most of your sentences—indeed, most sentences in English—begin with the subject, proceed to the verb, conclude with any objects or complements, and include a sprinkling of modifiers along the way. Such sentences are fine; in fact, they are the staple of good writing. But an unrelieved diet of anything, even a staple, can become tiresome after a while. Think about livening up your style by beginning your sentences in more unusual ways. But use these techniques sparingly—overusing them can be less effective than not using them at all.

Opening sentences with transitional expressions

The following sentences illustrate one variation on standard sentence openings.

1. Nevertheless, computers have changed forever the way people write.
2. In fact, my entire argument with Mario was based on a misunderstanding.

These two sentences open with conjunctive adverbs, sometimes called transitional expressions, that provide both a clear transition from the preceding sentence and some variation in sentence pattern. You can find a complete discussion of using transitional expressions to provide coherence in 8a. Punctuating such expressions is explained in 33c.

Opening sentences with introductory phrases

The box on the facing page illustrates how various phrases can be used to open a sentence.

Opening sentences with adverb clauses

Sentences 3 and 4 illustrate the use of adverb clauses (see 20j) as openers.

SENTENCE OPENERS

Sentence	Type of Opening	Reference
After a sleepless night, Susan anxiously called her psychologist.	Prepositional phrase	20f
Laughing hard, Micah fell off his chair.	Participial phrase	27b, 13c
To let my cat out, I had to get completely dressed.	Infinitive phrase	27a
Defiant and angry, the mob marched into the Administration Building.	Pair of adjectives	19d
Slowly and cautiously, Maxine lifted the cover off the ticking box.	Pair of adverbs	19e
Gracefully, Gina danced her way off the stage.	Single adverb	19e
Our minds made up, we knocked on the boss's door.	Absolute phrase	20i

Remind students that a sentence opener, especially a participial phrase, can become a dangling modifier if the opener doesn't clearly modify what follows it. Advise them to review 13c if they are in doubt.

14c
var

3. When Beatrice called, I was just finishing my assignment.
4. Because Marc lives in the city, he pays much more than I do for car insurance.

Adverb clauses can be located in many positions in a sentence, including at the very end. Opening a sentence with an adverb clause can provide sentence variety.

To summarize, you can achieve sentence variety through the use of sentence openers, including transitional expressions, various phrases, and adverb clauses.

14c   Using inverted word order

Natural word order in English usually requires that the subject be followed by the verb. However, it is possible to provide variety in sentence style by occasionally reversing this natural order and writing a sentence with **inverted word order**.

14c
var

Otherwise known as periodic sentence structure, inverted word order is evident in many literary masterpieces. You might quote such famous lines as "Of arms and the man I sing" (translated from the *Aeneid* 1.i), "The infernal serpent; he it was . . ." (Milton's *Paradise Lost* 1.34), or "St. Agnes' Eve— Ah, bitter chill it was!" (Keats's "Eve of St. Agnes") as examples.

      Subject Verb   Prepositional phrases

1. A dozen lilies were in a vase on the dining room table.

    Prepositional phrases   Verb   Subject

2. In a vase on the dining room table were a dozen lilies.

Sentence 1 is in natural word order and is perfectly correct. Sentence 2 expresses the same meaning in inverted word order. The verb *were* occurs before the subject *lilies*. This order is just as correct and provides a little variety in sentence style.

     Subject   Verb   Adjective

3. Paul's performance on the parallel bars was particularly impressive.

    Adjective Verb   Subject

4. Particularly impressive was Paul's performance on the parallel bars.

In sentence 4, the adjective *impressive,* which would normally be at the end of the sentence (as in sentence 3), has been moved to the front of the sentence, and the subject has been moved to the end.

       Subject   Verb Particle

5. The Christmas tree and all the ornaments fell down.

  Particle Verb   Subject

6. Down fell the Christmas tree and all the ornaments.

In sentence 6, the writer has inverted sentence 5 by moving the particle *down* to the beginning of the sentence followed by the verb *fell.*

  Subject   Verb

7. Donna called last night at midnight.

 Expletive Verb Subject

8. It was Donna who called last night at midnight.

In sentence 8, the subject follows the verb because an expletive, *it,* begins the sentence. Although this kind of inversion is correct and does result in sentence variety, it is generally out of favor because the expletive *there* or *it* is a meaningless placeholder, making the

sentence wordier and delaying the meaning-bearing words until later in the sentence.

Use inverted word order sparingly. Overuse will make your writing seem artificial and self-conscious.

14d Using commands, questions, and quotations

The following passages illustrate the use of commands, questions, and quotations to provide sentence variety. The first paragraph begins with a command, *Consider the environment.*

> Consider the environment. If people insist on continuing to drive gas-guzzling cars at sixty-five miles per hour on the interstate highways of this country, we are all going to end up breathing air that is filled with more carbon dioxide than is good for us. If people continue to use nonbiodegradable products, we are going to end up with nowhere to put the garbage of our society.

The next selection achieves sentence variety through the use of a question.

> From its very inception the purpose of the kibbutz movement, for both sexes, was first and foremost to create a new way of life in a very old and hostile land. True, the raising of a new generation to this new way of life was soon of crucial importance, but of necessity it took second place. Because unless the first generation created the society, how could it shelter any new generations? It was this older generation that subjected itself to great hardships and dangers, that first reclaimed the land, wresting harvests from barren soil, and later fought the war that gained them statehood.
>
> —Bruno Bettelheim, "Why Kibbutzim?"

The final selection makes use of a quotation to provide variety.

> Some people say the business about the jolly fat person is a myth, that all of us chubbies are neurotic, sick, sad people. I disagree. Fat people may not be chortling all day long, but they're a hell of a lot *nicer* than the wizened and shriveled. Thin people turn surly, mean and hard at a young age because they never learn the value of a hot-fudge sundae for easing tension. Thin people don't

like gooey soft things because they themselves are neither gooey nor soft. They are crunchy and dull, like carrots. They go straight to the heart of the matter while fat people let things stay all blurry and hazy and vague, the way things actually are. Thin people want to face the truth. Fat people know there is no truth. One of my thin friends is always staring at complex, unsolvable problems and saying, "The key thing is . . ." Fat people never say that. They know there isn't any such thing as the key thing about anything.

—Suzanne Britt, "That Lean and Hungry Look"

In summary, use commands, questions, and quotations when appropriate to provide variety in the sentence structure of your writing.

Mixed constructions are among the more serious grammatical errors found in college writing. Their widespread and repeated appearance in a student's work may signal the need for tutoring in addition to regular classroom instruction. Encourage writers who have special difficulties to review this chapter carefully and to ask questions about its examples.

RESOURCES

Krishna, Valerie. "The Syntax of Error." *Journal of Basic Writing* 1.1 (1975): 43–49.

Leki, Ilona. *Understanding ESL Writers: A Guide for Teachers.* Portsmouth: Boynton/Cook, 1992.

Shaughnessy, Mina P. *Errors and Expectations: A Guide for the Teacher of Basic Writing.* New York: Oxford UP, 1977.

15 AVOIDING MIXED AND INCOMPLETE CONSTRUCTIONS

Have you ever written a sentence that just doesn't "sound right"? It happens to all of us. In this chapter we will consider several causes of these awkward-sounding sentences.

15a Revising mixed grammatical constructions

The following fragment illustrates a problem known as mixed grammatical construction:

Subject   Dependent clause

1. **INCORRECT:** The fact that Jacqueline was late for work

Dependent clause

which made the manager furious.

This fragment starts with a subject, *fact,* which is followed by the dependent clause *that Jacqueline was late for work.* One would expect the next part of the sentence to be a verb that goes with the subject *fact.* Instead, the sentence continues with another dependent clause, *which made the manager furious.* This un-

expected ending causes the sentence to sound funny, to confuse the reader, and therefore to be ineffective—in fact, it isn't even a sentence; it is a fragment (see 32b). One way to correct the problem is to provide an ending for the sentence that fits the beginning, with a verb to go with the subject *fact*.

2. **CORRECT:**   The fact that Jacqueline was late for work made the manager furious.

Below is another example of a mixed grammatical construction.

3. **INCORRECT:**   By going to the movie last night meant that I did not finish my algebra homework.

4. **CORRECT:**   Going to the movie last night meant that I did not finish my algebra homework.

When *By* is removed from sentence 3, the result (sentence 4) is an effective sentence.

In summary, a **mixed grammatical construction** occurs when a sentence starts out with one kind of grammatical structure and changes to a different one someplace in the middle. Mixed constructions must be revised to eliminate the problem.

15b Revising mixed meaning

A slightly different problem with mixed sentences occurs when the subject and the verb don't fit together or don't make sense together. This problem is known as mixed meaning or faulty predication.

1. **INCORRECT:**   The purpose of this course is designed to improve your writing skills.

This sentence says that *the purpose is designed,* but surely the writer intended to say that *this course is designed* or that *the purpose is to improve your writing skills.* To eliminate the mixed meaning, the sentence could be revised in either of two ways:

2. ~~The purpose of~~ ͭ this course is designed to improve your writing skills.

15b
mixed

You might remind your class that economy is a virtue in writing. Students sometimes slip into faulty predication when they are trying to compose longer sentences than necessary. By having them search their drafts for words or phrases that can be deleted in the interests of economy, you may help them overcome the mixed meaning syndrome.

3. The purpose of this course is ~~designed~~ to improve your **writing skills.**

Take a look at some other examples of mixed meaning or faulty predication.

4. My long-range goal is ~~I hope~~ to become a legal secretary.

5. ~~The rules of~~ the college ~~expect~~ *expects* that students will miss no more than three classes in a semester.

The following sentences represent common constructions that often result in mixed meanings or faulty predication.

6. Success in this course is ~~when you get~~ *getting* a C.

Success is not a *when*; it is a *what*. *Success* is something you achieve, not a *time* when you achieve it. So be careful when you write that anything *is when*. Make sure that the something you are talking about is actually a time.

7. The best kind of revenge is ~~where you get~~ *getting* even with someone who isn't even aware of it.

A *kind of revenge* cannot be a *where* because it is not a place. Use *where* only to refer to nouns that are places.

8. The reason for the breakup of our relationship is ~~because~~ *that* Laura can't ever make a commitment.

There is something illogical about saying *the reason is because*. On the other hand, it is perfectly logical to say *the reason is Laura's indecisiveness* or to say *we broke up because of Laura's indecisiveness*.

In summary, **mixed meaning** or **faulty predication** occurs when the subject and the verb are mismatched—when they don't make sense together. Such problems must be revised to eliminate the awkwardness. Be especially careful with sentences that include the patterns *something is when, something is where,* and *the reason is because.*

15c Revising sentences of the pattern "My brother, he . . . "

The following sentences illustrate a kind of awkwardness caused by adding a pronoun subject that merely repeats the noun subject.

1. My brother/he enlisted in the army.

2. The essay question on the final exam/it caused me a lot of problems.

Do not include a pronoun with the subject if it merely repeats the meaning of the noun subject of the sentence.

15d Revising errors with *in which*

The phrase *in which* has many perfectly good uses in English, but it frequently is used in a way that just doesn't make sense, as the following sentences illustrate.

1. The novel in which I read over the weekend has a disappointing ending.

   In which in the original didn't make sense because you don't read *in* a novel.

   But notice that *in which* in the following sentence is fine.

2. The first movie in which Meryl Streep starred was *The French Lieutenant's Woman*.

   In which makes sense here because a person *can* star *in* a movie.

In summary, be careful to use *in which* to modify only nouns that you can put something *in*.

15e Revising incomplete sentences

Elliptical constructions

Writers can sometimes make their sentences more concise by omitting certain words in compound constructions rather than repeating them. For example, the following sentences could

15e
inc

15e
inc

be effectively revised by removing the words that would otherwise be repeated.

1. The first test in my math course was difficult, and the second test was even harder.
2. My older daughter is good at math, but my younger daughter can't even add simple numbers.

However, words may not be omitted if the omitted words are different from those at the beginning of the sentence.

3. That movie's characters are unconvincing, and the plot ^is pre-dictable.

The verb cannot be omitted in the second half of sentence 3 because it must be *is*, which is not the same as *are* in the first half.

4. Houng was afraid ^of and mad at his landlord.

Of must follow *afraid* because without it, the sentence would say Houng was *afraid at his landlord*. *Afraid at* is not acceptable English.

5. My husband and ^my accountant will be arriving at seven.

My must be repeated to indicate that the writer's husband and her accountant are two different people. If they were the same person, the second *my* should be omitted.

Comparisons

Comparisons should be stated fully enough so that no ambiguity is created.

6. **AMBIGUOUS:** My mother always liked me more than my sister.

Sentence 6 is ambiguous. It may mean that my mother liked me more than she liked my sister, or it may mean that my mother liked me more than my sister liked me. To clear up this ambiguity, the sentence should be revised as either sentence 7 or sentence 8.

7. **CLEAR:** My mother always liked me more than she liked my sister.
8. **CLEAR:** My mother always liked me more than my sister did.

When comparing an item with all the others in the same class, use the word *other*.

Students should notice how faulty comparisons can lead to embarrassing misunderstandings. In the example shown here, the ambiguity could result in confusing impressions of the mother, the sister, and especially the writer.

other

9. The ginkgo tree is older than any˄tree that still exists.

The word *other* had to be inserted to indicate that the ginkgo is older than any tree *other than a ginkgo*.

Comparisons must always be made with something. It is confusing or even deceptive to say that something is cheaper or larger or more nutritious without specifying what it is cheaper or larger or more nutritious than.

10. The new Parcel is safer and more economical.

Omitting *that*

The subordinating conjunction *that* can often be omitted, but not if omitting it makes the sentence hard to read.

that

11. Chinva has discovered˄a car is necessary in America.

In sentence 11, *that* must be inserted to ensure that the reader doesn't misread the sentence and think that Chinva discovered a car.

12. I am afraid Mikelle has missed the bus.

In sentence 12, it is not necessary to insert *that* because there is no possibility of misreading the sentence.

Adding missing subjects

In some languages—Spanish and Italian, for example—writers can omit the subject of a sentence or clause. English, however, allows you to omit the subject only if the sentence is imperative—if it gives a command (see 19c).

I went

13. Went to the dean's office to interview her for the school paper.

it

14. If a country uses raw materials from another country,˄has to pay for them.

Adding missing expletives

Whenever you place your subject after a linking verb (see 19c), you must put either *there* or *it* in front of the verb to make the sentence complete. (The expletives *there* and *it* are discussed in 16d.)

15e
inc

ESL

ESL ADVICE

Missing subjects and other omissions may occur in the writing of ESL students whose native-language syntax does not correspond to that of English. To make new syntax patterns habitual, students may need to practice the English constructions by rote, using a notebook or journal for that purpose. Consider giving extra credit to students who do such work independently, as well as to native speakers who might benefit from the same type of exercise.

15. *There are*
∧ ~~Are~~ a large number of books about the Vietnam War.

16. *It is*
∧ ~~Is~~ widely known that cats are fierce predators.

In 14c and 16d, we caution against wordiness caused by the use of expletives; however, sometimes the context makes an expletive necessary. In such cases, do not omit the expletive.

15e
inc

ESL

DRAFTING AND REVISING: EFFECTIVE WORD CHOICE

This chapter is concerned with effective self-expression. Though usage is an area in which the "do's" and "don'ts" change over time, students should nevertheless be advised to express themselves as clearly as possible. Carrying out that advice usually means avoiding common mistakes in usage and getting the prepositions right, as well as overcoming such ordinary problems as wordiness, awkwardness, and imprecision. It may also mean getting to know one's dictionary well. Encourage students to view this chapter as a means to improving both coherence and style.

16a
usage

RESOURCES

Seltzer, Hubert H., Jr. *Basic Idioms in American English.* Chicago: Science Research Assoc., 1981.

Simpson, Mary Scott. "Teaching Writing: Beginning with the Word." *College English* 39 (1978): 934–39.

Whitford, Harold C., and Robert J. Dixson. *Handbook of American Idioms and Idiomatic Usage.* New York: Regents, 1953.

See also reference works listed in 16i.

16 CHOOSING EFFECTIVE WORDS

In this chapter we discuss **word choice**—selecting just the right words to express the meaning and create the effect you intend. Word choice is often referred to as **diction** or **expression.** You can find a list of words that are frequently misused in the Glossary of Usage at the end of this book.

16a Avoiding mistakes in usage

Study this first set of sentences and see if you can figure out the kind of mistake they all have in common.

1. I remembered everything accept my swimsuit.
   except

   Accept is a verb meaning "to receive willingly or approve." *Except* is a preposition meaning "with the exclusion of" or "other than."

2. She is a better writer then he is.
   than

   Then is an adverb meaning "at that time." *Than* is a conjunction used to make comparisons.

3. I hope Amy will be able to come to New York to.
   too

   To is a preposition meaning "in the direction of." *Too* is an adverb meaning "also" or "more than enough," as in "This soup is too hot."

4. Automobiles have a negative affect on the environment.
   effect

   Affect is a verb meaning "to change or influence." *Effect* is a noun meaning "result." These terms also have less common meanings: *Affect* can also be a noun meaning "a person's feeling or emotion," as in "Her *affect* was very calm." *Effect* can be used as a verb meaning "to cause to occur," as in "We need to *effect* a change in the way things are done in this company."

These first four sentences all include errors that result from confusing two words that sound alike but have different meanings. These words are often called **homonyms** or, more accurately, **homophones.**

The next group of sentences illustrates a slightly different problem with choosing effective words.

a lot
5. We read alot while we were at the beach.
to
6. My chemistry teacher will try and call me tonight.
regardless
7. Kevin does whatever he wants, irregardless of the effect it will have

on the rest of us.
have
8. Jake should of called by now.

In sentences 5 through 8, the writer used words or phrases that don't exist in Standard Written English. Even though you may have heard people use them or may even have seen them in print, *alot, try and, irregardless,* and *should of* are not acceptable in formal English.

The next group of sentences illustrates a more subtle problem.
profane
9. I was shocked by the profuse language being used.

10. If you are going to file a discrimination suit, documenting your ac-
utmost
tivities is of the upmost importance.
bought
11. Andrew brought a new sweater at the mall.

In each of these sentences, the writer has used a word incorrectly. *Profuse* means "plentiful." *Upmost* means "on top." Merchandise is *bought,* not *brought.* In each case, the writer's error resulted from the confusion of an unfamiliar word with a similar sounding word. To prevent this kind of error, check the meaning of words you are not familiar with in the dictionary.

The next group of sentences illustrates the most difficult word choice errors to eliminate. They arise from slight misuses of ordinary words—words that the writers of these sentences know well. You can find a fuller listing in the Glossary of Usage at the end of the book.
number
12. So far this month, we have not had a large amount of complaints.

Use *amount* to express a quantity of something that cannot be counted (like *anger* or *gasoline*); use *number* to express a quantity of

Even careful writers may occasionally mix up words that sound alike, otherwise known as "mirror words." Advise students that such words are one good reason to allow time for proofreading. You might also call attention to style-check software programs that catch minor usage errors (see 16j).

16a
usage

something that can be counted (like *complaints,* in this case, or *marbles* or *apostrophes*).

13. The director suddenly put a spotlight on the dancers, ~~therefore~~ *thereby*

    causing one of them to fall.

Thereby is preferable here because the rest of the sentence is not an independent clause (see 20j). Notice that if the remainder of the sentence *is* an independent clause, *therefore* is preferred:

14. The director put the dancers in a spotlight; therefore, one of them fell.

Punctuation with *therefore* is discussed in 33c.

15. ~~Hopefully,~~ *I hope* I will graduate in one more year.

Mistakes in using *hopefully* are currently at the top of most English teachers' lists of irritating errors. Although the use of *hopefully* to mean "I hope" is very common in spoken English and in informal writing, this use is generally not acceptable in formal writing. *Hopefully* means exactly what it says: "full of hope." It *would* be correct to use it in a sentence like the following:

16. Hopefully, the girl scout, carrying sample boxes of cookies, walked up the sidewalk and rang the bell.

Here the sentence means that the girl scout was "full of hope," not that the writer of the sentence hopes that something will happen.

16a usage ESL

ESL ADVICE

Non-native speakers often have difficulty learning the idiomatic usage of these two key verbs. Those who need help should study the boxed checklists in this section carefully and perhaps do some rote practice in their notebooks. Encourage students to ask you about particular contexts they find troublesome.

Do and *make*

Do and *make* are verbs with similar meanings, but in most cases you cannot use one in place of the other. Forms of the verb *do* are highlighted in the following examples.

17. Did you go to the party last night?
18. I do not like cranberries with my Thanksgiving dinner.
19. Peter pretends to procrastinate, and so does Amy.

In these sentences, the verb *do* is acting as a *helping verb* (see 19c), sometimes called an *operator.* Helping verbs are used in questions (sentence 17), negatives (sentence 18), and sentences with repeating verbs (sentence 19). The verb *make* cannot be used as a helping verb.

Forms of the verb *make* are highlighted in the following examples.

20. The thunderstorm made Shane very nervous.
21. My boss makes me work on Saturdays.

In sentences 20 and 21, *make* is a *causative verb*. The verb *do* cannot be used as a causative verb.

Aside from these distinctions, there are only general guidelines you can use to decide when to use *make* and *do*; however, be aware that there are many exceptions.

22. Rick does the laundry and the cooking in the house.
23. Gloria makes a turkey dinner every Sunday.

The verb *do* is used for situations related to actions or routine tasks done primarily around the house, as in sentence 22. *Make* is usually used when the writer is referring to meals or food, however, as in sentence 23.

One use of the verb *do* is shown in the following examples.

24. You will do harm to your body if you smoke.
25. Ibrahim didn't do anything over the weekend.

The verb *do* is usually used with words or phrases expressing abstract ideas such as *harm* in sentence 24 or *anything* in sentence 25.

16a
usage

ESL

DO AND MAKE

Do	Make
Routine Tasks or Activities: do work do dishes do housework do laundry do cleaning	*Food or Meals:* make breakfast, lunch, dinner make a cake make spaghetti make a snack make a salad
Abstract Ideas: do business do the best you can do one's duty do a favor do well do justice	*Creating or Producing Something:* make a choice make a mistake make noise make a statement make a decision make a mess

16a
usage

ESL

The verb *make* is used for the following kinds of sentences.

26. President Kennedy made a very famous inaugural address.
27. Alice makes her breakfast every morning before leaving for school.

The verb *make* often means "to create or produce something that wasn't there before." In sentence 26, the speech by President Kennedy was such a creation. In sentence 27, the food was already there, but Alice has prepared the meal.

Another and *other*

Another and *other* are used as either adjectives or pronouns. The type of noun you are using in a sentence will help you decide whether to use *another* or *other,* which are highlighted in the following sentences.

28. Perot might want another chance at becoming president.
29. Other houses on the block have bigger yards.
30. The judge needed other information to make a decision.

Another means "one more" in addition to what is mentioned. *Other* means "several more" than what is mentioned. When these words are used as adjectives, *another* is used with singular countable nouns, like *chance* in sentence 28. *Other* precedes plural countable nouns (*houses* in sentence 29) and noncountable nouns (*information* in sentence 30).

The following sentences show an exception to these rules.

31. I need another twenty dollars to buy a stereo.
32. It's another fifty miles to Detroit.
33. It will take Bill another ten minutes to wash the car.

Another is always used with money, distance, or time, even if the noun is a plural countable noun.

In the following examples, *another* and *other* are used as pronouns.

34. An avalanche occurred in Colorado. Another is expected soon.
35. Avalanches have occurred in Colorado. Others have occurred in California.

Another is used to replace singular countable nouns, as in sentence 34, and *others* replaces plural countable nouns, as in sentence 35.

Certain determiners in a sentence will also help you decide when to use *another* or *other*. The determiners are highlighted in sentences 36–38 (see 29b).

36. One of my accounts is overdue; all others are balanced accurately.
37. Every other person in my family has balanced accounts.
38. The other account that isn't balanced is my roommate's.

> *Other* is used following *all, every,* and *the*. When the word *other* is preceded by *the,* as in sentence 38, it means "all that remains of a specific group."

The following sentences show some special meanings of expressions with *another* and *other*.

39. Dina and I telephone each other every month.
40. Dina and I telephone one another every month.

> In these examples, *each other* and *one another* convey a reciprocal relationship: sometimes I call Dina; sometimes Dina calls me.

16a
usage

ESL

Yet and *already*

The following sentences contain the word *already,* which is highlighted.

41. The ice cream has already melted.
42. Has the ice cream already melted?

> *Already* implies that something has happened by this time. *Already* is used with positive statements (but not negative), as in sentence 41, and with questions, as in sentence 42.

Compare the use of *already* in sentences 41 and 42 with the use of *yet* in the following examples.

43. The ice cream hasn't melted yet, even though I took it out of the freezer fifteen minutes ago.
44. Has the ice cream melted yet?

> *Yet* implies that an event hasn't happened but will happen. In sentences 43 and 44, the writer expects the ice cream to melt because it isn't in the freezer. *Yet* is used with negative statements and questions.

16b Getting the prepositions right

For many students, choosing the correct preposition is a problem. Few general principles exist to help with this decision, and the correct choice is often quite arbitrary, based more on custom than logic. Nevertheless, errors in this area can mar otherwise effective writing. If you have doubts about a particular word, consult the Glossary of Usage in the back of this book. The following examples illustrate some common mistakes.

1. I am writing in regard *to* of the position you advertised in last Sunday's paper.

2. I don't want my children to develop a dependence *on* for me.

3. That behavior isn't consistent *with* to our friendship.

4. We devised a plan *through* in which we could make a lot of money.

   (See discussion of *in which* in 15d).

5. They had not given any thought *to* on how their funds were being expended.

   Mistakes in which *on* is used in place of some more appropriate preposition are especially common, as sentences 5 and 6 illustrate.

6. My mind was churning out ideas *about* on the opportunities that existed.

7. Max was getting bored *by* of the discussion, so he suggested that we leave.

 Prepositions are particularly troublesome for many international students. In this section we will discuss prepositions in considerable detail, focusing on the problems unique to international students.

Each preposition may have several meanings. A dictionary will list these various meanings. However, we suggest that you keep a journal of sentences that you come across with prepositions so that you can remember their meanings within context.

16b
prep

ESL

The nine most common prepositions are explained in the accompanying chart.

NINE COMMON PREPOSITIONS

Preposition	Meaning	Examples	
in, on, at	Time	▪ The earthquake occurred in the evening. ▪ The earthquake occurred on October 22. ▪ The earthquake occurred at 5:04 P.M.	General ↑ ↓ Specific
	Place	▪ I was living in Monterey, California. ▪ I lived on Eighteenth Street. ▪ I lived at 216 Eighteenth Street.	General ↑ ↓ Specific
from	Source or origin	▪ I got the book from my friend. ▪ I was tired from working out. ▪ Nora just got back from an exciting European vacation. ▪ Juan studied at the library from 6:00 to 12:00.	
to	Direction toward a place	▪ We drove to Grand Rapids.	
	Direction toward a person	▪ Laura gave some chocolate eggs to Kathy.	
by	How or when something happens	▪ *Silent Spring* was written by Rachel Carson. ▪ We went to the baseball game by bus. ▪ I have to complete Chapter 12 by next week.	
	Location	▪ The chair is by the table.	

(continued)

ESL ADVICE

Because of their idiomatic usage, prepositions can be a major hurdle for ESL students to overcome. Suggest rote notebook practice of sentences that use the nine key prepositions correctly. Also, encourage non-native speakers to refer to this checklist often during the editing process.

16b
prep

ESL

16b
prep

ESL

NINE COMMON PREPOSITIONS (continued)

Preposition	Meaning	Examples
for	Purpose	■ Joe had to study for his chemistry final.
	Length of time	■ I was traveling in Asia for six months.
	In favor of	■ The Republican candidate is for lowering taxes.
	To be given to someone	■ Carlos baked a cake for Lucy.
	Cost	■ Susan bought new shoes for seventy dollars.
of	Relation-ship between part and whole	■ Many of the people in Somalia were starving.
	Reference to some-thing else	■ She is afraid of heights.
with	Associa-tion	■ Annette has long conversations with her mother. ■ Donald often eats dinner with me.
	Imple-ment	■ The Japanese usually eat with chopsticks.
	Descrip-tion	■ Catherine's dress was purple with small blue flowers.
	Manner	■ She spoke with grace and poise.

A common problem with prepositions occurs when a writer has to choose between a prepositional phrase beginning with *of* and the possessive formed with an apostrophe and an *s*.

Judy's car
8. The car of Judy was damaged in the accident.

Although the original version of sentence 8 was not technically wrong, it was stilted and awkward. In English, it is preferable to form the possessive *for nouns referring to humans* with an apostrophe and an *s*.

9. The pencil's tip is not very sharp.
10. The tip of the pencil is not very sharp.

> Sentences 9 and 10 are both correct. However, traditionally the apostrophe and an *s* were not used with inanimate nouns like pencil. More recently, some writers have abandoned this preference. If you are writing for a traditional audience, though, you should probably avoid using an apostrophe and *s* to form a possessive with inanimate nouns. (See 35a for a detailed discussion on forming possessives.)

Certain prepositions can be used only with certain verbs, adjectives, or nouns. The accompanying charts contain verb + preposition combinations and *be* + adjective or noun + preposition combinations. Do not memorize this list. Instead, keep a list in your journal of sentences you hear that contain these phrases, and try to remember each phrase in context.

VERB + PREPOSITION COMBINATIONS

account for	blame (something)	disapprove of
accuse (someone) of	on (someone)	dream about, of
adapt to	borrow from	excuse (someone)
add to	care about	for (something)
agree on (something)	catch up with	explain (something)
agree to (something)	come from	to (someone)
agree with	comment on	forgive (someone)
(someone)	communicate with	for (something)
apologize for	compare with	get along with
(something)	complain about, of	get back from
apologize to	compliment (some-	get rid of
(someone)	one) on (something)	get through with
apply for	concentrate on	get used to
approve of	congratulate	graduate from
argue about	(someone)	happen to
(something)	on (something)	have an
argue with (someone)	consent to	opportunity for
arrive at	consist of	have a reason for
ask for	convince (someone)	have a talent for
become of	of (something)	have confidence in
believe in	decide between	have influence over
belong to	decide on	have patience with
blame (someone) for	depend on	hear about, of

(continued)

ESL ADVICE

Verb phrases with prepositions are among the most difficult English idioms for ESL students to master. Studies show that new language acquisition occurs more slowly after childhood, so you may need to have special patience with older students struggling to use these idioms correctly. Frequent reading may help individuals acquire new habits of syntax. Students might also use their journals or notebooks for rote practice of phrases in sentence contexts.

16b
prep

ESL

16b
prep

ESL

VERB + PREPOSITION COMBINATIONS *(continued)*

hear from	pay for	stop from
help (someone) with (something)	plan on	substitute for
	prefer to	subtract from
hope for	prepare for	succeed in
insist on	prevent from	take advantage of
introduce to	protect from	talk about
invite (someone) to	provide for	talk over
keep for	provide (someone) with	talk to
keep from		thank (someone) for (something)
know about	recover from	think about
laugh about	refer to	think of
laugh at	relate to	throw away
learn about	rely on	travel to
listen for	remind (someone) of	vote for
listen to	search for	wait for
look at	see about	wait on
look for	send for	waste (money) on
look forward to	separate from	wish for
matter to	show up at	worry about
object to	spend (money) on	
participate in	stare at	

BE + ADJECTIVE OR NOUN + PREPOSITION

be absent from	be content with	be faithful to
be accustomed to	be dedicated to	be familiar with
be acquainted with	be delighted at, with	be famous for
be afraid of	be devoted to	be fed up with
be angry at, with	be different from	be finished with
be appropriate for	be disappointed by, in, with	be fond of
be ashamed of		be friendly to, with
be aware of	be divorced from	be frightened by, of
be bad for	be done with	be generous about
be bored by, with	be dressed in	be glad about
be capable of	be engaged to	be good at, for
be certain of	be enthusiastic about	be grateful for, to
be clear to	be envious of	be guilty of
be committed to	be equal to	be happy about, for, with
be composed of	be essential to	
be concerned about, by	be excited about	be incapable of
	be exhausted by, from	be in charge of

(continued)

BE + ADJECTIVE OR NOUN + PREPOSITION *(continued)*

be in danger of	be opposed to	be sensitive to
be in favor of	be out of	be sorry about, for
be innocent of	be patient with	be suitable for
be interested in	be polite to	be sure about, of
be in touch with	be prevented from	be surprised at, by
be jealous of	be proud of	be terrified of
be known for	be relevant to	be thankful for
be lazy about	be responsible for, to	be tired from, of
be made from, of	be satisfied with	be used to
be married by, to	be scared by, of	be worried about

16c   Avoiding unintended repetition

The following sentences illustrate a different problem with word choice, one that has more to do with awkwardness than with meaning.

1. We argued for about three hours about this until I realized how

   nearly

   stupid the argument was.

   Notice that each of the *about*'s is perfectly correct by itself, but having the two of them in the same sentence creates an awkward sound, so one of them must be changed to a different word. This awkward sound is sometimes called an *unfortunate chime*.

2. The room will also be large enough so that nonmembers will also

   In addition, the

   be welcome at the meeting.

   Each of the *also*'s is correct here, but the two of them together create an unfortunate chime.

3. Before I used to do aerobics, I used to go to work depressed.

   started doing

   The repetition of *used to* is another unfortunate chime.

16d   Avoiding wordiness and redundant expressions
Wordiness

Wordiness is a more complicated subject than one might suppose. The following examples are wordy.

16d
w

1. For people who don't want a big meal, there are vending machines ~~that they can use.~~

2. I recognized that she ~~had a higher level of maturity in comparison~~ *was more mature than* with my two brothers.

3. He ~~proceeded to escort~~ me on a tour of the paper mill. *escorted*

4. The first step ~~begins~~ with realizing that no one is perfect. *is*

From sentences 1–4, you might conclude that whenever you can reduce the number of words in a sentence, you should. Such a conclusion, however, would be an oversimplification, as the following examples illustrate.

16d
w

5. She climbed into her car and drove away. *shiny red Porsche*

6. Bruce was wearing a hat. *green beret*

7. The strawberries came in a container. *green plastic crate*

The revised versions in sentences 5–7 are clearly more effective than the originals even though they are longer. Each of the words added to sentences 5–7 contributed meaning by making the sentence clearer, more descriptive, or more powerful. By contrast, the words deleted from the first four sentences did not add meaning or increase effectiveness. Taking them out did not reduce the meaning or the power of those sentences.

Eliminating wordiness, then, involves editing out words that add nothing to a sentence—revising the sentence so that it says the same thing just as powerfully in fewer words.

Intensifiers

The italicized words in the following sentences raise another question about wordiness. Words like these, which increase the intensity of the adjectives or adverbs they modify, are called **intensifiers.**

8. It was *extremely* cold in January last year.
9. I was *very* tired by three o'clock.

Many writers would think that both words contribute nothing to the sentences and would therefore remove them. Other writers might

disagree. If the normal temperature in January for the area where the writer of sentence 8 lives is in the low thirties and the average temperature last January was in the twenties, perhaps *extremely* is unnecessary. Temperatures in the twenties are certainly cold, but perhaps not *extremely* cold. However, if the temperature never got out of the single digits for the entire month of January, that is *extremely* cold.

Extremely is not always wrong, then, but most of us have a tendency to use intensifiers such as *extremely* and *very* unnecessarily. Sometimes intensifiers are appropriate, but most of the time the adjective alone is strong enough to convey the meaning intended.

Redundancy

The following sentences illustrate a kind of wordiness that is less debatable than the use of intensifiers. Most careful writers would agree with the revisions in the following sentences.

10. She had no idea of the ~~boundaries and~~ limitations on behavior at

    a dinner party.

    In this case, the meanings of *boundaries* and *limitations* are similar; the writer had said the same thing twice. Either one word or the other can be eliminated without losing any meaning.

When a sentence says the same thing twice, it is **redundant.** Writers should avoid redundancy.

11. My sister's perception of men changed as she entered ~~into~~ college.

    Entered means "went into," so *into* is redundant.

12. ~~Often~~ m̃any marriages break up as a result of the financial pressure when one spouse becomes unemployed.

    Here *often* and *many* convey the same meaning, so one of them had to go.

Expletive constructions

The following sentences illustrate another source of wordiness.

13. ~~There were~~ T̃hree police officers *were* waiting to arrest Mr. Bowles.

    There added no meaning to this sentence. It simply held the normal subject position so that the subject could be moved to a position

following the verb. The revised version is clearly less wordy; it is also more direct and more forceful.

14. It is required that students pay their bills before the first day of classes.

> *It* in this sentence served the same purpose as *there* in sentence 13. It held the subject position while the true subject moved to a position after the verb. Again, the revised version, with the subject in the usual subject position, is more effective and less wordy.

There and *it* as they are used in sentences 13 and 14 are known as **expletives.** In most cases, an expletive construction is less concise, less forceful, and less direct than a sentence with the true subject in the subject position.

16e Avoiding awkward word choices

In the following sentences, the problem is not using the wrong word for the meaning intended, an unfortunate chime, or wordiness; instead, the wording of the sentence is simply awkward.

1. Opening the oven door can be a harmful effect on a cake that isn't ready to be taken out.

> The original sentence stated that *opening the door* was *an effect* when what the writer really meant was that *opening the door* can *have* an effect.

2. Jenny and I felt the same way about marriage being a sacred bond between a man and a woman.

> *Felt the same way about marriage being* was both wordy and awkward.

3. The outcome of this inquiry could have resulted in the loss of my job.

> The *outcome could have been* or the *inquiry could have resulted,* but you can't say that the "outcome could have resulted in something."

16f Avoiding prefab phrases

The following examples illustrate another kind of problem with word choice.

1. My job at drama camp wasn't really work; ~~it was a challenge.~~ *I enjoyed acting*

> Certain phrases in English come to be used over and over to express the same idea. Because they exist ready-made like a window frame you can buy off the shelf at a lumber yard, we call them *prefab phrases. It was a challenge* is one such expression. Because it has been used too often by too many writers and speakers, you would be wise to cast the sentence in a fresher way.

The word work has several meanings.

2. ~~Work means different things to different people.~~

> This prefab phrase, *means different things to different people,* is especially common in the writing of beginning writers.

3. I was glad to find that the rest rooms were located right around the corner. ~~for our convenience.~~

> *For your convenience* is a prefab phrase that comes from the business world. One bank actually cut back its hours from 9:00 to 5:00 to 9:30 to 4:00 and announced "new hours for your convenience."

16g Avoiding excessive humility

A certain amount of humility is undoubtedly a good thing in all of us, but the writer of sentence 1 surely has too much of a good thing.

1. ~~It is only my opinion, but I think that perhaps~~ *T*his course requires too much work.

> The writer of the original sentence indicated a lack of confidence in three different ways. That is clearly excessive. In truth, when you write an opinion about something, it is usually quite clear that you are stating your opinion, and to say so merely points out the obvious. To do so three times is overkill.

ESL ADVICE

Phrases that sound shopworn to native speakers may sound new and lively to ESL writers who are unfamiliar with English idioms. It would be unreasonable to expect such students to identify clichés easily. Make allowances for those students whose developing awareness of time-honored expressions may facilitate their language acquisition and fluency.

16g
wc

16h
wc

2. ~~In my opinion,~~ the Orioles will win the pennant next year.

Here the phrase *in my opinion* is more debatable. If you think about it, however, you will realize that there is no way you could know who is going to win the pennant. So to point out that you are giving your opinion states the obvious and makes you sound less sure of yourself.

3. ~~I feel that~~ we should hold an election within the next six months.

I feel should not be used to mean *I think*, and here either expression is probably unnecessary because it is perfectly clear without it that the writer is stating an opinion.

In some cultures, expressions of humility are expected of a writer, but in English they should be used sparingly. If it won't be clear to your reader that a statement is just your opinion, say so. But when it is clear, don't use these qualifying phrases to point out the obvious.

FOR DISCUSSION

Distinguishing between connotation and denotation might be the basis for class discussion. Assign a passage from an essay in a college reader. Have students focus on one adjective or one noun that figures prominently in the passage. Encourage students to discuss shadings of difference between the denotative (or abstract) meaning provided by a dictionary and the connotative (or emotional) meaning provided by the passage itself.

16h Being aware of connotation

The explicit meaning of a word, the meaning you find if you look the word up in a dictionary, is referred to as the *denotative meaning* or **denotation.** But words also have emotional colorings or associations that contribute to their meanings; these emotional colorings are called **connotations.** The denotative meanings of *lasting* and *endless* are nearly identical, but their connotations are quite different. *Lasting* has positive connotations; you would use it to describe something that you want to last. *Endless* has a negative connotation and would be used to describe something you wish would be over. Another example is *proud* and *vain.* The words are similar in denotation, but the connotations of *vain* are more negative.

The accompanying chart compares the denotations and connotations of a number of words, all having the general meaning of "not giving way to pressure or persuasion." Notice how different the connotations of these words can be.

DENOTATIONS AND CONNOTATIONS

Word	Denotation	Connotation
firm	Constant; steadfast; unyielding to pressure	Neutral to positive
determined	Marked by or showing fixed purpose; resolute; unwavering	Positive, especially when applied to the pursuit of a goal
faithful	Adhering strictly to a person or cause; dutiful; loyal	Positive, especially when applied to a person or a cause
single-minded	Having one overriding purpose; steadfast	Slightly negative, especially in connection with a particular goal
unyielding	Not giving way to pressure or persuasion; steadfast	Neutral to negative
stubborn	Not easily persuaded; persistent; unduly determined	Negative

16i
wc

When you write, it is important to use words with appropriate denotative meanings, but you must also think about connotations. To describe a man as *skinny* is quite different from saying he is *slender*. To describe a friend as *childish* creates a different impression from saying he or she is *childlike*.

A number of reference books are available to assist you in choosing words with just the right connotations (see 16i).

16i Using reference books

The more writing you must do, the more reference books you will need to assist you. Here we describe different types of reference books you may want to acquire. Writers who must worry

about correctness should own a dictionary and a handbook. If they can afford additional references, a usage guide, a thesaurus, and a research style manual are also useful.

Dictionaries

Types of dictionaries. Two basic types of dictionaries are available: unabridged and abridged. *Abridged* means "shortened"; *unabridged* means "not shortened." Unabridged dictionaries can be as large as twenty volumes and are rapidly becoming available on disks for computer use. They attempt to include all words currently in use in the English language (but, of course, they cannot because new words come into use every day). They are particularly useful for providing the history of words—what words have meant and how they have been used at various times in the past. Most writers will not need an unabridged dictionary of their own; when the need for one arises, they can find one at the local library.

Abridged dictionaries can be divided into two groups. *College* or *desk dictionaries* are a sensible compromise between the expense and bulkiness of an unabridged dictionary and the incompleteness of a pocket dictionary. College dictionaries contain between 150,000 and 200,000 entries and are designed for writing tasks such as those you will encounter in college. *Compact, concise,* or *pocket dictionaries* contain far fewer entries and less information about each entry. They are usually inadequate for the purposes of a college-level writer.

A word about *Webster's*. Noah Webster was a nineteenth-century American scholar who wrote many popular writing textbooks and spelling guides. His *American Dictionary of the English Language,* published in 1828, was immensely successful primarily because it included words and meanings common to *American* English. However, because the word *Webster's* is not protected by copyright, it can be used by anyone who wants to publish a dictionary. In fact, there are many dictionaries on the market today that include the word *Webster's* in their title, even though they have no connection with Noah Webster or his origi-

nal dictionary. If you wish to cite a dictionary definition, you must give the full name of the dictionary; "according to *Webster's*" will not suffice.

Using a dictionary. Every dictionary includes a section in the front where you will find material on such matters as usage, dialects, grammar, spelling, lexicography, and the history of the language, as well as a guide to pronunciation and a guide to the dictionary. This last section is one you may want to spend some time studying, especially if you are inexperienced with dictionaries or with this particular dictionary. There you will find out whether your dictionary lists meanings in chronological order or according to frequency of use, whether geographic and biographical entries are integrated into the word listings or included in special sections in the back, and how endings on words are indicated.

Because dictionaries must condense a large amount of information into a limited space, they make use of various abbreviations and conventions, which sometimes make them difficult to read. The following sample entry from *The American Heritage Dictionary of the English Language* illustrates how various kinds of information are represented. Your dictionary will probably use slightly different abbreviations and formats, but the general approach will be similar to that discussed here. The specifics about your dictionary will be explained in the front of that dictionary.

ACTIVITY
Consider sending students to the library as part of an extended definition assignment. Have them use *Webster's Third Unabridged* or the *Oxford English Dictionary* to research information about words individually chosen in class. Ask each student to jot down points about the history and varied definitions of a selected word. Such research can become the basis for an extended definition essay in which students consider synonyms, etymology, and personal examples to reveal the writer's own connotative experiences with the word.

16i
wc

① ② ③ ④

op·po·site (ŏp′ ə -zĭt) *adj.* *Abbr.* **op., opp.** 1. Placed or located directly across from something else or from each other; lying in corresponding positions from an intervening space or object: *opposite sides of a building.* **2.** Facing the other way; moving or tending away from each other: *opposite directions.* **3.** Contrary or antithetical in nature or tendency; diametrically opposed; altogether different. **4.** *Botany.* Growing in pairs on either side of a stem. Said especially of leaves. Compare **alternate**. —*n.* **1.** A person or thing that is opposite or contrary to another. See Usage note below. **2.** *Archaic.* An opponent or antagonist. —*adv.* In an opposite position or positions: *They sat opposite at the table.* —*prep.* **1.**

⑤

③ ③ ③

⑤ Across from or facing: *Park your car opposite the bank.* **2.** In a complementary dramatic role to: *She played opposite him.* [Middle English, from Old French, from Latin *oppositus,* from the past ⑦ participle of *oppōnere,* OPPOSE.]

—*ŏp po·site·ly* adv. —*ŏp po·site·ness* n.

⑧ *Synonyms: opposite, contrary, antithetical, contradictory.* These adjectives have the common meaning of being irreconcilably set apart. When two things have a definite relationship and yet differ to the extent of revealing marked contrast, they are *opposite: opposite sides of the street; opposite points of view. Contrary* stresses extreme divergence and may imply stubbornness. *Antithetical* emphasizes sharp, diametrical opposition, usually intellectual. *Contradictory* implies denial of one view by another.

⑨ *Usage: Opposite,* as a noun, may be followed by *of,* as in *The opposite of right is wrong.* As an adjective it may be followed by *to* or *from,* as in *This is opposite to* (or *from*) *my belief.* It is never followed by *than.*

① **Spelling and syllabication.** The main entry, in bold type, gives the correct spelling of the word and indicates whether it should be capitalized or not. (For example, *German shepherd* appears with a capital *G* and a lowercase *s,* which is how it should be written.) In addition, any optional spellings are also indicated, with the preferred spelling given first: the entry for *theater,* for example, begins like this: **the·a·ter** (thē′ə-tər) *n.* Also **the·a·tre.**

The syllables of the word are indicated by raised dots (·) in the main entry. Use this information when you are dividing words at the end of a line with a hyphen (see 42a). If an entry is spelled as a hyphenated word or as two words, that will also be indicated in the main entry. (For example, a hyphenated word looks like this: **bat·tle-ax**; a two-word entry, like this: **book review.**)

② **Pronunciation.** In parentheses, the entry indicates how the word is pronounced. The symbols used to represent pronunciation are explained at the bottom of each page or on the inside front and back covers. The accent mark (′) indicates the syllable that is stressed.

③ **Part of speech.** Dictionaries use a series of abbreviations to indicate parts of speech. In English, most words can be used as more than one part of speech. Notice that *opposite* is defined first as an adjective, but farther down, following bold dashes, it is also defined as a noun, an adverb, and a preposition. When looking up an unfamiliar word, be sure to look for definitions appropriate to its part of speech in the context. Dictionaries also indicate whether verbs are transitive or intransitive.

④ **Inflected forms and abbreviations.** Following the pronunciation guide, dictionaries generally indicate how the word is inflected—how its form changes, usually by changing the ending, to indicate different uses. *Opposite* is not inflected, so there is no indication of inflected forms. For the verb *finish*, for example, the beginning of the entry is as follows: **fin·ish** (fĭn′ ĭsh) *v.* **-ished, -ishing, -ishes.** The three items in bold type and preceded by hyphens indicate the principle parts of the verb (see 25a and 25b). For nouns, dictionaries usually indicate the form for plurals (see 19a); for adjectives, they give the comparative and superlative forms (see 28c). Some dictionaries include the inflections only when the word is irregular; others indicate inflections for all words, regular and irregular. Some dictionaries also indicate standard abbreviations for words that have them. In our example, *The American Heritage Dictionary* indicates that *opposite* can be abbreviated as *op.* or as *opp.*

⑤ **Meanings.** The largest portion of most entries is devoted to a list of definitions of meanings of the word. These may be arranged in chronological order (the earliest definition first, the most recent last) or in order of frequency (the most common first, the least common last) or, as in the *American Heritage* example, in "a psychologically meaningful order" so that the definitions form logical clusters rather than a string of unrelated meanings. To clarify the definition, dictionaries often give a brief example of the word used with that meaning. In the entry for *opposite*, the first definition is followed by the example *opposite sides of a building* to illustrate the first meaning.

ESL ADVICE

Second-language learners can benefit greatly from knowing how English dictionaries identify principal parts of verbs. If a student is familiar with the basic formulas for major tenses (see 25), he or she can learn to edit verb phrases by checking the dictionary's entries for past, past participle, and present participle spellings.

16i
wc

16i
wc

Some definitions will be labeled with a word indicating the usage appropriate for the word with that definition. In our example, the fourth definition is preceded by the word *Botany,* indicating that the term *opposite* is used by botanists with the definition that follows. Other labels might indicate the level of appropriate usage; these include *Nonstandard, Informal, Slang, Vulgar, Obsolete, Archaic, Rare,* and *Poetic.* Still other labels, such as *British* or *Southwestern U.S.,* indicate that a definition is more appropriate in a certain geographic region. If a word has no usage labels, it is considered standard English and can be used in most writing situations, even the most formal.

⑥ **Idioms.** Some dictionaries will also provide definitions of idioms that use the word being defined. For example, if you didn't understand the idiom *an iron in the fire,* you could look up its chief word, *iron,* in *The American Heritage Dictionary* and find that it means "an undertaking or project." If you are not sure which is the chief word, you may have to look up each of the important words in the idiom.

⑦ **Etymologies.** Most dictionaries provide a brief *etymology,* or history of words, either following the definitions or following the inflected forms. In our example, after the definitions the dictionary explains, in brackets, that *opposite* comes from Middle English, which took it from Old French, in which it evolved from the Latin word *oppositus,* derived from the past participle of the Latin verb *opponere,* which meant "to oppose."

⑧ **Synonyms.** Many dictionaries not only provide lists of synonyms for particular words but, more important, discuss the shades of differences among the various synonyms. In our example, *The American Heritage Dictionary* points out, for instance, that *opposite* things "have a definite relationship and yet differ to the extent of revealing marked contrast." On the other hand, *contrary* "stresses extreme divergence and may imply stubbornness."

⑨ **Usage notes.** Many dictionaries provide separate usage notes for words that are frequently misused or about which there is some controversy. The usage note in our example points out that you must never follow *opposite* with *than.*

Handbooks

Handbooks like this one are general reference works that provide guidance about many aspects of writing. They are important tools for writers.

Usage guides

A number of books contain guidance strictly about the use of problematic words. These do not contain nearly as complete a listing of words as standard dictionaries, only words that cause writers problems—words like *number* and *amount, disinterested* and *uninterested, literally* and *figuratively,* and *flaunt* and *flout.* Usually they feature long discussions of the distinctions among words, the contexts in which each is correct, and the reasons for such recommendations. After a good dictionary and a handbook, a usage guide is probably the next most useful reference tool for anyone who writes regularly.

The following are reputable usage guides. We especially recommend Bernstein's *Careful Writer.*

- Theodore M. Bernstein, *The Careful Writer*
- Theodore M. Bernstein, *Miss Thistlebottom's Hobgoblins*
- Roy H. Copperud, *American Usage and Style*
- Bergen Evans and Cornelia Evans, *A Dictionary of Contemporary American Usage*
- Wilson Follett, *Modern American Usage*
- William Morris and Mary Morris, *Harper Dictionary of Contemporary Usage*
- *Webster's Dictionary of English Usage*
- Kenneth G. Wilson, *The Columbia Guide to Standard American Usage*

ACTIVITY

If possible, arrange for a librarian to introduce your class to the reference collection at the campus library. The occasion should give students an opportunity to view not only the books listed in this section, but also other materials that could prove useful in future research.

16i
wc

16j
wc

Thesauri

A *thesaurus* lists common words in alphabetical order and gives synonyms for them. Some thesauri include near synonyms and antonyms, some give definitions of the entry words, and some list idioms as well as single-word synonyms. Most thesauri do not explain distinctions among the synonyms listed for each word; you need a good dictionary for that.

The best time to consult a thesaurus is when you can't think of a word to express a certain idea, but you know a word that means something close to what you want. Look that word up in the thesaurus; chances are good that the word you can't remember will be listed as a synonym. A thesaurus is excellent for helping writers *recall* words they know but can't think of.

However, some writers use a thesaurus to find a word that "sounds good" or perhaps "sounds literary" and may select a word they have never heard before. There is a great danger in using an unfamiliar word you found in a list of synonyms in a thesaurus: the word may have connotations (see 16h) you are not aware of, or it may have a slightly different meaning from what you intend. If you decide to use an unfamiliar word in your writing, discuss it with someone who is familiar with it, or look it up in a dictionary to make sure its meaning fits your intention.

Many word processing programs on computers now include an on-line thesaurus. If yours does, use it with the same caution you would when using a printed thesaurus.

16j Using the computer to edit for word choice

Certain computer programs can assist you in revising for word choice, among other things. These programs, called *style checkers* or *grammar checkers,* are based on lists of words that writers frequently have trouble with, words like *to/too, then/than,* and *its/it's.* The program *cannot* tell whether you have used each word correctly. It merely moves through your text, highlighting each word you have used that is on its list. *You have to decide, in each instance, whether the word is used correctly or not.* If you use a style checker, resist the temptation to change every word that is high-

lighted by the computer—you may be changing words that are correct, sometimes for the worse. For this reason, writers often conclude that they can revise their writing more quickly by reading it over carefully themselves than by using a style checker. However, if you have access to such a program, give it a try. Just be sure that you don't change every word the computer highlights. Evaluate each one.

If you don't have access to a style checker but do write your papers using a word processing program, you can still use the computer to assist you in revising for word choice. Most of us have a fairly limited list of words that we sometimes use incorrectly. Keep a list of such words handy, and use your word processor's search or find function to help you locate them in your writing. Just invoke the function and ask the computer to find every use of the first word on your list. You can then evaluate the correctness of each instance. Continue until you have checked every occurrence of each word on your list. If you have access to a sophisticated word processor that will allow you to search for more than one word at a time, you can type your entire list of words into the request and check them all in one pass.

17a
wc

17 USING APPROPRIATE WORDS

In Chapter 16 we discussed ways to avoid using words *incorrectly.* In this chapter we will consider the more subtlequestion of how to use words *appropriately.*

17a Avoiding sexist language

Language that expresses unwarranted assumptions about people based simply on their gender is sexist. Sexist language should be avoided for two reasons, one principled and one practical. First, most people these days agree that stereotyping people by gender is simply unjust, so we wish to avoid doing that. Second, some

Distinguishing between appropriate and inappropriate diction calls for a close awareness of audience as well as familiarity with the wide range of diction levels used in various kinds of writing. By way of general introduction to the problem of appropriateness, this chapter addresses such timely issues as sexist language, necessary and unnecessary jargon, pretentiousness, and profanity. It also reviews the importance of figurative language.

RESOURCES

Labov, William. *Language in the Inner City: Studies in the Black English Vernacular.* Philadelphia: U of Pennsylvania P, 1972.

Miller, Casey, and Kate Swift. *The Handbook of Non-Sexist Writing.* 2nd ed. New York: Harper-Collins, 1988.

Nilsen, Don L. F. "Clichés, Trite Sayings, Dead Metaphors, and Stale Figures of Speech in Composition Instruction." *College Composition and Communication* 27 (1976): 278–82.

Stotsky, Sandra. "Teaching the Vocabulary of Academic Discourse." *Journal of Basic Writing* 2.3 (1979): 15–39.

17a
wc

people who do not share this view still avoid sexist language because it may offend their audience and thus reduce the effectiveness of their writing. We hope you share our philosophical objection to sexism, but even if you don't, we advise you to avoid sexist language so that your writing will be more effective.

The following sentences illustrate the most extreme form of sexist language.

1. Two chicks were playing basketball when we arrived at the gym. *(women)*
2. My company hired three babes. *(women)*
3. Please call my girl and make an appointment to meet with me. *(secretary)*
4. I was pleased to find out that my dentist was a lady. *(woman)*

Words such as *chicks* and *babes* are so offensive as to be unacceptable to almost all readers, even those who do not agree with other aspects of feminism. *Girl*, when used to refer to an adult woman, is unacceptable to most people these days, and many find that *lady* evokes an image of a woman so delicate as to need the protection of a man.

The next sentences illustrate a more subtle form of sexist language.

5. Men have struggled to end injustice throughout history. *(People)*
6. Some people have criticized the American space program for putting too much emphasis on manned flights. *(that carry human beings)*

Referring to the entire human race by words that recognize only the male half is sexist.

Many instances of sexist language involve words referring to work or jobs.

7. The mailman delivered a package to our neighbors. *(letter carrier)*
8. This advertising campaign is aimed at businessmen. *(people)*

Most job titles now avoid the word *man: police officer, firefighter, chair* or *chairperson, diplomat* (rather than *statesman*).

Pronouns are another source of potentially sexist language. When these errors occur, there is usually more than one way to correct them.

9. A doctor should put *his or her* instructions in writing.
10. *Doctors* ~~A doctor should put his~~ *their* instructions in writing.
11. A doctor should put *all* ~~his~~ instructions in writing.

Some people find the use of *his or her* awkward, so it is usually better to recast the sentence in the plural (see 23b) or in a form that requires no personal pronouns.

The desire to avoid faulty parallelism as well as sexism would lead a writer to correct the next example of sexist language.

12. Mr. Hiroshige *and Mrs.* ~~and his wife~~ Margaret are meeting us at the movie.
13. Mr. Hiroshige *Sam and Margaret* ~~and his wife Margaret~~ are meeting us at the movie.

When referring to men and women, be consistent in the form by which you identify them.

Finally, thinking about who your audience is should help you avoid the next kind of sexist language.

14. At the end of this course, we will all go to the National Gallery; you may bring your *spouse or a friend* ~~wives~~ if you wish.

Unless this sentence is addressed to an all-male class, its author is making the sexist assumption that everyone reading it is male.

17b Using jargon effectively

Groups such as police officers, nurses, and motorcyclists develop specialized language that helps them communicate efficiently and clearly *within the group*; this specialized language shared by the members of a profession or other group is known

Students may suspect that an ability to wield jargon is necessary to their advancement in higher education. From our own academic experience, we know that this suspicion is not entirely unjustified. Point out, however, that the "best" jargon is that which has been coined in the interest of simplifying complex concepts. For example, *interface* as a computer science term conveniently represents an elaborate technical process. On the other hand, jargon can become gibberish if used excessively or pretentiously (see 17c).

17b
wc

ACTIVITY

Have students gather examples of sentences with jargon from textbooks or articles they may be reading. Put some of the examples on the board and ask students to try paraphrasing the sentences in simpler language. Depending on whether more or fewer words are required for a paraphrase, students may recognize whether the author of a given quotation uses jargon effectively or is merely wordy.

17b
wc

as **jargon.** (Sometimes the term *jargon* is also used to describe an elevated, pretentious style of writing, but we will discuss problems with that style in 17c.)

Believe it or not, each of the following passages speaks clearly to the group of readers for whom it was intended. The intended audience is identified in brackets following each passage.

> Macintosh menus are pulled down from the top of the screen and overlay whatever is being displayed (fig. 1.1). The menu options are highlighted as the cursor passes over them. You select an option by letting up the mouse switch when the right option is highlighted. The menu then rolls back up so that you can proceed with the program. By selecting and activating a menu option, you either get another menu requiring additional information or the entry window. [Macintosh computer users]
>
> —John Hannah, *Using Dollars and Sense*

Unless you are a Macintosh user, you probably won't understand this paragraph. Jargon can provide efficient and precise communication among professionals who share a vocabulary. For the general audience, however, it often approaches incomprehensibility. Extreme caution is therefore necessary when using jargon in writing intended for an audience that is not familiar with the specialized vocabulary. When experts in a field forget that they are not always writing for other experts, they often fail to communicate their ideas.

The following passage is taken from the application for a guaranteed student loan, a form that must be completed (and presumably understood) by students before they receive government-insured loans.

> The maker and comakers of this note hereby waive presentation, protest and notice of dishonor, and the benefit of the Homestead Exemptions as to this obligation and agree that the holder's right of recourse against them is expressly reserved and shall not be affected by extending the time of payment without their assent.

The problem with this passage is that it is written with a heavy dose of jargon. It is probably perfectly clear to the author of the passage, but it is incomprehensible to the intended audience.

Does this mean that you should never use jargon when writing to an audience that may not be familiar with it? No. Sometimes, if used thoughtfully and introduced clearly, technical jargon can be effective even for a general audience. For one thing, it demonstrates your qualifications as an expert; you know the jargon, the language of insiders. And some jargon serves the useful purpose of expressing a complicated idea succinctly. So you may want to use *a little* technical jargon, carefully selected and thoroughly explained, even when writing to an audience that is unlikely to be familiar with it. If you use jargon with a general audience, you should follow three guidelines:

- Keep the jargon to a minimum.
- Use technical terms primarily when no general term exists.
- Explain each technical term you use clearly and completely.

17b
wc

The following passage, taken from physicist Stephen Hawking's book *A Brief History of Time,* makes careful use of jargon to explain Newton's first and second laws to a general audience.

Notice that when Hawking does use a technical term (each instance is highlighted), it is followed by a clear explanation (shown in italics). Using technical jargon in this way can be quite effective. Notice also that Hawking makes repeated use of examples to illustrate the principles he is explaining.

> In Galileo's experiments, as a body rolled down the slope it was always acted on by the same force (*its weight*), and the effect was to make it constantly speed up. This showed that the real effect of a force is always to change the speed of a body, rather than just to set it moving, as was previously thought. It also meant that whenever a body is not acted on by any force, it will keep on moving in a straight line at the same speed. This idea was first stated explicitly in Newton's *Principia Mathematica,* published in 1687, and is known as Newton's first law. What happens to a body when a force

17c
wc

does act on it is given by Newton's second law. This states that the body will accelerate, or *change its speed,* at a rate that is proportional to the force. (For example, the acceleration is twice as great if the force is twice as great.) The acceleration is also smaller the greater the mass (or *quantity of matter*) of the body. (The same force acting on a body of twice the mass will produce half the acceleration.) A familiar example is provided by a car: the more powerful the engine, the greater the acceleration, but the heavier the car, the smaller the acceleration for the same engine.

17c Avoiding pretentious language

Closely related to the use of jargon is the use of unnecessarily pretentious and ornate language that seems to be designed more to impress than to communicate. Such language is sometimes known as *bureaucratese.* Consider the following passage.

The aim of the periodic management-staff interfacing sessions is to maximize communication and to ensure dissemination of company policies as well as to promote peer interaction.

This passage could have been written much more clearly, as follows.

We hold weekly meetings to allow management to tell the staff about new policies, to answer questions about these policies, and to let the staff discuss them among themselves.

The following list identifies words that can create a pretentious style and suggests some simpler alternatives.

PRETENTIOUS TERM	EFFECTIVE TERM	PRETENTIOUS TERM	EFFECTIVE TERM
ameliorate	improve	indicator	sign
author	write	interface	meet
(*as a verb*)		optimal	best
commence	begin	proceed	go, walk,
endeavor	try		move
exit	leave	prior to	before
facilitate	help	utilize	use
finalize	finish	viable	workable
impact on	affect		

17d Using slang effectively

In the discussion of dictionaries in 16i, we point out that dictionaries label some words as slang. You may have thought that such labeling means you should never use these words, but that's not quite true. Slang is frequently lively, forceful, and colorful. It is jarring in most formal writing, such as that done in college or in business, but it can be effective under certain circumstances.

1. The shopper asked her daughter, "Do you like the blue one, Doreen, dear?" to which Doreen answered, "Ooh, it's, like, totally rad!"

   The slang here is appropriate because it occurs in a quotation from spoken English. When you are trying to capture the flavor of a conversation, it is appropriate to use the exact words spoken.

2. The ballet was brilliantly conceived, beautifully choreographed, dramatically staged, powerfully danced. At points it became downright steamy.

   Steamy, meaning "provocative, sensual," is slang. Here it is being used in a passage that is otherwise quite formal to provide a little extra punch.

A word of caution is in order. Getting slang to work in a given context requires a good ear. Don't use slang in otherwise formal passages unless you are certain that the effect justifies the violation of norms. And don't use it very often. If you are unsure of whether it works or whether you are using it too often, leave it out.

17e Recognizing the perils of using obscenity and profanity

Obscenity is language that is offensive to standards of decency or modesty; **profanity** is language that shows contempt or irreverence toward God or sacred things. The legal establishment has struggled for centuries to define obscenity and profanity, and we will not try to achieve anything like legal rigor in discussing the concepts here. Nevertheless, users of English are aware of a group of words that are widely considered to fit in one of these two categories. Obscenities are graphic or blunt words that stand

17e
wc

for sexual or excretory organs or functions; clinical terms for these same organs or functions are not obscene. Profanities are words, usually involving names for God or references to hell or damnation, which are used as oaths or exclamations. *Damn, hell, Jesus Christ,* and similar words used to express anger, hostility, or strong emotion are profanities; the same words used to discuss religious concepts are not profane. If you are in doubt about the status of a word, check usage labels in a dictionary. Labels like *Obscene, Vulgar, Profane,* or *Offensive* will identify words that you should use only with caution.

Both obscenities and profanities are offensive to many readers. You should use them in only a few situations:

- When you are trying to express great emotion and believe that the risk of offending the audience is worth taking.
- When you know your audience well and are certain that such language won't offend. Even then, you should be aware that sometimes writing reaches audiences other than the one intended.

Even in these situations, obscenity and profanity have the desired effect only if used sparingly. At the end of the movie *Gone with the Wind,* when Rhett Butler says, "Frankly, my dear, I don't give a damn," the profanity is powerful because such language was not often heard in movies of the 1930s and was never used in the presence of women at the time Butler was supposed to be speaking.

Language that is intended to shock loses its force if used too frequently. If you are sure that it will be effective, you may use obscenity or profanity on the rare occasions when it is justified.

17f Using figurative language

Sometimes the difference between merely competent writing and vibrant, brilliant writing is the presence of figurative language, especially similes and metaphors. Too many writers wrongly assume that these figures of speech belong only to poets and novelists. Many writers, even those writing in freshman English classes, have experienced the pleasure of expressing an idea or a feeling metaphorically.

Similes

The following are similes.

1. They sat immobile on their antique bench like a row of crusty oysters and ingested with their eyes everything that passed.

   —John Barth, *The Floating Opera*

John Barth compares a bench full of retired oystermen to a row of oysters taking in everything that floats into view. The comparison helps us understand and feel the presence and significance of the old men. Notice that Barth makes the comparison clear by using the word *like*.

2. Over she went in the ditch, like a little puff of milkweed.

   —Eudora Welty, "A Worn Path"

Here Eudora Welty compares a frail older woman to the puffy flower of the milkweed, and the comparison helps us picture the woman. Again, the comparison makes use of *like*.

A comparison made with the word *like* (or sometimes *as*) is a **simile.** Notice how these figures of speech give us a better sense of the person or thing being described. We get a truer sense of Barth's old men by thinking of them as crusty oysters lined up and breathing in everything that floats near them. Something of the delicacy and fragility (and perhaps even the white hair) of Eudora Welty's old woman comes across in the comparison to the milkweed.

Similes, then, are comparisons that help us see and feel the person or thing being described and compared. The comparison is made explicit by the use of *like* or *as*.

Metaphors

The following sentences feature metaphors.

3. She felt that merely to go so far away from home was a kind of death in itself.

   —Richard Wright, "Long Black Song"

Richard Wright's young woman thinking about her lover who is overseas at war explains her feelings about his absence by compar-

17f
wc

ACTIVITY

To sharpen students' appreciation of figurative language, you might read aloud a favorite poem that does wonders with metaphor. Alternatively, distribute copies of a poem or prose passage for class analysis. Ask students to rewrite the same lines, eliminating the figures of speech and replacing them with ordinary diction. Then discuss differences between the two versions.

17f
wc

ing it to death. Instead of using *like* or *as*, Wright says that to be so far away "*was* a kind of death." Wright makes the comparison stronger by *equating* the two concepts instead of saying one is *like* the other. This kind of comparison, without the presence of *like* or *as*, is a **metaphor.** Wright's character really knows that absence and death are not the same thing, but by writing that her lover's being far away was a kind of death, Wright helps us understand the immensity of her sadness and sense of loss.

4. The words balloned from the lips and hovered about our heads—silent, separate, and pleasantly mysterious.

—Toni Morrison, *The Bluest Eye*

The metaphor here is a little more subtle, but if you think about the sentence, you will realize that it says that Claudia's mother's words seem to hang in the air *like balloons*. The comparison of her words with balloons is not *stated* but merely *implied*. This form is known as an *implied metaphor*. The implied comparison serves the same purpose as the more directly stated one in sentence 3: it helps us understand something better by comparing it with something else.

A metaphor, then, is a figure of speech that helps the reader understand a concept by comparing it with something the reader is likely to be familiar with. Though a metaphor states that one thing *is* another, this equating is not to be taken literally, only metaphorically. Absence in sentence 3 isn't the same as death, but by comparing it to death, we can better understand how the young woman feels about it. Metaphors can either be stated, as in sentence 3, or implied, as in sentence 4.

Although metaphors and similes can enliven your writing, there are two pitfalls in their use. The first is that in trying to use a lively metaphor or simile, writers sometimes employ expressions that have been used so often that they are no longer fresh. (This problem, the use of clichés, is discussed in 17g.) The second pitfall is known as a *mixed metaphor*.

Mixed metaphors

This second error writers sometimes make with metaphors and similes is illustrated in the following sentence.

5. Like a sailboat pushed by a strong wind, the bill sailed through Congress under a full head of steam.

> The problem here is that the bill's passage through Congress is being compared with *two different things*: a sailboat and a steamboat (or perhaps a steam locomotive). The confusion makes the sentence seem contradictory or even unintentionally humorous.

This kind of construction is known as a **mixed metaphor** because it mixes the comparison between two different objects. When using metaphors, make sure you do not "mix" them.

17g Avoiding clichés

The expressions in the chart below are all clichés. When they were new and fresh, clichés were effective expressions, but they have been used so often that they are worn out. At one time, they seemed to say something in a surprising way, but now they are so predictable that they fail. So don't use them. Normally, you can either eliminate them or replace them with ordinary words that don't try so unsuccessfully to be original.

CLICHÉS

acid test	face the music
all boils down to	few and far between
as luck would have it	hit the nail on the head
avoid like the plague	hour of need
beating around the bush	jumping on the bandwagon
between a rock and a hard place	knock your socks off
beyond the shadow of a doubt	the ladder of success
bring back to reality	last but not least
crushing blow	moving experience
crystal clear	ripe old age
deep, dark secret	rotten to the core

(continued)

ESL ADVICE

You might temper the advice given in this section by pointing out that a term can become a cliché only to an audience that has heard or read the same phrase a great many times. Because ESL students are relatively new to English, many of the phrases listed here may not seem trite at all. Non-native speakers may even improve their fluency by acquiring some of these expressions that are so common in everyday English discourse.

17g
wc

COLLABORATIVE ACTIVITY

Have students read one another's drafts and make suggestions concerning the kinds of usage reviewed in this chapter. Besides hunting for sexist language, unnecessary jargon, clichés, mixed metaphors, and archaic diction, writers might also compliment each other on well-phrased figures of speech.

18a
exact

Style is a topic to which all parts of this book relate. This chapter focuses on the aspects of style that most affect the power and clarity of expression: namely, concrete nouns and strong verbs. Encourage students to become aware of how the authors they read employ those key parts of speech to bring language alive.

CLICHÉS *(continued)*

sadder but wiser	this day and age
shoulder the burden	tried but true
sigh of relief	uphill battle
slowly but surely	

17h **Avoiding archaic language**

Dictionaries usually indicate that certain words, such as *betwixt, anon,* and *affright,* are archaic or obsolete. Unless for a particular rhetorical purpose you intend to sound exceedingly old-fashioned, avoid all words that are either obsolete or archaic.

18 WRITING WITH STYLE

18a **Choosing concrete words**

It would seem that words can be either abstract and general or concrete and specific. For example, *thing* is abstract and general, whereas *book* is much more concrete and specific. *Car* is fairly general and abstract; *Mazda Miata* is more concrete and specific. But the language is more complicated than it might seem. Consider the following dialogue.

HELEN: Laura, will you step across the hall and get that thing off the desk in my office.
[*Laura goes across the hall but returns a few minutes later.*]
LAURA: Helen, what "thing" do you mean? There are lots of things on your desk.
HELEN: I'm sorry, Laura. I meant the book on my desk.
[*Laura leaves and returns again a few minutes later.*]
LAURA: Helen, there are a dozen books on you desk. Which one do you mean?

HELEN: For heaven's sake, Laura. What a fool I am. I mean the blue book on my desk.
         [*Laura leaves and returns empty-handed again.*]
LAURA: Helen, do you know there are three blue books on your desk?
HELEN: Oh, no. The blue dictionary, please.
         [*Laura makes another trip to the office and returns.*]
LAURA: Two of the blue books on your desks are dictionaries. Which do you mean?
HELEN: Silly me. The blue *American Heritage Dictionary.*
LAURA: Helen, this has gone too far. Both of the dictionaries are *American Heritage.*
HELEN: Laura, I'm sorry. Please get me the blue *American Heritage Dictionary* with the coffee stain on the front of it.

This conversation shows that words do not simply fall into one of two categories: abstract and general or concrete and specific. The series of words Helen uses to tell Laura what she wants move gradually from the very abstract and general to the very concrete and specific. The following chart illustrates the continuum on which words can be placed.

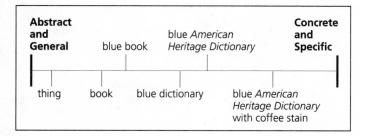

What does this continuum have to do with your writing? First of all, most beginning writers tend to use words from the abstract and general end of the spectrum too often. Frequently, writers need to shift their language toward the concrete and specific end of the spectrum. The following two paragraphs illustrate how

RESOURCES

Johnson, Donna M., and Duane H. Roen, eds. *Richness in Writing: Empowering ESL Students.* New York: Longman, 1989.

Lanham, Richard. *Revising Prose.* New York: Macmillan, 1987.

Strunk, William, Jr., and E. B. White. *The Elements of Style.* 3rd ed. New York: Macmillan, 1979.

Williams, Joseph M. *Style: Ten Lessons in Clarity and Grace.* 3rd ed. New York: Harper-Collins, 1989.

Zinsser, William. *On Writing Well.* 4th ed. New York: Harper-Collins, 1990.

18a
exact

substituting concrete and specific terms for more general and abstract ones can improve the effectiveness of a piece of writing.

> When we returned to our campsite, we discovered that the rain had caused our tent to collapse into a pile of equipment. After we managed to reerect the tent, we found that everything inside the tent was soaked.

> When we returned to our campsite, we discovered that the downpour had caused our tent to collapse into a pile of green canvas and aluminum poles. After we managed to reerect the tent, we found that our sleeping bags and clothes were soaked and a box of Saltines had gotten so wet it had split open, spilling soggy crackers everywhere.

One way to improve your writing is to move your language toward the concrete and specific end of the continuum. Another way is to be careful about the kind of concrete language you use. The following paragraphs both have plenty of concrete language, but the first one is a much better description of the process of cleaning strawberries than the second.

PARAGRAPH 1

I took the little green plastic basket of strawberries out of the refrigerator and dumped the berries on the counter. Most of them were perfect—a deep red with little greenish seeds all over them. A few had light green tips. I picked up each one, grasped the stem and leaves between my fingers, and attempted to pull out the stem and core. Most of the time the stem snapped off, and I had to slice off the top portion with a paring knife. Next I sliced all of the strawberries in half, exposing their whitish inner parts, placed them in a bowl, poured milk over them, and set them on the table. On the countertop, I left behind a gory pile of green and red debris in a bloody pool of juice.

PARAGRAPH 2

I took the package of strawberries out of the almond-toned GE refrigerator, which we had purchased just a few months earlier, and dumped them on the beige Formica counter. Most of them were perfect—red and plump and delicious. A few were less ripe. I cleaned the berries using a plastic-handled paring knife with a

serrated blade. Then I sliced each berry in half with the same knife, placed them in a white cereal bowl with a blue stripe around it, poured low-fat milk from Greenfield Dairy over them, and set them on our maple drop-leaf table. On the countertop, I left behind the leaves and stems, a puddle of juice, the container the berries had come in, and the plastic-handled knife.

Why is the first paragraph more effective? There are two reasons. First, the concrete details in the first paragraph are all closely related to the subject of the paragraph, strawberries: green basket, deep red, green seeds, stems, leaves, whitish inner parts, red and green debris. In the second paragraph, almost all the details are related to objects other than the strawberries—the refrigerator, counter, knife, bowl, milk, and table. When you use concrete language, select details that are focused on the subject of your writing. Concrete language that is unrelated to your subject can distract your reader.

Second, where the paragraphs contain corresponding details, those from the first paragraph seem much more perceptive and descriptive.

Paragraph 1	Paragraph 2
little green plastic basket	package
deep red with greenish seeds	red and plump and delicious
light green tips	less ripe
green and red debris	leaves and stems
a bloody pool of juice	a puddle of juice

Both of these descriptions are correct, but the ones from the first paragraph are the result of careful observation and thorough recall. The adjectives used in paragraph 2, *red and plump and delicious,* are unimaginative and unconvincing. For one thing, they are not very distinctive descriptions of strawberries; they could just as easily be applied to cherries, tomatoes, or plums. Further, the last adjective, *delicious,* is illogical: How would the writer know that the strawberries were delicious, having just taken them out of the refrigerator? A strictly visual description makes more sense at this point.

18a
exact

In summary, both paragraphs present concrete details, but those in the first paragraph are consistently more accurate, more observant, and more focused on the subject. As a result, paragraph 1 is more effective. Time after time, it makes you think, "That's right. Strawberries do have little greenish seeds, and they are whitish in the middle. This person really knows strawberries." Details that really make a difference, like those in paragraph 1, have been called *telling details* by an influential teacher and writer named Ken McCrorie.

While it is important to make your writing more concrete, to choose details that support the focus of the essay, and to strive for telling details, you also need to be aware of the complex relationship between the concrete and the abstract, between the general and the specific. Good writing usually involves an interplay between the two, beginning with a broad statement that is both abstract and general and then supporting that statement with examples that are concrete and specific (see 3b). Moving back and forth between the two ends of the continuum is usually a most effective style.

In the following passage, Hank Lopez describes growing up as a Chicano in Denver, Colorado. We have underlined his general and abstract expressions and then connected them to the concrete language (in boxes) that accompanies them. Notice how Lopez weaves back and forth between the two ends of the continuum, between concreteness and generality.

> My personal Mexican-ness eventually produced serious problems for me. Upon entering grade school I learned English rapidly, and rather well, always ranking either first or second in my class; yet the hard core of me remained stubbornly Mexican. This chauvinism may have been a reaction to the constant racial prejudice we encountered on all sides. The neighborhood cops were always running us off the streets and calling us "dirty greasers," and

18a
exact

FOR DISCUSSION

Choose a paragraph from an essay in a college reader or other source. Have the class read the paragraph carefully and then discuss its nouns and verbs. Ask whether they would suggest any changes in the paragraph.

most of our teachers frankly regarded us as totally inferior. I still remember the galling disdain of my sixth-grade teacher, whose constant mimicking of our heavily accented speech drove me to a desperate study of *Webster's Dictionary* in the hope of acquiring a vocabulary larger than hers. Sadly enough, I succeeded only too well, and for the next few years I spoke the most ridiculous high-flown rhetoric in the Denver Public Schools. One of my favorite words was *indubitable*, and it must have driven everyone mad.

—Enrique "Hank" Lopez, "Back to Bachimba"

In your writing, first make sure you have not relied completely on words that are abstract and general. Whenever possible, substitute more concrete and specific language. Second, try to weave back and forth between the two ends of the continuum to make your writing convincing.

18b
exact

18b Choosing strong verbs

In 18a, most of the examples involved concrete nouns and adjectives, but it is also important to use strong verbs. In general, the more specific a verb is, the stronger it is.

Think of the verbs you could use to describe the fact that someone moved from one place to another: *moved, walked, traveled.* Then think of the more specific, more descriptive verbs you could also use: *ambled, sauntered, sidled, sneaked, stormed, slammed, hurried, stumbled.* In general, stronger verbs are more effective. However, it is possible to overuse strong verbs. Try to use verbs that are appropriate for the subject, audience, and purpose of your writing.

Look at how substituting strong verbs strengthens the following passage.

Professor Jimenez walked into the room and put her books on the desk. She looked at the class and asked, "Who ruined the hard disk on the computer in my office?" We sat in our seats and looked down at our desks. No one raised a hand. After a few minutes of silence, a small woman in the back row said, "I may have done it."

Professor Jimenez stormed into the room and slammed her books on the desk. She glowered at the class and barked, "Who ruined the hard disk on the computer in my office?" We cowered in our seats and looked down at our desks. No one raised a hand. After a few minutes of silence, a small woman in the back row squeaked, "I may have done it."

18b
exact

GRAMMAR: UNDERSTANDING BASIC CONCEPTS

Even if your students learned parts of speech in grade school, you may find that memories have lapsed. As your class studies this chapter's concise treatment of the subject, stress the practical importance of recognizing parts of speech. Much as a driver can detect repair needs more easily by becoming familiar with the mechanical parts of a car, so a writer can edit and proofread more efficiently by knowing the basic components of language itself.

19 RECOGNIZING PARTS OF SPEECH

Each word in a sentence can be categorized as one of eight **parts of speech**: noun, pronoun, verb, adjective, adverb, preposition, conjunction, or interjection. A word may be a different part of speech in different sentences, depending on how it is used. For example, the word *cup* is most commonly used as a noun (*Would you like a cup of coffee?*), but it can also be used as a verb (*They cup their hands over their eyes to look toward the sun*) or as an adjective (*He bought an antique cup rack at the auction*). To know what part of speech a word is, one must consider the sentence in which it is used.

Becoming familiar with these eight parts of speech and how they are used will help you understand many of the rules of grammar and punctuation.

19a Nouns

Identifying nouns

In the following sentences, the nouns are highlighted.

1. Juan Bellancourt took *A Farewell to Arms* with him to New York.

   Notice that the nouns in this sentence stand for the *names* of persons, things, or places.

Name of a person:	Juan Bellancourt
Name of a thing (a book):	*A Farewell to Arms*
Name of a place:	New York

2. My teacher gave a test before she left for the beach.

   In sentence 2, the nouns are not *names,* but they do stand for persons, places, or things.

A person:	teacher
A thing:	test
A place:	beach

From these examples, you can conclude that a noun is a word that stands for a person, place, or thing. A noun may or may not be the *name* of the person, place, or thing.

3. A letter had fallen into the green basket.

Notice in sentence 3 the word *a* in front of *letter* and the word *the* in front of *basket*. The presence of the words *a* (or *an*) and *the*, which are articles (see 19d), are clues that a noun follows, although there may be one or more adjectives (see 19d) before that noun.

In sentences 4 and 5, a slightly different type of noun is highlighted.

4. Her honesty has got her in trouble.
5. The cause of his defeat was his arrogance.

The highlighted nouns in these sentences are a little harder to recognize because even though they are things, they are not *concrete* objects like *A Farewell to Arms, test, ocean, letter,* or *basket. Honesty, trouble, cause, defeat,* and *arrogance* are *abstract* things, more like concepts. But in the grammar of the English language, they are just as much things as *apples* or *tables* and are therefore nouns.

The highlighted nouns in the following sentences sometimes confuse people.

6. Her jump was higher than mine.
7. I took a long run.
8. I would love to take a drive.

These words, *jump, run,* and *drive,* are usually used as verbs to express actions (see 19c); in these sentences, however, they are used as nouns: a *jump,* a *run,* and a *drive* are all things. When checking for whether a word is a noun or a verb, consider how it is used in the sentence in question, not whether it is usually a noun or a verb. Notice the presence of the word *a* before *run* in sentence 7 and before *drive* in sentence 8; the presence of *a* (or *an* or *the*) is a clue that a noun follows.

RESOURCES

Enos, Theresa, ed. *A Sourcebook for Basic Writing Teachers.* New York: McGraw, 1987.

Kolln, Martha. "Closing the Books on Alchemy." *College Composition and Communication* 32 (1981): 139–51.

Methods of formal grammar instruction have been widely debated in recent years. Enos's sourcebook contains useful articles relating to the controversy. Kolln's influential article argues the value of formal grammar instruction.

19a
gr

DEFINITION OF A NOUN

A **noun** is a word that stands for a person, place, or thing. A noun may or may not be the *name* of the person, place, or thing. The thing that a noun stands for may be concrete (like *table* or *letter*) or abstract (like *trouble* or *arrogance.*). Words that are usually verbs can sometimes be used as nouns (as in "a *drink* of water" or "a *drive* in the country").

Insofar as nouns stand for things, you might point out that a noun is also identified by its ability to answer the question "What?"

19b ### Pronouns

Defining pronouns

In the following sentences, the pronouns are highlighted.

1. Geraldine read the newspaper before she left for work.
2. Before Melvin eats the plums, he should wash them.
3. Because Dawn studied hard for the test, she got an A on it.

From these sentences, you can see that a pronoun is a word that stands for or takes the place of a noun.

But look at the following pair of sentences:

4. INCORRECT: Margaret placed the small red book on the table when she finished reading the small red it.
5. CORRECT: Margaret placed the small red book on the table when she finished reading it.

Sentence 4 is quite unnatural. Even though it is unlikely that anyone would ever write it, we have included it here to illustrate an additional fact about pronouns. In sentence 4, the pronoun *it* takes the place of the noun *book,* and the result is incorrect. In sentence 5, *it* takes the place of the noun *book and all its modifiers (a small red),* and the result is correct. A noun and all its modifiers are referred to as a **noun phrase.**

Now you can see why it is not entirely accurate to say that a pronoun takes the place of a noun. A more accurate statement would be that a pronoun takes the place of a noun and all its modifiers.

The highlighted pronouns in the following sentence illustrate a slightly different function of pronouns.

6. I told Marcie about you.

These pronouns do not exactly stand for or take the place of *a particular noun* or *noun phrase.* They do, however, stand for a person: *I* stands for the person speaking the sentence, and *you* stands for the person being spoken to.

To include the type of pronouns in sentence 6 in our definition, we would add that a pronoun is a word that stands for a particular person, like the speaker or the person spoken to.

Look at the highlighted pronouns in the following sentences.

7. Someone spilled something sticky all over the kitchen floor.
8. No one bought anything at the auction.

Notice that these pronouns to not stand for any noun or specific person; they stand for an *unknown or unspecified* person or thing.

DEFINITION OF A PRONOUN

A **pronoun** is a word that stands for
- a noun and its modifiers (*he, they*)
- a particular person, like the speaker or the person spoken to (*I, you*)
- an unknown or unspecified person or thing (*someone, nothing*)

Antecedents of pronouns

Take another look at sentences 1 through 3. This time we have drawn arrows from the pronouns to nouns in the sentences.

1. Geraldine read the newspaper before she left for work.
2. Before Melvin eats the plums, he should wash them.
3. Because Dawn studied hard for the test, she got an A on it.

The noun that a pronoun stands for is its **antecedent.** Every pronoun must have a clear antecedent (see 23).

Types of pronouns

Pronouns can be classified into seven basic types, which are described in the accompanying chart.

19b
gr

TYPES OF PRONOUNS

Type	Function	Example	List of Pronouns
Personal pronouns	To stand for particular people or things	■ I gave him my best necktie. ■ They bought three of them.	*I, you, he, she, it, we, they, me, him, her, us, them*

(continued)

According to strict grammatical distinctions, the words *my, your, her, our,* and *their* are viewed as possessive adjectives, while *mine, yours, hers, ours,* and *theirs* are regarded as true possessive pronouns. Many grammar texts now treat both sets as belonging to the pronominal category, however.

TYPES OF PRONOUNS *(continued)*

Type	Function	Example	List of Pronouns
Possessive pronouns	To indicate ownership	■ My brother can never remember his social security number.	*my, your, yours, his her, hers, its, our, ours, their, theirs*
Reflexive pronouns	To stand for someone who is both receiver of and doer of an action	■ Roxanne should not blame herself for what happened. ■ We hurt ourselves in the final minutes of the game.	*myself, yourself, himself, herself, itself, ourselves, yourselves, themselves*
Intensive pronouns	To emphasize a noun or other pronoun	■ The teacher himself broke the overhead projector. ■ He himself solved the puzzle.	*myself, yourself, himself, herself, itself, ourselves, yourselves, themselves*
Relative pronouns	To introduce dependent clauses	■ The woman who chaired the meeting did not recognize me. ■ The car that I bought was a Chevrolet Caprice.	*who, whom, whose, which, that, whoever, whomever, whichever, whatever*
Interrogative Pronouns	To ask questions	■ What did she mean by that remark? Who ordered a pizza?	*who, whom, whose, what, which*
Demonstrative pronouns	To identify or point out specific persons, places, or things	■ This is the best minestrone I've ever eaten. ■ Those are not your shoes.	*this, that, these, those*

(continued)

19b
gr

TYPES OF PRONOUNS (continued)

Type	Function	Example	List of Pronouns
Indefinite pronouns	To stand for unknown or unspecified persons, places, or things	■ Each of the students gave something to the children. ■ Everyone knows someone who suffered from the storm.	*all, another, any, anybody, anyone, anything, both, each, either, everybody, everyone, every-thing, few, half* (any fraction), *many, more, most, much, neither, nobody, none, no one, nothing, one* (any number), *several, some, somebody, someone, something*

19c   gr

19c   Verbs (and verbals)

Identifying action verbs

In the following sentences, the verbs are highlighted.

1. Juan runs five miles every morning.
2. Xenia Tinios dances with the California Ballet.
3. A police officer walks past our house every evening around eleven.

From these sentences, you can see that a verb can express an action—something someone or something is *doing*. In sentence 1, *run* is something Juan is doing; in sentence 2, *dance* is something Xenia Tinios is doing; and in sentence 3, *walk* is something the officer is doing. This kind of verb is known as an **action verb.**

Frequently, verbs express actions that are not happening right now but happened at some time in the past.

4. Juan ran five miles every morning.
5. Xenia Tinios danced with the California Ballet.
6. A police officer walked past our house every evening around eleven.

The following section offers a general introduction to verb types. Related topics appear at several points in the book, including 9a (avoiding tense shifts), 20 (recognizing verbs in sentences), 21 (subject-verb agreement), 25 (verb forms), 26 (tense, voice, and mood), and 27 (verbals).

So a verb can express something someone or something is doing or was doing. In fact, a verb can also express something someone will be doing in the future.

The next group of sentences illustrates how subtle the action that a verb expresses can be.

7. Hank thinks Donna charged him too much.
8. My dog sleeps in the basement.
9. A terrible accident happened last night.

There is not much *action* going on in these sentences. *Think, sleep,* and *happen* are verbs that don't really indicate much action, but they are verbs nevertheless. In fact, they are action verbs. They do indicate what someone or something is *doing.* Hank is *thinking*, my dog is *sleeping*, and an accident *happened*.

The verbs in the next group can be a little confusing.

10. Maxine chaired the first half of the meeting.
11. We telephoned our parents over the weekend.

The verbs in these sentences are words that are usually nouns (*chair, telephone*), but in these sentences they express what someone is doing, so in these sentences they are verbs.

Identifying linking verbs

This next group of sentences contains an entirely new type of verb—a linking verb.

12. Warren Chin was an accountant.
13. April is the cruelest month.
14. Marcy sounded angry.

These verbs are known as **linking verbs** because they link the subject of the sentence (see 20b) with something that comes after the verb. The following diagrams illustrate this linking.

12. Warren Chin was an accountant.

13. April is the cruelest month.

14. Marcy sounded angry.

19c
gr

FOR DISCUSSION

Students may be confused about what "linking" means in grammar. You might offer them the analogy of the equal sign in math. For example, "She is a student" could be written "She = student." Similarly, in cases where a verb links a subject to a predicate adjective, there is at least an equivalence of condition. "You look unhappy" suggests "You are unhappy," or "You = unhappy."

LINKING VERBS

Forms of the Verb *be*			Sensory Verbs		
am	been	was	appears	seems	sounds
are	being	were	feels	smells	tastes
be	is	will be	looks		

Identifying helping verbs

The highlighted verbs in the following sentences illustrate another function that verbs can serve—as helping or auxiliary verbs.

15. Kelly was swimming at seven-thirty this morning.
16. The library is closing in five minutes.
17. My parents will be angry with me.
18. There must have been something wrong with my car.
19. Sven will have been sleeping for ten hours by now.

These sentences contain action verbs (*swimming* and *closing*) and linking verbs (*be* and *been*). These verbs, known as **main verbs**, have one or more **helping verbs** (*was, is, will, must have,* and *will have*) in front of them. Main verbs are always the last of the verbs in a group and can be action verbs or linking verbs; helping verbs precede the main verb.

The chart below lists the helping verbs, sometimes called **auxiliary verbs,** in English.

HELPING VERBS

Always Helping Verbs			Either Helping Verbs or Main Verbs		
can	might	should	am	did	have
could	must	will	are	do	is
may	shall	would	be	does	was
			been	had	were
			being	has	

Warn students that the sensory verbs are linking verbs only when those verbs identify the subject with the predicate (e.g., "This looks wonderful" could be restated "This is wonderful"). When sensory verbs such as *look, feel,* and *smell* are used to express action, they are no longer linking ("Look out the window" or "Smell the roses").

19c
gr

Using modals

Modals are a subgroup of helping verbs. They include all the verbs in the left column of the first section of the chart that follows (pp. 204–205) (true modals) and another group composed of two or more words (quasi-modals) in the left column of the second section of the chart (pp. 205–206). The chart will help you understand the meaning of various modals in English and how they are used in sentences.

MODALS

Modal	Sense	Tense	
		Present and Future	Past
True Modals can	Ability	I can bowl well.	I could sing well when I was young.
	Permission	Can I have some ice cream?	Maggie said I could go.
could	Advisability	You could use a haircut.	
	Polite questions	Could you wash my car now?	
may	Permission	May I go to the party?	
	Possibility	I may go to the Bahamas.	I may have been dreaming.
might	Possibility	I might go to the Bahamas.	I might have been dreaming.
	Advisability	You might want to sweep the floor.	
must	Probability	She must be sick.	She must have been sick.
	Advisability	She must go to the doctor.	

(continued)

MODALS (continued)

Modal	Sense	Tense	
		Present and Future	**Past**
shall	Polite offer	Shall I open a window?	
should	Advisability	He should clean his house.	He should have cleaned his house last week.
	Expectation	He should be here soon.	He should have been here by now.
will	Certainty	I will go to work next week.	
	Polite request	Will you baby-sit tomorrow?	
would	Question	Would you like some coffee?	
	Preference	I would rather have tea.	I would rather have ordered tea.
	Repeated action in the past		When I was little, I would always go to the park.
	Polite request	I would like a cup of coffee.	
Quasi-Modals			
be able to	Ability	I am able to bowl.	I was able to sing well when I was young.
be about to	Probability	I am about to leave for work.	I was about to leave for work when the phone rang.
		Are you about to leave for work?	Were you about to leave for work?

(continued)

ESL ADVICE

Because they are essentially idiomatic expressions, the quasi-modals offer a special challenge to ESL students. Encourage those for whom these terms are unfamiliar to practice the quasi-modals in notebook sentences, varying the examples offered in this box. Offer to check the students' sentences for coherence.

19c
gr

ESL

19c
gr

ESL

MODALS *(continued)*

Modal	Sense	Present and Future	Past
		Tense	
Quasi-Modals			
be allowed to	Permission	Am I allowed to go to the party? I am allowed to go to the party.	
be going to	Certainty	I am going to shop today. Are you going to shop today?	
be supposed to	Expectation	I am supposed to begin work at eight o'clock.	I was supposed to clean my car tomorrow.
had better	Advisability (strong)	You had better go to the doctor.	
have got to	Necessity	I have got to go to class.	
have to	Necessity	I have to go to class.	I had to go to class.
ought to	Advisability	You ought to wear a raincoat.	
	Expectation	You ought to begin work at eight o'clock.	
used to	Condition or state in the past		I used to like spinach.

DEFINITION OF A VERB

There are three kinds of verbs in English:
- **Action verbs** express something that someone or something is doing, has done in the past, or will do in the future. The action in action verbs is sometimes quite subtle (as in the action verbs *decide, think,* and *sleep*), but it is nevertheless something that someone is "doing."
- **Linking verbs** link the subject of a sentence with a noun or adjective that comes after the verb. (See list on p. 203.)
- **Helping verbs** are used in front of main verbs. (See list on p. 203.)

Identifying verbals

In English, it is possible to use verbs as nouns or adjectives in sentences by changing their form slightly. When verbs are used in this way, they are no longer verbs; they are **verbals.** The highlighted words in the following sentences are examples of verbals. It is important to recognize the difference between verbs and verbals so that you can use each correctly.

20. The point of the game is to collect as much money as possible.
21. To lose my gloves was irritating.

These sentences illustrate one type of verbal: **infinitives,** which are made up of verbs with the word *to* in front of them. Infinitives can be used as nouns (as they are in these sentences) or occasionally as adjectives or adverbs but never as verbs. (For a discussion of the use of infinitives, see 27a.)

A second type of verbal is highlighted in sentences 22 and 23.

22. Odysseus warned his men against opening the bag of winds.
23. A moving target is difficult to hit.

These verbals, composed of verbs with *-ing* endings, are either **gerunds** or **participles,** depending on their use in the sentence. If they are used as nouns, as in sentence 22, they are gerunds. If they are used as adjectives, as in sentence 23, they are participles. (For a discussion of the use of gerunds, see 27a. For a discussion of the use of participles, see 27b.)

A verb with an *-ing* ending can be also be used as a verb, as the following sentences demonstrate. The verbs are highlighted.

ACTIVITY

Write *swim* (or another common verb) on the board. Have students suggest sentences in which forms of the verb appear as infinitive, gerund, participle, and predicating verb, respectively. For example: *I like to swim. Swimming is easy. We saw them swimming in the pool. The lifeguard was swimming fast.*

19c
gr

24. Lew was swimming every Saturday morning.
25. The manager of the apartment is returning our deposit.

These sentences show that a verb with an *-ing* ending can be used as a verb *if it has a helping verb in front of it.*

To complement the general discussion of adjectives in this section, refer students to 28a (avoiding confusion between adjectives and adverbs), 28c (comparative and superlative forms), 34e (punctuating adjectives), and 38c (capitalizing proper adjectives).

19d **Adjectives**

The most common use of adjectives is represented by the highlighted words in the following sentences.

1. A yellow bus stopped in front of the elegant hotel.

   Yellow describes the noun *bus; elegant* describes the noun *hotel.*

2. Helene saw two birds sitting in the first tree on the walk.

   Two quantifies the noun *birds*—it tells how many. *First* identifies the noun *tree.*

19d
gr

Questions are especially helpful in determining parts of speech. Stress the value of the questions "What kind?" "Which?" and "How many?" by illustrating how adjectives in a particular sentence respond to those questions. You might write the following sentence on the board and ask which questions the underlined words answer: "The inexpensive afternoon snack satisfied the three students." The answers should be easy: "What kind?" "Which one?" and "How many?"

DEFINITION OF AN ADJECTIVE

An **adjective** is a word that modifies a noun. Adjectives can modify by describing, identifying, or quantifying (telling how many). They almost always answer one of these questions: What kind? Which? How many?

Note that the adjectives in sentences 1 and 2 precede the nouns they modify. The following sentences illustrate two other positions adjectives can occupy in a sentence.

3. The young child, alone and afraid, walked slowly up the path.

   Adjectives can follow the noun they modify.

4. She was dirty.

   Adjectives that follow the verb are called **predicate adjectives.** Note that the adjective modifies a pronoun.

   In the following sentence, adjectives that form a special group called **articles** are highlighted.

5. The mayor's car was parked next to a truck that was carrying an orangutan.

A, an and *the* are the only articles in English. Their use follows very complex rules, which are explained in 29.

19e Adverbs

Identifying adverbs

In the following sentences, the adverbs are highlighted and arrows have been drawn to indicate the words they modify.

Verb

1. The old cowboy walked slowly across the street.

Verb

2. When we heard about the accident, we called you immediately.

Verb   Verb

3. Mabel gently lifted the land mine and placed it carefully in the back of the truck.

Notice that these adverbs all modify (describe, intensify, limit, or place in time) a verb and they all end in *-ly*. Adverbs frequently modify verbs and frequently end in *-ly*, but they sometimes modify other parts of the sentence and take other forms.

Adjective

4. The accused senator gave his testimony in a barely audible voice.

The adverb *barely* is modifying an adjective, *audible*.

Adverb

5. The young cab driver walked very slowly over to the car.

The adverb *very* is modifying another adverb, *slowly*.

19e
gr

Prepositional phrase

6. When I saw Mr. Diego, he had climbed almost to the top of the hill.

The adverb *almost* is modifying a prepositional phrase, *to the top.*

Dependent clause

7. My knees bother me a lot, especially when it rains.

The adverb *especially* is modifying the dependent clause *when it rains.*

Sentence

8. Undoubtedly, Rajani is looking out for her own interests.

The adverb *undoubtedly* is modifying the entire sentence *Rajani is looking out for her own interests.*

Note that some adverbs (*barely, slowly, especially, undoubtedly*) end in *-ly* and others (*very, almost*) do not.

DEFINITION OF AN ADVERB

> An **adverb** is a word that modifies a verb, an adjective, another adverb, a prepositional phrase, a clause, or a sentence. Many adverbs end in *-ly*; others do not. Adverbs answer one of the following questions: In what manner? When? Where? To what extent?

Special types of adverbs

Negatives. The negative words *not* and *never* are always adverbs, as in the following sentences.

9. Martin Luther King, Jr., was not murdered in Atlanta.
10. I've never seen such a large pumpkin.

Conjunctive adverbs. *Conjunctive* adverbs modify the independent clause (see 20i) they are part of by indicating its relationship to the preceding independent clause.

11. We hoped to take a long walk this morning; however, it is raining too hard.

> *However* indicates that the information in its independent clause, *it is raining too hard,* in some sense contradicts or disagrees with the information in the preceding independent clause, *We hoped to take a long walk this morning.*

12. Rebecca lost her wallet. Consequently, she had to cancel her credit cards.

> *Consequently* indicates that the information in its independent clause, *she had to cancel her credit cards,* results from the information in the preceding independent clause, *Rebecca lost her wallet.*

The accompanying chart lists the most common conjunctive adverbs. Some grammarians call conjunctive adverbs made up of two or more words *transitional expressions.*

Also known as "adverbial coordinating conjunctions" or "transition words," conjunctive adverbs often lead to comma splices, one of the more common punctuation errors. Students should learn to recognize conjunctive adverbs in order to avoid misplaced commas. The correct punctuation of sentences containing conjunctive adverbs is covered in 33c.

CONJUNCTIVE ADVERBS

also	for instance	in fact	still
as a result	furthermore	instead	then
consequently	however	meanwhile	therefore
finally	in addition	nevertheless	thus
for example	indeed	of course	

19f Prepositions

A **preposition** is a word that indicates a connection between the noun that follows it and another word in the sentence.

1. The restaurant is near the movie.

> *Near* indicates the relationship between *movie* and *restaurant.* Often, but not always, these relationships are spatial—the preposition indicates where one thing is in relation to another.

2. Tamiko borrowed a book of Larry's.

> The preposition indicates possession (the fact that someone owns or is connected to something) rather than a spatial relationship. Here *of* indicates that Larry owns the book.

19f
gr

19g
gr

3. This picture was painted by Henri Matisse.

The preposition *by* indicates agency (the fact that someone is the performer of an action). In this sentence, *by* indicates that Matisse performed the action of painting.

The chart below lists the most common prepositions. Using the most effective preposition is discussed in 16b. Prepositional phrases are discussed in 20d.

PREPOSITIONS				
about	before	except	off	throughout
above	behind	except for	on	till
according to	below	excepting	onto	to
across	beneath	for	opposite	toward
after	beside	from	out	under
against	besides	in	out of	underneath
along	between	in addition to	outside	unlike
along with	beyond	inside	over	until
among	but	in spite of	past	unto
apart from	by	instead of	plus	up
around	concerning	into	regarding	upon
as	considering	like	respecting	with
aside from	despite	near	round	within
at	down	next to	since	without
because of	during	of	through	

19g Conjunctions

In the following sentences, the conjunctions are highlighted.

1. Biology and chemistry are required in my program.
2. Melia can store her comic books in the attic or in the basement.
3. Matisse wanted to keep painting in his old age, but his hands weren't steady enough.

Notice that these conjunctions are used to join words (*biology* and *chemistry* in sentence 1), phrases (*in the attic* and *in the basement* in sentence 2), or clauses (*Matisse wanted to keep painting in his old age* and *his hands weren't steady enough* in sentence 3). Conjunctions like these, which join items that are grammatically equal, are called **coordinating conjunctions.** There are only seven of them: *and, but, or, for, so, yet,* and *nor.*

Like coordinating conjunctions, **correlative conjunctions** also join terms that are grammatically equal.

4. Either Brussels sprouts or asparagus will be fine with me.
5. Both the reception and the wedding were filled with joy.

Correlative conjunctions always work in pairs: *either . . . or, both . . . and, neither . . . nor, not only . . . but also,* and *whether . . . or.*

In the following sentences, the subordinating conjunctions are highlighted.

6. When Tyrone gets here, we'll make him tell us what happened.
7. If you have the money, you should buy that computer.
8. I am not going out for the baseball team because I need the time for studying.
9. Hank made dinner while Elvira watched television.

These **subordinating conjunctions** join subordinate clauses to the rest of the sentence. The most common ones are listed below.

SUBORDINATING CONJUNCTIONS

after	even though	once	unless
although	how	provided (that)	until
as	if	rather than	when
as far as	if only	since	whenever
as if	in case	so that	where
as long as	in order that	supposing (that)	whereas
as soon as	insofar as	than	wherever
as though	in that	that	whether
because	lest	though	while
before	no matter how	till	why
even if	now that		

19h Interjections

The interjections are highlighted in the following sentences.

1. Oh! What have you done to my cat?
2. Great! Now my car won't start.

Interjections are words that express surprise or strong emotion.

ACTIVITIES

By way of summarizing this chapter, offer students a sentence or two to analyze for parts of speech. Write the sentences on the board and have students jot down responses individually before you review the correct answers. The following is one possibility: "Hey! I really need a ride to the downtown airport, and I have to be on time. Can you help me?" (Answers: Interjection; personal pronoun, adverb, verb, indefinite article, noun, preposition, definite article, adjective, noun, coordinating conjunction, personal pronoun, helping verb, infinitive [preposition + verb], preposition, noun; modal, personal pronoun, verb, personal pronoun.)

Another summary activity might be useful in pointing out the differences among parts of speech. Students need to keep in mind that a word can change its part of speech depending on context. Try writing the word *well* on the board. Ask students to write sentences in which *well* appears as a noun, an adjective, an adverb, and an interjection (e.g., "The well is dry." "I am well, thank you." "She writes well." "Oh, well! That sort of thing happens.").

Remind students that there are practical reasons for recognizing the parts of sentences. Correct punctuation depends on a working knowledge of syntax, as do other grammatical functions such as pronoun usage and modifier placement. A working knowledge of sentence structure minimizes the risk of inadvertent fragments, run-ons, and other mishaps. Besides the defensive advantage of knowing about sentence parts, there is also the stylistic advantage a writer gains from knowing how to reconstruct sentences to suit his or her purposes.

20a
gr

RESOURCES

Enos, Theresa, ed. *A Sourcebook for Basic Writing Teachers.* New York: McGraw, 1987.

Holt, J. R. "In Defense of Formal Grammar." *Curriculum Review* 21 (1982): 173–78.

Kroll, Barbara, ed. *Second Language Writing: Research Insights for the Classroom.* New York: Cambridge UP, 1990.

Lunsford, Andrea A. "Cognitive Development and the Basic Writer." *College English* 41 (1979): 36–48. Rpt. in Enos 449–59.

Noguchi, Rei R. *Grammar and the Teaching of Writing: Limits and Possibilities.* Urbana: NCTE, 1991.

20 RECOGNIZING PARTS OF SENTENCES

Becoming familiar with the parts of the sentence will help you understand many of the rules of grammar and punctuation. The two most essential parts of any sentences, and the only two that every sentence *must* have, are the subject and the verb. We will discuss verbs and subjects first and then consider the nonessential sentence parts.

20a Verbs

Identifying main verbs and helping verbs is discussed in 19c, as is the difference between action verbs and linking verbs. Action verbs themselves can be divided into two types: **transitive** and **intransitive.**

Transitive verbs

1. Nachelle broke her glasses.

   The *glasses* receive the action of the verb *broke*.

2. Maria read a novel over the weekend.

   The *novel* receives the action of the verb *read*.

Transitive verbs are always followed by a noun (see 19a) or a pronoun (see 19b) that receives the action that the verb expresses.

Intransitive verbs

3. Ms. Tan slept at my house last night.

   No word receives the action of the verb *slept*. Ms. Tan did not "*sleep* anything," so *slept* is an intransitive verb.

4. Brian rose at the sound of the bell.

   Again, no word receives the action of the verb, so *rose* is intransitive.

Most verbs can be transitive or intransitive depending on the sentence:

5. **INTRANSITIVE:**   The bank opens at 10:00 on Saturdays.
6. **TRANSITIVE:**   Veronica opened the letter with great anxiety.

The following sentences illustrate two different ways in which transitive verbs can be used. These two ways are known as *active* and *passive voice.*

7. Einstein discovered relativity.

> Sentence 7 is in *active voice.* The subject, *Einstein,* is the performer of the action expressed by the transitive verb, *discovered. Relativity* is the receiver of the action of the verb.

8. Relativity was discovered by Einstein.

> Sentence 8 is in *passive voice* because the subject is not the performer of the action of the verb. In fact, the subject, *relativity,* is the receiver of the action of the verb; *relativity* is what *was discovered.* The performer of the action, *Einstein,* has been placed in a prepositional phrase (see 19f) beginning with *by.*

Of the two voices, active voice is the more common and more direct. Use it unless passive voice expresses the meaning better. For a discussion of when to use active and when to use passive voice, see 26g.

9. My favorite cup was broken.

> Sentence 9 is also in passive voice. This time the subject, *cup,* is again the receiver of the action of the verb, but the performer of the action is not mentioned in the sentence.

You should use the construction in sentence 9 only on rare occasions: when the performer of the action is unknown or being concealed or is unimportant and therefore not worth mentioning.

It is also possible for a sentence to have more than one verb.

10. The doctor opened the door and walked into the office.
11. Traditional marriage vows require that you love, honor, and obey your spouse.

Sternglass, Marilyn. "Composition Teacher as Reading Teacher." *College Composition and Communication* 27 (1976): 378–82.

The works listed are among those addressing current issues in grammar instruction. Kroll's book includes timely research articles on ESL writing. Lunsford's article offers exercises designed to enhance students' awareness of basic sentence patterns. Noguchi's book explores the strengths and limitations of formal grammar instruction. The article by Sternglass advocates analytical reading as a method of teaching syntax.

COLLABORATIVE ACTIVITY

Have students study examples of verb phrases in an assigned essay from a college reader. Discuss in class the variety and effectiveness of the verb phrases used in the essay.

20a
gr

Two or more main verbs joined by a coordinating conjunction (see 19g) are known as **compound verbs.**

20b Subjects

Basic procedure for identifying subjects

In the following sentences, the subjects are highlighted.

1. Freud discovered the existence of the unconscious.
2. A rock broke the window on my car.
3. They left on the six o'clock bus.

Notice that the subject in each of these sentences is the person or thing *doing* the verb. *Freud* did the discovering of the unconscious, a *rock* did the breaking of my window, and *they* (whoever *they* are) did the leaving on the bus. Although in these sentences the subject is a noun or a pronoun, it can also be any one of several other constructions.

4. Smoking can cause cancer of the lungs.

The subject, *smoking,* is a verbal—more specifically, a gerund. See 19c for more discussion of verbals.

5. To speak in front of a large crowd makes me nervous.

The subject, *to speak,* is also a verbal, this time an infinitive. Infinitives are also discussed in 19c.

6. Whoever found my watch did not try to return it.

The subject is the entire clause, *whoever found my watch.* See 20i and 20j for a discussion of clauses.

Whatever the construction, the easiest way to find the subject is first to find the verb and then to ask who or what is *doing* (or *being,* in the case of a linking verb) the verb. In sentence 2, if you ask who or what *broke (the window on my car),* the answer is *a rock,* so that is the subject. In sentence 6, if you ask who or what *did not try (to return my watch),* the answer is *whoever found my watch,* so that clause is the subject.

20b
gr

ACTIVITY

Have students locate complete subjects and predicates in selected sentences from an assigned reading. Briefly review the findings in class.

Subjects in sentences with unusual word order

Usually, as in sentences 1 through 6, the subject precedes the verb in the sentence, but not always. In the following examples, the subjects are underlined once and the verbs twice.

7. Did your father send you any money?

> Sentence 7 is a question that can be answered with "yes" or "no." As a result, the helping verb *did* is moved to the beginning of the sentence.

8. Whom was Maggie arguing with on the phone?

> Sentence 8 is also a question, but it cannot be answered with "yes" or "no." The helping verb *was* has been moved in front of the subject but not to the very beginning of the sentence.

In questions, a helping verb is often moved to a position at or near the beginning of the sentence.

The next set of examples reveals another type of sentence in which the normal order of subject then verb is reversed.

9. There were three reasons for his mistake.

> The sentence begins with the expletive *there,* and the subject has been moved to a position following the verb.

10. In the closet was a large basket of pears.

> The sentence begins with a prepositional phrase (see 19f), and the subject has been moved to a position following the verb.

11. In the closet, Li found a basket of pears.

> The sentence begins with a prepositional phrase, but this time the subject appears in its normal position before the verb.

In sentences beginning with *there,* the subject is always moved to a position following the verb. *There* itself can never be the subject of a sentence. In sentences beginning with a prepositional phrase, the subject *may* appear in a position following the verb.

ESL ADVICE

Because many languages do not share the English syntax for interrogative word order or the "there" transformation, ESL students may need to practice writing questions and other sentences modeled on the examples shown here. Placing the subject in an intervening position between auxiliary and main verb is not an easy habit for non-native speakers to acquire.

20b
gr

Subjects in sentences with words between subject and verb

12. The <u>color</u> of her eyes <u>was</u> hazel.

Notice that in this sentence, the subject is *color* and not *eyes*. The subject can *never* be part of a prepositional phrase (see 19f). *Of her eyes* is a prepositional phrase, so *eyes* cannot be the subject.

You understood as subject

Imperative sentences give commands. The subjects in these sentences are quite different from the subjects we have been looking at.

13. Close that door.
14. Bring a dollar to the meeting on Saturday.

In each of these sentences, the person who will "do" the verb is the person being spoken to. In sentence 13, the person being addressed will *close the door,* and in sentence 14, the person being addressed will *bring a dollar.* If the speaker were to use a pronoun, it would be *you,* so the subject of these imperative sentences in fact is *you.* English speakers *understand* that *you* is the subject without its being spoken or written, so we say the subject is *you* understood.

Compound subjects

When a sentence has more than one subject, the subject is said to be **compound.**

15. Mushrooms and onions are good in a salad.
16. Anatomy, chemistry, and biology are required in my program.

20c **Direct and indirect objects**

The direct objects in the following sentences are highlighted.

1. The ball struck a telephone pole.

The *telephone pole* received the action of the verb; the *telephone pole* is what was *struck.*

2. I love her.

Her stands for the woman who is receiving the *love.*

FOR DISCUSSION

Another way of explaining the role of the direct object is by means of a simple test. Have students notice that a direct object answers the question "What?" about the action of a verb. (*What* did the ball strike? The telephone pole.) If the verb does not express action, but only a state of being, the answer to "What?" may be a subjective complement (e.g., "It remains a sure thing").

A **direct object** is a noun or pronoun that stands for the person or the thing that *receives the action of the verb.* Only transitive verbs take direct objects. Participle, gerund, and infinitive forms of transitive verbs can also take direct objects.

In English, a second type of object is the *indirect object.* Both indirect objects and direct objects are highlighted and labeled in the following sentences.

    Indirect object   Direct object

3. Stu gave Amy a necklace for her birthday.

    Amy received the *necklace,* which is the direct object, so *Amy* is the *indirect object.* The *necklace* is what received the action of the verb— the *necklace* is what was *given*—so it is the *direct object.*

        Indirect object   Direct object

4. The army sent Rod an official letter ordering him to report for active duty.

    Rod received the direct object, the *letter,* so *Rod* is the indirect object.

An **indirect object** is a noun or pronoun that stands for the person or thing that is receiving the direct object. Only transitive verbs take indirect objects. Participle, gerund, and infinitive forms of transitive verbs can also take indirect objects.

The third and final type of object in English, the *object of the preposition,* will be discussed in 20d.

20d Prepositional phrases

In the following sentences, the prepositional phrases are highlighted.

1. The woman with the baby is Ms. Gonzales.
2. The clapboard house near the First National Bank used to be a tavern.

    Prepositional phrases can serve as adjectives, as in sentences 1 and 2. Note that prepositions used as adjectives generally follow immediately after the noun they are modifying. Prepositional phrases used as adjectives usually answer the questions "Which?" or "What kind?"

20d
gr

To recognize prepositional phrases, students must be able to spot prepositions on sight. Encourage those who are having trouble to review 19f.

3. We placed the dishes in the sink.
4. Hank mailed a donation to the local NOW chapter.
5. With an angry shout, she stomped out of the room.

Prepositional phrases can also function as adverbs, as in sentences 3, 4, and 5. If they are used as adverbs, their position in the sentence is quite flexible. Notice that in sentence 5 one adverbial prepositional phrase is located at the beginning of the sentence and one at the end, but both modify the verb *stomped.* Prepositional phrases functioning as adverbs generally answer the questions In what manner? Where? When? Why? or Under what conditions?

A **prepositional phrase** starts with a preposition (see 19f) and ends with a noun or pronoun. In between, a number of adjectives may modify the noun. The noun or pronoun at the end of the prepositional phrase is known as the **object of the preposition.**

Warn students not to confuse the word *complement* with its mirror word, *compliment.*

20e
gr

20e **Complements**

The *subject complements* (sometimes called *predicate nouns, predicate nominatives,* or *predicate adjectives*) in the following sentences are highlighted.

1. Charlotte's mother is a firefighter.

   Charlotte's mother is being equated with the subject complement, *a firefighter.* The sentence could be viewed as an equation with the linking verb serving as an equal sign: Charlotte's mother = a firefighter.

2. This house was a station on the underground railroad.

   This house is being equated with *a station.*

The next two sentences illustrate a different kind of complement, sometimes called a *predicate adjective.*

3. The teacher was proud of us.

   The complement *proud* modifies the subject, *teacher.*

4. The test seems easy.

   The complement *easy* modifies the subject, *test.*

A **subject complement** is a noun, a pronoun, or an adjective that comes after a linking verb (see 19c) and is being equated with the subject (in the case of nouns and pronouns) or modifies the subject (in the case of adjectives).

20f   Appositive phrases

The appositive phrases in the following sentences are highlighted.

1. My teacher, a country music fan, is taking some of us to the Randy Travis concert this weekend.

   The appositive *country music fan* is a noun with several modifiers that stands for the same person as *my teacher*.

2. Josie's boyfriend, the biggest mistake of her life, has never held a job.

   The appositive *the biggest mistake of her life* is a noun with several modifiers that stands for the same person as *Josie's boyfriend*.

An **appositive** is a noun that, together with its modifiers, follows another noun and stands for the same person or thing as the first noun.

20g   Parenthetical expressions

The parenthetical expressions in the following sentences are highlighted.

1. Nathaniel Hawthorne is, according to most literary scholars, a major American novelist.
2. The Greek philosopher Plato wrote—surprisingly—that women should be given an equal opportunity to rule.
3. The student government voted seven to five (with three abstentions) against the new smoking policy.

Parenthetical expressions are words or phrases that are not essential to the meaning of a sentence but add extra information, facts, examples, comments, or digressions. They may be set off by commas, dashes, or parentheses.

FOR DISCUSSION

Another way to explain the appositive is by means of the mathematical equal sign. Have students note that in the second example Josie's boyfriend = the biggest mistake of her life.

20g
gr

20i
gr

20h Absolute phrases

The absolute phrases in the following sentences are highlighted.

1. His nose bleeding profusely, the young camper ran into the house.
2. I did not enjoy Jean's jokes about "flat cats," my own cat having been run over by a car.

An **absolute phrase** consists of a noun or pronoun and a participle (see 19c) together with any modifiers or objects of the participle. An absolute phrase modifies the entire sentence rather than any particular word or phrase and can usually be located anywhere in the sentence.

20i Independent clauses

The *independent clauses* (sometimes called *main clauses*) in the following examples are highlighted.

1. **INDEPENDENT CLAUSE:** Bells ring.
2. **INDEPENDENT CLAUSE:** The small yellow bird with black wings is a goldfinch.
3. **INDEPENDENT CLAUSE:** After he learned to read, Frederick Douglass began to plan his escape.

Note that the following are *not* independent clauses.

4. *NOT* **INDEPENDENT CLAUSE:** The small yellow bird with black wings.
5. *NOT* **INDEPENDENT CLAUSE:** Began to plan his escape.

What these five examples show is that independent clauses must have subjects and verbs, as sentences 1, 2, and 3 do. Example 4 is not an independent clause because it is missing a verb. Example 5 is not independent because it is missing a subject.

Sentences 6, 7, and 8 are also *not* independent clauses, but for a different reason. Notice that they *do* have subjects and verbs.

6. *NOT* **INDEPENDENT CLAUSE:** After he had learned to read.
7. *NOT* **INDEPENDENT CLAUSE:** If it rains on the weekend.

8. **NOT INDEPENDENT CLAUSE:** Until you receive her check in the mail.

Notice that at the end of each of these, the reader is "left hanging." There is a sense of incompleteness. We expect something to be added. This sense of incompleteness keeps these from being independent clauses.

But notice that some incompleteness is present in the following.

9. **INDEPENDENT CLAUSE:** She left it on the front porch.
10. **INDEPENDENT CLAUSE:** They were late for their own wedding.

Although sentences 9 and 10 do feel a little incomplete, this is *not* the kind of incompleteness that prevents them from being independent clauses. The incompleteness comes from the presence of pronouns—*she, it,* and *they*—and incompleteness caused by pronouns does *not* prevent a group of words from being an independent clause. (See 32a, on how to recognize sentences, for more on independent clauses.)

The following are *not* independent clauses.

11. **NOT INDEPENDENT CLAUSE:** Crying at the top of his lungs.
12. **NOT INDEPENDENT CLAUSE:** The car speeding around the curve.
13. **NOT INDEPENDENT CLAUSE:** A corkscrew to open the wine with.

There are two reasons why examples 11, 12, and 13 are not independent clauses. First, they have no verbs. *Crying, speeding,* and *open* may look like verbs, but they are *verbals* (see 19c). Second, they leave you hanging; they are incomplete. Don't be fooled by groups of words that contain verbals like these.

The following sentences reveal another interesting fact about independent clauses. The independent clauses are highlighted.

14. My phone has been disconnected, and the power company is threatening to turn off my electricity.
15. I wanted to order chocolate cake for dessert, but I am on a diet, so I just ordered coffee.

From these sentences, you can see that a sentence can contain more than one independent clause. Punctuating independent clauses is discussed in 33. Fragments are discussed in 32.

Stress that independent clauses, like sentences, must have subjects and predicates and make sense by themselves. Students should also keep in mind that all clauses are different from all phrases in that phrases do not have subjects and predicates.

20i
gr

You might remind your class that the three kinds of dependent clauses have the same functions as three parts of speech—the adjective, the adverb, and the noun. Students who are still uncertain about those parts of speech should review 19a, 19d, and 19e.

20j gr

20j **Dependent clauses**

Definition

The dependent (or subordinate) clauses in the following sentences are highlighted.

1. I rolled over and went back to sleep when my alarm went off.

   The dependent clause has a subject—*alarm*—and a verb—*went*—but if it stood alone, it would leave you hanging or expecting more, so it is not an independent clause.

2. The woman who made the speech used to live on my block.

   This dependent clause also has a subject—*who*—and a verb—*used*—but it too would leave you hanging, so it is not an independent clause.

3. Whoever answers the door will receive a big surprise.

   Again, the dependent clause has a subject— *whoever*—and a verb—*answers*—but would leave you expecting more if it stood alone, so it is not an independent clause.

From these examples you can see that a **dependent clause** contains a subject and a verb but cannot stand as a sentence by itself. If it did, it would leave you hanging.

Adjective clauses

Three types of dependent clauses can be distinguished in English according to the way they are used in sentences. Some dependent clauses are used as adjectives.

4. The car that Maurice bought was a real lemon.

   The adjective clause *that Maurice bought* modifies the noun *car*—it tells you which car—so it is an adjective (or *adjectival* or *relative*) clause.

5. The man who looked like he was drunk was the coach of the tennis team.

   The adjective clause *who looked like he was drunk* is modifying the noun *man*—it describes the man—so it is an adjective clause.

An **adjective clause** is a dependent clause that modifies a noun or a pronoun. Adjective clauses usually begin with *who, whom, whose, which,* or *that,* but they can begin with *when, where,* or *why* as well.

 For more information on forming adjective clauses, see 11c.

Adverb clauses

Another type of dependent clause can be used to modify the verb.

6. When it started to rain, the children ran into the garage.

   The adverb clause *when it started to rain* modifies the verb *ran.* It answers the question When?

7. Sanchez lifted the suitcase as though it were full of bricks.

   The adverb clause *as though it were full of bricks* modifies the verb *lifted.* It answers the question How? or In what manner?

20j
gr

Dependent clauses that modify the verb are called **adverb** (or *adverbial*) **clauses.** Adverb clauses generally modify the verb, although they can modify adjectives or other adverbs. They usually answer one of these questions: "In what manner?" "When?" "Where?" "Why?" "To what extent?"

For more information about forming adverb clauses, see 11d.

8. Sad because his dog had died, Larry did not enjoy the baseball game.

   In this sentence, the adverb clause modifies the adjective *sad.*

9. Lynn swims faster than Peter can.

   Here the adverb clause modifies the adverb *faster.*

The words that can begin adverb clauses are called **subordinating** (or **subordinate**) **conjunctions** (see the box on p. 226).

Refer students to 19e for a review of how simple adverbs function. Stress that adverb clauses answer the same questions that adverbs do: When? Why? How?

You might stress that subordinating conjunctions have important consequences for punctuation (see 33a and 34a). Recognizing them can be easy if one keeps in mind that subordinating conjunctions signal answers to these questions: When? Why? How?

SUBORDINATING CONJUNCTIONS			
after	even though	once	unless
although	how	provided (that)	until
as	if	rather than	when
as far as	if only	since	whenever
as if	in case	so that	where
as long as	in order that	supposing (that)	whereas
as soon as	insofar as	than	wherever
as though	in that	that	whether
because	lest	though	while
before	no matter how	till	why
even if	now that		

Students often confuse noun clauses with adjective clauses because relative pronouns signal both types. Stress that noun clauses answer the same questions nouns answer: What? Who? or Whom? Adjective clauses, like simple adjectives, answer the questions What kind? Which one?

20j
gr

COLLABORATIVE ACTIVITY

Assign discussion groups to locate examples of independent, adjective, adverb, and noun clauses in an assigned essay from a college reader. Each group might specialize in finding a particular type of clause. Briefly discuss the findings in class.

Noun clauses

A third type of dependent clause is used as a noun in a sentence.

10. Whoever phoned me at midnight last night has a warped sense of humor.

The noun clause is used as the subject.

11. Dr. Li was willing to speak with whoever was available.

The noun clause is the object of the preposition *with*.

A **noun clause** can be used for any function usually filled by a noun: subject, direct object, indirect object, object of a preposition, or complement. Noun clauses usually begin with a relative pronoun such as *who, whom, whoever, whomever, what, where,* or *that*.

For more information about noun clauses, see 11e.

PART VI

EDITING: GRAMMAR

This and subsequent chapters in Part VI take up common grammatical errors. We begin by focusing on subject-verb agreement. Encourage students to pay close attention to such issues as the -*s* ending, forms of *be,* helping verbs, intervening phrases, compound subjects, collective nouns, and other matters affecting basic predication. Writers who have special difficulties with verbs might be advised to study 25 concurrently.

RESOURCES

D'Eloia, Sarah. "The Uses—and Limits—of Grammar." *Journal of Basic Writing* 1.3 (1977): 1–48.

Enos, Theresa, ed. *A Sourcebook for Basic Writing Teachers.* New York: McGraw, 1987.

Shaughnessy, Mina P. *Errors and Expectations: A Guide for the Teacher of Basic Writing.* New York: Oxford UP, 1977.

The influential book by Shaughnessy analyzes how students and teachers perceive error in writing courses. D'Eloia's article (rpt. in Enos 373–416) is concerned with methods of grammar instruction and includes useful approaches to teaching the verb phrase.

21 FINDING AND REVISING SUBJECT-VERB AGREEMENT ERRORS

Subject-verb agreement requires using the form of the verb that agrees with the subject in a sentence. Some writers have trouble with the basic concept; others have trouble with just one or two special cases. In this chapter we will start with the basic principles of subject-verb agreement and then discuss a series of special situations.

If you don't know what we mean by *agreement,* take a close look at 21a. If you're not sure what is and what is not a verb, review 19c and 20a. If you need help with the many forms of regular and irregular verbs as they are used to indicate different tenses, take a look at 25 and 26.

In the examples in this chapter, subjects are underlined once and verbs twice to assist you in seeing how subject-verb agreement works.

21a Basic subject-verb agreement

The following sentences illustrate the basic rule for subject-verb agreement in English:

1. One dog barks every morning.
2. Two dogs bark every morning.
3. That student looks angry.
4. Those students look angry.

> Notice the -*s* endings on the verbs in sentences 1 and 3; notice that there is no -*s* ending on the verbs in sentences 2 and 4. The subjects in sentences 1 and 3 (*dog* and *student*) are singular; we are talking about *one* dog and *one* student. The subjects in sentences 2 and 4 (*dogs* and *students*) are plural; we are talking about more than one dog and more than one student in these sentences.

From these observations we can develop the basic rule: if the subject is singular, the verb must have an -*s* ending; if the subject if plural, the verb must *not* have an -*s* ending. We call this principle **subject-verb agreement.**

Note that for verbs, the -*s* ending works just the opposite of the way it works for nouns. For verbs, an -*s* ending makes the verb *singular*; for nouns, an -*s* ending makes the noun *plural*. It might help you remember this if you think that *for verbs* the -*s* ending stands for "singular."

21b Subject-verb agreement with verb endings that are difficult to pronounce

The -*s* endings on the following verbs are difficult to pronounce:

asks	exists	masks	risks
basks	frisks	mists	wastes
boasts	lasts	resists	whisks
costs	lists		

As a result, many people just don't pronounce the final -*s*. When they write the same verbs, they may mistakenly omit the -*s* ending. Even though it is difficult to pronounce the final -*s* on the verbs in sentences like the following, you must include it in order for the verb to agree with the singular subject.

1. My <u>daughter</u> often <u>asks</u> for avocados for dinner.
2. A <u>seal</u> <u>basks</u> in the sun for up to fourteen hours a day.
3. This <u>car</u> <u>wastes</u> too much gasoline.

21c Subject-verb agreement with *I* and *you* as the subject

The following sentences illustrate an exception to the basic rule for subject-verb agreement.

1. One <u>student</u> <u>leaves</u> early every Friday.
2. Two <u>students</u> <u>leave</u> early every Friday.
3. <u>I</u> <u>leave</u> early every Friday.
4. <u>You</u> <u>leave</u> early every Friday.

Sentences 1 and 2 follow the basic rule for subject-verb agreement, but sentences 3 and 4 illustrate an exception. Even though the subjects *I* and *you* are singular, the verbs used with them do

ESL ADVICE

The -*s* ending is a common problem among ESL writers. Encourage those who leave off endings to practice third-person constructions in a notebook. Students who have trouble "hearing" the -*s* endings might also benefit from reading verb phrases aloud with a tutor or in a peer group.

21c
agr

not have -*s* endings. Even though *I* and *you* are singular, they require the same verb endings as plural subjects.

BASIC SUBJECT-VERB AGREEMENT

- If the subject is singular, the verb must have an -*s* ending.
- If the subject is plural or *I* or *you,* the verb must *not* have an -*s* ending.

21d **Subject-verb agreement with the verb** *be*

The most common verb in the English language is also the most irregular: the verb *be*. The various forms of the verb *be* follow hardly any of the standard rules.

The following sentences illustrate how subject-verb agreement works for the various forms of the verb *be* in the present tense.

1. <u>She</u> <u>is</u> tired of feeling helpless.
2. <u>Max</u> <u>is</u> tired of feeling helpless.
3. <u>They</u> <u>are</u> tired of feeling helpless.
4. <u>Students</u> <u>are</u> tired of feeling helpless.

When the subject is singular, as in the first two sentences, the correct form of the verb is *is,* which at least ends in an -*s* just like the regular verbs with singular subjects. But sentences 3 and 4 reveal that you don't just take the -*s* ending off when the subject is plural; instead, you use the word *are*—an entirely different form of the verb.

The following sentences demonstrate how to use the verb *be* with the pronouns *I* and *you* as subjects.

5. <u>I</u> <u>am</u> tired of feeling helpless.
6. <u>You</u> <u>are</u> tired of feeling helpless.

For agreement with the pronoun *I* as subject, use the form *am,* as in sentence 5. For agreement with the pronoun *you* as subject, use the form *are,* as in sentence 6.

21d
agr

21e Subject-verb agreement with helping verbs

The following sentences illustrate subject-verb agreement when you use a form of the verb *be* as a helping verb in front of a main verb.

1. <u>One</u> of my neighbors <u>is helping</u> my mother.
2. <u>Two</u> of my neighbors <u>are helping</u> my mother.

   Notice that only the helping verb is changed to agree with the subject. The main verb does not change form.

   Two other common helping verbs work in much the same way.

3. <u>Suzanne</u> <u>does live</u> in the city.
4. <u>Suzanne</u> and <u>Stephen</u> <u>do live</u> in the city.

   You should use *does* as a helping verb with singular subjects, *do* with plural ones. Again, the main verb does not change form when there is a helping verb.

5. Paula <u>Skolnik</u> <u>has played</u> extremely well this year.
6. Paula <u>Skolnik</u> and Yuri <u>Sher</u> <u>have played</u> extremely well this year.

   You should use *has* as a helping verb with singular subjects, *have* with plural ones. Again, the main verb does not change when there is a helping verb.

   The following sentences show how to handle subject-verb agreement when more than one helping verb is used with a main verb.

7. The <u>airplane</u> <u>has been searched</u>, and no bomb was found.
8. The <u>airplanes</u> <u>have been searched</u>, and no bombs were found.

   When more than one helping verb is used, the ending of only the first helping verb is changed to reflect subject-verb agreement.

   In the English language, there are nine other helping verbs—*can, could, may, might, must, shall, should, will,* and *would*—known as *modals,* which work somewhat differently from *be, do,* and *have*.

9. That <u>nurse</u> <u>can take</u> blood without the patient even feeling the needle.
10. Many <u>nurses</u> <u>can take</u> blood without the patient even feeling the needle.

Helping verbs are more formally termed *auxiliary verbs.* Refer students who are unfamiliar with the basic terminology of verb construction to 25 and 26.

21e
agr

11. <u>Ms. de Hoyos</u> <u>might buy</u> my car this weekend.

12. <u>Mr. and Ms. de Hoyos</u> <u>might buy</u> my car this weekend.

From sentences 9 through 12 you can see that modals add no *-s* when the subject is singular. They are an exception to the basic rule for subject-verb agreement.

 For more information about modals, see 19c.

21f Subject-verb agreement in past and future tenses

So far in this chapter, we have discussed subject-verb agreement in the present tense. Now we will discuss subject-verb agreement with tenses other than the present.

1. One <u>dog</u> <u>barked</u> last week.

2. Two <u>dogs</u> <u>barked</u> last week.

Verbs do *not* change form to agree with their subjects in the past tense.

3. One <u>dog</u> <u>will bark</u> tomorrow morning.

4. Two <u>dogs</u> <u>will bark</u> tomorrow morning.

Verbs also do not change form to agree with their subjects in the future tense.

The one exception to this generalization is illustrated by the following sentences.

5. One <u>dog</u> <u>was barking</u> last week.

6. Two <u>dogs</u> <u>were barking</u> last week.

The only verb that changes its form to indicate subject-verb agreement in the past tense is the verb *be,* which takes the form *was* for singular subjects, *were* for plural subjects. Note that even this irregular verb ends in an *-s* with singular subjects.

21g Subject-verb agreement with phrases that come between subject and verb

What makes the following sentences a little tricky is the presence of a second noun between the subject and the verb.

Students can review tenses in more detail by referring to 26.

21g
agr

1. The cause of these incidents has not been discovered.

There are two ways to avoid mistakes with subject-verb agreement in this kind of sentence. First you can ask "what is *doing* the verb?"—in this case, "What has not been discovered?"—and you will find that *cause* (and not *incidents*) is the subject. Second, you can remember that *the subject can never be in a prepositional phrase* (see 20d for a discussion of prepositional phrases). Because *of these incidents* is a prepositional phrase, *incidents* cannot be the subject.

2. The losses of my mother's company are not as large as expected.

When you ask the question "What are not as large as expected?" you find that the subject is *losses,* not *company.* Also, because *of my mother's company* is a prepositional phrase, you know that *company* cannot be the subject.

The second noun in these sentences can be mistaken for the subject if you are not careful. Notice that in each of these sentences, identifying the wrong word (*incidents* or *company*) as the subject would have resulted in a subject-verb agreement error.

A second type of phrase that can come between subject and verb is illustrated by the following sentences.

3. The nurse, as well as the patients, was confused by the sounding of the alarm.

Here common sense will actually get you in trouble. It would seem that the subject is plural, that it includes a nurse *and* some patients. The problem is that the sentence doesn't say "and the patients." The phrase *as well as the patients* is not part of the subject. Only *nurse* is the subject, and the subject is therefore singular. If this makes the sentence seem awkward to you, as it does to many writers, change *as well as* to *and* to form a compound subject (see 21h).

4. The nurse and the patients were confused by the sounding of the alarm.

Other phrases that work this way include *along with, in addition to, including, together with,* and *not to mention.*

21h Subject-verb agreement with compound subjects

The following examples illustrate another type of sentence that sometimes causes trouble.

21h
agr

ACTIVITY

Using examples shown here as models, have students practice writing sentences in which phrases separate subject from verb. Alternatively, write five or more simple subject + verb combinations on the board and ask students to supply intervening prepositional phrases, for example, "The crate is broken. The crate of apples is broken."

1. <u>Cardinals</u> and <u>kingfishers</u> <u>are</u> my favorite birds.

   When subjects are composed of two or more words joined by the conjunction *and,* they are said to be *compound.* Notice that compound subjects joined by *and* are ordinarily treated as plural. Cardinals and kingfishers *are,* not *is.*

   One exception to this principle is illustrated by sentence 2.

2. The <u>winner and new champion</u> of the world <u>is</u> Bouncing Bill Bennett.

   The subject is *winner and new champion,* which would seem to be plural but is not because the two terms form a single idea and refer to a single person.

   Another exception is illustrated by sentence 3.

3. Each <u>man</u> and <u>woman</u> <u>receives</u> a sterling silver lapel button as a souvenir of this night.

   When a compound subject joined by *and* is preceded by the word *each* or *every,* the subject is treated as a singular.

   But note the following example:

4. <u>Sam</u> and <u>Carrie</u> each <u>ride</u> with a neighbor to work every morning.

   When a compound subject is *followed* by *each,* it is still treated as a plural subject.

   The following sentences show how subject-verb agreement works when compound subjects are joined by *or.*

5. <u>Langston</u> or <u>Reggie</u> <u>drives</u> me to work every Friday.

   Logically enough, if two singular subjects are joined by *or,* the subject is singular. Whether it is Langston *or* Reggie, only *one person* drives me.

6. <u>Raisins</u> or <u>bananas</u> <u>are</u> good in cream of wheat.

   If two plural nouns are joined by *or,* the subject is plural. This is completely logical. In sentence 6, we are going to use *either* raisins *or* bananas, not both, but whichever we use, we will be using *more than one* of them, so the subject is plural.

   The following pair of sentences illustrates a slightly more complicated and less logical situation.

21h
agr

FOR DISCUSSION

Another way of explaining the "or" rule is to demonstrate elliptical construction. For example, "Either the table or the chairs need fixing" can be written on the board as follows: "Either the table [*needs* fixing] or the chairs *need* fixing." Conversely, "Either the chairs [*need* fixing] or the table *needs* fixing."

7. The teacher or the students have to apologize.

8. The students or the teacher has to apologize.

When one singular and one plural subject are joined by *or*, there is no logical way to know whether the subject is singular or plural, so the rule is fairly arbitrary: the verb agrees with the nearer subject. In sentence 7, the nearer subject to the verb is *students*, so the plural verb *have* is used. In sentence 8, the singular *teacher* is the nearer subject, so the singular verb *has* is used.

21i Subject-verb agreement with indefinite pronouns

The following sentences illustrate subject-verb agreement involving indefinite pronouns. (Indefinite pronouns are defined in 19b).

1. Someone in the next booth is listening to us.

2. Anyone in this class is welcome to come to the lecture.

As you can see, most indefinite pronouns are singular and require the singular form of the verb. See the chart on page 236 for a complete list of singular indefinite pronouns.

3. Each of these plants requires watering twice a week.

4. Everyone likes to receive flowers.

Be especially careful with the pronouns *each* and *everyone*, which seem plural in meaning but are grammatically singular.

A much smaller group of indefinite pronouns are always plural.

5. Many are called, but few are chosen.

6. Two of my brothers play professional baseball.

A third group of indefinite pronouns are singular or plural depending on the noun in the prepositional phrase that follows the pronoun.

7. Some of the wine is cabernet sauvignon.

8. Some of the cookies are chocolate chip.

In sentence 7, the indefinite pronoun *some* is followed by a prepositional phrase ending in the singular noun *wine*, so *some* is singular and takes the singular verb *is*. In sentence 8, *some* is followed by a prepositional phrase ending in the plural noun *cookies*, so this time *some* is plural and takes the plural verb *are*.

21i
agr

9. <u>All</u> of Melia's personality <u>does</u> not <u>come</u> from her father.
10. <u>All</u> of Melia's sweaters <u>do</u> not <u>fit</u> in the closet.

In number 9, *all* is followed by the singular *personality,* so *all* is singular and takes the singular verb *does.* In sentence 10, *all* is followed by the plural *sweaters,* so *all* is plural and takes the plural verb *do.*

NUMBER WITH INDEFINITE PRONOUNS

Always Singular	Always Plural	Singular or Plural
another	both	all
each	few	any
either	many	more
every	several	most
neither	two (*any number*	much
one	*greater than one*)	none
every- ⎫ ⎧ -thing		some
any- ⎬ + ⎨ -one		half (*any fraction*)
no- ⎭ ⎩ -body		

The bracketing at the bottom of the left-hand column is just a shorthand way of remembering twelve different pronouns: *everything, everyone, everybody, anything, anyone, anybody, nothing, no one,* and *nobody,* all of which are always singular.

21j **Subject-verb agreement with collective nouns**

The subjects in the following sentences belong to a group of words known as **collective nouns.** Some common collective nouns are *army, audience, class, committee, crowd, family, group, jury,* and *team.* How they work in subject-verb agreement is illustrated by the following sentences.

1. The <u>jury</u> <u>is</u> <u>waiting</u> for the lawyers' closing arguments.
2. The <u>class</u> <u>wants</u> to take the final exam on Friday.
3. A <u>group</u> of bicyclists <u>rides</u> past my house each Saturday morning.

Notice that each of these subjects, *jury, class,* and *group,* is singular even though it involves a number of people. In each case, the

people are being considered *as a unit*. They are acting not as individuals but rather as *one* group; therefore, each is singular.

Occasionally, a collective noun is used in such a way that the members of the group are being considered as individuals. When this happens, it is correct to consider the collective noun plural.

4. The committee are not able to agree on a meeting time.
5. My family seem to be unable to communicate with each other.

   Even in these cases, it seems awkward to most writers to use these nouns as plurals. A less awkward solution is to edit the sentence to make the subjects more clearly plural:

6. The committee members are not able to agree on a meeting time.
7. My parents and my sisters seem to be unable to communicate with each other.

   The word *number* is an unusual collective noun:

8. The number of students who drop out of school is too large.
9. A number of students are planning to quit school this spring.

   The phrase *the number* is always singular; the phrase *a number* is always plural.

21k Subject-verb agreement when the subject follows the verb

The normal word order in English sentences is for the subject to come first in the sentence and the verb to follow. The following sentences illustrate some exceptions to normal word order.

1. There are three cups of coffee left.
2. There is a reason for his sudden absence.

   In these sentences, the subject follows the verb. Both sentences start with the word *there*. When sentences start with *there,* the subject almost always follows the verb. In these cases, subject-verb agreement works exactly the way it does in any other sentence, but the subject is a little harder to find.

The following sentences represent a second type of sentence in which the subject follows the verb.

ESL ADVICE

Foreign students who first studied English abroad may have acquired different habits with regard to collective noun agreement. For example, British usage may treat corporations and sports teams as plurals ("Argentina have won the tournament") in circumstances where American usage calls for singular agreement. You may need to make allowances for such minor differences.

21k
agr

3. In the closet on the left <u>are</u> my best <u>suits</u>.

4. Under that bed <u>live four</u> of the cutest kittens in the Western Hemisphere.

In sentences 3 and 4, the subject comes after the verb. Notice also that each sentence starts with a prepositional phrase. Subject-verb agreement works the same as it has in earlier examples, once the subject has been identified.

Now look at the following sentences, which also begin with prepositional phrases.

5. In the closet <u>Greg found</u> several new suits.

6. Under that bed <u>four</u> of the cutest kittens in the Western Hemisphere <u>were born</u>.

These sentences begin with prepositional phrases, but the subject does not follow the verb. It occupies its normal position. To make sure that the verb agrees with the subject in sentences that begin with prepositional phrases, you must be careful to find the actual subject of the sentence—whatever is "doing" the verb. It can come either before or after the verb.

21l **Subject-verb agreement with linking verbs**

Subject-verb agreement in sentences with linking verbs can be a little confusing.

1. My favorite <u>dessert</u> <u>is</u> strawberries and cream.

Even though *strawberries and cream* is plural, the verb is *is* because the subject is *dessert,* which is singular.

2. A major social <u>problem</u> in America <u>is</u> the many people who are homeless.

Even though *people* is plural, the subject is *problem,* which is singular.

Nouns that follow linking verbs are called *complements* (see 20e).

21l
agr

Remind students that linking verbs show equivalence or state of being. Besides the examples shown here, linking verbs include forms of *seem, look, smell,* and *feel* (when those forms are used intransitively). See also 20f.

21m Subject-verb agreement in clauses beginning with *who, which,* or *that*

The following sentences demonstrate a difficulty in subject-verb agreement that occurs with clauses in which the subject is *who, which,* or *that.*

Dependent clause

1. A student who is late for class should enter the room quietly.

Dependent clause

2. Students who are late for class should enter the room quietly.

> *Who is late for class* in sentence 1 and *who are late for class* in sentence 2 are dependent (adjective) clauses (see 11c and 20j) modifying the nouns *student* and *students. Who* in both sentences is a relative pronoun used as the subject of the dependent clause that it introduces. It is difficult to tell whether *who* is singular or plural by the form of the word. It is singular in sentence 1 and plural in sentence 2.

The only way to determine whether *who* is singular or plural is to determine what its antecedent is and whether that antecedent is singular or plural. An *antecedent* is the noun or pronoun that a pronoun stands for or refers to (see 19b and 22a). In sentences 1 and 2, arrows have been drawn from the pronouns to their antecedents.

In sentence 1, the antecedent for *who* is *student. Student* is singular, so *who* is singular, and the verb that agrees is *is.* In sentence 2, the antecedent for *who* is *students. Students* is plural, so *who* is plural, and the verb that agrees is *are.*

Which and *that* are also relative pronouns that do not change form to indicate whether they are singular or plural.

The following sentences illustrate a situation in which subject-verb agreement with *who, which,* and *that* is particularly complicated.

21m
agr

Dependent clause

3. This is one of those problems that are easy once you know the answer.

Sentence 3 is saying that there are many problems that are easy once you know the answer, and this is one of them, so the antecedent for *that* is *problems,* not *one.* Therefore, *that* is plural and takes the verb *are.*

Dependent clause

4. This is the only one of those problems that is easy once you know the answer.

Sentence 4, on the other hand, does not say that there are *many problems* that are easy once you know the answer; it says that there is *only one.* Therefore, the antecedent for *that* is *one,* not *problems,* making *that* singular. It takes the verb *is.*

If you don't want to reason all this out every time you use one of these expressions, you may just want to remember to use a plural verb with the expression *one of those* and to use a singular verb with the expression *the only one of those.*

21n
agr

21n Subject-verb agreement when the subject is plural in form but singular in meaning

The following sentences illustrate subjects that are plural in form but singular in meaning.

1. Mathematics is an easy subject for me.

   Mathematics ends in -*s* but is singular in meaning and takes a singular verb.

2. The news was very bad when I called the doctor.

   News ends in -*s* but is singular in meaning and takes a singular verb.

Other words that are plural in form but singular in meaning include *athletics, economics, ethics, mumps, physics, politics, sports,* and *statistics.*

The following sentences contain a different kind of word that is plural in form but singular in meaning.

3. <u>General Motors</u> <u>is</u> located in Detroit, Michigan.

4. *<u>Hard Times</u>* <u>is</u> a novel about working conditions in nineteenth-century England.

These sentences demonstrate that *names* and *titles* are singular in meaning even if they are plural in form.

The following sentences are one more example of subjects that are plural in form but singular in meaning.

5. Two <u>miles</u> <u>is</u> the distance from my house to my work.

6. Twenty <u>dollars</u> <u>is</u> a good price for that sweater.

Subjects that indicate quantities (of money, distance, weight, or time) are considered singular.

22 FINDING AND REVISING PRONOUN REFERENCE ERRORS

A **pronoun** is a word that stands for or takes the place of a noun and its modifiers, or (in the case of *I* and *you*)that stands for the speaker or the person spoken to, or (in the case of indefinite pronouns) that stands for an unknown or unspecified person or thing (see 19b). The specific noun or pronoun that the pronoun refers to is called the **antecedent** (see 19b).

Because the antecedent is essential to the reader's understanding of the pronoun, the relation between the two must be absolutely clear. If it is difficult for the reader to figure out exactly what the antecedent is, there is a problem with **pronoun reference,** which we will discuss in this chapter. If the pronoun is in the wrong form for the antecedent, there is a problem with *pronoun agreement,* which will be discussed in 23.

This chapter should sharpen students' awareness of pronoun reference errors, thereby helping them improve their editing skills. Stress the importance of the clear antecedent as a key factor in grammatical coherence.

22 ref

RESOURCES

Moskovit, Leonard. "When Is Broad Reference Clear?" *College Composition and Communication* 34 (1983): 454–69.

The author examines effective and ineffective uses of this *and other broad reference pronouns.*

22b
ref

22a Making sure that a pronoun has one clear antecedent

In 19b you learned that pronouns usually have antecedents as in the following sentences.

1. Richard Rodriguez wrote a novel about his childhood.

   Richard Rodriguez is the antecedent for *his.*

2. I read Kelly's essay, and it didn't seem bad to me.

   Essay is the antecedent for *it.*

   The following sentences illustrate errors in pronoun reference.

3. INCORRECT: My brother gave Mr. Williams a package before he left.

   It is not clear whether *he* refers to *brother* or *Mr. Williams.*

4. CORRECTED: Before my brother left, he gave Mr. Williams a package.

5. INCORRECT: Nancy bought some cookies from the Girl Scout, and then she walked across the street.

   It is not clear whether *she* refers to *Nancy* or *Girl Scout.*

6. CORRECTED: Nancy walked across the street after she bought some cookies from the Girl Scout.

22b Making sure that a pronoun has a specific antecedent

The following sentences illustrate another type of error involving pronoun reference.

1. INCORRECT: The tires on my car are worn, and the road was a little slippery. This made me worry all the way home.

   What does *this* refer to? The worn tires? The slippery road? Both?

2. CORRECTED: The tires on my car are worn, and the road was a little slippery. This combination made me worry all the way home.

3. INCORRECT: My committee decided to revise the by-laws, but it took us about a month.

   Does *it* refer to deciding on the revision? Actually doing it? Something else?

4. **Corrected:** My committee decided to revise the by-laws, but the revision took us about a month.

22c Avoiding the use of a pronoun with an implied antecedent

In the following sentences, the pronouns do not refer to a specific noun or pronoun.

1. **Incorrect:** After we camped in Baxter State Park this weekend, I knew it was something I would like to do more often.

   It seems to refer to *camping,* but *camping* doesn't appear in the sentence; it is merely implied by the first part.

2. **Corrected:** After we camped in Baxter State Park this weekend, I knew camping was something I would like to do more often.

22d Avoiding pronouns that are too distant from their antecedents

The following sentences illustrate a final problem with pronoun reference.

1. **Incorrect:** Richard Wright wrote a powerful autobiographical novel called *Black Boy,* who was a leading figure in the Harlem Renaissance.

   The pronoun *who* is too far away from its antecedent, so it is difficult for the reader to figure out what its antecedent is.

2. **Corrected:** Richard Wright, who was a leading figure in the Harlem Renaissance, wrote a powerful autobiographical novel called *Black Boy.*

A vague and careless *it* can lead to serious incoherence. Remind students, however, that indefinite reference is permissible in such idioms as "It's raining" or "It seems that. . . ."

COLLABORATIVE ACTIVITY

Editing groups can meet to search drafts for pronoun reference errors. Have students help one another revise sentences in which pronouns lack clear antecedents.

23
agr

23 FINDING AND REVISING PRONOUN AGREEMENT ERRORS

A **pronoun** is a word that stands for or takes the place of a noun and its modifiers, or (in the case of *I* and *you*) that stands for the speaker or the person spoken to, or (in the case of indefinite pro-

Pronoun agreement errors have come to have social as well as grammatical implications. This chapter enables students to avoid not only those slips having to do with person and number, but also those that might imply sexism or tactlessness.

RESOURCES

Kolln, Martha. "Everyone's Right to Their Own Language." *College Composition and Communication* 37 (1986): 100–02.

Miller, Casey, and Kate Swift. *The Handbook of Non-Sexist Writing.* 2nd ed. New York: Harper-Collins, 1988.

nouns) that stands for an unknown or unspecified person or thing (see 19b). The specific noun or pronoun that the pronoun refers to is called the **antecedent** (see 19b). In 22, we discussed the need for a clear and unambiguous relationship between a pronoun and its antecedent. If the relationship between a pronoun and its antecedent is not clear, the sentence has a problem with *pronoun reference.*

In this chapter we will discuss a second group of problems that can arise with pronouns and their antecedents: **pronoun agreement** errors.

23a Basic pronoun agreement

In the following sentences, the editing indicates changes necessary to make sure that the pronouns agree with their antecedents.

1. Julio worked until ten every night at a record store, but ~~they~~ ^{he} still came to class every morning at eight.

> In the incorrect sentence, the antecedent for *they* was *Julio.* Because the original pronoun *they* was plural and its antecedent *Julio* was singular, the pronoun did not *agree* with its antecedent, so the pronoun was changed to *he.* Now it agrees with its antecedent.

Example 1 demonstrates that pronouns must agree with their antecedents in *number.* If the antecedent is singular, the pronoun must be singular; if it is plural, the pronoun must be plural.

The next example illustrates a second problem in pronoun agreement.

2. We prefer a mature manager because ~~you~~ ^{he or she will} often have to close the store alone late at night.

> The agreement problem between the pronoun *you* and its antecedent *manager* is not the result of a problem in number; both *you* and *manager* are singular. The problem is that the correct pronoun to agree with *manager* is *he or she.* (We'll talk about the use of *he or she* instead of just *he* in 23b.) *You* didn't agree with its antecedent in *person.*

23a
agr

You can find a complete discussion of person in 9b.

To review, pronouns exist in three persons in English. *I, me, my, mine, we, us, our,* and *ours* are first-person pronouns and are used to refer only to the person actually speaking or writing. *You, your,* and *yours* are second-person pronouns and are used to refer only to the person being spoken or written to. *He, him, his, she, her, hers, it, its, they, them, their,* and *theirs* are third-person pronouns. They are used to refer to anyone or anything being spoken about who is not the speaker or writer or the person being spoken or written to. In general, once you begin using one person, you should not shift to another.

                                        his

3. George talked to ~~her~~ mother and father about the possible pro-

motion.

> The original pronoun *her* did not agree with its antecedent, *George.* They are both singular and third person, but *her* is feminine and *George* is masculine, so *her* was changed to *his.* Pronouns must agree with their antecedents in number (singular or plural) and person (first, second, or third person) as well as gender (masculine, feminine, or neuter). In many languages, possessive pronouns like *her, his, its, their, my, your,* and *our* agree with either the word they modify and the antecedent, or just the word they modify, but in English they must agree with their antecedents.

23b Avoiding sexism with pronouns

The following examples illustrate three methods of revision to eliminate sexism.

                                        he or she

1. A writer should think for a while before ~~he~~ starts to write.

> The original *he* is the pronoun that would have been used in the past, but in recent years writers have recognized that using the pronoun *he* to refer to all human beings can be interpreted as excluding women. To avoid any such implications, most writers no longer use *he* to refer to an antecedent that may in fact be male or female.

The phrase *he or she* can be a little awkward, especially if it is used repeatedly in a short piece of prose. To avoid such awkwardness,

ESL ADVICE

Advise students whose first languages differ from English in gender usage to study the examples given in this section carefully. ESL writers may benefit from writing sample sentences containing pronouns that agree in gender with antecedents.

23b
agr

ESL

FOR DISCUSSION

The advice given in this section reflects a generational change that your students are living through. Because it was uncommon for literature published earlier than fifty years ago to use "he or she" for indefinite reference, you might discuss the implications of the change. To what extent do students agree that using *he* or *his* alone in unspecific reference to persons is (or has been) evidence of male bias?

the following sentences illustrate two additional methods for eliminating sexist use of pronouns.

2. Sometimes, however, the best way for a writer to think is to start
   s
   them
   writing and see what ideas come to him.

   Here the sexism in the original sentence has been eliminated by making *writer* plural and using the plural pronoun *them,* which does not indicate any gender.

3. A writer should use the technique that makes it possible for him

   to come up with good ideas.

   In this example, the words *for him* were deleted, making the sentence more concise and eliminating the need to use any pronoun.

   writers are
4. When a writer is writing about good ideas, they will find their task

   much easier.

   The original *they* does avoid sexism, but only through an error in pronoun agreement. The plural *they* cannot be used to refer to the singular antecedent *writer.* This problem has been corrected by making the antecedent plural.

5. When a student is unsure of an assignment, he/she should discuss it with the instructor.

   He/she is used as a substitute for *his or her,* but many readers find it clumsy and distracting. We recommend *he or she* (if one of the other solutions is not possible).

23c Pronoun agreement with compound antecedents

The following sentences illustrate the basic rule for pronoun agreement with compound antecedents joined by *and.*

1. W. E. B. Du Bois and Booker T. Washington wrote books in which
   they
   he discussed the African-American experience.

   The antecedent for the original pronoun *he* was *W. E. B. Du Bois and Booker T. Washington.* Because the antecedent consists of two singular nouns joined by *and,* it is plural, so the pronoun was changed to *they.* If the antecedent consists of two words joined by *and,* it is plural.

The following sentences illustrate two exceptions to the basic rule.

2. The author and educator spoke frequently to audiences in the
   North and the South, but ~~their~~ *his* book *Up from Slavery* was what really
   made ~~them~~ *him* famous.

   Even though the antecedent consists of two words, *author* and *educator,* joined by *and,* the antecedent is not plural because the two words refer to one person, Booker T. Washington.

3. Every man and woman who reads W. E. B. Du Bois's *Souls of Black Folk* will be moved by the force of the language; ~~they~~ *he or she* will never think about the historical role of African-Americans in the same way again.

   Compound subjects joined by *and* but having *every* in front of them are treated as singular, so the plural pronoun *they* has been changed to *he or she.*

The next sentences illustrate pronoun agreement when compound subjects are joined by *or* or *nor.*

4. Du Bois argued that a man or a woman could be free only if ~~they~~ *he or she* ~~were~~ *was* educated.

   Here two singular nouns, *man* and *woman,* are joined by *or.* Common sense tells us that even though we don't know whether the antecedent is a man or a woman, we do know that it will be one or the other, and hence that it will be singular. Consequently, the original plural pronoun *they* was changed to the singular pronoun *he or she.*

5. Neither Du Bois nor Washington believed that ~~their~~ *his* people were being educated satisfactorily.

   Nor works just like *or;* when it joins two singular nouns, in this case *Du Bois* and *Washington,* the combined antecedent is singular. *Neither* at the beginning of the sentence works with *nor* to join the two nouns. *Either* and *or* are used as a pair in the same way.

23c
agr

6. Washington argued that men or women should be educated in order that he or she *they* can perform useful work.

In this sentence, *men or women* is a plural antecedent because both nouns, *men* and *women,* are plural. Therefore, the original singular pronouns *he or she* have been changed to the plural pronoun *they.*

7. Du Bois argued that neither the teacher nor the students should be satisfied if the final goal of his or her *their* work was simply a job and the income it would provide.

In this sentence, the antecedent is *teacher nor students.* Notice that of the two words joined by *nor,* one, *teacher,* is singular, and one, *students,* is plural. When one singular noun and one plural noun are joined by *or* or *nor,* the pronoun refers the noun that is closer to the pronoun. In this sentence, the plural word *students* is closer to the original pronouns *his or her,* so they have been changed to the plural pronoun *their.*

8. Du Bois argued that neither the students nor the teacher should be satisfied if the final goal of their *his or her* work was simply a job and the income it would provide.

Sentence 8 is the same as sentence 7 except that the order of the two nouns in the antecedent has been reversed. Now the singular *teacher* is closer to the pronoun, so the correct pronoun is the singular *his or her.* Readers, however, tend to find sentences like 8 awkward. In most sentences with one plural and one singular antecedent, the sentence will be less awkward if the plural antecedent is placed nearer the pronoun.

23d
agr

Some authorities now excuse the informal use of *their* in relation to the indefinite pronoun *everyone.* See, for example, Martha Kolln, *Understanding English Grammar,* 3rd ed. (New York: Macmillan, 1991), page 390. In general, however, formal usage continues to support singular agreement, as illustrated by the examples given here.

23d **Pronoun agreement with indefinite pronoun antecedents**

The following sentences illustrate the way pronoun agreement works most of the time when the antecedent is an indefinite pronoun (see 19b).

his or her
1. Everyone should bring their disks to class this week.

    The indefinite pronoun *everyone* is always singular, so the plural pronoun *their* was changed to the singular *he or her*.

    Sentences of this type might be revised in two other ways.

All students
2. Everyone should bring their disks to class this week.

    The singular antecedent *everyone* was changed to the plural *all students*.

two
3. Everyone should bring their disks to class this week.

    The sentence was edited to eliminate the pronoun *their*.

A complete list of the indefinite pronouns that are always singular can be found in 21i.

A few indefinite pronouns are always plural; however, these do not cause most writers much trouble because their plural sense is obvious. A complete list of these can also be found in 21i.

their
4. A few of the students in this class have used computers in his or her writing before.

    It's clear that *few* is plural; it means more than one. Originally, the singular pronoun *his or her* referred to the plural antecedent *few*, so the sentence was revised by replacing *he or she* with the plural *their*.

their
5. Several of these students have volunteered to share his or her expertise with anyone who is having trouble.

    Several also is plural. The singular pronoun *his or her* originally referred to the plural antecedent *several*. This agreement problem was corrected by replacing *his or her* with the plural *their*.

To understand a third group of indefinite pronouns, you first need to be able to identify antecedents of pronouns.

6. Some of the students will write their papers on IBM computers.

    The antecedent for *their* is *some*, not *students*.

23d
agr

7. One of the students will write his or her paper on an IBM computer.

> The antecedent for *his or her* is *one*, not *students*.

The antecedent, then, is usually the noun preceding a prepositional phrase rather than the noun at the end of the phrase. (Prepositional phrases are discussed in 19f and 20d).

Now let's look again at sentence 6. We now know that the antecedent for the pronoun *their* is *some*, but is *some* singular or plural? The following two sentences will help answer this question.

8. Some of the computers are Macintoshes, but they are older models.

> *Some* in this sentence is plural, so we have used the plural pronoun *they* to refer to it. In fact, *some* can be singular or plural. You determine which it is by looking at the noun at the end of the following prepositional phrase. In sentence 8, that noun is *computers*, which is plural, so *some* is plural and takes the plural pronoun *they*.

9. Some of the writing in this essay is quite good, but it is not very effective because of the frequent grammatical errors.

> In this sentence, *some* is singular; we use the singular pronoun *it* to refer to it. The noun at the end of the prepositional phrase is *writing*, which is singular, so *some* is singular and takes the singular pronoun *it*.

Now let's look one more time at the sentence that started us on all this discussion of *some*, sentence 6.

6. Some of the students will write their papers on IBM computers.

> We now know that *some* is the antecedent for *their*. Further, we know that *some*, in this case, is plural because *students*, the noun in the following prepositional phrase, is plural. So the pronoun that refers to *some* must be the plural *their*.

23d
agr

A list of indefinite pronouns that can be singular or plural depending on the noun in the prepositional phrase that follows can be found in 21i.

23e Pronoun agreement with collective noun antecedents

Collective nouns are nouns that refer to a group of people—a collection. These nouns are usually singular because they represent a collection of people *who are being discussed as a single unit.* For a list of common collective nouns, see 21j.

1. The audience roared their̶ approval of Elana Marshello's singing. *(its)*

   Audience is the antecedent for the original pronoun *their.* However, the audience here is being considered as a unit: the whole group of people shouted out its approval. Therefore, the original plural pronoun *their* has been changed to the singular pronoun *its* so that it agrees with its singular antecedent *audience.*

2. Her singing group got their̶ start at Cuyahoga County Community College. *(its)*

   The original plural pronoun *their* has been changed to the singular *its* to agree with its singular antecedent *group.*

   Collective pronouns are considered plural in some cases.

3. The committee that had invited her to sing had argued among itself̶ about whether she was good enough to appear in the Annual Spring Concert. *(themselves)*

   Here *committee* is clearly plural because the members are arguing among themselves. If it was being considered as a single unit, it would not be able to argue; only the individuals could argue. In these fairly rare cases, collective nouns are considered plural.

23e
agr

Pronoun usage often reflects life-long habits. Students lucky enough to have unconsciously acquired the conventions of Standard Written English may have little need of the advice in 24. In many instances, however, writers will need to modify old habits if they are to conform to academic usage. You might need to propose memorization and a good deal of practice to supplement the guidelines in this chapter.

RESOURCES

Celce-Murcia, Marianne, and Diane Larsen-Freeman. *The Grammar Book: An ESL/EFL Teacher's Course.* Rowley: Newbury House, 1983.

Shaughnessy, Mina P. *Errors and Expectations: A Guide for the Teacher of Basic Writing.* New York: Oxford UP, 1977.

24a
case

Students would be well advised to memorize the pronouns *by case,* especially if misuse is habitual. You might warn your class that, aside from habit or guessing, the only way to know if one is using a pronoun correctly is to know which case a given pronoun belongs in and to recognize which case is called for within a particular context.

24   FINDING AND REVISING PRONOUN CASE ERRORS

Almost every speaker of English is familiar with the concept of pronoun case. Hardly anyone would make the following mistakes.

1. *I*
   Me am going to the movies.
2. Hand that stapler to ~~I~~. *me*
3. That is ~~me~~'s stapler. *my*

Changing the form of a pronoun to indicate how it is functioning in a sentence (*I* in sentence 1 and *me* in sentence 2, for example) is what we mean by pronoun **case.** *I* is in the subjective case, *me* is in the objective case, and *my* is in the possessive case. These three are the only cases in English.

In English the pronouns *I, we, he, she, they, who,* and *whoever* have different forms for all three cases. Other pronouns and nouns have only subjective and possessive forms.

24a   Subjects versus objects

The chart on the facing page shows the subjective, objective, and possessive case forms for pronouns that have both subjective and objective forms.

The basic principle for choosing between subjective and objective cases is illustrated by the following sentences.

Subjective case

1. She is not sure what kind of job to pursue.

   Because *she* is used as the subject (see 20b), it is in the **subjective case.**

2. Emily wanted to be an architect when she was younger.

   The highlighted *she* is the subject of the dependent clause (see 20j), so it is in the subjective case.

FORMS FOR PRONOUN CASE

Subjective	Objective	Possessive
I	me	my, mine
he	him	his
she	her	her, hers
we	us	our, ours
they	them	their
who	whom	whose
whoever	whomever	

Objective case

3. I urged her to think it over carefully.

   Because *her* is the direct object (see 20c) in the sentence, it is in the **objective case.**

4. I gave her a book about careers.

   Here *her* is the indirect object (see 20c), so it is in the objective case.

5. I also asked my mother to talk to her.

   Her is the object of the preposition *to* (see 19f), so it is in the objective case.

24b Subjective case after linking verbs

In 24a you learned about the basic uses for the subjective and objective cases. In the rest of this chapter, you will learn about some more unusual uses of these cases.

The following sentence illustrates another use for the subjective case.

> Even though Elsie didn't think she sang very well, it was she who won the talent contest.

In this sentence, *she* is a subject complement (see 20e) rather than an object, so it is in the subjective case. Subject complements always come after a linking verb. (See 19c.)

You might point out that the correct use of object pronouns in these examples reflects two computer-like operations in the writer's mind. First, the writer knows (if so programmed by habit) that the context position is objective rather than subjective (even if the writer isn't consciously aware of those terms). Second, the writer automatically uses the pronoun associated with object position. An error would occur if the writer had been "misprogrammed" by habit, either with regard to recognizing object positions or, as is more often true, with regard to knowing which case a pronoun belongs to. Students who find themselves misusing pronouns need to do some reprogramming, usually by memorizing the pronoun categories and studying basic sentence structure.

24b
case

Linking verbs call for subjective case because they do not convey action but merely equate the subject with something else (e.g., "It was she" means "It = she"). If students object that people are more likely to say "It's me" than "It is I," tell them they have a point. In formal written discourse, students may have to differentiate their written usage of linking verbs from their habits of usage as speakers.

College instructors regard the use of *me* in a subject position as a very serious error. Yet students who misuse the pronoun often do so from long habit. You might advise those who have that habit to practice freewriting numerous sentences beginning with compound subjects that include *I*.

24c Case in compound structures

Even though the same principles that you learned in 24a and 24b apply, some writers have difficulty with sentences like the following.

1. Franklin and ~~me~~ *I* are going to talk to the Dean.

> Because the subject is compound (see 21h), some writers make the error of using *me* instead of *I*. However, since *Franklin and I* is the subject, the subjective case must be used for the pronoun.

A good way to figure out the correct case in sentences with compound constructions is to split the sentence mentally into two sentences without compound structures. If we split sentence 1 into two sentences without a compound subject, we get the following:

2. Franklin is going to talk to the Dean.
3. *I* am going to talk to the Dean.

> Clearly it would be incorrect to say "Me is going to talk to the Dean." Since *me* is incorrect in the split sentence, it is also incorrect in sentence 1, where it would appear as part of the compound subject.

Mistakes are even more common with compound constructions involving prepositional phrases, particularly when those phrases come at the beginning of the sentence.

4. According to Walter and ~~she~~ *her*, Julie's house is not for sale.

> Because *her* is the object of a preposition, it must be in the objective case. If the sentence is split to eliminate the compound construction, it becomes clear that the pronoun must be *her:*

5. According to Walter, Julie's house is not for sale.
6. According to ~~she~~ *her*, Julie's house is not for sale.

The most frequent error with pronoun case involves the phrase "between you and me," as in sentence 7.

me
7. Just between you and I, this restaurant's prices are very reasonable.

Because *me* is the object of the preposition *between*, it must be in the objective case.

24d Case in appositives

Appositives are defined in 20f. The case of a pronoun used as an appositive is the same as that of the noun or pronoun it is in apposition to.

me
1. Professor Starr gave the book to the only person in the room, I.

Me is in apposition to the noun *person*, which is the object of a preposition, so *me* must be in the objective case.

Sometimes compound constructions are used in appositives.

I
2. The winners, Janice and me, are going to compete in the national

tournament next month.

Because *Janice and I* is in apposition to the subject *winners*, the pronoun must be in the subjective case.

me
3. Trophies were presented to the winners, Janice and I.

Because *Janice and me* is in apposition to *winners*, the object of the preposition *of*, the pronoun must be in the objective case.

24e *We* and *us* before a noun

Occasionally in English, the pronouns *we* and *us* are used before a noun for emphasis.

We
1. Us students must insist that the requirements not be changed.

Because *we* is used before the subject *students*, it must be in the subjective case.

You might remind students that appositives represent equations, much as linking verbs do. With linking verbs, however, the term to the left of the verb will always be subjective, whereas the case of an appositive depends on the case of the noun phrase it restates.

24e
case

2. The administration should consider how the new requirements
   will affect we *us* students.

   Here *us* is used before *students,* which is the direct object, so the objective form *us* is correct.

When *we* or *us* is used before a noun, the form corresponding to the case of that noun should be used.

24f Case in sentences with *than* and *as*

1. Wilson can swim better than me *I*.

   Notice that this sentence really means the following:

2. Wilson can swim better than I (can swim).

   The phrase *can swim* is not actually written following the pronoun *me* in sentence 1, but it is understood to be there. Once you fill it in, it is clear that the pronoun should be *I*.

In sentences that make a comparison using *than* or *as,* the phrase that would be repeated is often omitted, but it is understood to be there. To figure out whether to use the subjective form or the objective form of the pronoun, mentally fill in the understood phrase; usually that will make the correct form clear.

3. Wilson is not as good a student as me *I*.

   When the understood word *am* is supplied, it is clear that the pronoun should be the subjective *I*.

4. Wilson likes Vivian better than I.

   Notice that sentence 4 has two possible meanings:

5. Wilson likes Vivian better than (he likes) me.
6. Wilson likes Vivian better than I (like Vivian).

   Of course, if you had written sentence 4, you would know which meaning you intended, and by mentally filling in the understood phrase, you would be able to select the correct form of the pronoun.

24g   *Who* and *whom*

Who and *whom* cause some writers a great deal of trouble. There are two things to keep in mind when choosing between *who* and *whom*.

- *Who* is the form for the subjective case, and *whom* is the form for the objective case.
- To decide which case to use, you must determine how the pronoun is being used *in its clause*.

1. Donald Johanson, whom is a paleontologist, discovered Lucy, the

    world's most famous fossil.

    The clause that *who* appears in is *who is a paleontologist*. In that clause, *is* is the verb, and *who* is the subject. Since *who* is the subject, the subjective form *who* is correct. (Clauses are discussed in 20i and 20j).

2. Johanson showed the fossil to Richard Leakey, who *[whom]* he admired.

    This time the pronoun *whom* appears in the clause *whom he admired*. In subordinate clauses beginning with *who* or *whom,* the word order is often changed to bring *who* or *whom* to the beginning of the clause. If you reorganize this clause into its natural order, you get, *he admired whom*. *He* is the subject, and *whom* is the direct object, the word that receives the action of the verb. Since *whom* is an object, it must be in the objective case.

3. Leakey, who *[whom]* people often showed fossils to, was not impressed.

    The natural word order for the subordinate clause here is *people often showed fossils to whom*. *Whom* is the object of a preposition and must therefore be in the objective case.

24h   Case before a gerund

A **gerund** is a verb form ending in *-ing* that is used as a noun (see 19c).

1. We didn't even hear him *[his]* whistling until he stopped.

    In this sentence, *whistling* is a gerund. When pronouns modify gerunds the possessive case should be used. In this sentence, the possessive form *his* is correct.

As with the personal pronouns treated earlier, students are well advised to memorize the cases involved. *Who* should be remembered as always subjective, *whom* as objective. Popular usage excuses the informal use of *who* as an object in such questions as "Who did you ask?" but formal usage calls for "Whom did you ask?"

24h
case

COLLABORATIVE ACTIVITY

Have members of peer editing groups examine one another's drafts for case errors involving pronouns. Invite students to ask you questions about problems they may be having.

Gerald's
2. We didn't even hear ~~Gerald~~ whistling until he stopped.

> Notice that the possessive case is also used for nouns that are modifying gerunds. In this case, the noun *Gerald's* is modifying *whistling*, so it is in the possessive case.

Occasionally, the objective case is used before a gerund, if the meaning requires it. Consider the difference in meaning between the next two sentences.

3. The teacher didn't notice him sleeping in the back of the room.
4. The teacher didn't notice his sleeping in the back of the room.

> In sentence 3, the teacher didn't notice *him*. In sentence 4, what she didn't notice was the fact that he was sleeping. When the emphasis is on the person and not the action, as in sentence 3, it is correct to use the objective rather than the possessive case.

Proper verb construction depends on a working knowledge of the principal parts of verbs. This chapter covers regular and irregular forms, as well as phrasal verbs and the suffixes *-ed* and *-s*. Encourage students to review this chapter carefully in anticipation of the tenses discussed in 26.

25a
vb

25 FINDING AND REVISING ERRORS WITH VERB FORM

Verbs are the most changeable words in the English language. They change their endings. They change their form. They add or change helping verbs. And all these changes indicate variations in the meaning they communicate.

In this chapter you will learn the various forms that a verb can take and how to create those forms with regular and irregular verbs. The distinction between regular and irregular verbs is discussed in 25b.

25a Regular verb forms

Verbs carry more information than any other words in a sentence. Look at the wide range of information conveyed by the verbs in the following sentences.

IF YOU WANTED . . .	YOU MIGHT SAY . . .
To indicate that Mary was involved in the act of jumping at the time that you yelled her name	Mary was jumping when I called her name.
To indicate that Mary was engaged in the act of jumping as a result of your calling her name	Mary jumped when I called her name.
To say something more tentative and conditional about what Mary did, perhaps because you're not quite sure	Mary may have jumped when I called her name.
To say that Mary was finished with her jump at the moment you called her name	Mary had jumped when I called her name.
To indicate that Mary jumps whenever you call her name	Mary jumps when I call her name.

RESOURCES

Courtney, Rosemary. *Longman Dictionary of Phrasal Verbs.* London: Longman, 1983.

Hopper, Vincent F. *English Verb Conjugations: 123 Irregular Verbs Fully Conjugated.* New York: Barron's, 1975.

Labov, William. *Language in the Inner City: Studies in Black English Vernacular.* Philadelphia: U of Pennsylvania P, 1972.

Leki, Ilona. *Understanding ESL Writers: A Guide for Teachers.* Portsmouth: Boynton/Cook, 1992.

25a
vb

   Writers express this complexity of information by making small changes in the ending of the verb, in the form of the verb, or in the helping verbs in front of the verb.

   To convey all this information, verbs exist in five different *forms*. These forms are then combined with various helping verbs to express shades of meaning. The five basic forms are indicated in the chart on page 260 using three regular verbs as illustrations. We'll discuss the various uses of these forms throughout this chapter and the next, but for now we want to make sure you see that these five forms of the verb, combined with various helping verbs, produce all the combinations that a verb can take in English.

   Notice that in the three examples in the chart, the past tense form and the past participle form are identical; this is true for all

You might stress that verb forms include what are often called the principal parts. Because the base form is the one listed alphabetically in dictionaries, students must know the base in order to be able to look up the other parts (past, past participle, and present participle) used in tense constructions reviewed in 26. Students also need to remember that while regular verbs have identical past and past participial forms, irregular verbs (see 25b) often do not.

FORMS OF REGULAR VERBS

Base Form	Past Tense (base + -*ed* [or -*d*])	Past Participle (base + -*ed* [or -*d*])	Present Participle (base + -*ing*)	-*s* Form (base + -*s* [or -*es*])
jump	jumped	jumped	jumping	jumps
love	loved	loved	loving	loves
pass	passed	passed	passing	passes

regular verbs in English, but, as you will see in 25b, it is frequently not the case with irregular verbs.

25b **Irregular verb forms**

The following sentences illustrate a complication in what you learned about the five verb forms in 25a.

	REGULAR VERB: *WALK*	IRREGULAR VERB: *GO*
Base form:	My neighbors *walk* to work at 7:00.	My neighbors *go* to work at 7:00.
Past tense:	My neighbors *walked* to work at 7:00.	My neighbors *went* to work at 7:00.
Past participle:	My neighbors have *walked* to work.	My neighbors have *gone* to work.
Present participle:	My neighbors are *walking* to work.	My neighbors are *going* to work.
-*s* form:	My neighbor *walks* to work at 7:00.	My neighbor *goes* to work at 7:00.

The **regular verb** *walk* follows the pattern you learned in 25a, but the verb *go* doesn't. If it followed the pattern, the past tense of *go* would be *goed*, but instead it is *went*; if it followed the pattern, the past participle would also be *goed*, but instead it is *gone*.

In Standard Written English, several hundred verbs, including *go*, do not follow the pattern of forms for regular verbs; these

are known as **irregular verbs.** Fortunately, you are probably already familiar with most of these. But if you do not know them all, it is worth the time it takes to learn the ones you don't know. Errors with verb form make your writing appear seriously flawed to many readers.

Some dialects of English use different verb forms, so speakers of these dialects may need to focus on irregular verb forms to master Standard Written English. The following sentences illustrate this problem; the original versions (before editing) were correct in some dialects but *not* in Standard Written English. (For a discussion of dialects and Standard Written English, see 5c.)

1. Victor ~~done~~ *did* his homework on Saturday afternoon.
2. When we ~~seen~~ *saw* him Saturday night, he was on his way to a movie.

The chart that follows lists the most common irregular verb forms. Because the present participle and *-s* forms are regular even for irregular verbs, we have not included them. Where two forms are acceptable, both are given, with the preferred form first.

FOR DISCUSSION
Stress that knowing the principal parts of irregular verbs is indispensable if one wishes to construct the tenses reviewed in 26. ESL and other students who have trouble with irregular verb forms may need a tutor's assistance. Encourage students to refer to the tables in this chapter whenever doubts arise as to a past or past participial form. ESL students may also benefit from the comprehensive reference work by Vincent Hopper, *English Verb Conjugations: 123 Irregular Verbs Fully Conjugated* (New York: Barron's, 1975).

25b
vb

FORMS OF IRREGULAR VERBS

Base Form	Past Tense	Past Participle
are	were	been
arise	arose	arisen
awake	awoke, awaked	awaked, awoke
bear	bore	borne, born
beat	beat	beaten
become	became	become
begin	began	begun
bend	bent	bent
bet	bet	bet
bind	bound	bound
bite	bit	bitten, bit
blow	blew	blown

(continued)

25b
vb

FORMS OF IRREGULAR VERBS *(continued)*

Base Form	Past Tense	Past Participle
break	broke	broken
bring	brought	brought
build	built	built
burst	burst	burst
buy	bought	bought
cast	cast	cast
catch	caught	caught
choose	chose	chosen
cling	clung	clung
come	came	come
cost	cost	cost
creep	crept	crept
cut	cut	cut
deal	dealt	dealt
dig	dug	dug
dive	dived, dove	dived
do	did	done
draw	drew	drawn
drink	drank	drunk
drive	drove	driven
drown	drowned	drowned
dwell	dwelt	dwelt
eat	ate	eaten
fall	fell	fallen
feed	fed	fed
feel	felt	felt
fight	fought	fought
find	found	found
flee	fled	fled
fling	flung	flung
fly	flew	flown
forbid	forbade, forbad	forbidden
forget	forgot	forgotten
forgive	forgave	forgiven
freeze	froze	frozen
get	got	got, gotten
give	gave	given
go	went	gone
grow	grew	grown

(continued)

FORMS OF IRREGULAR VERBS (continued)

Base Form	Past Tense	Past Participle
hang (an object)*	hung	hung
have	had	had
hear	heard	heard
hide	hid	hidden
hit	hit	hit
hold	held	held
hurt	hurt	hurt
is	was	been
keep	kept	kept
know	knew	known
lay (an object)	laid	laid
lead	led	led
leave	left	left
let	let	let
lie (recline)	lay	lain
light	lighted, lit	lighted, lit
lose	lost	lost
make	made	made
mean	meant	meant
meet	met	met
pay	paid	paid
prove	proved	proved, proven
put	put	put
quit	quit	quit
read	read	read
rid	rid	rid
ride	rode	ridden
ring	rang	rung
rise	rose	risen
run	ran	run
say	said	said
see	saw	seen
seek	sought	sought
sell	sold	sold
send	sent	sent
set	set	set
shake	shook	shaken

*Hang (a person) is regular.

25b
vb

(continued)

FORMS OF IRREGULAR VERBS (continued)

Base Form	Past Tense	Past Participle
shine (cast light)*	shone	shone
shoot	shot	shot
shrink	shrank	shrunk
sing	sang	sung
sink	sank	sunk
sit	sat	sat
slay	slew	slain
sleep	slept	slept
slide	slid	slid
speak	spoke	spoken
spend	spent	spent
spin	spun	spun
spring	sprang	sprung
stand	stood	stood
steal	stole	stolen
sting	stung	stung
stink	stank, stunk	stunk
stride	strode	stridden
strike	struck	struck, stricken
swear	swore	sworn
sweep	swept	swept
swim	swam	swum
swing	swung	swung
take	took	taken
teach	taught	taught
tear	tore	torn
tell	told	told
think	thought	thought
throw	threw	thrown
understand	understood	understood
wake	woke, waked	waked, woken
wear	wore	worn
win	won	won
wring	wrung	wrung
write	wrote	written

*Shine (polish) is regular.

Dictionaries also list the forms of verbs. The entry for a verb in most dictionaries starts like the following example, taken from *The American Heritage Dictionary of the English Language.*

walk (wôk) *v.* **walked, walking, walks.**— *intr.* **1.** To go or advance on foot; move by steps. . . .

The first item in the dictionary entry is always the base form of the word, usually printed in boldfaced type and divided into syllables. The next item, usually in parentheses, is the phonetic spelling to indicate pronunciation. The third item is an abbreviation to indicate the part of speech; verbs are indicated by the abbreviations *v, vb, vi* (verb, intransitive), or *vt* (verb, transitive). The next series of items is what we are interested in: the forms of the verb. In our example, the forms are *walked, walking, walks*—the past tense and past participle, present participle, and -*s* form.

Here is the entry for the irregular verb *go.*

go (gō) *v.* **went** (wĕnt), **gone** (gon, gön), **going, goes.**— *intr.* **1.** To move along; proceed. . . .

Notice that pronunciations are inserted after each of the forms that are pronounced differently from the base form. Notice also that because the past tense and past participle are different, both are listed.

Here is the entry for *walk* from *Webster's New World Dictionary of the American Language,* which follows a different format.

walk (wôk) *vi.* [ME *walken* <OE *wealcan,* to roll, journey . . .] **1.** to go along or move about on foot at a moderate pace. . . .

This dictionary organizes its entries differently in two ways. First, between brackets it indicates the history of the word. Second, the forms of the verb are not listed. The verb *walk* is regular, and all regular verbs form their past tense by adding -*ed.* Since the forms are the same for all regular verbs, many dictionaries don't list them.

Here is the same dictionary's listing for an irregular verb.

drive (drīv) *vt.* **drove, driv´en, dri´ving** [ME *driven* <OE *drifan,* akin to Goth *dreiban* . . .] **1.** to force to go. . . .

Because *drive* is an irregular verb, all dictionaries will list the various forms, starting with the past tense.

ACTIVITY

25b
vb

ESL ADVICE

Because of their idiomatic nature, phrasal verbs are often difficult for ESL learners to acquire. Encourage students who may be in doubt as to the meanings of any of the phrasal verbs listed here to ask you for help. Giving an example or two of how a verb is used in written sentences may be preferable to reviewing abstract definitions. Also, members of editing groups should be on the lookout for phrasal verb errors in one another's drafts.

25c vb

ESL

25c Phrasal verbs

Phrasal verbs are two- and three-word combinations that contain a verb and a **particle** (a preposition or an adverb). Because phrasal verbs are usually idiomatic, it is almost impossible to determine the meaning by looking at the verb and particle separately. Also, a phrasal verb can have several meanings. For example, the phrasal verb *put down* can mean, among other things, "to write down," "to criticize," "to assign to a category," or "to consume." The best way to learn these verbs is to pay attention when reading or listening to English. When you hear or read a phrasal verb, note it in your journal and look up the meaning in a dictionary. Then try using these phrasal verbs when you write or speak in English to reinforce your comprehension.

Phrasal verbs can also cause problems because they can be placed in different locations in a sentence.

1. INCORRECT: She was slow to catch to the game on.
2. CORRECT: She was slow to catch on to the game.

In this case, the phrasal verb *catch on* is an intransitive verb (a verb that cannot take a direct object; see 20a), so the verb and particle cannot be separated in a sentence. See the chart on the facing page for a list of intransitive phrasal verbs.

In the next two sentences, the phrasal verb is highlighted and the preposition is underlined.

3. INCORRECT: I decided to break with my boyfriend up.
4. CORRECT: I decided to break up with my boyfriend.

Some transitive phrasal verbs (those that can take a direct object; see 20a) can be either separated or together, some *must* be separated, and some *must* be together in a sentence. Unfortunately, there is no rule for determining this. The only solution is to check a grammar book or dictionary. In sentence 3, the phrasal verb *break up* cannot be separated, and it also requires the preposition *with* to mean "end a romantic relationship." See the chart on the facing page for a list of phrasal verbs that cannot be separated and require prepositions.

PHRASAL VERBS

Intransitive Phrasal Verbs (cannot be separated)

boil over	give in	look away
break out	go ahead	pass away
catch on	go back	play around
come away	go up	show up
come in	grow up	sit down
come out	hold off	stay up
get by	look ahead	talk back
get up		

Transitive Phrasal Verbs (cannot be separated)

Requiring prepositions:

break up with	end up with	look down on
catch up with	get along with	look in on
check out of	get away with	look up to
check up on	get back to	make away with
close in on	get down to	pick up on
come up with	get out of	put up with
cut down on	give in to	run out of
drop in on	go in for	stand up for
drop out of	keep up with	walk out on

Not requiring prepositions:

call on	get off	look after
check into	get over	run into
come across	go over	take after
get into	look into	

Transitive Phrasal Verbs (may be separated; must be separated if direct object is a pronoun)

ask out	bring up	check out
blow up	call back	cheer up
break in	call in	clean up
break down	call off	cross out
bring about	call up	cut out
bring on	carry out	do over

(continued)

25c
vb

ESL

PHRASAL VERBS *(continued)*

drop by	name after	take out
drop off	name for	take over
figure out	pass out	take up
fill out	pick out	tear down
find out	pick up	tear up
give back	point out	think over
give out	pull up	throw away
give up	put away	throw out
hand in	put back	throw up
hang up	put off	try on
have on	put on	turn down
hold up	put out	turn on
leave out	show off	turn out
look over	shut off	turn up
look up	take back	wear away
make up	take off	

5. INCORRECT: Yesterday, I called my neighbor on.
6. CORRECT: Yesterday, I called on my neighbor.

The transitive phrasal verb *call on* cannot be separated in a sentence, but it does not require a preposition. The chart lists these types of phrasal verbs.

The next group of sentences contains another kind of phrasal verb. In these sentences, the phrasal verb is highlighted, and the direct object is underlined.

7. CORRECT: We called the baseball game off because of rain.
8. CORRECT: We called off the baseball game because of rain.

In these sentences, the direct object of the transitive verb *call off* is a noun (*baseball game*). When this is the case, the parts of the phrasal verb can be either separated or together.

9. INCORRECT: I decided to call off it.
10. CORRECT: I decided to call it off.

In sentence 10, the direct object for the transitive phrasal verb *call off* is a *pronoun*. When this is the case, the phrasal verb must always be separated. See the chart for a list of phrasal verbs that can or cannot be separated, depending on whether the direct object is a noun or a pronoun.

25c
vb

ESL

25d   *Lie* and *lay*

Lie and *lay* may be the hardest words in the English language to use correctly. The following sentences illustrate the basic difference between the two words.

1. I often ~~lay~~ *lie* down for a few minutes after dinner.

2. A flannel nightgown was ~~laying~~ *lying* on the bed.

   Lie means "to recline or rest on a horizontal surface." It is an intransitive verb (see 20a)—that is, it cannot take an object; it cannot be done *to* something.

3. I always ~~lie~~ *lay* my wallet and keys on my nightstand before I undress for bed.

4. I was ~~lying~~ *laying* out towels for Tim and Gail when they called to say they weren't coming.

   Lay means "to place something in a horizontal position." It is normally a transitive verb (see 20a)—that is, it must be done *to* something. In sentence 3, it is being done to the wallet and keys; in sentence 4, it is being done to the towels.

Some of the confusion over these two words stems from their similar appearance; they are both three-letter words starting with *l*. Their meanings are fairly similar; both have to do with things in horizontal positions. Note that after you *lay* the towels on the bed, they just *lie* there until someone picks them up. The key difference between them is that *lay* is something you do to something (like towels); *lie* is what they do by themselves but not *to* anything else.

Lay and *lie* are even more confusing when they are used in the past tense.

5. Yesterday, I ~~laid~~ *lay* down for a half hour after dinner.

6. Yesterday, a flannel nightgown ~~laid~~ *lay* on the bed all afternoon.

   The past tense of *lie* is *lay*! So the past tense of *lie* is spelled exactly like the base form (present tense) of the other word *lay*.

To fix in mind the differences between *lie* and *lay*, you might have students practice putting the following sentences into past tense: "This morning I lie in bed for hours." "They lay their books on the desks." Then have everyone change the following to present tense: "She couldn't remember where she laid her car keys." "The old cat was lying by the fire."

25d
vb

No wonder people have trouble with these words! This is the hardest part of getting these two pesky words straight. Remember that if you are talking about reclining on a horizontal surface (as opposed to placing something on a surface) in the past, the verb you want is *lay*.

7. Yesterday, I ~~lain~~ *laid* my wallet and keys on the dresser before I undressed for bed.

8. Yesterday, I ~~lain~~ *laid* towels on the bed for Tim and Gail.

The past tense of *lay* is *laid*. If you did it to something else (like a towel) and you did it in the past, the correct verb form is *laid*.

The following sentences reveal that the past participle form is not quite as confusing as the past tense.

9. I had just ~~laid~~ *lain* down when the phone rang.

10. A flannel nightgown has ~~laid~~ *lain* on the bed all day.

The past participle of *lie* is *lain*.

11. I had ~~lain~~ *laid* my wallet and keys on the dresser before I undressed for bed.

12. I have ~~lain~~ *laid* towels on the bed for Tim and Gail.

The past participle of *lay* is *laid*.

The forms of these two confusing verbs are summarized in the chart.

25d
vb

THE FORMS OF *LAY* AND *LIE*				
Base Form	**Past Tense**	**Past Participle**	**Present Participle**	**-s Form**
lie	lay	lain	lying	lies
lay	laid	laid	laying	lays

Lie is intransitive and means "to recline or rest on a horizontal surface." You cannot do it *to* something.

Lay is transitive and means "to place something or someone in a horizontal position." You can do it *to* something else like a towel.

25e Omitted *-s* (or *-es*) endings

In some dialects of English, the *-s* ending on regular verbs is omitted; in Standard Written English, however, it is required whenever the subject is third-person singular (see 21a). If you regularly omit *-s* endings when you speak, be especially careful to include them in formal writing situations such as the following.

1. My sister ~~walk~~ *walks* her dog every morning.
2. Her dog usually ~~bark~~ *barks* at everyone they pass.

Once you become aware of the need to add these endings, there is another danger you need to watch out for: overcorrection. You are overcorrecting if you start putting *-s* endings on verbs when the subject is *not* third-person singular. The following sentences were overcorrected before they were revised.

3. The neighbors complains about the dog, but my sister can't stop his barking.
4. They really gets mad if she walks him on weekends when they are sleeping late.

25f Omitted *-ed* endings

Many speakers of English leave the *-ed* endings off past-tense verbs, especially when they are difficult to pronounce. Nevertheless, in writing, the *-ed* ending must be included for regular verbs in the past tense. The following sentences illustrate this problem.

1. My sister ~~use~~ *used* to walk her dog about seven o'clock on Saturday and

   Sunday mornings.
2. Now she is ~~suppose~~ *supposed* to wait until at least nine o'clock.

The following words and phrases are sometimes pronounced without the *-ed* ending in casual speech. When you *write* any of these, be careful that you do not leave off the *-ed* ending.

asked	fixed	pronounced
basked	frightened	risked
concerned	improved	supposed to
developed	prejudiced	used to

ESL ADVICE

Problems with *-s* (or *-es*) endings may reflect a combination of grammatical uncertainty and mispronunciation, especially among ESL learners. Students who have trouble with these endings should practice verb-agreement exercises in their notebooks and should also practice reading aloud.

Because pronunciation is sometimes responsible for omitted *-ed* endings, encourage students who have this difficulty to read drafts aloud to themselves slowly and pay close attention to past and past participial verb forms.

25f
vb

25g **Problems with linking and helping verbs**

The following sentences illustrate a problem some writers have with linking verbs.

1. Whenever my grandparents *are* in a restaurant, they order fish.
2. If the restaurant *is* out of fish, they go somewhere else.

Although some dialects omit linking verbs in some sentences, in Standard Written English they cannot be omitted.

The following illustrate a similar problem with helping verbs. (For a discussion of helping verbs, see 19c.)

3. They *have* been known to try three or four restaurants before finding one serving fish.
4. If they *are* going out to eat, they sometimes call restaurants first to see if fish is being served.

In the uncorrected version of these sentences, the helping verbs were omitted. Although this omission may occur in some dialects of English, it is not permitted in Standard Written English.

Another difference between some dialects and Standard Written English is illustrated by the following sentences.

5. Most of the restaurants in their neighborhood *are* be aware of their desires.
6. My grandmother *is* be afraid to cook fish at home.
7. I *am* be embarrassed when I eat out with them because they are so crazy about fish.

Some dialects use *be* in place of *are, am,* or *is,* as these sentences did before they were corrected.

COLLABORATIVE ACTIVITY

Members of peer editing groups can review one another's drafts for errors involving verb construction. Encourage students to use dictionaries and the boxed tables in this chapter for reference.

26 FINDING AND REVISING ERRORS WITH VERB TENSE, VOICE, AND MOOD

Verbs take different forms to indicate when the action or state of being of the verb is taking place. We call this quality of verbs their tense. English verbs have three simple tenses (present, past, and future) and three perfect tenses (present perfect, past perfect, and future perfect). In addition, there are progressive forms of each tense, three moods (indicative, imperative, and subjunctive), and active and passive voice forms. This chapter explains the meaning of each of these tenses, moods, and voices and how they are used.

26a Present, past, and future tenses

The **present** tense is used to describe actions that are taking place at the time of speaking or writing, but it also has many more uses, as the chart demonstrates.

USES FOR THE PRESENT TENSE

Describing Events Happening at the Time of Speaking or Writing
I understand why you are angry.

Describing a Habitual or Regularly Occurring Action
I leave for school at 7:30 every morning.

Stating General Truths or Scientific Facts
The capital of Montana is Helena.

Light from the sun takes eight minutes to reach the earth.

Discussing Literary or Artistic Works or the Actions of Characters in Them (see 48f)
Hester Prynn reminds us that strong women are often condemned by their communities.

The author of this article argues that birth control devices should be distributed in high schools.

Describing Future Events for Which There Is a Fixed Time
Classes begin on September 6.

Mastering tense, voice, and mood is the most difficult task in grammar. The complexity of English verb usage reflects many idiosyncrasies of the language, in turn causing special problems for ESL learners and those who have acquired habits inconsistent with Standard Written English. Advise students to read this chapter carefully and to make it a useful reference when they are editing the drafts of their essays.

26a
vb

To be prepared for the following review of tenses, students should be aware of the principal parts of verbs. Encourage anyone who is unfamiliar with basic verb elements to review 25.

RESOURCES

Ehrlich, Eugene, and Daniel Murphy. *HarperCollins Dictionary of English Usage.* New York: HarperCollins, 1991.

Hopper, Vincent F. *English Verb Conjugations: 123 Irregular Verbs Fully Conjugated.* New York: Barron's, 1975.

Quirk, Randolph, Sidney Greenbaum, Geoffrey Leech, and Jan Svartvik. *A Comprehensive Grammar of the English Language.* London: Longman, 1985.

Shaughnessy, Mina P. *Errors and Expectations: A Guide for the Teacher of Basic Writing.* New York: Oxford UP, 1977.

FOR DISCUSSION

26b
vb

You might introduce the complexity of English tenses by asking a few questions of your class. For example, does the present tense always represent the present? (No, as 26a shows.) Does the past tense always represent the past? (No, as the discussion of conditional mood in 26H shows.) What is the difference between present perfect and past perfect? (That is explained in 26b and 26c.) Native speakers of English should become aware of how complex their own habits are in using verbs, and non-native speakers should become aware of the need to practice a variety of verb phrase patterns.

The **past** tense is used to describe events that occurred in the past and do not extend into the present.

We arrived fifteen minutes after the wedding had begun.

Around the turn of the twentieth century, a large section of Baltimore burned to the ground.

The **future** tense is used to describe events taking place at some time in the future or events that are predictable.

The dean will retire at the end of this year.

If you soak that in vinegar, the stain will come out.

26b Past perfect tense

The highlighted verbs in the following sentences are in the **past perfect** tense.

1. The movie had started when we arrived.

   Two events are being discussed in this sentence: the start of the movie and our arrival. Both events happened in the past, but the start of the movie happened first and was completed prior to our arrival. Note that the past perfect form consists of *had* plus the past participle *started*.

2. By 1980, we had lived in California for ten years.

   Again two different events are indicated by this sentence: 1980 and our living in California for ten years. Both happened in the past, but one, our living in California for ten years, happened before the other. This time, however, the earlier event continued right up to the later event, as the diagram at the top of the facing page indicates. Notice again that the past perfect form consists of *had* plus the past participle *lived*.

Past	Present	Future
we had lived in California for ten years		

1980

26c Present perfect tense

The **present perfect** tense has two uses in English, represented by the following sentences.

1. Jason has worn braces for three years.

   The verb *has worn* describes an action that began in the past and continues to the present. Notice that the present perfect form of the verb consists of *has* plus the past participle *worn*.

Past	Present	Future
Jason has worn braces for three years		

2. I have seen that movie.

   The verb *have seen* describes an action that began in the past and was completed in the past. I saw that movie in the past and completed seeing it some time before now. Note that the present perfect form of the verb consists of *have* plus the past participle *seen*.

Past	Present	Future
I have seen that movie		

26d Future perfect tense

The following sentence illustrates the use of the **future perfect** tense.

Like a flashback, the past perfect represents a time farther back than the simple narrative past. You might help students grasp the general relation of tenses by writing the following continuum on the board: *past perfect—present perfect — present—future perfect—future*. If tenses were always used according to this continuum, verb usage might be simple. But as illustrated in this chapter, there are many exceptions.

Speakers sometimes confuse present perfect with past perfect, incorrectly believing that both tenses relate past to present. Remind students that while the past perfect relates the past to a deeper past, only the present perfect tense relates past to present. The present perfect may be especially confusing to non-native speakers whose first languages do not have a tense corresponding to the English present perfect. Refer ESL students to 26f, examples 14–16, for more about this tense.

26d
vb

You might point out that the future perfect is similar to present perfect except that time is projected into the future instead of retrieved from the past.

ACTIVITY

To summarize the perfect tenses, ask students to try writing out formulas for those tenses. Correct answers should resemble the following:

Past perfect
had + past participle

Present perfect
has/have + past participle

Future perfect
shall/will + *have* + past participle

In 1996, I will have worked for this company for twenty years.

The future tense verb *will have worked* indicates that the action, working, will be completed by another time in the future, in this case, by 1996. Note that the future perfect tense consists of *will have* plus the past participle *worked*.

Past	Present	Future
	I will have worked for this company for twenty years	
		in 1996

26e Progressive forms

Each of the six tenses discussed in 26a through 26d has a corresponding progressive form. The following sentences illustrate these.

1. Noriko is studying accounting at the library this afternoon.

   The **present progressive** verb *is studying* indicates an action that is taking place in the present and is in progress (hence the term *progressive.*) Note that the verb consists of a present-tense form of the verb *be,* in this case, *is,* together with the present participle of the main verb *studying.*

2. She was working on her biology project last night when I called her.

   The **past progressive** verb *was working* indicates an action in the past that was in progress; Noriko was in the middle of working on that biology project when I called. Note that the past progressive verb consists of a past-tense form of the verb *be*—in this case, *was*—combined with the present participle *working.*

3. Tonight she will be reading the assignment for English class.

   The **future progressive** verb *will be reading* indicates an action that will be in progress at some time in the future. It consists of the helping verb *will be* combined with the present participle *reading.*

26e
vb

Have ESL students take note of this usage point. You might encourage them to write practice sentences using the indicated verbs in simple rather than progressive forms.

ACTIVITY

Sometimes known as "continuous" forms, the progressive forms of verbs have formulas that students might benefit from learning. Have them review 26e, then try writing out the formulas for each progres-

4. I think she has been working too hard on her courses.

The **present perfect progressive** verb *has been working* indicates an action that began in the past and is continuing at the present. It consists of the helping verb *has* (or *have*) *been* plus the present participle *working*.

5. Until last week, she also had been working twenty hours a week at Wendy's.

The **past perfect progressive** verb *had been working* indicates an action that was in progress and ended prior to some other time or event in the past. In this case, the working began before last week and was in progress for some time before it stopped. The past perfect progressive consists of the helping verb *had been* plus the present participle *working*.

6. Next year, my parents will have been arguing for twenty-five years.

The **future perfect progressive** verb *will have been arguing* expresses an action that is in progress up to a specific point in the future. The future progressive consists of the helping verb *will have been* plus the present participle *arguing*.

The following sentences illustrate a problem encountered by some speakers of English as a second language when using the future tense in sentences with dependent clauses.

7. She will do well on the test if she ~~will~~ remain *remains* calm.

As this sentence shows, when the independent clause is in the future tense it is not correct to use the future tense for dependent clauses.

26f Tense and aspect for ESL writers

The English tense and aspect system is used to describe three different time frames: past, present, and future. The **tenses** indicate the time when an activity or state occurs. **Aspect** refers to the distinction between the *simple tenses* (present, past, and future) and the **progressive tenses.** (The tenses in English are discussed in 26a through 26e. See 19c for a review of modals and 9a for a discussion of tense shift.)

sive tense. Correct answers are as follows:

Past progressive
Past form of *be* + present participle (*-ing* word)

Present progressive
Present form of *be* + present participle

Future progressive
will/shall + *be* + present participle

Past perf. prog.
had + *been* + present participle

Present perf. prog.
has/have + *been* + present participle

Future perf. prog.
will/shall + *have* + *been* + present participle

ESL ADVICE

For some writers the chief problem in using future perfect may lie less in the tense itself than in the tense of an accompanying clause. ESL students in particular may have trouble understanding why future tense is not juxtaposed with future tense when we speak of future events. Why, for example, don't we say "I'll have taken the test before the hour will be ending"? Point out that it is simply characteristic of English to use present tense to indicate a future event that has been anticipated by future perfect: "I'll have waited in line for an hour when the ticket office *opens*."

26f
vb

ESL

ESL ADVICE

It is of course important that ESL students become familiar with the English tenses. But the task of learning such complex usage can be arduous and at times frustrating for them. Encourage those having difficulty to study the following section carefully and to write practice sentences that can be checked for correctness. Invite students to ask you for help if they have problems understanding any of the matters reviewed in 26f.

ESL ADVICE

Have students practice writing sentences that illustrate the uses of present tense given in examples 1–6. You might call special attention to example 6 (i.e., the use of present tense to indicate a scheduled future event, also illustrated below in example 50).

26f
vb

ESL

TENSE AND ASPECT IN ENGLISH

Present Time	
Simple present tense:	I brush my teeth every day.
Present progressive tense:	I am reading a good book.
Past Time	
Simple past tense:	I ate dinner at 5:00.
Past progressive tense:	I was eating dinner at 5:00.
Present perfect tense:	I have been to New York.
Present perfect progressive tense:	I have been running for two hours.
Past perfect tense:	I had been to New York.
Past perfect progressive tense:	I had been living in California until the earthquake.
Future Time	
Simple future tense:	I will go to the dentist.
Future progressive tense:	They will be arriving at six.
Simple present tense:	I have a date next week.
Present progressive tense:	They are coming for dinner later.
Future perfect tense:	I will have finished by noon.
Future perfect progressive tense:	I will have been working exactly ten years next July.

The present time

The verb forms used to express present time are the simple present and the present progressive.

Simple present. The **simple present** tense is used for many purposes as illustrated by the highlighted verbs in the following examples.

1. I live in Santa Fe. (to state a condition that has been true in the past, is true now, and will continue to be true in the future)
2. I go to class every day at 8:30. (to describe a habitual action)
3. The earth revolves around the sun. (to describe a general truth)
4. Faulkner often writes about the South. (to make statements about writers, composers, artists, or their works; see 48f)
5. Elway passes to Johnson. He catches the ball and runs twenty yards. (to describe events as they happen or as they happened in the past—often used for sporting events)
6. The semester ends on May 15. (to make statements about events scheduled to happen in the future.)

Occasionally writers use the modals *can* and *will* to express general truths.

7. Oil will float on water.
8. Annie can sing beautifully.

Present progressive. The next two examples demonstrate two meanings expressed by the **present progressive.**

9. I am typing on my computer.

   Am typing expresses an action that is ongoing and is actually occurring at the present moment.

10. Lynn is studying advertising at Michigan State University.

    Is studying also indicates an action that is ongoing but may not be occurring at the present moment.

The present progressive is used to represent an event or action that is ongoing at the present time.

The past time

The verb forms used to indicate past time are the simple past, the present perfect, the past progressive, the present perfect progressive, the past perfect, and the past perfect progressive.

Simple past and present perfect. The **simple past** is used to indicate an action or state that occurred in the past, in three different ways.

11. Susanna walked to work when she first moved to Cleveland. (to express an action that occurred habitually, that is over and over, but not continually)
12. Hector Ochoa liked to work in his garden. (to express a state of affairs that existed continually in the past)
13. My car blew up on the way home last night. (to expresses a single event that happened at a particular time in the past)

The **present perfect** also expresses three different kinds of actions or states but implies that the action or state continues up to (and perhaps beyond) the present.

ESL ADVICE

Students may have trouble recognizing when to use present progressive instead of the simple present tense. You might stress that present progressive is usually not appropriate for a more or less permanent or long-term action. For example, it would sound strange to say "I am being a student" rather than "I am a student"— or "She is liking you" instead of "She likes you" (see the discussion of progressive forms in 26e).

26f
vb

ESL

Refer students who have trouble with irregular past-tense verb forms to 25b.

ESL ADVICE

As the examples show, present perfect tense can be complicated because it does not always refer to action still taking place. (If the question "Have you lived outside the United States?" is posed, the answer may be "Yes, I have." But the respondent is not living outside the United States now.) To help ESL students grasp this tense more easily, you might help them to define and use such common phrases as *so far, up to now,* and *as of now*—all of which tend to call for present perfect verb phrases.

26f
vb

ESL

14. My committee has met every Thursday evening this semester. (to express a habitual action that started in the past and continues to the present)
15. Chinua has lived in America for three years. (to express a state of affairs that existed continually in the past and continues to the present)
16. My math professor has given only one quiz so far. (to express a single event that may still occur again)

The simple past and the present perfect are often interchangeable; however, there are a few instances where one or the other is required to express the correct meaning.

17. INCORRECT: Stefan has visited the company in Philadelphia last week.
18. CORRECT: Stefan visited the company in Philadelphia last week.

Sentence 17 is incorrect because the event does not continue up to the present. It was completed last week, so the present perfect is inappropriate. The simple past tense in sentence 18 is correct.

The following sentences show the various uses of the present perfect and compare the present perfect with the simple past.

19. I have lived in Michigan since 1991.
20. I have lived in Michigan for two years.

When the present perfect is used with *since* or *for,* it expresses an action, emotion, or event that started in the past and continues to the present. Note the difference between *since* and *for* in these sentences. *Since* is used with a specific point in time, whereas *for* is used with an expression for a span of time—in this case, *two years.*

The simple past tense causes problems in sentences with *since* or *for.*

21. INCORRECT: I lived in Michigan since 1991.
22. CORRECT: I have lived in Michigan since 1991.

The simple past can never be used with *since,* as this word implies that an action or event started in the past and continues up to the present.

The simple past tense can be used with *for,* but doing so changes the meaning.

23. I lived in Michigan for two years.

Sentence 23 means that the writer lived in Michigan for two years in the past but is no longer living there today. (Compare this sentence with sentence 20.)

24. I have already mailed the letter.

With the words *just, already,* and *recently,* the present perfect tense expresses an action that occurred in the past and finished recently—close to the moment of speaking.

25. I already mailed the letter.

You can also use the simple past with *just, already,* and *recently* without a change in meaning, but the present perfect is slightly clearer.

26. Divorce rates have increased dramatically.

The present perfect tense is also used to express an action that happened at an *indefinite* time in the past.

27. Divorce rates increased dramatically in 1968.

When the tense is changed to the simple past, the reader would expect to be told when the event happened.

28. I haven't done my homework yet.

Use *yet* and *still* in negative sentences with the present perfect tense when you want to emphasize that an action has not yet happened but that you expect the action to occur some time in the future.

29. I didn't do my homework yet.

If you use the simple past tense, the sentence does not imply as strongly that you *do* expect to complete the action in the future.

30. Eduardo has always been good at fixing cars.

Use the present perfect tense of the verb *be* with adverbs such as *always, often,* and *sometimes* that imply that an action is repeated frequently.

26f
vb

ESL

31. Eduardo was always good at fixing cars.

If you use the simple past tense, you imply that the meaning expressed by the verb is no longer true—Eduardo may have once been good at fixing cars, but he is no longer.

32. The Batistas haven't been skiing this year.

Use the present perfect tense with time expressions using *this* (*this morning, this year*) when the time frame is still possible. In sentence 32, the writer is saying that it is still possible to go skiing this year.

33. The Batistas didn't ski this year.

Using the simple past tense communicates that skiing is no longer possible, perhaps because it is now summer.

Past progressive. In the following sentences, the verb in the **past progressive** tense is highlighted.

34. Yesterday Rajani was reading about the latest events in Sri Lanka.

Use the past progressive tense for an action or activity that was in progress at a specific point in time in the past. *In progress* means it was going on before the specific point and continued after it.

35. Ms. Acosta was washing her car this morning when the real estate agent arrived.

Often the past progressive is used for an event that was in progress as another event happened, as in sentence 35. The washing was going on at the point when the real estate agent arrived.

Present perfect progressive. The **present perfect progressive** tense is used for an activity that began in the past and continues up to the present.

36. It has been snowing since yesterday.

The snowing started at some time in the past and continued up to the time when these words were spoken or written. The present perfect progressive tense is often used with words expressing a period of time such as *for* a number of *minutes, hours,* or *days; since* some time in the past; *all morning; all day;* or *all week.*

26f
vb

ESL

You might point out that the present perfect progressive is easier to define than simple present perfect. The progressive form of present perfect *does* always indicate action continuing in the present, whereas the simple present perfect may not. "Have you studied calculus?" doesn't presuppose that the answer ("Yes, I have studied it") expresses a present activity. But the reply "I have been studying calculus" confirms that the action goes on more or less in the present.

37. Andrea's boss has been giving her too much work.

This sentence has no specific mention of time. It expresses a general activity in progress up to the present.

38. Tyrone has been working at Leigh's for seven years.
39. Tyrone has worked at Leigh's for seven years.

With certain verbs like *live, work,* and *teach,* there is no difference between the present perfect or the present perfect progressive when *since* or *for* is used.

Past perfect. The **past perfect** tense is used for an action or activity that has been completed in the past prior to some event that also occurred in the past.

40. By the time Annette arrived home, the puppy had destroyed the house.

The puppy destroyed the house *before* Annette arrived home.

41. Wayne had shaved off his beard before he went to Chicago.
42. Wayne shaved off his beard before he went to Chicago.

Either the simple past or the past perfect is correct in sentences with *before.*

Past perfect progressive.

43. I had been living in California before I got a job in Michigan.

The **past perfect progressive** indicates that an action or activity took place for a period of time in the past (living in California) prior to some action or activity also in the past (getting a job in Michigan).

Modals that express past time. Modals can be used to express past time. (See 19c for more discussion of modals.)

44. My dog could climb through the fence when he was a puppy.

Use *could* + verb to indicate something that the subject *could do* in the past. In this sentence, *could* + the verb *climb* is used to indicate what the puppy could do in the past.

26f
vb

ESL

Have students note that the modals *could* and *would* are, in effect, the past forms of *can* and *will.*

45. Mary would jump off the fence when the children gave her money.

   Would + verb represents an action or event that happened habitually or regularly.

46. Rafael would have gone to the store, but his car was stolen.

   A *would have* + past participle represents actions or events that were not completed in the past because of some condition.

47. The Acostas must have gone on vacation, because their house is totally dark.

   Must have + past participle can be used to express guesses or assumptions about the past.

The future time

The verb forms that can be used to represent future time are the simple future, the simple present, the present progressive, the future perfect, the future progressive, and the future perfect progressive.

Future tense. While all of the modal auxiliaries can be used to express actions or events that occur in the future, the most common modals used with future time are *will* and *going to*.

48. Kelly will be off probation on Sunday.

   The simple future tense represents an action that takes place at some definite time in the future. Kelly will be off probation at a definite time—Sunday.

49. I am going to ride my bike to work every day.

   The simple future can also be used to express an action that will happen habitually or regularly. Sentence 49 indicates that I plan to ride my bike to work.

Present tense.

50. The plane leaves at 6:45.

   The simple present tense can be used to indicate future events that are certain to happen, events that are planned or scheduled. Verbs

often used in this way include *arrive, be, begin, close, end, leave, open,* and *start.*

51. When Ms. Esenbel graduates, she will move to Turkey.

Verbs in the simple present tense are also used in the subordinate clause to express actions or events that will happen in the future. (See 11b for a discussion of subordinate clauses.)

Present progressive tense.

52. My parents are coming next week.

The present progressive can be used to represent scheduled or planned events in the future. Usually these sentences include a word or phrase indicating when the event will occur, such as *next week.*

Future progressive tense.

53. I will be leaving my house in a few minutes to catch the train.

The future progressive is used to express an action that will be in progress at a specific time in the near future.

54. Don will be working on his doctorate for the next three years.

Future progressive can also be used in sentences that indicate the duration of some specific future action.

Future perfect.

55. I will have finished my research paper by tomorrow.

The future perfect tense expresses an action that will be completed prior to a specific time in the future. In this sentence, my research paper *will be finished* prior to *tomorrow.*

56. Laura will have run ten kilometers before Juan gets out of bed.

The future perfect can also represent a state or an action that will be completed in the future prior to some other future time or event. In this sentence, Laura's *running* will be completed prior to Juan's *getting out of bed.*

The words *by, at,* and *before* are used often in sentences with the future perfect tense.

26f
vb

ESL

ACTIVITY

Encourage ESL students to practice using the tense forms reviewed in 26f. Repetition is an effective means of acquiring new language habits. If your campus has a learning resource center, you might advise ESL students to find out about ESL drill books, tutoring, and other aids. Also encourage students to practice freewriting in the various tenses, using sentences in 26f as models for transformation.

Future perfect progressive.

57. Jim will have been training for six months by the time the race begins next May in Boston.

The future perfect progressive indicates a habitual or regular action that is taking place in the future and will continue up to or
through a specific future time. Jim's *training* will be taking place in
the future and will continue up to (and perhaps through) *the race
next May.*

26g Active and passive voice

Verbs that take objects (transitive verbs; see 19c) can appear in
two voices in English: active and passive.

Subject Verb Direct object

1. Eve ate the apple.

In an active-voice sentence, the subject "does" the action of the
verb, and that action is received by another noun or pronoun known
as the direct object (see 20c). Sentence 1 is in active voice; the subject, *Eve,* does the eating, and the direct object, *apple,* receives the
action of the verb.

Subject   Verb

2. The apple was eaten by Eve.

Sentence 2 is sentence 1 rewritten in passive voice. Now the subject is *apple,* which is the receiver of the action of the verb, not
the performer of it. *Eve,* the performer of the verb, is now moved
to a prepositional phrase.

3. The apple was eaten.

Sentence 3 demonstrates that in passive-voice sentences, it is even
possible to omit the performer of the verb altogether.

Note that passive voice is formed by making the direct object into the subject, using the past participle of the verb, and
adding the appropriate form of the verb *be* as a helping verb. The
next two sentences are in passive voice.

4. Eve was tricked by the serpent.
5. Adam and Eve were expelled from the garden.

Your writing will be stronger and more readable if you write most of your sentences in active voice. Reserve passive voice for situations when it is especially appropriate. For example, if you don't know who performed the action or wish to conceal that person's identity, you might use passive voice.

6. Two computers were stolen over the weekend.
7. The illegal donations were revealed by a high-ranking White House official.

Passive voice can also be used when you want to emphasize either the action itself or the receiver of that action.

8. Dozens of people were forced out of their homes in the middle of the night.

The writer of sentence 8 is emphasizing both the *dozens of people* and the fact that they were *forced* from their homes. What did the forcing is not even mentioned.

9. A bouquet of lilies was delivered to her office on the afternoon of the performance.

Here the writer is emphasizing the bouquet of flowers.

26h Conditionals and hypotheticals

Conditional and hypothetical sentences are similar in that they are introduced by an *if* clause. Each of the following sentences represents a relationship between two ideas. Each asserts that if one thing happens, another will also.

1. If too many trees are cut down, soil erosion will increase.

In sentence 1, the statement is **conditional**; if the first thing happens, the second thing is *likely* to happen.

2. If Francesca had lots of money, she would never work.

Sentence 2, however, is a **hypothetical** statement because the first thing is unlikely to happen.

Conditionals

Conditional sentences are formed by combining a conditional clause with a main independent clause (the result clause).

26h
vb

ESL

ESL ADVICE

Mixing conditional constructions in complex sentences is an error that many ESL students make. Stress that when an *if* clause uses present tense, the independent clause calls for future (e.g., "If it rains, I'll bring an umbrella), but that when an *if* clause uses past tense, the independent clause also calls for past (e.g., "If it rained, I brought an umbrella"). The auxiliaries *would* and *could* are also de facto past tense forms appropriate to the second conditional (e.g., "If it rained, I would bring an umbrella"). Writers get into trouble by confusing the first and second patterns (e.g., "If it rains, I brought . . ." or "If it rained, I will bring . . .").

26h
vb

ESL

VERB FORMS WITH CONDITIONAL STATEMENTS

Meaning	Verb Form in *if* Clause	Verb Form in Result Clause	Example
General truth (present time frame)	Simple present	Simple future	If you heat water to 212 degrees Fahrenheit, it will boil.
Habit (present or past time frame)	Simple present or past	Simple present or past	If I eat dinner early, I sleep well. If we came to class late in my grade school, we needed a note from our parents.
Prediction (future time frame)	Simple present	*Will, be going to, should, may, might, can,* or *ought to* + base form of verb	If the population increases, there might not be enough food to feed the people.

The verb form in each of these clauses will change, depending on the meaning of the sentence.

The following examples illustrate conditional sentences with subordinators other than *if.* The subordinator is highlighted. (For more information about subordinators, see 11b, 20j, and 34a.)

3. When you heat water to 212 degrees Fahrenheit, it will boil.
4. Whenever I eat dinner early, I sleep better.

Statements about general truths or habits can be introduced by the words *when* or *whenever.* The grammar of the sentence remains the same, and these words simply replace the word *if.* (For a discussion of punctuation with these clauses, see 34a.)

Sentences 5 through 7 illustrate another subordinator.

5. Unless water is heated to 212 degrees Fahrenheit, it will not boil.

The subordinator *unless* means "if not" and can be used with general truth, habit, or prediction statements. In this example, because

unless is negative, the result clause must also be negative. Therefore, the verb in the result clause is *will not boil*.

However, the result clause does not always have to be negative.

6. **Incorrect:** Unless you put antifreeze into your radiator, the water won't freeze.

Sentence 6 is incorrect because the verb in the result clause must have a positive meaning to make sense.

7. **Correct:** Unless you put antifreeze into your radiator, the water will freeze.

The following sentence illustrates another subordinator with conditional clauses.

8. There might not be enough food to feed the people in the event that the population increases.

The subordinator *in the event that* is in a category with *in case, given that, on condition that, provided that, providing that,* and *supposing that.* These subordinators can be used with general truth, habit, or prediction statements. Usually, the result clause is followed by the conditional clause, as in sentence 8. (Punctuation with subordinate clauses is discussed in 34a.)

Hypotheticals

The following sentences illustrate two types of hypothetical statements, using the word *wish.*

Speculation

9. I wish I knew more about computers so I could get a job. (present or future time)

Hindsight

10. I wish I had known more about computers so I could have got the job I applied for last week. (past time influencing the past)
11. I wish I had learned more about computers in college so I could find a job. (past time influencing the present)

Wish statements (*wish* + noun clause) are used when the speaker wants reality to be different or exactly the opposite of what it is. The verb forms in *wish* statements are similar to those

26h
vb

ESL

Students may wonder which "tense" hypothetical verb phrases represent. Stress that hypotheticals have to do with actions that exist outside of time. That is, the actions haven't happened—and may not. Past and past perfect tenses in hypothetical contexts do not allude to the past but only to the imagination.

26h
vb

ESL

VERB FORMS WITH HYPOTHETICALS

Meaning	Verb Form in *if* Clause	Verb Form in Result Clause	Example
Speculation (what might be in the present or the future)	Past tense: *were (to)*, *should*	*would, should, might, ought to, could* + base form of verb	If more people voted, election results would change. Were more people to vote, election results would change. Should more people vote, election results would change.
Hindsight (what might have been in the past and would have affected the present)	*had* + participle	*would, could, might, should, ought to* + base form of verb	If I had not stayed out late last night, I would not be tired now.
(what might have been in the past and would have affected the past)	*had* + participle	*would have, could have, might have, should have, ought to have*	If Sabine had found a horse, she could have entered the competition. If the president had been stronger in his campaign, he might have been reelected.

in conditional statements. One difference is that only the modals *could* and *would* follow wish statements.

12. I wish that I could fly.

The use of *could* gives the meaning of hypothetical ability or possibility.

13. I wish my boyfriend would buy me some jewelry.

The use of *would* implies hypothetical promises or certainties. (See also 26i for the use of the subjunctive mood.)

26i Subjunctive mood

The English language has three moods for verbs: indicative, imperative, and subjunctive. The **indicative** mood is used to state facts or opinions and to ask questions. It accounts for all but a small percentage of sentences. The **imperative,** used for commands and requests, causes no particular trouble. So here we will discuss the seldom used and slightly complicated **subjunctive** mood.

The subjunctive differs in form from the indicative in only three ways, as demonstrated by the first three sentences.

1. Each day the instructor requests that Mike stops leaving class early.

   In the present-tense subjunctive mood, verbs do *not* add an *-s* ending when the subject is singular.

2. It is important that Mike is *be* on time for the next few weeks.

   In the present-tense subjunctive mood, the verb *be* always takes the form *be* rather than *am, is,* or *are.*

3. If I was *were* Mike, I would not be late the rest of the semester.

   In the past-tense subjunctive mood, the verb *be* always takes the form *were,* never *was.*

The subjunctive mood used to be required in many more cases, but today we use it in only four situations.

Clauses beginning with *if* and expressing a condition contrary to fact

4. If I was *were* the instructor in this class, I would have failed Mike.

   The verb *were* is used in the first clause of this sentence because the clause begins with *if* and expresses an idea that is contrary to fact.

5. If Mike had been punctual, he would have passed.

   The verb *were* is not used in *if* clauses that refer to the past. Here we have used *had been.*

Stress that, like the conditionals and hypotheticals, subjunctive verb forms represent action outside of time—that is, they have nothing to do with the past. The subjunctive mood may confuse students because it calls for the use of *were* in singular agreement and for the use of *be* without a *to* preceding. Encourage your class to remember how subjunctive mood alters ordinary (i.e., indicative) subject-verb agreement.

26i
vb

Do not use the subjunctive mood in all clauses beginning with *if,* only in those that express a condition contrary to fact.

Clauses beginning with as *though* or as *if*

6. However, Michael acts as though he ~~was~~ *were* unaware that any struggle is going on.
7. He acts as if he ~~was~~ *were* oblivious to the problem.

Use the subjunctive verb *were* rather than *was* when it appears in a clause beginning with *as though* or *as if.*

Clauses expressing requirements, recommendations, demands, suggestions, or wishes

8. Common decency requires that Michael not challenges the instructor's authority.
9. I recommend that he attends class on time from now on.

Use the subjunctive mood in *that* clauses following clauses that express a requirement, a recommendation, a demand, a suggestion, or a wish.

Expressions that have become idioms

Finally, certain set expressions or idioms in English are traditionally formed with the subjunctive: *as it were, be that as it may, come rain or come shine, far be it from me, let me be, the people be damned.*

27a
verbal

ESL

The correct use of verbal phrases is basic to coherent grammar. Yet in this area, usage tends to reflect some arbitrary conventions of the language. ESL students should find the following chapter especially helpful as a guide to rules governing infinitives, gerunds, and participles.

27 VERBALS

Verbals are defined in 19c. In this chapter we discuss problems in using the three types of verbals in English: infinitives, gerunds, and participles.

27a Choosing between gerunds and infinitives

Both gerunds and infinitives can be used as nouns in sentences, but deciding whether to use a gerund or an infinitive is sometimes difficult. It may help to think first about the different functions these verbals perform in sentences, as outlined in the following chart.

Before proceeding with this chapter, be sure students can define and recognize the main categories of verbals (infinitives, gerunds, and participles). A general introduction to verbals is provided in 19c. The function categories listed in this chart are also reviewed earlier in the book as follows: subject (20b), subjective complement (20e), object (20d), appositive (20g), adjective (19d), object of a preposition (20f), noun modifier (19a), and verb phrase modifier (19c).

INFINITIVES AND GERUNDS

Function	Example
Infinitives	
Subject	To study for a test is important for a good grade
Subject complement	He seems to like going to the movies.*
Object of a verb	Students don't like to study.
Appositive	His reason, to earn a better salary, was convincing.
Adjective modifier	I was happy to lend her a hand.
Object of a preposition	I was about to leave.†
Noun modifier	Her decision to go to the doctor was a good one.
Verb phrase modifier	I quit smoking (in order) to save my health.
Special Uses of the Infinitive	
With *what, who, whom, where,* or *when* in a noun clause as object	She wasn't sure what to take to the party.
With *too* and *enough*	He is rich enough to afford a new car. It is too cold to go outside.

*The infinitive is often used with the verbs *be, seem,* and *appear.*
†Use the gerund but not the infinitive after the prepositions *but* and *after.*

(*continued*)

27a
verbal

ESL

RESOURCES

Quirk, Randolph, Sidney Green-baum, Geoffrey Leech, and Jan Svartvik. *A Comprehensive Grammar of the English Language.* London: Longman, 1985.

Shaughnessy, Mina P. *Errors and Expectations: A Guide for the Teacher of Basic Writing.* New York: Oxford UP, 1977.

Whitford, Harold C., and Robert J. Dixson. *Handbook of American Idioms and Idiomatic Usage.* New York: Regents, 1953.

27a
verbal

ESL

INFINITIVES AND GERUNDS (continued)

Function	Example
With *make, let,* or *have* (bare infinitive)*	She made me go to bed.
	They let us watch television.
	They had me grade the papers after school.
With *force, allow,* or *got*	She forced me to go to bed.
	They allowed us to watch television.
	They got me to grade the papers at school.
With *help* (*to* is optional)	They helped him (to) work in the yard.
With verbs of command or request	The teacher told the class to sit down.
	She asked the man to give her money.
Gerunds	
Subject	Working in a bank is not very exciting.
Subject complement	She doesn't like working in a bank.
Object of a verb	She loved singing in a choir.
Appositive	The next step, writing the conclusion, is easy.
Adjective modifier	It's hard drinking hot coffee.†
Object of a preposition	They were good at telling secrets.‡

*A bare infinitive is the verb part of the infinitive without *to.*
†The gerund can function in this position after certain adjectives, such as *difficult, easy, hard, miserable, uncomfortable,* and *worthwhile.*
‡Sometimes *to* is a preposition and not part of an infinitive. When it is a preposition, *to* can be followed by the *-ing* form. Some typical expressions in which *to* is a preposition are *adapt to, adjust to, admit to, agree to, be accustomed to, be used to, change to, get accustomed to, get used to, limit to, look forward to, put a stop to,* and *submit to.*

As you can see, infinitives and gerunds can both function as subjects, subject complements, appositives, adjective modifiers, objects of prepositions, and objects of verbs.

1. **GERUND:** Eating spaghetti is fun.
2. **INFINITIVE:** To eat spaghetti is fun.

Gerunds and infinitives can both function as subjects of sentences. The meanings of sentences 1 and 2 are the same, and they are both grammatically correct. However, it is more common to use gerunds as subjects.

3. **GERUND:**   The next step, writing the conclusion, is easy.
4. **INFINITIVE:**   The next step, to write the conclusion, is easy.

Gerunds and infinitives can also both function as appositives. In sentences 3 and 4, the meaning is the same, and both sentences are grammatically correct. However, it is more common to use gerunds as appositives.

5. **GERUND:**   It's hard drinking hot coffee.
6. **INFINITIVE:**   I am happy to lend her a hand.

The gerund *drinking* and the infinitive *to lend* modify the adjectives *hard* and *happy*, respectively.

When the infinitive is used to modify an adjective, the meaning suggests future time. When the gerund is used, however, it indicates something that is a general truth or happening at that time.

7. **GERUND:**   You can seal an envelope by licking the flap.
8. **INFINITIVE:**   I was about to leave when the phone rang.

The gerund *licking* and the infinitive *to leave* are objects of the prepositions *by* and *about*, respectively. Only infinitives can follow the preposition *about*.

9. **GERUND:**   They enjoy going to the movies.
10. **INFINITIVE:**   She wants to eat ice cream.

Gerunds and infinitives can both function as objects of verbs. Some verbs can be followed only by a gerund (sentence 9); some verbs can be followed only by an infinitive (sentence 10). Many verbs can be followed by either a gerund or an infinitive, however, as shown in the following two sentences.

11. **GERUND:**   He stopped buying a newspaper.
12. **INFINITIVE:**   He stopped to buy a newspaper.

The verb *stop* can take either a gerund or an infinitive, but the meaning is not the same. In sentence 11, the man no longer buys a newspaper. In sentence 12, the man stopped and bought a newspaper.

27a
verbal

ESL

Some verbs, however, can be followed by infinitives or gerunds without any effect on the meaning.

13. **GERUND:** I like going swimming.
14. **INFINITIVE:** I like to go swimming.

The meaning is the same. Both sentences tell us the person enjoys swimming.

The chart that follows indicates which verbs can be followed only by an infinitive, which verbs can be followed only by a gerund, which verbs can be followed by either an infinitive or a gerund without a change in meaning, and which verbs can be followed by either a gerund or an infinitive but with a different meaning.

VERBS THAT TAKE VERBAL OBJECTS

Verbs That Take Infinitives as Objects
Infinitive follows these verbs immediately:

agree	hope	pretend	swear
appear	intend	refuse	wish
decide	offer	seem	

    Verb Infinitive Object
She agreed to see the doctor.

Infinitive either follows immediately or follows an intervening noun or pronoun:

Different meaning: *ask, expect, get, need, want*

    Verb Infinitive
He asked to go. (He requested permission to leave.)

    Verb Pronoun Infinitive
He asked me to go. (He wants me to go.)

Same meaning: *promise*

    Verb Infinitive
He promised to go. (He gave his word that he would go.)

    Verb Pronoun Infinitive
He promised me to go. (He gave me his word that he would go.)

(continued)

ESL ADVICE

Here we come to a key difficulty faced by ESL writers. It is important for them to learn which verbs take infinitive objects, which take gerunds, and which can take either infinitive or gerund objects. Ideally students should memorize the verbs by category. But if that is impractical, encourage students to write practice sentences using verbs and objects correctly.

VERBS THAT TAKE VERBAL OBJECTS (continued)

With these verbs, infinitive *must* follow a noun or pronoun:

command	force	order	require
compel	instruct	persuade	tell
encourage	invite	remind	warn

Verb   Noun   Infinitive

He invited a friend to study in the library.

Verbs That Take Gerunds as Objects

admit	deny	escape	mind
appreciate	discuss	finish	postpone
avoid	endure	imagine	put off
delay	enjoy	keep	risk

Verb Gerund   Object

He finished baking the cookies an hour ago.

Verbs That Take Either Gerunds or Infinitives as Objects

Same meaning: *begin, continue, hate, like, prefer, stand, start*

Verb Gerund   Object

I hate playing the piano.

Verb Infinitive Object

I hate to play the piano.

Different meaning: *forget, quit, remember, stop, try*

Verb   Gerund   Object

I remember winding my grandfather's watch when I was little. (I recall winding the watch in the past.)

Verb   Infinitive   Object

I remember to wind my grandfather's watch every night. (I don't forget to wind the watch in the present.)

ACTIVITY

You might write several of the verbs reviewed in 27a on the board and have students make up impromptu sentences containing objects for those verbs. If problems or mistakes are revealed by this exercise, you can assign additional exercises for those students who need extra practice.

27a
verbal

ESL

Stress that participles are so named depending on how they are used in sentences. Remind students that an *-ing* word (*swimming*, for example) is called a gerund if used in a noun position (e.g., *Swimming is fun*), but the term *participle* denotes present or past participles used as adjectives, adverbs, or in predicating verb phrases. You might advise students to review 27a if they have trouble distinguishing between gerunds and present participles.

COLLABORATIVE ACTIVITY

If students are reading an essay from a college reader, have them underline or otherwise take note of the author's use of verbal phrases. Discuss the effectiveness of gerunds, infinitives, and participles to convey images or abstract ideas.

27b
verbal

ESL

27b Using participles

Participles are used to form tenses or to serve as adjectives. They are also used to modify adjectives and adverbs (see 13c for discussion of placement of these modifiers). Present participles are formed by adding *-ing* to the present-tense form of the regular verb. The past participle form of the verb ends in *-ed*, *-en*, or *-t*.

In the following sentences, the participles are highlighted.

1. Johnson was talking on the phone to the president. (past progressive tense)
2. He has talked to the president many times. (present perfect tense)
3. He will have seen the president by now. (future perfect tense)

In sentences 1, 2, and 3, the participles are used to form tenses. For a complete discussion of the use of these verb forms in tenses, see 25.

In sentences 4, 5, and 6, the participles are used as adjectives.

4. We had an exciting day at the casino.

   The participle *exciting* is modifying the noun *day*.

5. My parents consider poker exciting.

   The participle *exciting* modifies *poker*.

6. My parents were exhausted at the end of the day.

   The participle *exhausted* is used after the verb *were* and modifies the noun *parents*.

For a closer look at problems using participles as adjectives, see 28a.

One common mistake when participles are used as adjectives is the following:

7. INCORRECT: I am amazing at the price of ski tickets.
8. INCORRECT: The price of ski tickets is amazed to me.

   Deciding which participle to use is difficult when the verbs show mental states or opinions (see the chart on the facing page). If the

adjective modifies the person or animal that experienced the mental state or opinion, as in sentence 7, use the past participle. If the adjective modifies the cause of the mental state or opinion, as in sentence 8, use the -*ing* form.

9. **CORRECT:** I am amazed at the price of tickets.

10. **CORRECT:** The price of the tickets is amazing to me.

FORMS OF VERBS SHOWING MENTAL STATES OR OPINIONS

amazing/amazed	frightening/frightened
amusing/amused	irritating/irritated
annoying/annoyed	interesting/interested
confusing/confused	satisfying/satisfied
depressing/depressed	surprising/surprised
disappointing/disappointed	worrying/worried
embarrassing/embarrassed	

The participle form can be used to introduce participial phrases.

Participial phrase

11. Mr. Johnson, wanting to end the conversation, coughed loudly.

Wanting to end the conversation is a participial phrase modifying the noun *Mr. Johnson*. Note that the participle *wanting* introduces the participial phrase.

Participial phrase

12. Speaking to the president, he lit his cigar.

Speaking to the president is a participial phrase that modifies the verb *lit* and tells us when the person lit his cigar. Again, the participle *speaking* is used to introduce the participial phrase.

See 13c for a discussion of dangling modifiers, a common error that occurs when adverbial modifiers begin a sentence.

27b
verbal

ESL

Remind students that participial phrases can accidentally lead to the kind of dangling modifier discussed in 13c. You might point out that in example 12 the participial phrase does not dangle because the pronoun following it (*he*) is the person doing the speaking.

Adjectives and adverbs can be tricky parts of speech for writers. This chapter reviews common problems associated with the use of modifiers, stressing the importance of the adjective/adverb distinction. Topics include how to use adjectives after linking verbs, how to write comparative and superlative forms of adjectives, and how to avoid double negatives.

Before studying this section, students might review the definitions of adjectives and of adverbs given in 19d–e.

28a
ad

RESOURCES

Bernstein, Theodore M. *The Careful Writer: A Modern Guide to English Usage.* New York: Atheneum, 1965.

Bartholomae, David. "The Study of Error." *College Composition and Communication* 31 (1980): 253–69.

Viera, Carroll. "Helping Students to Help Themselves: An Approach to Grammar." *College Composition and Communication* 37 (1986): 94–96.

Bernstein's famous reference work contains useful articles on adjectives and adverbs, as well as on a great

28 FINDING AND REVISING ADJECTIVE AND ADVERB ERRORS

Because adjectives and adverbs perform similar functions in sentences, some writers have difficulty with them. Both adjectives and adverbs modify other words or groups of words. The term *modify* can imply a number of similar functions: to describe (a *yellow* dress; walking *slowly*), to identify (the *first* customer), to quantify (*three* mistakes), to intensify (a *very* large spider), to limit (*slightly* damaged), or to place in time (arrived *early*). In this chapter you will learn to distinguish between adjectives and adverbs and to use the correct one in various situations. You will also learn about several special problems with adjectives and adverbs.

28a **Distinguishing between adjectives and adverbs**

Although both adjectives and adverbs serve as modifiers in sentences, the parts of speech they can modify are completely distinct.

Adjectives

In the following sentences, the *adjectives* are highlighted, and arrows indicate the words they modify.

1. Ralph Ellison is a contemporary novelist.

   The adjective *contemporary* is modifying the noun *novelist* and is located right in front of it. Notice that it answers the question "What kind of?" and therefore *describes* the noun.

2. His first novel is titled *Invisible Man.*

   The adjective *first* is modifying the noun *novel* and is located right in front of it. It answers the question "Which?" and therefore *identifies* the noun.

3. Ellison has written only one novel.

   The adjective *one,* located right in front of the noun, answers the question "How many?" and therefore *quantifies* the noun *novel.*

4. Everyone in my English class thought it was very interesting.

   In this case, the adjective *interesting* is modifying the pronoun *it* and is located after the linking verb *was* (linking verbs are discussed in 19c). In this position, after the linking verb, the adjective is a *predicate adjective* or *subject complement* (see 20e). The adjective *interesting* answers the question "What kind of?" and therefore *describes* the pronoun *it* (the novel).

5. The hero of the novel, completely alone, sets out for New York City.

   The adjective *alone* is modifying the noun *hero.* Note that in this sentence, the adjective follows the noun it is modifying. This position, while correct, gives the sentence a formal, literary, and even melodramatic quality that might be inappropriate for many types of writing. *Alone* answers the question "What kind of?" and therefore *describes* the hero.

6. The speed and confusion of life in New York make the young man tense.

   Here the adjective *tense* also follows the noun it is modifying, *man,* but the style is quite different from sentence 4. After certain verbs (*call, consider, create, drive, find, keep, make*), the direct object is followed by an adjective (known as an *object complement*). The adjective *tense* answers the question "What kind of?" and therefore *describes* the young man.

   Although adjectives can appear in different positions in sentences, they always modify either nouns or pronouns. As modifiers, they answer the questions "What kind of?" (they *describe*), "Which?" (they *identify*), or "How many?" (they *quantify*).

   ### Adverbs

   In the following sentences, the *adverbs* are highlighted and arrows indicate the words they modify.

7. In an early scene in the novel, the young African-American man who is the main character nervously gives a speech to a group of white men.

   The adverb *nervously* modifies the verb *gives.* It answers the question "How?" or "In what manner?"

many other aspects of contemporary usage. The two listed articles suggest techniques for helping students discover errors on their own. Bartholomae discusses the value of reading drafts aloud to hear mistakes. Viera emphasizes the importance of handbook research and suggests ideas for group work.

28a
ad

8. They are exceedingly cruel to him.

   Here the adverb *exceedingly* modifies the adjective *cruel.* The adverb answers the question "To what degree?" Note that the adjective *cruel* is itself modifying the pronoun *they.*

9. The narrator very innocently uses a phrase that is interpreted incorrectly by the white men.

   Here the adverb *innocently* modifies the verb *uses* and answers the question "How?" In addition, the adverb *very* modifies (*intensifies*) the adverb *innocently.*

10. The narrator moves to New York, and when he arrives there, he tries to get a job.

    The adverb *there* modifies the verb *arrives.* It answers the question "Where?"

11. At first he lives in a boarding house; then he moves to an apartment.

    The adverb *then* modifies the verb *moves.* It answers the question "When?"

12. In New York, he frequently thinks about returning to college.

    Here the adverb *frequently* modifies the verb *thinks.* It answers the question "How often?"

13. Unfortunately, the young man never is able to return to college.

    Here the adverb *unfortunately* modifies *the entire sentence* and answers the question "How?"

    The position of adverbs is quite flexible in English.

14. Anxiously, he opened the envelope containing the last letter from Dr. Bledsoe.

15. He anxiously opened the envelope containing the last letter from Dr. Bledsoe.

16. He opened the envelope containing the last letter from Dr. Bledsoe anxiously.

But not *all* positions are acceptable for adverbs.

17. **INCORRECT:**   He opened anxiously the envelope containing the last letter from Dr. Bledsoe.

As a rule, avoid placing the adverb between the verb and the direct object.

The surest way to tell the difference between adjectives and adverbs is to figure out whether the word is modifying a noun or pronoun (in which case it is an adjective) or a verb, an adjective, or another adverb (in which case it is an adverb). It is also possible to distinguish between adjectives and adverbs by thinking about the questions they answer. The chart below summarizes these differences.

ADJECTIVES AND ADVERBS

Words Modified	Examples	Questions Answered
Adjectives		
Nouns	contemporary novelist	What kind?
Nouns	first novel	Which?
Nouns	one novel	How many?
Pronouns	it was very interesting	What kind?
Nouns	the hero, completely alone	What kind?
Nouns	made the young man tense	What kind?
Adverbs		
Verbs	nervously gives a speech	How? In what manner?
Adjectives	exceedingly cruel	To what degree?
Other adverbs	very innocently	To what degree?
Verbs	arrives there	Where?
Verbs	then he moves	When?
Verbs	he frequently thought	How often?
Clauses	Unfortunately, he was unable to return to college	How? In what manner?

ACTIVITY

To make your class more aware of the way modifiers answer questions, you might do the following. Have students locate some adjectives and adverbs within a passage from an assigned reading. Focusing on particular examples, ask which question each adverb or adjective answers within its sentence. In this way, you will demonstrate the usefulness of questions in testing the correctness of modifiers.

Forms of adjectives and adverbs

Once you know whether you need an adjective or an adverb in a particular sentence, you have to be able to choose the correct form. For many pairs of adjectives and adverbs, the distinction is quite easy:

ADJECTIVE FORM	ADVERB FORM
angry	angrily
beautiful	beautifully
perfect	perfectly
quick	quickly
rapid	rapidly
serious	seriously
slow	slowly
thorough	thoroughly

For these regular forms, the adverb form is the adjective form with an -*ly* ending. Unfortunately, however, many of the most common adjectives and adverbs in English are irregular, as the following list demonstrates.

ADJECTIVE FORM	ADVERB FORM
good	well
fast	fast
hard	hard
late	late
lovely	—
—	here
—	very
—	often

The most frequent error with adjectives and adverbs occurs when writers use an adjective in a situation requiring an adverb.

18. When he became a political leader in New York, he would always
    carefully
    speak careful to the crowds.

    Because *speak* is a verb, it must be modified by an adverb. Therefore, the writer has changed *careful* to *carefully*.

28a
ad

19. Even though the narrator spoke *well* ~~good~~, he could not prevent a riot.

Here also an adverb is called for because the word is modifying the verb *spoke*. The adverb form of *good* is *well*. (There is also an adjective *well*, which means "in good health," as in "The patient is not feeling well this morning." These two meanings for *well* make it a little tricky, but you should remember that *good* can never serve as an adverb.)

20. The ending of the book is *surprisingly* ~~surprising~~ optimistic.

Here an adverb is called for because the word is modifying the adjective *optimistic,* and the adverb form is *surprisingly.*

28b Using adjectives after linking verbs

The following sentences illustrate another source of error involving adjectives and adverbs.

If students have forgotten how to identify a linking verb, refer them to 19c.

1. Naomi behaved badly in class today.

This sentence is fine. The adverb *badly* modifies the verb *behaved*.

2. Naomi was *bad* ~~badly~~ in class today.

Here the adverb *badly* would definitely be wrong, but why? The verb *was* is a different kind of verb from *behave* in sentence 1; *behave* is an action verb, but *was* is a linking verb. Linking verbs (see 19c) always link a noun or adjective after the verb with the subject at the beginning of the sentence. In this case, *bad* is being linked to *Naomi*; it is modifying *Naomi*. Because *Naomi* is a noun, the word that modifies it must be the adjective *bad* and not the adverb *badly*.

3. Naomi feels *bad* ~~badly~~ about the way she has behaved.

Many people, including some fairly experienced writers, make this mistake. Besides the various forms of the verb *be* (like *was* in sentence 2), there is also a group of linking verbs that refer to the senses. *Feels* is one of these. Because it is a linking verb, it links the adjective following it, *bad,* to the noun *Naomi*.

After a linking verb, use the adjective form and not the adverb form.

28b
ad

To refresh your memory, the linking verbs that refer to the senses include *appears, feels, looks, seems, smells, sounds,* and *tastes.* To make things even more complicated, these linking verbs can also be used as action verbs.

4. Because it was dark, we didn't really look well for the hubcap last night.

   Here *look* is an action verb; it is describing something we did, using our eyes to examine the ground for a hubcap. Because it represents something we did, it is an action verb. If it is an action verb, it does *not* link *well* back to the subject *you.* Instead, *well* modifies the verb. Words that modify *verbs* must be *adverbs,* not *adjectives.*

5. We look good in our tuxedos.

   Here the same verb, *look,* is being used as a linking verb. We are not talking about using our eyes to search for something; in fact, *we* are not *doing* anything. Instead, a statement is being made about our appearance. Therefore, in this sentence, *look* is a linking verb, linking *good* back to the pronoun *we.* Because words that modify pronouns are adjectives, we use the adjective form *good.*

To help you tell the difference, remember that when *look* is used as an action verb, it is usually followed by a preposition, as in sentence 4. When *look* is a linking verb, it is not accompanied by *for* or *at,* as in sentence 5.

To keep this straight, you need to learn to distinguish between sensory verbs used as linking verbs or used as action verbs. After linking verbs, use an adjective; after action verbs, an adverb.

28c Using comparative and superlative forms

Most adjectives have alternative forms that are used for making comparisons.

1. Julio is tall.

   Here we use the regular form of the adjective *tall* because no comparison is being made.

2. Of the two men in my chemistry class, Julio is the taller.

   Here we are using a form known as the **comparative** because we are comparing *two* items: the two men in the chemistry class.

3. Of the six men in my chemistry class, Julio is the tallest.

This time we have used a form called the **superlative** because we are comparing more than two items, in this case, six.

Use the regular form when you are not making a comparison, the comparative when you are comparing two items, and the superlative when you are comparing more than two.

COMPARATIVE AND SUPERLATIVE FORMS OF ADJECTIVES AND ADVERBS

Regular	Comparative	Superlative
Short Adjectives		
big	bigger	biggest
smart	smarter	smartest
Long Adjectives		
beautiful	more beautiful	most beautiful
terrible	more terrible	most terrible
Adverbs		
carefully	more carefully	most carefully
sadly	more sadly	most sadly
soon	sooner	soonest

28c
ad

Regular adjectives and adverbs form the comparative and superlative in fairly predictable ways. Comparatives of adjectives are formed by adding an *-er* ending to the regular form; superlatives are formed by adding an *-est* ending. Note, however, that this applies only to adjectives and adverbs that are one or two syllables long. For longer adjectives and adverbs, form the comparative by placing the word *more* before the adjective or adverb. Form the superlative by using the word *most*.

The principle that adjectives and adverbs of one or two syllables add *-er* and *-est* is generally true, but there are many exceptions. In addition, many two-syllable adverbs take *more* or *most* rather than the *-er* and *-est* endings. If you are in doubt, consult a dictionary. If the word takes the *-er* and *-est* endings, these forms will appear in the definition; otherwise, use the words *more* and *most*.

You might mention that exceptions to the rule about adding *-er* or *-est* to two-syllable adjectives include words ending in *-ful*, such as *awful* and *helpful*, as well as a few words ending in *-id* such as *valid*. There are generally no exceptions to the rule about *not* adding *-er* to three-syllable adjectives, though there is the famous "Curiouser and curiouser" remark in Lewis Carroll's *Alice in Wonderland*.

It is also possible to compare things downward, as the following chart shows.

DOWNWARD COMPARISON OF ADJECTIVES AND ADVERBS

Regular	Comparative	Superlative
Adjectives		
expensive	less expensive	least expensive
impressive	less impressive	least impressive
Adverbs		
hurriedly	less hurriedly	least hurriedly
angrily	less angrily	least angrily

And as the chart below demonstrates, a small group of fairly common adjectives and adverbs form their comparatives and superlatives in irregular ways.

FORMS OF IRREGULAR ADJECTIVES AND ADVERBS

Regular	Comparative	Superlative
Adjectives		
good	better	best
bad	worse	worst
many	more	most
much	more	most
some	more	most
little	less, littler	least, littlest
Adverbs		
well	better	best
badly	worse	worst
little	less	least

Although there are two different ways to form comparatives and superlatives and there are even some words like *steady* that can be formed either way (*steady, steadier, steadiest* or *steady, more*

steady, most steady), it is never correct to combine both forms for the same word, as you can see from the following sentences.

4. She was a more steadier player than he was.

The following examples illustrate another possible problem with adjectives:

dead	*but not*	more dead
infinite	*but not*	more infinite

You probably find that the comparative forms in the right-hand column sound odd. When you think about it, it is just not logical to say someone is *more dead. Dead* is an absolute concept—you either are dead or you aren't. The same is true of *infinite*—it means "unlimited" or "without bound." If something is *unlimited,* it has *no* limits, so it would be impossible for something else to be *more limitless.*

The adjectives listed below are also **absolute**—the comparative forms are incorrect, although they are not as obviously illogical. Nevertheless, most experienced writers agree that these words, like *dead* and *infinite,* should never be used in the comparative or superlative forms.

impossible	*but not*	more impossible
perfect	*but not*	more perfect
pregnant	*but not*	more pregnant
unique	*but not*	more unique

In speech and casual writing, many writers continue to compare these terms, even though to do so defies logic. To be formally correct, you should avoid using comparative or superlative forms with absolute adjectives.

28d Avoiding double negatives

The following sentences illustrate another problem some writers have with adjectives and adverbs.

1. I do not understand ~~nothing~~ *anything* about nuclear energy.

The problem here is that the writer intends to indicate that he or she doesn't understand anything about nuclear energy, but the logic of the words indicates just the opposite. The words logically say that

28d
ad

Old habits are hard to break. If one is accustomed to using double negatives, overcoming the tendency may take much more than a review of the rules. Encourage students whose drafts show evidence of double negatives to practice writing sentences modeled on the corrected examples in 28d.

he or she does *not* understand *nothing*; in other words, he or she *does* understand *something*. This confusion between what the writer intends and what the words say is caused by the use of a double negative. *Not* conveys a negative meaning, and so does the *no* in *nothing*. These two negatives cancel each other out, creating the unintended meaning that the writer *does* know something.

2. It does not make no̲ sense to me to produce poisonous materials that we don't know how to dispose of.

[handwritten: any]

Again, the writer intends to say that it doesn't make sense, but the two negatives (*not* and *no*) cancel each other out, creating the opposite meaning.

There are ten negatives in English: *neither, never, no, nobody, none, no one, nor, not, nothing,* and *nowhere.* In addition, the five frequency adverbs *barely, hardly, rarely, scarcely,* and *seldom* are considered negative and create double negatives when used with each other or with any of the ten negative words.

3. We can't hardly keep the environment safe as it is without creating tons of highly toxic materials in nuclear power plants.

Here *not* (in the contraction *can't*) cancels out the negative meaning of *hardly*, so the sentence means that we *can* keep the environment clean, the opposite of the writer's intention.

Sometimes a double negative is acceptable in English.

4. I would not be unhappy to learn that all nuclear power plants were being closed down.

Here the two negatives cancel each other out to create the meaning that I would not be sad, which is apparently what the writer intends, so the double negatives are correct. In other words, you may use double negatives only when the positive meaning created by the two negatives canceling each other out is what you intend.

The desire to avoid double negatives leads many experienced writers to stay away from the phrase *can't help but.* It can be avoided by wording sentences as follows.

5. I can't help but wonder whether our greed for energy is going to lead us into poisoning the planet.

[handwritten: wondering]

28e Determining the order of adjectives

When a series of modifiers comes before a noun, the modifiers should be placed in order according to the accompanying chart. (The order is actually somewhat more flexible than this chart indicates; however, this order will generally be correct.) For example, you might say *the first expensive large green felt hat,* but you could not say *the felt green large expensive first hat.* You might talk about *a simple green picture frame,* but you could never say *a picture simple green frame.*

ORDER OF ADJECTIVES

Determiner	Number	Quality or Characteristic	Size or Shape	Color	Other Noun	Main Noun
the	one	expensive	large	green	bamboo	chair
these	six	impressive	small	red	picture	frames
this	first	Scandinavian	round	black	dining room	table
a	third		over-sized		automobile	tire
his		simple			felt	hat
Jose's		new				pen
some						chickens
many						students

29 USING ARTICLES

29a *A versus an*

Three very common adjectives—*a, an,* and *the*—make up a special group known as **articles** (or *determiners* or *noun markers*).

ESL ADVICE

Whereas the order of adjectives is habitual for most native speakers, it is by no means natural for those whose first language is not English. Encourage ESL students to study the order shown in the chart and to write practice phrases modeled on the sequence shown there (e.g., "the first inexpensive small red handbag").

COLLABORATIVE ACTIVITY

Have members of peer editing groups search one another's drafts for errors involving adjectives or adverbs. If students work independently, invite them to see you about any questions they have concerning adjectives following linking verbs, about adjective forms, or about double negatives.

29a
art

The words *a, an, the,* and other determiners can cause problems for writers. Owing to the complexity of the rules governing the use of these words, ESL students as well as native speakers may need to refer on more than one occasion to the specific explanations offered in this chapter.

RESOURCES

Leki, Ilona. *Understanding ESL Writers: A Guide for Teachers.* Portsmouth: Boynton/Cook, 1992.

Mohan, Bernard A., and Winnie Au-Yeung Lo. "Academic Writing and Chinese Students: Transfer and Developmental Factors." *TESOL Quarterly* 19 (1985): 515–34.

Wiener, Harvey S. *The Writing Room: A Resource Book for Teachers of English.* New York: Oxford UP, 1981.

Leki offers extensive advice for teachers of ESL, while Mohan and Lo focus on the particular difficulties faced by Chinese students. Wiener's book includes helpful resources, including exercises for mastering possessive determiners (175–80).

29a
art

ESL

ACTIVITY

Those who have trouble following the *a/an* rules might benefit from reading noun phrases aloud. Have ESL students pay special attention to the sound of *an* before nouns beginning with vowels.

For most native speakers of English, the biggest problem with articles involves the choice between *a* and *an*. The following examples illustrate the basic principle:

a banana	an apple
a notebook	an elephant
a taxi	an automobile

You can see from these examples that you use *a* before words starting with consonants and *an* before words starting with vowels. The following examples reveal one more aspect of this rule:

a blue umbrella	an old book
a wilted iris	an uncomfortable chair

These examples show that the choice of *a* or *an* is dictated by the next word, not the next noun. Even though *umbrella* starts with a vowel, *a* is the correct article because the next word is *blue*, which starts with a consonant.

The following list reveals one more twist to this rule:

a uniform	an hour
a one-dollar bill	an L-shaped room

Notice that *a* is used with *uniform*, even though it begins with a vowel. This is because the vowel *u* in *uniform* is pronounced "yoo," which begins with a consonant sound. Conversely, even though *hour* starts with a consonant, the letter *h*, the article *an* is used with it. This is because the *h* is silent, so the word is pronounced as if it begins with an *o*. From these two examples, we can conclude that we use *a* before words that start with a consonant *sound*, regardless of what *letter* they begin with. We use *an* before words that start with a vowel *sound*.

In the second pair of examples, *a* is used in front of *one-dollar* bill because even though *one* starts with a vowel, it is pronounced as if it began with the letter *w*, a consonant. *An* is used before *L-shaped room* because, even though *L* is a consonant, it is pronounced "el," as if it began with the vowel *e*.

29b Determiners

Whereas most native speakers of English have little trouble with articles, writers for whom English is a second language often find articles one of the most difficult aspects of English to master. The rules for determining when not to use an article, when to use *the,* and when to use *a* or *an* are surprisingly complex and subtle. To make the matter even more problematic, many languages, such as Chinese, Japanese, Korean, most Slavic languages, and most African languages, do not use articles at all. And those that do, such as French, Spanish, and most Semitic languages, use articles in ways that are quite different from the way English uses them.

Determiners are a category of words that precede nouns and modify their meaning. Only one determiner can be used for each noun. Articles are in this group; so are a number of other words, as shown in the following chart.

ESL ADVICE

Those learning English as a second language may find determiners doubly difficult. First there is the problem of recognizing where determiners are used. Then there is the equally difficult problem of understanding the order of determiners. Have students review this section carefully.

DETERMINERS IN ENGLISH

Articles	Other Determiners			
a, an	any	this	my	possessive nouns
the	each	that	his	
	either	these	her	which
	enough	those	its	whose
	every		your	whichever
	neither		our	whatever
	no		their	
	some			

29b
art

ESL

The rules concerning article use will help you determine when to use an article in front of a noun. But you also need to remember that each noun can have no more than one determiner. This means that if you use one of the other determiners, you should not also use an article.

To select the correct article (or the option of using no article), you must first decide whether the noun that the article modifies is proper or common. Articles that modify proper nouns are discussed in 29c; articles that modify common nouns are discussed in 29d and 29e.

29c Articles with proper nouns

A **proper noun** is the *name* of a particular person, place, or thing. The distinction between proper and **common nouns** is explained in detail in 38b. If you are not sure of this distinction, read that section first and then continue with the discussion here.

The following examples illustrate the basic rule for using articles with proper nouns.

a Central Park	~~an~~ *the* Alaska-Canada Highway
a Notre Dame	an Indiana State University

RULE 1: **Singular proper nouns do not take the article *a* or *an*.**

The following examples illustrate the rule for using the definite article *the* with *singular* proper nouns.

the Charles Street	the Lansing Community College
the Doctor Hernandez	the Mount Fuji

RULE 2: **In general, singular proper nouns do not take the definite article *the*.**

The following examples illustrate the basic rule for using articles with plural proper nouns.

the Williams   *the* Rocky Mountains   *the* Great Lakes

RULE 3: **In general, plural proper nouns take the definite article *the*.**

The following categories are exceptions to these general rules.

Geographic names

Geographic names present special problems because they often do not follow the general rules for articles with proper nouns. The following examples illustrate one exception.

Although proper nouns may seem easy to recognize because they are capitalized, students would be well advised to review the definition of a proper noun in 33b.

| *the* United States of America | *but not* | the America |
| *the* Republic of China | *but not* | the China |

Although the names of nations do not generally take an article, when the name includes a noun that would otherwise be common, such as *states* or *republic,* the name requires the definite article *the.*

Certain other names of nations require the article *the* by convention and not because of any discernible rule.

the Netherlands   *the* Philippines   *the* Sudan

The following examples illustrate several exceptions to this rule.

the Caucusus	*the* Crimea	*the* American South
the Sahara	*the* Mojave	*the* Gobi
the Monterey peninsula	*the* Iberian peninsula	*the* Baja peninsula
the Indian Ocean	*the* Pacific Ocean	*the* Mediterranean Sea
the Persian Gulf	*the* Gulf of Mexico	*the* Gulf of Suez
the Red River	*the* Yellow River	*the* Nile River
the Suez Canal	*the* Erie Canal	*the* English Channel

As these examples show, even singular names of regions, deserts, peninsulas, oceans, gulfs, rivers, and canals take the article *the.* One explanation is that large, hard-to-define areas (regions, oceans, gulfs, peninsulas) or bodies of *flowing* water (rivers, channels, canals) must take the article *the.* These generalizations may help you remember which geographic names require the article *the,* but note that names of capes (Cape Cod) and points (Point Lookout) do not fit this rule; they do *not* take an article.

29c
art

ESL

Colleges and universities

The use of articles with names of colleges and universities also causes difficulty. The general patterns are illustrated by the following names.

| *the* University of Hawaii | *the* University of California | *the* University of Texas |
| the Michigan State University | the Kansas State University | the Oregon State University |

The general pattern for universities and colleges is as follows:

> the University of _____; _____ University

Other exceptions

The following examples are also exceptions to the general rule that singular proper nouns do not take an article.

the Roman Empire	*the* British Common- wealth	*the* Ottoman Empire
the Louvre	*the* Boston Museum	*the* Library of Congress
the Empire State Building	*the* Hyatt Hotel	*the* White House

Even though they are singular, the names of empires, dynasties, museums, libraries, and other buildings usually take the definite article *the*. The names of organizations and religions, like nations, take *the* if they include a word that otherwise would be a common noun (the Roman Catholic Church, the Red Cross) but take no article otherwise (Islam, Christianity).

Languages are also an exception to the rule that singular proper nouns do not take an article.

The English language	*but not*	~~the English~~
The Spanish language	*but not*	~~the Spanish~~

29d Common nouns: four distinctions

If a noun is not proper, it is common. A common noun is a word that represents a person, place, or thing but not its name. The complicated set of rules governing article use with common nouns depends on four distinctions:

1. Is the noun countable or noncountable?
2. Is the noun singular or plural?
3. Is the noun definite or indefinite?
4. Is the noun definite or generic?

Countable versus noncountable

One concept essential to understanding the use of articles with common nouns is the distinction between countable nouns and noncountable nouns. As the name implies, you can count or

quantify countable nouns but not noncountable nouns. Also, countable nouns have separate singular and plural forms, but noncountable nouns do not.

For example, you could count *marbles* but not *sand.* Of course, if you wanted to, you could count *grains of sand,* but that makes *grains* a countable noun, not *sand.* You could count *bottles* but not the *wine* that is in them; that would make *bottles* a countable noun, but not *wine.* You could *measure* the amount of wine in bottles, but measuring is not the same as *counting.*

The distinction between countable and noncountable nouns is difficult for some students because nouns that refer to the same type of item may be countable in one language but not in another. *Furniture,* for example, is noncountable in English but countable in Spanish. *Chalk* is a noncountable noun in English but is countable in Japanese. Because of the complexity of this distinction, it would be a good idea to keep a list of noncountable nouns as you discover them. It is easier to list the noncountable nouns because there are fewer of them; most nouns in English are countable.

Singular versus plural

This distinction applies only to countable nouns. A singular noun represents only one of the item represented; a plural noun represents more than one.

SINGULAR NOUNS	PLURAL NOUNS
one hat	two hats
a car	six cars

As you can see, singular nouns represent one thing or person; plural nouns represent more than one. You also may have noticed that the plural form of these nouns is simply the singular form with an *-s* ending. This is the rule for forming the plural of *regular* nouns; however, many nouns in English are *irregular* and form their plurals in unpredictable ways (see 44g). Check the dictionary if you are not sure.

Definite versus indefinite

A third distinction important to the use of articles is whether the item named by a specific noun is known to the writer and

29d
art

ESL

ACTIVITY

Have students locate definite and indefinite articles in one paragraph from an assigned reading. After discussing the specificity criterion illustrated here in examples 1–6, ask individuals to explain briefly why the respective types of articles were used before particular nouns in the passage being examined.

reader. A noun is already known to the writer and reader if it fits one of the categories represented by the following examples.

1. Last week Tranh looked at a car that was advertised in the newspaper. The car was a 1989 Pontiac.

   The noun has already been mentioned in a previous sentence or earlier in the sentence in question. In sentence 1, at first mention, *car* is a noun not specifically known to the reader, so the indefinite article *a* is used. The second time *car* is mentioned, however, it is known to the reader, so the definite article *the* is used.

2. The car that he is driving now is ten years old.

   A specific noun is identified by a phrase or clause that follows it. In sentence 2, the clause *that he is driving now* identifies the noun *car* as a specific one, so it is known to the reader.

3. The most expensive car that he looked at this weekend was a Buick Riviera convertible for $18,000.

   The noun is modified by a comparative or superlative adjective. (See 28c for a discussion of superlative adjectives.) In sentence 3, *car* is known to the reader because it is specifically identified by the phrase *most expensive*. Only one car can be the *most expensive*.

4. The convertible would be great when the sun was shining.

   The noun stands for a unique and therefore specific person or thing. In sentence 4, *the sun* is definite because it refers to something that is known to everyone as a unique object.

5. As he looked at the Buick, Tranh noticed that the windows were power-operated.

   Nouns that stand for the parts of a whole that is being discussed are definite. In sentence 5, *the windows* are part of the whole car that is being discussed.

6. Tranh is now looking at cars at Russell Ford. I hope the salesperson realizes that he cannot spend more than $10,000 for a car.

   The context or situation makes the specific identity of the noun clear. In sentence 6, because of the situation—we know that Tranh is at a car dealership—it is clear that *salesperson* stands for whoever is helping him look at those Fords. Even though we don't know who

that is, because of the context, the noun does stand for a specific person who is therefore known to the reader.

The six situations described here make a noun definite. If none of these apply to a particular noun, it is either indefinite or generic. Generic nouns are discussed next.

Definite versus generic

7. The automobile is a part of many households in America.
8. The automobile was parked in Tranh's driveway.

Note the difference in the meaning of *the automobile* in sentences 7 and 8. In sentence 7, it is referring to automobiles *in general,* not to a specific vehicle; this kind of noun is generic because it refers to all members of a group *in general.* In sentence 8, *the automobile* is referring to a specific one—perhaps the ten-year-old car that Tranh owns. It is *not* referring to automobiles in general, so it is a definite noun.

9. Automobiles are a necessary expense for many families.
10. The automobiles involved in the accident were not badly damaged.

Here again, the same word is used in both a generic and a definite sense. In sentence 9, *automobiles* refers to automobiles *in general;* it is generic. In sentence 10, *automobiles* refers to specific ones—the ones involved in an accident—so it is definite, not generic.

Nouns, then, are **generic** when they refer to all the things or persons in a group in general.

29e Articles with common nouns

We will now use the four distinctions discussed in 29d to explain the rules for articles with common nouns.

RULE 1: **Always use an article with singular countable nouns.**

1. Tomorrow Tranh is going to look at ^*a* car.

Because *car* is a singular countable noun, we use an article. Which article to use will be discussed under rules 2 and 3.

Make sure students understand the meaning of *generic* in reference to nouns. Some reference to Plato's philosophy might even be in order here, for the concept of the generic noun is much like the concept of a generalized ideal that specific examples imperfectly represent.

29e
art

ESL

ESL ADVICE

Non-native speakers of English might find it helpful to write practice sentences imitating several of the examples given in the following section.

RULE 2: **Use the article *a* or *an* with singular countable nouns that are not definite—that is, not specifically known to the writer and the reader.**

2. Tranh has to buy ^a^ car this weekend so that he can drive to work on Monday.

The noun *car* is countable and not specifically known to the reader. We don't know which car Tranh will buy.

RULE 3: **Use the article *the* with singular countable nouns that are definite—that is, specifically known to the writer and reader.**

3. *The building* Building where he works is not located near a bus line.

The noun *building* is definite because of the clause *where he works*, which follows it.

RULE 4: **Use the article *the* with definite plural nouns.**

4. He looked at ^the^ keys that Jan had given him.

Use the article *the* in front of the noun *keys* because it is plural and definite. *The keys that Jan had given him* refers to a specific set of keys.

RULE 5: **Do not use an article with generic plural nouns.**

5. ~~The~~ ^C^ car dealers expect customers to bargain with them.

Car dealers is generic; we are talking about all the dealers in a group.

RULE 6: **Use the article *the* with definite noncountable nouns.**

6. Tranh was aware of ^the^ reputation of car dealers for driving hard bargains.

Reputation is noncountable, and it is definite. We are referring to a particular reputation—that of car dealers for their ability to bargain—so we use the article *the*.

RULE 7: **Use no article with generic noncountable nouns.**

7. The dealer assured Tranh that nervousness is a normal reaction.

Here the noncountable noun *nervousness* is not indefinite; it is generic. The dealer is talking about *nervousness* in general and not just the kind that Tranh had experienced.

EXCEPTION 1: Diseases

Diseases use articles in unpredictable ways. Those with formal names (*pneumonia, AIDS, influenza*) are frequently referred to by the singular noun and no article. Those with more informal names sometimes take *the* (*the flu, the plague*) and sometimes take *a* or *an* (*a cold, an earache*). Those with informal names and plural forms can often be used with no article (*measles* or *the measles; chicken pox* or *the chicken pox*). Note also that names of diseases are not capitalized.

EXCEPTION 2: Body parts

Remember that generic common nouns normally take one of two forms. If they are countable, like *marbles* or *lions,* the generic form is the plural with no article. If they are noncountable, like *wine* or *pollution,* the generic form is the singular with no article. However, the parts of the body are an exception to these rules.

8. The heart is the most common organ to malfunction.
9. The eyes of a child are not fully developed at birth.

For generic use, body parts take the form *the* + noun. The noun is singular or plural depending on whether the human body has one or more than one of the part.

EXCEPTION 3: Appliances

It is common for English speakers to use the definite article *the* instead of *a* or *an* when referring to radios and telephones.

CORRECT BUT UNCOMMON:

10. I listened to the baseball game on a radio.
11. I talked with my father on a telephone.

CORRECT AND MORE COMMON:

12. I listened to the baseball game on the radio.
13. I talked with my father on the telephone.

29e
art

ESL

With *telephone* and *radio,* the definite article *the* is more widely accepted even though the noun is not a specific one known to the writer and reader. However, note the following usage.

14. More than 100,000 people watched the soccer match on **the** television.

Television does not require the definite article *the* the way *radio* and *telephone* do.

EXCEPTION 4: **Trains and buses**

15. Mr. Alvarez came to San Francisco on **the** train.
16. Ms. Alvarez rides **the** bus to work every day.

Train and *bus* can take the definite article *the* even when a specific train or bus is not known to the reader and writer.

EXCEPTION 5: **Destinations**

Destinations are also an exception to the rule about the use of the definite article *the.*

17. Uche is going to a̶ store. *the*
18. Uche is going to a̶ library. *the*

In each case, the *preferred* form is with the definite article *the,* even if the reader is unfamiliar with the particular store, beach, or library that Uche is going to. But note the difference in the following sentences.

19. Uche is going to the school.
20. Uche is going to the church.

School and *church* are exceptions, perhaps because we think of them primarily as activities rather than buildings. Notice what happens when we do think of them as buildings.

21. Uche took a picture of *the* school. (specific school in mind)
22. Uche took a picture of *a* school. (no specific school in mind)
23. Uche took a picture of *the* church. (specific church in mind)
24. Uche took a picture of *a* church. (no specific church in mind)

ESL ADVICE

Some common activity expressions such as "going to school" or "going to work" are idioms that can be memorized. Have students practice them in written sentences. But check to see that those sentences do not confuse the idiomatic general usage with the kind of specific references illustrated in examples 21–24.

When *school* and *church* are used to denote buildings rather than the activity that takes place in them, they follow the regular rules for articles with common countable nouns.

EXCEPTION 6: **Items in a series**

25. I looked for my dog in the kitchen, basement, and back yard.
26. At the hardware store, she purchased a hammer, saw, and screwdriver.

When a series of items is joined by *and* or *or* and the same article is needed for each of them, it can be placed in front of the first item and omitted from the others.

30 EDITING FOR GRAMMAR ON A COMPUTER

After you have finished drafting a paper and revising it for organization, development of ideas, and style, it is time to worry about errors: those little problems with grammar, spelling, and punctuation that detract from an otherwise well written essay. For most writers, editing is much easier if they are writing their papers on a computer.

In this chapter we explain techniques for using the computer to improve your ability to eliminate errors in your writing. We do not discuss the specific commands for any particular computer program because there are so many and their commands are so different, but we do explain general techniques for using computers to eliminate errors. To figure out how to carry these techniques out on the computer, we suggest three sources of help:

- Consult the manuals that came with the particular word processing program you are using.
- Consult one of the many independently produced books that can be purchased in most bookstores and that explain the intricacies of your word processing program, sometimes with greater lucidity than the manuals.

Technology is changing the way writing is taught in college. Though some instructors still discourage the use of software editing features, many of us concede that the computer is now as inevitable an accessory to composition as the calculator is to mathematics. The conservative among us can remind students that Hemingway wrote with pencils at Paris café tables, and that today's writers can still use pencils and work outdoors. But we also need to point out that for editing a manuscript—whether that manuscript was originally drafted in pencil or on a computer screen— the computer can save time, detect mistakes, and help students learn.

30a
edit

RESOURCES
Software

Microsoft Word. Microsoft Corp.

PFS: Professional Write. Software Publishing Corp.

The 53rd Street Writer. The Daedalus Group.

WordPerfect. WordPerfect Corp.

Microsoft Word *and* WordPerfect *are among the most widely used brands of word-processing software, though many other specialized programs are being developed.* PFS *and* The 53rd Street Writer *are offered through the auspices of this book's publisher, HarperCollins.*

- Consult a friend who is proficient with the word processing program and computer you are using. (This is often the cheapest, fastest, and most user-friendly source of help.)

The effect of the computer on the writing process is discussed in 1d.

30a Editing on the screen versus editing on paper

First a warning. The printed page that comes out of your computer sometimes looks so good with its straight margins, centered titles, and absence of erasures that it may seem impossible that any errors could be lurking in it. Don't be fooled into thinking that your writing is perfect because it *looks* good when the computer prints it out. Instead, use the computer to ensure that the quality of the writing is as good as its appearance.

One of the first decisions you'll face when writing on a computer is whether to edit on the screen or on paper. Experienced computer users tend to edit their papers by reading them on the screen and making corrections as they find them. Others find they are better editors if they print out a copy of their paper, mark changes on the printed copy, and later enter the changes into the computer.

Which technique should you use? It's up to you; both are effective. Some writers edit on screen for some writing situations and on paper for others. Some writers edit on paper when they first start writing on the computer and later, when they are comfortable with the machine, switch to editing on the screen. Perhaps a discussion of the strengths and weaknesses of each approach will help you decide which to employ.

30b Using style-checking programs

One type of program that you may find helpful in editing is a style checker. These programs take a few minutes to whirr through your paper and then provide you with a printout or screenful of information about your writing. Until fairly recently, style checkers were good only at checking for things like whether you have a closing parenthesis to match every opening paren-

thesis, the reading level of your writing, the length of your sentences and paragraphs, and the use of unacceptable expressions like *alot* or *suppose to*. Such programs could not catch errors involving more sophisticated concepts because they could not parse sentences; that is, they could not determine whether a group of words was a sentence. Nor could they identify the parts of a sentence like the subject and verb. Without the ability to parse sentences, style checker programs could not identify fragments, comma splices, run-on sentences, or basic errors in subject-verb agreement or pronoun agreement.

Recently, however, style checkers have been developed that are capable of parsing sentences with some accuracy. These newer programs can find punctuation and agreement errors. Nevertheless, such programs should be used with great caution for the following reasons:

- When style checkers identify a potential problem, it is essential that you see it as just that: a *potential* problem. Often style checkers identify expressions that are perfectly correct and effective. It is important that you not assume that everything the program catches is an error; rather, think of it as something to check for a *possible* error.
- Style checkers miss many errors. You cannot assume that everything that the style checker *doesn't* flag is correct. After using the style checker, you must still proofread the paper carefully for other errors.
- Style checkers usually give far more information about your text than is really helpful. Use only what you find useful. For example, the information on reading levels is often thought to be quite unreliable because it is a mechanical judgment based mainly on word length and sentence length.

30b
edit

Style checkers may be available in the computer lab on your campus and can be purchased in most computer stores.

In addition to style checkers, computer programs that check spelling are available for most computers and can be extremely helpful, especially to students with learning disabilities. These programs are discussed in detail in 44h.

FOR DISCUSSION

You might spend some time discussing software with your students. Chances are that not all the members of the class are at the same level of computer literacy. Some may never have used a computer at all, while others may be regular hackers. Those who are new to software may feel less uncomfortable if they can hear from others about first experiences and get advice about working on screen. If you teach in a computer lab, or have access to one, try matching up the old hands with the less proficient, encouraging students to help one another develop basic knowledge of computerized editing.

30c
edit

ACTIVITY

Consider inviting a lab assistant or member of your school's computer science faculty to serve as a guest lecturer. Keeping the specific aims of your course in mind, arrange for the lecturer to cover topics that might prove especially useful to students—for example, style-check programs, search-and-replace functions, macros, and so on.

30c **Using the search or search-and-replace function in editing**

Almost every word processing program includes a search and a search-and-replace function. Learn the commands for these, as they can be helpful in editing your writing.

If you know that certain words, expressions, or punctuation marks cause you trouble, you can use the search or search-and-replace function to help you with editing. Suppose, for example, that you often confuse *then* and *than*. You could tell the computer you want to search for every instance of *then* and, if you decide it should be *than*, to replace it with *than*. The computer will search through your text, highlight the first instance of *then*, and ask you whether you want to replace it with *than*. You then study the sentence in question, decide whether you want to replace this particular *then*, and tell the computer. If you say "yes," the computer makes the change, moves on to the next place you have used a *then*, and asks you the same question. You and the computer continue through the document until every *then* has been checked.

You can use the same procedure for whatever words, phrases, or punctuation marks you habitually make errors with. Any words you sometimes make mistakes with (like *accept* and *except, too* and *to, it's* and *its,* or *past* and *passed*) can be checked in this way. See 16a for a complete discussion of these confusing words. In addition, the search-and-replace function can be used to locate every place you've used the pronoun *you* (allowing you to check for point-of-view shifts), to find every apostrophe (allowing you to check the correctness of their use), or to find every quotation mark followed by a period or comma (allowing you to move the punctuation inside the marks; see 36j).

Note that most word processors allow you to have the computer automatically replace every instance of a particular word or punctuation mark with something else or to have it locate each instance and ask you whether you want to replace this one or not. We recommend that you always choose the latter option. When the computer changes every instance automatically, there are too many possibilities for it to change things that are correct.

EDITING: PUNCTUATION

Part VII of this book considers the rules of punctuation, beginning with the important endings—that is, proper uses of the period, the question mark, and the exclamation point. A novice writer worries about how to begin sentences, while an experienced one worries how and where to end them. You might warn students that the key to successful punctuation is a knowledge of sentence parts, as reviewed in 20.

ESL ADVICE

Many foreign languages do not share the same punctuation marks used in English. Some ESL students may need not only to study the rules for these marks, but also to practice drawing the marks evenly on lined paper. Otherwise known as a "full stop," the period mustn't be written as a comma. The question mark never appears inverted at the beginning of a sentence, as it does in Spanish, for example. The exclamation point must be positioned correctly so that it doesn't look like a semicolon. Be prepared for basic questions about the visual form as well as the uses of these punctuation marks.

31b

?/!

USING PERIODS, QUESTION MARKS, AND EXCLAMATION POINTS TO END SENTENCES

In this chapter we will consider the punctuation used to indicate the boundaries of sentences. The concept of the *independent clause* is essential to understanding this chapter; if you need to review independent clauses, refer to 20i.

31a   Basic rules for punctuating sentences

Note the punctuation at the end of each of the following sentences.

1. A snake entered the garden.

   This sentence makes a statement, so it ends with a **period**. Because most sentences make statements, most end with periods.

2. Could this be the same snake that tempted Eve?

   This sentence is a question, so it ends with a **question mark** instead of a period.

3. The snake asked me my name!

   Use an **exclamation point** to end a sentence that you would emphasize strongly if you said it aloud.

31b   Fine points with question marks and exclamation points

1. Next he asked if I was hungry?

   This kind of sentence contains what is called an **indirect question**. The question the snake asked was "Are you hungry?" In sentence 1, that *direct* question does not appear, but an *indirect* version of it—"if I was hungry"—does. However, an indirect question does not make the *sentence* a question. In fact, the sentence itself makes a statement—that the snake asked me if I was hungry. Because the sentence makes a statement rather than asks a question, use a period, not a question mark.

2. Will you please accompany me to that tree in the middle of the

   garden?

   After a polite request, even when it is framed as a question, a question mark is optional. If an actual answer of *yes* or *no* is expected, use a question mark. If there is little or no expectation that the response will be negative, the request is not a question but rather a command, so a period is more appropriate.

3. Should I say yes. Say no. Run away.

   In the unusual case of questions in a series, use question marks to separate the questions even if they are not complete sentences. The use of capital letters to begin each of the questions is optional (see 38g).

4. I finally responded, "Are you talking to me"?

   Here the quoted material is a question, so the question mark goes inside the quotation marks. Note that although the entire sentence is a statement, it is not correct to place a period after the question mark. (For a fuller discussion of punctuation with quotation marks, see 36j.)

5. Hadn't I read a sign that said, "Don't eat the fruit of the tree in the

   middle of the garden?" ?

   Here the entire sentence is asking a question—Didn't I read a sign?—so the question mark goes *outside* the quotation marks. As in sentence 4, do *not* use a period with a question mark.

6. "No!" I yelled! "I will not eat any of the fruit!"

   When overused, exclamation points lose most of their punch. Save them for the rare occasion when the intensity of what you have to say cries out for them. Many professors frown on the use of exclamation points in any college writing.

7. At this moment I noticed that it was 3:00 P.M.

   When a sentence ends with an abbreviation, the period also serves as the end punctuation for the sentence; never use two periods in succession. If the abbreviation does not require a period, however, you will have to add one at the end of the sentence (see 39e).

RESOURCES

Meyer, Emily, and Louise Z. Smith. *The Practical Tutor.* New York: Oxford UP, 1987.

This book includes cogent advice on teaching punctuation (see esp. 177–201), as well as useful exercises for students.

31b
?/!

COLLABORATIVE ACTIVITY

In reading one another's drafts, students should look for problems with end punctuation. Have your writers check to see that periods follow complete sentences, that question marks haven't been omitted, and that exclamation points serve only where needed.

This chapter teaches writers to avoid three common errors resulting from mispunctuation: the sentence fragment, the fused sentence, and the comma splice. Because those errors often result from a faulty understanding of basic sentence structure, you might advise students to review the definitions of clauses given in 20i–j.

32a
sent

8. Had I been in this garden since 11:00 A.M. ?

   If a sentence that ends with an abbreviation is a question, you will have to add a question mark. If the sentence is an exclamation (see 31a), you should add an exclamation point.

9. I had been out in the hot sun for four hours!!! No wonder I was talking with snakes.

   Use more than one exclamation point in succession only in the most informal writing, and never in college or business writing.

32 AVOIDING FRAGMENTS, FUSED SENTENCES, AND COMMA SPLICES

This chapter explains what a sentence is and how to avoid three major errors involving the boundaries of sentences: fragments, fused sentences, and comma splices. The concept of the *independent clause* is essential to understanding this chapter; if you need to review independent clauses, refer to 20i.

32a Recognizing sentences

In 20i we explain that an **independent clause** must meet three criteria:

- It must contain a **subject** (see 20b).
- It must contain a **verb** (see 20a).
- It must express a complete thought—it must not leave you hanging or expecting more.

In this section, you will discover how a sentence is similar to an independent clause and how it is different.

Independent clauses must have subjects and verbs:

1. INDEPENDENT CLAUSE: Bells ring.

2. INDEPENDENT CLAUSE: The small yellow bird with black wings is a goldfinch.

3. INDEPENDENT CLAUSE: After he learned to read, Frederick Douglass began to plan his escape.

4. **Not an Independent Clause:**   The small yellow <u>bird</u> with black wings. (no verb)

5. **Not an Independent Clause:**   <u>Began</u> to plan his escape. (no subject)

The following examples are not independent clauses either, but for a different reason; note that they do have subjects and verbs.

6. **Not an Independent Clause:**   After <u>he</u> <u>had learned</u> to read.

7. **Not an Independent Clause:**   If <u>it</u> <u>rains</u> on the weekend.

8. **Not an Independent Clause:**   Until <u>you</u> <u>receive</u> her check in the mail.

At the end of each of these, the reader is left hanging with a sense of incompleteness. The reader expects something to be added. This sense of incompleteness keeps these from being independent clauses.

The following example reveals the major difference between a *sentence* and an *independent clause*.

Independent clause

9. Rita danced two pieces in the performance last night, and

Independent clause

Ramon watched her.

Here there is *one sentence* but *two independent clauses*.

The difference between a sentence and an independent clause, then, is that a sentence *may* contain more than one independent clause. In fact, a sentence can contain more than two independent clauses.

Independent clause   Independent clause

10. Rita's knee was sprained, and her toe was swollen, but

Independent clause   Independent clause

she danced anyhow, and she didn't feel any worse at the end

of the performance.

RESOURCES

Bamberg, Betty. "Periods Are Basic: A Strategy for Eliminating Comma Faults and Run-on Sentences." *Classroom Practices in Teaching English, 1977–1978: Teaching the Basics—Really!* Ed. Ouida Clapp et al. Urbana: NCTE, 1977. 97–99.

Brosnahan, Irene Teoh. "A Few Good Words for the Comma Splice." *College English* 38 (1976): 184–88.

Daiker, Donald A., et al., eds. *Sentence Combining: A Rhetorical Perspective.* Carbondale: Southern Illinois UP, 1985.

Harris, Muriel. "Mending the Fragmented Free Modifier." *College Composition and Communication* 32 (1981): 175–82.

Kline, Charles R., Jr., and W. Dean Memering. "Formal Fragments: The English Minor Sentence." *Research in the Teaching of English* 11 (1977): 97–110.

Meyer, Emily, and Louise Z. Smith. *The Practical Tutor.* New York: Oxford UP, 1987.

Noguchi, Rei R. *Grammar and the Teaching of Writing: Limits and Possibilities.* Urbana: NCTE, 1991.

32a
sent

32a
sent

A sentence can also include an independent clause and one or more dependent clauses (see 20j).

Independent clause · Independent clause

11. When Rita finished her performance, she wrapped her knee in ice,

Dependent clause

which kept it from swelling.

Sentences with pronouns

Knowing that an independent clause must have a subject and a verb and must express a complete thought, some students have trouble recognizing independent clauses that contain pronouns.

Dependent clause · Independent clause

12. When Picasso painted *Guernica,* he wanted it to express the horrors of war.

The independent clause *he wanted it to express the horrors of war* clearly has a verb, *wanted,* and a subject, *he,* but still feels a little incomplete. If it appeared by itself, the reader would wonder who *he* was and what *it* was. However, this is an independent clause because it contains both a subject and a verb. The slight sense of incompleteness that results from the use of pronouns (see 19b) like *he* or *it* does *not* prevent groups of words from being *grammatically* complete. The meaning of the clause is clarified by context. So if your common sense tells you that groups of words like *he wanted it to express the horrors of war* is incomplete, you are not wrong, but *incompleteness that results simply from the presence of pronouns does not count grammatically.*

You understood as the subject

Independent clause

13. Look at the paintings in a local art gallery.

At first glance, this sentence may seem like a fragment. It has a verb, *look,* but it doesn't seem to have a subject. Notice, however, that it gives a command; it tells someone to do something.

A command always has a subject that doesn't appear in the sentence: *you*. Because English speakers understand that the subject is *you* without the word itself being present, we say that the subject is "*you* understood." Commands are sentences because they *do* have a subject (understood rather than expressed) and a verb and are hence complete. (For further discussion of *you* understood as subject, see 20b).

Elliptical sentences

Perhaps one of the most difficult kinds of independent clauses to recognize is the type represented by sentence 14.

Independent clause   Independent clause

14. Matisse frequently painted the human form, and Picasso did too.

It would be easier to see why *Picasso did too* is an independent clause if we looked at a different, and less graceful, way of writing the same sentence.

Independent clause

15. Matisse frequently painted the human form, and

Independent clause

Picasso frequently painted the human form too.

It is clear that *Matisse frequently painted the human form* is an independent clause in both example 14 and example 15. It is equally clear that *Picasso frequently painted the human form too* in example 15 is also an independent clause.

Look more closely at the independent clause *Picasso did too* in example 14. Is there any doubt what Picasso did too? Could the sentence mean that he ate pizza too? Of course not. It is clear that Picasso *painted the human form too*. We know that because in English, when a second clause repeats a verb phrase from an earlier clause, it is customary to substitute *did too* for the verb phrase in the second clause. *Did too* always means that the subject in the second clause did the same thing as the subject in the first clause. Sentences of this type are called **elliptical** and *are* independent clauses.

32a
sent

ACTIVITY

Using examples 14 and 16 as models, you might have your class freewrite a few elliptical sentences to get the sense of how these sentences work. Make sure students practice transforming the elliptical clauses into ones with complete verb phrases.

32b
frag

Example 16 illustrates another form of elliptical sentence.

Independent clause   Independent clause

16. Matisse was interested in shape, and so was Picasso.

Here *so was* serves the same purpose as *did too* in example 14. We understand that the second half of the sentence means *and so was Picasso interested in shape. So was Picasso* is therefore an independent clause.

32b Finding and revising fragments

Defining fragments

The conventions of Standard Written English require that a *sentence* begin with a capital letter (see 38a) and end with a period or other end punctuation (see 31a). The following illustrates a serious problem some students have with this convention.

Fragment

1. Although most people think they know what art is.

Example 1 is not a sentence because it does not contain an independent clause. The group of words is not an independent clause because it does not express a complete thought; it leaves the reader hanging, expecting more. In fact, it is a *dependent* clause, more specifically an adverbial clause (see 20j), but the important fact is that it is *not* an independent clause; therefore, this group of words is *not* a sentence. (On page 337, we explain techniques for *correcting* fragments; here, we concentrate on *recognizing* them.)

Fragment

2. A fence running across the California countryside and into the ocean.

Example 2 does seem to have a subject: *fence*. At first glance, it also seems to have a verb: *running*. However, it is important to recognize that words ending in *-ing* are verbs only when they are preceded by a helping verb (see 19c); when they are not preceded by

a helping verb, they are *verbals*, which are *not* the same as verbs. Since there is no verb, there is no independent clause, so example 2 is not a sentence.

Each of these examples begins with a capital letter and ends with a period—the conventions for indicating a sentence in Standard Written English—but neither of them is a sentence. This violation of the conventions is called a **fragment** and is considered a serious error.

Recognizing fragments

If you have a great deal of trouble with fragments, this section is for you. In it we will discuss a wide range of fragments. The kinds you have trouble with should be covered somewhere in this section.

The first fragments we will look at are perhaps the easiest to recognize. They do not include verbs or even verbals.

Noun phrase   Prepositional phrase

3. **Fragment:** Matisse's painting of a pink nude

Prepositional phrase

against a checked background.

This fragment does not include an independent clause or even a dependent clause, for that matter. It starts with a noun phrase, *Matisse's painting,* which might be the subject if there were a verb to go with it. But instead of a verb, the rest of the example consists of two prepositional phrases. Not only does it leave the reader hanging, but it also has no verb.

4. **Fragment:** The stages or periods Picasso went through were quite

Conjunctive adverb   List

diverse. For example, his blue period, rose period,

classical period, and cubist period.

The fragment in example 4 is just a list introduced by the conjunctive adverb *for example* (see 19e for discussion and a list of conjunctive adverbs). It does not include a subject or a verb, and it leaves the reader

ACTIVITY

You might compose a handout with several numbered examples that contain independent clauses next to fragments such as "I was late. Because the traffic was heavy." Have students correct the examples to make complete sentences. Review solutions in class.

32b
frag

hanging. For some reason, some writers mistakenly treat any group of words introduced by a conjunctive adverb as if it were an independent clause. When you use a conjunctive adverb, the group of words that follows it must be an independent clause to form a sentence.

5. **Fragment:**   Picasso's art developed through many stages.

Verb phrase

And influenced almost everyone else painting in the twentieth century.

The fragment in example 5 is the second half of a compound verb; the noun *art* is the subject for two verbs, *developed* in the first part of the example and *influenced*, which has been separated incorrectly into its own "sentence." Since this "sentence" has no subject and leaves the reader hanging, it is a fragment.

The next two examples are a little more confusing because they include verbals (see 19c). A **verbal** is a word that would normally be a verb but is being used as an adjective or a noun. There are two kinds of verbals: gerunds (and participles) and infinitives. Gerunds and participles are forms of the verb that end in *-ing* and do not accompany helping verbs. Infinitives are verbs with the word *to* in front of them. Verbals are *never* verbs.

Noun Verbal Prepositional phrase

6. **Fragment:**   A dog sitting under a table.

This is a common type of fragment because it *seems* to have a subject, *dog*, and a verb, *sitting*, and the sense of incompleteness is not terribly strong. In this example, however, there is no helping verb, so *sitting* is a verbal, not a verb. Because it has no verb, the group of words is a fragment.

Verbal Prepositional phrase   Prepositional phrase

7. **Fragment:**   To look at this painting for more than thirty seconds.

This fragment consists of a verbal (more specifically, an infinitive, see 19c), and two prepositional phrases. It has no verb (remember, a verbal is not a verb), so it is incomplete. Without an independent clause, it cannot be a sentence.

32b
frag

The last group of fragments cause trouble because although they do include both subjects and verbs, those subjects and verbs are located in dependent clauses, usually adjective clauses (see 20j).

8. **FRAGMENT:** Many people would recognize a painting by Matisse.

Adjective clause

Who is one of the greatest painters of this century.

The highlighted portion is a fragment because it is not an independent clause; it is incomplete and leaves the reader hanging. In fact, it is a dependent clause, more specifically, an adjective clause. To recognize it as a fragment, all you need to know is that it does not contain an independent clause.

9. **FRAGMENT:** The best-known twentieth-century paintings are by

Noun   Adjective clause

Pablo Picasso. The artist who defined modern painting.

The fragment here is an appositive phrase (see 20f); the noun, *artist*, restates or renames a preceding noun, *Pablo Picasso*. This appositive is modified by an adjective clause, *who defined modern painting*.

Correcting fragments

You can correct fragments in two ways. The first is illustrated by examples 10 and 11.

10. Picasso painted *Guernica*./, A representation of the horrors of war.

Here the writer corrected the fragment by joining it to the preceding sentence.

11. Although Matisse was not a religious man./, The Catholic chapel

he designed at Vence, France, is one of his masterpieces.

The writer corrected this fragment by joining it to the following sentence.

32b
frag

One way to correct a fragment, then, is to join it to a nearby independent clause. When doing this, however, you must be careful that the more complex sentence you create actually makes sense. You may have noticed that the writer used a comma in examples 10 and 11 to join the fragment to the preceding or following sentence. The rules concerning this use of the comma are discussed in 34a and 34d.

The following sentence illustrates the kind of awkward or illogical sentence that can be created when writers attempt to join fragments to independent clauses without paying attention to meaning.

12. **FRAGMENT:**   In the 1940s, Matisse was stricken with a debilitating illness. As a result, making paintings out of cut-out pieces of colored paper.

This example contains a fragment, which the writer tried to correct in example 13.

13. **ILLOGICAL:**   In the 1940s, Matisse was stricken with a debilitating illness, as a result, making paintings out of cut-out pieces of colored paper.

In example 13, the writer has attempted to correct the fragment by joining it to the preceding independent clause. The result, however, is unsatisfactory because the fragment doesn't make sense joined to the preceding independent clause. It is not logical to say that being stricken with a debilitating illness causes one to make paintings out of cut-out pieces of paper.

14. In the 1940s, Matisse was stricken with a debilitating illness. As a

he began

result, making paintings out of cut-out pieces of colored paper.

In example 14, the writer has added the words *he began* to make the fragment a complete sentence. A second method for fixing fragments, then, is to add, delete, or change words to turn the fragment into an independent clause.

32b
frag

He wanted to

15. Matisse knew what he wanted to do with his life. To spend it mak-

ing art.

Here the writer has revised the fragment by adding a few words to make a sentence. In this case, the fragment was missing both subject and verb (*to spend* is a verbal). The writer added a subject, *he*, and a verb, *wanted*.

Intentional fragments

Take a look at the fragments in the following paragraph from a catalog of the J. Crew clothing company.

The relaxed flannel jacket. The silhouette is overscaled: cut very generously through the shoulders and back. See p. 4 for coordinating shorts. Wool and cashmere, with just a touch of nylon. Fully lined. Import. Dry-clean. Sizes 2–14.

Look at all those fragments! Can't the people at J. Crew write? Of course they can. Good writers frequently and consciously use fragments to create an informal, telegraphic style. Novelists and poets use intentional fragments for the same reasons. But they only use fragments that "work"—that achieve their desired effect without any possibility of misunderstanding.

How do you know when fragments work? The rules of formal English say that we should not use fragments; there are no guidelines for violating this rule. Writers just develop a sense of when fragments work. Unless you are confident of your sense of when fragments work, it is best to avoid them.

32c
cs/fs

32c Avoiding comma splices and fused sentences

As you learned in 32b, a fragment is an error that occurs when you punctuate as a sentence a group of words that is *less* than a sentence. An equally serious problem, a fused sentence, occurs when you punctuate as a sentence a group of words that is *more* than a sentence, as the following example illustrates.

ACTIVITY

Using exercises of your own or exercises in the HarperCollins Resources for Writers ancillary package, have your class practice correcting several examples of fused sentences and comma splices. If students wonder why avoiding such errors is important, you might offer a highway patrol analogy. If by definition a sentence is a unit of complete thought that must come to an end, a fused sentence is like a head-on collision between two vehicles of thought. A comma splice is, at best, a rolling stop at an intersection. Both violations of sound driving, or writing, can lead to grief.

Independent clause

1. **FUSED SENTENCE:** Chincoteague Island is my idea of a perfect place

Independent clause

for a vacation it has something for everyone.

This example contains two independent clauses that are run together without any punctuation. Such a construction is called a **fused sentence** (also known as a **run-on sentence**) and is a serious error. The following diagram may help you to remember what a fused sentence is.

FUSED SENTENCE: Independent clause ✗ independent clause .

Some writers attempt to correct a fused sentence as follows.

Independent clause

2. **COMMA SPLICE:** Chincoteague Island is my idea of a perfect place

Independent clause

for a vacation, it has something for everyone.

As you can see from example 2, correcting a fused sentence by joining the two independent clauses with a comma creates another error, known as a **comma splice**. A comma splice, like a fused sentence, is a *serious* error.

COMMA SPLICE: Independent clause ✗ independent clause .
                                        ,

To correct fused sentences or comma splices, you have a number of choices (see also 33).

3. Chincoteague Island is my idea of a perfect place for a summer vacation ꟾt it has something for everyone.

Here the writer has corrected the fused sentence by creating two separate sentences, using a period and a capital letter (see option 1 in 33a). Be careful with this approach. If used too often, it results in a choppy, immature style of writing because of an excessive number of short, simple sentences.

32c
cs/fs

4. Chincoteague Island is my idea of a perfect place for a summer vacation ˌˌ*for* it has something for everyone.

   Here the fused sentence was eliminated by adding a comma and the coordinating conjunction *for* (see option 2 in 33a).

5. Chincoteague Island is my idea of a perfect place for a summer vacation ˌ; it has something for everyone.

   This time the writer corrected the fused sentence by using a semicolon (see option 3 in 33b).

6. Chincoteague Island is my idea of a perfect place for a summer vacation ˌ; *indeed,* it has something for everyone.

   Here the writer used a semicolon and a conjunctive adverb (see option 4 in 33c) to correct the fused sentence.

7. Chincoteague Island is my idea of a perfect place for a summer vacation ˌ*because* it has something for everyone.

   The writer corrected the fused sentence by converting the second independent clause into a *dependent* clause (see 20j).

Even writers who never have problems with fused sentences under normal circumstances sometimes have trouble with sentences like the following.

Independent clause

8. **COMMA SPLICE:** "I love to go to Chincoteague," he said, "the restau-

Independent clause

rants there are excellent and inexpensive."

In sentences like 8, don't let the presence of quotations confuse you. Two independent clauses may not be run together without punctuation or joined by just a comma, even if they include quotations. (For further help with punctuating quotations, see 36j).

Failure to understand the role of conjunctive adverbs often leads to comma splices. Refer students to 33c for more about this problem.

32c
cs/fs

COLLABORATIVE ACTIVITY

Students reading essay drafts in groups may be able to help each other spot fragments, comma splices, and run-on sentences. Circulate among the groups, offering suggestions as needed.

Example 8 is corrected as follows.

9. "I love to go to Chincoteague," he said, "*The* the restaurants there are excellent and inexpensive."

33 USING COMMAS AND SEMICOLONS TO PUNCTUATE INDEPENDENT CLAUSES

In this chapter we will consider four options writers have for punctuating sentences with more than one independent clause. The concept of the independent clause is essential to understanding this chapter. If you need to review independent clauses, refer to 20i. Punctuation with smaller units within the sentence is covered in 34.

33a Using commas and coordinating conjunctions to join independent clauses

Writers have four options for punctuating two independent clauses. You're probably already familiar with option 1, to separate the two independent clauses into two sentences by placing a period at the end of the first clause and starting the second one with a capital letter.

OPTION 1: | Independent clause | . | Independent clause | .

A second option for punctuating independent clauses is illustrated by the following example.

1. Lin is moving into the city to be nearer the university, *and* she is looking for a housemate.

   The two independent clauses were originally joined by nothing but a comma, creating the error known as a comma splice (see 32c). The writer revised the sentence so that the two independent clauses are joined by a comma and the coordinating conjunction *and*.

There are only seven coordinating conjunctions in English: and, but, or, for, so, yet, and nor. It may help you to remember these, if you notice that each of them contains two or three letters. Or it may help to remember the fantasy word *fanboys,* which contains the first letter of each of the coordinating conjunctions:

F | or
A | nd
N | or
B | ut
O | r
Y | et
S | o

OPTION 2: | Independent clause | , | and
but
or
for
so
yet
nor | independent clause | .

Option 2, using a comma with a coordinating conjunction to join two independent clauses, is fairly inflexible, as the following example illustrates.

2. Lin rented the apartment, and invited her brother to share it with her.

   Note that in example 2, it is incorrect to use a comma with the co-ordinating conjunction *and* because the second half of the sentence, *invited her brother to share it with her,* is *not* an independent clause. In other words, you *must* use a comma with a coordinating conjunction when it is joining two independent clauses. If a coordinating conjunction is *not* joining two independent clauses, you usually should *not* use a comma.

A second way to correct sentence 2 is as follows.

RESOURCES

Daiker, Donald A., et al., eds. *Sentence Combining: A Rhetorical Perspective.* Carbondale: Southern Illinois UP, 1985.

Meyer, Emily, and Louise Z. Smith. *The Practical Tutor.* New York: Oxford UP, 1987.

Shaughnessy, Mina P. *Errors and Expectations: A Guide for the Teacher of Basic Writing.* New York: Oxford UP, 1977.

Encourage students to memorize the coordinating conjunctions. Knowing these words by heart can help writers recognize compound sentences, use commas correctly, and avoid simple comma splices that result from omitted conjunctions.

33a
,

Though the rule about coordinating conjunctions between independent clauses is fairly inflexible, you might point to an exception: sentences that contain three or more independent clauses. In such a sentence, the clauses are treated as items in a list, and the final clause is joined with a comma (e.g., "We went to the beach, we enjoyed our picnic, and then we went home"). Another exception occurs in short sentences where the clauses are parallel and imply a contrasting or correlative relation (e.g., "The bigger they are, the harder they fall").

               she
3. Lin rented the apartment, and invited her brother to share it.

    This correction, though perfectly acceptable, is somewhat less concise than that illustrated in sentence 2.

Sometimes writers make an exception to the rule when the coordinating conjunction *but* joins the two parts of the sentence:

4. Her brother wanted to share the apartment, but wasn't sure he could afford the rent.

    Even though the second half of the sentence, *wasn't sure he could afford the rent,* is not an independent clause, a comma is permissible before *but* to emphasize that what follows will be in contrast or contradiction to what went before. This exception applies only to the conjunction *but* and is not mandatory; it is perfectly correct to omit the comma before *but.*

For sentences in which there are internal commas within one or both of the independent clauses, another exception is allowed:

5. Each month he had to make a payment on his car loan, his education loan, and his Visa card, so he didn't have much money left for rent.

    In example 5, the comma that normally would be used before *so* to join the two independent clauses has been upgraded to a semicolon because there are commas within the first independent clause. This upgrading is optional; the sentence would also be correct with a comma before *so.*

33b
;

33b Using semicolons to join independent clauses

The following sentence illustrates a third option for joining independent clauses.

1. Michelangelo painted a series of frescoes on the ceiling of the Sistine Chapel in Rome, these frescoes are among his most famous works.

Here the two independent clauses are joined with a semicolon.

OPTION 3: | Independent clause | ; | independent clause | .

Note that a semicolon cannot be used unless the sentence contains *two* independent clauses.

2. **The frescoes depict a series of scenes from the Bible; including**
   scenes of the creation and of the life of Noah.

   The semicolon was incorrect because the second half of the sentence was not an independent clause.

Of course, whenever you use a semicolon in this way, you could use a period and a capital letter instead. Many writers use a semicolon when they want to signal that the next independent clause will be *closely related* to the first one. Of course, every independent clause is somewhat related to the one that comes before it; if it weren't, the passage would not make sense. However, a semicolon indicates that the independent clauses are more closely related than most. Sometimes the second clause *explains* the first one; sometimes it *gives an example* to support it.

3. **The paintings of the creation are the more famous. One of these**
   is among the most famous paintings in the world. It depicts the
   creation of Adam.

   The first two sentences are not closely related, but the second and third are, so they have been joined with a semicolon.

33c **Punctuating sentences with conjunctive adverbs or transitional expressions**

The final option for joining independent clauses is illustrated by the following.

1. **Bird watching is not an expensive hobby, however, you do need to**
   invest in a pair of binoculars.

   You may be wondering why a semicolon rather than a comma is required before *however*. If *but* were used instead of *however*, a comma would be correct.

33c
,/;

Conjunctive adverbs are also discussed in 19g.

2. Bird watching is not an expensive hobby, but you do need to invest in a pair of binoculars.

But is a coordinating conjunction; *however* isn't. Only the seven coordinating conjunctions—*and, but, for, nor, or, so,* and *yet*—can be used with a comma to join independent clauses.

Actually, a period and a capital letter (option 1) could also be used in this case. We chose to use a semicolon, however, because the two sentences are fairly closely related, making option 4 suitable for joining the independent clauses.

ACTIVITY

There is some danger that students will begin using semicolons in front of *however* and other conjunctive adverbs wherever those words appear. To head off that overreaction, you might advise students to carry out the following test with a number of examples: When a conjunctive adverb appears, first look to the left and ask, "Is this an independent clause?" Then look to the right and ask the same question. Only if independent clauses appear on either side of the conjunctive adverb is the semicolon needed; otherwise, only commas may be required. Further discussion of independent clauses appears in 20i. To get students used to punctuating sentences containing conjunctive adverbs, you might use the supplemental exercises in the Harper-Collins Resources for Writers package or develop handout exercises of your own.

33c
;/;

OPTION 4: Independent clause ; { however / therefore / for example / for instance / consequently / in fact / moreover / nevertheless / furthermore / then / indeed / also / as a result / after all / instead / still / in general / subsequently / accordingly } , independent clause .

You may be wondering what *however* is in sentence 1. Note that the word *however* is movable in the sentence; it could be placed in any of the following locations.

3. Bird watching is not an expensive hobby; you do need to invest in a pair of binoculars.

This movability within the sentence is another difference between *however* and *but*. Note that *but* in the following sentence is not movable; it can go in only one place.

but
↓

4. Bird watching is not an expensive hobby, you do need to invest in a pair of binoculars.

Words and phrases that are movable, like *however*, are **conjunctive adverbs.**

    In general, conjunctive adverbs must be set off with commas. If they appear at the beginning of a clause, they are followed by a comma; if they appear at the end of a clause, they are preceded by a comma.

5. Bird watching is not an expensive hobby; however, you do need to invest in a pair of binoculars.
6. Bird watching is not an expensive hobby; you do, however, need to invest in a pair of binoculars.
7. Bird watching is not an expensive hobby; you do need to invest in a pair of binoculars, however.

33c
,*I*;

    The most common conjunctive adverbs are listed in the following chart. The two- and three-word phrases on the list are sometimes called *transitional expressions*, but because the words and phrases are all used in the same way, we will refer to all of them as *conjunctive adverbs*.

    Each conjunctive adverb is used in the same way as *however* in sentence 1:

CONJUNCTIVE ADVERBS

accordingly	for example	in other words	on the other hand
after all	for instance	instead	otherwise
also	further	likewise	similarly
anyway	furthermore	meanwhile	still
as a result	hence	moreover	subsequently
besides	however	nevertheless	then
certainly	in addition	next	thereafter
consequently	incidentally	nonetheless	therefore
even so	indeed	of course	thus
finally	in fact		

8. Songbirds are the most common; therefore, you will probably want to start with them.
9. Sandpipers and plovers are brown shorebirds that must be distinguished by subtle differences in the shape of their bills and the color of their legs; they are, as a result, quite difficult to identify.
10. Hawks and other birds of prey are even more difficult to identify; nevertheless, many birders enjoy attempting to identify them during the fall migration.

Remember that you may *not* use a semicolon unless you are joining two independent clauses. You do not *always* need a semicolon in front of a conjunctive adverb—only when it is joining two independent clauses.

11. Songbirds include a wide variety of species; for example, woodpeckers, swallows, warblers, and flycatchers.

33d **Punctuating compound-complex sentences**

Various combinations of independent and dependent clauses are possible within the same sentence, as the following examples illustrate.

33d

Dependent clause

1. When Ralph Ellison finished his second novel,

Independent clause   Independent clause

he was living in Massachusetts, and his house caught fire.

A dependent clause precedes the first independent clause in sentence 1 and is set off by a comma (see 34a). The two independent clauses are joined by a comma and a coordinating conjunction (option 2), just as if the dependent clause weren't there.

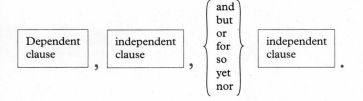

Independent clause   Dependent clause

2. He did not have a second copy because this was before the popu-

Independent clause

larity of personal computers, and he has never rewritten the novel.

Here a dependent clause follows the first independent clause. The comma and coordinating conjunction are still used to join the two independent clauses—as if the dependent clause weren't there.

Optional but
usually omitted

| Independent clause | , | dependent clause | , | { and but or for so yet nor } | independent clause | . |

33d
,

Independent clause   Independent clause

3. Ellison has never written another novel, but his first novel is still

Dependent clause

very popular because it is beautifully written.

In this sentence, a dependent clause follows the second independent clause. Note that the presence of the dependent clause has no effect on the punctuation joining the two independent clauses.

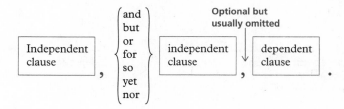

Independent clause

4. The second novel started with a boy being raised out of a coffin,

Dependent clause   Independent clause

and when it reached the final chapter, an old man found a coffin

full of termites.

Here a dependent clause precedes the second independent clause. Note that a comma and a coordinating conjunction are still used to join the two independent clauses, even though a dependent clause appears between them.

33d
,

34 OTHER COMMA RULES

In 33 we discuss how to use commas to join independent clauses. In this chapter we will discuss other uses of commas within the sentence. Commas with quotations are discussed in 36j.

Before beginning, however, we need to discuss a common misconception related to the use of commas. When asked why they put a comma in a particular place, many students respond, "Because I paused there." This is not an illogical answer; after all, commas were invented to represent pauses. However, adding a comma wherever you pause is risky. First, a number of other punctuation marks were also invented to represent pauses: periods, semicolons, colons, and dashes. Putting a comma wherever you pause may mean that you are using a comma when you should be using another punctuation mark. Second, you may pause more or less often than the average person and therefore put in too many or too few commas. So using the pause theory *alone* to decide where to place commas is not a good idea.

However, the pause theory is not completely worthless. It is a good way to locate places where you *may* need a comma. Ask yourself whether any rule requires a comma at that point. If so, put one in; if not, leave the comma out. In this chapter you will learn a series of rules about when a comma is required. When you locate a place in a sentence where you pause, use these rules and the ones in 33 to decide whether or not a comma is needed.

34a Commas with introductory elements

An **element** is any group of words in a sentence: a clause, a phrase, even a single word. Sentence 1 contains two elements.

Independent clause	Dependent clause

1. Angel didn't go to the soccer game | because it was raining.

The first element of the sentence is the independent clause (see 20i); the second is a dependent clause (see 20j). Many sentences in English follow this pattern, but sometimes a writer reverses it:

Students need to be aware that comma placement is a far more complex matter than simply marking pauses in a sentence. Besides the comma splice problem reviewed in 33, important rules concern introductory phrases, adjectival lists, and restrictive and nonrestrictive modifiers, as well as the punctuation of dialogue and the avoidance of unnecessary commas. Getting to know those rules takes practice. Students should anticipate using this chapter for future reference as they make decisions about where commas are needed—or not needed—in their writing.

34a
,

RESOURCES

Chafe, Wallace. "What Is Good Punctuation?" *Quarterly of the National Writing Project and the Center for the Study of Writing* 10.1 (1988): 8–11.

Christensen, Francis. "Restrictive and Nonrestrictive Modifiers Again." *Notes Toward a New Rhetoric: Nine Essays for Teachers.* Ed. Francis Christensen and Bonniejean Christensen. 2nd ed. New York: Harper, 1978. 117–32.

Collignon, Joseph. "Why Leroy Can't Write." *College English* 39 (1978): 852–59.

Meyer, Charles F. "Teaching Punctuation to Advanced Writers." *Journal of Advanced Composition* 6 (1985–86): 117–29.

The articles by Chafe and Meyer consider the relations between punctuation and style. Christensen's analytical chapter analyzes the various ways commas are used with modifiers. Collignon discusses the value of oral reading as a means to improve punctuation.

34a
^
,

Sentence parts that can act as introductory elements are defined in 20.

Dependent clause , Independent clause

2. Because it was raining, Angel did not go to the soccer game.

The dependent clause (see 20j) has been moved to a position in front of the independent clause. This order in a sentence is somewhat less common but perfectly correct.

Any element of the sentence that comes in front of the independent clause is called an **introductory element.** An introductory element is generally set off with a comma in order to alert the reader that something comes before the independent clause.

Dependent clause , Independent clause

3. When I saw my professor, she was having a cup of coffee.

The introductory element is a clause.

Verbal phrase , Independent clause

4. Glancing at her watch, Juanita realized she was late for class.

The introductory element is a verbal, more specifically a participial phrase (see 19c).

Prepositional phrases , Independent clause

5. In the booth next to us, two young men were having a loud argument.

The introductory element in this sentence is a succession of prepositional phrases.

Word , Independent clause

6. Yes, you may have a ride home with us this afternoon.

The introductory element is the single word *yes*.

No matter what the introductory element is—clause, phrase, or word—it is set off with a comma, with the one exception illustrated by sentence 10. The only thing that *can't* be set off as an introductory element is an independent clause, as sentence 7 shows.

Comma splice

Independent clause   **,**   Independent clause

7. Tyrone did well on the midterm exam, he had studied all weekend.

One independent clause appears at the beginning of the sentence and another at the end, with nothing but a comma joining them. Joining two independent clauses with just a comma is a comma splice (see 32c), a serious error.

Independent clause   **, but**   Dependent clause   **,**

8. Lynn wanted to go for a bicycle ride, but when she got her bike out,

Independent clause

its tires were flat.

Sentence 8 has two independent clauses, with the introductory element coming before the second one. Because it is an introductory element, it must be set off by a comma, even though it comes in the second half of a sentence with two independent clauses.

Dependent clause   **and**   Dependent clause **,** Independent clause

9. If you work hard and if you are lucky, you could win this audition.

When you use two introductory elements, place a comma after the second one; the comma indicates the end of all introductory material and the beginning of the independent clause. You do not use a comma before *and* because it is joining *dependent* clauses (see 34k).

Under some circumstances, the comma following an introductory element *may* be omitted.

34a

,

Prepositional phrase   Independent clause

10. In December we had eight inches of snow.

The comma after an introductory phrase *may* be omitted if the phrase is short (three words or less) and there is no danger of misreading. Some writers also omit the comma after short introductory clauses. However, the comma is almost never omitted after conjunctive adverbs, transitional phrases, interjections, or *yes* or *no*.

Participial phrase **,**   Independent clause

11. When studying, Susanna needs complete silence.

> Even though the introductory element is short, the writer needed to add a comma because of the possibility that a reader might misunderstand the sentence. Without the comma, a reader might at first think the writer is talking about "studying Susanna."

Many writers always use commas in sentences like 10 and 11 so that there is no possibility of misreading. The option is yours, but a comma is *always* correct after an introductory element, even a short one.

Not all phrases and clauses at the beginning of the sentence are introductory.

Infinitive phrase   Verb phrase

12. To drive to Kansas City takes about four hours.

> In sentence 12, the phrase is not introductory because what follows it is *not* an independent clause. In fact, *to drive to Kansas City* is the subject of the sentence.

Only *introductory* elements are set off by commas. In sentence 12, a comma would be wrong.

34b Commas with items in a series

The following sentences illustrate how to punctuate a series of words, phrases, or even clauses.

1. Strawberries, blueberries, and plums are in season right now.
2. You can buy them from the supermarket, from a roadside stand, or from a health food store.
3. I eat blueberries for breakfast, I eat strawberries for dessert, and I eat plums as a snack.

These examples illustrate the rules for punctuating items in a series, whether the items joined are words, phrases, or clauses. In general, items in a series are separated with commas. It is optional to omit the final comma, the one before the conjunction, but we recommend that you use it to eliminate any possibility of misreading.

The following diagram may help you remember the basic rule.

It is *always incorrect* to put a comma *after* the final item in a series. A comma after the word *plums* in sentence 4 would be incorrect.

4. Strawberries, blueberries, and plums, are in season right now.

If the items in a series are long or contain internal commas of their own, use semicolons instead of commas to separate them.

5. Recently, some unusual fruits have come on the market, such as kiwi fruit, which originated in New Zealand; papayas, which are grown in Hawaii; and mangoes, which come from Mexico.

34c Commas with restrictive and nonrestrictive clauses, phrases, and appositives

Restrictive and nonrestrictive clauses

The following two sentences are both correct, but they describe different circumstances.

Restrictive

1. Edith's brother who lives in Alaska is getting married.

Edith must have two or more brothers; the clause *who lives in Alaska* serves to clarify which one of these brothers is getting married—the one who lives in Alaska (see 20j for a discussion of dependent clauses).

Nonrestrictive

2. Jane's brother, who lives in Alaska, is getting married.

Jane has only one brother. The clause *who lives in Alaska* merely provides extra information about Jane's brother. It does not identify a particular brother because Jane has only one.

FOR DISCUSSION

On the theory that comma breaks slow down the reader, popular journalism often omits the comma before *and* in such lists. Academic writing, however, typically includes the comma in the interest of precision. You might offer the following example: "While shopping I bought spinach, macaroni and cheese." Ask students whether they envision the macaroni and cheese as separately packaged or already mixed. Then ask this: If a comma were included after *macaroni*, would the impression be different? Academic and technical writing use commas to minimize confusion over the separation of listed items.

34c
,

The clause in sentence 1 is called a **restrictive clause** because it restricts the word it is modifying—in this case *brother*—from all of Edith's brothers to a particular one. In sentence 2, the same clause, *who lives in Alaska,* is **nonrestrictive** because it does *not* restrict the word *brother* to a particular one—Jane has only one brother.

Restrictive

3. Americans who live in Alaska tend to be interested in nature.

In sentence 3, the clause *who live in Alaska* restricts the noun *Americans* from all Americans to only those who live in Alaska.

Nonrestrictive

4. Americans, who have one of the highest standards of living in the world, do not eat the healthiest diet.

Here the clause *who have one of the highest standards of living in the world* does *not* restrict the noun *Americans* to a more limited subgroup. Sentence 4 does *not* say that a subgroup of Americans—those with a high standard of living—do not eat the most healthful diet. It says that *all* Americans have one of the highest standards of living and that *all* of them do not eat a very healthy diet. Because the clause *who have one of the highest standards of living in the world* does not restrict the noun it modifies, *Americans,* to a smaller group, it is a nonrestrictive clause.

Note the commas in sentence 1 through 4. The restrictive clauses (sentences 1 and 3) are *not* set off by commas; the nonrestrictive clauses (sentences 2 and 4) are.

Because restrictive clauses can make a significant difference in the meaning of a sentence, they are considered essential and are therefore *not* set off with commas. The information that nonrestrictive clauses contribute to the meaning of the sentence is less important. In many cases, nonrestrictive clauses can be eliminated without changing the meaning. To indicate the fact that they are not essential to the meaning of the sentence, they are set off with commas.

Restrictive and nonrestrictive phrases

Phrases can also be classified as restrictive or nonrestrictive (see 20d, 20f, 20g, and 20h).

34c

,

Restrictive

5. Spring weather in upstate New York can be unpredictable.

The prepositional phrase (see 20d) *in upstate New York* narrows down the noun *spring weather* from all spring weather in the world to just that in upstate New York. Because it narrows down or restricts the noun it modifies, it is restrictive and is *not* set off with commas.

Nonrestrictive

6. San Francisco, in the middle of an earthquake zone, is the home of the San Francisco Giants.

The prepositional phrase *in the middle of an earthquake zone* does not narrow down or restrict the noun *San Francisco;* in fact, *San Francisco* indicates a specific place, so it is already restricted to one city. Because the phrase is nonrestrictive, it is set off with commas.

Restrictive

7. Women running for political office are often asked about their husbands.

The participial phrase (see 19c) *running for political office* restricts or narrows down the noun *women* from all women to just those running for office. Because it is restrictive, it is *not* set off with commas.

Nonrestrictive

8. My mother, driving home from work, did not notice the protest.

The participial phrase *driving home from work* does not restrict or narrow down the noun phrase *my mother*. Because I have only one mother, the noun phrase cannot be narrowed down any further. Because the participial phrase is nonrestrictive, the writer set it off with commas.

Restrictive and nonrestrictive appositives

The following sentence illustrates what an appositive is.

Appositive

9. My father, the mayor, is running for reelection.

The appositive *the mayor* is a noun; it follows another noun, *father,* and explains or clarifies that first noun (see also 20f).

Appositives also can be either restrictive or nonrestrictive.

Restrictive appositive

10. The movie *Dr. Strangelove* was popular during the 1960s.

The noun *movie* stands for all movies that have ever been produced. It is followed by another noun, *Dr. Strangelove,* which narrows or restricts it to one specific movie. Because the appositive *Dr. Strangelove* restricts the noun it modifies, it is *not* set off with commas.

Nonrestrictive appositive

11. John Barth's first novel, *The Floating Opera,* is set in Maryland.

The phrase *John Barth's first novel* is already restricted to one novel, so the appositive *The Floating Opera* is nonrestrictive and is set off with commas.

PUNCTUATING RESTRICTIVE AND NONRESTRICTIVE CLAUSES AND PHRASES

Type of Element	Function	Punctuation
Restrictive	Narrows down the noun	*Not* set off with commas
Nonrestrictive	Provides additional information but does *not* narrow down the noun	Set off with commas

34d
,

34d **Commas to set off parenthetical expressions, nouns of direct address, *yes* and *no,* interjections, and tag questions**

In this section we will discuss five uses of the comma to set off expressions that are not essential parts of the sentence.

Parenthetical expressions

Parenthetical expression

1. This camera, in my opinion, is overpriced.

   In my opinion is a **parenthetical expression**—a supplementary or explanatory word or phrase inserted in a sentence but not really a part of it. Sometimes parenthetical expressions are actually placed in parentheses (see 37c), which is why they are called parenthetical. Parenthetical expressions, when they are not placed in parentheses, are set off with commas.

Parenthetical expression

2. Cora Lee can come to the party, I suppose.

   Here the parenthetical expression *I suppose* appears at the end of the sentence, so a comma is placed before it, but not after it.

Nouns of direct address

Noun of direct address

3. Jose, do you wish you were back in California?

Noun of direct address

4. With a little luck, Monica, you will be in England in June.

   Each of these sentences contains a noun that is the name of the person being addressed. Nouns used this way are called **nouns (or nominatives) of direct address** and are set off with commas. Note in the next sentence that a noun of address does not have to be the actual name of a person.

Noun of direct address

5. The time has come, fellow bird lovers, to demand restrictions on the cats of America.

   Because the phrase *fellow bird lovers* is used in place of an actual name, it is a noun of direct address and is set off with commas.

34d
,

Yes and *no*

6. Yes, I have gotten better at using commas since I read this book.
7. No, I cannot go to the movies tonight.

When you use *yes* or *no* at the beginning of a sentence, set it off with a comma.

Interjections

Interjections are words or phrases placed at the beginning of a sentence to express surprise or strong emotion (see 19h).

Interjection

8. Well, I suppose I should stay home and study this weekend.

Interjection

9. Oh, I spent about eighty dollars on the party.

Mild interjections like *well* and *oh* should be set off with commas. Stronger interjections, such as the one in sentence 10, are sometimes set off with exclamation points (see 31a).

Interjection

10. Damn! I broke my fingernail.

Tag questions

In English, one way to ask a question is illustrated by the following sentences.

Tag question

11. You were born in Hawaii, weren't you?

Tag question

12. Tony is good at head stands, isn't he?

Tag questions are formed by repeating the verb in the main clause and adding the word *not* (or the contraction *n't*). The verb is then followed by a pronoun that stands for the subject of the sentence. In sentence 11, the pronoun *you* is repeated. In sentence 12, the pronoun *he* stands for *Tony*.

34d

,

When the verb in the main clause is followed by a *not* (or *n't*), *not* is omitted in the tag question.

Tag question

13. You didn't hurt yourself, did you?

Because the verb in the main clause, *didn't*, is already negative, *not* is omitted in the tag question.

34e Commas with coordinate and cumulative adjectives

When two or more adjectives (see 19d) precede a noun, they can be categorized as one of two types: *coordinate* or *cumulative*. The distinction is important because the two types are punctuated differently.

Coordinate adjectives

1. Anneke was carrying a wet, muddy kitten into the kitchen.

   Kitten is being modified separately by the two adjectives *wet* and *muddy*. The sentence asserts that the kitten is *wet* and the kitten is *muddy*. When two or more adjectives modify the same noun in this parallel way, they are coordinate.

Cumulative adjectives

2. The gray, electric blanket was folded up at the end of the bed.

   The word *blanket* is *not* being modified separately by each of the two adjectives, *gray* and *electric*. The writer asserts that the blanket is *electric* and that the *electric blanket* is *gray*. The adjective *gray* modifies the combination of two words—*electric blanket*—and not just *blanket*. Because these adjectives do not modify the noun *blanket* separately, they are cumulative rather than coordinate.

Note the punctuation in sentences 1 and 2. In sentence 1, a comma is correct between the two adjectives; in sentence 2, a comma between the adjectives would be wrong. Even with coordinate adjectives, however, you do *not* use a comma *after* the final adjective.

Students may find cumulative adjectives tricky. You might stress the importance of recognizing whether or not an adjective is necessary to the categorical meaning of the noun phrase (e.g., as in the case of *electric blanket, ice cream, ocean liner,* etc.), in which case commas do not normally precede the adjectives. ESL students might find this problem especially difficult. You might encourage them to keep a list of two-word noun phrases they encounter and to review the order of adjectives explained in 28e.

34e
,

The rule for punctuating two or more adjectives before a noun is this: Use a comma between coordinate adjectives but not after the final one. Do not use a comma between cumulative adjectives.

The distinction between coordinate and cumulative adjectives is subtle. Fortunately, there are two tests to help determine whether adjectives are coordinate or cumulative. First, if the word *and* can be inserted between them, they are coordinate. Second, if their order can be reversed without the sentence sounding odd, they are coordinate. Notice that both of the following revisions to sentence 1 sound fine.

3. Anneke was carrying a wet and muddy kitten into the kitchen.

   Placing *and* between the adjectives does not make the sentence sound strange.

4. Anneke was carrying a muddy, wet kitten into the kitchen.

   The sentence sounds fine even after the order of the adjectives is reversed.

Because we can insert *and* between the adjectives in sentence 1 and we can reverse their order, they have passed the tests for coordinate adjectives. But look at what happens when we apply the same tests to sentence 2.

5. INCORRECT: The gray and electric blanket was folded up at the end of the bed.

6. INCORRECT: The electric gray blanket was folded up at the end of the bed.

   Sentences 5 and 6 sound odd. They don't work as English sentences. Applying the tests for coordinate adjectives shows that the adjectives are cumulative, not coordinate. (For a discussion of the order of adjectives in English, see 28e.)

34f Commas with absolute phrases

Absolute phrases are somewhat unusual but can be quite effective.

Absolute phrases are further discussed in 20h.

34f

,

Absolute phrase

1. Her homework finished, Samona went for a bicycle ride.

   The noun *homework* and the past participle *finished* form an absolute phrase. In this case, the absolute phrase comes at the beginning of the sentence.

An **absolute phrase** consists of a noun and the *-ed* or *-ing* form of a verb (past or present participle) used to modify the whole sentence rather than any specific word in it.

Absolute phrase

2. Samona drove off to Gunpowder State Park, her bicycle firmly mounted on the back of her car.

   Besides the noun *bicycle* and the *-ed* verb *mounted,* the absolute phrase also includes an adverb, *firmly,* and two prepositional phrases, *on the back* and *of her car.* Note also that the absolute phrase is located at the end of the sentence. In fact, absolute phrases can be located just about anywhere in a sentence.

Absolute phrase

3. Her bicycle, its tires pumped up, was ready for an all-day ride.

   Here the absolute phrase occurs in the middle of the sentence. Wherever they occur, absolute phrases are set off with commas.

34g Commas with contrasted elements

A **contrasted element** is a phrase or clause set off from the rest of the sentence and introduced by a negative word such as *not,* *but,* or *unlike.*

Contrasted element

1. Paula, unlike her sister, is a good athlete.

Contrasted element

2. Stan is teaching level three, not level two, on Saturday mornings.

Contrasted elements are set off with commas.

34g
,

34h Commas with quotations

We discuss punctuation with quotations in more detail in 31 and 36, but we will summarize the major rules involving *commas* with quotations here.

1. "Get out of here before I throw you out," said Arnie Becker.

2. I asked Professor Blumenthal for an extension. She replied, "You've known about this deadline since September."

   Phrases like *said Arnie Becker, she replied, he said,* or *Emerson wrote* are separated from the quoted material with a comma.

3. "My mother," said Francine, "does not sound like she is from the South."

   When the explanatory phrase like *said Arnie Becker, she replied, he said,* or *Emerson wrote* appears in the middle of an independent clause, it is set off with commas.

4. "I am going to tell you of Sundiata," said the griot. "ʰᵉ he was great among kings."

   When more than one sentence is quoted and the explanatory phrase follows the first sentence, use a comma to separate the first sentence from the explanatory phrase and put a period after the phrase. Start the next sentence of the quotation with a capital letter.

34i Commas with dates, places, numbers, and personal titles

Dates

The following sentence illustrates the basic rule for punctuating dates.

1. May 15, 1993, was a day I will always remember.

   Use commas between the day and year *and after the year*.

A diagram may help you remember this rule.

· · · 　month　day　**,**　year　**,**　· · ·

The following sentences illustrate several variations on the basic rule for punctuating dates.

2. My grandmother was born on April 30, 1922.

   If the year comes at the end of the sentence, follow it with a period rather than a comma.

3. The warranty on my Plymouth Sundance expired on Monday, March 29, 1993.

   If you use the name of the day of the week before the date, use a comma following it.

4. I was discharged from the army on 30 November 1988.

   If you invert the month and day (as is common in the military and in some businesses), do not use a comma.

5. My loan will be paid off in December 1998.

   When you use the month and year, a comma is not required. We recommend that you not use it.

Places

The following sentence illustrates the basic rule for punctuation with places.

6. Kansas City, Missouri, was the first stop on our tour of the Midwest.

   Use a comma between the city and the state and after the state.

   A diagram may help you remember this rule.

   . . . | city | , | state | , . . .

7. My aunt lives in Birmingham, Alabama.

   Do not use a comma after the state if it appears at the end of a sentence.

FOR DISCUSSION

To summarize comma placement, you might have students look at commas used in a paragraph or two from an assigned reading and explain which rules are being applied.

34i
,

8. Ms. Jennifer Johnson, 11308 South Street, Stockton, CA 95202, was the address on the envelope.

Separate the items in an address by commas when it is written in sentence form. Do *not* use a comma between the state and zip code.

• • • [city] **,** [state] [ZIP] **,** • • •

Of course, use a period after the zip code if it comes at the end of the sentence.

Numbers

The conventions for the use of commas with numbers are illustrated by the following examples.

64,000   10,000,000   398,754,230,819

For numbers of more than four digits, use commas to separate the digits into groups of three, starting from the right.

3,000   3 000

In four-digit numbers, the comma is optional.

Do not use commas, regardless of the number of digits, in telephone numbers, street numbers, zip codes, social security numbers, or years more recent than 10,000 B.C.

Personal

Use commas with titles and degrees, as in the following:

9. Martin Luther King, Jr., was buried in Atlanta, Georgia.
10. Donald L. Hart, Ph.D., will be the next president of the college.

Titles or degrees that follow names are set off with commas.

34j Commas to avoid misreading

Even when no rule requires it, use a comma if it will help the reader avoid misreading.

1. Students who are able to, write their papers on computers.
2. My uncle stormed in, in a seersucker jacket and plaid pants.

34k Unnecessary commas

In general, you should use a comma only when required by one of the rules in 33 or 34. Many errors result from using commas when they are unnecessary.

COLLABORATIVE ACTIVITY

Encourage students to read one another's essay drafts to check for unnecessary commas.

■ Do not use a comma with a coordinating conjunction unless it is joining two independent clauses (see 33a).

1. Sabrina jumped out of bed, and answered the phone.

   Answered the phone is not an independent clause.

2. I found out that I passed the course, and that I got an A on the final exam.

   That I got an A on the final exam is not an independent clause.

■ Do not separate the subject and verb, the verb and its object, or a preposition and its object with a comma unless one is required by a specific rule (see 34a, 20a, 20c, and 20d).

3. Making a list of every idea I have on a topic, is the way I start my papers.

   Making is the subject, and *is* is the verb. No rule requires a comma after *topic*, so it should be removed.

4. I had forgotten, the meeting that I was supposed to attend at nine o'clock.

   Had forgotten is the verb, and *meeting* is its object, so the comma should be removed.

5. We found the phone number in, a leather-bound book hidden under Stacy's bed.

   In is a preposition, and *book* is its object, so the comma separating them should be removed.

6. The top of the dirty, scratched table could not be restored.

   The comma comes between the subject *top* and the verb *could*, but it should not be removed because it is required by the rule for punctuating coordinate adjectives (see 34e).

■ Do not use a comma after a prepositional phrase at the beginning of a sentence with inverted word order (see 20b).

34k
no ,

7. In the back of the closet, was a large box full of old shoes.

No comma is needed after the two prepositional phrases at the beginning of this sentence with inverted word order.

- Do not set off *restrictive* elements with commas (see 34c).

8. The student, who gave me a ride, lives in my neighborhood.

- Do not use commas before the first or after the last item in a series (see 34b).

9. Mr. Lopez gave, a typewriter, a television, and a refrigerator, to the recreation center.

The comma before the first item and the one after the last item in this series are incorrect.

- Do not use a comma before an indirect quotation (see 36i).

10. The manager reminded us, that the store would open at 8:00.

That the store would open at 8:00 is an indirect quotation, so it should not be set off with commas.

- Do not use a comma after a coordinating conjunction (see 33a).

11. We opened the refrigerator and, took out some bottles of wine.

- Do not use a comma after *such as* or *like*.

12. We should order a bunch of unusual flowers such as, alstroemerias and rubrum lilies.

35a
poss

Is the apostrophe really important? George Bernard Shaw didn't think so, having tried to divest English punctuation of what he viewed as an anachronism. Still often regarded as a trivial mark whose misuse can be blamed on typewriters or absent-mindedness, the apostrophe challenges the proofreader's eye. Writers who make flawless use of the apostrophe must owe their skill to an indelible memory of the rules covered in this chapter.

35   FINDING AND REVISING ERRORS WITH APOSTROPHES

35a Forming possessives of nouns

What is a possessive?

The most common use of apostrophes in English is to show possession. Most writers are aware that possessive words show ownership, but many writers are not aware of how many situa-

tions beyond literal ownership are included in the grammatical concept of **possession**. The following sentences illustrate the range of situations that are considered grammatically possessive in the English language.

1. I found Carmella's umbrella under some dirty clothes in the back seat of my car.

   This is the basic possessive situation. That umbrella belongs to Carmella, so the word *Carmella* is possessive. Note that the noun that is doing the owning is possessive, not the noun being possessed; it is *Carmella* and not *umbrella* that is possessive.

2. Jeff's back has not bothered him for the past six months.

   Here the concept of possession is a little different. Jeff does not "own" his back the way Carmella owns her umbrella. Nevertheless, grammatically Jeff possesses his back. It belongs to him in that it is part of him. Thus grammatical possession is not limited to things that are literally owned; it also includes the parts of the body.

3. Corretta's grandmother is coming to visit.

   Although Corretta does not own her grandmother, in a sense the grandmother belongs to her. Family relationship is also considered grammatically possessive.

4. Al's sense of humor makes the office a pleasant place to work.

   Again, Al doesn't own that sense of humor the way Carmella owns her umbrella, but the situation is grammatically possessive. It is possible to say that Al's sense of humor belongs to him, is part of him. People's qualities or characteristics are grammatically possessed by them.

5. Alyce's essay was the best in the class.

   Here what Alyce produced—her essay—is possessed by Alyce. Grammatical possession includes the relationship between a person and a product that person has produced.

6. The university's policy on plagiarism is summarized in the catalog.

   Here an organization, a *university,* possesses its policy.

RESOURCES

Wiener, Harvey S. *The Writing Room: A Resource Book for Teachers of English.* New York: Oxford UP, 1981.

This book contains useful suggestions for teaching students to recognize and properly write possessive nouns (175–80).

You might further illustrate the difference between literal ownership and grammatical possession by drawing examples from nature (e.g., the tree's branches, a bird's wing, the day's weather, etc.).

35a
poss

7. Today's students are likely to hold jobs and may also be parents.
8. One hour's delay will not wreck our plans.

Periods of time can also be possessive. Note that you could also write *a one-hour delay,* but without the article *a,* you must use the possessive. (For more discussion of articles, see 29.)

Choosing between *of* form and possessive form

The following sentences illustrate a general principle in English for choosing between the possessive formed with the preposition *of* and the possessive form using an apostrophe and an *s* (*'s*).

9. The haircut of Lon made him look different. *Lon's haircut*
10. The bowl of my dog has his name on it. *My dog's bowl*
11. The pencil's tip is very sharp. *The tip of the pencil*

In general, when the noun that is possessing something is a human being like *Lon* or an animal like *my dog,* use the apostrophe and *s* to show possession. When the noun that is possessing something is inanimate, like *pencil,* use the preposition *of* to show possession.

Forming possessives

Once you have determined whether a word is possessive or not, your next task is to figure out how to make it possessive—should it end in *'s* or *s'*? The procedure for making this decision is outlined in the chart on the facing page. To illustrate how this procedure works, we will now use it to edit a sentence.

12. **INCORRECT:** Two mens hats were hanging in the cloakroom.

   (1) You note that *mens* is possessive; those hats belong to those men.

   (2) You determine that *mens* is a noun.

   (3) You determine that you are using the word in a plural sense: you are talking about *two* men. You write the *plural* form of the word: *men.*

   (4) You note that the word in its plural form does *not* end in *-s;* it ends in *-n.* Since the plural form does *not* end in *-s,* you add an apostrophe and an *s: men's.*

13. **CORRECTED:** Two men's hats were hanging in the cloakroom.

PROCEDURE FOR FORMING POSSESSIVES WITH NOUNS

1. Ask yourself whether the word in question is possessing anything. Is it in a possessive situation? If not, do not make it possessive.
2. Ask yourself whether the word in question is a noun or an indefinite pronoun. If not, do not use an apostrophe and an *s* to make it possessive. Pronouns other than indefinite pronouns never form their possessives with an apostrophe (see 19b for a discussion of pronouns).
3. Ask yourself if the word is singular or plural. Write the word on scrap paper or in your head in its singular or plural form, as appropriate. Remember that at this point you are *only* making the word singular or plural; do *not* make it possessive until step 4.
4. Form the possessive as follows:
   a. If the word is singular, add an apostrophe and an *s: 's.*
   b. If the word is plural and ends in *s,* add just an apostrophe: *'.*
   c. If the word is plural and ends with a letter other than *s,* add an apostrophe and an *s: 's.*

ACTIVITY
You might use the blackboard to help students practice forming possessives. In one column, write several ordinary nouns (e.g., *accuracy, food, condition,* etc.). Then, to the left, write a column of singular and plural nouns ending in *-s* or *-es* (e.g., *notes, octopus, empress,* etc.). Have students tell you where the apostrophes should be placed to make the left column possessive (e.g., "the notes' accuracy").

This procedure will always work with singular nouns. However, there are a few singular proper nouns for which the possessive *may* be formed by adding just an apostrophe (without the *s*).

Note that we normally pronounce the apostrophe and *s* as an additional syllable: *Doris's* is pronounced *Dor-is-is,* with the final *is* actually pronounced. But for a few proper nouns, we do not pronounce apostrophe and *s* as a separate syllable. *Moses's tablets* is usually pronounced *Moz-es tab-lets,* not *Moz-es-es tab-lets.* Other words of this type include *James, Los Angeles, Texas, Jesus,* and *Euripedes.*

It is *always* correct to add an apostrophe and *s* to a singular word to make it possessive. Some writers, however, add just an apostrophe to words like *Moses* in which the apostrophe and *s* are not usually pronounced as an extra syllable. Whichever way you choose to punctuate these words, be sure you are consistent.

Forming possessives with hyphenated and compound nouns and groups of words that function as single nouns

Occasionally you will need to form the possessive of a hyphenated word (such as *sister-in-law*) or a group of words that function as a unit (such as dean of faculty).

35a
poss

You may wish to stress that writers have the choice of adding either *'s* or the apostrophe alone to short proper (i.e., capitalized) nouns ending in *s*. While it is probably more convenient simply to use the apostrophe, adding *'s* can head off accidents such as "John Keat's [instead of *Keats'* or *Keats's*] poetry."

14. Her sister-in-law's house is on the same block as mine.

15. The dean of faculty's policy is quite clear.

> To form a possessive with a hyphenated word or a group of words that function as a unit, attach the apostrophe and *s* to the final word in the group.

The rule for forming possessives with two or more words joined by *and* or *or* is more complicated.

16. Polly Walker and John Schumaker's business has really taken off.

> Polly and John own the business together, so the apostrophe goes on the last noun only.

17. Polly Walker's and John Schumaker's businesses have really taken off.

> In this case, Polly and John each own a separate business, both of which have taken off. When nouns joined by *and* or *or* are possessive but each of the nouns is doing its possessing separately, you should place an apostrophe and *s* after each noun.

35b
poss

35b Forming possessives with pronouns

Up to this point, we have discussed forming possessives with nouns. In this section, we will discuss forming possessives with pronouns.

1. Carmella has lost ~~she's~~ *her* notebook.

> *She's* is incorrect because *she* is not a noun; it is a pronoun.

The rules for forming possessives that you learned in 35a do not apply to pronouns, with one exception (which we will discuss shortly). Pronouns do not use apostrophes to form possessives. Instead, each pronoun has a slightly different form that indicates that it is possessive. For example, in sentence 1, the possessive form of *she* is *her*.

Possessive forms for pronouns are indicated in the chart on the facing page. Always use these possessive forms for pronouns rather than attempting to add an apostrophe and *s*.

Pronouns that have two possessive forms use these forms as indicated in the following sentences.

2. Min has lost her notebook.
3. That notebook is hers.

You might remind students that possessive pronouns are by definition possessive and therefore don't require added apostrophes.

POSSESSIVE FORMS OF PRONOUNS

Singular		Plural	
I →	my (mine)	we →	our (ours)
you →	your (yours)		
he →	his (his)	they →	their (theirs)
she →	her (hers)		
it →	its (its)	who →	whose

When the possessive pronoun appears before the noun, the first form is used. When the possessive pronoun is a predicate adjective (see 20e), the form in parentheses is used.

The rule that you don't use apostrophes to form possessives of pronouns has one exception.

4. I found someone's wallet behind the bookcase.

Someone is an *indefinite pronoun*. You *do* use an apostrophe and *s* to form the possessive of indefinite pronouns, but only in the case of *indefinite* pronouns. (See 19b.)

35c Apostrophes with contractions

The following sentences show another use of the apostrophe.

1. Nicole should not wear such expensive clothes to work. *shouldn't*
2. We will join you for coffee. *We'll*

In each of these sentences, two words have been joined and, in the process, a letter or two has been left out. The writer used an apostrophe to indicate the omission. Note that the apostrophe goes where the letter or letters were omitted, *not* necessarily where the two words were joined.

35c
,

ESL ADVICE

Non-native speakers should learn that pronoun contractions cannot be used in certain positions (for example, at the end of a clause). "It's my kind of car" is standard, but not "I know what kind of car it's" or "What kind of dinner do we've?"

3. The class of 92 made a large donation to the scholarship fund.

The apostrophe can also indicate that numbers have been omit-ted—in this case the first two digits of the year 1992.

Contractions are common in spoken English and in all but the most formal written English. If you are in doubt about your instructor's or boss's attitudes toward contractions, ask him or her before using them in your writing.

35d Apostrophes with plurals of letters, numbers, signs, abbreviations, and words used as words

A third use of apostrophes is to form the plurals of numbers, signs, and abbreviations. In general, writers use an apostrophe and *s* any time -*s* alone might cause confusion. However, usage of the apostrophe for this purpose varies. The only firm rules are that your usage should avoid confusion or awkwardness and that it should be consistent throughout any single piece of writing. Here we present our *recommendations* and the reasons for them.

1. Ned dotted his *i*'s with little circles.

If an *s* were added without an apostrophe, it would be easy for the reader to read the word as *is* and thus to become confused, so an apostrophe is strongly recommended.

In general, use an apostrophe and *s* to form the plural of *lower-case* letters.

Note that when a letter is used to represent itself as a letter (as opposed to being used as part of a word), it is italicized. If you are writing on a typewriter or by hand, underline the letter to indicate italics. (See 41c.) When an *s* is added to an italicized letter, number, or word to make it plural, the *s* is not italicized.

2. Angela had received *A*'s on all the quizzes.

Because the capital *A* followed by a lower-case *s* is not likely to be read as a word in the middle of a sentence, there is not as much need for an apostrophe as there is with lower-case letters.

To form the plural of capital letters used as letters, add just *s* (without an apostrophe).

3. Gertrude made her 7*s* with little crossbars.

   Because there is no chance of misreading a number and an -*s* as a single word, an apostrophe is not necessary in plurals of numbers.

4. I certainly hope that the economy improves before the end of the 1990*s*.

   As with numbers, it's not necessary to use an apostrophe to form the plural of years.

5. Constance Coyle always used &*s* instead of writing out the word *and*.

   Again, because there is little chance of misreading without the apostrophe, adding just -*s* to form the plural of symbols such as *&* and *$* is recommended.

6. Very few R.N.'*s* work on the night shift at Union Memorial Hospital.

   Because a simple *s* following the punctuation mark looks awkward, use an apostrophe and *s* to form plurals of abbreviations ending with a period. (For a discussion of capitalization and periods with abbreviations, see 39.)

7. Two BMW*s* were parked in front of Nancy Percovich's house.

   We recommend adding just -*s* to form the plural of upper-case abbreviations that do not end with a period—the result will be neither awkward nor confusing.

8. Professor Schwartz's collection of lp'*s* from the 1950s was destroyed in the fire.

   Because a simple -*s* added after an abbreviation spelled with lower-case letters might be misread (the -*s* in *lps* could easily be read as part of the abbreviation), use an apostrophe and *s* to form the plural of lower-case abbreviations.

It is not uncommon for students with severe writing problems to be in the habit of adding apostrophes to ordinary plurals (e.g., "There were two book's on the table"). For the benefit of those students as well as others, you might emphasize that the use of apostrophes to form plurals occurs only in the limited circumstances reviewed here, that even in these circumstances it is a rare and possibly dying convention, and that in general the apostrophe mark should be used only for showing possession or contraction.

35d
,

9. The opening paragraph of Donna's essay contained five *conse-*
   quently's.

   A simple -*s* used to form the plural of a word used as the word itself could be easily misinterpreted, making the word hard to read.
   Use an apostrophe and *s* to form the plural of words when they are
   used to represent themselves. A word used to represent itself is italicized. (See 41c.)

35e Common errors with apostrophes
Confusion of contractions and possessives

It is important to remember that apostrophes are not used
to indicate possession with pronouns (except for indefinite pronouns). Apostrophes are, however, used with pronouns to form
contractions.

1. My dog was chasing it's tail.   *[its]*

   It's was wrong because this is a possessive situation—the tail belongs to it (the dog)—and apostrophes are not used to show possession with pronouns.

2. My dog thinks its time for dinner.   *[it's]*

   Here *its* is wrong because *its* is the possessive, but this is *not* a possessive situation—the time does *not* belong to it (the dog). *It's*—the
   contraction formed from *it is*—is the correct form.

This confusion between possessives and contractions
formed with pronouns causes headaches for many writers, and
its and *it's* is not the only problem pair. Almost as troublesome
are *your* and *you're, their* and *they're,* and *whose* and *who's.*

Many writers find it helpful to remember that contractions
actually stand for two words. If they say the sentence to themselves with the two contracted words spelled out in full, they can
usually hear whether they've got the correct form or not. For example, consider the following sentence.

your

3. I have not mailed you're package.

The writer wasn't sure whether she needed *your* or *you're*, so she said the sentence to herself with the contraction *you're* split into the two words that make it up: *I have not mailed you are package.* As soon as she said it, she knew that the sentence made no sense, so she changed the word to the possessive form, *your.* As a check, she asked herself whether this is a possessive situation: are we talking about a package that belongs to *you?* The answer was yes, so she knew in two different ways that the form she wanted was *your.*

who's

4. I have an aunt whose running for Congress.

Here the writer tried splitting the contraction form *who's* into its two parts: *I have an aunt who is running for Congress.* Since the sentence sounded fine, the writer knew the form he wanted was *who's,* the contraction for *who is.*

Using apostrophes with plural nouns that are not possessive

Once writers start thinking about apostrophes, sometimes a new problem crops up: they overuse them. If you have this problem, it probably means that you are using apostrophes with most nouns that end in -*s. Possessive* nouns do need an apostrophe, but many nouns that end in -*s* are not possessive; they are simply plural. Consider the following.

boats

5. Three boat's were wrecked by the storm.

Here the word *boats* is not possessive; nothing belongs to those boats. So there is no need for an apostrophe. The *s* on the end of *boat* is there because the word is plural, not possessive.

After reading this chapter, do not become so focused on apostrophes that you start using them with words that have no need for them.

35e
'

COLLABORATIVE ACTIVITY

Have members of editing groups check one another's drafts for errors involving apostrophes.

Because correct use of quotation marks is tied to the serious issue of plagiarism, students need to pay very careful attention to the rules covered in 36. Encourage anyone who has trouble understanding or following these rules to check with you immediately.

ACTIVITY

In order to clarify for students the difference between direct and indirect quotations, you might perform the following exercise. Write a direct quote on the board (e.g., *"It is important," she said*), calling attention to the positions of quotation marks and other punctuation. Then rewrite the sentence as an indirect quotation (e.g., *She said that it was important*), calling attention to the use of *that* and to any tense changes that occur. Have students imitate the same procedure with a different statement (e.g., *I know just what you mean*). Ask a volunteer to write the resulting direct and indirect quotes on the board. (*I know just what you mean, she said. She said that she knew just what I meant.*) Make corrections as needed.

36b
quote

36 QUOTATION MARKS

Quotation marks are used to indicate words spoken or written by someone other than the writer or written by the writer at another time. They can also be used to mark titles, words used in a special sense, and definitions.

36a Direct quotations

The following examples illustrate how quotation marks are used to indicate **direct quotations**. (For information on how to document quotations, see 46.)

1. Tran Thi Nga wrote to her mother in Vietnam, "Here we are materially well off, but spiritually deprived."

   Quotation marks indicate where the exact words of the person being quoted begin and end. When using quotation marks, be careful to ensure that the words of the original are reproduced exactly, including spelling, capitalization, and interior punctuation.

2. "To be equal to men," writes Marilyn French, "does not mean to be like them."

   Here the quoted material is split into two parts by the phrase *writes Marilyn French*. Quotation marks are used to mark the beginning and end of each section of quoted material.

36b Quoting longer passages and poetry

Quotations of longer passages (more than four lines) and of poetry are indicated by the conventions discussed in this section rather than by quotation marks.

Quoting longer passages

Quotation marks are used for passages that are relatively short—that can be written in four lines or less. Example 1 shows how to quote longer passages.

Sylvia Plath opens her novel, The Bell Jar, with her
narrator's thoughts about the execution of the
Rosenbergs:

> It was a queer, sultry summer, the summer
>
> they electrocuted the Rosenbergs, and
>
> I didn't know what I was doing in New
>
> York. I'm stupid about executions. The
>
> idea of being electrocuted makes me sick,
>
> and that's all there was to read about
>
> in the papers—goggle-eyed headlines staring
>
> up at me on every street corner
>
> and at the fusty, peanut-smelling mouth
>
> of every subway. It had nothing to do
>
> with me, but I couldn't help wondering
>
> what it would be like, being burned alive
>
> along your nerves. (1)

Because the quoted material is more than four lines long, it is not
put in quotation marks. Instead, the quotation is set off by double-
spacing and indenting ten spaces from the left margin if you are following MLA style (see 46d). Indent five spaces if you are following
APA style (see 46e). If you want to emphasize a passage of fewer
than four lines, set it off in this same manner.

If the quoted material is more than one paragraph long, indent the first line of each paragraph an additional three spaces.
If the material is more than one paragraph but the first section is
not a complete paragraph, indent the first line of the first paragraph ten spaces; indent the first line of succeeding paragraphs
an additional three spaces.

RESOURCES

Gibaldi, Joseph, and Walter S.
Achtert. *MLA Handbook for
Writers of Research Papers.* 3rd
ed. New York: Modern Lan-
guage Association, 1988.

*This manual includes rules for the use
of quotation marks with direct quotes,
titles, etc., as well as many models of
MLA documentation procedure.*

36b
quote

Quoting poetry

The following example illustrates the punctuation of *short* passages of poetry.

```
When Robert Frost wrote the lines, "The woods are
lovely, dark and deep, / But I have promises to
keep," I think he was explaining why he would not
consider suicide.
```

> —Robert Frost, "Stopping by Woods
> on a Snowy Evening"

Up to three lines of poetry may be quoted this way, within the existing text, with a slash (/) separating the lines. Leave a space before and after the slash.

Longer quotations from poems are handled in the following manner.

```
In "Ode on a Grecian Urn," John Keats writes the
following:
```

```
            When old age shall this generation waste,
                Thou shalt remain, in midst of other woe
            Than ours, a friend to man, to whom thou
                say'st,
        "Beauty is truth, truth beauty,"—that is all
            Ye know on earth, and all ye need to know.
```

You should indent poetry of more than three lines ten spaces from the left margin and double-space it. Do not use quotation marks unless they appear in the original. In addition, you should attempt,

FOR DISCUSSION

Warn students that the block indenting of quotes is a risky though legitimate procedure. It must be done exactly according to the rules if they wish to avoid the impression of plagiarism. Stress that quotation marks may be omitted *only* if the entire passage is clearly indented from normal paragraph margins. If any portion of the passage without quotation marks is extended to the same left-hand width as standard paragraphs in the paper, the result will be an instance of plagiarism. Another difficulty students often have is with the accuracy of the quotation itself. Warn students that it is harder than it seems to copy a passage word for word and punctuation mark for punctuation mark. Quotations of any length deserve careful proofreading. Refer students to 45f for more about handling quotations in research.

to the extent possible, to reproduce the look of the poem on the page; notice, in the excerpt on page 380, that the first, third, and fifth lines are indented an extra three spaces (as they are in the original). Notice also that the second line is indented an extra six spaces (again, as in the original).

36c **Using quotation marks with dialogue**

The following conversation between Sid and Sam illustrates how dialogue (the representation of conversation between two or more people) should be handled.

> "I told you I don't have any advice." He poured coffee for both of them. "Do me a favor, Sam. Whatever happens between your Mom and me, or between your Mom and Dad, stick with me. Will you? Like a brother—I haven't got a brother."
>
> "Sure. But that's a funny idea."
>
> They looked into each other's eyes, maybe for the first time. The intimacy was a shock and a joy.
>
> Sid told him, "Your Mom's coming back."
>
> "She was terrible yesterday. Really out of control."
>
> "She'll be okay. I really think so."
>
> "I guess. He hit her. He hit me a couple of times last week. He doesn't mean it. He's okay. I feel lousy for him."
>
> "You love your father."
>
> "I guess so."
>
> "It's all right," Sid said. "I guess so do I. Love my father, I mean. I think you're allowed to."
>
> —John Jacob Clayton, *What Are Friends For?*

In dialogue, place the words of each speaker in quotation marks and start a new paragraph each time the speaker changes. This makes it unnecessary to use a phrase like "he said" each time the speaker changes. Place text that is not spoken by either character right in the paragraphs along with the spoken text, but use no quotation marks with it. (See the first paragraph in the example above.)

36c
" "

36d Using a quotation within a quotation

The following example illustrates how to punctuate a quotation that occurs within a larger quotation.

> In his book *Working,* Studs Terkel describes Dolores Dante, a waitress whose "pride in her skills helps her make it through the night. 'When I put the plate down, you don't hear a sound.' "

When a quotation occurs within a quotation (in this case, the words of Dolores Dante within the words of Studs Terkel), the inner quotation is set off with single quotation marks rather than double. Use the apostrophe key for single quotation marks on a typewriter or computer. At the end of the quotation, the writer has used both a single and a double quotation mark. The single quotation mark shows the end of the quotation from Dante; the double marks are for the end of the quotation from Terkel. (See 36j for a discussion of periods with quotation marks.)

36e Using quotation marks with titles of short works

1. I've just finished reading "O Yes" by Tillie Olsen.

   The title of the short story "O Yes" is set off with quotation marks. Note that no commas are used with these quotation marks. Short works are pieces that are included in books, journals, or newspapers or are of such length that they could be included in a book. Examples of short works are short stories, most poems, one-act plays, chapters, articles, essays, songs, and episodes of radio and television programs.

2. Larzer Ziff's article "The Ethical Dimensions of 'The Custom House' " argues that Hawthorne was dissatisfied with his novel *The Scarlet Letter.*

   The writer of sentence 2 has placed the title of Ziff's article in quotation marks and the title of the Hawthorne short story "The Custom House," which is a part of the larger title, in single quotation marks.

Titles of longer works are italicized (or underlined if you do not have access to italics). Longer works include books, plays, newspapers, magazines, journals, book-length poems, films, television or radio programs, paintings, and sculpture. (See 41a.)

36e
" "

36f Using quotation marks with words used as words

Words used as words are illustrated by the following sentence, written two ways.

1. Professor Chavez used *hegemony* fourteen times in her speech.
2. Professor Chavez used "hegemony" fourteen times in her speech.

> The word *hegemony* in both sentences is being used to stand for the word itself, not for the concept of domination, which is its meaning. This is what we mean by the phrase "a word used as a word."

Most commonly, words used as words are italicized (as in sentence 1 and in this handbook), but it is also correct to place them in quotation marks (as in sentence 2). Whichever style you choose, be consistent within a single piece of writing.

36g Using quotation marks with words used ironically

> Alvin's "limousine" was actually a Volkswagen Rabbit.

> In this sentence, the word *limousine* is being used ironically. It doesn't stand for what it usually represents—a large, luxurious car—but instead stands for something almost the opposite: a small, economical car. You may indicate that words are being used ironically by setting them off with quotation marks.

Warn students not to overdo the use of quotation marks for irony. Sometimes readers misinterpret the ironic use of quotation marks as indicating a quoted source. In general, the marks are best reserved for direct quotations and for titles of short written works.

36h Using quotation marks with definitions

> Ms. Lewis is using *affect* to mean "a feeling or emotion."

> Definitions of words may be set off with quotation marks.

36i Misuses of quotation marks

Do not overuse quotation marks.

1. My "brother" convinced me to "help" him with his homework.

> If the person being talked about in sentence 1 actually *is* the brother of the writer and if what he asked for was indeed help, there is no reason to put either word in quotation marks.

36i
no " "

Sometimes writers who learn about quotation marks start putting words in quotation marks when there is no reason to do so. Such excess should of course be avoided.

2.   "Light and Dark Imagery in Hawthorne's Fiction"

This second example represents the title of a work as written on the title page or at the top of the first page of an essay (see 46g). The quotation marks are a mistake. Do not use quotation marks with your own title at the beginning of your paper.

                                    stop where we were
3. About midnight we decided to "hunker down" and wait for day-

break.

Hunker down is slang, meaning "to stop where you are and abandon efforts to make progress." If slang is appropriate for the piece of writing in which sentence 3 appears, there is no reason to put quotation marks around *hunker down*. If slang is not appropriate, putting quotation marks around the expression doesn't make it appropriate; instead, the writer should revise to eliminate the slang.

4. Jason said "he would not be able to join us for the trip to

Reading."

"He would not be able to join us for the trip to Reading" is an indirect quotation. These are *not* the exact words Jason said. (He probably said something like, "*I* will not be able to join *you* for the trip to Reading.") Do not use quotation marks to set off *indirect* quotations.

36j Other punctuation with quotation marks

Periods

1. My aunt said, "I believe that Malcolm X was a great leader."

Periods go *inside* quotation marks in American English. In other parts of the world, the convention may be different.

36j

" "

Students may occasionally encounter British or other foreign works in which periods do fall outside quote marks, but the practice is uncommon in American publishing except when a parenthetical citation follows the quote and the quote is not block indented. Advise students also to read 42b for more about how ellipses, periods, and parenthetical citations are used according to MLA guidelines.

2. It is clear, as Michael Millgate points out,
   that "the doom of the Compson family seems
   about to be finally accomplished" (107).

The only time that periods do not go inside quotation marks is when you use parenthetical documentation for a quotation within the text. In these cases, the period goes after the parenthetical documentation. (See 46d, 46e, and 46f for a discussion of parenthetical documentation.)

Commas

3. "I would like a cup of coffee," said Mr. Chang.

Place commas *inside* quotation marks.

Colons and semicolons

4. The letter from the Department of Motor Vehicles said, "You owe a total of $129 for overdue fines"; I've never gotten a ticket in my life, so I know there is some mistake.

Place colons and semicolons *outside* quotation marks.

Question marks, exclamation points, and dashes

5. Nan asked, "What did you get on the test?"
6. Was it Joan who said, "I don't care about grades"?

Place question marks inside the quotation marks when the quoted words are a question (sentence 5); place them outside the quotation marks when the whole sentence is a question (sentence 6).

7. When the couch fell on her foot, Corretta shouted one word: "Damn!"
8. I will never use the words "I give up"!

Place exclamation points inside quotation marks when they apply to the quoted material (sentence 7) and outside if they apply to the whole sentence (sentence 8).

36j
" "

9. "I will not open my—" began Mitchell, until Carlos's look silenced him.
10. Peter said to the teacher, "I missed the final because my grandmother died"—the oldest excuse in the book.

Place dashes inside the quotation marks if they belong to the quoted material (sentence 9); otherwise, place them outside (sentence 10).

This chapter examines punctuation marks that students sometimes find mysterious: the colon, ellipses, parentheses, brackets, dashes, and slashes. Encourage your class to study how these marks can bring precision and variety to a writer's prose style.

RESOURCES

Meyer, Emily, and Louise Z. Smith. *The Practical Tutor.* New York: Oxford UP, 1987.

Shaughnessy, Mina P. *Errors and Expectations: A Guide for the Teacher of Basic Writing.* New York: Oxford UP, 1977.

Winterowd, W. Ross. "The Grammar of Coherence." *College English* 31 (1970): 828–35.

See Meyer's book for suggestions on teaching punctuation (177–201), including reading aloud, asking analytical questions, and using unpunctuated sentences as models. Shaughnessy discusses how unfamiliarity with punctuation limits the development of writers (14–43). Winterowd's article reveals the importance of the colon in establishing inclusive relations within sentences.

37a
:

37 OTHER PUNCTUATION MARKS

37a Colons

When to use a colon

1. Two issues mark her campaign: employment and health care.

In this sentence, the independent clause specifies two issues; these issues are then *named* following the colon.

One use for a colon is to introduce specific instances or examples of general ideas mentioned in the independent clause preceding the colon. Often the number of examples is specified in the independent clause preceding the colon.

2. I could never live in a big city: I grew up on a farm.

The material following the colon explains or gives a reason for the fact stated in the first independent clause.

3. The museum will be exhibiting one of the world's most famous paintings: van Gogh's *Starry Night.*

The material following the colon is an appositive phrase (see 20f), a noun phrase that restates or renames a noun phrase in the independent clause. In this case, *van Gogh's Starry Night* renames (and clarifies) the noun phrase *one of the world's most famous paintings.*

4. At times like these, we should remember the words of Winston Churchill: "We have nothing to fear but fear itself."

A colon may be used to introduce a quotation.

5. When Rafael heard the phone ring, he; turned off the television, turned off the dishwasher, and picked up the phone.

Use a colon only if it is preceded by an independent clause. In this example, *When Rafael heard the phone ring, he* is not an independent clause, so the colon was incorrect.

From these examples you can see that a colon can be used only after an independent clause. It indicates a break between two grammatical elements greater than that marked by a semicolon but less than that indicated by a period. A colon is a fairly formal punctuation mark that points to the second element as an illustration or amplification of the initial independent clause.

What can follow a colon

6. There was one explanation for her success: luck.
7. Max was hiding in the one place we never thought to look: under his bed.
8. My collection included three kinds of recipes: salads, appetizers, and desserts.
9. You should remember what Thoreau said about being in jail: "Under a government which imprisons any unjustly, the true place for a just man is also in prison."
10. The teacher did the only thing he could under the circumstances: he dismissed the class.

These five examples demonstrate that a colon is used *following an independent clause* to introduce other material. The other material may be a word (as in sentence 6), a phrase (as in sentence 7), a list (as in sentence 8), a quotation (as in sentence 9), or an independent clause (as in sentence 10). For the rule regarding capitalization following a colon, see 38a.

Unnecessary colons

15. The two aspects of yoga we teach are: prāṇāyāma and āsana.

16. We saw lots of birds, for example: indigo buntings, northern orioles, and scarlet tanagers.

Sentences 15 and 16 contained a common error: they used a colon following a group of words that is not an independent clause. For example, before it was corrected, sentence 15 read "The two forms

You might stress the difference between the colon, which introduces material, and the semicolon, which separates material. The use of the semicolon between clauses is explained in 33b–c.

37a
:

of yoga we teach are:" which is incorrect because the group of words preceding the colon is not an independent clause. A comma is needed in sentence 16 because *for example* is a conjunctive adverb (see 33c).

There are two ways to correct this error. In sentences 15 and 16, we corrected it by removing the colon. It would also be correct to revise the first half of each sentence so that it *is* an independent clause:

17. ~~The~~ two aspects of yoga We teach ~~we teach are:~~ prāṇāyāma and āsana.

18. We saw lots of birds, ~~for example:~~ indigo buntings, northern orioles, and scarlet tanagers.

Colons with *the following* and *as follows*

19. You should bring the following: a pen, a pad, and a dictionary.
20. The ingredients are as follows: corn, flour, salt, and milk.

A colon is required after *the following* and *as follows* when they introduce a list.

Other uses of the colon

The colon is often used in special situations to separate elements.

21. The train arrived at 6:38 P.M.

Use a colon to separate hour and minutes in clock time.

22. Dear Mr. Vasquez:

Use a colon after the salutation of a business letter.

23. The text for my psychology course is *Understanding Human Behavior: An Introduction to Behavioral Psychology.*

On title pages of published books, titles—in this case *Understanding Human Behavior*—are usually on one line, with subtitles—in this case *An Introduction to Behavioral Psychology*—on the line below, perhaps in a different typeface or in smaller type. When the com-

37a

:

plete title and subtitle are referred to elsewhere, however, a subtitle is separated from the title by a colon.

24. The ratio of water to salt is 10:1 in this solution.

Use a colon to separate the two terms or numbers in a ratio or proportion.

25. We preferred the version of creation in Genesis 1:27 to that in Genesis 2:22.
26. We preferred the version of creation in Genesis 1.27 to that in Genesis 2.22.

Traditionally, writers have used a colon to separate the chapter number from the verse in references to the Bible and other holy books, as in sentence 25. However, the Modern Language Association's *MLA Style Manual* and the *Chicago Manual of Style* now recommend using a period rather than a colon, as in sentence 26.

37b Ellipses

Ellipses to show omissions in quotations

An **ellipsis** is a series of three periods separated by spaces used to indicate that some material has been left out of a direct quotation. The plural of *ellipsis* is *ellipses*. To make an ellipsis, you first press the space bar, then type a period, then the space bar again, then another period, then the space bar once more, then a third period, and finally the space bar.

A quote from Annie Dillard's *Pilgrim at Tinker Creek* will illustrate the use of ellipses. The original passage appeared as follows:

> When I was six or seven years old, growing up in Pittsburgh, I used to take a precious penny of my own and hide it for someone else to find. It was a curious compulsion; sadly, I've never been seized by it since. For some reason I always "hid" the penny along the same stretch of sidewalk up the street. I would cradle it at the roots of a sycamore, say, or in a hole left by a chipped-off piece of sidewalk. Then I would

37b
• • •

take a piece of chalk, and, starting at either end of the block, draw huge arrows leading up to the penny from both directions. After I learned to write I labeled the arrows: SURPRISE AHEAD or MONEY THIS WAY. I was greatly excited, during all this arrow-drawing, at the thought of the first lucky passer-by who would receive in this way, regardless of merit, a free gift from the universe. But I never lurked about. I would go straight home and not give the matter another thought, until, some months later, I would be gripped again by the impulse to hide another penny.

Sentence 1 shows the basic method of quoting and omitting a section from the original.

1. Annie Dillard tells about hiding a penny along the sidewalk near her home in Pittsburgh. "Then I would take a piece of chalk, and . . . draw huge arrows leading up to the penny from both directions."

The writer of this sentence has omitted the phrase *starting at either end of the block* from the original and has indicated this omission by inserting an ellipsis.

2. After hiding her penny, Dillard reports that she never waited to see who would find it, but "would go straight home and not give the matter another thought. . . ."

Here the writer has quoted a section with an omission at the beginning and at the end. Note that an ellipsis is not used to indicate omitted material at the beginning of a quotation. Note also that the omission at the end coincides with the end of the writer's sentence. A period (*not* preceded by a space) indicates the end of the sentence and is placed immediately after the final word; this period is followed by a traditional ellipsis (three spaced periods).

3. Telling about her childhood prank of hiding a penny and then marking the path to it with arrows, the author observes that she "was greatly excited, during all this arrow-drawing . . ." (Dillard 14).

The end of the quotation coincides with the end of the writer's sentence, but the presence of a citation (*Dillard 14* in parentheses; see

37b
. . .

46c) requires that the final period be placed after the citation. Note that no space follows the final period of the three spaced periods making up the ellipsis.

4. Annie Dillard tells a story about a curious activity she engaged in when she was a child. "When I was six or seven years old, growing up in Pittsburgh, I used to take a precious penny of my own and hide it for someone else to find. . . . For some reason I always 'hid' the penny along the same stretch of sidewalk up the street."

In this sentence, a period and ellipsis are used because a complete sentence has been omitted.

5. INCORRECT: "I would go straight home and . . . would be gripped again by the impulse to hide another penny."

Sentence 5 is *not* a legitimate use of ellipsis because even though it reproduces the original words accurately and indicates where words have been omitted, it distorts the meaning of the original passage. In this case, the quoted passage implies that Annie would go home and immediately be gripped by the desire to hide another penny. In fact, the original passage indicated that months would pass before she would again feel such a compulsion. Distorting the original author's meaning through the use of ellipses is unethical.

Omissions of lines of poetry

In quoted poetry of more than three lines, a full line of spaced periods is used to indicate the omission of one or more lines of the original poem.

6. Let me not to the marriage of true minds
   Admit impediments. Love is not love
   Which alters when it alteration finds,
   Or bends with the remover to remove.
   . . . .
   Love alters not with his brief hours and weeks,
   But bears it out even to the edge of doom.
      If this be error, and upon me proved,
      I never writ, nor no man ever loved.

   —Shakespeare, Sonnet 116

The dotted line indicates that one or more lines of poetry have been omitted.

37b
· · ·

Because ellipsis points may also indicate a deliberate omission of words from a quotation, some writers prefer to use a dash for signifying discontinued speech (e.g., "Yes, but—").

You might warn students that excessive use of parentheses can make a writer's prose style look choppy. As demonstrated in 34d and 37e, students have the option of using commas or dashes instead. Many academic writers reserve parentheses for use in situations illustrated by examples 2–6.

37c
( )

Ellipses to indicate interrupted speech

An ellipsis may be used to indicate hesitation or an interruption in the words of a speaker or writer or to suggest speech or writing left unfinished.

7. I wonder what would happen . . .

The ellipsis indicates that the speaker's voice trails off without finishing the sentence.

37c Parentheses

1. Mayor Schmidt (now in his third term) announced a 20 percent budget cut.

    Parentheses are used to set off information that is supplementary to the main idea of the sentence. In sentence 1, the fact that the mayor is in his third term is not essential to the main idea—that he has announced a budget reduction. Material in parentheses could be omitted without serious loss to the sentence. It is included parenthetically, however, because it may be of interest to the reader.

2. The Modern Language Association (MLA) publishes a guide to research and documentation.

    An acronym is an abbreviation, usually written with capital letters and without periods. If you are going to use an acronym throughout a piece of writing, introduce the reader to it, as the writer of sentence 2 has, by first using the spelled-out name and including the acronym in parentheses. Thereafter, you can use the acronym alone to refer to the organization.

3. The interest on this debt amounts to six thousand four hundred dollars ($6,400) per year.

    In some business writing, it is common to spell out amounts of money and then to indicate the same amount parenthetically in numbers.

4. The causes of the accident were (1) excessive speed, (2) faulty brakes, and (3) foggy conditions.

    When presenting a numbered or lettered list within a sentence, it is conventional to place the numbers or letters in parentheses.

5. My mother never learned how to drive an automobile. (She grew up in rural China.) She did, however, get her pilot's license in 1972.

When an entire sentence is used parenthetically, begin the sentence with a capital letter and end it with a period. Do not place an entire sentence parenthetically inside another sentence.

6. Wagenknecht observes that Hawthorne was "a solitary, introspective man" (5).

—Edward Wagenknecht, *Nathaniel Hawthorne: The Man, His Tales and Romances*

Use parentheses to set off citations indicating the sources of quotations and paraphrases in your writing. (For discussion of parenthetical documentation, see 46c.)

37d Brackets

1. John Dean reports that "within a month of coming to the White House, [he] had crossed an ethical line."

—John Dean, *Blind Ambition*

Use **brackets** to indicate places within direct quotations where the writer has inserted material or made minor changes in the wording. In the original text quoted in sentence 1, John Dean wrote, "I had crossed an ethical line." The writer using this quotation placed *he* in brackets to indicate that it has been changed from the original word, *I*. Many writers prefer to avoid such changes.

2. I had to meet with a representative of the neighborhood organization (a man who was rumored to work for the Central Intelligence Agency [CIA] and whom I had avoided for years).

Normally, the acronym CIA would be placed in parentheses. In sentence 2, however, it is placed in brackets because it appears within a larger element already in parentheses.

If words that would normally be placed in parentheses should occur within a larger element that is already in parentheses, change the parentheses around the inner element to brackets.

You might stress the practical difference between brackets and parentheses. To careful readers, especially those who study research papers, whatever is enclosed by parentheses appearing within a quotation is understood to have been written by the quoted author, whereas brackets indicate an interpolation by the writer who did the quoting.

37d
[ ]

You might point out that dashes are preferable to commas or parentheses in circumstances where commas intervene within an interrupter. To illustrate, you could put the following example on the board: "Three members of the club — Betty, Jack, and Leslie — showed up for the meeting." Students should realize that using commas instead of dashes after the words *club* and *Leslie* might confuse the reader as to how many people (three or six?) attended the meeting. Dashes, on the other hand, make the meaning clear.

37e Dashes

A **dash**—more precisely, an *em dash* (because it is the width of the letter *M*)—is not the same as a hyphen. It is longer than a hyphen. On a typewriter, use two hyphens to represent a dash. In most word processing programs there is a key combination that will produce a true dash. Do not place spaces at either end of a dash.

1. The president—with only three weeks remaining in his term—should not appoint a new Supreme Court justice.

   Dashes are used here to set off parenthetical information because the writer wants to emphasize that information. Use dashes to set off parenthetical information that you want to emphasize.

Supplemental material, asides, and minor digressions can be set off with commas, parentheses, or dashes. Dashes give the material the most emphasis, indicating that it is important. Commas give less emphasis, and parentheses give even less, indicating that the material can be skipped if the reader is in a hurry.

2. Frank returned slowly to the study—a room he had added to the house only three years earlier.

   The dash here indicates a break in the sentence, a discontinuity of thought.

Don't confuse a dash with a hyphen; a hyphen is an entirely different mark of punctuation. It is about half the length of a dash. The hyphen is used to join words or to break words. Details of its use are discussed in 42.

37f Slashes

A **slash**—also called a *virgule* or a *solidus*—is useful for separating certain specific kinds of expressions in English.

1. Emily Dickinson's self-effacing style can be seen in her lines, "I'm nobody. Who are you? / Are you nobody too?"

   The slash is used to separate lines of poetry when they are run into the text instead of set off from it. Add a space before and after the slash. (See 36b for more discussion of quoting poetry.)

2. An error of 1/32 of a millimeter can make the tool inoperable.

   The slash is also used to form fractions.

3. The memo was dated 3/12/93.

   In informal or brief communications, slashes are sometimes used in abbreviating dates.

4. Your mother and/or your father may also attend the banquet.

   Two words may be joined by a slash to indicate that either is appropriate. In sentence 4, the student's mother *or* father or mother *and* father are invited to the banquet.

5. A student should always make sure he/she understands an assignment before beginning to work on it.

   To avoid sexism, the third-person pronoun is sometimes written *he/she* (or *s/he*), indicating that it is referring to either a man or a woman. However, opinion is divided over this usage. Many readers find it clumsy or distracting. We recommend that you either use a plural form or write *he or she* (see 23b).

COLLABORATIVE ACTIVITY

Have students consult this chapter as they check one another's drafts for proper use of the colon, ellipses, parentheses, brackets, dashes, and slashes.

37f
/

EDITING: MECHANICS

This chapter covers standard rules of capitalization applied in academic writing. The discussion assumes that students already know the different forms of capital and small letters. In some instances, ESL or remedial students may need to do handwriting exercises or otherwise practice the standard printed and cursive forms. Calligraphy books and close attention to printed typefaces can help those who need that kind of review, as can tutoring.

RESOURCES

The American Heritage Dictionary. 2nd College Edition.

Webster's New World Dictionary of the English Language. 3rd College Edition.

Wiener, Harvey S. *The Writing Room: A Resource Guide for Teachers of English.* New York: Oxford UP, 1981.

Dictionaries are useful aids for students working on capitalization. The American Heritage, for example, alphabetizes letter models (upper-case and lower-case) in both print and cursive styles throughout the dictionary. It also includes a review of capitalization rules as part of its prefatory style manual. See Harvey Wiener's book for a discussion of the causes of capitalization errors, as well as for exercises to help students recognize where capitals are needed.

38a
cap

38 CAPITALIZATION

Capital letters are larger than regular or lower-case letters. On a typewriter or a computer, you can type a capital letter by pressing the shift key, usually located in the lower left or right corner of the keyboard, at the same time you strike a letter key.

38a First word of a sentence or a line of poetry

The most basic use of a capital letter is illustrated by the following sentence.

1. This coffee is great.

    This is the first word in the sentence.

RULE 1: **Capitalize the first word in every sentence.**

The lines of the following poem illustrate a second use of capital letters.

2. To fling my arms wide
    In the face of the sun,
    Dance! Whirl! Whirl!
    Till the quick day is done.
    Rest at pale evening . . .
    A tall, slim tree . . .
    Night coming tenderly
        Black like me.

    —Langston Hughes, "Dream Variations"

RULE 2: **Each line of a poem begins with a capital letter.**

Some contemporary poets do not capitalize the first word in every line of their poetry. When quoting poetry, reproduce the capitalization exactly as the poet has used it.

The next two sentences illustrate an option in capitalization.

3. My mother is a determined woman: she went back to college at the age of forty-five.

4. My mother is a determined woman: She went back to college at the age of forty-five.

RULE 3: **When an independent clause follows a colon, it is correct to begin the independent clause with either an upper-case or a lower-case letter.**

Whichever style you choose, be consistent throughout a single piece of writing.

5. Early in "Civil Disobedience," Thoreau makes a paradoxical observation: "that government is best which governs not at all."

RULE 4: **If a quoted sentence follows a colon, it must begin with a capital letter.**

6. My boss treats me well: he listens to my suggestions. He gives me credit when I do well. Most important, he explains what I've done wrong when I make a mistake.

RULE 5: **When a colon introduces material that consists of more than one sentence, each sentence must begin with a capital letter, including the one following the colon.**

38b Proper nouns versus common nouns

An important use of capitalization involves proper nouns. The following lists indicate the basic difference between proper and common nouns.

PROPER NOUN	COMMON NOUN	PROPER NOUN	COMMON NOUN
Doctor Williams	my doctor	James Miller	that man
Arkansas	the state	Boise State University	the university
the Arctic Ocean	the ocean	Rover	my collie
Physics 101	a physics course	Uncle Jake	her uncle

FOR DISCUSSION

Some discussion of the history of capital letters and of the terms *upper-case* and *lower-case* may be in order. You could explain that the word *capital* derives from the Latin word for "head," thus implying importance, and possibly height. For centuries typesetters kept their type moldings arranged in encased trays. The upper parts of the type cases traditionally held the capital letters, the lower parts the small letters. Because the terms *upper-case* and *lower-case* are still used by teachers in referring to capitalization rules, students should know what those terms mean.

With respect to capitalization rules in general, you might call students' attention to exceptions and variances, particularly those having to do with lines of poetry and the use of the capital after the colon.

38b
cap

ESL ADVICE

Non-native speakers may have some difficulty grasping the rationale behind English capitalization. German speakers, for example, will be in the habit of capitalizing *all* nouns. One way to explain English capitalization is to stress that proper nouns denote "one of a kind"—in other words, the unique—whereas common nouns signify categories of things. English usage seems to imply that in an ideal world each person or special place would have a capitalized name all its own (there would be only one John, one Mary, one town called Riverdale). In practice, of course, there aren't enough unique names to go around. Students should realize, however, that when they speak of "John" or "Mary" or refer to "Riverdale," they are signifying objects that, in the immediate context at least, are unique.

FOR DISCUSSION

Many people associate capitalization with status. They are therefore reluctant to use lower-case letters for nouns denoting job classifications, college majors, and so on. To some it may seem a matter of self-esteem to write, "I plan to become an Engineer." In dealing with this tendency, you might concede that professions and job titles can be legitimately capitalized "in house" by corporations and other institutions, though not in generalized dis-

38b
cap

A proper noun not only *refers* to a specific person, place, or thing but must also be the *name* of that specific person, place, or thing. *My doctor* refers to a specific person, but it is not that person's name, so *doctor* is a common noun. *Doctor Williams* is my doctor's name, so it is a proper noun. *Her uncle* may refer to a specific person, but it is not a proper noun because it is not that person's name; *Uncle Jake* is his name and is consequently a proper noun.

> RULE 6: **Capitalize proper nouns—nouns that are the *names* of specific persons, places, or things.**

Although the general principle for proper nouns is easy to state, its application to specific cases can be complicated; the most troublesome cases are discussed here.

Names

PROPER NOUN	COMMON NOUN
Julie Moriarty	my neighbor
Tracey Robertson	a freshman
Professor Scheper	the professor
Colonel Adams	a colonel
Dean Snope	the dean

The titles of important figures such as presidents and deans were traditionally capitalized, even when used without the person's name; however, the trend is toward using lower case in these circumstances. Whichever style you choose, be consistent within a single piece of writing.

Groups

PROPER NOUN	COMMON NOUN
African American	aborigine
Black	disabled
Caucasian	gay
Chicano	lesbian
Hispanic	minority
Jew	northerner
Muslim	retiree

Proper Noun	Common Noun
Native American	yuppie
Thai	
Vietnamese	
White	

This is an area about which there is much disagreement. The general principle is to capitalize the names of racial, religious, national, and ethnic groups. Although many writers think that terms like *Black* and *White* and *Native* in *Native American* should not be capitalized because they are not names of groups but are merely words describing members of groups, we think that they clearly have become names of racial or ethnic groups and therefore should be capitalized. Whichever convention you use, make sure you are consistent.

The words in the right-hand column refer to groups of people but are not *names* of racial, religious, national, or ethnic groups and therefore should not be capitalized.

Place names

Proper Noun	Common Noun
the Delaware River	the river
the Indian Ocean	the ocean
the Middle East	northern Iraq
California	this state
Southeast Asia	southeast Arkansas
the South	walking south
the West Coast	the western coast of Africa

Capitalize the *name* of a geographic region. When a generic term (for example, *river, lake,* or *state*) is used alone, however, do *not* capitalize it. Use capitals for the *name* of a region (the South, the Middle East, the West Coast) but not for a direction (walking south).

Also, do not capitalize terms that *specify* an area but are not a *name*. In the phrase *the western coast of Africa, Africa* is capitalized because it is the name of a continent. *The western coast* specifies a certain piece of terrain, but it is not the *name* of that

course. For example, an executive assistant may be rightly titled "Executive Assistant" on the staff roster. Students should keep in mind the difference between common nouns and proper nouns, noting that one can become the other, depending on context.

ESL ADVICE

Some students may repeatedly capitalize all letters of the name of the country from which they come (e.g., IRAN, ISRAEL), just as others, not necessarily ESL, may have religious reasons for capitalizing all letters of words synonymous with God (e.g., JEHOVAH). If you wish to point out the exceptional nature of such practices, be careful not to oppose an individual's freedom of cultural or religious expression.

38b
cap

area. Southeast Asia is the name of an area; southeast Arkansas is not. If you are in doubt, consult a dictionary or an atlas.

Organizations

PROPER NOUN	COMMON NOUN
the Boy Scouts	my club
New York Court of Appeals	traffic court
the House of Representatives	the lower house of the legislature
Eastman Kodak Company	the company
Miami-Dade Community College	the college
the Department of Psychology	the psychology department
Groveton High School	my high school

Words for organizations (court, company, college, school, and the like) are capitalized only when they are used as part of the *name* of the organization. When used alone, they are *not* capitalized.

Historical periods

PROPER NOUN	COMMON NOUN
the Great Depression	the next depression
the Vietnam War	the war
the Age of Enlightenment	the eighteenth century
the Middle Ages	the baroque period
the Roaring Twenties	the sixties
the Renaissance	the romantic period

The rules for capitalizing historical periods are fairly subtle. The tendency is to capitalize terms for periods that have developed an individual identity like the Roaring Twenties or the Middle Ages but to lower-case other terms that are more generic. If you are in doubt, consult a dictionary.

Time

PROPER NOUN	COMMON NOUN
Wednesday	winter
March	the thirteenth of June

Though it is generally true that *the* is not capitalized before titles, there are exceptions (e.g., The Johns Hopkins University, The Hartford, etc.). You might advise students who are corresponding with organizations to consult letterheads or other sources to determine whether the definite article is part of the incorporated title.

Students who read widely may discover some variance among publications when it comes to capitalizing decades or centuries. You might stress that the rules presented here are consistent with standard practice in academic writing.

38b
cap

Students used to leafing through bulletins advertising "Spring Classes" may fall into the incorrect but understandable habit of capitalizing seasons of the year. Be sure to stress the difference between "Spring" as a word in a title and *spring* as a common noun.

Because the names of days of the week and months are derived from the names of Greek, Roman, and Norse gods and goddesses, they are capitalized. Wednesday comes from Woden; March from Mars. The words for seasons and numbers representing days are not derived from the names of gods or goddesses and so are not capitalized.

Religious terms

Proper Noun	Common Noun
God	a statue of a god
Allah	a Greek god
the Prophet (Muhammad)	the god worshiped by Christians
Buddha	the words of a prophet
the Koran	priest
the Talmud	a hymnal

Capitalize the names of deities and holy writings, but not the word *god* when used generically. It was once conventional to capitalize pronouns that refer to the deity, but the practice is less common today. For example, in the expression "God's in his heaven," it was traditional to capitalize *his*. Today, most writers would write *his* with a lower-case *h*.

Scientific terms

Scientific Name	Common Name
Homo sapiens	oak tree
Quercus palustris	poodle
E. coli	iris
	German shepherd

For scientific names of plants and animals, the genus is capitalized and the species is lower-cased. Because these are Latin words, they are also italicized. Vernacular names (everyday names) for plants and animals are lower-cased, except for any words that are otherwise proper nouns, such as *German* in *German shepherd*.

Proper Noun	Common Noun
Mars	planet
the Milky Way	star
Crab Nebula	galaxy

38b
cap

Names of heavenly bodies are capitalized; words that refer to heavenly bodies but are not *names* are lower-cased. *Earth, sun,* and *moon* are generally not capitalized; however, when they are used in a discussion of other capitalized heavenly bodies, they frequently are.

COMMON NOUNS

uranium
sulfuric acid
the second law of thermodynamics
cancer
pneumonia
Kaposi's sarcoma
Newton's second law

Words referring to chemicals, scientific laws, or diseases are not considered names and so are not capitalized. However, words such as *Kaposi's* or *Newton's* that are proper nouns or adjectives (see 38c) and are used as part of a term referring to a chemical, scientific law, or disease *are* capitalized.

Trademarks

TRADE NAME	GENERIC NAME
Kleenex	tissues
Coca-Cola	soda, pop, soft drink
Advil	aspirin
Xerox	photocopier

Registered trade names should be capitalized, but generic names should not. If in doubt, check a dictionary.

School courses

FORMAL NAME	GENERIC NAME
Sociology 101	mathematics
Early Childhood Psychology	psychology
	English literature

Capitalize names of specific courses offered by a school but not words that describe subject areas, except words that are proper

38b
cap

FOR DISCUSSION

Because many students associate capitalization with status, they may fear that not capitalizing the name of a college discipline will seem disrespectful. You might stress the difference between the uncapitalized

nouns or adjectives (see 38c). The word *English,* as in *English literature,* is capitalized even when it refers only to a general subject area because it is a proper adjective.

38c Proper adjectives

The following are proper adjectives; all are derived from proper nouns.

Asian	Jewish
Buddhist	Moslem
Christian	Roman
French	Shakespearean

RULE 7: **Capitalize proper adjectives, that is, adjectives that are derived from proper nouns.**

38d *I* and *O*

The following sentences illustrate the treatment of *I* and *O* when they are used as words by themselves.

1. When I heard the phone ring, I answered it.
2. I replied, "I will do whatever you wish, O mighty one."

RULE 8: **Capitalize the pronoun *I* and the interjection *O*.**

38e Capitalization with quotations

1. My father asked us not to "besmirch the family's name."

   Besmirch the family's name is not a sentence by itself. It is a part of a larger sentence. Because it is not a complete sentence, the first letter is not capitalized.

2. My father said, "Be home by midnight," as we walked out the door.

   In sentence 2, *Be home by midnight* is a sentence by itself, so it is capitalized.

discipline as a common noun (e.g., "I am majoring in sociology") and the capitalized term as it appears in a course title or on the department office door. You might also point out the exception in the case of language departments (i.e., one always majors in *E*nglish!)

Stress that adjectives of religion or nationality should always be capitalized. Warn students that failure to observe this rule can be insulting to readers.

38e cap

FOR DISCUSSION
Stress that capitals within quotes occur where and if the original quotation contains them.

3. "When you get home," my father said, "don't wake me up."

In sentence 3, the second half of the quotation is not capitalized because it is not a sentence by itself; it is the continuation of the sentence begun in the first half of the quotation.

RULE 9: **Capitalize the first word of quotations that are sentences by themselves.**

38f Titles

Titles of books, poems, paintings, plays, musical compositions, movies, radio and television programs, and periodicals are capitalized, as in the following:

The Floating Opera
Paradigms Lost: Images of Man in the Mirror of Science
Sundiata: An Epic of Old Mali
"The Artist of the Beautiful"

RULE 10: **Capitalize the main words in titles. Articles, prepositions, coordinating conjunctions, and *to* in infinitives are not capitalized (regardless of their length) unless they are the first or last word of the title or subtitle. Follow this rule regardless of how the title appears on the title page of the work itself.**

Note that some conventions require the capitalization of prepositions with five or more (or sometimes four or more) letters. If you are in doubt, check with your instructor or the style manual for your organization.

38g Questions in a series

1. What will the government tax next? Our children? Our underwear? Our garbage?
2. What will the government tax next? our children? our underwear? our garbage?

The convention for capitalizing a series of questions that are not complete sentences varies. Use either style, but be consistent throughout a single piece of writing.

Remind students that if they are to capitalize titles correctly they must first be able to recognize the parts of speech reviewed in 19.

38g
cap

COLLABORATIVE ACTIVITY

Have members of editing groups refer to this chapter as they check the capitalization in one another's drafts.

39 ABBREVIATIONS AND ACRONYMS

39a Personal titles

The following illustrate the use of abbreviated titles and degrees with names.

Ms. Hillary Clinton   Dr. Marie Williams
Mr. Jacob Miller   Ms. Tanaka
George Scheper, Ph.D.   Nancy Hume, M.A.
Ursula Gudrun, D.D.S.   Martin Villanueva, M.S.W.
Henry Gonzalez, Jr.   Kent G. Stockdale III

Common personal and professional titles are normally abbreviated; in fact, there is no spelled-out version of *Ms.* These titles are used with a person's entire name or with the family name alone.

Other titles, including religious, military, academic, and government titles, are used as follows:

Prof. Ralph Stephens   Professor Stephens
Sen. Barbara Boxer   Senator Boxer
Col. L. Dow Adams   Colonel Adams

The abbreviated form may be used before the full name. When using only the last name, write out the full title. In most academic writing, titles should be spelled out even when the full name is given.

The following examples illustrate some errors with abbreviations for titles.

Professor Lynda Salamon, ~~Ph.D.~~

~~Dr.~~ Stephen Howard, Ph.D.

Do not use a title both before and after a name; choose one or the other.

professor   *doctor*
I explained to my ~~prof.~~ that I had an appointment with my ~~Dr.~~

Abbreviate personal and professional titles only when used with a full name.

Abbreviations play an important role in contemporary writing. This chapter can help make your students aware of how to use acronyms and other abbreviated forms. It can also serve as a reference guide to several of the standard abbreviations used in college.

Though titles normally do not both precede and follow person's names, you might point out that exceptions occur in the case of block-form addresses, where a position title may appear on a line beneath a name preceded by a title:

Ms. Janet Rogers
Sales Manager
Global Industries, Inc.
Los Angeles, CA 90024

39a
abbr

RESOURCES

Acronyms, Initialisms, and Abbreviations Dictionary. 3 vols. Detroit: Gale, 1976.

The American Heritage Dictionary. 2nd College Edition.

Dictionary of Foreign Phrases and Abbreviations. 3rd ed.

Desk dictionaries are often the most convenient sources for students to use in looking up abbreviations and acronyms. The American Heritage, *for example, has a well-detailed appendix on abbreviations that includes many timely acronyms. More specialized sources, such as the* Dictionary of Foreign Phrases and Abbreviations, *should be available in your college library reference collection. You might also remind students that Postal Service abbreviations of the fifty states (possibly the abbreviated forms most often sought) are listed in standard telephone books.*

39b **Abbreviations with numbers**

Periods have traditionally been used for many abbreviations but not for others. In recent years, the trend has been toward using fewer periods with abbreviations, a trend we encourage. Nevertheless, for those who prefer a more conventional approach, the examples here show periods where they have been traditionally required. The trend toward omitting periods is especially strong in technical writing.

10:30 P.M. or 10:30 p.m.	Typesetters normally use small caps—letters the size of lower-case letters but in the form of capital letters. If your typewriter or computer doesn't permit small caps, use lower case for A.M. or P.M.
400 B.C. or 400 B.C.	Again, use small caps, if you can; if not, use *upper case*.
A.D. 1492 or A.D. 1492	B.C. follows the date; A.D. precedes it. B.C. is the abbreviation for *before Christ* and indicates the number of years before the birth of Christ that an event occurred. A.D. stands for *anno Domini,* Latin for "in the year of the Lord." It is used to indicate dates of events after the birth of Christ.
400 B.C.E. or 400 B.C.E.	B.C.E. stands for "before the Common Era" and is the equivalent of B.C. It is used to avoid the Christian orientation of B.C.
1492 C.E. or 1492 C.E.	C.E. stands for "Common Era" and is the equivalent of A.D. It is used to avoid the Christian orientation of A.D. Note that C.E. follows the date rather than preceding it, as A.D. does.

39b
abbr

No. 10 or no. 10	The abbreviation for *number* may be either capitalized or lower-cased.
$19.95	Use a dollar sign with numbers and a decimal point to indicate dollar and cent amounts. Never use a dollar sign and a cent sign (¢) with the same numbers.
32°F 0°C 273 K	A small superscript circle stands for the word *degrees.* The capital *F* indicates that the temperature is being measured on the Fahrenheit scale; the capital *C,* that the Celsius (centigrade) scale is being used; the capital *K,* that the Kelvin scale is being used.

afternoon

1. I will meet you in the P.M.

The abbreviations A.M. and P.M. should be used only with times expressed in numbers and should not substitute for the word *morning* or *afternoon* in other contexts.

dollar

2. I found a $ bill in my pocket.

Use a dollar sign only with a number amount, not to indicate the word *dollar* or *dollars* by itself.

number

3. We have ordered a no. of spare parts for the computer.

Use the abbreviation for number only in conjunction with a number, not to represent the word *number* by itself.

Abbreviations for weights and measures (qt., lb., cc, km) are commonly used *with numbers* in scientific and technical writing but should be avoided in other writing.

39c Organizations, companies, and government agencies

Use accepted abbreviations for organizations, companies, and government agencies, as illustrated in the list on the next page.

39c
abbr

ACTIVITY

Have students take note of some acronyms found in the lead section of a daily newspaper (e.g., NASA—National Aeronautics and Space Administration). Discuss the reported examples, making sure that the students who bring in the acronyms are ready to explain what those acronyms stand for.

CIA	Central Intelligence Agency
NAACP	National Association for the Advancement of Colored People
IBM	International Business Machines
NOW	National Organization for Women
CBS	Columbia Broadcasting System
GM	General Motors

These abbreviations are acceptable in most writing. Today they are almost always written without periods. Be careful, however, not to use an abbreviation with which your reader may be unfamiliar, unless you introduce it first, as in the following sentence.

> We sent a grant proposal to the National Endowment for the Humanities (NEH), and we expect to be funded. NEH is giving a priority to proposals related to cultural diversity this year.

Use abbreviations such as *Inc., Co., Corp.,* or the ampersand (&) only if they appear in the official name of the company or organization.

39d Abbreviations of Latin terms

In general, avoid Latin terms and the abbreviations for them in your writing. They are intended primarily for use in documenting sources (see 46).

cf.	compare (*confer*)
e.g.	for example (*exempli gratia*)
et al.	and others (*et alii*)
ibid.	in the same place (*ibidem*)
i.e.	that is (*id est*)
loc. cit.	in the place cited (*loco citato*)
N.B.	note well (*nota bene*)
op. cit.	in the work cited (*opere citato*)
q.v.	which see (*quod vide*)

In written text, use the English translation in place of the Latin term.

Because your class may encounter a number of other abbreviated terms during future research, you might stress the usefulness of a desk dictionary (such as the *American Heritage*) for locating lists of standard abbreviations.

39d
abbr

for example
This college has many support services for students, ~~e.g.,~~ counseling, job placement, tutoring, and assessment.

39e Periods with abbreviations

The use of periods with abbreviations varies greatly, although the trend is strongly away from the use of periods with most abbreviations. If there is a principle behind current use, it is illustrated by the following:

ABBREVIATIONS	ACRONYMS AND INITIAL ABBREVIATIONS
St.	CARE
Blvd.	UNICEF
Nov.	IRS

In general, true **abbreviations**—words shortened by the omission of letters—are often followed by a period. An **acronym,** which consists of the first letter of a series of words used as a shortened version and pronounced as though it were a word (CARE, UNICEF, MIRV), is generally used without periods. *Initial abbreviations,* which are made up of the first letter of a series of words and are pronounced by saying each letter (IRS, IBM, AFL-CIO), are also commonly written without periods.

When periods are used with abbreviations (as in A.M., U.S.A., or B.C.), do not leave a space between the period and the next letter. For initials in a personal name (G. K. Chesterton), however, *do* leave a space between the period and the next letter.

ACTIVITY

Encourage your class to notice examples of abbreviations and acronyms in phone books, textbooks, technical manuals, and research articles. Recommend that students jot down any abbreviations they don't understand. Have them consult dictionaries or ask you for help to find out the meanings.

40 NUMBERS

To decide whether you should use numerals (*73*) or words (*seventy-three*) to express a number, you must first decide which of two types of writing you are doing. If your writing contains few numbers, follow the examples in the left-hand column of the list on page 412. If your writing contains many numbers—particularly if it is scientific, technical, or business writing—follow the examples in the right-hand column.

Numbers (or numerals) are more commonly used in scientific disciplines than in the humanities, but all students need to be aware of basic rules concerning the formal use of numbers in writing. Encourage students to ask questions about any of the specific examples given in this chapter.

40 num

RESOURCES

Gibaldi, Joseph, and Walter S. Achtert. *MLA Handbook for Writers of Research Papers.* 3rd ed. New York: Modern Language Association, 1988.

This manual includes MLA guidelines for using numbers to cite acts and scenes in plays, volumes and editions of books, and periodicals. See its index listings under "numbers" and "numerals."

Stress the importance of using hyphens in spelled-out numbers from twenty-one to ninety-nine. You might also refer students to 42 for more about hyphens in general.

For Writing That Contains Few Numbers	For Writing That Contains Many Numbers
zero	zero
six	six
fourteen	14
ninety-nine	99
104	104
one thousand	1,000
1,352	1,352

In writing with few numbers, use words for all numbers that can be expressed in one or two words. Use numerals for numbers that require three or more words.

If you do have occasion to write out lengthy numbers in words, use *and* only to indicate where a decimal point would go; do not use *and* between the hundreds and the tens in a number:

one hundred and twenty-two   thirty-one and nine-tenths

In writing that includes many numbers, use words for the numbers zero to nine; use numerals for all others.

When you use words for numbers from *twenty-one* to *ninety-nine,* hyphenate the two words. When deciding whether to use words or numbers, count such hyphenated constructions as two words.

1. We sold eight mugs on Monday, 19 on Tuesday, and 22 on Wednesday.

When you are following these guidelines, be consistent. If one number in a series requires that you use numerals, then use numerals for all numbers in that sequence.

The following examples illustrate how to handle numbers at the beginning of a sentence.

2. *One hundred twenty-six* 126 people applied for this job.
3. *There were 126 applicants for this job.* 126 people applied for this job.

Do not begin a sentence with a number expressed in numerals. Either write the number out in words (even if this makes for inconsistency with other numbers in a series), or recast the sentence so that the number appears later.

40 num

Round numbers greater than one million may be expressed as follows:

four million   780 million

When expressing time of day, use numerals when you use A.M. or P.M.; use words otherwise:

9:00 P.M.   nine o'clock
11:15 A.M.   eleven-fifteen in the morning

Even when you are writing a text that otherwise uses words for most numbers, use numerals for the following purposes:

Dates: May 8, 1956   A.D. 1056   1607

Divisions of
books, plays,
or poems: Chapter 4   pages 33–41   Act 3

Decimals: 3.1416   0.5   0.0001

Money: $4.50 $1.2 million $1,187.25

In writing with few numbers, however, write out amounts of money that can be expressed in two words or fewer: *ten dollars, one thousand dollars, fifty cents.*

Fractions: $8\frac{1}{2}$ $32\frac{3}{4}$ 99 98/100

In writing with few numbers, however, fractions that can be written in two words or fewer should be written out: *one-half, three-fourths.*

Addresses: 10 Downing Street
                   11308 South Road, Apartment 12J

Scores and statistics: the odds were 3:1
                         the Rangers won 6–2
                         the ratio of wounded to killed was 5 to 1

When writing two numbers next to each other, express one of them in words, one in numerals.

4. We saw 10 two-masted sailboats.
5. Last year, they made three 1,000-mile trips.

ESL ADVICE

Encourage ESL students to practice writing amounts of money in several common ways ($5.25, five dollars and twenty-five cents, five and a quarter, five twenty-five, etc.).

COLLABORATIVE ACTIVITY

As they read drafts of one another's essays, have students check to see that numbers have been used according to the rules covered in this chapter.

40
num

Research reports and other kinds of college writing often require the use of italicized (or underlined) terms. This chapter reviews several key factors that students must consider when deciding when and where to use italics.

RESOURCES
Computer-Assisted Instruction

Software manuals normally explain how to change the style of fonts. Suggest that students who use computers become familiar with procedures for underlining text and setting on-screen italics. Those who have difficulty may need to ask for help from a computer lab assistant.

41 ITALICS

Most printing is done with letters that are vertical. This standard style is known as *roman. There is, however, a second style of typeface in which the letters are slanted to the right, as they are in this sentence.* This style of printing is known as **italics.** Italics are used to emphasize certain words. As with everything else in English, there are conventions about when to use italics to emphasize text. This chapter will explain these conventions.

Most typewriters and many computers are not capable of producing italics, and you should never attempt italics if you are handwriting your paper. <u>If you are not able to produce italics, underline the words that you intend to italicize, just as we have underlined this sentence.</u> Underlining has exactly the same effect as italicizing text.

41a Titles of works

Use italic type or underlining to indicate the titles of longer works and works in the visual arts. Titles of shorter works are placed in quotation marks (see 36e). The following examples should help clarify this principle:

WORKS THAT SHOULD BE ITALICIZED OR UNDERLINED

Books:	*A Brief History of Time*	<u>A Brief History of Time</u>
Plays:	*King Lear*	<u>King Lear</u>
Long musical works:	Haydn's *Creation*	Haydn's <u>Creation</u>
Long poems:	*The Waste Land*	<u>The Waste Land</u>
Visual art:	Matisse's *Pink Nude*	Matisse's <u>Pink Nude</u>
Magazines:	the *Atlantic Monthly*	the <u>Atlantic Monthly</u>
Newspapers:	the *St. Louis Post-Dispatch*	the <u>St. Louis Post-Dispatch</u>
Television programs:	*60 Minutes*	<u>60 Minutes</u>

41a
ital

Films:	*Rebel without a*	Rebel without a
	Cause	Cause
Journals:	*Modern Fiction*	Modern Fiction
	Studies	Studies

Legal documents, religious books such as the Bible or the Koran, and parts of these works are not italicized, underlined, or placed in quotation marks.

the Bible	the Declaration of	the Talmud
	Independence	
the Book of Tao	the Constitution	Exodus

Note that for titles of newspapers, magazines, or journals, an initial *the* is not italicized or underlined even when it is part of a title.

| the *New York* | the *American History* | the *Baltimore Sun* |
| *Times* | *Review* | |

In citations of such works, the initial *the* is usually omitted.

41b Names of spacecraft, ships, airplanes, and trains

The *names* of spacecraft, ships, airplanes, and trains are italicized or underlined.

Apollo IX	Apollo IX	the *Titanic*	the Titanic
the *Orient*	the Orient	*Air Force One*	Air Force One
Express	Express		

Italicize or underline only the *names* of specific spacecraft, ships, airplanes, and trains. Do *not* italicize or underline types or models of such vehicles.

| space shuttle | Boeing 747 | aircraft carrier |

41c Words used as words, letters used as letters, numbers used as numbers

Use italics or underlining to indicate a word, letter, or number used, not with its normal meaning, but because you are dis-

RESOURCES

Gibaldi, Joseph, and Walter S. Achtert. *MLA Handbook for Writers of Research Papers*. 3rd ed. New York: Modern Language Association, 1988.

See this manual for definitive MLA rules concerning the use of italics.

The rule about italicizing book titles reflects MLA style guidelines. However, you might mention that editorial practices vary among magazines and other publications. Newspapers, for example, still often use quotation marks in referring to books. Nevertheless, college students should follow the academic guidelines presented here. The use of quotation marks is discussed further in 31e.

Ships' names are capitalized because they are proper nouns. Students who have trouble recognizing proper nouns should review 38b.

FOR DISCUSSION

You might point out that a word's "foreign" status depends on ever-changing popular usage. Food is a case in point. The word *pizza* would have been italicized in the decades before pizza parlors sprang up across America. Now few words are more American. Sushi and falafel are probably already domesticated, at least in the vernacular of large cities. A test might be whether the food item can be bought from a large supermarket chain or whether it is found only in a specialty store. By that criterion, *baklava,* now offered at supermarkets, wouldn't be italicized, whereas the Greek deli's *kataifi* still would be. Owing to the fast pace of change, even dictionaries may not keep up with every term newly qualified for a place in English vocabulary. Encourage students to think of their own examples.

FOR DISCUSSION

41d
ital

To summarize a lesson on italics, you might call attention to some italicized words that appear in an essay from a college reader. Ask students to identify the rules that cover the use of italics in examples you've cited.

cussing it *as a word, letter,* or *number.* For example, look at the following sentences:

1. My boss gave me some advice about how to organize the brochure.

   Advice is used with its normal meaning, so it is not italicized or underlined.

2. My boss uses *advice* the way other people use *command.*
3. My boss uses advice the way other people use command.

   In sentences 2 and 3, the word *advice* is used to stand for the word itself; in fact, sentences 2 and 3 could be worded as follows:

4. My boss uses the word *advice* the way other people use the word *command.*
5. My boss uses the word advice the way other people use the word command.

From sentences 4 and 5, you can see what we mean by *a word used as a word* rather than with its normal meaning. Letters used as letters and numbers used as numbers are also italicized or underlined.

41d **Words from other languages**

When used in English sentences, foreign words are italicized or underlined.

1. *Adios* was all she said as she drove away.
2. Adios was all she said as she drove away.

However, words or phrases from other languages that have been used so often they have become a part of the English language, such as *burrito, chutzpah, sushi,* and *wigwam,* are not italicized or underlined. If you are in doubt, consult a dictionary, where words from other languages that should be italicized or underlined are identified by a symbol, italicized, or marked with their language of origin.

41e Emphasis

Italics or underlining may be used to indicate stress or emphasis on a word or phrase, but do not overuse italics for this purpose. When italics or underlining is used too often, it quickly loses its force and becomes just a distraction.

Notice how the meaning in these sentences changes as the emphasis changes.

1. I can't believe that *you* did that.
2. I can't believe that you *did* that.
3. I can't believe that you did *that*.

42   HYPHENS

42a Using a hyphen to divide a word at the end of a line

A hyphen and a dash are not the same thing; a hyphen is about half the length of a dash. The hyphen is usually available on the top row of a keyboard on the right, often just to the right of the zero key. Dashes are discussed in 37e.

When you come to the end of a line while typing, occasionally there won't be enough room for a word, but if you put it on the next line, a big blank space will be left at the end of the line.

```
1. On the evening of Saturday, August 21, Barbara

   checked into the Refuge Motor Inn on

   Chincoteague Island.  She wasn't sure how long

   she was going to stay, but she knew she would

   have fun while she was there.
```

The blank space at the end of the second line of sentence 1 happens because *Chincoteague* is too long to fit and so has to be

Is the hyphen disappearing from the language? At a time when computers "wrap" text to avoid syllable breaks and each newly edited dictionary shows more prefixes merging with words from which they were once detached, it might seem so. But style conventions change slowly. Your students need to learn hyphenation principles if they are to avoid violating rules that editors and teachers still uphold. Besides, as you might point out, the hyphen can be a mark of distinction. Correctly used, this tiny vestige of old typography can attest to a writer's grammatical knowledge. Encourage students to pay careful attention to this chapter.

RESOURCES

The American Heritage Dictionary. 2nd College Edition.

Gibaldi, Joseph, and Walter S. Achtert. *MLA Handbook for Writers of Research Papers.* 3rd ed. New York: Modern Language Association, 1988.

Many dictionaries and style manuals contain advice on hyphenation. The MLA Handbook *demonstrates the use of the hyphen in bibliographies and in general usage. See also the style manual section of* The American Heritage Dictionary.

42a
-

Because punctuation habits vary according to linguistic background, be prepared to counsel students who write a hyphen at line bottom (_) instead of midway up (-). You might also advise students never to place a hyphen at the left margin following a syllable break.

FOR DISCUSSION

Computers automatically "wrap" lines of text, thus making right-margin syllable breaks a virtual thing of the past. However, students who use typewriters should be advised to keep line-ending hyphens to a minimum. As professional writers have discovered to their chagrin, a transcriber of the manuscript might accidentally preserve an unnecessary hyphen during the printing process. (One doesn't want "col-lected" showing up in the middle of a page!)

Stress that the hyphen must be placed between syllables when a word is broken at the right margin. In general, syllables reflect changes in the position of the tongue as a word is pronounced. But because the dictionary must be the final authority, make sure students know about those dots that dictionaries use to indicate *syl • la • ble* breaks.

42b

placed on the next line. The large blank space gives an awkward look to the right margin. To correct this problem, the word *Chincoteague* can be split between the two lines, using a hyphen to indicate the division:

2. On the evening of Saturday, August 21, Barbara
   checked into the Refuge Motor Inn on Chincoteague Island. She wasn't sure how long she
   was going to stay, but she knew she would have
   fun while she was there.

Now the blank space at the end of the line has been eliminated.

When you use a hyphen to divide a word at the end of the line, you must observe certain conventions:

- Divide words only between syllables. If you have any doubt about where the syllables divide, consult a dictionary.
- Never divide one-syllable words.
- When you divide a word, never leave a single letter at the end of one line or fewer than three letters at the beginning of the next line.
- When dividing a word that already is hyphenated, always divide it at the hyphen.

42b **Compound words**

Compound words are words that are made up of a combination of two or more other words. Compounds take three different forms: two words, hyphenated words, and run-together words. Usage may vary for some words, but if you are in doubt, consult a dictionary. If the compound word is not in the dictionary, it should be written as two words. Unfortunately, dictionaries do not always agree on these conventions. However, if you consis-

tently follow the guidance of a single reputable dictionary, you will have no problems.

The following list includes common examples of all three types of compound words according to *The American Heritage Dictionary* (3rd edition).

Run-Together	Hyphenated	Two Words
blueberry	blue-collar	nurse practitioner
crosswalk	cross-reference	cross section
waterproof	water-repellent	high school
textbook	city-state	parking meter
extraterrestrial	go-between	floppy disk
notebook	self-government	guinea pig
		attorney general

42c Compound adjectives

The following examples illustrate the use of compound adjectives.

a well-known actor   a late-starting movie

When two or more words modify a noun *as a unit,* they should be hyphenated. The parts of a compound adjective cannot be separated without changing its meaning. If you write *a known actor who is well,* it means something very different from *a well-known actor.* The following are examples of adjectives that are *not* used as a unit and are therefore not hyphenated.

a young Vietnamese woman   the rusty old Chevrolet

These adjectives could be separated without affecting the meaning. *A Vietnamese woman who is young* has the same meaning as *a young Vietnamese woman.*

Note also that when two or more adjectives come *after* the noun, they are not hyphenated even if they are used as a unit.

1. That actor is not well known.
2. Tyrone's paper was well written.

Adverbs ending in *-ly* and words in comparative or superlative forms (see 28c) are not hyphenated.

a carefully ironed shirt   the most expensive ring

Remind students that hyphenation rules are evolving. You might give the example of the word *today,* which, your class might be surprised to learn, was *to-day* earlier in this century.

ACTIVITY

Have students practice moving a hyphenated compound adjective from in front of a modified noun to a position following the noun, where the hyphen must be removed. For example, "twentieth-century technology" can be rewritten as "technology of the twentieth century."

42c

Refer students to 40 for more about hyphenated numbers.

42d Using hyphens with fractions and numbers

Hyphens are also used when writing out numbers in words. (See 40 for a discussion of when to write numbers as words.) Use a hyphen for two-word numbers under one hundred.

twenty-one   ninety-nine

When writing out fractions in words, use a hyphen between the numerator and the denominator. The numerator is the first number; the denominator is the second. In their fraction form, numerators are on the top; denominators are on the bottom:

one-half $\frac{1}{2}$ three-fourths $\frac{3}{4}$

You should not use a hyphen between numerator and denominator, however, if either of them already contains hyphens.

three thirty-seconds $\frac{3}{32}$ sixty-four hundredths $\frac{64}{100}$

42e Using hyphens with prefixes and suffixes

Usually, when words are formed with prefixes or suffixes, they are written as one word: *antiwar, semisweet, naturalize*. However, in a few cases, prefixes and suffixes are hyphenated.

Use a hyphen with the prefixes *self-, all-, ex-* (when it means "former"), and *quasi-* and with the suffix *-elect*.

self-confident   ex-wife
president-elect   all-inclusive

Hyphenate prefixes when either the base word or the prefix begins with a capital letter.

un-American   post-Bush era
A-frame   non-African

Sometimes a hyphen is used to clarify meaning.

re-creation / recreation   re-cover / recover

Re-creation means "creating something again"; *recreation* is what we do on weekends. To *re-cover* is to replace the cover on something; to *recover* is to get well.

42e
-

ACTIVITY
You might have students look up *pre-* or *anti-* in desk dictionaries to see which terms using the prefix are still hyphenated. Stress the importance of consulting up-to-date dictionaries, for hyphens tend to be dropped as the years go by.

Sometimes prefixes and suffixes are hyphenated to prevent misreading, especially when the prefix or suffix results in the repetition of a vowel or a triple consonant.

deemphasize   antiintellectual   belllike

42f Suspended hyphens

Sometimes two or more modifiers requiring hyphens are used to modify the same word. In these cases, each modifier retains its hyphen even though the base word appears only once. Leave a space after all but the last hyphen.

> full- and part-time employees
> English- or Chinese-speaking students

COLLABORATIVE ACTIVITY

Have members of editing groups check one another's drafts for correct hyphenation. Urge students not to overlook line-end syllable breaks, compound adjectives before nouns, two-word numbers, and prefixes that might call for hyphens or suspended hyphens.

43 MANUSCRIPT FORM

43a Instructors' preferences

The appearance of your paper does matter. Take care to ensure that your paper looks neat and does not send the message that you prepared it hurriedly or carelessly.

Instructors' preferences for the format of your papers will vary from class to class. So will the preferences of your bosses in the workplace. This does not mean that format isn't important; it *is* important, but it will vary depending on what you are writing and who your audience is. Make sure you understand the format that is expected for each piece of writing. In college, that may mean asking questions of your professor to find out just what he or she expects. Once you understand the format expected, follow it carefully.

Preparing a final draft for submission can be a nerve-racking ordeal for some students, especially those who competitively aim for high marks. This chapter should lower the anxiety level by offering basic advice and useful guidelines. You might set aside time to discuss the chapter's main points with your class, adding ideas drawn from your own experience.

43a
ms

FOR DISCUSSION

You might discuss the practical importance of consulting an instructor about manuscript guidelines. Students who are afraid to ask for advice when they are in doubt may find themselves lost in misunderstanding. Point out that each college discipline has its own style guidelines for research papers. While it is the student's responsibility to follow the procedures of the discipline in which he or she is working, instructors usually welcome questions about those procedures. You might also remind students that they are free to discuss with you any concerns having to do with writing projects in your course.

RESOURCES

The Chicago Manual of Style. 14th ed. Chicago: U of Chicago P, 1993.

Gibaldi, Joseph, and Walter S. Achtert. *MLA Handbook for Writers of Research Papers*. 3rd ed. New York: Modern Language Association, 1988.

Publication Manual of the American Psychological Association. 3rd ed. Washington, DC: American Psychological Association, 1983.

Turabian, Kate L. *A Manual for Writers of Term Papers, Theses, and Dissertations*. 5th ed. Chicago: U of Chicago P, 1987.

43b
ms

The style manuals listed above are among the most widely used guides

In the absence of guidelines from your instructor, the guidelines in the following section are generally acceptable for college writing.

43b Manuscript guidelines

Paper

For typed papers, use standard-size ($8\frac{1}{2}$- by 11-inch) white paper. Unless your instructor indicates otherwise, do not use onionskin or erasable paper. Such paper is difficult to write comments on. Double-space your writing. Use only one side of the paper.

Most college instructors do not accept handwritten papers, but if yours does, use ruled standard-size ($8\frac{1}{2}$- by 11-inch) white paper. Skip lines. Do not use colored paper or paper torn from a spiral-bound notebook.

If you are printing on a computer, use standard-size ($8\frac{1}{2}$- by 11-inch) white paper. If you are using continuous-feed computer paper, after you have printed, remove the perforated strips from both sides of the paper and separate the pages at the perforations.

Some instructors will not accept papers printed on low-quality dot-matrix printers. Try to find a good printer for producing your papers, and print them on the highest quality setting (usually this setting is called *near letter quality* or *NLQ*). A laser printer would be even better.

Ink

On a typewriter or printer that uses a ribbon, use a good black ribbon. For handwritten papers, use black, blue-black, or blue ink.

Typeface

If you are using a typewriter, use a standard size of type, either pica or elite. Avoid typefaces that are hard to read, particularly those that attempt to reproduce script. Clean the type regularly. Do not use all capitals.

If you are using a computer, use a standard type size, 10 or 12 point. Avoid typefaces that are unnecessarily ornate and difficult to read, especially those that attempt to imitate script. Do not use all capitals. Do not overuse the flexibility of the computer. Once you choose a font, stick to it. Change type fonts or sizes within a single document only under rare conditions.

Handwritten corrections

In final drafts, keep corrections to a minimum. If you are working on a computer, make corrections and reprint the revised pages. If you are working on a typewriter, use either the correction ribbon or correction fluid to make corrections. If there is not sufficient room for the correction, you may make neat corrections by hand; however, if you need to make more than two or three of these on a page, that page should be retyped. If handwriting, make corrections neatly by hand.

Title page

For most college papers, unless your instructor states otherwise, a cover sheet is unnecessary. (See page 499 for an example of a title page in MLA style; see page 533 for an example of one in APA style.)

First page

If you don't use a title page, certain identifying information will have to appear on the first page of the paper. If you have not received guidance from your instructor, we suggest that you place—each on a separate line—your name, your professor's name, your course number and section number, the date, and any identification of the assignment that seems appropriate (such as "Paper #3") in the upper left-hand corner. This information should be double-spaced and should begin one inch down from the top of the page and one inch in from the left edge. (See page 505 for an example of the first page of a paper using MLA style.)

Following this information, double-space again and then type your title, centered on the page. Do not underline or italicize your title; do not place it in quotation marks or in all capi-

FOR DISCUSSION

Are handwritten corrections okay with you? If so, you might advise your class not to worry. Some students are shy about making last-minute corrections, believing that the pristine appearance of a manuscript is a key factor in the grade. You might explain that while you can't speak for all of your colleagues, you do appreciate evidence that the writer of a submitted draft has taken time to proofread carefully.

43b
ms

tals. Follow the rules for capitalizing titles explained in 38f. If your title includes a subtitle, separate it from the main title with a colon or type it on a separate line; do *not* use both a colon and a separate line.

Double-space again and begin the first line of your paper.

Page numbering

Number all pages starting with the first one in the upper right-hand corner. One-half inch down from the top of the paper and flush against the right margin, type your last name with no punctuation and the page number in arabic numerals. Do not write out the page number in words or use the word *page* or the abbreviation *p.* in front of it. Do not use any punctuation following the page number.

If your paper is one or two pages long, you need not number the pages.

 If you are writing on a computer, use the computer's built-in page-numbering capability to number your pages following the recommended format.

Binding

Although a plastic folder or a brightly colored cardboard one may seem like a nice touch to contain your paper, most professors prefer that papers be turned in without any binding or folder. Unless your professor tells you otherwise, turn your paper in fastened only with a paper clip in the upper left-hand corner. Do not staple or bend the corner. Do not fold the paper.

44a
sp

44 SPELLING

44a Spelling as a state of mind

Like errors in grammar, punctuation, and capitalization, spelling errors can greatly detract from an otherwise well-written paper. It is important that you do all you can to reduce the number of

spelling errors in your writing. However, like the other errors, spelling is something you should not focus on until the major parts of your paper are as you want them. In other words, you should work on spelling primarily in your final draft.

The most important factor in reducing spelling errors is your state of mind. As with someone trying to lose weight or quit smoking, the most important factor is desire. If you are determined to improve your spelling, this chapter can help you do it.

44b Spelling rules

Several rules are of some help in spelling. Because English spelling is so irregular, however, there are always exceptions to each rule. Nevertheless, in this section you will learn the most useful spelling rules and the most common exceptions to each one.

RULE 1: Use *i* before *e* except after *c* or when sounded like *ay* as in *neighbor* or *weigh*.

This is probably the best-known spelling rule. Almost everyone has heard the basic rule before, and many people even remember the exceptions. A few examples will demonstrate exactly how this rule works.

believe [The *i* comes before the *e*.]

receive [The *e* comes before the *i* because they follow *c*.]

eight [The *e* comes before the *i* because they sound like *ay*.]

Those examples all follow the rule; however, even this fairly complicated rule doesn't cover all the cases in English. The following exceptions must be memorized:

either	leisure	seize
foreign	neither	their
height	protein	weird

RULE 2: When a suffix (ending) that begins with a vowel (such as *-er*, *-est*, *-ed*, or *-ing*) is added to a word, the final consonant is doubled if all of the following are true: (1) the word ends in a single consonant; (2) the final consonant before ending is preceded by a single vowel; (3) the accent (stress) is on the last syllable or the word

insecure about spelling. In fact, embarrassment can prevent improvement in this area. We have known students who are afraid to write home owing to their shame over poor spelling. Others have trouble writing fluently because they dread orthographic mistakes. Then again, some simply don't care. Whatever the circumstances, students need motivation and encouragement if they are to become competent spellers. This chapter addresses the spelling issue as a matter of attitude as well as of rules. Encourage your students to keep dictionaries handy, to set aside time for practice, and to be brave about spelling.

FOR DISCUSSION

Motivate students to take responsibility for correct spelling. Some may have grown complacent over the years, believing that errors are inevitable, that poor spelling habits are insurmountable, or that computer spelling checkers and meticulous secretaries will always be there to intervene. Point to situations where writers are on their own, as in the case of quick handwritten memos or other off-the-cuff correspondence. Stress that poor spelling *is* surmountable, given time and a willingness to acquire new habits.

44b
sp

RESOURCES

Bartholomae, David. "The Study of Error." *College Composition and Communication* 31 (1980): 253–69.

Clark, Roger, and I. Y. Hashimoto. "A Spelling Program for College Students." *Teaching English in the Two-Year College* 11.1 (1984): 34–38.

Dobie, Ann B. "Orthographical Theory and Practice, or How to Teach Spelling." *Journal of Basic Writing* 5.2 (1986): 41–48.

McClellan, Jane. "A Clinic for Misspellers." *College English* 40 (1978): 324–29.

Shaughnessy, Mina P. *Errors and Expectations: A Guide for the Teacher of Basic Writing.* New York: Oxford UP, 1977.

ACTIVITIES

Standard strategies for teaching spelling include phonetics (i.e., listening to oral pronunciation), memorizing and applying rules (as listed in 44b), and kinesthesia (i.e., rote writing of correctly spelled words, preferably in cursive handwriting so that movement is unconsciously memorized). We recommend a combination of all three approaches. Phonetic practice may be especially helpful to ESL students who make errors reflecting vowel pronunciation (e.g., "this"/ "these"); this practice may include mnemonic ploys to prompt memory (e.g., "He *ought* not to *cough*"). As for rules and kinesthesia, it is

44b

'sp

has only one syllable (if you are uncertain where the stress falls, check a dictionary).

Let's look at how this rule applies to some specific cases.

WORD	APPLICATION OF RULE
occur	This word ends in a single consonant *r*. This consonant is preceded by a single vowel, *u*. The accent is on the final syllable (oc-CUR). Since all the conditions under rule 2 are met, the final consonant must be doubled when a suffix beginning with a vowel is added: *occurred*.
listen	This word ends in a single consonant, *n*, preceded by a single vowel, *e*. However, the accent is not on the final syllable (the word is pronounced LIS-en). Since one of the three conditions of rule 2 is not met, the final consonant is not doubled: *listening*.
meet	This word ends in a single consonant, *t*, that is not preceded by a single vowel (it is preceded by two vowels, *ee*), so the final consonant is not doubled: *meeting*.

RULE 3: **When a word ends in a silent *-e*, the *-e* is dropped before adding a suffix that begins with a vowel. The *-e* is retained before a suffix that begins with a consonant.**

Let's apply this rule to a few examples:

SUFFIXES BEGINNING WITH VOWELS	SUFFIXES BEGINNING WITH CONSONANTS
move + -ing = moving	*move + -ment = movement*
love + -ing = loving	*love + -less = loveless*

This rule is fairly straightforward; however, it is complicated by a number of exceptions, which can only be memorized:

argument	courageous	mileage
canoeing	judgment	noticeable
changeable	manageable	truly

RULE 4: **When adding a suffix to a word ending in *-y*, change the *-y* to *i* if both of the following conditions are met: (1) the letter preceding the *-y* is a consonant; (2) the suffix is not *-ing*.**

Let's look as some examples:

WORD	APPLICATION OF RULE
happier	*Happy* ends in *-y,* and the preceding letter, *p,* is a consonant. The suffix *-er* is not *-ing,* so the *-y* is changed to *i.*
worrying	*Worry* ends in *-y,* and the preceding letter, *r,* is a consonant. However, the suffix is *-ing,* so the *-y* is retained.

This rule, too, has exceptions, among them *said, paid, laid,* and *daily.*

44c Frequently misspelled words

Here is a list of words whose spelling gives many people trouble; sometimes these are known as "spelling demons." You might want to have a friend test you on these words (or use a tape recorder). Add the ones you don't know to your spelling list.

absence	beginning	definite
accidentally	behavior	dependent
accommodate	believe	desert
actually	benefited	desperate
adequately	bureaucracy	dessert
adolescence	business	develop
amateur	calendar	development
among	category	dilemma
analyze	changeable	dining room
annually	cigarette	disappoint
answer	coming	disastrous
appreciate	committee	discussion
apologize	completely	disease
applying	conscience	eighth
appropriate	condemn	eligible
argument	conscientious	embarrass
assassination	controlled	environment
athlete	convenience	exaggerate
attendance	courtesy	excitable
available	criticize	exercise
beautiful	cruel	familiar
becoming	deceive	fascinate

a good idea to ask students to keep a record of their misspellings, either in a notebook or on index cards. Index cards can be grouped according to types of mistakes covered by the rules in 44b so that students can diagnose their own problem areas and concentrate on relevant rules. You might check to see that individuals have practiced writing repeated corrections of words previously misspelled. After all, there is no substitute for habit where spelling is concerned.

ACTIVITY

Though many spelling rules are fraught with exceptions, learning those rules can be helpful. You might ask students to keep spelling error lists, either in notebooks or on note cards, as recommended in the preceding annotation. Have students refer to the rules in 44b that relate to particular mistakes. Keeping track of spelling slips as they occur should help students to learn rules and correct erroneous habits.

44c
sp

ACTIVITY

Should you give a spelling quiz? Students tend to enjoy that sort of exercise, especially if the quiz is informal and ungraded. You might think of twenty words that you want students to learn by heart. Compose a multiple-choice quiz along the following lines: "*Directions:* Choose the letter of the correctly spelled word. 1. (*a*) ocured; (*b*) occurred; (*c*) occured. . . ." Allow fifteen minutes for completing the exercise, then review answers in class. Encourage students to use their notebooks for rote practice of words that were missed.

favorite
February
finally
financially
foreign
forty
fulfill
genius
government
grammar
guarantee
guidance
happened
height
heroes
hoping
humorous
illogical
immediately
independence
innocuous
inoculate
intelligent
interest
interruption
jewelry
judgment
knowledge
laboratory
leisure
length
library
license
losing
luxury
lying

marriage
mathematics
medicine
necessary
nickel
ninety
nuclear
nuisance
omission
oppressed
parallel
paralyze
personnel
persuade
possess
preferred
prejudice
privilege
probably
proceed
professor
psychology
pursue
quarrel
receipt
receive
recommend
recommendation
religion
religious
repetition
rhythm
ridicule
ridiculous
roommate
sacrilegious

sandwich
schedule
seize
separate
similar
sincerely
skiing
sophomore
speech
studying
succeed
sufficient
surprise
swimming
technique
temperature
thoroughly
though
thought
together
tragedy
transferred
truly
twelfth
unnecessary
until
usually
vacuum
valuable
villain
visibility
vitamin
weather
Wednesday
writing
written

44c
sp

44d Finding words in the dictionary when you don't know how to spell them

The most important tool for improving your spelling is a dictionary. If you are going to improve your spelling, you need to own a dictionary and keep it within reach when you are proofreading.

Certain strategies will allow you to find a word in the dictionary even if you don't know how to spell it. The most straightforward strategy is merely to write down two or more ways in which you think the word might be spelled and then look up each possibility. Chances are, one of them will be correct.

More difficult words—ones you have no idea how to spell—require a more complicated strategy. Focus on the first three to five letters of the word. Figure out as many options for spelling those sounds as you can think of. Then look each option up to see if there is a word beginning with that set of letters. If there is, check its definition to see if it means the same thing as the word you want. Continue until you have found the word you are seeking.

As you sound out the word, trying to think of possible ways it could be spelled, pay particular attention to the vowel sounds—that is where there are usually the most possible variations. Also watch for the following alternative consonant sounds:

1. The letters *c* and *sc,* as well as *s,* can represent the *ss* sound (for example, *bicycle* and *science*).
2. The letters *ch* and *ss,* as well as *sh,* can represent the *sh* sound (for example, *chauffeur* and *tissue*).
3. The letters *k, ck, qu,* and *ch,* as well as *c,* can represent the *k* sound (for example, *kill, lick, liquor,* and *school*).
4. The letters *s,* and *ss,* as well as *z,* can represent the *zz* sound (for example, *his* and *scissors*).
5. The letters *ph* and *gh,* as well as *f,* can represent the *ff* sound (for example, *phone* and *rough*).
6. Watch for double letters that sound like one (as in *alloy, giddy,* or *inning*).

44d
sp

There are many more alternative spellings in English, but this list will help you with the most common ones.

Using one of these strategies, you should be able to find most words in the dictionary. However, if you are still having trouble, you will need to buy what is known as a "bad speller's dictionary." In such a dictionary, words are listed according to the way they are usually *misspelled* as well as by the correct spelling. If you look a word up under the wrong spelling, the dictionary will give you the correct spelling.

44e Commonly confused words

Many spelling errors happen because the writer confuses **homophones**—two words that are pronounced the same or nearly the same but have different meanings. These mistakes are particularly troublesome because the spelling checker on a computer (see 44h) will not catch them.

Study the following lists, and make sure you understand the differences among these commonly confused words.

Words	Definitions
accept	to receive
except	excluding
advice	suggestions about a course of action (noun)
advise	to give advice (verb)
affect	to influence (verb); in psychology, feeling or emotion (noun)
effect	result of something (noun); rarely, to bring about a change (verb)
allusion	indirect reference
illusion	false idea
already	by now
all ready	completely prepared
altar	platform for religious ceremony (noun)
alter	to change (verb)
altogether	completely
all together	all in one place or at one time

44e
sp

Words	Definitions
always	forever
all ways	every way
ascent	climb
assent	agreement
bare	nude, naked
bear	to carry (verb); an animal (noun)
board	slab of wood
bored	uninterested
brake	device for stopping a vehicle
break	to damage, to fracture
breath	air from the lungs (noun)
breathe	to take in air (verb)
buy	to purchase
by	near, next to, through the agency of
capital	city where government is located
capitol	building where government meets
choose	to make a choice, (present tense)
chose	made a choice (past tense)
cite	to quote, to make reference to (verb)
sight	view, something to be seen (noun)
site	location (noun)
coarse	rough
course	path, college subject
complement	something that completes
compliment	praise or flattery
conscience	moral sense
conscious	awake, alert
council	governing body
counsel	advice
dairy	place with cows
diary	personal journal
descent	downward movement
decent	following accepted behavior
dissent	disagreement

44e
sp

Words	Definitions
dessert	sweet food at end of meal
desert	dry, barren area (noun); to abandon (verb)
discreet	modest, not showy
discrete	separate, individual
elicit	to ask for or draw out
illicit	illegal
eminent	prominent
immanent	inherent
imminent	about to happen
fair	light in color; just; a festival
fare	cost of transportation
formally	seriously, officially
formerly	previously
forth	forward
fourth	in position number four
gorilla	an animal
guerrilla	irregular soldier
hear	to use one's ears
here	in this place
heard	used one's ears
herd	group of animals
hole	opening, gap
whole	complete, entire
human	of people
humane	compassionate
its	belonging to it
it's	it is
know	to be mentally aware of
no	opposite of *yes*
later	subsequent in time
latter	second of two things
lead	a heavy metal (noun)
led	past tense of *lead* (verb)
lessen	to make less (verb)
lesson	something learned (noun)

44e
sp

WORDS	DEFINITIONS
loose	not tight
lose	to misplace
maybe	perhaps
may be	might be
miner	person who works in a mine
minor	person who is under age
moral	having to do with right and wrong; lesson from a fable or story
morale	attitude, spirit
pair	two of a kind
pare	to slice
pear	fruit
passed	past tense of *pass*
past	previous, earlier
patience	calm endurance
patients	people in a hospital
peace	opposite of *war*
piece	part of a whole
personal	intimate
personnel	employees
plain	simple, not fancy (adjective); flat land (noun)
plane	to shave wood (verb); an airplane (noun)
precede	to come before
proceed	to continue
presence	attendance
presents	gifts
principal	foremost, main (adjective); school administrator (noun)
principle	basic truth (noun)
quiet	opposite of *noisy*
quite	very
quit	to give up; to resign
rain	precipitation (noun)
reign	to rule (verb)
rein	strap to guide a horse (noun)

44e
sp

Words	Definitions
raise	to lift up (verb); an increase in pay (noun)
raze	to tear down (verb)
respectfully	with respect
respectively	in the order indicated
right	correct; opposite of *left* (adjective)
rite	ritual (noun)
write	to put words on paper (verb)
road	path (noun)
rode	past tense of *ride* (verb)
scene	place of action; section of a play (noun)
seen	past tense of *saw* (verb)
sense	perception; meaning
since	from the time of; because
stationary	standing still
stationery	writing paper
straight	not bent
strait	waterway between two landmasses
taught	past tense of *teach*
taut	tight, rigid
than	compared to
then	at that time
their	belonging to them
there	in that place
they're	they are
through	finished; passing into and out of
threw	past tense of *throw*
thorough	complete
to	toward; in the direction of; particle in verbals
too	also; excessively
two	one more than one
waist	area above the hips (noun)
waste	to use excessively and carelessly (verb); **material to be thrown away (noun)**
weak	not strong
week	seven days

44e
sp

Words	Definitions
weather	atmospheric conditions
whether	if
where	in which place
were	past-tense form of *be*
we're	we are
wear	to have on one's body, as clothes
which	what; that
witch	sorcerer
whose	belonging to whom
who's	who is
your	belonging to you
you're	you are
yore	long ago

44f Spelling plural nouns

The following examples illustrate the basic rule for forming plurals of nouns in English.

one girl / two girls
one computer / many computers

Basic Rule: **To make a noun plural, add -*s* to the singular form.**

Nouns that do not follow the basic rule are considered irregular. The following examples illustrate one group of irregular nouns.

one bush / six bushes
one church / three churches
one class / three classes
a hero / two heroes
one tomato / two tomatoes

Exception 1: **When a word ends in -*ch*, -*sh*, -*ss*, -*x*, or -*z*, add an -*es* ending instead of just an -*s* to make it plural.**

In addition, most words that end in -*o* form their plurals by adding -*es;* however, the examples on page 436 are exceptions and form their plurals by adding just -*s*.

COLLABORATIVE ACTIVITY

Members of editing groups might check the spelling of plural nouns in one another's drafts.

44f
sp

one lasso / two lassos
one piano / two pianos
one radio / two radios
one soprano / two sopranos

The following examples illustrate a second way in which irregular nouns form their plurals.

half / halves	self / selves
knife / knives	thief / thieves
life / lives	wolf / wolves

EXCEPTION 2: **To pluralize a noun that ends in -*f* or -*fe*, change the -*f* or -*fe* to *v* and add -*es*.**

There are several exceptions to this exception:

one belief / two beliefs	one roof / two roofs
one chief / two chiefs	one safe / two safes
one cuff / two cuffs	

The following examples illustrate another variation on the rule for forming plural nouns:

one enemy / two enemies	this sky / these skies
one French fry / two French fries	one study / two studies
one lily / two lilies	one try / two tries

EXCEPTION 3: **To pluralize a noun that ends in a consonant and -*y*, change the -*y* to *i* and add -*es*.**

The following group illustrates an exception to exception 3:

one boy / two boys	one Monday / two Mondays
one day / two days	one ray / two rays

EXCEPTION 4: **To pluralize a noun that ends in a vowel and -*y*, just add -*s*.**

The following examples illustrate yet another group of irregular noun plurals:

one deer / two deer	one moose / two moose
one fish / two fish (or fishes)	one sheep / two sheep

EXCEPTION 5: **Some very irregular nouns do not change their form from singular to plural.**

44f
sp

44g American versus British spelling

The British spelling of some words is different from the American spelling. This can be particularly confusing for students who have previously studied British English. The most common of these words are listed here. When writing for an American audience, you should use the American spelling.

AMERICAN	BRITISH
acknowledgment	acknowledgement
anesthetic	anaesthetic
apologize	apologise
behavior	behaviour
canceled	cancelled
center	centre
check	cheque
civilization	civilisation
color	colour
connection	connexion
criticize	criticise
defense	defence
dreamed	dreamt
endeavor	endeavour
fetus	foetus
honor	honour
humor	humour
inflection	inflexion
judgment	judgement
labor	labour
licorice	liquorice
mold	mould
neighbor	neighbour
realize	realise
smolder	smoulder
theater	theatre
traveled	travelled
vigor	vigour

44h Using computer spelling checkers

Most word processing programs feature a "spelling checker." After you have finished a draft of a paper or other writing on a

44g
sp

ESL

ACTIVITY

word processor, you can just run it through the spelling checker. This program highlights each word that might be misspelled and gives you a chance to change it. You decide whether or not it is spelled the way you want it to be. The screen lists suspect words and may suggest alternative choices. These programs can be a real blessing for people who are weak spellers. If your office or school has computers, ask about spelling checkers.

Unfortunately, the computer cannot tell when a misspelled word actually forms a correctly spelled word. For example, if you mistakenly write *effect* when the word you mean is *affect,* the computer cannot detect the error. Similarly, if you type in *king* when you mean *kind,* the computer will not recognize the error. You will have to catch such errors when you proofread your writing.

Spelling checkers can also be an excellent tool for improving your spelling skill. Each time you finish checking the spelling in a document, many computers ask if you want a list of the words you corrected. Tell the computer "yes." Then save the printouts it gives you, and you will have a list of the words you have trouble spelling.

44h
sp

WRITING: SPECIAL SITUATIONS

A research paper may be the most demanding project assigned in a composition course. For many students it may also be a worrisome challenge. Developing an original viewpoint, gathering sources competently, and maintaining control of the developing paper are all necessary if writers are to avoid the pitfalls of plagiarism and disorganized reporting. This chapter can help teach your class to think of original topics. Also, its general introduction to library sources identifies many useful points of departure for exercising research skills.

FOR DISCUSSION

Spend some time discussing the difference between merely summarizing available material and developing an original research report. Students sometimes wonder how anything called research can be original if it must be based on sources. You might point out that the originality consists in the researcher's way of discussing and evaluating those sources. In general, a research project is bound to be original if it focuses on a question that is still open to debate or interpretation. Depending on the topic, the researcher may discover a number of different views on the issue, which he or she will call attention to by way of quotation, summary, or paraphrase. But in the final analysis, the researcher must contribute his or her own ideas to the discussion of the issue.

45a
res

45 THE RESEARCH PAPER: IDENTIFYING A TOPIC AND GATHERING INFORMATION

There was a time when students could expect to do most of their writing in humanities and literature classes. Today, however, writing is taught and practiced in every discipline, and you are likely to encounter all types of writing and research assignments across the curriculum. Getting comfortable with the process by which you move from assignment to finished product in a research paper will certainly improve your chances for success in college. Although some aspects of the research process vary from discipline to discipline, the basic strategies for conducting research remain the same.

45a What is a research paper?

A research paper is an entirely new work that you create by consulting several sources to answer a research question. The paper is a synthesis of your interpretation and evaluation of the information you discover, with complete documentation of where these discoveries came from (see 46c for a discussion of documentation). It is *not* a summary of an article or book or a collection of summaries of articles or books.

The entire process of writing a research paper can take a great deal of time, depending on the assignment. The following timetable is a guide based on an assignment given on November 15 and due on December 15.

Assignment:	Write a ten- to twenty-page research paper on a current issue, using a minimum of five sources.

DEADLINE	PHASE	ACTIVITIES
Nov. 18	Narrowing the topic, forming a tentative thesis	Brainstorming, visiting the library, preliminary reading, talking with people, forming tentative thesis

Deadline	Phase	Activities
Nov. 23	Gathering information	Locating primary and secondary information (see 45c for more information about primary and secondary sources)
Nov. 30	Recording information, refining and revising the thesis as necessary	Compiling bibliography cards; preparing summary, paraphrase, quotation, and personal-comment notes; refining thesis statement
Dec. 2	Organizing ideas	Making an outline
Dec. 15	Writing the paper	Drafting, revising, editing, drafting, revising, and so on; preparing a Works Cited or References page

45b Selecting and narrowing a topic: identifying your purpose

Depending on the situation, your instructor will either assign a topic for research or ask you to develop one. In either case, you will need to do three things right away:

- Interpret your assignment
- Refine your topic
- Develop a working hypothesis

If your professor provides a topic, get as much clarification as you can regarding purpose, style, and form. If you are allowed to choose the topic, consider only research that will sincerely interest you—that will answer a question, satisfy your curiosity, or further an interest. Nothing is less productive or more tedious than conducting research that bores you. (See 2b for a complete discussion of choosing and narrowing your topic).

Once you have decided on a topic, you will need to narrow your focus by identifying your purpose. Keep in mind, however,

COLLABORATIVE ACTIVITY

Depending on the nature of your research assignment, you might have groups gather for brainstorming sessions having to do with the assignment and with the problem of limiting topics to focused issues. Students who are working to narrow a topic may find a review of 2b useful.

45b
res

RESOURCES

Esch, Robert M. "Research Paper Paranoia." *College Composition and Communication* 26 (1975): 42–43.

Marshall, Colleen. "A System for Teaching College Freshmen to Write a Research Paper." *College English* 40 (1978): 87–89.

Martin, R. G. "Plagiarism and Originality: Some Remedies." *English Journal* 60 (1971): 621–28.

Schwegler, Robert A., and Linda K. Shamoon. "The Aims and Processes of the Research Paper." *College English* 44 (1982): 817–24.

The articles listed above offer useful and often entertaining advice for teachers assigning term papers. Bibliographical indexes and other resources available to student researchers are listed separately throughout this chapter.

FOR DISCUSSION

Stress the importance of beginning research early. Warn students that last-minute library searches can be frustrating because needed materials can be checked out of the library and unavailable within the time allowed for the project.

45c
res

that your paper will likely change as you work on it, and at every stage of the writing process, your paper should become more focused and your purpose clearer.

45c Gathering information

After you have narrowed your topic and developed a tentative thesis, you will engage in the most time-consuming part of planning your paper: reading, collecting, and assembling information. In a general sense, you will have two sources other than personal experience from which to draw this information. First, you will have the library, with its varied print and multimedia resources; second, you may have the results of field research, including informal and formal discussions with your professor, other faculty members, and fellow students.

Primary and secondary sources

Most of the materials you will consult in the library will be secondary sources, but you should also consider using primary sources when they are available.

Primary sources. The Sears, Roebuck catalog for a particular year is an example of a primary source. Other primary sources include letters and diaries; transcripts of interviews; government statistics; photographs; and video or audio recordings. In the sciences, the results of experiments and data from field observations are considered primary evidence. Evidence from primary sources means little in itself—it's raw data that need to be analyzed and interpreted in order to be meaningful.

Secondary sources. When scholars and scientists analyze and interpret data from primary sources and publish the results of their analyses, these books or articles are secondary sources. For example, if a sociologist analyzed all mention of the activities of children in Sears, Roebuck catalogs from 1900 to 1910 and published the results of that study in a scholarly journal, the article would be a secondary source that the student could consult while gathering evidence.

Using the library

The library is an intimidating place for many students—for obvious reasons. Your college or university library is undoubtedly different from the one in your hometown. Further, advances in technology have turned what once seemed a simple search-and-retrieval process into a highly sophisticated treasure hunt. With the introduction of the compact disc read-only memory system (CD-ROM), computerized databases, and increased reliance on multimedia resources, students must achieve a new type of research sophistication.

Given this wide array of information, a student must first research the library before researching a topic. Your composition class may tour the research facilities at your campus. If so, take notes and ask questions. Especially at larger institutions, where there are often many specialized subject-specific campus libraries, it's quite possible that the library itself will offer an orientation program.

Upon entering the library, locate the information or circulation desk and the reserve room. Also acquaint yourself with the following sources of information:

- Card catalogs (subject, author, and title) and shelflist (catalog file of periodical holdings)
- On-line catalog of the library's holdings
- CD-ROM and on-line database facilities
- Interlibrary loan desk
- Current periodicals, both bound and unbound
- Microfilm or microfiche of older periodicals
- Reference room

One of the most helpful resources in writing your research paper will be your reference librarian. Students are often reluctant to ask reference librarians questions; however, that is why they are there. Reference librarians can help you narrow the focus of your topic, locate a source, or give you information about preparing a bibliography.

The diagram on page 444 traces the procedure for using the library in order to narrow your topic and conduct your research.

The diagram on page 444 traces the procedure for using the library

ACTIVITY

Most college libraries offer staff lectures and introductory tours by appointment. Consider arranging for a librarian to meet with your class to discuss library materials. Be sure to notify the lecturer in advance of your class research project so that he or she can focus on materials relevant to that assignment.

45c
res

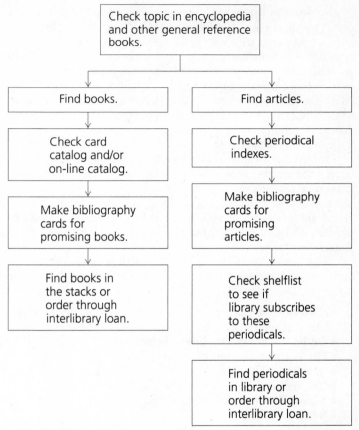

Adapted from Ellen Strenski and Madge Manfred, *The Research Paper Workbook*, 2nd ed.

The reference area

When you have a topic in mind (or if you are choosing among several possible topics), your first step might be to explore your subject by reading about it in encyclopedias and other general-reference books. The library's reference room holds generalized and subject-specific dictionaries, almanacs,

and encyclopedias loaded with definitions, statistical information, and article summaries. Though instructors may frown at reliance on these reference tools due to their limited scope and currency, few would object to their use early in the research process, when you are choosing and narrowing your topic. Use them sparingly to define and classify your subject and to confirm facts and figures.

Here's what you can expect to find in your library's reference room:

General encyclopedias. General encyclopedias contain entries about famous people, historical events, places in the world, scientific discoveries, and natural phenomena, among other subjects. They are a good starting place as you begin to explore a topic.

- *Encyclopedia Americana.* 30 volumes. Reprinted yearly.
- *New Encyclopaedia Britannica.* 32 volumes. 1990.
- *Collier's Encyclopedia.* 24 volumes. 1988.

Specialized encyclopedias. These sources contain articles about a wide variety of topics in a given field. Not only can these encyclopedias help you narrow your topic and develop your tentative thesis, but they can also provide you with leads to pursue for further information. Authors of signed articles in specialized encyclopedias are experts in their fields, and it's often useful to look for other sources written by them.

- *CRC Handbook of Chemistry and Physics.* Since 1913.
- *Britannica Encyclopedia of American Art.* 1976.
- *Encyclopaedia Judaica.* 16 volumes. 1972 and decennial book 1973–1982.
- *Encyclopedia of Biological Sciences.* 1970.
- *Encyclopedia of Black America.* 1981.
- *Encyclopedia of Management.* 1982.
- *Encyclopedia of Business Information Sources.* 1992.
- *Encyclopedia of Community Planning and Environmental Protection.* 1983.

45c
res

- *Encyclopedia of Economics.* 1982.
- *Encyclopedia of Educational Research.* 1992.
- *Encyclopedia of Geographic Information Sources.* 1986.
- *Encyclopedia of Pop, Rock, and Soul.* 1990.
- *Encyclopedia of Psychology,* 1984.
- *Encyclopedia of Social Work.* 1987 and supplements.
- *Encyclopedia of World Architecture.* 1982.
- *Encyclopedia of World Art.* 1959–1968; supplements 1983 and 1987.
- *Guide to American Law.* 1945–1985 and annual supplements.
- *International Encyclopedia of the Social Sciences.* 1977. Biographical supplement 1979.
- *McGraw-Hill Encyclopedia of World Drama.* 1984.
- *McGraw-Hill Encyclopedia of Science and Technology.* 1992.
- *The Oxford Companion to American Literature.* 1983.
- *The Oxford Companion to Art.* 1970.
- *The Oxford Companion to English Literature.* 1985.

Dictionaries. Unabridged dictionaries provide definitions of most words in a given language. Specialized dictionaries provide definitions of the terms used within a particular field or subject area.

- *Dictionary of American History.* 1976.
- *Dictionary of Computing.* 1990.
- *The New Grove Dictionary of Music and Musicians.* 20 volumes. 1980.
- *The Oxford English Dictionary,* 2nd ed. 20 volumes. 1989.
- *The Random House Dictionary of the English Language,* 2nd ed. 1987.
- *Webster's Third New International Dictionary of the English Language.* 1986.

Yearbooks and almanacs. These books are compilations of facts and statistics, usually updated yearly. For example, *Statistical Abstracts of the United States* provides social, political, and economic statistics gathered by the U.S. Census Bureau. The *Facts on File Yearbook* provides factual information and statistics

45c
res

for a wide variety of subjects, including sports, government, and science.

- *Americana Annual.* Annually since 1923.
- *Facts on File Yearbook.* Annually since 1941.
- *Information Please Almanac.* Annually since 1974.
- *Statesman's Yearbook.* Annually since 1964.
- *Statistical Abstracts of the United States.* Annually since 1878.
- *World Almanac and Book of Facts.* Annually since 1868.

Biographical references. These sources provide brief biographies of important people. A biographical reference such as *Current Biography* deals with contemporary public figures in a wide variety of fields, whereas the *Dictionary of Literary Biography* confines itself to authors of fiction and nonfiction.

- *Biology and Geneology Master Index.* 8 volumes. 1980. Annual supplements since 1986.
- *Current Biography.* Since 1940.
- *Dictionary of American Biography.* 17 volumes (supplements). 1927–1984.
- *Dictionary of Literary Biography.* 38 volumes (supplements). 1978.
- *McGraw-Hill Encyclopedia of World Biography.* 16 volumes. 1989.
- *Notable American Women. 1607–1950.* 1974.
- *Notable American Women: The Modern Period.* 1980.
- *Webster's New Biographical Dictionary.* 1988.
- *Who's Who in America.* Since 1899. (See also *Who's Who* for subject group and geographical locations.)
- *World Authors, 1950–1970.* 1975; supplements 1979 and 1985.

Atlases. Atlases are books of maps. Often they also include tables with statistical information, such as the populations of countries, the heights of mountains, and the lengths of rivers.

- *Goode's World Atlas,* 18th ed. 1992.
- *New York Times Atlas of the World,* 9th ed. 1992.
- *Rand McNally Historical Atlas of the World.* 1981.

45c
res

Your general reading on your topic should help you narrow it to a more specific subject. Perhaps you started with a topic such as the section of New York City known as Harlem. After reading about Harlem in several general encyclopedias, you decide to narrow your topic to the African-American jazz musicians who played in music clubs there during the 1920s. After doing some more background reading in the *Encyclopedia of Black America* and the *New Grove Dictionary of Jazz*, your next step is to look for books and articles on this subject in the catalogs of the library's holdings and in the periodical indexes.

One caution: if you find that your library has a limited number of sources on a given topic, you may want to reconsider your subject and choose another one for which your library has adequate resources.

Catalogs of the library's holdings

Many libraries, especially larger ones, will have both a card catalog and an on-line catalog. It may be that newer records will be available only on the on-line catalog and older records will be found only in the card catalog. If your library has both, it's a good idea to ask the reference librarian for the *cutoff date*—the date when the library began entering its new holdings only into the on-line catalog. If the source you are looking for was published before this date, you'll have to look for it in the card catalog. If it was published after the cutoff date, you'll have to consult the on-line catalog.

Searching the on-line catalog. Once you have learned to use your library's on-line catalog, searching it for books on your topic can save you a great deal of time. If you have never used one, ask the reference librarian for assistance. Usually, instructions on how to use the catalog will also be available either on-screen or near the computer terminal. If you are searching for books on a particular subject, you'll have to enter key words related to that topic. The computer will provide a list of the library's holdings on the subject you enter.

One valuable source of key words is the *Library of Congress Subject Headings* (LCSH). The LCSH lists headings and sub-headings used by the Library of Congress in cataloging books. A quick look at your topic heading in the LCSH can spare you hours of time searching for books with a key word that isn't used by your library. The LCSH can also help you find out if you have narrowed your topic sufficiently. If your heading has a large number of subheadings in the LCSH, chances are it's too broad for the scope of your paper.

The card catalog. Because many libraries—even larger ones—still record a book's author, subject, and title information on indexed and cross-referenced cards, it helps to be familiar with the format of these cards.

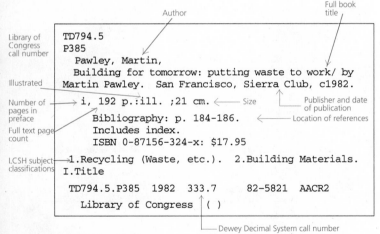

Sample author card.

```
TD794.5
P385
  RECYCLING
  Building for tomorrow: putting waste to work/ by
Martin Pawley.  San Francisco, Sierra Club, c1982.

    i, 192 p.:ill. ;21 cm.
      Bibliography: p. 184-186.
      Includes index.
      ISBN 0-87156-324-x: $17.95

  1.Recycling (Waste, etc.).   2.Building Materials.
I.Title
TD794.5.P385    1982    333.7    82-5821    AACR2
    Library of Congress  ( )
```

Sample subject card.

```
TD794.5
P385
  Building for tomorrow
  Pawley, Martin, Building for tomorrow: putting
waste to work/ by Martin Pawley.  San Francisco,
Sierra Club,   c1982.

    i, 192 p.:ill. ;21 cm.
      Bibliography: p. 184-186.
      Includes index.
      ISBN 0-87156-324-x: $17.95

  1.Recycling (Waste, etc.).   2.Building Materials.
I.Title
 TD794.5.P385    1982    333.7    82-5821    AACR2
    Library of Congress  ( )
```

Sample title card.

When you are looking through the entries for your topic in the on-line or card catalog, keep your working thesis (see 2b) in mind, and ask yourself the following questions:

1. When was the book published or reprinted? (Will the information be current or out of date?)

2. Am I using more than one work by the same author? (You may of course use any number or works by the same author, but sound research maintains a necessary balance. Avoid reliance on a single source.)
3. Does the book have a bibliography and an index? (Will reviewing this book lead me elsewhere?)
4. What other Library of Congress subject headings have been assigned to the book? They can serve as cross-references.

Make bibliography cards for all books that appear to be potentially useful (see 45g).

The stacks (and special collections)

The official term for the area in which books are shelved is the *stacks*. Most libraries allow you to walk freely through this area; others insist that you request books from library attendants. In addition to the stacks, many libraries include special collections (often noncirculating). These contain rare and often irreplaceable primary source items, such as letters, diaries, and manuscripts. Consider using all available resources, including these special collections.

Interlibrary loan

In this age of comprehensive indexing, you may uncover a number of books or journals in your search that are not part of your library's permanent collection. If such is the case, you may turn to interlibrary loan services. Most colleges are linked through the On-line Computer Library Center (OCLC) with libraries in their own and neighboring states. Occasionally, institutions charge for the privilege of borrowing through interlibrary loan; most do not.

Getting books from other libraries is often a time-consuming procedure, however. Ask how long you'll have to wait before the book arrives, the length of the borrowing period, and other possible restrictions. Also, *be sure that you really want what you request.* It is cumbersome and impractical to review a large number of books through interlibrary loan. Should you decide

45c
res

against interlibrary loan, choose alternate texts, or check your city or town library. Also find out if your college has a reciprocal agreement with schools nearby. If your library is networked with others via an on-line database, you can in most cases even determine if a book has been checked out or is available in the stacks.

Periodical indexes and computerized databases

In addition to books, you'll also need to locate relevant articles in periodicals (journals, magazines, and newspapers). There are literally thousands of printed and on-line indexes to articles in periodicals published and updated on a regular basis.

Your library will probably have bound indexes as well as computerized databases to help you find information on your topic. The library may have indexes stored on compact discs that can be read but not amended. These are known as *CD-ROM indexes,* and they usually consist of a computer terminal with a drive for inserting the compact discs. Print and CD-ROM indexes are updated monthly or quarterly.

In addition, the library may have access to one or more commercial databases. Check with your reference librarian regarding the particulars (including possible cost) of a computerized or on-line search. Whereas libraries usually won't charge for the use of a CD-ROM product, gaining access to an on-line database such as MEDLINE involves connecting the library's computer to a vendor by modem and can be expensive. Usually, the search is conducted by a librarian to keep the expense down. Although some libraries subsidize the cost, others may charge you for computer time.

As with the library catalogs, searching either a print or computerized index also involves using key words related to your topic. For example, a student doing a paper on African-American jazz musicians in Harlem during the 1920s might decide to search the magazine index for relevant articles. If, following the instructions on the computer screen, he or she enters the word *Harlem,* a number of subheadings will appear, including three promising ones: *history, popular culture,* and *1920–1929.* Selecting any of these subheadings will generate a list of one or more articles. The key words *jazz music* produce another possibly help-

You might check with your library to find out whether computerized databases must be used by appointment. If appointments are required, let your class know.

45c
res

ful subheading, *history*. A look at the *Library of Congress Subject Headings* might give the student other key words to try.

General indexes, newspaper indexes and databases, and bound indexes and computerized databases for a number of academic fields are listed below—in many cases, an index will be available in both print and computerized form.

GENERAL SOURCES

- *Biography Index*. Since 1946. Indexes biographies, autobiographies, memoirs, journals. Also available as CD-ROM.
- *InfoTrac*. Since 1984. CD-ROM system that catalogs business, popular, and academic periodicals; expanded academic index.
- *Magazine Index*. Available both on-line and as a CD-ROM system. Indexes over four hundred popular magazines, with annotations.
- *Poole's Index to Periodical Literature*. 1802–1906. Subject index to British and American periodicals of the nineteenth century.
- *Popular Periodical Index*. Since 1973. Index of contemporary and regional issues.
- *Public Affairs Information Service* (Bulletin). Since 1915. Indexes over fourteen hundred international publications in native languages. Areas include business, education, law, and social work (CD-ROM, on-line).
- *Readers' Guide to Periodical Literature*. Since 1900. American periodical index, concentrating on high-circulation magazines. Also available as a CD-ROM system.
- *Vertical File Index*. 1935. Subject and title index to pamphlet material with summary description. (For congressional publications, see *Congressional Information Service Annual*.)

INDEXES TO NEWSPAPERS AND WIRE SERVICES

- *National Newspaper Index*. Available on-line, as a CD-ROM system, and on microfiche and microfilm reels. Does not have annotations.
- *New York Times Index*. Since 1913. Includes *Personal Name Index to the New York Times, 1851–1979*. Indexes articles throughout the twentieth century. Brief abstract of each article. Available on-line with full text.

45c
res

- AP (Associated Press) News. Computerized database.
- Reuters. Computerized database.
- UPI (United Press International) News. Computerized database.

Sources for Specific Academic Fields

Art

- Art Bibliographies Modern.
- *Art Index*. Since 1929. Indexes over two hundred periodicals, yearbooks, and other manuscripts (CD-ROM, Wilsonline).
- Art Literature International.

Business

- *Business Periodical Index*. Since 1958. Index of over three hundred business periodicals; includes management, marketing, personnel (CD-ROM, Wilsonline).
- D&B Dun's Financial Records.
- D&B Electronic Yellow Pages.
- *Wall Street Journal Index*. Since 1958. Index of business-related topics. Published annually.

Computing

- INSPEC.

Economics

- *Index of Economic Articles*. Since 1961. Index to articles in theoretical and applied economics.

Education

- *Current Index to Journals in Education*. Since 1969.
- *Education Index*. Since 1929. Indexes over 350 periodicals, books, reports, and other publications (CD-ROM, Wilsonline).
- ERIC.
- *State Education Journal Index*. Since 1963. A regional perspective on education.

Engineering

- *Engineering Index*. Since 1906. Index of technical engineering periodicals.

45c
res

Ethnic Studies

- Social SCISEARCH.

History

- Historical Abstracts.

Literature and Language

- *Abstracts of English Studies*. Since 1958. Abstracts, monographs, and index of journal articles.
- *Humanities Index*. Since 1974. Indexes material across the humanities. Provides subject/author access to over three hundred English titles (CD-ROM).
- *MLA International Bibliography of Books and Articles on the Modern Languages and Literatures*. Since 1921. Indexes articles on ethnic languages and literature, including French, German, Latin, Spanish, and Russian (CD-ROM).
- *Book Review Digest*. Since 1905. Index to excerpted book reviews (CD-ROM).
- *Index to Book Reviews in the Humanities*. Since 1960. Suited for research of nonliterary works.

Medicine

- *Cumulative Index Medicus*. Since 1958. General index to medical journals.
- MEDLINE.

Music

- *Music Index*. 1949. Index of band issues, music therapy, instrumentation, and composition.

Philosophy

- *Philosopher's Index*. Since 1967. Indexes journals across the spectrum of philosophical inquiry (CD-ROM, on-line).

Psychology and Sociology

- Sociological Abstracts.
- *Social Sciences and Humanities Index*. 1965–1974. (Replaced by *Social Science Index*. 1974.) Provides subject/author access to over three hundred English periodicals (CD-ROM, Wilsonline).

45c
res

Sciences

- *Applied Science and Technology Index.* Since 1958. Wide-ranging index of subjects in aerospace technology, robotics, data processing, computer science, telecommunications, and electronics (CD-ROM, Wilsonline).
- *Current Physics Index.* Since 1967. Index of physics studies, both applied and theoretical.
- *Environmental Index.* Since 1971. Indexes general environmental periodicals and those concerned with environmental psychology, philosophy, and application.
- *General Science Index.* Since 1978. Especially valuable index of science periodicals for the lay researcher. Provides subject access to over one hundred English periodicals (CD-ROM).
- NTIS.
- SCISEARCH.

As with books, make bibliography cards for all promising articles that you turn up in your search (see 45g).

45d Other forms of research

In many fields, particularly psychology and sociology, your goal as a researcher will be a thoughtful integration of information from books and articles with information gathered in the field. Your effort will not only improve your credibility as a researcher and writer, but it will also make for a more effective essay, report, or term paper.

Of the numerous varieties of field research strategies, the most widely used are undoubtedly the *interview* and the *questionnaire.*

Interview

A sound formal interview—one that yields important, useful, and verifiable information—is well conceived, well planned, and well documented. As opposed to an impromptu or on-the-spot interview, the well-conceived interview requires that you ask yourself the following questions:

45d
res

1. What is the purpose of the interview?
2. Whom shall I interview to achieve this purpose?
3. How shall I prepare the text of my interview to address both my purpose and the personality of the person or persons being interviewed?

The purpose of introducing interview material into any research project is mostly to achieve a balanced presentation. Beyond that, the content of an interview is important for its currency (interviews are, after all, up-to-the-minute accounts), its immediacy (interviews tend to get to the heart of the matter in ways that published material cannot), and its texture (interviews often provide a refreshing human touch to research).

Having considered the purpose, you'll want to locate worthy interview subjects. When evaluating prospective candidates, consider their availability, reliability, and authority. Also consider the issues of fair and equal representation; that is, don't interview too many subjects with similar points of view. The most difficult aspect of the interview process, however, is determining not why or whom but *how* to interview.

Successful interviewers prepare by reading background materials. Make sure that you're familiar with your own research goals and appropriately acquainted with the personal or professional life of the subject of the interview. It's also a good idea to draft a tentative list of questions or an outline for use during the interview. It's often difficult to think of questions under pressure. While conducting the interview, however, do not hesitate to ask impromptu follow-up questions requesting clarification, elaboration, or illustration as necessary. Ask fair, balanced, open-ended questions designed to elicit telling responses, not to impose your own opinions or values. Avoid yes-no and fill-in questions and anything that suggests your personal bias.

If possible, take handwritten and tape-recorded notes of the interview (if you plan to tape-record the interview, be sure to get your subject's permission in advance). These notes will serve as a permanent and verifiable record of your conversation. As soon as you have the time, go back and examine your notes.

Groups might gather to practice the techniques reviewed here. Participants can interview one another about selected issues of public interest, such as drug abuse, taxes, fee or tuition increases, or freedom of speech. An interview dialogue may begin with a question such as "What is your position on . . . ?" Circulate among the groups to make sure that individual interviewers are recording answers accurately.

45d
res

If you cannot decode a response or find it unclear, call and ask the person for further explanation. Be faithful and accurate. Finally, express your appreciation by calling or sending a thank-you note.

Questionnaire

When it's essential to gather the opinions of many people, interviews are often not possible and are certainly less convenient than questionnaires. Though you sacrifice some of the currency, immediacy, and texture of an interview, a questionnaire allows for a measure of comprehensiveness. It also provides your subjects with increased privacy and the opportunity for reflection.

As with the interview, to construct an effective questionnaire, you'll have to consider purpose (what), audience (who), and method (how). You must also be sure to gather information from a sufficient number of people to be able to generalize from your results (see 3c).

Because few people will willingly respond to an exhaustive document, narrow your concerns and limit your questions. Some people find writing a chore; therefore, it makes sense to provide a mix of open-ended, multiple-choice, comparison, and short-answer questions. Strive to make your questions as objective as possible. If you can, ask a friend to complete your questionnaire—the friend's responses will help you spot weak, inappropriate, or confusing questions.

Once you have collected your questionnaires, you'll have to sort, select, and interpret the information according to your needs.

45e A research journal

Writing a research paper requires a great deal of organization. Keeping a research journal is one way to help you in your task. Here is an excerpt from Ken Mitchell's research journal, used while he was composing "Don't Throw It Out" for Professor Gina Zirinsky's composition class (see 46g for an outline, partial draft, and revision of the complete research paper).

Research Journal

<u>Zirinsky's assignment to class</u>: Write a research paper
on a current issue using a minimum of five sources.

<u>Deciding on a topic</u>: Having spent my summers working in
the city of Ithaca's curbside recycling program, I
decided to write not on recycling--which didn't seem to
be working out as well as the city had hoped--but on a
related area, reusing or remanufacturing.

<u>Questions to myself</u>: Is there a way to turn used things
into new without the energy, bother, and complications of
this kind of recycling effort?

<u>Asking teachers and friends</u>: Because this is such a hot
subject, everyone suggested that I combine library and
field research (interviews). That suits me fine--I can
get out and walk around!

<u>In the library</u>: Found nothing useful under the term
<u>remanufacturing</u> in the on-line catalog, so checked for
terms other than <u>remanufacturing</u> to widen my search. The
reference librarian suggested that I use an unabridged
dictionary for a more detailed definition of the word and
a thesaurus for possible synonyms. She then directed me
toward the <u>Library of Congress Subject Headings</u> (LCSH)
listing. This allowed me to locate other subject

classifications under which <u>remanufacturing</u> could be listed. The two most promising major headings in the LCSH were "Salvage (Waste, etc.)" and "Recycling (Waste, etc.)."

*Sample LCSH Classification**

Salvage (Waste, etc.) *(May Subd Geog)*
    [HD9975 (Economics)]
    [TP995–TP996 (Technology)]
    Here are entered works on reclaiming and reusing equipment, parts, structures, etc. Works on the processing of waste paper, cans, bottles, etc. are entered under Recycling (Waste, etc.).
   UF Conversion of waste products
       Industrial salvage
       Recovery of waste products
       Solid waste management
       Utilization of waste products
       Waste management
       Waste reclamation
   BT Waste products
   RT Recycling (Waste, etc.)
       Refuse and refuse disposal
   NT Airplanes—Salvaging
       Barns—Salvaging
       Buildings—Salvaging
       Locomotives—Scrapping
       Resource recovery facilities
       Scrap metals
       Ships—Scrapping
       Water reuse
 —Computer programs

Recycling (Waste, etc.) *(May Subd Geog)*
    [TD794.5}
    Here are entered works on the processing of waste paper, cans, bottles, etc. Works on reclaiming and reusing equipment, parts, structures, etc. are entered under Salvage (Waste, etc.)
   UF Conversion of waste products
       Recovery of natural resources
       Recovery of waste materials
       Resource recovery
       Waste recycling
       Waste reuse
   BT Conservation of natural resources
       Pollution control industry
       Refuse and refuse disposal
   RT Energy conservation
       Salvage (Waste, etc.)
       Waste products
   SA *subdivision* Recycling *under subjects,*
       e.g. Waste paper—Recycling;
       Glass waste—Recycling
   NT Agricultural wastes—Recycling
       Animal waste—Recycling
       Copper—Recycling
       Deposit-refund systems
       Fish-culture—Water-supply—Recycling
       Metals—Recycling
       Organic wastes—Recycling
       Pavements, Asphalt—Recycling
       Pavements, Concrete—Recycling
       Recycling industry
       Resource recovery facilities
       Scrap metals—Recycling
       Waste products as road materials
       Water reuse
 —Law and legislation *(May Subd Geog)*
Recycling industry *(May Subd Geog)*
    [HD9975]
   BT Recycling (Waste, etc.)
   NT Scrap metal industry

---

*Abbreviations used: UF = "used for"; BT = "broader topic"; RT = "related topic"; SA = "see also"; NT = "narrower topic."

Finally, she sent me to the <u>Readers' Guide to Periodical</u>
<u>Literature</u>, the <u>Encyclopedia of Community Planning and</u>
<u>Environmental Protection</u>, the <u>Encyclopedia of Business</u>
<u>Information</u>, and the <u>World Almanac and Book of Facts</u>.

Sample from **Readers' Guide.**

SALVAGE (WASTE)
       See also
       Recycling (Waste, etc.)
       Scrap metal
Prospectors mine landfills for profit. D. E. Loupe. *Science*
  News 138:219 0 6 '90
            Anecdotes, facetiae, satire, etc.
A place of splendid dreams, R. L. Welsch. *Natural History*
  p78+ My '90

After this portion of his search, Ken turned up a number of
other headings to pursue, including "conversion of waste products," "recovery of waste materials," "waste reuse," and "utilization of waste products." While in the library, he sought out the
InfoTrac system and made a printout of what he found:

InfoTrac listings.

```
Heading:   RECYCLING INDUSTRY
             -Innovations

   1.      Recycling Britain. (recycling of domestic waste in
           Great Britain)(includes related article on US
           recycling of waste) by John Newell il v127 New
           Scientist Sept 8 '90 p46(3)

   2.      Natural plastics. (Special issue: The Endless
           Cycle - producing biodegradable plastics with
           bacteria) by R. Clinton Fuller and Robert W. Lenz il
           v99 Natural History May '90 p82(3)
           55L1741
               LIBRARY SUBSCRIBES TO JOURNAL

   3.      New method for recycling plastics. by Mindy B.
           Horowitz v31 Environment May '89 p23(2)
               LIBRARY SUBSCRIBES TO JOURNAL

   4.      New paths for old tyres to tread. by John Emsley
           il v121 New Scientist March 4 '89 p34(1)
```

45e
res

The InfoTrac database revealed a number of possible articles for Ken to review. In many subject areas where extensive indexes or bibliographies are not available, however, researchers must begin to create lists of this information on their own. Often one resource will lead to another. When you review an article, a book, or a pamphlet on your topic, always check the References or Works Cited section for other possible avenues of research.

45f Evaluating sources

Once you have found a source, you must decide if it is worth using. The following guidelines will help you evaluate your sources.

- If the source is a book, skim the table of contents and the index.
- Survey chapters or periodical articles by reading captions under pictures and looking quickly at any charts, graphs, or tables. Then skim them by reading the first line of every paragraph.
- Decide if the source contains the appropriate information. Does it support your purpose? Is it understandable, or is it too technical? (See 3b for guidelines on evaluating evidence.)

45g Recording information

After they've had some initial success at the library, writers often scan and discard irrelevant material and begin studying what remains. Depending on the scope of your topic, your research may include a large number of sources. Experienced researchers often use bibliography and note cards for recording information because they are easy to hold, rearrange, and read. Choose three-by-five, four-by-six, or five-by-eight-inch cards, as you see fit. The smallest size is often most appropriate for bibliographic

cards, as you usually don't need to record much information on them; the larger sizes are more suitable for notes.

Researchers use bibliography cards to keep publication information for later use in the Works Cited or References section (see 46d and 46e). Taking time and care with your bibliography cards will save you trouble in the end. Follow some simple guidelines.

Bibliography cards

- Indicate call number (if a library text), name of library, and shelf location.
- Using the appropriate format (MLA, APA, CBE, or other—see 46c through 46f), provide the complete citation, including name of author or editor, title of work, place of publication, publisher, and date of publication.
- For articles, include relevant periodical data, with page numbers.
- Prepare a card for *every* source, even those you consult but do not use.

Stress the importance of recording all bibliographical information that may later be needed for the "Works Cited" listing in the research paper. Students who are required to follow MLA or another standard style should preview bibliographic requirements illustrated in 46.

333.7/P289B

Columbia College Main Library

Pawley, Martin. Building for Tomorrow: Putting
        Waste to Work. San Francisco: Sierra Club Books, 1982.

Sample bibliography card (book), MLA format.

45g
res

Reference Room

Columbia College Main Library

Langone, John. "Waste: A Stinking Mess."
Time 2 Jan. 1989: 44-47.

Sample bibliography card (periodical), MLA format.

FOR DISCUSSION

As a point of fact, not all researchers have the patience to classify material on cards as paraphrases, summaries, or quotations, as suggested in 45g. No matter how research information is arranged, however, direct quotations must be identified as such. Inadvertent plagiarism often results from sloppy research notes. Warn students to keep direct quotations marked off from paraphrases and summaries, even if they do not use separate cards. Stress that the simplest way to keep track of direct quotes is to enclose them within quotation marks immediately. Also, remind students to proofread each transcription for accuracy and to record the page number(s) for future reference.

45g
res

Note cards

As you read your sources, you will choose either to summarize or to paraphrase information that supports your thesis or that may lead you to revise or change it. You will also want to copy direct quotations that you may want to use in your paper or record personal ideas on note cards. A well-executed note card system will make writing your paper easier. Follow these guidelines:

- Note only one thought, paraphrase, summary, or quotation per card. Focusing the material on each card will simplify your search for specific material later on.
- Use a recognizable keyword or title at the top of each card. Use this word or phrase to reference the source or idea.
- Write down the author's name (or if none, the work's title) and the page number for future reference.

As you conduct your research, you'll generally use four types of note cards: summary cards, paraphrase cards, direct-quotation cards, and personal-idea cards. It is a good idea to indicate which type of note card you are writing in the top right-

hand corner. A system of abbreviations should do the trick: *Sum* for summary, *Par* for paraphrase, *Idea* for personal idea, and "*Q*" for direct quotations. Keep asking yourself, "What's mine, and what have I borrowed?"

Summary cards. Summary cards allow you to condense original material into a few sentences that capture the main idea of a text. These few sentences must be original, not copied from your source. Phrases that appear in the source should be in quotation marks in your summary. Here you will find both the source and a summary passage Ken Mitchell used in taking notes:

ORIGINAL

Long Islanders are no strangers to environmental nightmares foisted upon them by big business. The Shoreham Nuclear Power Plant—now the subject of intense controversy and local opposition—was first lauded as the inexpensive, clean solution to Long Island's energy problems. Now the myth of nuclear power's benefits has been exposed by disasters such as Three Mile Island and Chernobyl and billions of dollars of cost overruns. Consequently, nuclear power is on the wane.

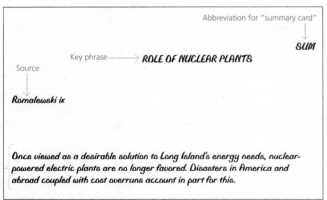

Summarized information

Sample summary card.

Paraphrase cards. Paraphrase cards allow you to explain the author's material in your own words. They are especially helpful because the notes on them are ready for use in your paper. Unlike a summary, a paraphrase includes all of the major and minor points from the source. A paraphrase should be the same approximate length as the original text. Expressing another person's ideas in your own language can be tricky, however. If it is done incorrectly, it can lead to serious problems. One of your goals in taking notes is to distinguish between personal ideas and borrowed material. The direct or indirect use of someone else's ideas or language without giving proper credit is **plagiarism.**

Neglecting to acknowledge your debt to others within the bounds of your paper is irresponsible and dishonest. Each school or department has its own response to plagiarism, ranging from simple grade reduction to expulsion. Most instances of plagiarism are inadvertent. But not knowing the rule is no excuse.

Often it is difficult to decide what needs to be documented and what doesn't. Information that is common knowledge to the well-informed does not have to be documented. For example, you would not have to document the statement that Bill Clinton was elected president of the United States in 1992. There are three types of information for which you must document your sources:

- Opinions, judgments, theories, and personal explanations
- Assertions of fact that are open to dispute and virtually all statistics regarding human behavior
- Factual information that has been gathered by a small number of observers

 Many cultures do not have strict rules regarding documentation. In fact, in a number of countries, it is perfectly acceptable to copy words from others without citing the source. In addition, many ESL students mistakenly think that if they paraphrase a passage, it is not necessary to document the source.

Students who are pressured by time constraints or worried about using language that is not idiomatic English must nevertheless guard against borrowing other writers' words without

ESL ADVICE

Foreign languages follow different conventions for punctuating direct quotations. ESL students who have trouble using quotation marks properly should study the sample research papers in 46, as well as the punctuation rules covered in 36.

45g
res

ESL

giving credit. Remember, using other people's words or ideas without documenting them is plagiarism, and it is treated as a serious offense at American colleges and universities.

Paraphrases that too closely parallel the original are the most common form of plagiarism. Therefore, it is *essential,* when paraphrasing, that you restate the meaning of the original *in your own words.* Not only is this intellectually honest, but it also makes sense stylistically. When you restate the original in your own words, the style of the material you are incorporating into your research paper will match your writing style.

The following example shows one way that a paraphrase could have become plagiarism in Ken Mitchell's paper. The highlighted words in the faulty paraphrase are also found in the original.

ORIGINAL

Americans produce 160 million tons of solid waste every year—more than 3 pounds per person each day—which is the highest per capita rate among industrialized nations. Along with the natural increase in population and the resulting increase in the volume of waste materials, the cost of traditional landfill disposal in some locations has skyrocketed, doubling and even tripling in recent years. These cost increases reflect the growing awareness that landfill sites around the country have already closed or will close soon.

FAULTY PARAPHRASE

Americans create 160 million tons of garbage every year—greater than 3 pounds per person per day—which is the most per person of any developed country. In addition to the rise in population and the increase in garbage, the expense of landfill disposal has increased by two or three times. This expense shows that people know that landfill areas have closed or will close shortly.

This is plagiarism in two senses: first, the writer does not credit the author as the original source of the information; second, the phrasing is too similar to the original. The sentence structure is almost identical, and words and phrases have been repeated

Many students are unaware of how difficult it is to copy a passage verbatim without mistakes. The determination to make sure one's quotes are accurate is a thankless scruple, for it is practically impossible for professors to check all student quotes against original texts. Nevertheless, accuracy *is* important. Major accidents and even deaths have resulted from faulty data, miscopied prescriptions, and other tricks of the human eye. To reveal the difficulty of accurate quotation, you might choose a paragraph from this or another textbook you are using. Give everyone in class ten minutes to copy the passage word for word, punctuation mark for punctuation mark. Then have students trade copies and check each other's work. When proofreading closely, students should read backward from end to beginning, using a pencil tip to mark the place. Discuss the results of the exercise. In our experience, 25 percent or more of the class will have made at least one minor mistake in copying the paragraph.

45g
res

without quotation marks. This passage would not be acceptable as paraphrase, even if it were correctly cited, because it is too similar to the original.

The following example shows a correct paraphrase of the original text.

Sample paraphrase card.

On the card, the writer has put the source information *completely* into his or her own words, except for statistical information, which is quoted. The writer has also added a citation in the MLA format (see 46d).

To avoid plagiarism when paraphrasing, follow these suggestions.

PROCEDURE FOR AVOIDING PLAGIARISM

- Read the passage carefully.
- Put the material aside; then write in your own words what you remember.
- Check your writing against the original by rereading the passage to make sure you have conveyed the same meaning.
- Cite the source.

FOR DISCUSSION

Plagiarism is often the result of confusion over how to handle sources rather than a deliberate effort to cheat. Be sure students understand that it is all right—even necessary at times—to cite other writers' ideas and words, provided that they acknowledge sources according to standard citation procedure.

Direct-quotation cards. There may come a point in your paper where summary and paraphrase pale in comparison to the words of the author, when nothing is as compelling or rings as true as the original. When you'd like to use the language of the source, be it for emphasis, clarity, or interest, record the quotation on a direct-quotation card.

Deciding whether to paraphrase or use direct quotations is sometimes difficult. The following guidelines should help you.

WHEN TO QUOTE THE ORIGINAL SOURCE

- When the language is written so eloquently that it shouldn't be changed.
- When you cannot find an effective way to paraphrase.
- When the original is a famous saying, such as, "To be, or not to be—that is the question" (*Hamlet* 3.1.56). (See 48f for information on documenting quotations from literary works.)
- If there is a danger that a paraphrase will change the original meaning.
- When you present expert testimony to support your opinions, especially when the person is highly regarded in that particular area.

Abbreviation for "direct-quotation card" → *"Q"*

Key phrase → *SUCCESSIVE USES*

Pawley 151 ← Source, with page number

"A much more efficient response to the rising tide of waste would be a design ethos based on prolonging product life, developing alternative and successive uses and exploring material substitutions that would enable products to tidy up after themselves."

Sample direct-quotation card.

You might call everyone's attention to the quotation marks used on the note card. Again, stress that direct quotes should be surrounded by quotation marks immediately to avoid any future confusion over whether or not the quote is verbatim.

45g
res

To save time and make sure that you get a source's exact words, you may decide to make a photocopy of the page on which a quotation appears. If you do so, write the author's name on the copy, make sure the page number appears on it (or write it in), and highlight in some way the material you want to use—don't rely on your memory.

Personal-idea cards. As you investigate your topic more thoroughly, you will probably arrive at ideas neither borrowed nor quoted but worth remembering just the same. This synthesized information should be recorded on personal-idea cards.

Indicates original idea ⟶ *IDEA*

RECYCLING MOTIVATION ⟵ Key phrase

Something more can be said to link recycling and remanufacturing. Consider what runs through people's minds as they recycle. Is the same motivation at work with large companies?

Sample personal-idea card.

COLLABORATIVE ACTIVITY

Have students meet in groups occasionally to share information and discuss progress on the term paper assignment. To focus discussion, ask each group to come up with relevant questions that you or a reference librarian might be able to answer.

45g
res

Computer note taking. Note-making programs are now available for many computers. These programs allow you to create note cards that can be nested inside one another to form a detailed outline. In fact, these programs usually allow you to switch back and forth from note card view to outline view. When you are ready to start drafting, the computer will also display your notes in a word processing format to form your first draft.

46 WRITING AND DOCUMENTING YOUR PAPER

46a The writing process

As discussed in 1, successful writers of all sorts understand, react to, and adapt to the contexts in which they write. They actively consider audience, purpose, assignment, and subject matter before, during, and after drafting. Of equal importance, they allow sufficient time for these activities. Writers weave in and out of planning, drafting, and revising, reacting as much to what they have written as to what they wish to write.

Writing research is no different. By researching a particular topic, you will learn a great deal about it, but you will also find that you learn even more about your subject as you draft and revise your paper. Most important, you will learn what *you* think about your topic (see 3).

Planning

If you have not formed a tentative thesis by the time you finish your research, you'll need to decide on one, at least tentatively, before you begin writing (see 2b). Once you have a thesis, your next step is to decide how to organize your paper. Because research papers tend to be more complex than shorter essays, you may want to use an outline to plan your paper. An informal outline may be all you need, especially if your instructor does not require an outline with your final paper. If a formal outline is required, you may still prefer to start with an informal outline and allow it to evolve as you write and revise your essay. Use your research notes to fill in specific examples and points in your argument. See 2c for more information on preparing an outline.

Drafting

As with any other kind of writing, research papers that are written as a series of drafts are apt to be more effective than papers written in one draft the night before they are due. When you write the first draft of your research paper, just concentrate on

This chapter considers two closely related aspects of research: writing an essay of one's own on the one hand, and documenting that essay according to traditional style specifications on the other. Advise students that writing successive drafts is often necessary to achieve a coherent research report, as demonstrated in 46b. They should also take note of differences in documentation procedures used in various disciplines. Be sure your class knows which of the style models—MLA, APA, or another—you want research papers in your course to follow.

ACTIVITY

Plan to consult with students individually about their research paper assignments, even scheduling office hours for that purpose. Invite questions about level of focus, tentative thesis statements, outlines, introductory paragraphs, gathering sources, documentation procedure, and other matters that may be of concern to students unaccustomed to college-level research.

Stress that introductions can change over the course of a paper's development. In fact, many writers rewrite introductions as a last step in the development of an essay. Urge students not to let themselves be blocked by worries over the introduction, but rather to get on with the overall exposition. One can always go back and make changes. Most of us do.

46a
res

RESOURCES

CBE Style Manual: A Guide for Authors, Editors, and Publishers in the Biological Sciences. 5th ed. Bethesda: Council of Biology Editors, 1983.

Gibaldi, Joseph, and Walter S. Achtert. *MLA Handbook for Writers of Research Papers.* 3rd ed. New York: Modern Language Association, 1988.

Publication Manual of the American Psychological Association. 3rd ed. Washington, DC: American Psychological Association, 1983.

The MLA and APA styles are often dealt with in detail by English composition handbooks, as is the case in this chapter. For a review of CBE style points, see 46f. For an additional list of style manuals used in college disciplines, see 46c.

getting all of your ideas down on paper or into the computer. Don't worry about errors in spelling, grammar, or punctuation. You may choose to use your notes at this stage, or you may prefer to put them aside and use them later, perhaps just indicating in brackets where information, statistics, or quotations will go. (See 4.)

As you write, you'll need to pay particular attention to your introduction (see 10a). A strong introduction should present your thesis in a way that will grab your reader's attention and hold it. Because writing a good introduction can be difficult, you might find it best just to write your thesis statement at the beginning of your first draft and wait until you have finished your draft before attempting to write your introduction. Chances are you'll want to modify your thesis as well.

Revising

After you've finished your first draft, put it aside for at least a day, then read it over, checking for any large-scale changes you'll need to make. (See 5a for a list of questions to ask yourself at this stage.) After you've revised in response to large-scale issues, read your paper again, this time focusing on small-scale issues (see 5b). In addition, check to be sure that you've documented all information that you've gotten from other sources (see 45g and 46c). Wait until your final reading to check for errors in grammar, punctuation, and mechanics. Don't neglect this last step—after all the work you've put into your research and writing, it would be a shame to spoil the impression your paper will make with easily avoided mistakes.

46b Writing your paper on a computer

Because research papers tend to be more complicated and more time-consuming than other types of writing, preparing them on a computer has obvious advantages. Instead of retyping every draft of your paper, you can just open the file that contains your first draft and revise. Use the techniques discussed in 5d to check your organization or experiment with your introduction or conclusion. If you're not sure that a way of reorganizing your text

46b
res

will be effective, you can copy your paper into another file and try out various approaches, leaving the original version intact.

If you have used a computer note-taking program (see 45g), you may be able to prepare your first draft by organizing your notes on the computer. Even if you type your draft out separately, you can easily cut and paste (or block and move) your notes into the appropriate places in your paper.

Finally, a number of commercial programs are available that will automatically format your bibliographic entries into the appropriate style (usually MLA or APA).

46c Different styles of documentation

To ensure uniformity and to simplify the reader's task, each academic discipline has its own strict rules for documentation. These rules dictate the ways in which quoted, paraphrased, or summarized material is acknowledged in notes and in bibliographies. For information on the particulars of manuscript preparation and parenthetical and bibliographic citations, consult the appropriate references from the following list:

Biology
- *CBE Style Manual: A Guide for Authors, Editors, and Publishers in the Biological Sciences.* 5th ed. Bethesda, MD: Council of Biology Editors, 1983.

Chemistry
- *Handbook for Authors of Papers in American Chemical Society Publications.* Washington, D.C.: American Chemical Society, 1978.

Geology
- *Geowriting: A Guide to Writing, Editing, and Printing in Earth Science.* Alexandria, VA: American Geological Institute, 1984.

Humanities, Language, and Literature
- *MLA Handbook for Writers of Research Papers.* 3rd ed. New York: Modern Language Association of America, 1988.

Law
- *A Uniform System of Citation.* 14th ed. Cambridge, MA: Harvard Law Review, 1986.

46c
docu

Linguistics
- "LSA Style Sheet." Appears annually in the *LSA Bulletin,* December issue.

Mathematics
- *A Manual for Authors of Mathematical Papers.* 7th ed. Providence, RI: American Mathematical Society, 1980.

Medicine
- "Uniform Requirements for Manuscripts Submitted to Biomedical Journals." *Annals of Internal Medicine* 90. 1(1979). [International Steering Committee of Medical Editors.]

Physics
- *Style Manual for Guidance in the Preparation of Papers.* 3rd ed. New York: American Institute of Physics, 1978.

Social Sciences
- *Publication Manual of the American Psychological Association.* 3rd ed. Washington, DC: American Psychological Association, 1983.

In the humanities (literature, language studies, art history, music appreciation, theater, film studies, and foreign languages), the style of the Modern Language Association (MLA) is most often used. Always consult your instructor before choosing a style guide.

FOR DISCUSSION

Students often have difficulty making MLA-style in-text citations. Part of the problem is deciding what to put in the citation. You might simplify matters by invoking common sense: The citation

46d MLA **style of documentation**

Scholars and researchers alike use a two- or three-tiered system of documenting borrowed information, whether that information is summarized, paraphrased, or quoted directly. Paying strict attention to this system will make you a more credible writer and prevent inadvertent plagiarism (see 45g).

46d
MLA

Level One (works cited list)

Writers following the guidelines of the MLA system of documentation call the list of sources for a paper *Works Cited*. Writers and researchers should be able to use this bibliographic record to re-create or expand on your research. The Works Cited list appears at the end of your research paper. Each entry contains information regarding authorship; title of text, article, or other work; place and date of publication; and related matters.

Level Two (parenthetical citations)

To acknowledge your debt to other authors properly, you should attribute material to sources and incorporate references within the body of your writing (see the discussion of plagiarism in 45g). The usual method for doing this is often called *parenthetical citation*. Your aim is to offer the reader enough information within the text to identify a particular entry in the Works Cited list and to specify the exact page location of the original material.

Unlike MLA, some style guides and some instructors require that the information about sources be placed at the end of the paper (as endnotes) or at the bottom of the page (as footnotes). A superscript (raised number) in the text alerts the reader to the citation.

If possible, introduce quoted material by acknowledging the author or both the author and source in your sentence. This makes referencing easier and adds authority to your own work:

> According to Martin Pawley, writing in his landmark book, Building for Tomorrow: Putting Garbage to Work, recycling's "chief drawback is that the energy that went into giving the bottle its distinctive shape or the can its remarkable dimensional shape is lost" (109).

If the quotation won't fit into your sentence easily, you may opt to acknowledge the source at the end of the borrowed material instead:

should contain the minimum information needed to allow the reader to locate the full reference on the "Works Cited" page. Thus, if the author of a book is introduced before the quote, the citation need only include the page number—e.g., "(23)"—because the reader knows that the author's name is listed alphabetically at the back. If the quote is not clearly identified by author in the context of the discussion, then the citation should provide the author's name—e.g., "(Smith 23)." A few other rules apply, as in cases involving more than one work by an author, but basically students should view the procedure as a matter of simple convenience, not of arcane complexity.

FOR DISCUSSION

If you are among the many English instructors who require students to follow MLA guidelines, consider setting aside time to discuss 46d with your class. It might be helpful to organize the discussion according to the three main problem areas covered in this section: the "Works Cited" list, in-text citations, and the sometimes optional notes. As you review specifics and invite questions about documentation procedure, you might also refer students to the model term paper in 46i.

46d
MLA

Many students are confused about how to separate their own viewpoints from those of sources, especially where summaries or paraphrases are involved. You might stress the value of transitional remarks such as "According to X, . . ." or "As X points out . . ." in identifying where summaries or paraphrases, as well as direct quotes, come into play. Even when a parenthetical citation follows a borrowing, the reader deserves to know at what point the borrowing begins.

"Today most of the design work in resource recovery is going to the development of doomsday machines capable of crushing and burying everything that we make," comments Pawley (151).

Acknowledgment of the author can also be made with such expressions as *according to, states that, in the words of, remarks that, points out that, says that, claims that,* and *concludes by saying that.*

If your Works Cited section contains more than one work by a single author, you'll have to give an abbreviated form of the title along with the page number, as follows:

According to Fenton, no mention is made of the plastic recovery process known as "reintegration" before 1990 (<u>Remanufacturing</u> 343).

If the author's name is not introduced within the text, it should appear in parentheses with the page number.

According to the author, "The remanufactured machines reportedly met or exceeded corporate expectations of uptime, utilization, and networkability" (Kirkland 45).

Level Three (explanatory notes)

Writers occasionally need to include explanatory footnotes at the bottom of the page or at the end of the paper. These notes may point readers to sources not listed in the Works Cited list or explain concepts, terms, or references essential to an understanding of the work. Some writers also use explanatory notes to go into detail about interesting but peripheral points. If you decide to use explanatory footnotes in a paper, use the superscript system:

Older students returning to college may find themselves befuddled by the updated meaning of "Notes." Before 1984, MLA style called for formal endnotes that included all bibliographical information about works cited. Since 1984, the separate "Works Cited" list has taken over the function of providing bibliographic detail. As shown here, the notes (in the newer sense) are simply digressions from the main essay; they refer to the "Works Cited" list in the same way the main essay does.

In the text: Tupperware engineers redesign their molding machinery on the basis of

46d
MLA

```
                          feedback they receive from workers who

                          use the machinery.²
At bottom of page         ²Although the Tupperware company has
(or end of paper):
                          not published a study of its machine

                          conversions or remanufacturing

                          processes, this information is

                          available to interested parties

                          through Tupperware's public relations

                          department.
```

MLA Works Cited

The Works Cited list provides readers with essential information that allows them to make sense of your research process. At minimum, an MLA Works Cited entry contains the following information:

- Names of all authors or editors
- Title of the work
- Place of publication, publisher, and date of publication
- Page numbers (for articles and works in collections)

The directory on page 478 will help you find most of the formats you'll need to set up the Works Cited list for a typical research paper in the MLA style.

The following guide explains and gives an example for each type of work.

Books (MLA format)

Single author. Invert author's name. Underline the complete title. Give both the city and state or country of the publisher when the city alone might not be clear. Obtain publication information from the title page of the book or the copyright page that follows. If more than one city is given, use the first; if more than one date, use the most recent. Use a shortened version of the

46d
MLA

Encourage your class to examine MLA "Works Cited" page requirements *before* doing library research. You might also suggest that students take this book with them when they go to the library. If, while taking notes, they are in doubt as to what bibliographic information they should record for later inclusion on the "Works Cited" page, they can check this format directory to locate model entries for sources of all kinds.

MLA FORMAT DIRECTORY

Books
Book by a single author, 477

More than one work by the same author, 478

Two or three authors or editors, 479

More than three authors or editors, 479

Corporate or group author, 479

Single editor, 479

Translation, 479

Republished book, 480

Edition other than the first, 480

Work in two or more volumes, 480

Work in an anthology, 480

Unpublished dissertation, 481

Periodicals
Article in a weekly or twice-monthly magazine, 481

Article in a monthly or bi-monthly magazine, 481

Article in a journal paginated continuously by volume, 481

Article in a journal paginated separately by issue, 481

Unsigned article in a periodical, 482

Book review in a periodical, 482

Signed article in a newspaper, 482

Letter to an editor, 482

Other Sources
Lecture, 483

Interview, 483

Dictionary entry, 483

Encyclopedia entry, 483

Audio recording, 483

Computer software, 484

Videotape or film, 484

Television or radio program, 484

Government publication, 484

publisher's name. Abbreviate *University Press* as *UP*. Note that when an entry is more than one line long, subsequent lines should be indented *five spaces*.

```
Piccione, Anthony.  Seeing It Was So.  Brockport, NY:
     BOA Editions, 1986.
```

More than one work by the same author. When citing two or more books written by the same author, indicate the au-

thor's name only in the first entry; thereafter, use three hyphens followed by a period in place of the name. List works by the same author alphabetically by title.

> Everwine, Peter. Collecting the Animals. New York:
>
>   Atheneum, 1976.
>
> - - -. Keeping the Night. New York: Atheneum, 1977.

Two or three authors or editors. Invert only the name of the first author. Give names as they appear on the book's title page.

> Knoblauch, C. H., and Lil Brannon. Rhetorical Tradi-
>
>   tions and the Teaching of Writing. Upper Mont-
>
>   clair, NJ: Boynton/Cook, 1984.

More than three authors or editors. Use the abbreviation *et al.* ("and others") after the initial author.

> Belanoff, Pat, et al. The Right Handbook. Upper
>
>   Montclair, NJ: Boynton/Cook, 1986.

Corporate or group author. Use the corporate author as both the author and publisher, if necessary.

> Environmental Defense Fund. Secondary Containment:
>
>   A Second Line of Defense. New York: Environmen-
>
>   tal Defense Fund, 1985.

Single editor. Use the single-author format, add a comma and the abbreviation *ed.*

> Franzosa, Bob, ed. Grateful Dead Folktales. Orono,
>
>   ME: Zosafarm Publ., 1989.

Translation. Highlight either the original writer or the translator, depending on the focus of your paper. (*UP* is the MLA abbreviation for *University Press.*)

46d
MLA

Botwinik, Berl. <u>Lead Pencil: Stories and Sketches by</u>
<u>Berl Botwinik</u>. Trans. Philip J. Klukoff. De-
troit: Wayne State UP, 1984.

Republished book. Add the date of the original publication after the title. End the citation with the current publication date.

Polyani, Michael. <u>Personal Knowledge: Towards a</u>
<u>Post-Critical Philosophy</u>. 1958. Chicago: U of
Chicago P, 1962.

Edition other than the first. Place the edition number and *ed.* after the full title.

Ruggiero, Vincent Ryan. <u>The Art of Thinking: A Guide</u>
<u>to Critical and Creative Thought</u>. 3rd ed. New
York: Harper, 1991.

Work in two or more volumes. Include the total number of volumes, whether you use more than one or not. Insert the volume information before the publication reference.

Bonfantamantin, Reginald. <u>The Jewish Mystique</u>.
3 vols. New York: Achshav, 1977.

Work in an anthology. Highlight the author of the selection, rather than the editor of the anthology. The editor's name follows the title of the anthology, preceded by the abbreviation *Ed.* Give the page numbers of the entire work, not just those pages you have cited.

Bettelheim, Bruno. "The Informed Heart." <u>Out of the</u>
<u>Whirlwind: A Reader of Holocaust Literature</u>.
Ed. Albert Friedlander. New York: Schocken,
1976 48-63.

Unpublished dissertation. Take care to put the dissertation title in quotation marks, followed by the abbreviation *Diss.*

```
Wilensky, Harold L.  "The Staff 'Expert': A Study of
     the Intelligence Functions in American Trade
     Unions."  Diss.  U of Chicago, 1953.
```

Periodicals (MLA format)

Article in a weekly or twice-monthly magazine. Give the periodical's complete date, in inverted abbreviated form, followed by a colon and the page range for the entire article.

```
Corliss, Richard.  "Do Stars Deliver?"  Time 26 Aug.
     1991: 38-40.
```

Article in a monthly or bimonthly magazine. Give the month and year. Use a hyphen between months for a bimonthly publication.

```
Murphy, Bob.  "Modern Neo-Pagans."  Utne Reader Nov.-
     Dec. 1991: 22-26.
```

Article in a journal paginated continuously by volume. In a periodical with continuous pagination, if the first issue for a year ends on page 216, the second issue will begin with page 217. In such a periodical, give the volume number, the year in parentheses, and the page numbers of the entire article, not just those you have cited.

```
Coles, Robert.  "Public Evil and Private Problems:
     Segregation and Psychiatry."  Yale Review 54
     (1965): 513-31.
```

Article in a journal paginated separately by issue. For a periodical that begins each issue with page 1, give the volume number and the issue number, separated by a period.

46d
MLA

```
Revell, Donald.  "'Abesces': The Oz and Sheol of

    James Tate."  Willow Springs 25.2 (1990): 63-89.
```

Unsigned article in a periodical. For anonymous articles, use the title in the author slot, and alphabetize the entry by its title.

```
"Dough Conditioners: Pizzeria Question Mark."

    Pizza World Jan. 1990: 23-24.
```

Book review in a periodical. Give author and title of review, followed by *Rev. of* and the title of the work reviewed. (Do not underline, italicize, or place inside quotation marks the words *Rev. of.*) Follow the title of the work with *by* and the name of the work's author. Include the name of the publication and appropriate publication information. If the name of the reviewer is not known, begin with the title of the review.

```
Smith, Raymond J.  "Some Poetic Self-Revelations."

    Rev. of American Poets in 1976, ed. William

    Heyen.  Ontario Review 5 (1976-77): 102-04.
```

Signed article in a newspaper. Include the author's name, the title of the article, the date and edition, and the section and page numbers if applicable. If the article is unsigned, leave the title of the article in the position usually occupied by the author's name and alphabetize by title.

```
Sullivan, Barbara.  "Burning Ambition."  Chicago Tri-

    bune 21 May 1992, late ed., sec. 7: 11.
```

Letter to an editor. Include the word *Letter* after the author's name.

```
Lovis, Adrian C.  Letter.  AWP Chronicle 24.1 (1991):

    17-18.
```

Other sources (MLA format)

Lecture. Use a description unless an organization, meeting, or title is available.

```
Anderson, Mary Victoria.  Class lecture, English 095.
     Loyola U of Chicago.  21 Oct. 1991.
```

Interview. If the interview is conducted by the researcher, indicate the name and date of the person interviewed and include a descriptive phrase such as *Personal interview.*

```
Avrahami, Nir, and Ilene Greenberg.  Personal inter-
     view.  6 July 1988.
```

Dictionary entry. Follow the rules for a work in an anthology.

```
"Experimental Design."  Modern Dictionary of Sociol-
     ogy.  Ed. George A. Theodorson and Achilles G.
     Theodorson.  New York: Crowell, 1969.
```

Encyclopedia entry. Follow the rules for a work in an anthology. If articles are arranged alphabetically, you may omit volume and page numbers.

```
Fussell, Paul.  "Meter."  Encyclopedia of Poetry and
     Poetics.  Ed. Alex Preminger.  Princeton, NJ:
     Princeton UP, 1965.
```

Audio recording. Your purpose will determine whether you highlight performer, conductor, composer, or title. Give catalog number, if possible.

```
Garcia, Jerry.  Jerry Garcia Band.  With John Kahn,
     Melvin Seals, David Kemper, Jackie La Branch,
     and Gloria James.  Arista, 07822-18690-2, 1991.
```

46d
MLA

Computer software. In the case of company authorship, indicate company name. Include as much description as possible: system, size, medium.

> Sweitzer, Keith. Backup Master: High Performance Hard
>
>   Disk Backup Utility. Computer software. Inter-
>
>   secting Concepts, 1986. IBM, 160kb, 5.25" disk.

Videotape or film. Include title, director, and other significant participants (such as writers or performers).

> Teenage Mutant Ninja Turtles: The Shredder Is Splin-
>
>   tered. Based on characters and comic books cre-
>
>   ated by Kevin Eastman and Peter Laird. Mirage
>
>   Studios, 1988.

Television or radio program. Generally, place the episode title in quotations first, followed by writer, title of program, other contributors, network, local station and city, and the date of broadcast.

> "Youth." Writ. Roseanne Arnold. Roseanne. Prod.
>
>   Marcy Carsey and Tom Werner. With John Good-
>
>   man. WABC, New York. 29 Oct. 1991.

Government publication. If no author is given, list the government first, followed by the actual agency. Cite the printer in the publisher slot (in the United States, usually *GPO*, the U.S. Government Printing Office).

> United States. Environmental Protection Agency.
>
>   Chemicals in Your Community: A Guide to the
>
>   Emergency Planning and Community Right-to-Know
>
>   Act. Washington, DC: GPO, 1988.

When following the MLA style of manuscript preparation and documentation, keep these basic considerations in mind:

MLA Style of Manuscript Preparation

- Type or print clearly on white paper. Check with your instructor before submitting copy prepared on a dot-matrix printer.
- For your protection, always keep a copy of the original.
- As a rule, double-space your text (including the Works Cited list and any notes). Indent five space to indicate the beginning of a paragraph. Indent ten spaces from the left margin to show a set-off quotation.
- Allow for one-inch margins at the top, bottom, and on both sides of your paper (page numbers appear at the right margin, half an inch below the top of the page).
- Provide a title page and report cover if you want to or if your instructor requires them. Otherwise, include all relevant information on the first page. Do not number the title page.
- Indicate your last name and page number of *all* pages beginning with the first (including notes, Works Cited list, and appendixes).

Always check with your instructors regarding their preferences for manuscript formatting and presentation.

46e   APA style of documentation

Parenthetical citations

Researchers following the system devised by the American Psychological Association (APA) link their parenthetical citations to a References section. In the APA system, the page number or range appears in parentheses at the end of a quotation, preceded by the abbreviation *p.* or *pp.* The author's name usually appears at the beginning of the sentence, the publication date, in parentheses, follows it immediately:

```
According to Kirkland (1991), "The remanufactured ma-
chines reportedly met or exceeded corporate expectations
of uptime, utilization, and networkability" (p. 45).
```

Students who are using APA documentation procedure should examine the model APA research paper in 46j.

46e
APA

If the author's name does not appear in the sentence, it is given in parentheses with the year and the page number, separated by commas:

```
According to the author, "The remanufactured
machines reportedly met or exceeded corporate
expectations of uptime, utilization, and networkability"
(Kirkland, 1991, p. 45).
```

In a summary or paraphrase, the page number is optional, but the author's name and the date of publication must be included.

```
Miller (1981) describes patients who were not
allowed to express their feelings as children because
they had had a narcissistic parent.
```

```
Patients were not allowed to express their feelings
as children because they had had a narcissistic parent
(Miller, 1981).
```

If a work has more than one author, both authors should be named in the text. Use an ampersand (&) if the names are given in parentheses: `(Thompson & Hickey, 1994, p. 48).`

APA references

The basic APA references entry contains the following information:

- Names of all authors or editors
- Title of the work
- Place of publication, publisher, and date of publication
- Page numbers (articles and works in collections)

The directory on the facing page will help you locate most of the formats you'll need to set up the References section for a typical research paper done in APA style.

46e
APA

APA FORMAT DIRECTORY

Books
Single author, 487
More than one work by the same author, 488
Two or more authors or editors, 488
Corporate or group author, 488
Edited book, 488
Work in an anthology, 488
Translation, 489
Edition other than the first, 489
Unpublished dissertation or manuscript, 489

Periodicals
Article in a weekly or twice-monthly magazine, 489
Article in a journal paginated continuously by volume, 489

Article in a journal paginated separately by issue, 490
Book review in a periodical, 490
Article in a newspaper, 490
Unsigned newspaper article, 490
Letter to an editor, 490

Other Sources
Published interview, 491
Government document, 491
Audio recording, 491
Videotape or film, 491
Computer software, 491

The following guide explains and gives an example for each type of reference.

Books (APA format)

Single author. Invert author's name, and reduce all given names to initials. Give year of publication next, in parentheses. Capitalize only the first word and proper nouns in the title (and the first word following the colon in a subtitle). When an entry is more than one line long, subsequent lines indent *three spaces*.

```
Kroeber, T.  (1961).  Ishi in two worlds: A biography
    of the last wild Indians in North America.  Berke-
    ley: University of California Press.
```

46e
APA

More than one work by the same author. Use author's name for each work. List in chronological order.

```
Cassirer, E. (1944). An essay on man. New Haven,
   CT: Yale University Press.
Cassirer, E. (1961). The logic of the humanities.
   New Haven, CT: Yale University Press.
```

Two or more authors or editors. Provide the names of all authors, inverted. Use an ampersand (&) before the last.

```
Kinsey, A. C., Pomeroy, W. B., & Martin, C. E.
   (1948). Sexual behavior in the human male.
   Philadelphia: Saunders.
```

Corporate or group author. When the author and publisher are the same, use *Author* in the publisher slot.

```
Environmental Defense Fund. (1988). Coming full
   circle: Successful recycling today. New York: Au-
   thor.
```

Edited book. After the name or names, insert *(Ed.)* or *(Eds.)*.

```
Cumming, R. D. (Ed.). (1965). The philosophy of
   Jean-Paul Sartre. New York: Random House.
```

Work in an anthology. Cite the author of the work, not of the anthology. Use no quotation marks. Give page numbers of the entire article.

```
Bettelheim, B. (1980). Eichmann: The systems, the
   victims. In B. Bettelheim (Ed.), Surviving (pp.
   258-273). New York: Vintage.
```

46e
APA

Translation. Show the original author and title, followed by the translator.

```
Neumann, E.  (1973).  Depth psychology and a new

    ethic (E. Rolfe, Trans.).  New York: Harper.

    (Original work published 1949)
```

Edition other than the first. Abbreviate edition *ed.* in parentheses after the title.

```
Evans-Wentz, W. Y. (Ed.).  (1960).  The Tibetan book

    of the dead (3rd ed.).  London: Oxford University

    Press.
```

Unpublished dissertation or manuscript. Describe the manuscript appropriately (*M.A. thesis, Ph.D. dissertation*, and so on).

```
Rosenbaum, G.  (1953).  An analysis of personaliza-

    tion in neighborhood apparel retailing.  Unpub-

    lished M.A. thesis, Department of Sociology,

    University of Chicago.
```

Periodicals (APA format)

Article in a weekly or twice-monthly magazine. Include issue date in parentheses after author's name. Page numbers (of the entire article) appear last.

```
Strykeer, P.  (1953, August).  How executives get

    jobs.  Fortune, pp. 182-194.
```

Article in a journal paginated continuously by volume. In a journal with continuous pagination, if the first issue of a volume ends on page 302, the next issue will begin on page 303. For such a journal, provide only the volume number (underscored) and pages; do not give issue information.

> Winnicott, D. W. (1969). The use of an object. Inter-
>
> national Journal of Psychoanalysis, 50, 700-716.

Article in a journal paginated separately by issue. For a journal that begins each issue on page 1, give volume number, issue number in parentheses, and page references.

> Hart, H. (1989). Seamus Heaney's anxiety of trust
>
> in field work. Chicago Review, 36(3), 87-108.

Book review in a periodical. Bracket *Review of* and the title of the book being reviewed. Complete periodical format.

> Homes, R. J. (1991, September). [Review of A reference
>
> guide to media bias]. Bloomsbury Review, p. 7.

Article in a newspaper. Cite full date in parentheses after author's name.

> Mateja, J. (1991, October 27). Chrysler planning a
>
> battery-powered mini-van. Chicago Tribune,
>
> pp. T3, T8.

Unsigned newspaper article. Provide the title of the article in first position; then follow newspaper article format.

> Reader's guide to the silver screen. (1991, October
>
> 25). Chicago Reader, pp. 33-36.

Letter to an editor. If the letter as published has no heading, use the first sentence as title. Bracket the description *Letter to the editor.*

> Smith, L. (1991, September). DAT deterioration?
>
> [Letter to the editor]. Stereo Review, p. 9.

Other sources (APA format)

Published interview. Bracket *Interview with* and the person's name. (APA does not reference unpublished interviews.)

Auer, T. (1991, July-August). Montana memories

    [Interview with Ivan Doig]. Bloomsbury Review,

    pp. 9-20.

Government document. Style as for a book with one author.

Environmental Protection Agency. (1988). Medical

    waste: EPA environmental backgrounder. Washing-

    ton, DC: EPA, Office of Public Affairs.

Audio recording. Provide catalog number, if available.

Youman, B. (Producer), & Rivers, B. (Narrator).

    (1991). TDK's ultimate guide to recording from

    CDs [Compact Disc Recording CDK 0100]. Port Wash-

    ington, NY: TDK Electronics.

Videotape or film. Use the name of producer, director, or writer as author, depending on your focus. Bracket the description *Videotape*.

Smith, G. W. (Producer). (1988). Your water, your

    life [Videotape]. Washington, DC: Public Interest

    Video Network.

Computer software. Indicate writer or group, followed by release numbers. Bracket description *Computer program*.

46e
APA

```
WordStar International.  (1989).  WordStar Release 5.5

    [Computer program].  San Rafael, CA: WordStar

    International.
```

46f CBE style of documentation

If you are writing a paper for a course in the natural sciences, one accepted guide for documentation and manuscript preparation is the *CBE Style Manual,* published by the Council of Biology Editors. CBE style includes two methods of documentation, one similar to APA style (see 46e) and another system that uses numbers. In the numbered system, sources are listed on the References page either in alphabetical order or in the order in which they are cited. Each reference has a number, and this number is given in parentheses in the text when a source is cited.

```
Thomas (1) maintains that our national fixation on

health is a symptom of our fear of dying.
```

In the References list, the entry for that source, the basic entry for a book with one author, would look like this:

```
1. Thomas, L.  The Medusa and the snail.  New

    York: Penguin; 1981.
```

Capitalize only the first word in the title and any proper nouns. Do not underline or italicize the title. Use a semicolon to separate the date from the publisher. If the note is more than one line long, subsequent lines should begin under the first letter of the author's last name.

Other CBE entries

Book with two or more authors. Use semicolons to separate all authors' names, regardless of number.

```
2. Minnich, J.; Hunt, M.  The Rodale guide to com-

    posting.  Emmaus, PA: Rodale Press; 1979.
```

Book with a corporate or group author. Place the corporation or group name in the author slot.

3. Natural Resources Defense Council. Cooling the
   greenhouse: vital first steps to combat global
   warming. Washington, DC: Government Printing
   Office; 1988.

Book with a single editor. Spell out the word *editor*; otherwise follow the rules for a book with a single author.

4. Busnel, R. G., editor. Acoustic behavior of
   animals. Amsterdam: Elsevier; 1963.

Work in an anthology. List the author of the work first, then the title followed by *In:*, and then the author or editor of the anthology, the title of the anthology, and publication information.

5. Wilson, E. O. Chemical systems. In: Seboek,
   T. A., editor. Animal communication: techniques of study and results of research.
   Bloomington: Indiana University Press; 1970:
   200-221.

Article in journal paginated continuously by volume.
In a journal with continuous pagination, if the first issue of a volume ends on page 228, the next issue will begin on page 229. A colon (but no space) is used between volume and page numbers.

6. Wiener, H. External chemical messengers. New
   York State Journal of Medicine 66:3153-3170;
   1968.

46f
CBE

Magazine article. Only the first word and any proper nouns are capitalized in the title of the article.

```
7. Bettelheim, B.  Surviving.  New Yorker.  1976
   August 2:31-52.
```

46g Sample research paper: a portion of Ken Mitchell's first draft

Reacting to his research assignment (see 45e), Ken Mitchell wrote an unedited and unrevised first draft for composition class, a portion of which is presented here. His instructor's comments appear in the margins. Because this was a first draft, Professor Zirinsky commented mainly on content, organization, and sentences that were difficult to understand. However, Ken will later need to proofread his final draft more carefully for grammatical errors and misspellings.

```
                Do It Again

            by Kenneth Mitchell
```

*Follow the MLA format
and documentation style
for research papers.*

```
        That the planet's capacity to handle the

   byproducts of a materially based culture is in

   danger is no longer open to speculation.  Towns,

   counties, states, and governments all over the

   world are all faced with the same problem--what

   to do with their garbage.

        Burying the garbage has always been the

   easiest solution, but in the 1990s landfill space

   is no longer an easy acquisition.  Talk to any
```

46g
res

e you
e you
nt this
ormal
e?

community that is trying to initiate a new one.
Nobody wants the garbage in their backyard. If
your geographic location is someplace like the
United States' Northeast corridor, or the
European continent, there just may not be any
available space left for your garbage heap.

Aren't there dangers greater than running out of space?

Burning the garbage is another solution, one
of the seemingly simplest methods of waste
management, and the method of choice for much of
Europe. But while incineration might have been a
viable method of waste management in nonindustrial cultures who only generated organic
debris, today's byproducts of industry and
technology, are not as easily or safely
dispersed. Proponents of incineration, often
fail to consider the toxic ramifications. Just
because you can't see it doesn't mean it isn't
there. In the 1990 edition of New York
Naturally, writer Steven Romalewski points out
that incineration has some obvious and major
drawbacks.

Aren't there safe ways to "incinerate" being used in industrial countries?

Use a colon to introduce quotations.

> When garbage is burned it doesn't just
> disappear. Instead, discarded
> materials, virtually all of which are
> recyclable, are converted to air
> emissions that can be tainted with
> literally thousands of toxic chemicals

46g
res

and ash residue that is typically so
contaminated that it qualifies as
hazardous waste under federal
regulations. (Romalewski, NY viii)

*When you
knowledge
author in t
text, you n
not reuse h
or her nam*

See its and it's.

But even if incineration were not such a
polluting method of waste disposal, it's
applicability is limited by practical physics.
You simply cannot burn large pieces of industrial
machinery or cars for that matter. The amount of
heat required to facilitate such a process on a
large scale makes its widespread utilization
prohibitive.

*What are y
referring to*

In the next four paragraphs, Ken describes the problems
with recycling garbage. He then continues:

tone? So with landfill space at a premium, the
toxic backlash of incineration, and the
reliability and efficiency of recycling programs
dubious at best, the need for alternatives in
waste management is critical. But what can be
done? *Has this become your guiding question?*

On a practical level there is simple reuse
and conservation. Still, our entire economy is
built around the ease of the throwaway cycle.
And while it is the byproducts of technology that
have brought us to our current crisis, it may
indeed be that technology coupled with innovative
thinking that must be our savior.

*Interesting
please exp*

*Do we nee
rescue? If
spell out th
urgency ea
and more
forcefully.*

46g
res

According to writers like Martin Pawley, it needn't necessarily be high-tech machinery that delivers more efficient means of use, disposal, or recovery. For Pawley, it starts on the philosophical side. "Today most of the design work in resource recovery is going to the development of doomsday machines capable of crushing, burying everything that we make." (Pawley 151)

He goes on to say that,

Okay, I'd like to know more about this "ethos" and the culture of "successive uses."

> A much more energy efficient response to the rising tide of waste would be a design ethos based on prolonging product life, developing alternative and successive uses and exploring material substitutions that would enable products to tidy up after themselves. (Pawley 151).

Is this your focus? Possible title for this paper.

An entire industry has sprung from at least one of Pawley's recommendations, "successive uses," albeit a variation on his vision.

Finding new ways of using products that have reached the conclusion of their life cycle was

ow are awley's ex- eriments rel- ant to your scussion?

the focus of Pawley's work, but the bricolage and garbage-building experiments that he and his associates initiated have not been picked up by the industrial and manufacturing sectors. The variation on Pawley's concept of "secondary use"

46g
res

that I alluded to is the technique of

remanufacturing, a process that is not new to our

environmentally sensitive era.

You won't find remanufacturing in your

trusty collegiate dictionary, but a search of the

current indexes for business periodicals will

bring up more than a handful of listings.

Companies in an interesting array of industries,

Are you adding an economic slant to your position? seeking an edge in a difficult economy, have

begun to employ this innovative and cost-saving

technique.

In the remainder of his paper, Ken defines *remanufacturing* and describes remanufacturing programs at three companies.

46h Student conference

Professor Zirinsky decided to have a conference with Ken before he wrote the second draft of his research paper. She suggested that he reorganize his paper to focus on remanufacturing, use headings to guide his readers, provide more examples, and contact and conduct interviews with people in the field. She also cautioned him to follow MLA guidelines more closely and to edit and proofread his final draft carefully.

46i Research paper in MLA form: Ken Mitchell's revision

Ken's research paper revision, with comments and explanations, follows. Although no paper is ever beyond additional revision, Ken felt that his was ready to submit to Professor Zirinsky.

Some instructors require a formal title page. If yours does and specifies the form it should take, then you should follow those specifications. If your instructor requires a title page but doesn't specify a format, you can follow this one. Note that the title page is not numbered, nor do you count it when numbering subsequent pages.

Not all instructors formally review interim drafts with students. If you plan to do so, be sure the research paper is assigned early enough in the term to permit convenient scheduling of progress conferences. Alternatively, you might invite students to see you during regular office hours about any specific difficulties that arise as the deadline approaches.

46i
MLA

Successive Uses: Waste Management and Remanufacturing

Place title 1/3 of the way down the page.

1 inch

All lines are centered.

By Ken Mitchell

1 inch

English 102, Section 74

Professor Zirinsky

24 November 1994

Separate title pages follow this format (compare alternative format on p. 505).

46i
MLA

Some instructors request a formal outline with the research paper. Note how Ken builds an outline using Roman numerals, capital letters, Arabic numbers, and, if necessary, lower-case letters to show the relationships of major and minor points. (For a discussion of outlining, see 2c.)

Note that outline pages are numbered in the upper-right-hand corner with the author's last name and a lower-case Roman numeral.

Mitchell i

Outline

Thesis: With increased attention to the environmental side effects of our unrestricted commercialism, remanufacturing simultaneously promises financial and ecological benefits to all concerned.

I. Although remanufacturing is not currently the preferred method of industrial production in this country, its popularity is increasing.

   A. Remanufacturing can cut production costs.

   B. Remanufacturing is naturally more efficient, resulting in less waste.

      1. Less waste limits our dangerously large waste stream.

      2. Less waste limits the negative environmental impact.

II. Specifically, remanufacturing is the combination of old and new parts, a process involving the refurbishing and often reengineering of older products.

   A. Necessity has driven remanufacturing over the years.

   B. Industries of all sorts, from fix-it shops to mass manufacturers, engage in remanufacturing in one form or another.

Not all instructors require students to include outlines. If you do, remind your class that standard outline form requires divisions that are at least binary: If there is a "I," there must be a "II,"; if there is an "A," there must be a "B"; and so on. Also have students check to be sure that their outlines show consistent form. The entire outline should be comprised either of sentences or of fragments, not a mingling of the two.

46i
MLA

III. The benefits of remanufacturing are great.

    A. Energy and material savings making it an environmentally sensitive strategy.

        1. Remanufactured products require between 10 and 20 percent fewer raw materials and energy expenditures.

        2. Consumers can expect to save 20 to 50 percent on these goods.

    B. These products are often of superior quality.

IV. The time for remanufacturing is now.

    A. Burying garbage is no longer an attractive solution.

        1. Landfill space is quickly disappearing.

        2. People don't want your garbage in their backyard.

    B. Burning the garbage is also a poor choice.

        1. Burned materials give off toxic emissions.

        2. Burning larger items is impractical.

    C. Recycling may sound good, but it has its drawbacks, too.

        1. New York City has had difficulty enforcing mandatory recycling.

        2. In the end, recycling is quite inefficient.

    D. Reuse and conservation don't go hand in hand with the prevailing "throwaway" mentality.

V. Can the same technology that got us into this trouble help us out?

A.   Reutilization or successive uses result in new
     ways of using old (and seemingly spent)
     products.

B.   Some industries are already engaged in the
     practice.

     1.   Arrow Automotive Industries remanufactures
          auto parts on a wide scale.

     2.   Tupperware uses employee feedback to
          remanufacture its own machinery to suit
          changing demands.

     3.   Others such as AT&T, the New York City
          Transit Authority, and furniture companies
          nationwide rely on remanufactured goods.

VI. We must find ways to change the minds of both
     manufacturers and consumers if the practice of
     remanufacturing is to be of continued benefit.

On left-hand pages and in the margins of Ken's paper, you will find commentary on his revision, as well as guidelines for following MLA format and documentation style.

Format

Title page. In lieu of a title page, Ken includes all necessary information in the upper left-hand corner of his first page. (A sample of a separate title page is found on page 499.) Your teacher may specifically request a cover page and possibly a folder. If not, the *MLA Handbook* suggests that you use the top left-hand corner to record necessary class information: your name, your professor's name, the class number or name, and the date, all double-spaced. Follow this with the paper's title, placed two lines below the date. Center the title and subtitle. Skip four lines, indent five spaces, and begin the first paragraph of the paper.

All subsequent pages. Using the MLA convention, number every page (including the first) in the upper right corner. Give your last name and the page number, separated by two spaces.

Approach

In recasting his paper, Ken chose to borrow Martin Pawley's term *successive uses* as his title. He chose to narrow and clarify the title further by adding the subtitle "Waste Management and Remanufacturing." Note how he uses a colon (:) to distinguish between general and specific titles. Although it can serve other purposes, the title usually introduces the subject of the research paper.

By introducing it early in his paper, Ken leaves no doubt that his focus will be the financial and environmental benefits of remanufacturing. Ken's thesis appears in the final sentence of paragraph 2.

1/2" 1"

Begin numbering → Mitchell 1
with the first page.

side

About 1" top margin

→ Ken Mitchell

Professor Zirinsky

English 102, Section 74

24 November 1993

Use title to
introduce and
focus paper.

Successive Uses: Waste Management and Remanufacturing

1   You won't find remanufacturing in your
trusty collegiate dictionary, but a search of the
current indexes for business periodicals will
bring up more than a handful of listings.
Companies in an interesting array of industries--
most seeking an edge in a difficult economy--have
begun to employ this innovative and cost-saving
technique.

2   Although cost cutting and efficiency have
long been the concerns of both the business and
consumer sectors, today's buyers and sellers have
other reasons to consider this revolutionary
technique. With increased attention to the
environmental side effects of our unrestricted
Thesis — commercialism, remanufacturing simultaneously
promises financial and ecological benefits to all
concerned.

46i
MLA

An inviting question such as this both draws the reader into the paper and further serves to introduce and define the topic at hand. Note how Ken uses the parenthetical documentation style with this direct quotation.

When paraphrasing—as Ken does in the final sentence of paragraph 3—it is necessary to acknowledge the authors, either in the body of the text or in the parenthetical citation. Here, because the authors' names are mentioned in the body of the text, only the page number is given in parentheses.

When you introduce quotations or paraphrases into your text, integrate them smoothly. Introduce each quotation or paraphrase with a "signal phrase" indicating the relationship of the author to his or her words:

> Composition specialist David Bartholomae concludes that . . .
>
> Environmental activist Edward Abbey points out that . . .
>
> Yasir Arafat claims that . . .
>
> As Senator Dole has steadily maintained, . . .
>
> . . . declares NAACP president Ben Chavis.

You can use a verb from the following list to introduce quoted or paraphrased material:

acknowledges	confirms	observes
adds	contends	points out
admits	declares	reports
agrees	describes	responds
alleges	emphasizes	reveals
argues	explains	says
asks	finds	suggests
asserts	implies	thinks
claims	insists	warns
concedes	maintains	writes
concludes	notes	

When no author is mentioned within a paraphrase, the author's name must be included in parentheses along with the page number(s), as Ken does in the last line: (Moore 77; Pawley 110).

Mitchell 2

3   So what is remanufacturing? According to
recent business periodicals, companies that
remanufacture don't just repair or refurbish older
products. "They combine old and new parts and
build versions that are as good [as] or better
than new" (Schulman and Sabin 69). Products are
typically taken apart and examined. Then
technicians, mechanics, or engineers determine
which parts are worn and replace or repair as
needed. The components are then reassembled,
tested, and either painted, refinished, or
cosmetically restored so that they can sit side
by side with similar new products. As Schulman
and Sabin remark, the remanufactured version is
often then sold at a fraction of the cost of the
original (69).

4   Throughout history, thrifty small-time
entrepreneurs have always been on the lookout for
salvageable items. Your neighborhood fix-it shop
is a good example. There you can find a rebuilt
blender or toaster oven, floor polisher or vacuum
cleaner. Nowhere is this spirit more prevalent
than in the Third World, where necessity-driven
scavengers have been defying the originally
intended life cycles of everything from bicycles
to agricultural machinery (Moore 77; Pawley 110).

When authors'
names don't ap-
pear in introduc-
tory phrase

When authors'
names do appear
in introductory
phrase

Authors not
introduced

Have your students check to see
that their own in-text citations are
punctuated like those in this paper.
For example, this paragraph shows
the form of a citation following a direct quote. There is no period inside the closing quotation marks,
but a period does follow the parentheses. Exceptions occur in the case
of block-indented quotations.

46i
MLA

Headings and subheadings can be of great convenience to your reader, dividing your paper into recognizable sections. Ken's use of five main headings, for instance, moves the reader from the general matter of "Some Benefits" and "Other Methods" through specific considerations in "The Case Book" and "Other Industries" to a final consideration of "The Future."

Having discussed energy and material expenditure in paragraph 5, Ken uses paragraph 6 to discuss enhanced product quality.

Mitchell 3

Remanufacturing expands on this spirit by enlarging the concept with modern assembly-line production techniques. It is precisely this emphasis on large-scale production that defines modern remanufacturing (Keller 3).

Some Benefits

5   Reduction in energy and material expenditure is what makes remanufacturing a significant and environmentally sensitive strategy. According to reports in trade magazines from the plastics, furniture, automotive, and transportation industries, remanufactured products are produced using approximately one-fifth the energy and one-tenth the raw materials (Kaelble 82-85). Thanks to this reduction in manufacturing overhead, consumers can usually expect savings of 25 to 50 percent (Schulman and Sabin 69).

6   But are the products of comparable quality? In some cases, the products are improved versions of the original. Instead of scrapping them, companies remanufacture from the original product's strength. Instead of merely rebuilding products to original specifications, they find ways to enhance and modify them (Kruglinski 74).

46i
MLA

In paragraph 7, when Ken uses the language of his interviewee, Susan Park Pritchard, he places it in quotation marks. Ken uses an explanatory note to acknowledge the special circumstances in which this information came his way (see pages 476–477). He places the note number above the line and slightly to the right of the sentence punctuation; this placement of a number is known as a *superscript*.

Paragraph 8 serves as a forecast of the upcoming section on other methods. Paragraph 9 deals with garbage burial and related landfill practices, paragraph 10 with the limitations and toxic consequences of incineration, and paragraphs 11 through 15 with the feasibility of recycling, recycling laws, and enforcement dilemmas.

Mitchell 4

7   Still, the special characteristics of the
remanufacturing process are more psychological
and philosophical than practical. Instead of
seeing worn and outdated products as waste,
remanufacturers look at the original products as
"cores." Instead of wasting energy in the
disposal of old manufactured products, one
spokesperson explained, remanufacturers can use
them as "building blocks for new products."[1]

Explanatory note

Methods of Waste Management

8   To understand remanufacturing's place in the
larger culture of waste management and
conservation, we must examine a few current and
favored methods of dealing with waste.

9   Burying garbage has always been the easiest
solution. There is little processing involved,
and once you bury it, it is easy to imagine that
it's gone. In the 1990s, however, acquiring
landfill space is no easy task. Talk to any
community trying to initiate a new landfill
program or site. People don't want the garbage
in their backyard (Romalewski viii). If you live
someplace like the northeastern corridor of the

46i
MLA

Because he paraphrases material from a number of pages, rather than a single page, Ken lists his source as pages x–xi of Romalewski's article.

Since he has already credited this author, Ken is not obliged to repeat his name after the set-off quotation in paragraph 10. The MLA guidelines require using this set-off style when a quotation takes up more than four lines. With a set-off quotation, no quotation marks are necessary (see 36b).

Mitchell 5

United States or the European continent, there
may not be any available space left for your
garbage.

10   Burning the garbage is another seemingly
simple solution, the method of choice for much of
Europe (Romalewski x-xi). Incineration might
have been a viable method of waste management in
nonindustrial cultures that generated only
organic debris, but today's industrial and
technological by-products are not as easily or
safely disposed of. Proponents of incineration
often fail to consider the toxic ramifications.
Seeing is not the only measure of believing.
In a recent New York Naturally article, Steven
Romalewski points out that incineration has some
obvious and major drawbacks: Source and author credited

> When garbage is burned it doesn't just
> disappear. Instead, discarded materials,
> virtually all of which are recyclable, are
> converted to air emissions that can be
> tainted with literally thousands of toxic
> chemicals and ash residue that is typically
> so contaminated that it qualifies as
> hazardous waste under federal regulations.
> (viii)

In the last line of paragraph 11, Ken indicates that his paraphrase is taken from the unsigned article "Trash into Cash: That's Only the Half of It." For the sake of convenience, you may abbreviate long titles in this manner.

Mitchell 6

But even if incineration were not such a polluting method of waste disposal, its applicability is limited by practical physics. You simply cannot burn large pieces of industrial machinery or cars. The amount of heat required to facilitate such a process on a large scale makes its widespread utilization prohibitive.

11   But what about recycling? Due to public pressure and the rising cost of traditional means of disposal, many municipalities and private industries have turned to recycling to cope with their waste management problems. Still, large cities like New York have recently considered shelving full-scale curbside recycling programs because of major budgetary constraints. As politically correct as it may seem, New York's problems reinforce the fact that recycling is not a panacea ("Trash into Cash" 12).

Format for unknown author

12   First of all, New York faces a problem with compliance, but perhaps an even greater problem is the cost of processing collected recyclables and finding markets for them. The mixed success of recycling-based legislation, like New York's "bottle bill"--which mandates five- or ten-cent deposits on soft drinks and beer--is a case in

46i
MLA

Mitchell 7

point. The 1990 edition of New York Naturally reports about the problems with this legislation: "When New York first enacted its bottle bill, the state amassed a tremendous quantity of beverage bottles, much of it to end up in landfills because the support network for dispersal had yet to be established" ("Trash into Cash" 12-13).

13   But even if mechanisms for processing recyclables were better established, there are inherent problems with recycling that even the most conservation-conscious individuals sometimes don't consider. According to Martin Pawley's statements in Building for Tomorrow: Putting Garbage to Work, recycling is by nature an inefficient technique. "Its chief drawback," he writes, "is that the energy that went into giving the bottle its distinctive shape or the can its remarkable dimensional shape is lost" (109).

14   To understand the recycling's inefficiency further, it is important to consider what is really involved. Although the meaning of the word recycle has often been enlarged to include all kinds of reuse, technically (and in most cases practically) speaking, recycling involves stripping back a product to its raw-material

Good touch to maintain flow

When author title of book c article are give in text, page number is sufficient.

46i
MLA

Mitchell 8

state. It is precisely in this stripping, or processing, that recycling's liabilities are most obviously revealed.

15   In the case of paper, this involves turning the paper back into pulp. With plastics, it involves melting the plastic and re-forming it. The process is similar for all kinds of metals, including aluminum and steel. In each instance, tremendous amounts of energy must be expended to bring the material back to a point where it can be used again. Moreover, recycling is not a nontoxic proposition. In paper recycling, for example, bleaching agents and chemical agents must be added to make the paper reusable; the same is true for other recycling processes ("Trash into Cash" 12-14).

16   Therefore, with landfill, incineration, and recycling programs dubious at best, the need for alternatives in waste management is critical. But what can be done?

17   On a practical level, there is simple reuse and conservation. Still, our entire economy is built around the ease of a throwaway cycle. And although it is the by-products of technology that have brought us to our current crisis, it may indeed

46i
MLA

Mitchell 9

be that technology coupled with innovative thinking will be our salvation.

18 According to writers like Pawley, it needn't necessarily be high-tech machinery that delivers more efficient means of use, disposal, or recovery. For Pawley, it starts with basic design philosophy. "Today most of the design work in resource recovery is going to the development of doomsday machines capable of crushing, burying everything that we make" (151).

19 He goes on to point out an alternative philosophy:

> A much more energy-efficient response to the rising tide of waste would be a design ethos based on prolonging product life, developing alternative and successive uses and exploring material substitutions that would enable products to tidy up after themselves. (151)

The entire remanufacturing industry has sprung from at least one of Pawley's recommendations, "successive uses," the simple reutilization of a product once it has reached the end of its originally intended life cycle.

20 Finding new ways of using products that have reached the conclusion of their life cycle

You might have your students check their own block-indented quotations against the one here. In each case, the proofreader might ask these questions: Are the lines consistently indented from the left? Are quotation marks omitted (given that the block indent shows that the passage is quoted)? Is the period placed *before* the parenthetical citation, not after as in the regular paragraphs?

46i
MLA

Mitchell 10

was the focus of Pawley's work, but the bricolage
and garbage-building experiments that he and his
associates initiated have not been seriously
adopted by the industrial and manufacturing
sectors.[2] The variation on Pawley's concept of
"secondary use" that has taken hold is the
technique of remanufacturing.

Ken has defined his
subject, refined his
focus, and prepared
the way for specific
examples of the re-
manufacturing
process and product.

The Case Book

21   Arrow Automotive Industries is considered
the pioneer in the remanufacturing field.
Founder Albert Howasser first began
remanufacturing automobile parts in 1929, when he
realized that instead of restricting his work to
fix-it operations, he could actually produce
first-quality remanufactured parts that could
compete with their new counterparts.

22   Arrow celebrated its sixtieth anniversary in
1989 and is now an integral player in a sophisticated
network of warehouse distributors, jobbers, and
installers of remanufactured products. According to
company spokesperson Susan Park Pritchard, Arrow has
expanded from automotive parts to heavy, industrial,
and construction equipment. In 1988, company sales
reached $106.5 million.

46i
MLA

Mitchell 11

23   According to Pritchard, Arrow's longevity
and success are attributable to the growth of the
"aftermarket," the sector of the automobile
industry that typically deals with cars once they
are no longer under the care of warranties or
factory-sponsored dealership service. Pritchard
explained that the end users of remanufactured
automobile parts are the neighborhood service
centers and mechanics: "If you had a car that
was, say, five years old and had substituted a
neighborhood shop for your dealer service, you
might very well end up with an alternator that we
remanufactured."

24   Arrow's network of junk dealers and
automotive parts suppliers keeps the cycle of
"cores" (the used parts that are the basis for
the manufacturing process) in motion. The same
alternator that your mechanic removed from your
car would be sent back to the supplier, who would
then credit the mechanic or service station on
the purchase of the next unit.

25   Arrow is using the promise of energy efficiency and environmental preservation as a selling point for its remanufactured products.
According to the company's promotional materials,

Mitchell 12

Arrow has launched major efforts to respond to
the "energy crisis" in particular. As their
literature explains: "Huge energy savings accrue
through elimination of many energy-intensive
operations required in new part production. By
reusing durable previously produced components of
cast iron and steel, remanufacturers eliminate
mining, transport, smelting, and casting of
metals" (Arrow 6). ——— Format for corporate author

26   Another of the leaders in remanufacturing is
the Tupperware company, whose entry into the
remanufacturing business was deliberate and
driven by a desire to maintain high-quality, if
somewhat outdated, injection molding machinery
that was specially made for it in the 1960s. As
reported by Carl Kirkland in Plastics World,
rather than have to buy entirely new machinery
when the company automated its production
facilities, its managers saw the opportunity to
build off the company's original investment (42).
But rather than bring outsiders to remanufacture
equipment that was unique to its operation,
Tupperware decided to remanufacture the equipment
itself--after all, who better to understand the
needs and demands of its own facility? And since

46i
MLA

Mitchell 13

the company was already in the manufacturing business to begin with, it was able to transfer skills and know-how to bring old equipment up to date.

27 By July 1991, Tupperware had remanufactured 89 of its 200 injection machines that were producing the company's well-known line of plastic storage containers: "The remanufactured machines reportedly met or exceeded corporate expectations of uptime, utilization and networkability. And they have allowed Tupperware to run newer, tougher parts more easily than ever before" (Kirkland 45).

28 What is significant about the Tupperware move is that it shows how a company can use remanufacturing for very specialized needs. Furthermore, because the process was handled internally, it produced equipment that was customized, without a customized price tag.

29 Tupperware actually redesigns and reengineers its equipment during the remanufacturing process based on feedback received from workers on the production line.[3] Instead of having to learn new procedures, workers can continue using what they are accustomed to while gaining the much desired

Mitchell 14

improvements (Kirkland 43). Anybody who has had
to work with poorly designed equipment on a
regular basis--where vital controls are missing
or misplaced--recognizes the value of a
remanufactured product of this.sort.

Other Industries

30   The American Telegraph & Telephone Company
(AT&T) is perhaps the best known of the earlier
remanufacturers. It started routinely
remanufacturing phones after World War II.
Typically, a remanufactured AT&T phone will sell
for 25 percent less than its virgin counterpart,
with no distinguishable cosmetic or performance
differences.

31   In the past two decades, remanufacturing has
spread not only to high-tech industries like
robotics and aviation but also to transportation.
For example, New York City regularly
remanufactures its subway cars. By 1995, two-
thirds of the New York City Transit Authority's
subway fleet will be of the remanufactured
variety (Schulman and Sabin 70).

32   Another industry that has strong ties to
remanufacturing is the office furniture business.

Mitchell 15

In a recession economy like that of the early
1990s, businesses just can't afford the outlay
for virgin office furniture. And why should
they, when they can get the same top-quality
furniture from top-shelf manufacturers like
Steelcase and Henry Miller in remanufactured
versions? All the corporate mergers, downsizing,
and reorganization have produced a surplus of
top-quality office furniture that has been a boon
to the remanufacturing business. Companies like
Remanufactured Business Furniture of St. Louis
scour the country in search of merchandise that
they can remanufacture. Once they acquire the
necessary "cores," they dismantle and refurbish
to customer specifications. "The previously
discarded furniture looks like it was delivered
off the assembly line of Henry Miller, Steelcase,
Knoll, or Westinghouse," according to owner Bill
Greytak, and the costs are 25 to 40 percent less
than retail (qtd. in Ezer 1C).

Use page number as it appears in the source.

Indirect source

33   Aside from saving money, the customer can
reap other benefits. "Another advantage to
buying remanufactured is that it takes less time
than new furniture for delivery and installation"
(Aragon 27). And according to the same article

46i
MLA

Mitchell 16

in the San Jose Business Journal, a company can
have its furniture remanufactured in a couple of
weeks, as opposed to waiting six to twelve weeks
for delivery from a traditional factory (27-28).

34   Another option for impatient businesses
wanting to reap the savings of remanufacturing is
literally to trade in their old furniture. The
San Jose report points out that whereas some
businesses are interested in the ecological
benefits of remanufacturing, the major incentive
for buying remanufactured is cost. It is
interesting to note that none of the literature
made mention of the environmental benefits of
remanufacturing.

The Future

35   Although in many cases it seems like a
logical step in the manufacturing-use-disposal
cycle, remanufacturing has failed to get the
widespread attention that other waste management
techniques have received. To some extent this is
attributable to the mindset of the manufacturers
and consumers, who consider a used product an
inferior product, one that will never be as

worthwhile. This is the same psychological
barrier that makers of recycled products face.
Still, if industries could be convinced--even on
a purely financial level--of the benefits of
remanufacturing, it could go a long way toward
making this economy more efficient and
productive. Furthermore, the positive
environmental side effects would be astonishing.
Through remanufacturing, businesses can realize
improved equipment and cost reduction and benefit
the world as well.

Number page. ———→ Mitchell 18

Set aside
separate
page for
notes.

Notes

↑
Center.

——— Indent first line five spaces.

[1]On November 9 I spoke with Susan Park

Maintain
double
spacing.
Pritchard of Arrow Automotive Industries. This

conversation and some of the company's

promotional literature represent my research on

Arrow.

[2]According to Pawley, bricolage is a French

word meaning "odd-jobbery, the work of an odd-job

man." The garbage-building experiments, in which

construction is done with refuse, junk, and

similar materials, are common in developing

nations.

[3]Although the Tupperware company has not

published a study of its machine conversions or

remanufacturing processes, this information is

available to interested parties through the

company's public relations department.

The Works Cited list starts on a separate page after the body and notes. Again, center the words *Works Cited*, and maintain double spacing throughout. If an entry exceeds a single line, indent the subsequent lines five spaces. Arrange entries alphabetically, author's or editor's last name first. When no author is listed, use the work's title for alphabetizing purposes.

- [Aragon] This is the form for an article in a weekly magazine, including date and page numbers.
- [Arrow] Because corporate authorship is assumed for the promotional literature, Ken uses the company name in the author's slot.
- [Keller] This is the form for edited books. If the city alone might be unclear, indicate state or country as well.
- [Kirkland] This is the form for articles in periodicals published monthly or every other month. Page numbers indicate the entire article, not just the section cited.

Number page. ⎯⎯⟶ Mitchell 19

Works Cited

Aragon, Lawrence. "New Is Not the Only Way to Buy
     Furniture." <u>San Jose Business Journal</u> 6 May
     1991: 27-28.

Arrow Automotive Industries. <u>Arrow: Leader in
     Remanufacturing</u>. Framingham, MA: Arrow
     Automotive Industries, 1989.

Ezer, Andrew. "Furniture Rehabber: Greytak Makes
     Used Furniture Look Like New." <u>St. Louis Busi-
     ness Journal</u> 27 July 1992: 1C.

Kaelble, Steve. "Franklin Power Products." <u>Indiana
     Business</u> Sept. 1991: 82-85.

Keller, Hans, ed. <u>Who Is Who in Service to the
     Earth: People, Projects, Organizations, and Key-
     words</u>. Waynesville, NC: Vision Link Educational
     Foundation, 1991.

Kirkland, Carl. "Remanufacturing--by Tupperware."
     <u>Plastics World</u> July 1991: 42-46.

Kruglinski, Anthony. "How Much Are Rebuilt Locomo-
     tives Worth?" <u>Railway Age</u> Jan. 1991: 74-75.

Moore, Walt. "Three Ideas for Saving Time, Money,
     and Trouble." <u>Construction Equipment</u> 15 Nov.
     1989: 76-79.

FOR DISCUSSION

Draw students' attention to the overall layout of this "Works Cited" page. Have them notice the major points first: i.e., the alphabetical listing of sources, the indentation of second and subsequent lines in the entries, and the periods ending all of the entries. Then you might call attention to the underlined titles of books and periodicals, the quotation marks around article titles, the placement of periods within the citations, and the way book entries list cities, publishers, and copyright dates. Refer students to 46b for further explanation of particular entry types appearing here.

46i
MLA

- [Pawley] This is the basic form for books with a single author.
- [Pritchard] The words *Personal interview* and the date of the interview are all that's required to credit an unpublished personal interview.
- [Romalewski] Articles found in reference books such as encyclopedias, guides, or directories are treated as pieces in a collection. Because this article was signed, Ken gave the author's name, the edition, and the page numbers.
- [Schulman...] When listing an article with more than one author, invert the first author's name but retain the normal order for each additional author.
- [Trash] When no author is listed, use the title of the work and follow other citation rules accordingly. Because "Trash into Cash" is taken from a reference work, Ken follows the rules for pieces in a collection (see Romalewski).

Mitchell 20

Pawley, Martin. Building for Tomorrow: Putting Waste
    to Work. San Francisco: Sierra Club Books,
    1982.

Pritchard, Susan Park. Personal interview. 9 Nov.
    1991.

Romalewski, Steven. "Long Island's Burning Issue."
    New York Naturally. 1990 ed. viii-xi.

Schulman, Roger, and Margaret Sabin. "A Growing Love
    Affair with the Scrap Heap." Business Week 29
    Apr. 1985: 69-70.

"Trash into Cash: That's Only the Half of It." New
    York Naturally. 1990 ed. 12-17.

46i
MLA

46j **Excerpt from a research paper in APA form**

On the following pages, you will find an excerpt from Ken Mitchell's research paper, prepared according to the manuscript preparation and documentation guidelines set forth by the American Psychological Association (APA).

Title or abbreviated
title begins on cover.

Successive Uses

1

Center title.

Successive Uses: Waste Management and Remanufacturing

Ken Mitchell   Author

Include all
information
requested by
your instructor.

English 102, Section 74, Dr. G. Zirinsky   Class information

November 24, 1994   Date

FOR DISCUSSION

As students examine the model here, ask them to contrast APA style with the MLA style demonstrated previously. What major differences are evident from the title page, the abstract, the information provided by in-text citations, and the arrangement of details on the "References" page? How do the differences between the two styles affect the tone and readability of the report? Which of the two styles, MLA or APA, would students prefer to use in future research?

46j
APA

Successive Uses

2

Paragraph of no more than 150 words presents
the thesis and summarizes key points.

Abstract

As an economically and environmentally sound waste
management and resource recovery strategy,
remanufacturing is far superior to traditional recycling,
incineration, and related practices. Remanufacturing
encourages successive uses of products that might
otherwise be thrown away. The process of remanufacturing
involves utilizing the "core" of the original product and
modifying or adding to it so that its specifications are
equal to or better than the original. Further,
remanufacturing enlarges the related techniques of
refurbishing and rebuilding to the level of production
manufacturing. Companies that remanufacture use the same
assembly-line techniques that manufacturers of virgin
products use.

46j
APA

Successive Uses: Waste Management and Remanufacturing

ple space

    You won't find remanufacturing in your trusty
collegiate dictionary, but a search of the current
indexes for business periodicals will bring up more than
a handful of listings. Companies in an interesting array
of industries--most seeking an edge in a difficult
economy--have begun to employ this innovative and cost-
saving technique.

    Although cost cutting and efficiency have long been
the concerns of both the business and consumer sectors,
today's buyers and sellers have other reasons to consider
this revolutionary technique. With increased attention
to the environmental side effects of our unrestricted
commercialism, remanufacturing simultaneously promises
financial and ecological benefits to all concerned.

    So what is remanufacturing? According to recent
business periodicals, companies that remanufacture don't
just repair or refurbish older products. "They combine
old and new parts and build versions that are as good
[as] or better than new" (Schulman & Sabin, 1985, p. 69).
Products are typically taken apart and examined. Then
technicians, mechanics, or engineers determine which
parts are worn and replace or repair as needed. The

46j
APA

components are then reassembled, tested, and either painted, refinished, or cosmetically restored so that they can sit side by side with similar new products. As Schulman and Sabin remark, the remanufactured version is often then sold at a fraction of the cost of the original (p. 69).

Throughout history, thrifty small-time entrepreneurs have always been on the lookout for salvageable items. Your neighborhood fix-it shop is a good example. There you can find a rebuilt blender or toaster oven, floor polisher or vacuum cleaner. Nowhere is this spirit more prevalent than in the Third World, where necessity-driven scavengers have been defying the originally intended life cycles of everything from bicycles to agricultural machinery (Moore, 1989, p. 77; Pawley, 1982, p. 110). Remanufacturing expands on this spirit by enlarging the concept with modern assembly-line production techniques. It is precisely this emphasis on large-scale production that defines modern remanufacturing (Keller, 1991, pp. 3-12).

Students should notice how the typical APA in-text citation at the end of this paragraph differs from MLA citations in the previous model. For example, APA style requires a comma after the author's name; MLA does not. APA includes the date of the source; MLA does not. APA uses the abbreviation "pp." before page numbers; MLA does not.

46j
APA

Some Benefits

Reduction in energy and material expenditure is what makes remanufacturing a significant and environmentally

Successive Uses

5

sensitive strategy. According to reports in trade
magazines from the plastics, furniture, automotive, and
transportation industries, remanufactured products are
produced using approximately one-fifth the energy and
one-tenth the raw materials (Kaelble, 1990). Thanks to
this reduction in manufacturing overhead, consumers can
usually expect savings of 25 to 50 percent (Schulman &
Sabin, 1985, p. 69). . . .

FOR DISCUSSION

Students should again note differences between APA procedure and MLA procedure. Among the most important is the title of the bibliography itself: "References" (not "Works Cited," as in MLA style). Although both styles alphabetize and space entries in much the same way, students should note that APA has a much different way of recording information within the entries. Publication dates follow authors' names. There are no quotation marks surrounding article titles, and the abbreviation "pp." is included before page numbers. Ask students to point out other differences.

Successive Uses

6

References

Aragon, L. (1991, May 6). New is not the only way to buy furniture. <u>San Jose Business Journal</u>, pp. 27-28.

Arrow Automotive Industries. (1989). <u>Arrow: Leader in remanufacturing</u>. Framingham, MA: Author.

Ezer, A. (1987, July 27). Furniture rehabber: Greytak makes used furniture look like new. <u>St. Louis Business Journal</u>, p. 1C.

Kaelble, S. (1990, Sept. 30). Franklin power products. <u>Indiana Business</u>, pp. 82-85.

Keller, H. (Ed.). (1991). <u>Who is who in service to the earth: People, projects, organizations, and keywords</u>. Waynesville, NC: Vision Link Educational Foundation.

Kirkland, C. (1991, July). Remanufacturing--by Tupperware. <u>Plastics World</u>, pp. 42-46.

Kruglinski, A. (1991, January). How much are rebuilt locomotives worth? <u>Railway Age</u>, pp. 74-75.

Moore, W. (1989, November 15). Three ideas for saving time, money, and trouble. <u>Construction Equipment</u>, pp. 76-79.

Successive Uses

7

Pawley, M. (1982). Building for tomorrow: Putting
      waste to work. San Francisco: Sierra Club Books.

Romalewski, S. (1990, January). Long Island's burn-
      ing issue. New York Naturally, pp. viii-xi.

Schulman, R., & Sabin, M. (1985, 29 April). A grow-
      ing love affair with the scrap heap. Business
      Week, pp. 69-70.

Trash into Cash: That's only the half of it. (1990,
      January). New York Naturally, pp. 12-17.

COLLABORATIVE ACTIVITY

If you permit collaborative proof-reading of final drafts, encourage students to check one another's papers for typographical errors and for mistakes having to do with documentation procedure (including the format and punctuation of "Works Cited" entries).

46j
APA

Chances are that many of your students are already facing essay exams or lab report assignments in other courses. This chapter provides basic advice for test takers and those who are engaged in writing scientific reports.

47 WRITING FOR OTHER PURPOSES IN COLLEGE

Although the research paper is a very important part of college writing, other kinds of writing will be expected of you as well. You may be asked to write a five-minute response to a quiz, a science lab report, a personal journal, an hour-long essay exam, a business report, a nurse's log, a report on an interview, or a procedure for doing some task. No matter what the format, style, or time limit, the writing principles that we discussed in Part I will help you write more effectively. Don't make the mistake of thinking that these principles apply only in your English class.

In every writing situation, spend some time planning what you are going to write and save some time at the end for proofreading what you have written. Make sure you take some time to think about your audience—who they are, what they already know, and what style of writing they will expect. Spend some time making sure you understand the assignment; if you have questions about it, ask your instructor. And spend some time thinking about the purpose of this piece of writing. What are you trying to accomplish? Time spent on these tasks will produce better writing in the long run.

This chapter will look at two common tasks: the essay exam and laboratory reports.

47a Learning to take essay examinations

All college writers face the likelihood of taking regular essay examinations. The two most familiar are open-book and closed-book tests. In the first, your instructor will usually allow you to prewrite, view notes and journals, and have annotated books at hand. In the second, you are expected to respond from memory.

47a
exam

Whenever you are required to take either variety, consider the issues raised here carefully.

Know your assignment

Nothing can substitute for reading the directions closely. Take a moment to decide what's called for. Are you being asked to respond? React? Analyze? Define? Describe? If you are unsure or troubled by the question, ask for clarification.

Here are two typical essay questions:

> Prove that the greenhouse effect does or does not exist. Illustrate your argument using the major points covered in class and in your text.

In this essay, you are asked to *prove,* which means to make a claim (the greenhouse effect does or does not exist) and then to give support with examples and information learned in class and in your textbook.

> Describe how the election process works, and comment on this process.

In this essay, you are asked to discuss the parts of the election process and then give your own personal opinion on it.

Manage your time

Given the time allowed and the questions at hand, you must decide the best way to manage your response. In an examination setting, your instructor will specify a time limit, so you must determine how to use every moment most effectively. It's a good idea to use all of the allotted time. Also, consider making a schedule of how you will use the available time before you begin.

Manage the material

Your next task is to use your response to convince your instructor that you have mastered the material at hand. How? Your best bet is to use the same process you would outside of class: prewrite, draft, revise, and edit. The box illustrates this process for a one-hour examination.

FOR DISCUSSION

Spend some time discussing essay exams with your class. Invite students to share their past experiences or future concerns. You might also point out that while test anxiety can strike anyone, for some it can develop into a serious problem. Make sure your class is aware of whatever professional counseling services your college offers to students.

ACTIVITY

You might schedule at least one impromptu essay to be written in class during the course. Students should benefit from the practice of taking what in effect is an hour-long exam. Encourage students to study the advice in 47a in order to prepare. After students have written the essay, follow up at the next meeting with a class discussion. Invite students to share their thoughts about how they responded to and dealt with the test directions.

RESOURCES

Elbow, Peter. *Writing with Power: Techniques for Mastering the Writing Process.* New York: Oxford UP, 1981.

Shamoon, Linda K., and Robert A. Schwegler. "Sociologists Reading Student Texts: Expectations and Perceptions." *Writing Instructor* 7 (1988): 71–81.

Vargas, Marjorie Fink. "Writing Skills for Science Labs." *Science Teacher* 53.8 (1986): 29–33.

47a
exam

PLAN FOR A ONE-HOUR ESSAY EXAMINATION

Task Analysis (5 minutes)

What's being asked? Do I understand all of the terms? Is there a single, unified question? Are there parts to the question? What does the teacher expect?

Planning (10 minutes)

Resist the urge to start writing. List and freewrite for a couple of minutes. Highlight important items. Sketch a quick plan or outline.

Drafting (35 minutes)

Write with your plan or outline in front of you. Triple-space with possible revision and editing in mind. Be purposeful; get to the point.

Revising (10 minutes)

Reread the question; decide how well you have answered. Play the role of the teacher and read your response: clarify, add definitions, explanations, and illustrations accordingly.

Editing (5 minutes)

Proofread and correct misspellings, punctuation, and other mechanical errors.

47b Writing in the sciences

Students in classes as diverse as chemistry, astronomy, psychology, and physics can regularly expect to write proposals, literature surveys, critiques, abstracts, and research reports. Perhaps the most common of all assignments in the sciences, however, is the laboratory report. Though the specific form and content of this type of report vary from class to class and assignment to assignment, the primary purpose of these reports is to present laboratory research findings in a manner and style consistent with the discipline.

47a
exam

Many instructors will provide laboratory manuals that detail specific research and writing requirements for these reports. In general, laboratory reports include a title page and report body; sometimes they include end matter as well.

- **Title page**. Laboratory reports include title and subtitle; researcher's name, class name, and number; instructor's name; and date of submission—all on a separate page.
- **Report body**. Most reports include a section devoted to purpose—a statement setting forth the research objectives; a section covering laboratory *procedures, methods,* and *materials* employed, complete enough to allow someone else to replicate the experiment; a *results* section, providing a summary of observations and data (often given in the form of tables, graphs, or charts); and a *discussion* section, featuring an interpretation of research findings. The body may also include sections devoted to a discussion of theoretical background and recommendations.
- **End matter.** Depending on the purpose and scope of your report, you may be expected to provide formal references, a glossary, and appendixes.

Unless your instructor states otherwise, it is a good bet that he or she will accept a report prepared according to the formatting and documentation guidelines provided by the Council of Biology Editors (see 46f).

Although stylistic conventions for scientific writing vary, the following guidelines generally apply:

- Write in the third person. Do not use the pronouns *you* or *I.*
- Emphasize concrete, observable events or results. Avoid the philosophical or speculative.
- Use precise, simple, and accurate language.
- Rely more on nouns and verbs—less on adjectives and adverbs.
- Use the passive voice when you want to emphasize results rather than causes.
- Use tables, graphs, and diagrams when they clarify your presentation.

ACTIVITY

Consider inviting a colleague who teaches a science course to visit your class. Ask him or her to discuss informally the problems faced by professionals who write scientific reports. Encourage your students to question the guest about the writing skills expected of students in his or her field.

47b
sci

As a college English instructor, you no doubt have plenty of experience in writing about literature. Your own advice and reminiscences should be of special interest to your class. This chapter, however, can serve as background for your discussion by introducing questions that literary essays tend to address. You might point out that more advanced types of literary commentary vary widely according to critical methodology and that each literature professor may have his or her own favorite avenue of approach. The advice offered in this chapter can help prepare students for the many challenges and pleasures of literary analysis.

If you are using a college reader that includes short stories, poetry, and drama, consider assigning at least one example from one of those genres to serve as a basis for class discussion. Encourage students to read the selected work carefully and to record first impressions in a journal or notebook.

48 WRITING ABOUT LITERATURE

Almost every undergraduate student will take at least one literature class during his or her academic career. In many ways, the process of writing about literature is no different from the process of writing about other subjects. Writers move from brainstorming through topic selection, thesis construction, outlining, drafting, revising, and editing. In some cases, they rely on their own interpretations of the work; in others, they consult outside sources.

48a Genre

Like other complex systems, literary works have been classified and divided into manageable categories. There are three major categories, or *genres*, in literary studies: *poetry, fiction,* and *drama,* with subdivisions such as lyrical and narrative poetry; novel, novella, and short story (fiction); and comic and tragic drama.

These categories are not exhaustive or exclusive. For instance, most scholars would acknowledge fiction's debt to drama, and lyrical poetry often contains elements of fiction.

48b Types of written assignments

In a literature class, you are likely to encounter the following types of assignments.

Type of Assignment	Definition	Example
Reaction	Calls for you to read and comment on a literary work without necessarily consulting secondary sources.	■ Read and react to Henry David Thoreau's *Walden*.

TYPE OF ASSIGNMENT	DEFINITION	EXAMPLE
Explication	Calls for an interpretation, either word by word or line by line (for poetry), paragraph by paragraph (for stories and plays), or section by section (for other works).	■ Prepare a line-by-line reading of Deborah Digges's "Milk."
Analysis	*Character analysis* requires that you get inside a character to question that character's motives, thoughts, attitudes, beliefs, and actions.	■ What makes Emily worthy of our continued attention in Faulkner's "A Rose for Emily"?
	Plot analysis requires that you consider and discuss the dynamics and arrangement of the events of a story.	■ In what ways can you compare the plot of Updike's "A&P" to a shopping list?
Comparison and contrast	Calls for an analysis of elements—imagery, diction, dialogue—in two or more works, focusing on similarities and/or differences.	■ Compare the ways in which Kafka ("A Hunger Artist") and Faulkner ("A Rose for Emily") use physical confinement.
Interpretation	Calls for an appraisal of the meaning and significance of a work or elements within that work.	■ What does Malamud's "Magic Barrel" have to say about magic, myth, and transformation?
Review	Requires that you advance and support an evaluation of a literary work.	■ Are the works you've read by William Stafford actually poetry?

RESOURCES

Barnet, Sylvan. *A Short Guide to Writing about Literature.* 5th ed. New York: HarperCollins, 1985.

Biddle, Arthur W., and Toby Fulwiler, eds. *Reading, Writing, and the Study of Literature.* New York: McGraw, 1989.

Peters, John. *The Elements of Critical Reading.* New York: Macmillan, 1991.

Barnet's book is a classic introduction to writing about literature, focusing mainly on rhetorical aspects of drama, poetry, and fiction. Biddle and Fulwiler have collected useful essays by scholars on topics ranging from genres to critical methodology. Peters' book shows how works from across the disciplines can be read and analyzed from social, emotional, ethical, and other basic perspectives.

48b
lit

Assignments may combine two or more of these tasks. For example, don't be surprised to run across an assignment requiring both explication and comparison and contrast. A worthy review will likely combine explication and analysis. An interpretation could easily make use of both character and plot analysis, perhaps combined with explication.

ACTIVITY

Invite a colleague who has published literary criticism to visit your class. Ask your guest to discuss his or her methods and critical philosophy, as well as how his or her approach may differ from those of other critics. Encourage students to ask questions.

48c **Important perspectives: critical approaches**

Whether you are asked to react to, explicate, analyze, interpret, or review a literary work, you'll be influenced not only by the work itself but also by who you are as a reader, what you have read, and how your teacher frames class discussions and assignments. In fact, the way one approaches writing about literature is often through already established interests. A historian, for instance, would view a piece differently from a psychologist, a linguist differently from a political scientist. Here you'll find some popular perspectives on literature.

The work at hand

Scholars of the school known as *the New Criticism* view a poem, play, or work of fiction as an artifact. In their estimation, the study and appreciation of a literary work should be confined to its essential elements: the language of the work and its patterns of arrangement, unity, symbolism, imagery, irony, ambiguity, and plot.

If you approach a literary work in this manner, your task as reader and critic is to uncover relationships within the literary work itself and steer away from such superficial questions as who wrote the work, when, and why. Understanding the meaning of a work can come only after close reading and analysis of its parts and their relation to the whole. Many introductory classes still favor this critical strategy. (The sample paper in 48f is an example of this approach.)

Origins of the work

Unlike adherents of the New Criticism, the *biographical* critic appreciates the creation for itself and then looks for mean-

48c
lit

ing in the relationship between the literary work and the author's personal history. Although there is never a one-to-one correspondence between an author's life and a given work, there are often important and illuminating parallels to uncover. A reader of Sylvia Plath's work may or may not wish to exploit the recurrence of death imagery in her poetry, but a biographical critic will likely consider the poet's own suicide in relation to many of her poems.

Historical critics derive meaning from considering the historical period in which a work was written. The core of their investigation concerns how and why certain cultures either adapt to or repudiate conventions and trends in both literary genres and the world at large.

Rather than focusing on external social trends, critics who employ *psychological* and *archetypal* criticism apply the theories of psychology and the study of myth to authors and their creations. Students of the psychoanalysts Sigmund Freud and Carl Jung link the study of literature to the dreams, myths, and psychic patterns of an individual or society.

Influences of the work

Still other critics consider issues of gender, economic or political status, and moral and ethical behavior as they read and analyze literature. *Feminist* critics, for example, argue against the traditionally male group of "great authors" dominating literary and critical circles and focus on literature that features female characters, concerns, and activities. The *Marxist* critic reacts to and evaluates literary efforts based on their depiction of the worker and the treatment of the working class by the ruling or dominant class. The *religious* or *moral* critic responds to literature as a vehicle for and representation of universal truth.

The reader and the work

Reader-response critics hold that there is no literary work until a reader completes it. In other words, without the reader, there is no meaning. These critics maintain that the meaning is to be found in the interplay between reader and material.

48c
lit

48d Reading for writing about literature

Poets, novelists, and playwrights do not always hold effective, efficient communication as their immediate priority. A poem communicates, to be sure, but it may speak to your emotions, not your intellect; a novel may instruct, but its lesson may be expressed through the use of symbols and may therefore require deep reflection.

To excel at critical and interpretive reading, and later at writing about reading, you must read the work several times. With this in mind, most instructors assign short works to beginning students and longer works to those who are more advanced. Still, even if you are assigned a lengthy novel, you should attempt to read it through twice.

Active reading

As you read, question and highlight areas crucial to understanding, analysis, and evaluation. Underline character names, mark abrupt shifts in time, use the margins for exclamations of joy and frustration. Summarize and paraphrase your reading after each session (see 45g). Interact with the text, and make the reading your own.

Reading and writing about fiction

Our days are full of stories, and our lives themselves are, in a sense, unfolding stories. When it comes to reading and writing critically about stories, though, many students are perplexed and frustrated. The key to a workable understanding of a short story or novel is simple: at first, don't look for mysterious and complex meaning. Trust your instincts. Ask the same questions as you would in almost any other situation:

Who? Who wrote the story? Who is telling the story? Who are the major and minor characters? Who are the agents of change?

What. What is going on (in each section, chapter, volume)? What is being done? What is being said? What is being

thought? What transformations or changes are taking place? What are your reactions to characters, events, and ideas?

When? When is the piece set? When do things happen? (Consider flashbacks and flashforwards.)

Where? Where is the piece set? Where do the various actions take place?

Why? Why do characters act and think as they do? Why are the pieces arranged as they are? Why am I reacting in the way I am to this work (or part of it)?

How? How does the story get me from beginning to end? How do the characters evolve in the work? How well does the piece hold together?

Obviously, you are free to add to or modify this list; merely considering these questions while reading will put you in a position to write about a given work.

You may also wish to consider the narrator's *point of view.* A story can be told in the first person by a character, or it can be told by an omniscient (all-knowing, all-seeing) narrator, a narrator of limited omniscience (all-knowing about certain issues), or a removed narrator.

Character study, too, may be central to your reading and writing. Writers of literary papers often consider heroes and anti-heroes, characters who act as agents of change, those who teach, and those who are overdeveloped or underdeveloped.

Readers often analyze *setting,* too. Where is the story set, and how do the customs, attitudes, and beliefs of that culture's inhabitants determine the outcome? *Style* is yet another departure point for study. What is the feel of the work, of the narrator's voice? Is the work cast as irony, sarcasm, humor, sermon?

There is no substitute for experience. Read as widely and deeply as you can. Read once for familiarity and appreciation; read the second time with questions in mind; read selectively again to test your interpretation.

COLLABORATIVE ACTIVITY

If you decide to have students write a paper on a short story, consider having them first meet in groups to discuss their responses to the work they've read. To help generate essay ideas, groups might also brainstorm a bit by answering several of the basic questions listed in 46d.

48d
lit

48d
lit

ACTIVITY

Does your college have a video collection available for classroom use? If so, you might arrange to show a one-act play by a noted playwright. As students watch, have them think about how they would answer the "Why?" and "How?" questions for analyzing fiction. After the showing, discuss the answers to those questions or have students write short response essays.

Reading and writing about drama

Most drama is written for performance. Yet often we read and analyze plays in much the same way we read and analyze fiction and poetry. Discussion of plot, character, conflict and resolution, structure, irony, symbolism, and the like are all common to dramatic analysis. When reading and analyzing a play, therefore, it is often appropriate for you to ask many of the same questions and probe many of same issues you would for short stories, novels, and poems.

As with fiction, understanding the plot of any drama is essential. After all, you must feel confident about the story's direction before beginning your search for meaning. Start by familiarizing yourself with the work's major and minor characters. Learn to distinguish among the characters' speeches, the playwright's comments, and stage directions.

As with poetry, appreciating the relationship of language, imagery, and structure to the whole is central. Having read the play once for a basic understanding and for flow, reread to uncover and examine appealing or unusual words and phrases, striking image patterns, and significant organizational choices— decisions regarding the order of episodes, scenes, and acts. In other words, read it again for critical understanding.

If possible, read the play and listen to it or view it. Many works are available on videotape and audiocassettes. Things that confuse you while reading the text are often clarified while watching or hearing a live or taped performance.

Reading and writing about poetry

To many of us, poetry is a difficult genre. At times, a poem will defy narrative logic, and often it requires a courageous and committed reader to discover its value and meaning. Here are some elements to consider while reading any poem.

Imagery. There are two basic kinds of literary imagery: *literal* (language or patterns that appeal to the senses) and *figurative* (metaphor and simile). You are encountering literal imagery

when you are drawn into a poem through descriptive patterns or the poet's use of the senses of smell, touch, hearing, taste, and sight. The astute reader of Deborah Digges's "Milk" (see 48e), for example, will notice the following image patterns: whiteness (dawn, egg, milk, milkman's shirt, lace wedding dress, bed-jacket, doctor's coat), cold (November mornings, warm breath into cupped hands, dressing under blankets, heating milk on the stove), and movements (from present tense to nostalgic remembrance, to the kitchen of youth, to a possible wedding, to a doctor's rounds).

When poets employ figurative imagery, they engage in comparisons, either stated explicitly or implied. Again, in "Milk," note how the speaker describes the morning light "like waking under the paper- / thin hood of a dream / or in an attic room" or later calls milk scum "a new skin rising" and "the milkman's shirt." In this way, figurative imagery allows readers to make connections that extend the perspective and consequently the meaning of the work.

Theme. *Theme* refers to the poem's purpose, its central idea—not the subject, but rather the *significance* of the subject. "Milk" is about childhood memories of a father on November mornings. Its purpose or theme, however, as Jill Simone suggests (48g), is maturity and the ever-evolving nature of relationships. Some literary scholars believe that theme is what gives work its meaning.

Other elements. In addition to imagery and theme, such elements as character, point of view, plot, setting, diction, organization, symbolism, rhythm, and sound all contribute to a reader's experience. For a more detailed treatment of literary analysis, consult your instructor or librarian. As with any type of college writing, no matter how you choose to read, view, and write about a work, you must be willing to understand your purpose, arrive at a subject, focus your concern, formulate a thesis, draft, revise, and edit.

COLLABORATIVE ACTIVITY

Studying poetic imagery can be a useful exercise for students even if your course emphasizes nonfiction. You might assign a short poem from a college reader or distribute one as a handout. Ask students to read the poem as well as the rest of this chapter, including the sample response paper. Students can then meet in groups to analyze the poem you've assigned. Have groups focus on the question of how particular images in the poem contribute to its overall theme. But warn students not to be surprised if members of the group disagree on precisely what the theme of the poem is. Point out that even professional critics often argue about how to interpret famous poems.

48d
lit

48e Writing assignment and sample poem

Here you will find a typical assignment from an American literature class. The student, Jill Simone, is asked to read and respond to a poem. Her instructor has said that she does not expect students to do any library research for this assignment. Some teachers, however, will insist on formal research; if yours does, follow the research and paper writing guidelines provided in 45 and 46.

JILL SIMONE'S ASSIGNMENT

Read and react to one of the poems in our class packet. Use the poem, only; do not use any secondary sources. Keep your paper to five typed pages or less. Follow MLA guidelines. No cover sheet is required.

If you are free to choose a topic, choose one based on long-standing interest, a burning curiosity, or a challenge. Never choose out of ease or convenience. To consider your choices, read the work carefully and jot down whatever comes to mind. After reading "Milk" a number of times, Jill Simone developed the following list of possible subjects from which to choose:

Cold imagery

Fathers and daughters

The female perspective

Narrative movement

The role of color

Growth and maturity

Poems of remembering

Nostalgia

A list of this sort could go on and on; stop when you are interested enough in a subject to continue with it, at least preliminarily. Don't feel locked into your first choice, however. If after a while you sense a dead end, begin anew.

Although arriving at a subject is essential, before proceeding with her paper, Jill had to translate her very general subject into a thesis. A thesis statement is the surest way of moving from a

48e
lit

MILK

> This morning the light seems
> smaller, like waking under the paper-
> thin hood of a dream
> or in an attic room.
>
> In other Novembers
> my father woke me near dawn.
> He said he wanted company before
> making
>
> his hospital rounds.
> He'd blow into my hands, give me
> a warm egg to hold after
> I dressed
>
> beneath the blankets.
> Then we stood by the stove while he
> heated the milk, a new skin rising
> to the surface.
>
> He called it the milkman's shirt
> and dipped his finger in.
> What came away looked more like lace
> from a wedding dress
>
> or a woman's bed-jacket,
> the one she'd slip on
> just before the doctor came, the first
> to see her, mornings.

Sample poem: "Milk" by Deborah Digges.

broad subject to a refined, compelling focus. A sound thesis indicates both a subject and an assertion about that subject. (For
more on thesis, see 2b.)

Here are theses Jill considered:

POSSIBLE THESES

Digges uses temperature images to show emotional transitions
and transformations in "Milk."

"Milk" is primarily a poem about living as a woman in a man's world.

The absence of color in "Milk" reveals sterile characters inhabiting a sterile landscape.

"Milk" is a chronicle of maturity and separation.

The key to "Milk" is understanding and appreciating the relationship between father and daughter.

Jill chose "'Milk' is a chronicle of maturity and separation" as her thesis and wrote a first draft. After receiving comments from her teacher and her peers, she rethought her paper and revised. Her final paper is reprinted in 48f.

48f Sample literature paper

Separation: Growth and Leave-Taking

in Deborah Digges's "Milk"

"Milk" is a chronicle of maturity and separation. While relating apparently commonplace remembrances of childhood, the poet muses about much larger concerns-- among them emotional nourishment, parental relationships, personal transformation, and awakening.

In stanza 1, the poet deftly alerts the reader that a dream journey will ensue, shuttling us from a morning scene set in the present tense to a morning scene somewhere in memory and beyond. She writes:

This morning the light seems

smaller, like waking under the paper-

thin hood of a dream

or in an attic room. (lines 1-4)

Attics are indeed places of dreams, nostalgia, stored memories. It is as if the poet asks us to follow her up a winding stair to an out-of-the-way and musty room where trunks of keepsakes are secreted, where she will whisper a story to us: the story of her transition from childhood to adulthood.

The next two stanzas reemphasize this mysterious journey into the attic of memory. "In other Novembers," she signals, "my father woke me near dawn" (5-6). Has she unlocked a cracked leather steamer trunk and extracted a letter or a photo? Is she looking longingly out a window across a leaf-strewn yard, reminiscing about the comfort of being young? Suddenly, the reader is with the remembered child as her father calls for her to take warm milk with him before his hospital rounds.

Once the poem is solidly located in dream or memory, the emphasis shifts to reveal a certain kind of father-daughter relationship. The narrator loves and admires this father. She depends on him, and he on her. There is no mother here. Milk is nourishment. And here it is emotional nourishment. This child is suckling at the breast of the home and father. She is not, but will soon be, weaned of her need for this type of relationship. Warm milk is comfort; it rids us of an inner chill. She is not warm but will soon be warmed and ready to go forth.

To this end, the father lovingly cares for this daughter, blowing a "warm egg" of air into her cold

If your class has worked with MLA style guidelines in discussing prose works, make sure students understand that the parenthetical citations in this paper refer to line numbers in the poem, not to pages.

48f
lit

hands. He teaches her, too, by pointing out "a new skin
rising / to the surface" (15-16) of heated milk--"the
milkman's shirt" (17), he calls it. What child cannot
recall a parent initiating her in similar ways and with
familiar folk wisdom?

At this point, the focus on the father-daughter
relationship lessens, however, as the issues of marriage,
womanhood, life, and death arise. "What came away looked
more like lace / from a wedding dress" (19-20), she
writes of the milk scum, and we are once more transported
from a scene we imagine featuring the young girl with
father huddled in the morning cold around a comforting
stove to years later: this daughter preparing for
marriage and separation from father, this father
preparing to give over this bride. We can imagine the
life lived in between: the daily and the special events,
the playgrounds, the boyfriends, the proms. We can
imagine the natural growth. She has drunk the milk and
is growing.

In some way beyond practical intelligence--one so
difficult to pin down--the father's finger dipped in the
skin of boiled milk punctures a kind of membrane. Time
itself seems to be altered. The girl is suddenly a
woman. The father's relationship with her has been
forever changed.

We are saddened, but there is a purity rather than a
sadness to this transformation--for everything is white,

white.   The morning light is clean and in its way white.
The warm egg's shell is white.   The doctor's hospital
coat, the milkman's shirt, the woman's bed-jacket, and
the milk are all white.   And in this whiteness there is
hope for many mornings to come.

　　　In this way, the poem can be seen as a cycle of
awakening growth, separation, and beginning anew.   At the
beginning, we imagine the speaker a dreaming adult
nostalgically reviewing the knickknacks and mementos
gathered through life.   In the middle section, we hear
the sentimental tale of a young girl bonding with her
father before work.   By the poem's end, the girl has
married, left home, and achieved a type of separation
from her father--who becomes "the doctor . . . ,
the first / to see her, mornings" (23-24).   We have come
full circle and begun another journey.

[The Works Cited list starts on a new page.]

Works Cited

　　Digges, Deborah. "Milk." Vesper Sparrows. New York:
　　　　　Atheneum, 1986. 28.

In writing her paper, Jill followed the MLA system (see
46d). She also followed the conventions for literary papers:

48f
lit

You might mention that the first convention listed in this box applies to writing about nonfiction works as well. In general, students should remember to use what is sometimes called "literary present tense" whenever they are analyzing or alluding to passages by other authors, even when those authors are dead.

We are teaching in a decade when vast numbers of college students cannot afford to wait for diplomas before their job search begins. Even the freshman year is not too soon for them to develop skills in résumé preparation and standard business communication. This chapter cannot guarantee future employment, but it does offer basic advice that might prove helpful to many students in your class.

CONVENTIONS FOR PAPERS ABOUT LITERATURE

- Use the present tense to talk about events in the work.
- Use examples and quotations from the work to support your thesis.
- When writing about a short story or a novel, give page numbers for quotations; when writing about a poem, give line numbers.
- For a play, provide references to acts and scenes using Arabic numbers, and to line numbers as well if the play is in verse: *Ham.* 3.2.1–4.
- At the end of the paper, include a list of Works Cited.

49 WRITING OUTSIDE OF SCHOOL: JOB APPLICATIONS AND MEMOS

At one time or another, you will have the occasion to apply for a full- or part-time job. Some companies are satisfied with having the candidate merely complete an employment application form; most, however, expect you to submit a letter of application in combination with a résumé. These documents are the first impression a company will have of you; together they will qualify or disqualify you for an interview and possible employment. Therefore, you'll want to take great care with each.

When you respond to an ad, it is likely that there will be many similarly qualified applicants. Therefore, it will help if your letter and résumé can somehow stand out from the rest; at the very least, they should be well written and neat in appearance.

49a The job application process

- **Consider your qualifications**. List your immediate and long-range goals, attitudes toward work, strengths and weaknesses.
- **Read advertisements carefully.** Consider company, job title, duties, special needs, and qualifications.
- **Write an ad for yourself.** If you keep a journal, formulate the ad there. Articulate everything in the first two points. Prepare questions to ask the interviewer.

49a
bus

- **Research the job and the company.** Call the personnel division of the company to request further information about the opening (person in charge of the search, specific duties, special considerations). Remember, print ads are by their very nature limited in size and scope. Companies are often willing to provide further information on request.
  —Drop by the company offices to collect company literature, speak with public relations staff, and generally ask around.
  —Use the library to investigate the nature, needs, and concerns of the company in question. See the reference librarian for sources.
- **Write a summary.** Use your journal to summarize your findings about the job and the company before you write.
- **Write your résumé and cover letter.** Using your research, create a résumé (or modify an existing one), and write a cover letter *specifically* related to the desired position. Using a generic, all-purpose résumé and cover letter will lessen your chances of being considered for an interview.
- **Follow up.** Call to confirm that the company has received your application materials. If you have been interviewed, call or write to thank the appropriate person for his or her attention and time.

If you choose to apply at a company that has not advertised, begin by writing your own ad; then follow the other steps listed.

Here is an ad that appeared in a local classified section (*Chicago Reader* 8 Nov. 1991):

> **Activist/Environmentalist.** Citizens for a Better Environment seeks an energetic person for its public outreach program. Salaried position. No canvassing or telemarketing. Contact: Ms. Verna Van Keuren, (312) 555-1699, ext. 252.

49b The résumé

Résumé literally means "summary," and writing one offers you an opportunity to do just that: cite your most important credentials in condensed form. The primary purpose of a résumé is to persuade an employer to grant you an interview. Imagine what

RESOURCES

Mehaffy, Robert, and Constance Warloe. "Corporate Communications: Next Step for the Community College?" *Technical Writing Teacher* 16 (1989): 1–11.

Mendelson, Michael. "Business Prose and the Nature of Plain Style." *Journal of Business Communication* 24.2 (1978): 2–18.

Odell, Lee, and Dixie Goswami, eds. *Writing in Nonacademic Settings.* New York: Guilford, 1985.

ACTIVITY

If your college has a career placement office, you might ask one of its representatives to provide your class with information about the services offered.

ACTIVITY

Consider inviting a business professor or corporate executive to visit your class. Ask your guest to discuss topics relevant to job placement and business writing. Encourage students to ask questions.

49b
bus

your job would be like if you were a personnel director and had to read the full life history of each applicant. Résumés vary in length, but few exceed two pages. They offer the reviewer the opportunity to glance and continue or glance and toss away.

A résumé is usually organized in reverse chronological order. In other words, your most recent job or school is listed first, and the rest are listed in descending order. However, this organization may not serve you well if you have been unemployed for a long time or if you wish to change career goals.

An alternative format is that of the functional résumé, which lists positions by job skills, such as "Administrative Experience" or "Marketing Skills." This format is most useful for those who are reentering the job market, those who wish to emphasize skills rather than prestigious positions, and those who are changing careers.

At a minimum, every résumé should include three sections:

- Identification (name, address, phone number)
- Education (institutions attended, degrees earned, and dates)
- Work Experience (part time, full time, volunteer)

Other sections often seen on résumés include "Career Objective," "Honors and Achievements," "Professional Affiliations," "Writing" or "Publications," "Computer Skills," "Language Skills," "Interests," "Travel," and "References." The order of this material will depend on what you wish to emphasize; however, education or experience should always come first. In each case, your goal is to select entries that demonstrate that your abilities and experience match the company's needs.

49c Writing the résumé

Like any writing assignment, a résumé will need to be drafted, revised, and edited. If possible, find the career development office on your campus, and see if someone there can critique your résumé. Remember, your résumé is often the only document a potential employer will evaluate, so it is important that it be written clearly and effectively.

49c
bus

Complete sentences are usually not used in a résumé. First of all, sentences that describe your experience do not begin with a subject because you are the implied subject. Instead, these sentences usually begin with action verbs—words that clearly express what you did in that position. Use the present tense if you are currently working at the job; use the simple past if you no longer have the position. Second, articles and pronouns are usually left out. (See 49d.)

An attractive and appropriate résumé is illustrated on page 562.

49d Letter of application (cover letter)

Your résumé summarizes your background; a letter of application addresses the specific job you seek, elaborates on your qualifications, and requests an interview. Like all writing, it allows your reader a glimpse of your personality and your writing abilities.

Before writing a cover letter, you should investigate the prospective organization, analyze the job description, and decide how your background matches the qualifications for the position. Remember, you want to tailor your letter to the company so that the people there know that you have gone beyond sending a standard form letter.

Your cover letter should be individually typed and should be no longer than one page. If possible, address the person who will review your application by name. If no name is available and you cannot obtain one through research, begin with a generic salutation, such as "Dear Personnel Director."

There are four basic issues (easily separated into paragraphs) to be discussed in a typical cover letter:

1. Begin with a reference to the job itself and how you learned of the position (for query letters, substitute a statement regarding the origin of your interest in the company or program).
2. Indicate why you are interested in working for this organization. This paragraph is your only chance to demonstrate that your letter is not a form letter. Use the information you learned from researching the organization.

49d
bus

Jeremy Mirskin
2603 Wasson Beltway Northeast
Madison, Wisconsin 53703
(608) 555-4943

CAREER OBJECTIVE

A career in a government or not-for-profit organization
advocating environmentally conscious policies.

EDUCATION

University of Wisconsin (Madison)
    Bachelor of Arts, Environmental Studies, expected May 1993

Relevant Coursework
 Advanced Ecology Studies, Environmental Pollution, Chemical
Analyses, Industrial Psychology, Government Relations, Issues
              in Modern Forestry, Oceanography

EXPERIENCE

Summer Internship
   Global Releaf, Washington, D.C., 1990

* Composed petitions regarding reforestation
* Raised funds through grassroots giving programs
* Directed local park planting projects

Summer Internship
   New York Public Interest Research Group, New York, 1989

* Assisted in establishing community plastic recycling
  programs
* Surveyed policy documents for court use
* Canvassed congressional districts on referendum issues

Group Leader (Assistant Teacher), After-School Program
    Beth Israel Synagogue, New Hyde Park, N.Y., 1983-1985

* Organized in-house community service seminars
* Taught regular classes in Hebrew language, grades 3-6
* Led workshops on materials reuse for faculty and staff

RELATED ACTIVITIES

Alternatives: The Madison Food Co-op
  * Member of the Board (1988-present)

Effington House (Sons without Fathers Program)
  * Student Member of Advisory Board (1990-Present)

REFERENCES   Available upon request

Sample résumé.

3. Give specific examples of experience, education, or interests in areas closely linked to the job, and make reference to the enclosed résumé by pointing out something interesting or important on it.
4. Request an interview, and thank the reviewer for his or her consideration of your application.

The letter of application on page 564 follows the above guidelines.

49e Memos

Once you've got a job, you'll begin to notice that business writing tasks are to a great extent specific to your company and the project at hand. The most common form of in-house writing, however, is the *memorandum,* or *memo.* Memos occasionally entertain and express a writer's emotion; most often, though, they are informative or persuasive. Usually they are written in response to a task, as a solution to a problem, in answer to a question, or in the cause of a program.

Often companies have established rules for style, but generally memos should be written in the block format, single-spaced, with no indented paragraphs and one line between paragraphs. Memos can include any or all of the following types of information:

- **Identifying information.** Indicate whom the memo is to, whom it is from, the date, and the subject.
- **Purpose statement.** Get right to the point of the memo. State it in clear, concise language.
- **Summary.** Give a brief summary of the point you are making.
- **Body.** Include any further detailed information that is needed for the reader; however, do not get into too many specifics—the purpose of most memos is to convey a purpose and call for action in a concise way.
- **Call for action.** Use the end of the memo to clarify your aim and the desired action.

The memo on page 565 follows the above guidelines.

49e
bus

FOR DISCUSSION

You might spend some time discussing this model letter with your students. First ask them to read the letter from the viewpoint of a prospective employer. Then ask them what they find most impressive about the application. How effective is the use of "you" in achieving a friendly tone? Are there any negatives? Given the information provided in the résumé in 49c, are there ways in which the content or emphasis of the letter might be changed for the better—or worse?

2603 Wasson Beltway Northeast
Madison, WI 53703
3 May 1993

Ms. Verna Van Keuren
Citizens for a Better Environment
623 South Wabash
Chicago, Illinois 60605

Dear Ms. Van Keuren:

In the May 1 issue of the Chicago Reader, you advertised an opening for an energetic activist to work in your public outreach program. My educational background in environmental studies, coupled with my field and office work for various not-for-profit public-interest groups, indicates my enthusiasm for environmental issues.

Citizens for a better Environment is just the type of organization I hope to work for after graduation. Your combination of commitment to the environment and willingness to seek compromises in order to make progress is the approach most likely to succeed in the nineties.

To follow up on my long-standing interest in the environment, I chose to enroll in the University of Wisconsin's Environmental Studies Program. Since my arrival, I have studied and written about garbage incineration, toxic disposal methods, and grassroots recycling efforts. I will be awarded my B.A. later this month--with departmental honors. While a summer intern for the New York Public Interest Research Group, I had the opportunity to work actively with local and national ecoeducation and recycling programs (see enclosed résumé). My experience included writing and circulating petitions and awareness literature, raising funds, and assisting at an on-site planning program.

I look forward to meeting with you to discuss further my qualifications and interest in becoming an activist for your organization. Thank you for your consideration.

Sincerely,

Jeremy Mirskin

Jeremy Mirskin

49e
bus

Sample application letter.

INTEROFFICE MEMORANDUM

TO: Mr. Joshua Rufus, Staff Assistant, Department of
English

FROM: Pamela Adam-Ross, Head of College Support Staff

DATE: 20 August 1993

SUBJECT: Rules for Deskside Office Paper Recycling Program

As you may recall, this semester marks the beginning of our
deskside office paper recycling program. Below you will find
the rules established for the program by Uptown Recycling
Services, our outside sponsor. Following these rules
precisely will ensure that we have a successful, ecologically
sound program here at the college.

WHAT CAN BE RECYCLED

Uptown's machines are set up to process only certain paper
items (of any color):

* Personal stationery
* Letterhead stationery
* Typing paper and tablet sheets
* Continuous-feed computer paper
* Index cards

Do not worry about staples or paper clips, as they pose no
problem during the sorting process; however, tape and rubber
bands of any sort should be removed.

WHAT CANNOT BE RECYCLED

Although our goal is eventually to recycle all paper
products, at present Uptown cannot process any of the
following:

* Glued or vellum (glossy) items, including Post-It
  notes, coated fax paper, and gummed labels
* Newspapers
* Photographic or blueprint paper
* Magazines
* Corrugated boxes

If you have any questions, call me at extension 2152.

Sample memo.

49e
bus

Glossary of Usage

a, an   The sound at the beginning of the next word determines which of these two to use. If the next word begins with a consonant sound, use *a;* if the next word begins with a vowel sound, use *an: a banana, an apple.* Notice *an hour* (the *h* in *hour* is silent, so the word starts with a vowel sound), *a one-hour delay* (*one* sounds like it begins with the consonant *w* rather than the vowel *o*), and *a uniform* (*uniform* sounds like it begins with the consonant *y* rather than the vowel *u*).

accept, except   *Accept* is a verb meaning "to receive" or "to agree to." *Except* is a preposition meaning "excluding": *Julia accepted my offer and returned everything except my deposit.*

ability   Takes the preposition *at* (doing something) or *with* (something).

abstain   Takes the preposition *from.*

accountable   Takes the preposition *to* (a person) or *for* (an act).

accuse   Takes the preposition *of.*

acquaint   Takes the preposition *with.*

adapt, adopt   *To adapt something* means "to modify it so it suits one's purposes": *The novel was adapted for television. To adapt to something* means "to adjust to it; to become comfortable with it": *April adapted to her new job within a few weeks. Adopt* means to make something your own, often as a parent: *Ms. Henry adopted a kitten.*

adjusted   Takes the preposition *to.*

adopt   See *adapt, adopt.*

advantage   Takes the preposition *of* or *over.*

adverse, averse   *Adverse* means "to be opposed or hostile to something or someone": *The Republicans are adverse to a tax increase. Averse* is a milder word meaning "to be reluctant or disinclined toward something, usually an activity": *Frederico is not averse to going swimming this afternoon.*

gl/us

advice, advise   *Advice* is the noun meaning suggestions for behavior or action: *Her advice has always been useful. Advise* is the verb meaning "to give advice": *She advised me not to write a paper about capital punishment.*

affect, effect   *Affect* is usually a verb meaning "to influence": *The new policy will not affect my job. Effect* is usually a noun meaning "the result of something": *The effect of the new policy on my job is that I have to work twice as hard.* Occasionally, most often in psychology, *affect* is used as a noun meaning "a person's feelings or emotions": *Her affect was quite subdued throughout the interview.* When used this way, *affect* is pronounced with the accent on the first syllable. *Effect* is occasionally used as a verb meaning "to bring about something": *The new manager hopes to effect some changes in our policies concerning returned purchases.*

African-American   The term now preferred by many Americans of African descent instead of "Black" or "Negro."

aggravate   A verb that means "to make worse." The use of *aggravate* to mean "to annoy or irritate" is colloquial and should be avoided in formal writing. Use *annoy* or *irritate* instead.

agree   Takes the preposition *with* (a person), *to* (a proposal or suggestion), or *on* (a course of action).

ain't   Despite the fact that you can find it in the dictionary, *ain't* is considered nonstandard and is heavily stigmatized. Use it in only the most informal and colloquial writing.

all ready, already   *All ready* means "completely prepared": *She is all ready for the trip. Already* means "by now" or "before now": *I have already seen that movie.*

all, all of   Before common nouns, *all* is generally preferred to *all of: All the students passed the test. All of* is generally preferred with pronouns and proper nouns. *All of them are angry.*

all right, alright   *All right* should always be written as two words. *Alright* is considered nonstandard.

all together, altogether   *All together* means "at one time" or "in one place": *My family was all together for the holidays for the first time in ten years. Altogether* means "entirely" or "in sum." *The party was not altogether a success.*

allude   A verb meaning "to make an indirect reference to something": *She alluded to a problem without spelling it out.* If someone makes a direct reference to something, he or she has not *alluded* to it; he or she has *referred* to it or *discussed* it.

allusion, illusion   *Allusion* means "an indirect reference to something": *Lynn made an allusion to her tendency to be late. Illusion* means "a misleading appearance": *She created an illusion of great opulence while living on a limited budget.*

a lot, alot *A lot* is always two words. It is used in informal writing to mean "many." *Alot* is not a word in formal English.

already See *all ready, already.*

alright See *all right, alright.*

altogether See *all together, altogether.*

among, between Use *among* to refer to three or more people or things: *The three students discussed their papers among themselves.* Use *between* to refer to two people or things: *Just between you and me, this coffee is too strong.*

amongst A form of *among* used in British English but generally considered overly fancy in American English.

amoral, immoral *Amoral* means "neither moral nor immoral" or "lacking a sense of morality": *I believe many people are amoral; they just don't think about questions of right or wrong.* *Immoral* means "morally wrong": *Georgia argued that child abuse is immoral as well as illegal.*

amount, number *Amount* is used with things that cannot be counted: *I spilled a small amount of sugar.* *Number* is used with things that can be counted: *I spilled a small number of marbles.*

amused Takes the preposition *at, by,* or *with.*

an See *a, an.*

and etc. Since *etc.* is the abbreviation for a Latin term meaning "and so forth," *and etc.* is redundant. Omit the *and.* See also *etc.*

and/or Generally, this construction is considered awkward and should be avoided. It is often misused when the writer intends either *and* or *or.* Use it only in technical or legal writing and only when you mean to imply three options: *The defendant and/or his counsel can raise an objection at this point.* Here three options are implied: the defendant, his counsel, or both.

angry Takes the preposition *with* or *at.*

ante-, anti- *Ante-* means "earlier" or "before." *An antebellum house was built before the Civil War.* *Anti-* means "against": *This magazine is not anti-intellectual.* When *anti-* is used before a proper noun or a word beginning with *i,* it is hyphenated.

anxious, eager *Anxious* means "nervous" or "worried," not "eager," and often takes the preposition *about: When my son is late getting home, I usually become anxious, even though he is twenty-two.* *Eager* means "looking forward to" and is usually followed by *to. Jake was eager to get started on the hike.*

anybody, any body *Anybody* is an indefinite pronoun meaning "any person": *Anybody can go to college these days.* *Any body* is an adjective and noun. Use the two-word version only when referring to an actual body: *The police did not find any body at the scene of the murder.*

anymore, any more   Use both these words in negative constructions. *Anymore* means "as of now": *Alice doesn't live here anymore. Any more* means "any additional": *Ina doesn't want any more wine.*

anyone, any one   *Anyone* is the indefinite pronoun meaning "any person": *Anyone can go to college these days.* Use *any one* only when you are using *one* to mean the number one: *I cannot part with any one of my baseball cards.*

anyplace, anywhere   *Anyplace* is informal. In formal writing use *anywhere.*

anyways, anywheres   Not acceptable words in formal English. Use *any way* or *anywhere.*

apart   Takes the preposition *from.*

approve   Takes the preposition *of.*

aroma   "A pleasant smell." If the smell is not pleasant, use *odor, smell,* or, in extreme cases, *stench.*

arrive   Takes the preposition *at* or *in.*

as   Means "because" or "when." Do not use *as* if the meaning is ambiguous. For example, the sentence *We left the restaurant as my former husband was arriving* could mean we left *when* he was arriving or *because* he was arriving. Use either *when* or *because* to make the meaning clear.

as, like   *As* is a subordinate conjunction and is used to introduce dependent clauses: *Sadek sings as if she had been doing it for years.* Note that *as if* is sometimes used instead of just *as. Like* is a preposition and should not be used to introduce clauses: *My son looks like a dancer* but not *My son looks like he was up all night.* Use *as if* instead: *My son looks as if he was up all night.*

as far as   This expression is a subordinate conjunction; therefore, a complete clause must follow it. Not *As far as reading poetry, I am just learning,* but *As far as reading poetry is concerned, I am just learning.*

assent   Takes the preposition *to.*

associate   Takes the preposition *with.*

assure, ensure, insure   *Assure* means "to promise," and it almost always is followed by a noun or pronoun representing a person: *The officer assured me I would not receive a ticket. Ensure* and *insure* both mean "to make certain," and they usually are followed by a thing or a subordinate clause beginning with *that: Ricardo wanted to ensure* (or *insure*) *that he passed the test.* Use *insure* when your meaning is "to protect against financial risk."

as to   Do not use as a substitute for *about: I questioned my sister about* (not *as to*) *her relationship with Max.*

astonished   Takes the preposition *at* when indicating disapproval; *by* when indicating approval.

gl/us

at   avoid the use of *at* in sentences with a *where: I don't know where she is living at.*

at this point in time   A wordy way to say *now* or *at this time* or *at this point*. Use one of these less wordy expressions.

averse   See *adverse, averse.*

awful, awfully   Strictly speaking, *awful* means "full of awe," but it has come to mean "bad" or even "terrible" in informal speech. *Awfully* has come to mean "very." Avoid both of these uses in formal writing: *Even though I had a terrible* (not *awful*) *time at the party, it was very* (not *awfully*) *late when I left.*

awhile, a while   *Awhile* is an adverb and so should be used to modify a verb: *My father stayed awhile. A while* is an article and noun and is usually used as the object of a preposition—usually the preposition *for: My father stayed for a while.*

bad, badly   *Bad* is an adjective and therefore modifies nouns and pronouns: *I feel bad about your accident.* Here *bad* follows a linking verb and modifies the pronoun *I. Badly* is an adverb and so modifies verbs, adjectives, and other adverbs: *I sing badly.* Here *badly* follows an action verb, *sing*, and modifies that verb.

based   Takes the preposition *on, upon,* or *in.*

being as, being that   These are both inappropriate in formal writing. Use *because.*

beside, besides   *Beside* is a preposition meaning "next to": *I parked my car beside the bank. Besides* is a preposition meaning "except" or "in addition to": *Who is coming to the party besides you and Susan?*

between   See *among, between.*

between you and I   The correct expression is *between you and me.* See 24c.

biannual   Twice a year.

biennial   Every two years.

bimonthly   Every two months.

biweekly   Either every two weeks or twice a week.

blend   Takes the preposition *with* or *in.*

bored   Takes the preposition *by* or *with* (but not *of*).

break   Takes the preposition *with* or *from.*

bring, take   *Bring* is used for movement toward the speaker: *Bring me a glass of water. Take* is used for all other movement: *Take this glass of water to your brother.*

bunch   A noun meaning "a group or cluster of things that grow or are fastened together such as bananas or grapes." In formal usage it is incorrect to use *bunch* to refer to other things or to people. Use *group* or *crowd* instead.

gl/us

burst, bursted, bust, busted   *Burst* is a verb meaning "to come open or fly apart suddenly and violently." The past tense of *burst* is *burst;* the form *bursted* is, therefore, incorrect in formal written English. *Bust* and *busted* are colloquial versions of *burst* and also should not be used in formal writing.

but yet   Do not use this wordy and redundant expression. Use just *but* or *yet.*

can, may   Although the distinction is fading, careful writers still distinguish between these two words. *Can* refers to one's ability to do something: *Lynn can ice skate. May* refers to having permission to do something: *Taxpayers may file anytime after the first of January.* See 19c.

cannot, can not   Generally *cannot* is the one you want, except in the rare case when you want to emphasize the *not: I can tolerate ignorance, but I can not tolerate prejudice.*

can't hardly, can't scarcely   *Hardly* and *scarcely* are negatives, so these expressions are redundant double negatives. Omit the *not (n't): I can hardly wait until the end of the semester.*

can't help but   A wordy and redundant expression. Use *I can't help worrying* or the more formal *I can't but worry.*

capable   Takes the preposition *of.*

capital, capitol   *Capital* is the word for a city where a government is located: *The capital of Kentucky is Frankfort. Capital* can also mean a sum of money. *Capitol* is the word for the building where a legislature meets: *The statue on top of the capitol was removed for cleaning in 1993.*

caution   Takes the preposition *against.*

censor, censure   *To censor* means to "edit or suppress material considered objectionable": *Henry Miller's novels were censored in the fifties. To censure* means "to criticize severely and, in many cases, officially": *The legislature censured one of its members.*

center around, center on   *Center around* is illogical; use *center on.*

cite, site, sight   *To cite* is "to quote as an authority" or "to issue a summons (or citation) to appear in court": *He cited Ernest Hemingway in his research paper. Site* means "a location": *This park was the site of a major civil rights demonstration. Sight* is the capability of seeing.

climactic, climatic   *Climactic* refers to *climax* which means "the dramatic high point in a sequence of events." *Climatic* is derived from *climate* and refers to weather.

coincide   Takes the preposition *with.*

commiserate   Takes the preposition *with.*

compare to, compare with   *Compare to* means to point out how one thing or person is similar to another: *Hazel compared the experience to*

being in a hurricane. Compare with is the more general expression meaning "to examine the similarities and differences between two things or people": *This paper will compare the poetry of Robert Frost with that of Sylvia Plath.*

compatible Takes the preposition *with.*

compendium A brief summary or outline; also a collection (not a large work containing everything but the kitchen sink, as many people believe).

complacent Takes the preposition *toward.*

complement, compliment *Complement* means "to make complete, whole, or perfect": *Li's yellow dress complemented her black hair. Compliment* means "to praise or flatter": *Melia complimented Albert on his new baseball hat.*

comprise, compose While the distinction between these words is eroding, careful writers still use *comprise* to mean "contain": *The United States comprises fifty states.* They use *compose* to mean "constitute" or "make up": *Fifty states compose the United States.*

conducive Takes the preposition *to.*

confide Takes the preposition *in.*

confident Takes the preposition *of.*

conscience, conscious *Conscience* is a noun meaning "the sense of right and wrong": *Katy should have a guilty conscience. Conscious* is an adjective that means "awake" or "aware": *Fernando was not conscious of the effect his decision would have on the rest of us.*

consensus of opinion *Consensus* means "general agreement of opinion": *Consensus of opinion* is therefore redundant. Use just *consensus.*

consent Takes the preposition *to.*

consequently "As a result" or "therefore." If you mean one thing caused another, use *consequently.* If you mean simply that one thing happened after another, use *subsequently.*

consistent Takes the preposition *with.*

contact In casual speech, *contact* can be used to mean "get in touch with." In formal writing, use a more precise verb like *telephone* or *write.*

continual, continuous *Continual* means "recurring regularly or repeatedly": *The continual sound of sirens reminded Ina of living in New York. Continuous* means "occurring over and over without interruption": *I have had a headache continuously for four hours.*

convict Takes the preposition *of.*

convince, persuade While the distinction is disappearing, careful writers use *convince* to mean "to use reason to cause someone to change his or her opinion." In order to honor this distinction, one should not use an infinitive after *convince: Horst convinced Ida that the world should adopt a single currency.* Use *persuade* to mean "to move

gl/us

someone to an action": *Persuade* can take an infinitive: *We persuaded the coach to cancel practice.*

correspond   Takes the preposition *with* or *to.*

could care less   An illogical expression that literally means the speaker does care some. If you mean to say that you care very little, use *couldn't care less.*

could of   Do not substitute *of* for *have* in the expression *could have.*

criteria, criterion   *Criteria* is plural; *criterion,* singular.

cured   Takes the preposition *of.*

data   *Data* has, in the past, been used as a plural word only. However, all but the most traditional have now come to accept *data* as both singular and plural.

defend   Takes the preposition *from* or *against.*

deficient   Takes the preposition *in.*

deprive   Takes the preposition *of.*

desert, dessert   *Desert* is a barren or desolate area, often arid and sandy. *Dessert* is a sweet eaten as the last course of a meal.

desirous   Takes the preposition *of.*

detract   Takes the preposition *from.*

deviate   Takes the preposition *from.*

different from, different than   Generally the preference is for *different from,* although many writers also find *different than* acceptable. If a clause follows the phrase, then *different than* is usually preferable to avoid awkwardness or wordiness. *Children are different than they used to be* is preferable to *Children are different from what they used to be.*

differ from, differ with   *Differ from* means "to be unlike": *My answer differs from yours by exactly 100 pounds. Differ with* means "to disagree": *I often differ with my history professor.*

disapprove   Takes the preposition *of.*

discourage   Takes the preposition *from.*

discreet, discrete   *Discreet* means "tactful," "prudent," or modest": *I discreetly told my boss that he had misspelled two words in his memo. Discrete* means "separate and distinct": *There are three discrete problems in the way we conduct this business.*

disinterested, uninterested   *Disinterested* means "impartial" or "unconcerned": *The police officer served as a disinterested witness. Uninterested* means "bored" or "lacking interest": *Ms. Ingres was uninterested in my excuse for missing the final exam.*

disqualify   Takes the preposition *from* or *for.*

dissatisfied   Takes the preposition *with.*

distrustful   Takes the preposition *of.*

divorce   Takes the preposition *from.*

due to   An adjective that should not be used in place of the preposition *because of. Because of* (not *due to*) *the hurricane, we canceled our trip to Cape Hatteras. Due to* is correct as a predicate adjective following a form of the verb *be: Her absence was due to a death in her family.*

due to the fact that   A wordy expression. Use *because.*

each   *Each* is always singular.

eager   See *anxious, eager.*

effect   See *affect, effect.*

e.g.   The trend is to use *for example* or *for instance* instead of this Latin abbreviation.

egoism, egotism   *Egoism* means "an excessive tendency to think of things as they affect oneself." *Egotism* is "an excessive tendency to talk about oneself": *Egotism* is the more common word today.

elicit, illicit   *Elicit* means "bring out" or "call forth": *His comment elicited boos from the audience. Illicit* means "illegal": *He made his money in illicit ways.*

emerge   Takes the preposition *from.*

emigrate, immigrate   *Emigrate* means "to leave one's original country." *Farouk emigrated from Egypt when he was six. Immigrate* means "to settle in a new country": *My family immigrated to the United States in 1955.*

eminent, imminent   *Eminent* means "prominent" or "outstanding": *Professor Rimini is an eminent classics scholar. Imminent* means "about to happen": *I worried that a change in the interest rates was imminent.*

endowed   Takes the preposition *with.*

end result   A redundant phrase. Use just *result.*

engaged   Takes the preposition *in* or *upon.*

ensure   See *assure, ensure, insure.*

enthralled   Takes the preposition *by.*

enthused   Informal. Use *enthusiastic* in formal writing.

envious   Takes the preposition *of.*

equal   Takes the preposition *to.*

especially, specially   *Especially* means "exceedingly" or "particularly": *My mother was especially pleased to hear from Tim. Specially* means "for a particular occasion" or "with unusual care": *Maya Angelou's poem was specially written for the inauguration.*

-ess   This suffix is widely considered demeaning when used to indicate a woman doing a job thought of as more appropriate for men. Avoid such constructions as *poetess* and *authoress.*

essential   Takes the preposition *to.*

estranged   Takes the preposition *from.*

gl/us

etc.   Many writers feel that ending a list with *etc.* or the spelled out version *et cetera* lacks emphasis. Include enough items in the list to make your point.

everyday, every day   *Everyday* is an adjective meaning "common" or "ordinary": *Finding a twenty-dollar bill is not an everyday occurrence. Every day* means "happening on each day": *I read the newspaper every day.*

everyone, every one   *Everyone* is an indefinite pronoun: *Everyone should bring a dish to the party tonight. Every one* means "each individual item in a group": *Every one of my dishes was broken when I unpacked.*

exam   Informal for *examination.* Avoid in formal writing.

except   See *accept, except.*

exclude   Takes the preposition *from.*

exclusive   Takes the preposition *of.*

expect   Takes the preposition *to* or *from.*

expel   Takes the preposition *from.*

experienced   Takes the preposition *in* or *at.*

explicit, implicit   *Explicit* means "openly stated" or "physically present": *I don't allow my children to see movies with explicit sex. Implicit* means "implied" or "present but not openly stated": *When my father didn't reply, I assumed that gave me implicit permission to use the car.*

farther, further   *Farther* is used for physical distances: *Denise jumped eight inches farther than I did. Further* is used for an abstract degree, amount, or time: *I don't expect further trouble from her.*

fatal, fateful   *Fatal* means "leading to death": *She drank a fatal dose of strychnine. Fateful* means "that which leads to major consequences— good or bad": *In 1980, Bill Clinton made the fateful decision that led to his presidency.*

feed   Takes the preposition *on* or *off.*

fewer, less   *Fewer* is used with countable items represented by a plural noun: *Ten dollars buys fewer groceries than it did when I was first married. Less* is used with noncountable items represented by a singular noun: *Ten dollars buys less gasoline than it did when I was first married.*

figuratively, literally   To speak or write figuratively is to use figures of speech that are not literally true: *When I said Mark was a sheep during our argument with the boss, I was speaking figuratively. Literally* means that your words are to be taken at their face value: *I literally fell asleep in the middle of class.*

finalize   Generally considered bureaucratic jargon. Use *end, complete, conclude,* or *make final.*

gl/us

firstly   Thought by many to sound pretentious and to force one to use the even more pretentious *fourthly* and *fifthly*. Because so many object to these terms, it is safer to use *first, second,* and so forth.

flaunt, flout   *To flaunt* is "to show something off": *Mr. Partridge flaunted his knowledge. To flout* is "to show contempt for": *Hank flouted the speed limit whenever he drove on the Interstate.*

flunk   Informal. In formal writing, use *fail.*

folks   An informal expression for *parents.* In formal writing, use *parents.*

fond   Takes the preposition *of.*

fondness   Takes the preposition *for.*

freedom   Takes the preposition *from* or *of.*

friend   Takes the preposition *of* or *to.*

friendly   Takes the preposition *to* or *toward.*

fugitive   Takes the preposition *from.*

full   Takes the preposition *of.*

fun   When used as an adjective, *fun* is informal. In formal writing, use *enjoyable* or *pleasurable.*

further   See *farther, further.*

good, well   *Good* is an adjective and should be used to modify only nouns and pronouns: *Gertrude is a good singer. Well* is the adverb: *Gertrude sings well.*

good and   *Good and* is informal for *very.* In formal writing, use *very.*

half   *A half a* is redundant. Use either *half a* or *a half.*

hanged, hung   *Hanged* and *hung* are both past participles of the verb *hang. Hanged* is used for executions: *The rustler was hanged at dawn. Hung* is for all other uses: *Mikhail hung the clothes on the line.*

hardly   See *can't hardly.*

have, of   Do not substitute *of* for *have* in expressions such as *should have, would have,* and *could have.*

he, he or she   Historically, *he* was used to represent both men and women. In recent years, most writers have avoided this masculine bias. When possible, recast the sentence in plural form. Otherwise, use *he or she.* See 23b.

he/she, his/her   These expressions, attempts to avoid a masculine bias, are generally viewed as awkward. When possible, recast the sentence in plural form. Otherwise, use *he or she.* See 23b.

help but   See *can't help but.*

hint   Takes the preposition *at* or *of.*

hisself   Nonstandard. Use *himself.*

hopefully   *Hopefully* means "full of hope" or "with hope": *Hopefully, Houng mailed his application for the job.* Do not, however, use *hopefully*

to mean "I hope" or "it is hoped": *I hope* (not *hopefully*) *that it will not rain on Saturday.*

how come   Informal. In formal writing, use *why.*

hung   See *hanged, hung.*

idea, ideal   An *idea* is a "thought" or a "concept": *Mr. Hernandez's idea seemed to be the most promising. Ideal* means "a model of perfection" or "a goal": *My ideal of a husband is nothing like Larry.*

identical   Takes the preposition *to* or *with.*

identify   Takes the preposition *with.*

if, whether   *If* is used to introduce clauses that are hypothetical: *If I were a poet, I would write poetry about nature. Whether* is used to introduce clauses that represent alternatives: *Whether you bring Elvira or come alone. . . .*

illicit   See *elicit, illicit.*

illusion   See *allusion, illusion.*

immigrate   See *emigrate, immigrate.* Takes the preposition *to* or *into.*

imminent   See *eminent, imminent.*

immoral   See *amoral, immoral.*

impact   *Impact* is both a noun and a verb referring to a "forceful and even violent collision": *The impact of the collision caused my daughter's head to crack the windshield.* Its use to mean "have an effect on" is faddish and imprecise and should be avoided; use *affect* instead: *The cuts in military spending will affect* (not *impact*) *our profits for the next five years.*

implicit   See *explicit, implicit.* Takes the preposition *in.*

imply, infer   *Imply* means "to suggest indirectly." Speakers and writers imply: *The president implied that it would be un-American to oppose his plan. Infer* means "to draw a conclusion." Listeners and readers infer: *I inferred from Lamont's comments that he would not be interested in dating my sister.*

impose   Takes the preposition *on* or *upon.*

impressed   Takes the preposition *by* or *with.*

improve   Takes the preposition *on* or *upon.*

in, into   *In* indicates that "something is located in the interior of something else": *The telephone is in the kitchen. Into* indicates "movement to the inside of something": *I got into the car and drove to Mollie's house.*

inconsistent   Takes the preposition *with.*

independent   Takes the preposition *of.*

individual, person   Refer to a person as an individual only when you are stressing that person's uniqueness in contrast to the group: *I hope to sell my business to an individual rather than to a corporation.* In all other cases, use person: *I hope that at least one person* (not *individual*) *will come forward as a witness.*

gl/us

indulge   Takes the preposition *in* or *with*.

indulgent   Takes the preposition *to* or *of*.

inferior   Takes the preposition *to*.

infested   Takes the preposition *with*.

ingenious, ingenuous   *Ingenious* means "extremely clever": *Her solution to the puzzle was ingenious. Ingenuous* means "naive and lacking in sophistication" or "frank and honest": *I don't think Maxwell was trying to deceive us; he is too ingenuous for that.*

in order to   Usually wordy. Use just *to*.

in regards to   A confusion of two idioms: *in regard to* and *as regards.* Use one of these and avoid the confusion. *About* is often a more effective substitute.

inside, inside of, outside, outside of   In most cases, the *of* is superfluous and should be omitted: *Rudy placed the bottle inside* (not *inside of*) *the box.*

insight   Takes the preposition *into*.

inspire   Takes the preposition *by* or *with*.

insure   See *assure, ensure, insure.*

interface with   Generally considered jargon. Use a more specific verb such as *talk with, meet with,* or *discuss with.*

intervene   Takes the preposition *in* (for disputes) or *between* (disputants).

in the near future   Wordy. Use *soon* instead.

in the vicinity of   Wordy. Use *near* instead.

introduce   Takes the preposition *to* or *into*.

invest   Takes the preposition *in* or *with*.

involve   Takes the preposition *in*.

irregardless   Not a word in standard English. Use *regardless.*

is when, is where   These expressions lead to faulty predication (see 15b) when used in definitions. Avoid them. Use *in which* instead.

its, it's   *Its* is a possessive pronoun: *My dog has spilled its water. It's* is a contraction meaning "it is": *It's too hot for tennis.*

kind of, sort of   Do not use these informal expressions in formal writing. Use *rather* or *somewhat* instead.

kind of, sort of, type of   These words are singular and should be preceded by the singular pronoun *this*, not the plural *these,* and followed by a singular noun: *This kind of mustard is very hot.* When used in their plural forms they should be modified by the plural pronoun *these* and followed by a plural noun: *These types of bicycles are hard to ride.*

laugh   Takes the preposition *at* or *over*.

lay, lie   The hardest pair in the entire list. *Lie* means "to recline or rest horizontally": *I like to lie down after lunch for a half hour. Lay* means

"to put or place something in a horizontal position": *I always lay my wallet on my dresser at night.* The past tense of *lie* is especially tricky because it is identical with the present tense of *lay: I lay down after dinner last night and fell asleep.* The past tense of *lay* is *laid: I laid my wallet on the dresser before I went to bed last night.* See 25d.

lean   Takes the preposition *on, upon,* or *against.*

leave, let   *Leave* means "to exit or depart." Do not use it in the informal sense of "permit." Use *let* to mean "permit": *Will you let* (not *leave*) *me ride your bicycle?*

less   See *fewer, less.*

liable   Means "obligated" or "responsible": *I am liable for any damages that my daughter causes.* Do not use it to mean "likely" except in informal writing: *I am likely* (not *liable*) *to forget my passport.*

libel, slander   Both refer to saying something harmful and untrue about another person. The difference is that when you slander someone, you do it orally. When you libel someone, you do it in some other medium, usually print.

like, as   See *as, like.*

literally   See *figuratively, literally.*

loan, lend   Some people object to using *loan* as a verb. To be safe, use *lend* as a verb: *My father will lend me the money for a down payment on a house.* Use *loan* as a noun: *The loan will be for five thousand dollars.*

loose, lose   *Loose* is an adjective meaning "not securely fastened" or "unfastened": *My rowboat had come loose during the night. Lose* is a verb meaning "to misplace" or "not to win": *I would hate to lose this game after being ahead by five runs.*

lots, lots of   Informal expressions. In formal writing, use *many* or *much.*

made   Takes the preposition *of, out of,* or *from.*

man, mankind   These traditional expressions are now out of favor because they use a masculine word to refer to the entire human race. To avoid this problem, use *humankind, the human race,* or *people.*

marred   Takes the preposition *by.*

may   See *can, may.*

maybe, may be   *Maybe* means "perhaps" or "possibly": *Maybe school will be canceled tomorrow. May be* is the verb *be* with the helping verb *may: I may be late for school tomorrow.* See 19c.

may of, might of, must of   Not idioms in formal English. Use *may have, might have,* and *must have.*

meddle   Takes the preposition *with* or *in.*

media, medium   *Media* is the plural of *medium.* The word you almost always want, when talking about radio and television is *media,* but

make sure you recognize that it is plural: *The media are* (not *is*) *waiting for confirmation from the White House.*

mediate   Takes the preposition *between* or *among.*

meditate   Takes the preposition *on* or *upon.*

mistrustful   Takes the preposition *of.*

moral, morale   *Moral* means "ethical" as an adjective and "an ethical conclusion or lesson" as a noun: *The moral of this story is not clear. Morale* refers to the "spirit" or "state of being" of a person or group: *Despite the loss, the debating team's morale was quite high.*

most, almost   Do not use *most* as a synonym for *almost* in formal writing.

motive   Takes the preposition *for.*

Ms.   A title created in the 1960s to be the equivalent for women of *Mr.* for men. Previously *Mrs.* and *Miss* were used for women and indicated their marital status. Some women still prefer the old-fashioned titles, but most today prefer *Ms.*

must of   See *may of, might of, must of.*

myself   *Myself* is a reflexive pronoun: *I gave myself a little pep talk.* It is also an intensifier: *I wallpapered this living room myself.* Do not use *myself* as a substitute for the objective pronoun *me: Helene thanked Jose and me* (not *myself*) *for our assistance.*

nauseous, nauseated   *Nauseous* means "tending to make one sick to one's stomach": *The seafood at Nick's has been nauseous in the past. Nauseated* means "to become sick to one's stomach": *I became nauseated the last time I ate there.*

necessary   Takes the preposition *for* or *to.*

necessity   Takes the preposition *of* or *for.*

neglectful   Takes the preposition *of.*

negligent   Takes the preposition *of* or *in.*

neither   Always singular. See 21i and 23d.

nowheres   Nonstandard for *nowhere.*

number   See *amount, number.*

obedient   Takes the preposition *to.*

observant   Takes the preposition *of.*

occasion   Takes the preposition *for* or *of.*

occupied   Takes the preposition *by* or *with.*

of, have   Do not substitute *of* for *have* in expressions such as *should have, would have,* and *could have.*

off of   The *of* is redundant. Use just *off.*

OK, O.K., okay   All three spellings are okay, but the term is considered informal. Use a more specific word in formal writing.

on, upon   In most cases, the simple *on* is preferable. *Upon* sounds a little stuffy and old fashioned.

gl/us

opportunity   Takes the preposition *for* or *of*.

opposition   Takes the preposition *to*.

oral, verbal   See *verbal, oral*.

originate   Takes the preposition *with* or *in*.

overwhelm   Takes the preposition *by* or *with*.

outside, outside of   See *inside, inside of, outside, outside of*.

parallel   Takes the preposition *to* or *with*.

partial   Takes the preposition *to*.

partiality   Takes the preposition *to, toward,* or *for*.

participate   Takes the preposition *in*.

passed, past   *Passed* is the past tense of the verb *pass,* meaning "to go beyond or ahead of": *I passed Professor Starr on the Interstate. Past* is a noun or adjective that means "a time before the present": *In the past, this coffee was much less expensive.*

percent, per cent, percentage   *Percent* (also spelled *per cent*) means "out of a hundred." It should be preceded by a specific number and should be written out (not expressed by the symbol %): *The principal estimates that 30 percent of students at this school do not graduate. Percentage* means "a fraction of one hundred." It should be preceded by a word indicating size such as *small* or *large: A small percentage of traffic accidents are caused by bees distracting the driver.*

persevere   Takes the preposition *in*.

persuade   See *convince, persuade*.

phenomena   The plural form of *phenomenon: Three phenomena convinced us that something extraordinary was taking place.*

phenomenon   Means either "any occurrence observable by the senses" or "an unusual occurrence": *Marcia observed a strange phenomenon last night.*

pleased   Takes the preposition *at, by,* or *with*.

plenty   Don't use *plenty* as a substitute for *very,* except in the most informal situations: *It was very* (not *plenty*) *hot this afternoon.*

plus   Should never be used to join independent clauses: *The price of a ticket was too high, and* (not *plus*) *there were only scattered single seats remaining, so we didn't go to the concert.*

possessed   Takes the preposition *by, with,* or *of*.

possibility   Takes the preposition *of*.

precede, proceed   *Precede* means "to occur before": *An awards ceremony will precede tonight's baseball game. Proceed* means "to go forward": *The police car proceeded down the highway.* Note that it is redundant to say *proceeded to drive* or *proceeded to walk.* Say just *drove* or *walked* instead.

precluded   Takes the preposition *from*.

prejudice, prejudiced   *Prejudice* is the noun: *Reducing prejudice should be one goal of a liberal education. Prejudiced* is the adjective. When using the word as an adjective, don't omit the final -*d: That is a very prejudiced* (not *prejudice*) *news report.*

preoccupied   Takes the preposition *with* or *by.*

preside   Takes the preposition *over* or *at.*

pretty   Use *pretty* as an adverb meaning *somewhat* only in very informal situations.

principal, principle   *Principal* is a noun meaning "the head of a school" or "a sum of money." As an adjective, it means "chief" or "most important": *The principal decided to expel Janet for one principal reason. Principle* means "a basic truth or law": *The idea that opposites attract is a basic principle of human relationships.*

proceed   See *precede, proceed.*

proficient   Takes the preposition *at* or *in.*

profit   Takes the preposition *by* or *from.*

prohibit   Takes the preposition *from.*

protest   Takes the preposition *against.*

qualify   Takes the preposition *for* or *as.*

quotation, quote   *Quotation* is a noun; *quote*, a verb. Use *quote* as a shortened version of *quotation* only in informal writing.

raise, rise   *Raise* is a transitive verb; it must have an object: *I raise the flag every morning. Rise* is an intransitive verb; it cannot take an object: *The fog rises off the lake by nine o'clock every morning.*

real, really   *Real* is an adjective; it can modify only nouns and pronouns: *I had my picture taken next to a real Swiss guard. Really* is an adverb; use it to modify verbs, adjectives, and other adverbs: *It was really hot this afternoon.*

reason   Takes the preposition *for.*

reason is because   The idiom is *reason is that: The reason I am late is that* (not *because*) *my car broke down.*

reason why   A redundant expression. Omit *why: The reason* (not *the reason why*) *I got an A on the midterm is that I studied all last weekend.*

relate to   An informal expression best avoided in formal writing.

rejoice   Takes the preposition *at* or *in.*

resemblance   Takes the preposition *to, between,* or *among.*

resentment   Takes the preposition *against, at,* or *for.*

respectfully, respectively   *Respectfully* means "with respect": *I respectfully suggest that we need to stockpile additional medical supplies. Respectively* means "in the order given": *Kevin, Lee, and Romeo were respectively a tenor, a baritone, and a bass.*

responsibility   Takes the preposition *for.*

gl/us

restrain   Takes the preposition *from*.

rise   See *raise, rise*.

round   No apostrophe. *Round* is a word by itself, not a contraction of *around*.

saturate   Takes the preposition *with*.

scarcely   See *can't hardly, can't scarcely*.

scared   Takes the preposition *at* or *by*.

sensitive   Takes the preposition *to*.

sensual, sensuous   *Sensual* means "affecting the sense organs, especially those associated with sexual pleasures": *The dance she performed was very sensual*. *Sensuous* means "pleasing to the senses, especially through art, music, or nature": *Listening to Tchaikovsky's music is always a sensuous experience*.

set, sit   *Set* is a transitive verb meaning "to place": *I set my coffee on the dining room table*. *Sit* is an intransitive verb meaning "to take a seat" or "to be seated": *Hermione sat on my couch for more than an hour without saying a word*.

shall, will   *Shall* used to be the required helping verb for future tense when the subject was *I* or *we*. Today, however, *will* is the preferred helping verb even with *I* and *we*. *Shall* is used only in polite questions and certain legal phrases: *Shall we go into the dining room?* See 19c.

should of   Do not substitute *of* for *have* in the expression *should have*.

since   *Since* can mean either "from a certain time" or "because." Don't use it to mean "because" if the meaning is ambiguous: *Because* (not *since*) *I got a new job, I have been celebrating*.

sit   See *set, sit*.

site   See *cite, site*.

so   Except in informal writing, *so* should not be used to mean *very: I was very* (not *so*) *angry*. Do use *so* as an intensifier if a *that* clause follows: *I was so angry that I couldn't speak*.

solution   Takes the preposition *of* or *to*.

somebody, someone   These two indefinite pronouns are singular.

sometime, some time, sometimes   *Sometime* is an adverb meaning "at an unspecified time": *We should get together for lunch sometime*. *Some time* means "a period of time—more than an instant": *I need some time to think your offer over*. *Sometimes* is an adverb meaning "now and again, at various times": *Sometimes I go to bed at eight o'clock*.

sort of   See *kind of, sort of, type of*.

sought   Takes the preposition *after* or *for*.

specially   See *especially, specially*.

stationary, stationery   *Stationary* means "standing still": *I get my exercise on a stationary bike. Stationery* means "writing paper": *I received a box of stationery for my birthday.*

strive   Takes the preposition *for, with,* or *against.*

subsequently   Indicates that one thing happened after another. If you mean one thing caused another, use *consequently.*

suitable   Takes the preposition *to, for,* or *with.*

superior   Takes the preposition *to.*

supposed to   Be careful to retain the *-d* on the end of *supposed* in this construction. It's hard to pronounce, but it must be there.

sure and   Nonstandard. In formal writing, use *sure to.*

surprised   Takes the preposition *by* or *at.*

take   See *bring, take.*

tendency   Takes the preposition *to* or *toward.*

than   See *then, than.*

that   See *who, which, that.*

theirselves   Not a word in standard English. Use *themselves.*

then, than   *Than* is a conjunction used to make comparisons: *Ibrahim is taller than Jake. Then* is an adverb that indicates time: *Kirsten opened the door; then she noticed the cat at her feet.* It may help if you notice that *than* has an *a* and so does *compare; then* has an *e* and so does *time.*

there, their, they're   *There* is either an adverb indicating place or an expletive (see 20b): *Your book is over there. Their* is a possessive pronoun: *My parents have sold their house. They're* is the contraction of *they are: They're building another shopping center in my neighborhood.*

therefore, thereby   *Therefore* is a conjunctive adverb meaning "consequently" or "for that reason": *I slept through class today; therefore, I need to borrow your notes. Thereby* has a similar meaning—"because of that" or "by that means"—but it is an adverb, not a conjunctive adverb, so it cannot be used to introduce an independent clause: *Emily dropped her flute, thereby waking up the man in the front row.*

thru   An informal spelling. In formal writing, use *through.*

till, 'til, 'till, until   *Till* and *until* have the same meaning and are both correct, although *until* is slightly more common when it is starting a sentence. *'Til* and *'till* are both now obsolete.

time period   Redundant. Use just *time.*

tired   Takes the preposition *of, from,* or *with.*

to, too, two   *To* is either a preposition indicating direction or the first word in an infinitive: *I walked to school to save money. Too* is an adverb meaning either "also" or "more than enough": *George is too tired to go out to dinner. Are you tired too?* Two is a number: *Two women are cutting my grass.*

tolerance   Takes the preposition *for, of,* or *toward.*

gl/us

tormented Takes the preposition *by* or *with.*

toward, towards These words mean the same thing, and both are acceptable. *Toward* is more common in American English; *towards* in British English. Whichever you use, be consistent.

trust Takes the preposition *to* or *in.*

try and Not an idiom in formal English. Use *try to.*

two See *to, too, two.*

type of See *kind of, sort of, type of.*

unique Means "the one and only." Therefore, such expressions as *more unique* or *most unique* are illogical and should be avoided.

uninterested See *disinterested, uninterested.*

use, usage *Use* is usually the word you want: *We should avoid the use of dangerous chemicals.* Use *usage* only to refer to conventions for the use of something, especially a language: Ain't *still violates the rules of usage in formal English.*

use, utilize Do not use *utilize* as a substitute for *use.* In most cases, *use* is the preferable word: *May I use your calculator? Utilize* has the special meaning of "to find a profitable or practical purpose for": *My grandmother was able to utilize every part of the slaughtered cow.*

used to Be careful to retain the *-d* at the end of *used* in this construction. It's hard to pronounce, but it must be there.

useful Takes the preposition *to, in,* or *for.*

verbal, oral *Oral* clearly refers only to spoken language (as opposed to written). *Verbal,* formally, means communication in words (as opposed to communication through signs, symbols, body language, or music, for instance). However, many good writers have used *verbal* to mean only spoken communication. Since this confusion concerning the meaning of *verbal* exists, we recommend you use *oral* to represent spoken language.

vary Takes the preposition *from.*

versus, v., vs. The abbreviation *v.* for *versus* is appropriate only in legal documents. In most formal writing, spell the word out. When it is necessary to abbreviate it in a nonlegal document, use *vs.*

very Avoid overuse of this adverb. Often it is unnecessary. At other times, the combination of *very* and a weak adjective can be replaced by a single stronger adjective. For example, *very cold* might be replaced by *frigid.*

vulnerable Takes the preposition *to.*

wait for, wait on *Wait for* means "await": *I am waiting for George. Wait on* means "to serve": *The woman who waited on us is in one of my classes.*

way, ways When referring to distances, use *way* not *ways*: *We had to walk a long way* (not *ways*).

wear, we're, where   *Wear* means "to have on one's body": *Ms. Yamaguchi always wears a hat. We're* is the contraction for *we are: We're not going to the movies tonight. Where* is an interrogative pronoun: *Where are my car keys?*

well   See *good, well.*

whether   See *if, whether.*

which   See *who, which, that.*

while   Can mean either "at the same time as" or "although." Don't use it to mean *although* if ambiguity results, as in the following sentence: *Although* (not *while*) *Margie made the salad and dessert, Carlos took credit for the entire dinner.*

who, which, that   Use *who* to refer to persons and *which* to refer to things; *that* is also used to refer to things and by some writers to refer to persons as well. Use *that* to introduce restrictive clauses only (see 34c): *The car that Susanna bought was a Geo Prism.* Use *which* to introduce nonrestrictive clauses (see 34c): *This salad, which is a day old, is a little limp.* Some writers also use *which* to introduce restrictive clauses, especially those beginning with the phrase *in which* or *of which: The hotel in which we are staying is very inexpensive.*

who, whom   Use *who* for subjects and complements, *whom* for objects. See 24g.

who's, whose   *Who's* is the contraction for *who is: I wonder who's pitching for the Orioles tonight. Whose* is a possessive pronoun: *I don't know whose umbrella this is.*

will   See *shall, will.*

worthy   Takes the preposition *of.*

would of   Do not substitute *of* for *have* in the expression *would have.*

yield   Takes the preposition *to.*

you   In formal writing avoid *you* in the sense of "anyone": *Any passenger* (not *you*) *would have gotten sick on that flight.*

your, you're   *Your* is a possessive pronoun: *Don't forget to bring your dictionary. You're* is the contraction for *you are: You're late again, Mr. Jackson.*

zeal   Takes the preposition *for* or *in.*

Glossary of Terms

abbreviation Strictly speaking, a single word shortened by the omission of letters and followed by a period: *etc., Blvd., Mr.* See 39.

absolute adjective An adjective, like *dead* or *infinite,* that cannot be compared. See 28c.

absolute phrase A noun or pronoun and a participle together with any modifiers or objects of the participle. An absolute phrase modifies the entire sentence rather than any particular word or phrase and can usually be located anywhere in the sentence: *Her work finished, Tabitha sat down in front of the fire.* See 20h.

abstract language Words that represent intangible ideas rather than concrete objects or acts. The opposite of concrete. See 18a.

acronym The first letter of a series of words used as a shortened version and pronounced as though it were itself a word: *NATO, OPEC, UNESCO.* See 39e.

action verb A verb that expresses an action—something someone or something is doing (or has done in the past or will do in the future). See 19c.

active voice The form of the verb in which the subject is the "do-er" of the verb; the direct object is the receiver of the action. See 26g.

adjective A word that modifies a noun by describing, identifying, or quantifying (telling how many). Adjectives almost always answer one of these questions: What kind of? Which? How many? See 19d.

adjective clause (also known as **relative clause**) A dependent clause that modifies a noun or pronoun. Adjective clauses usually begin with *who, whom, whose, which,* or *that* but can also begin with *when, where,* or *why.* See 11c, 20j.

adverb A word that modifies a verb, an adjective, another adverb, a prepositional phrase, a clause, or a sentence. Adverbs often but not always end in *-ly.* They answer one of the following questions: In what manner? When? Where? Why? To what extent? See 19e.

adverb clause A dependent clause that modifies a verb, an adjective, or another adverb. It usually answers one of these questions: In what

manner? When? Where? Why? To what extent? Adverb clauses begin with subordinate conjunctions such as *although, because, if, since,* and *when.* See 20j.

agreement   When a word is in a form appropriate in number, person, and gender for another word in a sentence. Subjects should agree with their verbs (see 21) and pronouns with their antecedents (see 23).

antecedent   The noun a pronoun stands for. See 22a.

APA style of documentation   The format established by the American Psychological Association for providing documentation in a piece of writing. The style commonly followed in the social sciences. See 46e.

apostrophe   The punctuation mark (') used to indicate that a word is a possessive (see 35a) or is a contraction (see 35c). Apostrophes are also used to form plurals in special cases. See 35d.

appositive   A noun that, together with its modifiers, follows another noun and stands for the same person or thing as the first noun: *My aunt, the well-known embezzler, will be released from prison next week.* See 20f.

appropriateness   The concept that there are many effective ways to write and that the choices you make should be those likely to be effective with the audience you are addressing and for the purpose you intend. See 5c.

archaic language   Words that are not in active use in contemporary English: *betwixt, anon, affright.* Such words are usually labeled in the dictionary. See 17h.

argument   Writing that attempts to persuade the reader to agree with a particular point. See 1c.

articles   A subgroup of adjectives including only the words *a, an,* and *the.* See 19d and 29.

aspect   A word denoting the difference between the six simple tenses and their progressive forms. See 26f.

assertion   A statement claiming that something is true. Assertions generally should be supported with evidence. See 3b.

assumption   A belief, usually unstated, that underlies an argument. See 3d.

audience   The person or people the writer anticipates will read what he or she is writing. See 1c.

auxiliary verbs   See *helping verbs.*

awkward   Describes a sentence that may not violate any rule, but nevertheless just doesn't sound graceful. See 16e.

base form   The form of the verb without inflection. The base form is used for present tense with a plural subject (or with *I* or *you* as subjects) or with *to* in infinitives.

gl/t

bibliography   A list of books and articles about a particular subject. Bibliographies often appear in books and articles. Writers generally include a bibliography with their research papers. If you are following the MLA style, such a list is called "Works Cited"; if you are following APA or CBE style, it is called "References." See 46.

brackets   Punctuation marks (**[]**) used to indicate places within direct quotations where the writer has inserted material or made minor changes in the wording. Also, words that would normally be placed in parentheses should be placed in brackets if they are part of a larger group of words that is already in parentheses. See 37d.

brainstorming   The process of writing down a list of ideas as fast as they occur to you—without censoring, organizing, or even worrying about spelling. Brainstorming is a method for coming up with ideas for subjects for papers or for details within the paper. See 2b and 2c.

case   The different forms of pronouns that indicate whether they are functioning as subjects or objects or whether they are indicating possession. Only pronouns change their form in English to indicate case: *She* (*subjective case*) *sent* _him_ (*objective case*) *to see* _her_ (*possessive case*) *therapist.* See 24.

cause and effect   The organizational pattern used to discuss the causes of a particular event or the results of an event. See 7e.

CBE style of documentation   The format established by the Council of Biological Editors for providing documentation in a piece of writing. The style commonly followed in the sciences. See 46f.

chronological organization   Organizing a piece of writing according to the time at which events occur or occurred.

citation   A notation in a text indicating the source of a quotation, paraphrase, or summary. Citations can take the form of footnotes, endnotes, or parenthetical notes. See 46c.

classification   The organizational pattern that takes a group of items and groups them according to some principle. See 7e.

cliché   Expressions that attempt to say something in a surprising way, but are so overused and predictable that they fail. See 17g.

clustering   (also called **mapping**) A highly visual technique that leads a writer to think about many different aspects of a topic and to generate ideas about it. See 2c.

coherence   The quality that allows writing to stick together and flow smoothly. Problems in coherence can make a piece of writing difficult for the reader to follow. See 8.

collaboration   In writing, the practice of two or more people working together to produce a written document. See 1b.

collective nouns   Nouns that are singular in form even though they refer to a group of people or things: *flock, class, team.* See 21j.

gl/t

colon   The punctuation mark (**:**) used after an independent clause
   to indicate a break between two grammatical elements that is greater
   than that marked by a semicolon, but less than that indicated by a
   period. A colon is a fairly formal punctuation mark that points to
   the second element as an illustration or amplification of the initial
   inde-pendent clause: *There were two causes of the accident: speeding
   and inattention.* See 37a.

comma   The punctuation mark (**,**) that is used to separate most elements within a sentence. See 33a and 34.

comma splice   A major error created when two independent clauses
   are joined by nothing but a comma. See 32c.

comparative form of adjectives   The form of adjective used to
   compare two people or things. In this form, adjectives either end
   in *-er* or, for longer adjectives, are preceded by *more: taller, more expensive.* See 28c.

comparison and contrast   Organizational patterns used to discuss
   two subjects either by comparing their similarities or contrasting their
   differences or, most commonly, by doing both. See 7e.

complex sentence   A sentence containing at least one independent
   clause and at least one dependent clause: *When Jose arrived at work,
   the building was locked.*

compound sentence   A sentence consisting of two or more independent clauses joined by a coordinating conjunction, a correlative conjunction, or a semicolon: *My father works for IBM, and my mother
   works for Apple.* See 11.

compound subject   A subject that consists of two or more nouns or
   pronouns joined by a coordinating conjunction: *Movies and television
   shows contain too much violence.* See 20b.

compound words   Two or more words joined by a conjunction like
   and. Nouns, pronouns, verbs, adjectives, and adverbs can be compound. See 21h.

concrete language   Words that appeal directly to the senses—words
   that represent solid objects or specific actions rather than broad, general categories. The opposite of *abstract.* See 18a.

conditional   A sentence that begins with an *if* clause and asserts that
   if one thing happens then another will also happen: *If Pandora had not
   opened that box, the world would be a more pleasant place.* See 26h.

conjunction   A word that joins two or more elements in a sentence.
   There are three kinds of conjunctions in English: coordinate (*and,
   so*), correlative (*either . . . or*), and subordinating (*when, if, because*).
   See 19g.

conjunctive adverbs   Words that both modify the independent clause
   they are in and indicate its relationship to the preceding independent

gl/t

clause. Common conjunctive adverbs include *however, therefore, for example,* and *nevertheless.* See 19e and 33c.

connotation   The emotional colorings or associations that contribute to a word's meaning. See 16h.

contrasted element   Phrase or clause that begins with *not* and is set off from the rest of the sentence: *Rosalie ordered a glass of wine, <u>not a bottle of wine</u>.* See 34g.

coordinating conjunctions   The seven conjunctions that are used to join words, phrases, or clauses of equal importance: *and, but, or, for, so, yet,* and *nor.* See 11a.

coordination   The use of coordinating conjunctions to link ideas that are of equal importance. These ideas may be independent clauses, phrases, or just single nouns. See 11a.

correlative conjunctions   The pairs of words *either . . . or, both . . . and, neither . . . nor, not only . . . but also,* and *whether . . . or.* These pairs are used like coordinating conjunctions to join elements of equal importance in a sentence. See 19g.

dangling modifier   A modifier (often a participial phrase) that does not modify any word in the sentence; it dangles all by itself, usually at the beginning of the sentence: *<u>Leaning out the window,</u> my hat blew off.* See 13c.

dash   The punctuation mark (—) used to set off material that is important. (Less important material is set off by parentheses or commas.) A dash is longer than a hyphen; on a typewriter it is created by typing two hyphens. See 37e.

deductive reasoning   An argument that uses a generalization to prove a particular case. See 3d.

definition   The organizational pattern used to clarify the meaning intended for a particular word or phrase in a particular piece of writing. See 7e.

demonstrative pronouns   Pronouns that identify or point out specific persons, places, or things: *this, that, these,* and *those.* See 19b.

denotation   The explicit meaning of a word, the meaning in a dictionary. See 16h.

dependent clause   A group of words that includes a subject and verb, but that leaves the reader "hanging" or feeling something is missing at the end. These clauses usually start with a subordinating conjunction or relative pronoun: *My mother, <u>who works for the government,</u> is worried about being laid off.* See 20j.

description   The organizational pattern used to create a picture of a person, a thing, or a place. The details are organized in a logical spatial order such as near to far. See 7e.

determiners   A category of words that precede nouns and modify their meaning. Only one determiner can be used for each noun. Determiners include articles, possessive nouns, possessive pronouns, demonstrative pronouns, and a few others. See 29b.

development of ideas   To develop an idea is to provide support for it. Which ideas need development and how much development they need is determined by your audience and purpose. See 7c.

dialogue   The written representation of a conversation between two or more people. See 10d and 36c.

diction   Selecting just the right words to express the meaning and create the effect you intend. Some choices are ineffective because a word simply doesn't mean what you think it means (using *then* for *than*). Most of the time, however, diction refers to choosing a word with just the right shade of meaning for what you are trying to express (choosing *sidled* instead of *skulked* to describe how a used car salesman approached you). See 16.

direct object   A noun or pronoun that stands for the person who or the thing that receives the action of the verb. Only transitive verbs take direct objects. See 20c.

direct quotation   Reporting the exact words of another person. Direct quotations are placed in quotation marks. See 36a.

division   The organizational pattern that analyzes a single item into its constituent parts. See 7e.

documentation   Providing information about the sources of quotations and ideas. See 46.

double negative   A sentence containing two negative words that cancel each other out, creating a positive meaning that is the opposite of what the speaker or writer intended. See 28d.

drafting   Writing with an awareness that you will later go back and revise what you have written—getting your ideas down on paper in a tentative way. See 4.

element   A word, phrase, or clause that acts as a unit in a sentence. See 34g.

ellipsis   A series of three periods separated by spaces that is used to indicate that some material has been left out, most often from a direct quotation. See 37b.

elliptical sentences   In elliptical sentences, words are omitted in the second half of compound constructions that would otherwise be repeated from the first half: *Martha went to the movie, and Albert did too.* See 15e and 32a.

evidence   The support you provide to convince your reader of each point in your essay. Evidence might consist of facts, of argument, of

gl/t

expert opinion, of narrative, or of anything else that will serve to convince your reader of the validity of your point. See 3.

excessive humility   The overuse of expressions like *it is only my opinion* or *I think*, creating the impression you are not very sure of yourself. See 16g.

exclamation point   The punctuation mark (!) used to end sentences expressing strong emotion. See 31a.

expletive   (1) *There* or *it* used at the beginning of a sentence, making it necessary to move the subject to a position following the verb—a construction often better avoided: *There were three seals swimming in the harbor.* See 16d. (2) A word considered profane or obscene.

expository writing   Traditionally, writing whose chief aim is to *explain* its subject. In recent times, however, the term commonly includes persuasive writing.

expression   Selecting just the right words to express the meaning and create the effect you intend. Similar to *diction.* See 16.

fallacy   (also called **logical fallacy**) Erroneous reasoning. See 3f.

faulty predication   (also called **mixed meaning**) A sentence in which the subject and the verb are mismatched—in which they don't make sense together: *The purpose of this meeting is because our business has declined dramatically since the first of the year.* See 15b.

field research   Research that is done outside the library. It may involve interviewing or surveying people; it may involve close observation of people, places, or things. See 45e.

focused freewriting   Like freewriting, but here you start with a general idea you want to write about or have been assigned, and you write about it for a set period of time. See 2b.

fragment   A group of words punctuated as if it were a sentence when it is not. A fragment does not contain an independent clause, which means it is missing a subject or a verb or it does not express a complete thought—it leaves the reader hanging or with a feeling of incompleteness. See 32b.

freewriting   Writing without rules, constraints, or even a goal. When you freewrite, you turn your mind loose and let whatever streams out appear on the page or screen. Freewriting is a method for generating ideas and even content for a paper. See 2b and 2c.

fused sentence   A major error created when two independent clauses are joined using no punctuation—they are just "fused" together. Sometimes called a **run-on sentence**. See 32c.

future perfect progressive tense   The form of the verb used to describe an ongoing event in the future that will be completed before some other action in the future or before some fixed time in the fu-

ture: *Ms. Sanchez will have been waiting for more than an hour by the time this movie is over.* See 26e.

future perfect tense   The form of the verb used to describe events in the future that will be completed before some other action in the future or before some fixed time in the future. The future perfect tense consists of *will have* plus the past participle. See 26d.

future progressive tense   The form of the verb used to indicate an action that will be in progress at some time in the future: *Takiko will be arriving home at midnight tonight.* See 26e.

future tense   The form of the verb used to describe events taking place at some time in the future or events that are predictable. See 26a.

generalization   A statement that is asserted as a truth about a set of people or things *generally,* but not necessarily about every member of the set. Because generalizations are so powerful, they must be used carefully. See 3b.

general language   Words that represent things in general rather than specific examples of those things. *Vehicle* is more general than *car,* which is more general than *Ford Escort.* The opposite of *specific.* See 18a.

gerund   A word that is normally a verb but is used as a noun; gerunds end in *-ing.* See 27a.

helping verbs   (also called **auxiliary verbs**) Verbs like *is, was, must, should,* or *has* that precede the main verb in a sentence. The initial helping verb indicates the tense, mood, and sometimes person for the clause and, when appropriate, must agree with the subject in number. See 19c.

homonyms   Two words having the same sound and the same spelling but different meanings: *book* (*something you read*) and *book* (*to make a reservation*). Also used (less precisely) for two words having the same sound but different spellings and meanings: *there/their/they're, to/too/two.* See 16a.

homophones   Two words having the same sound but different spellings and meanings: *there/their/they're, to/too/two.* See 16a.

hyphen   The punctuation mark (-) used to divide words at the end of a line, to form compound words, and to write out numbers between twenty-one and ninety-nine. Hyphens are about half as long as dashes. See 42.

hypothetical   A sentence beginning with an *if* clause that asserts that if one thing happens, a second will follow. A hypothetical statement is different from a conditional in that the event in the *if* clause may or may not ever happen. See 26g.

gl/t

imperative mood   The form of verb used in sentences that give commands. See 26h.

indefinite pronouns   Pronouns that stand for unknown or unspecified persons, places, or things. See 19b.

independent clause   A group of words containing a subject and a verb and expressing a complete thought. An independent clause cannot "leave you hanging," cannot feel incomplete at the end. See 20i.

indicative mood   The form of verb used in sentences that make statements. See 26h.

indirect object   The noun or pronoun that stands for the person or thing that receives the direct object. Only transitive verbs take indirect objects. See 20c.

indirect question   A question reported by someone other than the speaker or writer and stated in that person's indirect words rather than the original speaker or writer's words: *Carmina asked whether most people in Columbus's day really believed that the world was flat.* See 31b.

indirect quotation   Reporting what someone else has said or written but in slightly different words than those the person used—different usually in tense and person. See 36i.

inductive reasoning   A form of argument in which data are examined and then a conclusion is reached. See 3c.

infinitive   A form of the verb with *to* in front of it. Infinitives can be used as nouns, adjectives, or adverbs. See 19c and 27a.

intensifiers   Words like *very* and *extremely,* which increase the intensity of the adjectives or adverbs they modify, are called intensifiers. Using intensifiers when they are not needed causes wordiness. See 16d.

intensive pronouns   Pronouns that take the same forms as reflexive pronouns but are used to emphasize a noun or another pronoun: *Liza Minnelli herself walked into the room.* See 19b.

interjections   Words that express surprise or strong emotion: *oh, wow.* See 19h.

interrogative pronouns   Pronouns that are used to ask questions: *who, whom, whose, what, which.* See 19b.

intransitive verb   A verb that does not take a direct object, a noun or pronoun that receives the action that the verb expresses. See 20a.

introductory element   A word, phrase, or dependent clause that appears before an independent clause. See 34a.

inverted word order   A reversal of the normal order of words in a sentence, as when the direct object precedes the subject and verb: *"Murder," she wrote.* The most common form of inverted word order is when the subject follows the verb: *In my pocket were two silver dollars.* See 21k.

gl/t

irony Words consciously used to mean the opposite of their normal meaning. See 36.

irregular words Words that take different forms from those prescribed by standard rules. For irregular verbs, see 25b.

italics Text printed in a slanted style to indicate that particular words are being emphasized for some reason. When you are writing in longhand or with a typewriter that cannot produce italics, underline words to emphasize them. See 41.

items in a series A group of words (or occasionally phrases or even clauses) that are joined by commas with a coordinating conjunction before the final one. See 34b.

jargon Specialized language shared by a profession or other group. See 17b.

journal An informal record of your thoughts. Many writers keep a journal in which they regularly write ideas that occur to them and that may or may not be useful in their future writings. See 2b and 2c.

limiting modifiers Modifiers that limit the meaning of the word following them; they include *almost, even, exactly, hardly, just, merely, nearly, only, scarcely,* and *simply.* They must be placed in front of the word they modify. See 13b.

linking verbs Verbs that link the subject of the sentence with something that comes after the verb. Linking verbs include various forms of the verb *be (am, is, are, was, were, will be, has been, have been, had been, will have been)* and a small group of sensory verbs (*looks, appears, seems, feels, sounds, smells, tastes*). See 19c.

logical fallacy Erroneous reasoning. See 3f.

main verb The linking or action verb(s) in a sentence. Main verbs can appear alone or with one or more helping verbs preceding them.

mapping (also called **clustering**) A highly visual technique that leads you to think about many different aspects of a topic and to generate ideas for that topic. See 2c.

metaphor A figure of speech that helps the reader understand a concept by comparing it with something familiar. While a metaphor states that one thing *is* another, this equating is not to be taken literally, only metaphorically. See 17f.

misplaced modifier Any modifier placed so that it could be interpreted as modifying more than one word: *I saw a man pushing a baby carriage in my rearview mirror.* See 13a.

mixed construction A sentence that starts out using one kind of grammatical structure and changes to a different one in the middle, resulting in writing that just doesn't "sound right": *By seeing the movie meant I never read the book.* See 15a.

mixed meaning   (also called **faulty predication**) A sentence in which the subject and the verb are mismatched—when they don't make sense together: *The purpose of this meeting is because our business has declined dramatically since the first of the year.* See 15b.

mixed metaphor   A problematic construction in which an object is likened simultaneously (and usually accidentally) to two different things: *Like a sailboat pushed by a strong wind, the bill sailed through Congress under a full head of steam.* See 17f.

MLA style of documentation   The format established by the Modern Language Association for providing documentation in a piece of writing. The style commonly followed in the humanities. See 46d.

modals or **modal verbs**   A subgroup of helping verbs consisting of the following: *can, might, should, could, must, will, may, shall,* and *would.* See 19c.

modifier   A word, phrase, or clause that describes or provides extra information about another word or phrase. Adjectives and adverbs are the simplest modifiers, but prepositional phrases, infinitives, participles, appositives, adjective clauses, and adverb clauses are other types of common modifiers. See 13.

mood   One of three forms of the verb in English sentences. Sentences that make statements are in indicative mood. Sentences that give commands are in imperative mood. Clauses that express conditions that are contrary to reality are in subjunctive mood. See 26h.

narration   The organizational pattern used to tell about something that happened—to tell a story or report an event. Narration is usually organized in chronological order. See 7e.

nonrestrictive clauses, appositives, and **phrases**   Clauses, appositives, and phrases that do not restrict or narrow the scope of a noun. To omit nonrestrictive clauses does not usually change the meaning of the sentence significantly. See 34c.

noun   A word that stands for a person, place, or thing. A noun may or may not be the name of the person, place, or thing. The thing that a noun stands for may be concrete (like *table* or *letter*) or abstract (like *trouble* or *arrogance*). Words that usually are verbs can sometimes be used as nouns (as in "a *drink* of water" or "a *drive* in the country"). See 19a.

noun clause   A dependent clause used in any function usually filled by a noun: subject, direct object, indirect object, object of preposition, or complement. Noun clauses usually begin with a relative pronoun such as *who, whom, whoever, whomever, what, where,* or *that.* See 20j.

noun of direct address   The name of the person being addressed embedded within a sentence. Sometimes called a *nominative of address.* Nouns of direct address are set off by commas. See 34d.

noun phrase   A noun and all its modifiers. See 19b.

objective case   The forms of pronouns used as direct objects, indirect objects, and objects of prepositions. See 24b.

object of the preposition   A noun or pronoun or a word, phrase, or clause that functions as a noun or pronoun and appears at the end of a prepositional phrase: *in the box, near the window*. See 20d.

obscenity   Language that is offensive to standards of decency or modesty. See 17e.

organization   The arrangement of ideas in an essay in order to best create the desired effect in the reader. Organization involves ordering ideas and clustering them into logical groups. See 5a.

paragraph   A group of sentences that support one point, usually indented or set off from the preceding paragraph by skipping a space. See 7.

paragraph unity   The focusing of a paragraph around one idea. See 7b.

parallelism   When words, phrases, or clauses joined by coordinate conjunctions are equivalent in structure. See 12a.

parentheses   The marks of punctuation (**( )**) used to set off information that is supplementary to the main idea of the sentence. See 37c.

parenthetical expressions   Words or phrases that are not essential to the meaning of a sentence but add extra information, facts, examples, comments, or digressions. They may be set off by commas, dashes, or parentheses. See 20g and 34d.

participle   The form of the verb used in verb phrases to form tenses; participles are also used by themselves as adjectives (see 12c). Present participles are formed by adding *-ing* to the present tense form of the regular verb. The past participle form of the verb ends in *-ed, -en,* or *-t*. See 27b.

particle   A preposition or adverb that follows a verb and is an integral part of it: *look up, catch on, fill out*. See 25c.

parts of speech   The eight categories into which most words in English can be placed: noun, pronoun, verb, adjective, adverb, preposition, conjunction, or interjection. The same word may be a different part of speech in different sentences depending on how it is used. See 19.

passive voice   The form of verbs in which the receiver of the action of the verb is the subject; the "do-er" of the verb, if present, is located in a prepositional phrase beginning with *by*. See 20a and 26g.

past perfect progressive tense   The form of the verb used to describe an ongoing event in the past that was completed before some other action in the past or before some fixed time in the past: *The phone had been ringing as I attempted to unlock the front door*. See 26e.

gl/t

past perfect tense   When two events that happened in the past are being discussed, the past perfect tense is used for the one that happened earlier. Past perfect verbs consist of *had* plus the past participle: *When the bus finally arrived, we had been waiting for an hour.* See 26b.

past progressive tense   The form of the verb used to indicate an action that was in progress at some time in the past: *The man was drinking heavily when the heart attack occurred.* See 26e.

past tense   The form of the verb used to describe events that occurred in the past and do not extend into the present: *Lorna jumped into the front seat of Leonard's car.* See 26a.

peer response groups   The practice, common in many writing classrooms, of having each student in a small group ask others in the group for reactions to or suggestions for a piece of writing. See 1b.

period   The punctuation mark (**.**) used to end sentences that make statements. Called a *full stop* in countries using British terminology. See 31a.

person   Pronouns exist in three persons in English. First-person pronouns (*I, me, we, us, my, our*) refer to the person actually speaking or writing. Second-person pronouns (*you, your*) refer to the person being spoken or written to. Third-person pronouns (*he, she, it, they, him, her, them, his, her, their, its*) refer to anyone or anything being spoken about who is not the speaker or writer or the person being spoken or written to. See 23a.

personal pronouns   Pronouns that stand for particular people or things: *I, you, he, she, it, we, they, me, him, her, us, them.* See 19b.

phrasal verbs   Two- and three-word combinations that contain a verb and a "particle" (a preposition or adverb) and function as a unit: *look up, catch up with, call off.* See 25c.

plagiarism   The direct or indirect use of someone else's ideas or words without giving that person proper credit. See 45f.

possession   A grammatical concept that includes ownership but also includes many other relationships in which one thing or person belongs to another. For example, people "possess" the parts of their bodies, their relatives, and aspects of their personalities, even though they don't own them in a literal sense. See 35a.

possessive pronouns   Pronouns that indicate ownership: *my, your, yours, his, her, hers, its, our, ours, their, theirs.* See 19b.

predicate adjectives   An adjective that comes after a linking verb and modifies the subject. See 20e.

predicate noun or nominative   A noun or pronoun that comes after a linking verb and is being equated with the subject. See 20e.

preposition   Words that indicate a connection between the noun at the end of the phrase and another word in the sentence. Prepositions

often indicate a relationship in time or space. Common prepositions include *of, in, by, with, to,* and *from.* See 19f.

prepositional phrase   A phrase beginning with a preposition and ending with a noun or pronoun. Any number of adjectives may occur between the preposition and the noun or pronoun: *in the corner, with a yellow hat.* See 20d.

present perfect tense   The form of the verb used to represent an action that began in the past and continues to or was completed before the present. The present perfect form of the verb consists of *has* plus the past participle: *The United Nations has become involved in a large number of conflicts.* See 26b.

present progressive tense   The form of the verb used to indicate an action that is taking place at the present and is in progress: *Paul is reading a book by Dave Barry.* See 26e.

present tense   The form of the verb used to represent an action or state of being that is happening at the time of speaking or writing or that is true at all times—past, present, and future: *Rome is the capital of Italy. Molly takes the seven-thirty train.* See 26a.

pretentious language   Unnecessarily ornate and elevated language that seems to be designed more to impress than to communicate. See 17c.

problem/solution   An organizational pattern common in business and technical writing but useful in most writing. In this pattern you first describe a problem and then propose one or more solutions; if you propose more than one solution, you may or may not recommend a particular one. See 7e.

process   The organizational mode used to describe a process—how to do something or how something was done. See 7e.

profanity   Language that shows contempt or irreverence toward God or sacred things. See 17c.

proper adjective   An adjective that is derived from a proper noun: *Chinese, South American.* See 38c.

proper noun   The name of a specific person, place, or thing. See 38b.

pronoun   A word that stands for a noun and its modifiers (*he, they*), a particular person like the speaker or the person spoken to (*I, you*), or an unknown or unspecified person or thing (*someone, nothing*). See 19b.

pronoun agreement   The principle that a pronoun must be the same gender, person, and number as its antecedent. See 23.

pronoun reference   The principle that a pronoun must unambiguously stand for a specific noun or other pronoun. See 22.

purpose   Traditionally, the purposes for writing have been defined as four: to explain, to persuade, to entertain, or to express yourself. The

gl/t

purpose of a piece of writing may also be thought of as what you hope or intend will happen as a result of this writing being read by the intended audience. See 1c.

question mark　The punctuation mark (**?**) used to end sentences that ask questions. See 31a.

quotation　Reporting the exact words of someone else—sometimes called direct quotation. See 36. Quotations are placed in quotation marks. See 36i.

quotation marks　The punctuation marks ("　") used to indicate when a writer is reporting the exact words of someone else. See 36.

redundant　When a sentence says the same thing twice, as in *The blouse is yellow in color.* See 16d.

References　A list of the works referred to in a research paper. *References* is the term used when following APA or CBE style of documentation. See 46e.

reflexive pronouns　Pronouns that stand for someone who or something that is the receiver of the same action for which he, she, or it is also performing: *myself, yourself, himself, herself, itself, ourselves, yourselves, themselves.* See 19b.

regular　Words whose different forms follow the rules for words of their type. For regular verbs, see 25a.

relative clause　(also known as **adjective clause**) A dependent clause that modifies a noun or pronoun. Adjective clauses usually begin with *who, whom, whose, which,* or *that* but can begin with *when, where,* or *why.* See 20j.

relative pronouns　Pronouns that introduce dependent clauses: *who, whom, whose, which, that, whoever, whomever, whichever, whatever.* See 19b.

research paper　In college, a paper in which a student consults several sources to gather information, which is integrated into the student's argument. See 45a.

restrictive clauses, appositives, and **phrases**　Clauses, appositives, and phrases that restrict or narrow the scope of a noun. To omit a restrictive clause usually changes the meaning of the sentence significantly. See 34c.

run-on sentence　A major error created when two independent clauses are joined using no punctuation—they are just "fused" together. Also called a **fused sentence.** See 32c.

semicolon　The punctuation mark (**;**) used to join closely related independent clauses. See 33b and 33c.

sentence　A linguistically coherent group of words containing at least one independent clause. See 32a.

sexist language   Language that expresses unwarranted assumptions about people based simply on their gender. See 17a and 23b.

shifts   The error in which a writer shifts from one tense to another with no reason (see 9a), changes from one number (singular or plural) to the other for no reason (see 9b), or changes from one person to another for no reason (see 9b).

simile   A comparison made with the word *like* (or sometimes *as*). A simile is used to express an insight about an unfamiliar term by comparing it to a more familiar one. See 17f.

slang   The lively, forceful, and colorful language of our informal conversations—inappropriate for most formal writing situations. See 17d.

slash   The punctuation mark (/) used to separate certain specific kinds of expressions in English. Sometimes called a *virgule* or *solidus*. See 37f.

specific language   Words that represent a narrow class of objects as opposed to a general group. *Red-headed woodpecker* is more specific than *bird,* which is more specific than *animal.* The opposite of *general.* See 18a.

split infinitive   An infinitive is said to be "split" when a modifier appears between the word *to* and the verb that follows. See 13e.

squinting modifier   A word or phrase that is unclear because it could be modifying either of two different words in a sentence. See 13d.

Standard Written English   The style of English used for formal situations such as most academic and business writing. See 5c.

stereotypes   The logical fallacy of generalizing inaccurately about a group of people—often a group identified by race, gender, or religion. See 3f.

subject (of an essay)   The topic or idea that the essay is "about." See 2a.

subject (of a sentence)   The person, place, or thing that is "doing" or "being" the verb. See 20b. The simple subject is the single word in question; the complete subject is that word together with all its modifiers.

subject complement   (sometimes called **predicate noun, predicate nominative,** or **predicate adjective**) A noun, a pronoun, or an adjective that comes after a linking verb and is equated with the subject (in the case of nouns and pronouns) or modifies the subject (in the case of adjectives): *Milton was a devout <u>Christian</u>. The sunset was <u>beautiful</u>.* See 20f.

subjective case   The forms of pronouns used for subjects and subject complements. See 24b.

gl/t

subject-verb agreement   Writing the form of the verb that agrees with the subject in a sentence. In regular present-tense verbs this means adding an -*s* to the verb when the subject is singular and leaving the -*s* off when the subject is plural. See 21.

subjunctive mood   An *if* clause that expresses something that the writer or speaker knows is not the case is in subjunctive mood: *If I were you....* See 26h.

subordinate clause   (also known as a **dependent clause**) A group of words that include a subject and verb, but which leave the reader "hanging" or feeling something is missing at the end. These clauses usually start with a subordinating conjunction or relative pronoun. See 20j.

subordinating conjunctions   Words used to introduce subordinate clauses. See 11b and 19g.

subordination   In a sentence with two or more ideas expressed in separate clauses, placing the less important idea in a subordinate clause is subordination. See 11b.

superlative forms of adjectives   The form of adjectives used to compare three or more people or things. Adjectives in the superlative form usually end in -*est* or, for longer adjectives, are preceded by *most*. See 28c.

tense   The form of the verb that changes to indicate when the action or state of being takes place. See 26.

thesis   A thesis is a subject and a point you make about that subject. A good thesis is not too broad, is not too narrow and factual, and is not a question. See 2b.

topic sentence   The sentence that states the main point of a paragraph. See 7a.

transitional expressions   Words and phrases, usually placed at the beginning of sentences, that explain the relationship between that sentence and the preceding one: *for example, as a result, in fact.* See 8 and 33c.

transitional paragraph   A paragraph, usually short, that signals to the reader that one section of the paper is over and informs him or her what to expect next. See 10c.

transitive verb   A verb that is followed by a direct object (a noun or pronoun) that receives the action expressed by the verb. See 20a.

unfortunate chime   When the same word appears twice in a sentence and creates an awkward sound. See 16c.

unity   That aspect of a piece of writing that makes it feel "whole." Unity is usually accomplished by focusing the paper on a single thesis and by ensuring that everything in the paper supports that thesis. See also 5a.

gl/t

verb   The word in a sentence that expresses action—something that someone or something is doing, has done in the past, or will do in the future—that links the subject of a sentence with a noun or adjective that comes after the verb, or that serves as a helping verb preceding the main verb. See 19c.

verbal   A word that is normally a verb but is changed into a noun or adjective by the addition of the ending *-ing* or the preceding word *to*. There are three kinds of verbals in English: infinitives, gerunds, and participles. See 19c and 27.

word choice   Selecting just the right words to express the meaning and create the effect you intend. See 16.

wordiness   Using more words than are necessary to express an idea. Adding words that sharpen or clarify meaning is not wordiness. See 16d.

Works Cited   A list at the end of a research paper of the various works quoted from, paraphrased, or summarized in the paper. *Works Cited* is the term used when the writer is following the MLA style of documentation. See 46d.

you **understood**   The subject of a sentence that gives a command—tells someone to do something—is always the person represented by the pronoun *you*. Since users of the English language understand this pronoun to be the subject, it is seldom present in the sentence. The subject of such sentences is, therefore, said to be *you understood*.

Exercises

EXERCISE 1-1 (1a) Write a paragraph describing how you went about writing a recent paper or an important piece of personal writing such as a letter of application or complaint. Describe how you planned, drafted, and revised your writing and how you felt about the result. Exchange papers with two or three classmates and discuss one another's paragraphs. If you had to write the same papers over again, discuss what you would each do differently.

EXERCISE 1-2 (1c) Read the following three paragraphs. Either by yourself or in a group, determine the audience that the writer of each paragraph is addressing, as well as each writer's purpose or purposes (remember that a writer may have more than one purpose).

1.   Children in poverty are in misery. We shouldn't play politics with their future. That means giving Head Start the financing it needs. [Edward Zigler, "Head Start: The Whole Story"]

2.   One could predict, but not with certainty, what a grizzly would do. Odds were very great that one touch of man scent would cause him to stop his activity, pause in a moment of absorbed and alert curiosity, and then move, at a not undignified pace, in a direction other than the one from which the scent was coming. That is what would happen almost every time, but there was, to be sure, no guarantee. The forest Eskimos fear and revere the grizzly. They know that certain individual bears not only will fail to avoid a person who comes into their country but will approach and even stalk the trespasser. It is potentially in-

EXERCISE 1-1 (1a)
Answers will vary.

EXERCISE 1-2 (1c)
Answers may vary. Possible answers:

1. *Audience:* general readers, policymakers, voters; *purpose:* to persuade
2. *Audience:* hikers, backpackers, people interested in the outdoors or in wildlife; *purposes:* to explain grizzly behavior, to persuade people likely to come in contact with grizzlies to be cautious

E-1

3. *Audience:* potential job applicants, general readers; *purposes:* to explain how to behave on a job interview, to entertain

accurate to extrapolate the behavior of any one bear from the behavior of most, since they are both intelligent and independent and will do what they choose to do according to mood, experience, whim. A grizzly that has ever been wounded by a bullet will not forget it, and will probably know that it was a human being who sent the bullet. At sight of a human, such a bear will be likely to charge. Grizzlies hide food sometimes—a caribou calf, say, under a pile of scraped-up moss—and a person the bear might otherwise ignore might suddenly not be ignored if the person were inadvertently to step into the line between the food cache and the bear. A sow grizzly with cubs, of course, will charge anything that suggests danger to the cubs, even if the cubs are nearly as big as she is. They stay with their mother two and a half years. [John McPhee, *Coming into the Country*]

3. The best job applicant is one who is able to sing his or her own praises without embarrassment, confident enough to steer an interview away from inappropriate areas, and persistent. When you would demur, socially, with "Oh, it was nothing really," you would, in business, say, "I graduated with honors, had the best sales record in my last job, and left because I felt the job wasn't really using my abilities." When you would tell a prospective host, "I would be simply delighted to be there," you tell a prospective employer, "I think your company would benefit from my contribution." To a dinner partner, you might say, "Why, yes, my husband is the one over there with the blond mustache, and we have four beautiful children from three marriages"; to a personnel person, you say, "Well, I really don't think my personal life will have any bearing on my work." [Judith Martin, *Miss Manners' Guide to Excruciatingly Correct Behavior*]

EXERCISE 2-1 (2b)
Answers will vary.

EXERCISE 2-1 (2b) Choose one of the following subject areas and, using either brainstorming or freewriting, narrow it down until you arrive at a subject with the characteristics listed on page 15.

1. Violence on television
2. The national park system
3. Advances in technology versus the right to privacy

4. Major-league sports
5. The Pacific Rim nations

EXERCISE 2-2 (2b) Develop a thesis statement for the subject you arrived at in Exercise 2-1. Either on your own or in a group, determine whether your thesis meets the requirements listed on page 21.

EXERCISE 2-3 (2c) Using one of the activities discussed on pages 22–29, generate ideas for the thesis you developed in response to Exercise 2-2.

EXERCISE 3-1 (3b) Study a catalog, popular magazine, or newspaper from before 1980 and make a list of ways in which American life was different then from what it is now. Underline the generalizations in your list; then rearrange the list, placing facts under the generalizations they support.

EXERCISE 3-2 (3f) Identify the logical fallacies in the following items, and explain the source of the faulty reasoning in each. Example:

(stereotyping)
One of my opponents in this election, a greedy corporate attorney,
(ad hominem attack)
works only for the benefit of his rich clients and friends.

1. His marriage ended in divorce, proving that he shirks responsibility whenever possible.
2. Eighty-five percent of voters state that crime ranks as the most important issue in this election; therefore, you should vote for the candidate with the most experience in prosecuting criminal cases.
3. A certain candidate in this election even admits that she sent her children to private school rather than public school.

EXERCISE 2-2 (2b)
Answers will vary.

EXERCISE 2-3 (2c)
Answers will vary.

EXERCISE 3-1 (3b)
Answers will vary.

EXERCISE 3-2 (3f)

1. Non sequitur
2. Bandwagon appeal
3. Ad hominem attack

4. Transfer, image over issue
5. Careless assumption of cause and effect
6. Circular reasoning, begging the question
7. Red herring
8. Either-or fallacy
9. Hasty generalization
10. False analogy

4. The most elite thinkers and intellectuals concur that my platform offers the best hope for social reform.
5. The increasing rate of unemployment is a direct result of the incumbent party's focus on foreign policy.
6. The average cost of health care in this country soared during the past four years because medical care suppliers dramatically increased their rates to balance expenditures.
7. My voting record on environmental issues may be dubious, but I have consistently supported the nuclear arms industry to help us survive the threat of military takeover.
8. Cast your vote for the honest candidate, or cast your vote away.
9. One trade union has already endorsed my candidacy; I am, therefore, the organized-labor candidate.
10. If we can train poodles to walk on their hind legs, we can teach our politicians to run honest campaigns.

EXERCISE 5-1 (5a)
Answers will vary.

EXERCISE 5-1 (5a) Either by yourself or in a group, examine Steve Shaver's first draft on pages 57–58 and decide what large-scale revisions are needed. Use the list of questions on pages 59–60 to help you.

EXERCISE 5-2 (5b)
Answers will vary.

EXERCISE 5-2 (5b) Examine one of your recent papers and decide what small-scale revisions you still could make to improve it. Use the list on page 61 to help you.

EXERCISE 7-1 (7a–d)
Topic sentences are in bold type.

Most biologists shy away from speculating what it must be like to see life through the eyes of an animal. . . . **But we need some understanding of the natural mind of an animal if we are to see how the human mind differs.**

EXERCISE 7-1 (7a–d) Read the following excerpt, divide it into five paragraphs, and then underline the topic sentence in each paragraph. Each paragraph should focus on one main point. Remember that a topic sentence presents both the subject of a paragraph and the point that is being made about the subject.

Most biologists shy away from speculating what it must be like to see life through the eyes of an animal. They stick strictly to observing an animal's behavior and do not concern themselves with its conscious experience of the world. But we need some understanding of the natural mind of an animal if we are to see how the human mind differs. The great physical similarity of the brains

of higher animals, such as birds and mammals, and man should show that our minds work in a broadly similar way. Perception would certainly seem to be much the same for a cat or kangaroo as it is for us. Animals have sense organs like ours, a cortex mapping of the world like ours, and a rising froth of impressions like ours, from which we would expect animals to be conscious of the world like ourselves. The mapping and processing of the world on the cortex is what creates raw consciousness in humans, so, given that the sensory and neural equipment of animals is the same, we can expect all vertebrates to show at least some degree of consciousness. An obvious difference between the human brain and most animal brains is size. Because the human brain has a tablecloth spread of cortex for sensations to dance across, compared with the handkerchief of an ape or postage stamp of a rat, we would expect human consciousness to be richer and sharper simply due to the extra neurons that can be devoted to mapping the detail of the world. But as we have said, the forming of raw impressions in the mind is only half the story of consciousness: To feel truly aware, we need to understand what passes through the mind. We need to forge a connection between sensation and memory; otherwise we would experience only a chaotic kaleidoscope of impressions. Animals can certainly do this too. There is no doubt that they have good memories for recognizing the familiar: All higher animals can recognize the cries of their children or the faces of their mates; they can find their way back to their burrows or learn a complex path through a maze. The memories of animals are often at their most impressive when it comes to food. Marsh tits hide caches of food through the day and can store several hundred grubs and insects to be collected up to a day later. Chimps also show very good memories. In one experiment, a scientist carried a chimp around while he hid eighteen pieces of fruit in an acre-sized compound. When he let the chimp free an hour later, it could remember its way back to about a dozen pieces—running straight to its favorite types of fruit first. Then, after eating most of the fruit and resting a few hours, it suddenly got up—presumably prompted by fresh hunger pangs—and ran off to gather some more, showing that the memory must have persisted. A purer test of the powers of animal memories can be made by teaching an animal to associate the showing of a colored card with the arrival of food a short time later. As might be expected, the duration of such memories was linked with brain size. If there was more than ten seconds' delay between card and food, goldfish would forget the significance of the signal, whereas pigeons and lizards could remember for two or three minutes and baboons would wait for the food to arrive up to half an hour later. However, the important

The great physical similarity of the brains of higher animals, such as birds and mammals, and man should show that our minds work in a broadly similar way. . . .

An obvious difference between the human brain and most animal brains is size. **Because the human brain has a tablecloth spread of cortex for sensations to dance across, compared with the handkerchief of an ape or postage stamp of a rat, we would expect human consciousness to be richer and sharper simply due to the extra neurons that can be devoted to mapping the detail of the world. . . .**

The memories of animals are often at their most impressive when it comes to food. . . .

A purer test of the powers of animal memories can be made by teaching an animal to associate the showing of a colored card with the arrival of food a short time later. . . .

point is that all animals—even the humble goldfish—show at least some memory ability. [Excerpt from *The Ape That Spoke* by John McCrone. Text copyright © 1991 by John McCrone. Reprinted by permission of William Morrow & Company and Macmillan Publishers, Ltd., London.]

EXERCISE 8-1 (8a–c)

First paragraph: sentences 7, 10, 13, 1, 14.
Second paragraph: sentences 8, 3, 9, 2, 11, 6, 4, 12, 5.

EXERCISE 9-1 (9a–b)

1. Mardi Gras festivities in the United States began well over a century ago. Groups of revelers, or krewes, first celebrated Carnival in New Orleans in 1857. They not only **organized** parades filled with decorated floats, costumed marchers, and lively bands, but **they held** elaborate costume balls as well.

2. Although the balls remain closed to the general public today, the parades entertain many people of all ages and backgrounds. The doubloons and colorful strings of beads tossed into the crowds from the floats are coveted prizes among schoolchildren in Louisiana. **They** can collect a surprising assortment of prizes in a short period of time.

EXERCISE 8-1 (8a–c) Read the following sentences carefully. Then reorder them into two coherently organized paragraphs. Note that transitional expressions may help. (*Hint*: The first paragraph contains five sentences.)

1. First, an automobile offers mobility into and out of the city, providing opportunities for brief and inexpensive reprieves from the bustle of metropolitan life.
2. Such difficulties are exacerbated during foul weather conditions.
3. For example, parking is consistently a hassle.
4. Each year, the frequency of auto theft and vandalism steadily rises in most cities.
5. It should be no surprise that most city dwellers decide to use public transit systems.
6. Besides these considerations, the continual threat of crime alarms many potential car owners.
7. Residents of rural and suburban areas rarely question whether or not they should own a car.
8. However, owning an automobile in a metropolitan area presents several problems.
9. The cost of private lots can be prohibitive, and finding spaces on the streets often seems impossible.
10. Like a home, an automobile is a basic requirement of life, and it comes with certain responsibilities, such as maintenance and insurance costs.
11. The very snowplows meant to clear lanes for drivers often bury their cars under deep banks of snow.
12. Finally, the percentage of automobile accidents in urban areas increases with the number of cars owned, so insurance rates generally exceed those in the suburbs.
13. When someone initially moves to an urban center, however, he or she must examine the advantages and disadvantages of keeping a car.

14. A car also allows one to travel to and from work with more comfort and privacy than buses or subways offer.

EXERCISE 9-1 **(9a–b)** The following paragraphs have coherence problems because of inconsistencies in number, person, and verb tense. Revise the passage to eliminate these inconsistencies. Example:

When most people think of Mardi Gras, ~~you~~ *they* automatically think of New Orleans. This city hosts the largest Mardi Gras celebration in the United States. Every year, tens of thousands of visitors from around the world ~~will~~ journey to "Fat City" to participate in the raucous festivities. Many tourists also attended the unique parades held in the smaller towns of southern Louisiana, where ~~you~~ *they* experienced a more personal version of Carnival.

1. Mardi Gras festivities in the United States began well over a century ago. Groups of revelers, or krewes, first celebrated Carnival in New Orleans in 1857. They not only organize parades filled with decorated floats, costumed marchers, and lively bands, but you hold elaborate costume balls as well.
2. Although the balls remain closed to the general public today, the parades entertain many people of all ages and backgrounds. The doubloons and colorful strings of beads tossed into the crowds from the floats are coveted prizes among schoolchildren in Louisiana. You can collect a surprising assortment of prizes in a short amount of time.
3. For many years, the krewes in New Orleans practice racial segregation. The city recently enacted laws to make selection to the secret societies more equitable. Most krewes also originally refused admission to women; however, a number of female krewes surfaced early in this century. Today, any resident can gain admission to a krewe, though they must pay the very high dues.
4. When you attend Mardi Gras in New Orleans for the first time, you should be prepared to face the dense crowds on the streets.

3. For many years, the krewes in New Orleans **practiced** racial segregation. The city recently enacted laws to make selection to the secret societies more equitable. Most krewes also originally refused admission to women; however, a number of female krewes surfaced early in this century. Today, any resident can gain admission to a krewe, though **he or she** must pay the very high dues.
4. When you attend Mardi Gras in New Orleans for the first time, you should be prepared to face the dense crowds on the streets. Once **you enter** the throngs of parade-watchers packing the sidewalks, you surrender a bit of your will to the masses. The crowd often exerts an uncanny control over the individuals in it. For this reason, **you** may find the parades more enjoyable from a distance; however, many people **find** losing themselves in these crowds an exciting aspect of the Carnival experience.

EXERCISE 9-2 (8a, 9a–b)

. . . Viewers generally meet this stock player in the first scene of any episode, and **they** rarely escape its monotonous influence before the end credits roll. In the brief span beween the punchline of the comfortingly familiar first gag and the lilt of the theme song over the opening montage, this character forcefully but subtly **introduces itself**. . . . The producers, it seems, have little faith in **their** audience's perceptive abilities.

Why do the studios insist on convincing viewers that the live audience **doubled** over at stale jokes? . . . Perhaps canned laughter causes an entirely different response in home viewers, assuring **them** that **they** need not think about the program at all.

Ultimately, the problem with canned laughter **stems** not so much from the illusion it attempts to promote, that real people are rolling with giggles in the studio, but from the producers' insistence that the viewers accept as humorous what the show tells **them is** humorous. Working under extreme time constraints and under the media's golden rule, "Never insult anyone who might be one of our sponsors," television sitcom writers rarely **find** producers interested in untried, complex, or controversial material. Producers want **them** to write scenarios and jokes

Once I entered the throngs of parade-watchers packing the sidewalks, you surrender a bit of your will to the masses. The crowd often exerts an uncanny control over the individuals in it. For this reason, they may find the parades more enjoyable from a distance; however, many people found losing themselves in these crowds an exciting aspect of the Carnival experience.

EXERCISE 9-2 (8a, 9a–b)

Read the following passage, searching for unnecessary shifts in number, person, and tense. As you read, look also for missing or misplaced transitional expressions and for inappropriate paragraph divisions. Revise the passage to eliminate these errors.

Most situation comedies share one common character. Viewers generally meet this stock player in the first scene of any episode, and you rarely escape its monotonous influence before the end credits roll. In the brief span between the punchline of the comfortingly familiar first gag and the lilt of the theme song over the opening montage, this character forcefully but subtly introduced themselves.

The laugh track chuckles its insidious assurance that what the viewer sees and hears is indeed humorous and possibly meaningful. The producers, it seems, have little faith in its audience's perceptive abilities.

Finally, why do the studios insist on convincing viewers that the live audience doubles over at stale jokes? Why not pay someone to write better scenes? Do the laugh tracks play a role other than telling the home audience when to grin? Perhaps canned laughter causes an entirely different response in home viewers, assuring you that you need not think about the program at all. The problem with canned laughter stemmed not so much from the illusion it attempts to promote, that real people are rolling with giggles in the studio, but from the producers' insistence that viewers accept as humorous what the show tells us was humorous. Working under extreme time constraints and under the media's golden rule, "Never insult anyone who might be one of our sponsors," television sitcom writers rarely found producers interested in untried, complex, or controversial material. Producers want you to write scenarios and jokes with proven marketability. Unfortunately, this unwritten policy doesn't lend themselves to creative writing or engaging viewing.

But why did canned laughter work? Even newcomers to television viewing can usually distinguish live studio laughter from canned chuckles if we are asked to differentiate between the two.

And almost anyone aware of this distinction will admit that they prefer either live response or none at all to the standard laughs tracks recorded over the action of the show. However, these same viewers also concur after watching two episodes of the same program, one with canned laughter and one without, that the show seems less humorous and less entertaining without the prerecorded tracks. In other words, the program itself may not be very interesting, but the laugh tracks make watching them more bearable. Canned laughter kept the viewer on the sofa, the advertisers in line, and the producers in business. Unfortunately, it did not improve the quality of television programming.

EXERCISE 10-1 (10d) Read the passage below carefully. Then divide it into paragraphs that format dialogue properly. Example:

"All right, everyone!" Julio shouted. "Whose turn was it to feed Toby?" He waited for an answer from upstairs. "Come on. I know you heard me." Juanita called, "It was Hector's turn." Bounding down the stairs, Hector quickly countered, "No, no! It was Juanita's month to feed him."

Juanita soon joined Hector and Julio in the basement. For a moment, they stared anxiously at Toby. Their pet lay resting a bit too quietly in his cage. "I fed him in January," Julio stated emphatically, "when I had so much trouble finding food after the holidays." "February was my month," Juanita exclaimed. "I tried to feed him chocolates from my Valentine box. Remember?" "Oh, yeah," the brothers answered simultaneously, rolling their eyes at each other. Their mother stepped into the doorway. "I minded him in March, while you were visiting your grandmother, though I'd sworn I would never do it," she said. "You're right. Thank you, Mother," Juanita responded. "You're welcome. But who forgot to feed Toby this month?" Everyone turned to Hector. "I never wanted a pet python anyway!" he yelled. "How can you say that, Hector? You begged Mama to get Toby for us," Julio argued,

with proven marketability. Unfortunately, this unwritten policy doesn't lend **itself** to creative writing or engaging viewing.

But why **does** canned laughter work? Even newcomers to television viewing can usually distinguish live studio laughter from canned chuckles if **they** are asked to differentiate between the two. And almost anyone aware of this distinction will admit that **he or she prefers** either live response or none at all to the standard laughs tracks recorded over the action of the show. . . . In other words, the program itself may not be very interesting, but the laugh tracks make watching **it** more bearable. Canned laughter **keeps** the viewer on the sofa, the advertisers in line, and the producers in business. Unfortunately, it **does** not improve the quality of television programming.

EXERCISE 10-1 (10d)

The following sentences start new paragraphs:

Juanita soon joined Hector and Julio in the basement. . . .

"I fed him in January," Julio stated emphatically, "when I had so much trouble finding food after the holidays."

"February was my month," Juanita exclaimed. . . .

"Oh yeah," the brothers answered simultaneously, rolling their eyes at each other.

Their mother stepped into the doorway. . . .

"You're right. Thank you, Mother," Juanita responded.

"You're welcome. . . ."

Everyone turned to Hector. . . .

"How can you say that, Hector? . . ." . . .

"I didn't know I'd have to feed him *live* mice," Hector whispered, wiping his eyes. . . .

EXERCISE 11-1 (11a–b)

Possible revisions:

1. In 1986, scientists discovered a stone monument covered with epi-Olmec hieroglyphics, **but no** one had yet successfully translated the language.
2. The basalt monument, or stela, contained the earliest complex writing found in the Americas, **so researchers** worked diligently. . . .
3. **Although the** Olmecs did not construct any major cities, they developed numerous trade routes, **many still in use today,** from the Gulf of Mexico to the Pacific Ocean.
4. The hieroglyphics tell the story of an Olmec king, Harvest Mountain Lord, **and** how he won the throne. . . .
5. The deciphering of the Olmec text, **a rare and exciting archaeological event,** helped researchers map important steps in the development of Native American language.

though he stopped when he saw that his brother was crying. "Are you okay?" he kindly asked. "I didn't know I'd have to feed him *live* mice," Hector whispered, wiping his eyes. "I thought we could buy snake food in cans."

EXERCISE 11-1 (11a–b) Combine the sentences in the following items by coordinating ideas of equal importance or by subordinating minor ideas. There are several possible revisions for each entry, and you must choose which points to emphasize. Example:

Archaeologists recently deciphered the written language of the ancient Olmecs. ~~Their~~ $\stackrel{\text{, whose}}{}$ civilization thrived along the southern Gulf of Mexico from the 1200 to 500 B.C.

1. In 1986, scientists in Veracruz discovered a stone monument covered with epi-Olmec hieroglyphics. No one had yet successfully translated the language.
2. The basalt monument, or stela, contained the earliest complex writing found in the Americas. Researchers worked diligently to decode the delicate carvings.
3. The Olmecs did not construct any major cities. They developed numerous trade routes from the Gulf of Mexico to the Pacific Ocean. Many of these are still in use today.
4. The hieroglyphics tell the story of an Olmec king. His name was Harvest Mountain Lord. They tell how he won the throne in a series of wars.
5. The deciphering of the Olmec text helped researchers map important steps in the development of Native American language. It was a rare and exciting archaeological event.

EXERCISE 11-2 (11a–e) Change the emphasis in each of the following items. That is, revise the sentences so that the subordinate idea becomes emphasized in an independent clause and the main idea becomes subordinated in a dependent clause. Example:

Though my
~~My~~ parents faced difficulties during the first years of their marriage, ~~though~~ they act like newlyweds today.

1. My mother, who finally received her bachelor's degree last year, quit college when she married my father.
2. They were building a new house in the suburbs when their business collapsed.
3. Mom's parents generously allowed my folks to live with them, although Dad and Grandpa argued every day the first two weeks.
4. My mother convinced the men to stop fighting by refusing to speak with either of them for a month.
5. Mom and Dad's dream house, which they finally completed two years ago, is an exact replica of the one they started building after their wedding.

EXERCISE 12-1 (12a–c) Revise the following sentences to eliminate errors in parallelism. Example:

My hobbies include roller-blading, skiing, and horses. *horseback riding*

1. I sometimes travel by roller blade to class, to work, and even church.
2. The resort where I ski offers lessons in downhill, cross-country, and in slalom.
3. The university stables employ student grooms for feeding the horses, polishing the tack, and the stalls are cleaned.
4. All three hobbies allow me to indulge my love for the outdoors, my passion for speed, and help me get needed exercise.
5. Unfortunately, my favorite pastimes—to skate, to ski, and riding—do not lend themselves to simultaneous enjoyment.

EXERCISE 12-2 (12d) Edit the following sentences to make the comparisons parallel. Example:

Myuko thinks changing her major would be easier than to take *taking*

Mr. Wasfi's course.

1. Henri assured her that passing the course would prove less difficult than to begin a new curriculum.
2. Her brother advised her to quit school rather than facing "Wacky" Wasfi's three-hour exams.

EXERCISE 11-2 (11a–e)
Possible revisions:

1. My mother, who quit college when she married my father, finally received her bachelor's degree last year.
2. Their business collapsed while they were building a new house in the suburbs.
3. Although Mom's parents generously allowed my folks to live with them, Dad and Grandpa argued every day the first two weeks.
4. My mother refused to speak with either of the men for a month, thereby convincing them to stop fighting.
5. Mom and Dad's dream house, an exact replica of the one they started building after their wedding, was finally completed two years ago.

EXERCISE 12-1 (12a–c)
Possible revisions:

1. I sometimes travel by roller blade to class, to work, and even **to** church.
2. The resort where I ski offers lessons in downhill, cross-country, **and slalom**.
3. The university stables employ student grooms for feeding the horses, polishing the tack, and **cleaning the stalls**.
4. All three hobbies allow me to indulge my love for the out-

Answers to Exercise 12-2 appear on page E-12.

doors, my passion for speed, and **my need for exercise**.

5. Unfortunately, my favorite pastimes—**skating**, **skiing**, and riding—do not lend themselves to simultaneous enjoyment.

EXERCISE 12-2 (12d)

Possible revisions:

1. Henri assured her that passing the course would prove less difficult than **beginning** a new curriculum.
2. Her brother advised her to quit school rather than **face** "Wacky" Wasfi's three-hour exams.
3. Myuko finally decided to leave the university **rather than** ruin her grade point average.
4. **Passing** quantum accounting seemed as likely as hurdling the moon.
5. Myuko will not only take your order at the burger stand, but **she will brag** about her perfect grades too.

EXERCISE 12-3 (12e)

Possible revisions:

1. Complete Section 1.
2. Have attending physician complete **Section** 2.
3. **Sign** on page 4, line 38.
4. **Attach** résumé detailing employment history for the past twelve years.
5. Enclose check for $75.

3. Myuko finally decided to leave the university instead of to ruin her grade point average.
4. To pass quantum accounting seemed as likely as hurdling the moon.
5. Myuko will not only take your order at the burger stand, but bragging about her perfect grades too.

EXERCISE 12-3 (12e) Edit the following items to eliminate parallelism errors. Example:

III. Guitar Heroes

   A. Rock

      1. Eric Clapton

      2. Stevie Ray Vaughn

      3. ~~Jimi Hendrix vs. Eddie Van Halen~~

        4. Eddie Van Halen

     5. 4. Steve Vai

   B. Jazz-fusion

      1. Wes Montgomery

      2. Al Di Meola

      3. John McLoughlin

      4. Stanley Jordan

      5. ~~Jazz guitar techniques~~ *(relocate)*

INSTRUCTIONS:

1. Complete Section 1.
2. Have attending physician complete section 2.
3. Signature on page 4, line 38.
4. attach résumé detailing employment history for the past twelve years.
5. Enclose check for $75.

6. We reserve the right to request additional information before issuing approval for compensation.

REQUIRED MATERIALS:

Two (2) Number 2 (#2) pencils, sharpened

Three (3) outside sources, including at least one (1) newspaper article.

Bring two (2) examination booklets, large.

Two reference books, unabridged.

EXERCISE 12-4 (12a–f) Revise the following passage to eliminate faulty parallelism.

International efforts to protect giant pandas and Asian tigers have proved less successful than those to some other species. Wildlife biologist George Schaller, who has written books on lions and gorillas and he lived among pandas in China for nearly a decade, argues that the conservation measures of the Chinese government, like those of many other nations, function more as a front for the exploitation of high-profile endangered species instead of a program for the protection of key natural habitats. For example, while less than a thousand giant pandas exist in the wild, China continues to trap, confine, and to relocate these animals as loans to zoos that are willing to pay approximately a million dollars per year for a mating pair. Similarly, the state-owned Chinese National Native Produce Corporation encourages the trapping and shooting of most wildlife species commanding an international market, including the Asian tiger. Some reports indicate that these great cats no longer exist in the wild, but thriving on commercial breeding farms. The species' survival now depends on a strong market for tiger by-products and the possibility of successfully reintroducing large numbers of the tigers to their former habitat.

Extinction through sanctioned exploitation once threatened the American bison, alligator, and the puma in the United States, but pressure by domestic and international environmental groups forced the government to enact tougher conservation guidelines that have substantially increased the odds of survival for these species. International conservation efforts must focus on convincing nations to strengthen poaching penalties, protect natural habitats, and to regulating captivity trapping if "marketable" endangered species are to escape extinction.

We reserve the right to request additional information before issuing approval for compensation.

Two (2) Number 2 (#2) pencils, sharpened

Three (3) outside sources, including at least one (1) newspaper article [no period]

Two (2) examination booklets, large [no period]

Two **(2)** reference books, unabridged

EXERCISE 12-4 (12a–f)
Possible revision:

International efforts to protect giant pandas and Asian tigers have proved less successful than those to **protect** some other species. Wildlife biologist George Schaller, who has written books on lions and gorillas and **who** lived among pandas in China for nearly a decade, argues that the conservation measures of the Chinese government . . . function more as a front for the exploitation of high-profile endangered species **than** a program for the protection of key natural habitats. . . . China continues to trap, confine, **and relocate** these animals as loans to zoos that are willing to pay approximately a million dollars per year for a mating pair. . . . Some reports indicate that these great cats no longer exist in the wild, **though they thrive** on commercial breeding farms. The species' survival now depends on a strong market for tiger by-products

and **on** the possibility of successfully reintroducing large numbers of the tigers to their former habitat.

Extinction . . . once threatened the American bison, **the** alligator, and the puma in the United States. . . . International conservation efforts must focus on convincing nations to strengthen poaching penalties, pro-tect natural habitats, and **regulate** captivity trapping. . . .

EXERCISE 13-1 (13a–b)

Possible revisions:

1. My sister, Meadow, inherited the Grateful Dead album collection that she listens to constantly from my Aunt Dove.
2. During her sophomore year, Aunt Dove traveled to almost a hundred of the band's concerts.
3. One of her boyfriends legally changed his name from Field Vitolito to Jerry Garcia because he loved the Dead so much.
4. A police officer arrested Dove and her roommate, Sunrise, while they danced across the stage during a show in Portland.
5. Returning to school in Dove's Volkswagen Beetle, Sunrise could not recall which band member she had kissed.

EXERCISE 13-2 (13c–d)

Possible revisions:

1. Recalling my awful dream, **I felt** my pulse **racing** wildly.

EXERCISE 13-1 (13a–b) Revise the following sentences by relocating the misplaced or awkwardly placed modifiers. Example:

I stood behind six barefoot Dead Heads ^*with Gold Cards* waiting in line for the automatic teller at the student union ~~with Gold Cards~~.

1. My sister, Meadow, inherited the Grateful Dead album collection from my Aunt Dove that she listens to constantly.
2. During her sophomore year, Aunt Dove almost traveled to a hundred of the band's concerts.
3. One of her boyfriends changed his name from Field Vitolito to Jerry Garcia because he loved the Dead so much, legally.
4. While dancing across the stage during a show in Portland, a police officer arrested Dove and her roommate, Sunrise.
5. Sunrise could not recall which band member she had kissed returning to school in Dove's Volkswagen Beetle.

EXERCISE 13-2 (13c–d) Revise the following sentences to eliminate dangling and squinting modifiers. Example:

Waking from a nightmare, ^*I saw* the full moon *glaring* ~~glared~~ eerily into my room.

1. Recalling my awful dream, my pulse raced wildly.
2. My psychologist advised me specifically to record the events in my dreams.
3. After reading Freud's *Interpretation of Dreams,* tranquilizers must be taken at bedtime.
4. I once awoke screaming from a nightmare in which Frankenstein's monster warned me immediately to wake up before Dracula bit me.
5. Sleeping only four hours a night, fatigue still seems preferable to my horrible dreams.

EXERCISE 13-3 (13e) Revise the following sentences to eliminate awkward split infinitives. In some sentences the split infinitive may not be awkward and revision may not be necessary. Example:

, after an hour's deliberation,
Mamut bought two pairs of boots because he was unable to, after

an hour's deliberation, choose which color looked best on him.

1. Mamut's indecisiveness dates from childhood, when he could not decide whether or not to loudly applaud with his sister at the end of *Sesame Street*.
2. His parents always dreaded taking him to Picadilly Cafeteria, his favorite restaurant, because he loved to ravenously sample every dish they offered.
3. After applying to more than three dozen colleges, Mamut was relieved to ultimately discover that he had been accepted by only one school.
4. Mr. Watkins, his academic adviser for three years, finally convinced Mamut to tentatively pursue a major course of study.
5. Mamut completes computer-graded examinations much more rapidly if he remembers to only take one pencil to a test.

EXERCISE 13-4 (13a–e) Revise the following passage to eliminate problems with modifiers and split infinitives. (Some revisions are optional.)

Gene therapy, a medical application of genetic engineering, promises to eventually eliminate many of our most incapacitating ailments. After three decades of intensive research, the complex structure of human chromosomes and the location of particular genes within those chromosomes are being illuminated. Every human chromosome houses over 100,000 genes, and each gene functions to individually define one or more traits in the body. Researchers can now pinpoint the location of only 2,000 genes, but they expect to precisely locate almost twice that number soon. The recently launched Human Genome Project will attempt carefully to chart the genetic composition of the human body during the next ten to twenty years. Including many birth defects, scientists have linked particular gene locations with a number of crippling and lethal diseases. Genes associated with muscular dystrophy, cystic fibrosis, and several forms of cancer have been isolated in laboratories, which baffled the medical profession for years. Once preventive and therapeutic techniques to replace or to perhaps mutate these genes are developed, humans may no longer fall victim to diseases lurking savagely in their inherited genetic structure.

2. My psychologist **specifically** advised me to record the events in my dreams.
3. After reading Freud's *Interpretation of Dreams*, **I needed to take** tranquilizers at bedtime.
4. I once awoke screaming from a nightmare in which Frankenstein's monster warned me to wake up **immediately** before Dracula bit me.
5. Sleeping only four hours a night, **I still prefer** fatigue to my horrible dreams.

EXERCISE 13-3 (13e)
Possible revisions:

1. . . . whether or not **to applaud loudly** . . . [or leave as is]
2. . . . he loved **to sample ravenously** . . . [or leave as is]
3. . . . Mamut was **ultimately relieved to discover** . . .
4. . . . convinced Mamut **to pursue tentatively** . . . [or leave as is]
5. . . . if he remembers **to take only** one pencil . . .

EXERCISE 13-4 (13a–e)
Possible revision:

Gene therapy, a medical application of genetic engineering, promises **eventually to eliminate** many of our most incapacitating ailments. After three decades of intensive research, **scientists are illuminating** the complex structure of human chromosomes and the location of particular genes

within those chromosomes. . . . Researchers can now pinpoint the location of only 2,000 genes, but they expect **to locate precisely** almost twice that number soon.

The recently launched Human Genome Project will attempt to chart the genetic composition of the human body **carefully** during the next ten to twenty years. **Scientists** have linked particular gene locations with a number of crippling and lethal diseases, **including many birth defects.** Genes associated with muscular dystrophy, cystic fibrosis, and several forms of cancer, **which baffled the medical profession for years,** have been isolated in laboratories. Once preventive and therapeutic techniques to replace or **perhaps to mutate** these genes are developed, humans may no longer fall victim to **savage** diseases lurking in their inherited genetic structure.

EXERCISE 14-1 (14a–d)

Answers will vary. Possible answers:

1. *Varying sentence length:* "He loved gum." (short), "If she didn't watch him closely . . ." (long); *varying sentence openings:* "When the train started moving . . . ," "If she didn't watch him . . ."; *quotations:* "That's right, Arnold. . . ."

EXERCISE 14-1 (14a–d) Read the following passages carefully, noting the techniques the authors use to achieve sentence variety, such as varying sentence length, varying sentence openings, using transitional expressions, using inverted word order, and using commands, questions, and quotations. Underline and label examples of these techniques.

1.　　He hadn't been on a train before and acted a little nervous, bouncing up and down in his seat and flipping the lid of his ashtray and craning forward to see the man ahead of them. When the train started moving, he crowed and pulled at her sleeve. "That's right, Arnold. Train. We're taking a trip," Bet said. She unwrapped a stick of chewing gum and gave it to him. He loved gum. If she didn't watch him closely, he sometimes swallowed it—which worried her a little because she'd heard it clogged your kidneys; but at least it would keep him busy. She looked down at the top of his head. Through the blond prickles of his hair, cut short for practical reasons, she could see his skull bones moving as he chewed. He was so thin-skinned, almost transparent; sometimes she imagined she could see the blood traveling in his veins. [Anne Tyler, "Average Waves in Unprotected Waters"]

2.　　Mrs. Turpin stood there, her gaze fixed on the highway, all her muscles rigid, until in five or six minutes the truck reappeared, returning. She waited until it had time to turn into their own road. Then like a monumental statue coming to life, she bent her head slowly and gazed, as if through the very heart of mystery, down into the pig parlor at the hogs. They had settled all in one corner around the old sow who was grunting softly. A red glow suffused them. They appeared to pant with a secret life. [Flannery O'Connor, "Revelation"]

EXERCISE 14-2 (14a–d) Revise the following paragraph to develop variety in sentence structure using techniques suggested in 14. Add information or phrases as needed to enhance the passage.

My cousin Stevie was mean. His father, Lewis, was my uncle. I called him Unc. Even Unc called Stevie the meanest child he

had ever seen. Stevie loved to shoot his pellet gun at anything that felt pain. He learned early that I acknowledged pain. He thought the funniest sound in the world was a pellet ricocheting off my skull. He said the sound of me crying ranked second on his list. He thought the crunching noise my toys made under his boots would make him laugh. He never found the right crunch. He kept trying. He worked diligently at amusing himself. He would demand my newest treasure. He made me feel like his best friend. Stevie was always happy to see me.

EXERCISE 15-1 (15a) Revise the following sentences to eliminate mixed grammatical constructions. Example:

The notion that a celebrity's face legally qualifies as property,

which means that commercial reproduction of its image must be

authorized.

1. Although laws have long protected celebrities from unauthorized publication of their names or images, but not from mere allusions to the celebrities themselves in advertising.
2. For instance, when a television show featuring a new star can be spoofed on a commercial without the star's authorization.
3. At least that seemed to be the case until Vanna White filing suit against an electronics company whose advertisement parodied *Wheel of Fortune.*
4. White's attorney's argument was when the company's advertisement featured a robot based on her identity.
5. By making fun of celebrities risk lawsuits that could eat into advertisers' profits.

EXERCISE 15-2 (15b) Revise the following sentences to untangle mixed meaning. Example:

According to sociologists, research on the degree of intolerance to alternative lifestyles is rising alarmingly in the United States.

1. Studies indicate that Americans who favor protecting the rights of homosexuals may be dwindling.

2. *Varying sentence openings:* "Then like a monumental statue . . . ," "A red glow . . ."; *transition words:* "Then," "until"; *varying sentence length:* "Then like a monumental statue coming to life . . ." (long), "A red glow suffused them." (short)

EXERCISE 14-2 (14a–d)
Answers will vary.

EXERCISE 15-1 (15a)
Possible revisions:

1. **Laws** have long protected celebrities from unauthorized publication of their names or images but not from mere allusions to the celebrities themselves in advertising.
2. For instance, **a** television show featuring a new star can be spoofed on a commercial without the star's authorization.
3. At least that seemed to be the case until Vanna White **filed** suit against an electronics company whose advertisement parodied *Wheel of Fortune.*
4. White's attorney **argued that** the company's advertisement featured a robot based on her identity.
5. By making fun of celebrities**, advertisers** risk lawsuits that could eat into **their** profits.

Answers to Exercise 15-2 appear on page E-18.

EXERCISE 15-2 (15b)

Possible revisions:

1. Studies indicate that **the number of** Americans who favor protecting the rights of homosexuals may be dwindling.
2. Some sociologists, **practitioners of** a fairly new science, admit that these figures may reflect the outspokenness of individual groups rather than their relative size.
3. **Though polygamy remains illegal in most Western countries, having** several wives **is an emblem** of financial and social status **in many other cultures.**
4. A particular society's view of socially acceptable behavior may change over time; **for example, most Americans' impression of cigarette smoking changed from positive to negative** in recent years.
5. **Society** once placed a social stigma **on divorce.**

EXERCISE 15-3 (15c–d)

Possible revisions:

1. Wollstonecraft, along with her sisters and a friend, opened a new school in 1784, **which allowed** her to develop her theories on the education of women.
2. The proceeds from her first book, *Thoughts on the Education of Daughters*, **which** Wollstonecraft used to relocate the family of a deceased friend, amounted to only ten guineas.

2. Some sociologists, a fairly new science, admit that these figures may reflect the outspokenness of individual groups rather than their relative size.
3. In many cultures, several wives are emblems of financial and social status, though polygamy remains illegal in most Western countries.
4. A particular society's view of socially acceptable behavior may change over time, as when Americans' impression of cigarettes were considered negative in recent years.
5. When a couple was divorced once placed a social stigma on them by society.

EXERCISE 15-3 (15c–d) Edit the following sentences to eliminate errors in the use of *in which* and problems resulting from inappropriate noun-pronoun constructions. Example:

> Mary Wollstonecraft, whose writings became important texts for women's rights movements, she wrote *A Vindication of the Rights of Woman* in 1792.

1. Wollstonecraft, along with her sisters and a friend, opened a new school in 1784, in which it allowed her to develop her theories on the education of women.
2. The proceeds from her first book, *Thoughts on the Education of Daughters,* in which Wollstonecraft used to relocate the family of a deceased friend, amounted to only ten guineas.
3. Wollstonecraft, whose translations and reviews earned her an outstanding reputation during the early 1790s, she composed several major political tracts in response to the French Revolution.
4. Her well-publicized love affairs, personal scandals, and suicide attempts threatened to overshadow her literary accomplishments, in which she was established as one of the great thinkers of her era.
5. Wollstonecraft died eleven days after the birth of her daughter, Mary Godwin, who as an adult she wrote the horror classic *Frankenstein.*

EXERCISE 15-4 (15e) Revise the following sentences to eliminate ambiguity caused by omitted words or incomplete comparisons. Example:

to
My eyes were drawn but repulsed by the works in the art show at the new campus gallery.

1. Several of the photographs were frightening, but the video dazzling.
2. The artist, whose name I've forgotten, suggested in an interview no one should eat prior to viewing her artwork.
3. The violent images were beautifully rendered, whereas the single landscape garishly tinted.
4. Some artists are more willing to risk alienating viewers than others.
5. When the painter failed to appear at the opening, the gallery director hinted the artist feared contact with humans.

EXERCISE 16-1 (16a) Revise the following sentences to eliminate mistakes in usage. Look for incorrect homophones, unacceptable phrases, and misuses of ordinary words. Example:

Although he had appeared as a peripheral character in other
accept
comics, Krazy Kat refused to except a title role in a comic strip before 1913.

1. Hearst Publications began running full-page Krazy Kat cartoons in its weekly magazine in 1916, therefore establishing George Herriman, the strip's creator, as the utmost cartoonist of his day.
2. Alot of readers found the longer weekly strip more confusing then the more concise and more conservative daily version.
3. Herriman lived in New Mexico, and he usually set his Krazy Kat weeklies in the magnificent desserts of that state to.
4. Often the geography of the landscape would transform magically behind the lovelorn feline as Ignatz Mouse would try and clobber the cat with a brick.
5. Krazy certainly must of been a masochist; ever week he waited hopefully for Ignatz's love brick to bounce off his skull.

EXERCISE 16-2 (16b) Revise the following entries to correct problems with prepositions. Example:

3. Wollstonecraft, whose translations and reviews earned her an outstanding reputation during the early 1790s, **composed** several major political tracts in response to the French Revolution.
4. Her well-publicized affairs, personal scandals, and suicide attempts threatened to overshadow her literary accomplishments, **which established her** as one of the great thinkers of her era.
5. Wollstonecraft died eleven days after the birth of her daughter, Mary Godwin, who as an adult **wrote** the horror classic *Frankenstein.*

EXERCISE 15-4 (15e)

Possible revisions:

1. Several of the photographs were frightening, but the video **was** dazzling.
2. The artist, whose name I've forgotten, suggested in an interview **that** no one should eat prior to viewing her artwork.
3. The violent images were beautifully rendered, whereas the single landscape **was** garishly tinted.
4. Some artists are more willing to risk alienating viewers than others **are**.
5. When the painter failed to appear at the opening, the gallery director hinted **that** the artist feared contact with humans.

Answers to Exercise 16-1 and 16-2 appear on page E-20.

EXERCISE 16-1 (16a)

Possible revisions:

1. thereby *instead of* therefore; pre-eminent *instead of* utmost
2. Many *instead of* Alot; than *instead of* then
3. deserts *instead of* desserts; too *instead of* to
4. to *instead of* and
5. have *instead of* of; every *instead of* ever

EXERCISE 16-2 (16b)

Possible revisions:

1. . . . a disorder **of** the growth hormones.
2. . . . and weighed **over** 275 pounds.
3. . . . the best opportunity **for** long-term public exposure.
4. . . . André became interested **in** acting.
5. Though he died **at** a young age, André led a full life highlighted **by** travel, fame, and leisure.

EXERCISE 16-3 (16c)

Possible revisions:

1. Frequent alcohol use has little impact on certain people, yet even moderate **consumption** can lead others to addiction.
2. **Approximately** thirty percent of college freshmen claim to have drinking problems, but only one-quarter of these students express concern about their potential for alcoholism.

André the Giant, one of the largest and most popular **professional** wrestlers in history, died in 1993 with *of* a heart attack.

1. Born in France, André René Roussimoff developed **acromegaly**, a disorder to the growth hormones.
2. At sixteen, he already stood six foot seven and weighed **above** 275 pounds.
3. A friend suggested that he might capitalize on his size by pursuing a career in professional sports, and André concluded that wrestling would offer him the best opportunity on long-term public exposure.
4. After achieving worldwide fame and accumulating a fortune in wrestling, André became interested by acting.
5. Though he died in a young age, André led a full life **highlighted** in travel, fame, and leisure.

EXERCISE 16-3 (16c) Rewrite the following sentences to eliminate awkward repetition. Example:

While *A* alcohol often serves as a social lubricant, *but* its effects can be fatal if experienced while driving.

1. Frequent alcohol use has little impact on certain **people**, yet even moderate use can lead others to addiction.
2. About thirty percent of college freshmen claim to have **drinking** problems, but only about one-quarter of these students express concern about their potential for alcoholism.
3. Most universities want to create an atmosphere for exploration and experimentation, but most report that alcohol- and drug-related incidents account for most of the violent crime and vandalism on their campuses.
4. Along with routine and emergency health care, most **universities** also offer counseling and therapeutic services for **students** experiencing problems associated with alcohol **and** also with other addictive substances.
5. Many universities used to offer few alcohol abuse **services** because the legal drinking age in most states used to be eighteen; as a result, the schools used to deem themselves less **responsible** for alcohol consumption among their **undergraduates**.

EXERCISE 16-4 (16d–e) Edit the sentences below to eliminate redundancy. Also, minimize wordiness by removing intensifiers and expletive constructions. Example:

> Horse races very often generate more excitement and thrills for gamblers than for people who are merely spectators.

1. Most Americans watch only one race each year, the annual running of the Kentucky Derby, held each year at Churchill Downs.
2. There were a number of racing accidents during the past several seasons that resulted in the death and destruction of several extremely valuable horses.
3. It was nearly twenty years ago that the uniquely outstanding filly Ruffian suffered a fatal fracture during a nationally televised match race at Belmont Park in 1975.
4. Following a series of unlucky and unfortunate racing accidents broadcast nationally on national television in the past several few years, many fans began to come to agreement that some type of racing reforms had become essentially necessary to protect mounts and jockeys from devastating racing injuries.
5. It was veteran jockey Ron Turcotte who guided the exceedingly talented Secretariat to Triple Crown fame, but it was also Turcotte who later suffered paralysis as a result of a racing accident.

EXERCISE 16-5 (16f–g) Revise the following sentences to eliminate prefabricated phrases and excessive humility. Example:

> *I   fair*
> In my humble opinion, it seems crystal clear that the winner of the
>
> class's weekly spelling bee should be exempt from Friday's quiz.

1. As you might have guessed, I feel that spelling proficiency reveals an honest measure of sophistication.
2. I think I earned my fifth consecutive spelling bee title through hard work and dedication and by bribing the teacher.
3. Calm and collected, I approach each week's trial with eager enthusiasm.
4. The ability to spell words properly under the most trying of circumstances may be my most impressive quality, if I do say so myself.

3. Most universities want to create an atmosphere for exploration and experimentation, but **many** report that alcohol- and drug-related incidents account for **much** of the violent crime and vandalism on their campuses.
4. Along with routine and emergency health care, most universities also offer counseling and therapeutic services for students experiencing problems associated with alcohol **and other** addictive substances.
5. Many universities **once offered** few alcohol abuse services because the legal drinking age in most states **was** eighteen; as a result, the schools **deemed** themselves less responsible for alcohol consumption among their undergraduates.

EXERCISE 16-4 (16d–e)
Possible revisions:

1. Most Americans watch only one race each year, the annual running of the Kentucky **Derby at** Churchill Downs.
2. **Racing** accidents during the past **few** seasons **led to the loss** of **several valuable** horses.
3. **Nearly** twenty years ago**, the outstanding** filly Ruffian suffered a fatal fracture during a nationally televised match race at Belmont **Park.**

Answers to Exercise 16-5 appear on page E-22.

4. Following a series **of unfortunate** racing accidents **broadcast on** national television in the **past few** years, many fans began **to agree that racing** reforms **were necessary** to protect mounts and jockeys from **devastating injuries.**

5. **Veteran** jockey Ron Turcotte **guided the talented** Secretariat to Triple Crown fame, **but he was later** paralyzed after a racing accident.

EXERCISE 16-5 (16f–g)
Possible revisions:

1. **Spelling** proficiency **reveals sophistication.**
2. **I** earned my fifth consecutive spelling bee **title by** bribing the teacher.
3. **I** approach each week's trial **with enthusiasm.**
4. The ability to **spell may** be my most impressive **quality.**
5. **If you want** my assistance in training for upcoming spelling **bees, I** have set up a telephone hot line.

EXERCISE 16-6 (16h)
Most logical choices:

1. secret
2. unsightly
3. firm
4. highlight; covering
5. scent

5. I have the sneaking suspicion that you might want to request my assistance in training for upcoming spelling bees as an investment in your future, so for your convenience I have set up a telephone hot line.

EXERCISE 16-6 (16h) Underline the word in brackets that offers the most logical connotation in each sentence. A dictionary and a thesaurus may prove helpful in this exercise. Example:

Mother claims that my rigorous personal hygiene regimen attests to our family's sense of [**pride/vanity/arrogance**].

1. I insist that my dentist fill my cavities with porcelain to prevent anyone from discovering my [**concealed/latent/secret**] history of tooth decay.
2. Adding mouthwash to your shampoo helps battle [**gross/ugly/unsightly**] plaque buildup on your roots.
3. When shaving, apply [**firm/intense/unyielding**] pressure to the skin.
4. Cosmetics can [**heighten/highlight/intensify**] one's best features while [**covering/masking/veiling**] one's flaws.
5. Never allow your cologne to overpower your natural [**odor/scent/smell**].

EXERCISE 16-7 (16i) Identify the incorrect use of idiom in the following sentences and rewrite using the correct form. You may need to consult a dictionary or other reference book. Example:

He had a difficult ditch to hoe as he tried to save enough money

for a three-week trip to Greece.

1. All his subtle stumbling around the bush failed to gain extra cash from his rich but self-absorbed uncle.
2. When a college friend in Salonika offered him a free place to stay, however, he decided to strike while the steel was hot.
3. He put his brow to the wheel, worked hard, and saved enough money to buy an airplane ticket.

4. The price of Turkish coffee in Greek restaurants really grabbed his goat.
5. After a week of overeating, he was slapped by a thought: any more Greek pastry, and he wouldn't be able to fit into the plane seat home.

EXERCISE 16-8 (16a–j) Edit the following paragraph, correcting any errors in word choice.

> "I'll admit that I'm so obsessed on food that alot of my friends call me Mr. Swine-out," he explained. "Because my hometown offers little in the way of restaurants in comparison to New York City, this weekend I'm planning to visit Greenwich Village and Brooklyn to. No doubt many delicious and luscious meals await for me. I'm certainly standing in need of some descent cheesecake, though no doubt native New Yorkers take such a desert for granite. Suspense bills: will my Southern ascent help waiters and waitresses except me as an endearing oddity, or will they deny me the pizza and tandoori chicken I want, need, and crave? There is little likelihood that my favorite drink, Dr Pepper, is being often ordered in a city so far north, so I'll try and make the best of Coca-Cola. It has less affect on my sensitive sinuses anyway." Drooling and waving goodbye, he moved at the door, a man obviously willing to give wild rein to his appetite.

EXERCISE 17-1 (17a) Revise the following sentences to eliminate sexist language. Example:

The town is so small and crime is so rare that the citizens employ few ~~policemen~~ *police officers*.

1. There is only a small squad of firemen as well.
2. Nevertheless, every mayor regards his position as one of great responsibility.
3. City councilmen have been meeting for generations in the Lazy Cow Café to discuss civic matters.
4. Despite a vociferous clamoring for refreshments, chairmen always insist on completing the business at hand before adjourning council meetings.

EXERCISE 16-7 (16i)
1. All his subtle **beating around the bush** . . .
2. . . . he decided to **strike while the iron was hot**.
3. He **put his shoulder to the wheel** . . .
4. The price of Turkish coffee . . . really **got his goat**.
5. After a week of overeating, he was **struck by a thought** . . .

EXERCISE 16-8 (16a–j)
Possible revision:
> "I'll admit that I'm so obsessed **with** food that **a lot** of my friends call me Mr. Swine-out," he explained. "Because my hometown offers **few** restaurants **compared to** New York City, this weekend I'm planning to visit Greenwich Village and Brooklyn **too**. No doubt many **delicious** meals **await me**. I'm **certainly in** need of some **decent** cheesecake, though no doubt native New Yorkers take such a **dessert** for **granted**. Suspense **builds**: will my Southern **accent** help waiters and waitresses **accept** me as an endearing oddity, or will they deny me the pizza and tandoori chicken **I crave**? **It's unlikely** that my favorite drink, Dr Pepper, is **ordered often** in a city so far north, so I'll try **to** make the best of Coca-Cola. It has less **effect** on my sensitive sinuses anyway." Drooling and waving goodbye, he moved **toward** the door, a man obviously willing to give **free** rein to his appetite.

Answers to Exercise 17-1 appear on page E-24.

EXERCISE 17-1 (17a)

Possible revisions:

1. firefighters *instead of* firemen
2. his or her *instead of* his
3. Members of the city council *instead of* City councilmen
4. chairs *instead of* chairmen
5. workers *instead of* girls; determinedly *instead of* manfully

EXERCISE 17-2 (17b–c)

Possible revisions:

1. Despite my cunning **use** of **rhythm**, I remained completely without fame.
2. **What contacts** must I **make** to **get** my poetry manuscript **accepted** for publication?
3. Literary magazines continued to reject my epic involving **evergreens** and **flowers**.
4. I decided that my only hope for **improvement** would be to **begin** lurking in coffeehouses, cultivating my beard, and hoping for some **lucky meeting** with a poetry editor.
5. Meanwhile, I'm sure you'll **enjoy** my latest lyric on **gardening**.

EXERCISE 17-3 (17d–e)

Possible revisions:

1. **His opinions are offensive**.
2. His views on the environment can hardly be considered **appealing**.
3. You've never seen such a **garish** wardrobe, with ties in col-

5. Rolling their eyes at the political rhetoric swirling through the café, the girls behind the lunch counter struggled manfully to repair the grease trap.

EXERCISE 17-2 (17b–c) Revise the following sentences to remove jargon or pretentious language. Use the dictionary to find simpler and clearer synonyms. Example:

I thought of all the unpublished poems I had ~~authored~~ *written* and wondered if I would ever ~~exit the state of~~ *escape* obscurity.

1. Despite my cunning utilization of spondees and trochees, I remained completely without fame.
2. With whom must I interface to facilitate the acceptance of my poetry manuscript for publication?
3. Literary magazines continued to reject my epic involving gymnosperms and corollas.
4. I decided that my only hope for amelioration would be to commence lurking in coffeehouses, cultivating my beard, and hoping for some fortuitous convergence with a poetry editor.
5. Meanwhile, I'm sure you'll find my latest lyric on floriculture most viable.

EXERCISE 17-3 (17d–e) Revise the following sentences by removing slang, obscenity, or profanity. Example:

Will that ~~old slob of a~~ politician ever retire?

1. I mean, like, he's got totally gross opinions.
2. His views on the environment can hardly be considered cool.
3. You've never seen such a tacky wardrobe, with ties in colors usually found on tropical blossoms.
4. Hell, even his speeches are boring, usually lasting for two hours.
5. In other words, it's time for someone to kick his butt.

EXERCISE 17-4 (17f–h) Rewrite these sentences by eliminating mixed metaphors, clichés, and archaic language. Example:

Fifi's coat was impressively groomed and as ~~white as snow~~.
(blindingly) written above "white as snow"

1. 'Twas fun to fit that poodle with a rhinestone collar and display her in the local obedience trials.
2. As Fifi competed, her purebred background bequeathed her a demeanor as cool as a cucumber.
3. I knew that if she and I pulled the oars together, we'd rise in triumph above the mongrel crowd.
4. By fall of even, Fifi had won a blue ribbon.
5. Only when Fifi's fangs turned on me with a paranoid petulance did I realize that beneath her prize-winning hide, she was rotten to the core.

EXERCISE 17-5 (17a–h) Revise the following paragraph to eliminate sexist language, mixed metaphors, pretentious language, slang, and clichés.

Any guy with taste would enjoy our local restaurant, the Basement. The aromas of feta-topped pizza certainly impact on a visitor's appetite, causing his stomach to commence growling. Prior to dinner, there is a plethora of imported beverages to choose from. The Evian is always selling like hotcakes. True, there's a lot of gross graffiti on the bathroom walls and the girls waiting tables are less than efficient, but the guitarist, reaching a full head of steam around midnight, hammers out some memorable melodies. Any dude can tell it's a killer place.

EXERCISE18-1 (18a) In each of the following sentences, identify each general and abstract expression; then rewrite the sentences using concrete language. (*Note:* The sentences can be corrected in a number of ways.) Example:

College is ~~different from~~ high school ~~in many ways~~.
(more demanding than) written above "different from"; *(academically as well as socially)* written above "in many ways"

1. If you want to get good grades in college, the main thing to keep in mind is that you must study hard.
2. In addition, putting extra work into assignments will pay off.
3. Writing well also helps.
4. Be a good student in class—or at least act like one.
5. Many students think that merely toeing the line will get them good grades, but most teachers reward independent thinking.

ors usually found on tropical blossoms.

4. **Even** his speeches are boring, usually lasting for two hours.
5. In other words, it's time for someone to **defeat him**.

EXERCISE 17-4 (17f–h)
Possible revisions:

1. **It was** fun to fit that poodle with a rhinestone collar and display her in the local obedience trials.
2. As Fifi competed, her purebred background **lent** her a **coolly controlled** demeanor.
3. I knew that if she and I **worked** together, we'd rise in triumph above the mongrel crowd.
4. By **evening**, Fifi had won a blue ribbon.
5. Only when Fifi's fangs turned on me with a paranoid petulance did I realize that beneath her prize-winning hide, she **possessed an evil nature**.

EXERCISE 17-5 (1a–h)
Possible revision:
Any **student** with taste would enjoy our local restaurant, the Basement. The aromas of feta-topped pizza certainly **whet visitors' appetites**, causing **their stomachs** to **begin** growling. **Before** dinner, there **are many** imported beverages to choose from. The Evian is always **popular**. True, there's a lot of **offensive** graffiti on the bathroom walls and
The answer to Exercise 18-1 appears on page E-26.

the **staff is** less than efficient, but the guitarist, **at best** around midnight, **strums** out some memorable melodies. **Certainly anyone** can tell it's a **festive** place.

EXERCISE 18-1 (18a)

Answers will vary.

EXERCISE 18-2 (18b)

Possible revisions:

1. Eighty-five major studies of television violence have **revealed** that violent television programs **cause** actual violence.
2. **In one study,** children in a town that had recently **been wired** for television **became** more violent **after watching** violent shows.
3. Another study **discovered** that murder rates **soared** after South Africa began to **receive** television programming in 1975.
4. A study **conducted** at the University of California at San Diego **revealed** that the national murder rate **climbed** to higher than normal levels for a week each time a boxing match was **televised**.
5. Almost all of the studies **concluded** that televised violence **desensitizes** viewers to real violence.

EXERCISE 18-2 (18b) Identify the weak, ineffective verbs in the following sentences and replace them with strong, evocative verbs. (*Note:* You may need to rewrite to eliminate wordy verb phrases or ambiguity.) Example:

Many people are ~~against~~ *oppose* violence on television.

1. Eighty-five major studies of television violence have shown that violent television programs have a direct causal relationship with actual violence.
2. One study showed that children in a town that had recently gotten television were negatively affected by violent shows.
3. Another study showed that murder rates in South Africa increased greatly after that country got television in 1975.
4. A study done at the University of California, San Diego, said that the national murder rate went up for a week each time a boxing match was shown on TV.
5. Almost all of the studies found that televised violence makes viewers insensitive to real violence.

EXERCISE 18-3 (18a–b) The following passage is a section of Annie Dillard's essay "Total Eclipse," rewritten in ambiguous, dull, weak language. Rewrite it to make it as concrete and evocative as you can; then compare your version with the original. Obviously, you will not write the same words as Dillard, but try to make your language as concrete as hers.

> The hotel lobby was a dark, narrow, stuffy room. We sat on a couch while the manager went upstairs to do something to our room. Beside us on a chair was a still, blond, middle-aged woman wearing a dress and a necklace. Her legs were crossed; she held her head on her hand. At the other side of the room sat some old men watching television. A couple of them seemed to be asleep. They were drunks. The man on the television said, "Number six!"

EXERCISE 19-1 (19a) In each of the following sentences, change the boldfaced noun so that it can be used first as a verb and then as an adjective. (*Note:* You do not have to retain the meaning of the original sentence.) Example:

I decided to go **hiking** in the Canadian Rockies this past summer.

Verb: I hiked in the Canadian Rockies this past summer.

Adjective: I bought new hiking boots before I went.

1. Many of the hiking trails in the Canadian Rockies pass through glacial basins, eerie valleys of gravel and ice created by thousands of years of **melting** and erosion.
2. **Climbing** on glaciers can be a dangerous sport unless one has the proper equipment.
3. At one easy-to-climb glacier, **warnings** placed around the bottom detailed the dangers of walking on glaciers, such as falling into the deep crevasses.

EXERCISE 19-2 (19b) As you read the following passage, underline each pronoun. If the pronoun has an antecedent, draw an arrow to that antecedent. Example:

Many people ignored the warnings, walking right past them and

climbing up onto the glacier.

Most of the people were wearing only light walking shoes; some of them were even wearing dress shoes! "Whoever gave them the idea that those would be appropriate for hiking on a glacier?" I thought to myself. However, I must admit that I myself followed them, and I was also wearing only light walking shoes. When I reached the first deep crevasse, I realized that I could easily fall into it without anyone seeing me disappear. I decided not to push my luck, so I got off the glacier as soon as I could, though not without scaring myself several times by slipping on the icy surface. Of course, only after I was on safe ground did I think that climbing the glacier had been fun.

EXERCISE 19-3 (19c) Insert the appropriate linking verb in the space provided. Example:

Though you will not often come upon the more dangerous wild animals while hiking in the Rockies, you ___*are*___ sure to find

EXERCISE 18-3 (18a–b)
The original version:

The hotel lobby was a dark, derelict room, narrow as a corridor, and seemingly without air. We waited on a couch while the manager vanished upstairs to do something unknown to our room. Beside us on an overstuffed chair, absolutely motionless, was a platinum-blond woman in her forties wearing a black silk dress and a strand of pearls. Her long legs were crossed; she supported her head on her fist. At the dim far end of the room, their backs toward us, sat six bald old men in their shirtsleeves, around a loud television. Two of them seemed asleep. They were drunks. "Number six!" cried the man on television, "Number six!" [Annie Dillard, "Total Eclipse"]

EXERCISE 19-1 (19a)
Possible answers:

1. *Verb:* Over thousands of years, glaciers **melted.** *Adjective:* **Melting** glaciers eroded the landscape.
2. *Verb:* Before people **climb** on glaciers, they should get the proper equipment. *Adjective:* Wear **climbing** shoes when you walk on glaciers.
3. *Verb:* At one easy-to-climb glacier, signs **warned** tourists of danger. *Adjective:* At one easy-to-climb glacier, **warning** signs detailed the dangers of walking on glaciers.

Answers to Exercises 19-2 and 19-3 appear on pages E-28 and E-29.

EXERCISE 19-2 (19b)

Most of the people were wearing only light walking shoes; some of them were even wearing dress shoes! "Whoever gave them the idea that those would be appropriate for hiking on a glacier?" I thought to myself. However, I must admit that I myself followed them, and I was also wearing only light walking shoes. When I reached the first deep crevasse, I realized that I could easily fall into it without anyone seeing me disappear. I decided not to push my luck, so I got off the glacier as soon as I could, though not without scaring myself several times by slipping on the icy surface. Of course, only after I was on safe ground did I think that climbing the glacier had been fun.

EXERCISE 19-3 (19c)

Possible answers:

1. sound *or* seem; is; is

plenty of "sign"—claw marks, paw or hoof prints, droppings, and other clues ___*are*___ everywhere.

1. It may _____ silly, but tracing wild animals _____ much more fun than actually seeing them—and it _____ certainly safer!
2. One day, we _____ hiking on a backwoods trail in Glacier National Park when we saw what _____ to be claw marks on a tree; the marks _____ long and deep.
3. The claw marks _____ like fresh pine sap; obviously, the bear had _____ there recently.
4. On the way back, we found what _____ like a fresh bear dropping, but since it _____ very fresh, we did not stop to investigate.
5. Thanks to the "bear bells" clipped to our jackets, we _____ safe; unfortunately, the bells made us _____ like cows, and we could not help _____ morbid and wondering whether we would _____ like a cow to a bear.

EXERCISE 19-4 (19c) Insert the appropriate helping verb, modal, or quasi-modal to accompany the boldfaced word. Example:

At all the campgrounds and information booths in the Rocky Mountains, you ___*will*___ **find** pamphlets warning, "This is bear country—all hikers ___*should*___ **be** extremely cautious.

1. The pamphlets tell you what you _____ **do** if a bear, especially a grizzly bear, approaches you.
2. You _____ not **run**—bears _____ **think** you are prey and chase you.
3. You _____ not **to look** the bear in the eyes, as it _____ **interpret** that as aggressive behavior.
4. You _____ **try** to slouch or bend at the knees and _____ **stand** sideways, as this _____ **make** you look less intimidating.
5. Walk slowly away from the bear until it _____ no longer **see** you.

6. Many people _____ rather **avoid** wilderness hiking altogether than risk meeting a grizzly.

EXERCISE 19-5 (19d) In the following sentences, underline the adjectives (including articles) and draw an arrow from each of them to the word it modifies. Examples:

The birds in this spectacular park are unusual and plentiful.

1. We saw beautiful black jays every morning.
2. In the fresh snow at the higher elevations, we saw white ptarmigans.
3. On a rocky cliff overlooking a glacial pool, purple finches were plentiful.
4. While we were picnicking beside a clear mountain stream, we saw a dipper walking on the bottom of the stream.
5. On the last day we were there, a glorious bald eagle soared over the park.

EXERCISE 19-6 (19e–f) In the following sentences, underline the adverbs and draw an arrow to the words or phrase they modify. Next, put parentheses around every prepositional phrase. Example:

Columbian ground squirrels, animals commonly seen (in the Canadian Rockies), visited our campsite almost every morning and waited patiently (for crumbs) to fall (from the table).

1. Determined to obey the strictly worded park rules, we steadfastly resisted the temptation to feed the squirrels.
2. This was difficult, especially when they stood on their hind feet gazing mournfully at us.
3. One day, having given up on us as a food source, a squirrel discovered a straw whisk broom and joyfully made off with it—with me hotly in pursuit.
4. Despite its hilariously unsuccessful attempts at getting the broom into its burrow, it was able to bite off a few straws for its dinner.

2. were; appeared; were
3. smelled; been
4. looked; seemed
5. felt; sound; being; taste

EXERCISE 19-4 (19c)
Possible answers:
1. should *or* ought to *or* had better
2. should; will *or* might *or* may
3. ought *or* are supposed; might
4. should; should *or* might *or* may *or* ought to *or* should
5. can
6. would

EXERCISE 19-5 (19d)

1. We saw beautiful black jays every morning.
2. In the fresh snow at the higher elevations, we saw white ptarmigans.
3. On a rocky cliff overlooking a glacial pool, purple finches were plentiful.
4. While we were picnicking beside a clear mountain stream, we saw a dipper walking on the bottom of the stream.
5. On the last day we were there, a glorious bald eagle soared over the park.

Answers to Exercise 19-6 appear on page E-30.

EXERCISE 19-6 (19e–f)

1. Determined to obey the strictly worded park rules, we steadfastly resisted the temptation to feed them.

2. This was difficult, especially when they stood (on their hind feet) gazing mournfully (at us).

3. One day, having given up (on us) (as a food source), a squirrel discovered a straw wisk broom and joyfully made off (with it)—(with me) hotly (in pursuit).

4. (Despite its hilariously unsuccessful attempts) (at getting) the broom (into its burrow), it was able to bite off a few straws (for its dinner).

EXERCISE 19-7 (19g)

Possible answers:

1. and; because
2. unless; whenever; and
3. After *or* When; and
4. Whether; but; as long as

EXERCISE 19-7 (19g)

In the following sentences, insert the correct coordinating or subordinating conjunctions. (See the box on page 213 for a list of subordinating conjunctions.) Example:

___*After*___ our experience with ground squirrels, we went to a new campground, ___*where*___ we were visited by a herd of elk.

1. The elk—nearly sixty mothers _____ their recently born calves—lived at the campsite _____ it was their traditional feeding ground.

2. _____ we wanted to be charged by a protective mother elk, _____ we wanted to get water, we had to scan the path to make sure it was clear _____ then walk as quickly as we could.

3. _____ campers had turned in at night, the elk would begin to feed around the tents, _____ some even slept only a few feet away from the sleepers in the tents.

4. _____ the elk minded sharing their space with humans, I don't know, _____ but they didn't seem to care _____ we humans behaved ourselves.

EXERCISE 20-1 (20a–h)

Read the following passage once; then read it again, looking for examples of each of the following sentence parts. (*Note:* There may be more than one example for each sentence part, but you need to choose only one. Do not choose the ones we have used in the example.) Example:

Subject: the Beatles (sentence 1)

Verb: were (sentence 1)

Subject	*Complement*
Verb	*Appositive phrase*
Direct object	*Parenthetical expression*
Indirect object	*Absolute phrase*
Prepositional phrase	

[1] In the music industry, the Beatles were the most commercially successful musical phenomenon in rock. [2] They became even bigger than Elvis Presley and eventually sold well over 100 million singles and 100 million albums. [3] A change made for the

better, their success turned the industry away from its preoccupation with individual singers who performed songs written by professional songwriters and toward music groups that performed original material. [4] The Beatles' rise, a spectacularly fast climb, enabled dozens of other English musicians to become popular and to express themselves musically. [5] This success, in the view of most critics, broke the American stranglehold on British popular music. [6] Perhaps most significant, the musical and songwriting advances that were pioneered by the Beatles gave critics a new view of rock music. [7] Critics considered rock music a valid art form. [Adapted from Brock Helander, *The Rock Who's Who* (New York: Shirmer Books, 1982), p. 29. Reprinted by permission.]

EXERCISE 21-1 (21a–b) Revise the following sentences to make subjects and verbs agree. Example:

When a tourist ask for a scenic, relaxing spot, I always recommend Hinton.

1. The mountains of southern West Virginia surrounds this small town on the New River.
2. The local farm vegetables—tomatoes, melons, corn—costs very little at roadside stands.
3. Often an angler risk the rapids of the New to fish for bass or bluegill.
4. Near the courthouse, Amy's Upper Crust, a restaurant in an old Victorian house, serve excellent Southern cooking.
5. At nearby Pipestem State Park, the contented visitor bask in the sun or play golf.

EXERCISE 21-2 (21c) Revise the following sentences so that subject and verb agree. Example:

The next time you visits Europe, be sure to see Vienna.

1. I loves to stop by the coffeehouses and absorb the relaxed atmosphere.
2. If you enjoys amusement parks, the Prater's Ferris wheel isn't far from the Danube.

EXERCISE 20-1 (20a–i)

Numbers indicate sentences in which words appear.

Subjects: 2–They; 3–success; 4–rise; 5–success; 6–advances; 7–Critics

Verbs: 2–became, sold; 3–turned, performed; 4–enabled; 5–broke; 6–were, pioneered, gave; 7–considered

Direct objects: 2–singles, albums; 3–industry, songs, material; 4–dozens; 5–stranglehold; 6–view; 7–rock music

Indirect objects: 6–critics

Prepositional phrases: 1–in the music industry, in rock; 2–than Elvis Presley [if *than* is considered as a preposition rather than a conjunction], over 100 million singles and 100 million albums; 3–for the better, from its preoccupation, with individual singers, by professional songwriters, toward music groups; 4–of other English musicians; 5–on British popular music; 6–by the Beatles, of rock music

Complements: 1–the most commercially successful musical phenomenon; 2–bigger

Appositive expressions: 4–a spectacularly fast climb

Parenthetical expressions: 5–in the view of most critics

Absolute phrases: 3–change made for the better

EXERCISE 21-1 (21a–b)

1. The mountains of southern West Virginia **surround** . . .

Answers to Exercise 21-2 appear on page E-32.

2. The local farm vegetables—tomatoes, melons, corn—**cost** very little . . .
3. Often an angler **risks** . . .
4. . . . Amy's Upper Crust, a restaurant in an old Victorian house, **serves** . . .
5. At nearby Pipestem State Park, the contented visitor **basks** . . .

EXERCISE 21-2 (21c)

1. I **love** to stop by the coffee-houses . . .
2. If you **enjoy** amusement parks . . .
3. At night, I **stroll** about the Hofburg Palace grounds . . .
4. When you **recover** your energy after jet lag . . .
5. At twilight, I **drive** up to the suburb of Grinzing . . .

EXERCISE 21-3 (21d–e)

1. He **is** usually out of bed around nine and lately **has** spent . . .
2. Until noon, he may **stay** at home . . .
3. At noon, Tom always feels he should **prepare** a decent lunch full . . .
4. He **has** lifted weights regularly for months and **has** worn tank tops to display his progress.
5. In the evenings, he might **sprawl** about . . .

EXERCISE 21-4 (21f)

1. Despite the Tidewater humidity, she **was** eager . . .

3. At night, I strolls about the Hofburg Palace grounds, trying to imagine how the imperial family must have lived.
4. When you recovers your energy after jet lag, climb the winding stairs to the top of the cathedral tower.
5. At twilight, I drives up to the suburb of Grinzing for the Wiener schnitzel and the violin music.

EXERCISE 21-3 (21d–e) Revise the following sentences to correct errors in subject-verb agreement. Example:

have
Tom's days this summer has followed a fairly simple schedule.

1. He are usually out of bed around nine and lately have spent a large part of the morning doing aerobics.
2. Until noon, he may stays at home to write journal entries or essays that no one will publish.
3. At noon, Tom always feels he should prepares a decent lunch full of carbohydrates to give him energy for his gym workout.
4. He have lifted weights regularly for months and have worn tank tops to display his progress.
5. In the evenings, he might sprawls about the humid house, watching television or playing with his pet ferret.

EXERCISE 21-4 (21f) Correct the following sentences by making subjects and verbs agree. Example:

If Cindy finishes this project, she will drives to Richmond for the weekend.

1. Despite the Tidewater humidity, she were eager to walk along the waterfront last summer.
2. The magnolias was still blooming on the grounds of the state capitol, and the many fountains was bubbling.
3. In the old House of Delegates were standing a statue of Robert E. Lee.
4. On this summer's visit, Cindy will tours the Poe House and its quaint sheltered gardens.
5. Along Monument Avenue was erected statues of Civil War generals.

EXERCISE 21-5 (21g) Revise the following sentences, correcting subject-verb agreement. Example:

Sylvia Plath, one of several confessional poets, refer often to the

New England coast in her works.

1. Plath, as well as her contemporary Anne Sexton, were from the Boston area.
2. The relentless fury of the Atlantic's rough waters are the subject of Plath's poem "Point Shirley."
3. A dead shark, together with other rubbish, were tossed into her grandmother's yard during a violent storm.
4. All attempts by her grandmother to keep order against such weather was doomed.
5. Plath seems to suggest that all civilization, including her grandmother's efforts, are fated for inevitable failure.

EXERCISE 21-6 (21h–j) Correct the sentences by eliminating problems with subject-verb agreement. Example:

In California, San Francisco and Berkeley each provides great entertainment for people watchers.

1. Purple beehive hairdos, scruffy beards, platform shoes, and many other oddities tends to surprise out-of-town visitors.
2. Burly men with silver earrings or a woman with a shaved scalp are likely to raise eyebrows in a city less cosmopolitan.
3. A group of neon-haired demonstrators waving big signs often frighten passers-by.
4. Nevertheless, most of the colorful locals is harmless, simply trying to escape boredom by shocking people.
5. Some of the local residents visits Market Street simply to watch the tourists react.

EXERCISE 21-7 (21k–l) Correct the following sentences so that subject and verb agree. Example:

There *are* several cats in our household: Noir, Shannon, and Chessy.

1. Under the spruce tree in the front sleep the surly black cat Noir.

2. The magnolias **were** still blooming . . . and the many fountains **were** bubbling.
3. In the old House of Delegates **was** standing . . .
4. On this summer's visit, Cindy will **tour** the Poe House . . .
5. Along Monument Avenue **were** erected statues . . .

EXERCISE 21-5 (21g)

1. Plath, as well as her contemporary Anne Sexton, **was** from the Boston area.
2. The relentless fury of the Atlantic's rough waters **is** the subject of Plath's poem "Point Shirley."
3. A dead shark, together with other rubbish, **was** tossed into her grandmother's yard during a violent storm.
4. All attempts by her grandmother to keep order against such weather **were** doomed.
5. Plath seems to suggest that all civilization, including her grandmother's efforts, **is** fated for inevitable failure.

EXERCISE 21-6 (21h–j)

1. Purple beehive hairdos, scruffy beards, platform shoes, and many other oddities **tend** to surprise out-of-town visitors.
2. Burly men with silver earrings or a woman with a shaved scalp **is** likely to raise eyebrows in a city less cosmopolitan.

Answers to Exercise 21-7 appear on page E-34.

3. A group of neon-haired demonstrators waving big signs often **frightens** passersby.
4. Nevertheless, most of the colorful locals **are** harmless, simply trying to escape boredom by shocking people.
5. Some of the local residents **visit** Market Street simply to watch the tourists react.

EXERCISE 21-7 (21k–l)

1. Under the spruce tree in the front **sleeps** the surly black cat Noir.
2. Shannon's favorite midnight snack **is** chicken and giblets.
3. Through the house **stalks** the lanky baby of the trio, Chessy, who loves to chase a snarling Shannon from room to room.
4. There **are** certain times when Chessy grows so obnoxious that we must spray him with a water pistol.
5. The cats' only fear **is** the Gross children, who run wild without discipline.

EXERCISE 21-8 (21a–n)

Possible revision:

One of those experiences that **are** impossible to forget **is** a weekend in Manhattan. Five or six miles of steady walking **is** not an unusual amount, for the famous sights of such a huge city **are** widely scattered about the island. Each of the neighborhoods **boasts** its own charms, which you discover if you remain observant. In Chelsea, one

2. Shannon's favorite midnight snack are chicken and giblets.
3. Through the house stalk the lanky baby of the trio, Chessy, who loves to chase a snarling Shannon from room to room.
4. There is certain times when Chessy grows so obnoxious that we must spray him with a water pistol.
5. The cats' only fear are the Gross children, who run wild without discipline.

EXERCISE 21-8 (21a–n) Edit the following paragraph for problems with subject-verb agreement.

One of those experiences that is impossible to forget are a weekend in Manhattan. Five or six miles of steady walking are not an unusual amount, for the famous sights of such a huge city is widely scattered about the island. Each of the neighborhoods boast its own charms, which you discover if you remain observant. In Chelsea, one can visits the Chelsea Hotel, where author Thomas Wolfe, poet Dylan Thomas, and musician Joni Mitchell has stayed. Nearby there is a number of great bagel shops for either tourists or any local who are famished for a solid snack. The area around New York University, in addition to Ukrainian diners and Italian espresso bars, offer quiet side streets as well. Cheap plastic items along Canal Street, Soho's granite sidewalks and art galleries, and the ginseng shops and fish markets of Chinatown each seizes your attention. Seven dollars are the average price of a spicy Indian dinner on Sixth Street. The view of the city from the Brooklyn Bridge's windswept heights are certainly one of the world's most impressive sights.

EXERCISE 22-1 (22a–b) Revise the following sentences by giving each pronoun one clear antecedent. Example:

On his vacation, Roberto visited Mountain Lake, a well-known resort; hiked to the Cascades, a nearby waterfall; and decided that *the week was worth the expense.* ~~it was all worth it.~~

1. The movie *Dirty Dancing* had been filmed at Mountain Lake, all around the old stone lodge, which impressed him greatly.

2. Enjoying the superb Sunday brunch and walking around the hemlock-edged lake—it was memorable indeed.
3. The Cascades were located high in the mountains, and Roberto found them the most beautiful sight of all.
4. On the fern-lined trail, he ran across only one other higher, and he pointed out the thimbleberries' violet blossoms.
5. Below the waterfalls' torrents, children splashed in the chilly pools, and they glistened in the sun.

EXERCISE 22-2 (22c–d) Rewrite the following sentences to eliminate implied or distant antecedents. Example:

Adrienne Rich*, who is one of the most respected poets today,* grew up in Baltimore, Maryland *who is one of the most respected poets today.*

1. Her third volume, *Snapshots of a Daughter-in-Law,* was published in 1962, which clearly reveals her budding feminism.
2. As I studied her in the early 1980s, I knew it would influence my own work.
3. "Living in Sin" is often anthologized in literature textbooks, which deals with the painful contrast between expectations and reality.
4. "Diving into the Wreck" is dominated by underwater imagery, which is the title poem of her 1973 volume.
5. When you analyze her poetry, it's certain to deepen your appreciation of her talent and social awareness.

EXERCISE 23-1 (23a) Edit the following sentences to correct pronoun agreement errors involving gender, number, or person. Example:

Yolanda loved to read stories from *The Arabian Nights' Entertainments,* but they *she* often found the character's names difficult to pronounce.

1. Yolanda asked several friends for assistance, but he could not pronounce the names either.

can **visit** the Chelsea Hotel, where author Thomas Wolfe, poet Dylan Thomas, and musician Joni Mitchell **have** stayed. Nearby there **are** a number of great bagel shops for either tourists or any local who **is** famished for a solid snack. The area around New York University, in addition to Ukrainian diners and Italian espresso bars, **offers** quiet side streets as well. Cheap plastic items along Canal Street, Soho's granite sidewalks and art galleries, and the ginseng shops and fish markets of Chinatown each **seize** your attention. Seven dollars **is** the average price of a spicy Indian dinner on Sixth Street. The view of the city from the Brooklyn Bridge's windswept heights **is** certainly one of the world's most impressive sights.

EXERCISE 22-1 (22a–b)
Possible revisions:

1. The movie *Dirty Dancing* had been filmed at Mountain Lake, all around the old stone lodge, **a building that impressed him greatly**.
2. Enjoying the superb Sunday brunch and walking around the hemlock-edged lake—**both meal and scenery** were memorable indeed.
3. The Cascades were located high in the mountains, and Roberto found **those waterfalls** the most beautiful sight of all.

Answers to Exercise 22-2 and 23-1 appear on page E-36.

4. On the fern-lined trail, **Roberto** ran across only one other hiker, **who** pointed out the thimble-berries' violet blossoms.
5. Below the waterfalls' torrents, children splashed in the chilly pools, **which** glistened in the sun.

EXERCISE 22-2 (22c–d)

Possible revisions:

1. Her third volume, *Snapshots of a Daughter-in-Law*, **which clearly reveals her budding feminism**, was published in 1962.
2. **In the early 1980s, as I studied her work**, I knew it would influence my own.
3. "Living in Sin," **which deals with the painful contrast between expectations and reality**, is often anthologized in literature textbooks.
4. "Diving into the Wreck," **which is the title poem of her 1973 volume**, is dominated by underwater imagery.
5. **An analysis** of her poetry **is** certain to deepen your appreciation of her talent and social awareness.

EXERCISE 23-1 (23a)

Possible revisions:

1. they *instead of* he
2. she *instead of* you
3. she *instead of* it
4. he or she *instead of* they
5. They *instead of* It; they *instead of* it

2. Her brother, Delroy, suggested that you check the dictionary.
3. Although Yolanda found *Scheherazade* listed in several dictionaries, it could not locate *Schahriar,* the name of the sultan.
4. Yolanda decided to ask a librarian if they knew of any annotated editions of *The Arabian Nights' Entertainments*.
5. The librarian suggested several helpful texts. It provided the proper pronunciation of the characters' names, and it explained the historical context of the tales.

EXERCISE 23-2 (23b) Revise the following sentences to eliminate sexism in the use of pronouns. Example:

or she

Before a student chooses a career, he should realize that in many

others their lives.

professions, a single mistake can cost someone his life.

1. A nurse closely monitors the progress of her patients to supply the doctor with the information he requires.
2. Many difficult decisions must be made by a police officer in the instant before he fires his weapon.
3. As part of a team, each firefighter knows the other firefighters depend on him for their safety.
4. While the jury decides the innocence or guilt of a defendant, the judge realizes that only he can sentence someone to death.
5. Even a grade school teacher or a flight attendant understands the pressure of people entrusting their lives to her every day.

EXERCISE 23-3 (23c) Revise the following sentences so that the pronouns agree with their antecedents. You will need to consider whether the pronouns should be singular or plural. Some sentences may be correct as written. Example:

Larry, Moe, and Curly, better known as the Three Stooges,

they

sparked laughter in millions of viewers, even though he employed

slapstick tactics that might be considered too violent today.

1. Moe, the leader and disciplinarian, was often the first to flee from danger, but they rarely escaped unscathed.

2. Every boy and girl who watched the Three Stooges learned to avoid anyone carrying a mop or a plank on their shoulder, or at least they learned to duck when he turned around.
3. A famous actor or actress would sometimes be cast in a small role, but they never altered the comedic formula of the film.
4. Directors often shot scenes several times because one of the Stooges or an extra could not stop laughing during their lines.
5. During the Stooges' later years, Curly was replaced, first by Shemp and later by "Curly Joe," but neither of the replacements was as popular as he had hoped.

EXERCISE 23-4 (23d) Revise the following sentences to make the pronouns agree in number with their antecedents. You may want to revise some sentences to avoid awkward pronoun constructions. Example:

Each of the teachers here creates their own grading system within

the guidelines of the department.

his or her

1. Everyone assumes that the policy granting teachers this right will adversely affect their grades.
2. Of course, few of the students consider the impact that an alternative policy might have on her education.
3. Several instructors favor a policy requiring uniform testing and grading criteria, because it would result in less work for him.
4. Most of the departmental policies are unfamiliar to the students, who have read only excerpts from it in the school newspaper.
5. Each of the instructors who favor the current policy has signed their name on a petition.

EXERCISE 23-5 (23e) Revise the following sentences to eliminate pronoun agreement errors. Examine the sentences carefully to determine if collective nouns are singular or plural. Example:

Elvis Presley rarely failed to please an audience, especially when

it

they consisted of loyal fans.

EXERCISE 23-2 (23b)

Possible revisions:

1. A nurse closely monitors the progress **of patients** to supply **doctors** with **required information**.
2. Many difficult decisions must be made by **police officers** in the instant before **they** fire **their weapons**.
3. As part of the team, each **firefighter depends on other team members for safety**.
4. While juries decide the innocence or guilt of a defendant, **judges realize** that only **they** can sentence someone to death.
5. Even grade school **teachers** and flight **attendants understand** the pressure of **being entrusted with people's lives** every day.

EXERCISE 23-3 (23c)

Possible revisions:

1. Moe, the leader and disciplinarian, was often the first to flee from danger, but **he** rarely escaped unscathed.
2. **All children** who watched the Three Stooges learned to avoid anyone carrying a mop or a plank on **his or her** shoulder, or at least they learned to duck when **that person** turned around.
3. A famous actor or actress would sometimes be cast in a small role, but **he or she** never

Answers to Exercises 23-4 and 23-5 appear on pages E-38 and E-39.

altered the comedic formula of the film.

4. Directors often shot scenes several times because one of the Stooges or an extra could not stop laughing during **his or her** lines.

5. (Correct as written.)

EXERCISE 23-4 (23d)

Possible revisions:

1. his or her *instead of* their
2. their *instead of* her
3. them *instead of* him
4. them *instead of* it
5. his or her *instead of* their

EXERCISE 23-5 (23e)

Possible revisions:

1. Elvis first sang publicly to his ecstatic high school **class-mates**, but **this acclaim** failed to fulfill his need for attention.
2. The crowd at the Louisiana Hayride covered **their** eyes when **they** saw Elvis swivel across the stage.
3. Elvis acknowledged his gospel roots by selecting a backup vocal group that took **its** name from the Bible.
4. After Elvis left the army, he continued to help **it** promote hand-to-hand combat and the use of firearms.
5. Although one Senate-appointed committee continues to argue among **themselves** ... **they have** unanimously declared

1. Elvis first sang publicly to his ecstatic high school class, but they failed to fulfill his need for attention.
2. The crowd at the Louisiana Hayride covered its eyes when it saw Elvis swivel across the stage.
3. Elvis acknowledged his gospel roots by selecting a backup vocal group that took their name from the Bible.
4. After Elvis left the army, he continued to help them promote hand-to-hand combat and the use of firearms.
5. Although one Senate-appointed committee continues to argue among itself over evidence suggesting that Elvis faked his fatal overdose, it has unanimously declared him "King for Life" should he be alive.

EXERCISE 23-6 (23a–e) Revise the following paragraph to eliminate pronoun agreement errors. You may want to recast some sentences to avoid awkward pronoun constructions.

Demonstrations erupted in several cities across the United States when the jury agreed among itself that the officers accused of unnecessarily beating Rodney King were innocent on all counts. Rioters in Los Angeles expressed its anger over the verdict by destroying property, looting businesses, and battering innocent victims. The violence spread to other cities, such as Portland and Las Vegas, but in some metropolitan areas where widespread violence was expected, particularly Chicago and New York, protesters organized peaceful demonstrations that allowed him or her to denounce the verdict publicly without harming others. Many people who saw the video footage of the police beating was forced to question the outcome of the trial and to decide whether he or she would voice an opinion on the release of the officers. Even King himself, however, spoke out against the brutal attacks and rioting that followed the announcement of the verdict, and their plea for peace may have helped contain further outbursts of violence around the nation.

EXERCISE 24-1 (24a–b) Underline the correct pronoun in each paired choice. Example:

After Alice had finished [**she/her**] draft, [**she/her**] gave it to [**I/me**] to read.

1. [**I/me/my**] read it and then returned it to [**she/her**] with [**I/me/my**] comments written in the margins.
2. [**I/me/my**] thought that [**she/her**] readers would not understand everything [**she/her**] had written.
3. Some of the sentences were worded ambiguously, so [**I/me/my**] pointed [**they/them/their**] out to [**she/her**].
4. Although [**I/me/my**] helped [**she/her**], it was [**she/her**] who did most of the work.
5. As a result, [**she/her**] finished paper was clearer than those of students [**who/whom/whose**] had not gotten any feedback.

EXERCISE 24-2 (24c–f) Underline the correct pronoun in each paired choice. Example:

After assigning *Jane Eyre,* our English teacher recommended that John and [**I/me**] read *Wide Sargasso Sea* for extra credit.

1. The main characters in *Wide Sargasso Sea* also appear in the more famous novel *Jane Eyre,* but just between you and [**I/me**], I think that *Wide Sargasso Sea* is better.
2. John reads faster than [**I/me**]; however, he doesn't read as carefully as [**I/me**].
3. *Jane Eyre* was a challenge for [**we/us**] students to read, but reading *Wide Sargasso Sea* helped [**we/us**]—John and [**I/me**]—understand the earlier novel better.
4. John and [**I/me**] thought that one of the main characters from *Jane Eyre,* Mr. Rochester, had more faults but was also more human in *Wide Sargasso Sea.*
5. When the film of *Wide Sargasso Sea* comes to town, [**we/us**] two plan to see it.

EXERCISE 24-3 (24g–h) Underline the correct word in each paired choice. Example:

A new award, called the Right Livelihood Award, honors people [**who/whom**] have done something to benefit humanity.

1. One of these awards was given to John Gofman, a scientist from the United States, and Alla Yaroshinskaya, a journalist from

him "King for Life" should he be alive.

EXERCISE 23-6 (23a–e)
Possible revision:

Demonstrations erupted in several cities across the United States when the **jurors** agreed among **themselves** that the officers accused of unnecessarily beating Rodney King were innocent on all counts. Rioters in Los Angeles expressed **their** anger over the verdict by destroying property, looting businesses, and battering innocent victims. The violence spread to other cities, such as Portland and Las Vegas, but in some metropolitan areas where widespread violence was expected, particularly Chicago and New York, protesters organized peaceful demonstrations that allowed **them** to denounce the verdict publicly without harming others. Many people who saw the video footage of the police beating **were** forced to question the outcome of the trial and decide whether **they** would voice an opinion on the release of the officers. Even King himself, however, spoke out against the brutal attacks and rioting that followed the announcement of the verdict, and **his** plea for peace may have helped contain further outbursts of violence around the nation.

Answers to Exercises 24-1, 24-2, and 24-3 appear on page E-40.

EXERCISE 24-1 (24a–b)
1. I; her; my
2. I; her; she
3. I; them; her
4. I; her; she
5. her; who

EXERCISE 24-2 (24c–f)
1. me
2. I; I
3. us; us; me
4. I
5. we

EXERCISE 24-3 (24g–h)
1. who
2. their
3. who
4. whom; who
5. his

EXERCISE 25-1 (25a–b)
1. lost; became
2. fought
3. enjoyed; overthrew
4. undergone; taken
5. led; caught; imprisoned

Ukraine, [**who/whom**] together investigated the Chernobyl disaster.
2. The award was given for [**them/their**] exposing the long-term, long-range health hazards of the disaster.
3. Helen Mack, [**who/whom**] is a human rights activist, received another of these awards for her work in Guatemala against government corruption.
4. The memory of her sister, [**who/whom**] Mack admired and [**who/whom**] was mysteriously murdered in Guatemala, spurred her on.
5. Dr. Zafrullah Chowdhury, from Bangladesh, known for [**him/his**] manufacturing of low-cost medicine, received an award on behalf of an organization he founded.

EXERCISE 25-1 (25a–b) Write the correct form of the verb in each blank. Example:

The history of Myanmar (formerly Burma) has ___*been*___ [**be**] a long and unsettled one.

1. In 1886, Burma _____ [**lose**] its independence and _____ [**become**] a British colony.
2. During World War II, the British and the Japanese _____ [**fight**] each other in Burma.
3. The country _____ [**enjoy**] fifteen years of peace until 1962, when the military _____ [**overthrow**] the government.
4. Since then, the country has _____ [**undergo**] severe economic troubles, and the government has _____ [**take**] the people's freedom from them.
5. In 1988, students and monks _____ [**lead**] a rebellion, but it was crushed, and the government _____ [**catch**] and _____ [**imprison**] the leaders.

EXERCISE 25-2 (25c) Underline the correct verb in each of the choices in the following sentences. (*Note:* Though more than one choice may be grammatically correct, only one is appropriate for the context of the sentence.) Example:

When Kim was deciding whether or not to [**break up/break up with/break down**] her boyfriend, she [**ran onto/ran into/ran over**] her good friend Sally.

1. Kim asked Sally to [**drop/drop in/drop in on**] her that night.
2. Sally offered to [**pick over/pick up/pick through**] some pizza and soda on her way over.
3. While they ate the pizza, they discussed whether Kim should [**get out of/get into/get by with**] the relationship.
4. Sally thought Kim should [**stand in for/stand up for/stand over**] herself and just [**walk into/walk over/walk out on**] her boyfriend.
5. Kim, however, worried that if she [**gave up on/gave back/gave out**] the relationship, she would only [**end up/end up on/end up with**] an even worse one.

EXERCISE 25-3 (25d) Underline the correct verb in each of the following sentences. Example:

The book [**lie/lay**] on the desk all weekend.

1. I [**lied/laid**] it there on Friday.
2. I was supposed to read it by Monday; instead, I [**lie/lay/laid**] in bed watching television.
3. While I was [**lying/laying**] there on Saturday, I watched five hours of football on cable.
4. All the time, that book [**laid/lied/lay**] there accusing me of not doing what I ought to be doing.
5. On Monday morning, I cracked it open and found a note I had [**lay/laid/lain**] inside reminding me to do my homework on time for once.

EXERCISE 25-4 (25e–g) Correct the following incorrect sentences. Check for incorrect use of -s, -es, or -ed endings and for problems with linking or helping verbs. Example:

In Latino communities, a *Quinceañera*, or Sweet Fifteen party, is
^often held for girls.

1. The family of the girl rent gowns for the girls, tuxedos for the boys, and limousines and throw an expensive party.
2. Often, the *Quinceañera* be more expensive than a wedding.
3. The birthday girl suppose to help her mother make the arrangements.
4. The girl escorted by attendants, who is called her "court."

EXERCISE 25-2 (25c)
1. drop in on
2. pick up
3. get out of
4. stand up for; walk out on
5. end up with

EXERCISE 25-3 (25d)
1. laid
2. lay
3. lying
4. lay
5. laid

EXERCISE 25-4 (25e–g)
1. The family of the girl **rents** gowns for the girls, tuxedos for the boys, and limousines and **throws** an expensive party.
2. Often, the *Quinceañera* **is** more expensive than a wedding.
3. The birthday girl **is supposed** to help her mother make the arrangements.
4. The girl **is** escorted by attendants, who **are** called her "court."
5. Before the party, the girl usually **goes** to Mass to be **blessed** by the priest.

5. Before the party, the girl usually go to Mass to be bless by the priest.

EXERCISE 26-1 (26a)

1. *Present:* catches; *past:* caught; *future:* will catch.
2. *Present:* does, goes over; *past:* did, when over; *future:* will do, will go over.
3. *Present:* stops; *past:* stopped; *future:* will stop.
4. *Present:* gets; *past:* got; *future:* will get.
5. *Present:* finds; *past:* found; *future:* will find.

EXERCISE 26-1 (26a) Rewrite the following sentences, changing the infinitive in brackets to the present, the past, and the future. Example:

Alan [**to go**] to school every day.

Present: Alan **goes** to school every day.

Past: Alan **went** to school every day.

Future: Alan **will go** to school every day.

1. He [**to catch**] the bus at the corner of Ninth and Sycamore.
2. On the way, he [**to do**] his homework—most likely he [**to go over**] it frantically.
3. Jumping off the bus at 8:10, he [**to stop**] at the corner restaurant for a quick cup of coffee and a doughnut.
4. He [**to get**] to his 8:30 class just in time.
5. After class, he [**to find**] a quiet corner in the library for a nap.

EXERCISE 26-2 (26b–e)

1. has developed
2. have separated; have decided
3. had undergone
4. had attended
5. will have been held

EXERCISE 26-2 (26b–e) Write in the correct perfect- or progressive-tense form for each of the verbs in brackets in the following sentences. Sometimes either form is appropriate, but in other cases, only the perfect *or* the progressive form is correct. Example:

Recently, some ethnic communities *have created* [**create**] coming-of-age rituals for their youths.

1. For example, an African-American community in Philadelphia _____ [**develop**] a process called Unyago that helps young people make the passage from childhood to adulthood.
2. Traditionally, coming-of-age rituals _____ [**separate**] males from females, but this community _____ [**decide**] that it would be better for modern youths to go through the process together.
3. After "graduating" from Unyago, young men and women who _____ [**undergo**] the process felt that they had a better understanding of adult life.

4. In Unyago, they _____ [**attend**] workshops on topics such as identity, relationships, and spirituality.

5. The first Unyago was held in 1991; the community hopes that by the turn of the century, many more Unyago ceremonies _____ [**hold**].

[Based on a case study from Balch Institute for Ethnic Studies, *Rites of Passage in America: Traditions of the Life Cycle* (Philadelphia: Balch Institute for Ethnic Studies), pp. 50–54.]

EXERCISE 26-3 (26g) Rewrite the following sentences, changing passive voice to active voice. Each passive verb has been boldfaced. Remember that sometimes passive voice is the better choice because you don't know who performed the action of the verb, or you don't want to reveal that person's identity, or you want to emphasize the receiver of the action of the verb or the action itself. Example:

Bruce Bethke coined the term
ᶜ*Cyberpunk,* ~~**was** a term~~ **coined** ~~by~~ Bruce Bethke in a 1983 science

fiction story about teenage computer hackers.

1. After Bethke's story, the term **was used** by many other writers.
2. Soon the term had become so popular that real-life computer hackers **were inspired** to exploit and often to subvert technology.
3. Now a cyberpunk "underground" subculture **is being pursued** by the government, which **is worried** that top-secret information is no longer safe.
4. Many cyberpunks **have been arrested** for breaking into corporate and government computer files.
5. In response, the Electronic Frontier Foundation **has been formed** by members of the computer community, and it argues that computerized information should be legally accessible to everyone.

EXERCISE 26-3 (26g)

1. After Bethke's story, **many other writers used the term.**
2. Soon the term had **become** so popular that **it inspired real-life computer hackers** to exploit and often to subvert technology.
3. Now **the government is pursuing** the cyberpunk "underground" subculture because **it worries** that top-secret information is no longer safe.
4. (No change; the writer wants to emphasize what has happened to these cyberpunks.)
5. In response, **members of the computer community have formed** the Electronic Frontier Foundation, **which** argues that computerized information should be legally accessible to everyone.

EXERCISE 26-4 (26h) Correct the errors in verb tense in the following sentences. (*Note:* Some sentences may be correct.) Example:

EXERCISE 26-4 (26h)

1. If I wanted a new sweater when I was growing up, my father **took** me to a department store.
2. (Correct as written.)
3. If I could avoid stores altogether, I **would be** very happy.
4. If I were home right now, I **would watch** television all afternoon.
5. If it weren't for soap operas, I **would** get a suntan at the beach.

EXERCISE 27-1 (27a)

1. looking
2. to make
3. leaving *or* to leave
4. to spend
5. to take

EXERCISE 27-2 (27b)

1. amazing
2. surprising
3. frightened
4. confusing
5. disappointed

will

If you shop at a discount store, you ~~would~~ find bargains.

1. If I wanted a new sweater when I was growing up, my father takes me to a department store.
2. Now when I need to shop, I watch the Home Shopping Network.
3. If I could avoid stores altogether, I would have been very happy.
4. If I were at home right now, I will watch television all afternoon.
5. If it weren't for soap operas, I will get a suntan at the beach.

🌐 **EXERCISE 27-1** **(27a)** Fill in the blank with the gerund or infinitive form of the verb in brackets. Example:

My sister Renata needed ___*to find*___ [**find**] day care for her two children when she got a job.

1. Because a good, affordable day-care center is hard to find, Renata put off _____ [**look**] for one for as long as she could.
2. Finally, events forced her _____ [**make**] a decision.
3. Renata hates _____ [**leave**] her children all day.
4. She feels guilty, so she tries _____ [**spend**] plenty of time with them on weekends.
5. This Saturday, she intends _____ [**take**] them on a canoe trip.

🌐 **EXERCISE 27-2** **(27b)** Underline the correct form of the participle in each sentence. Example:

In the United States, some people are [**depressing/depressed**] about changes in the economy.

1. During the past ten years, the country has experienced [**amazing/amazed**] changes.
2. Computers have become part of everyday life with [**surprising/surprised**] speed.
3. Often people are [**frightening/frightened**] by the pace of technological change.
4. They think having too much change at once is [**confusing/confused**].
5. Once people learn to use computers, though, they are seldom [**disappointing/disappointed**] by the results.

EXERCISE 28-1 (28a–b) Edit the following sentences to correct errors with adjectives or adverbs. Example:

Hamlet is Shakespeare's longest play, but the entertaining plot
reads quick. *[quickly]*

1. As the play opens, Claudius has brutal murdered his brother, the king, and seduced Gertrude, the queen.
2. Hamlet feels unsurely about what to do to avenge his father's death.
3. Hamlet reacts angry when he learns of his uncle's treachery; then he hesitates.
4. His indecision causes, direct or indirect, the deaths of several other characters.
5. You will probably feel badly after reading this play.

EXERCISE 28-2 (28c–d) In the spaces provided, write the correct comparative or superlative form of the adjective. Also, correct any double negatives. Example:

The Mississippi is one of the _longest_ [long] rivers in the world.

1. In my opinion, not nowhere is there a _____ [pretty] river.
2. Last summer, I went with my family to the source of the Mississippi, Lake Itasca, in Minnesota; getting up _____ [early] than the rest of the family, I walked to the shore at dawn.
3. The river is, of course, _____ [powerful] at the source than it is downstream, yet I thought it was _____ [impressive].
4. No one who lives along the river's shores doesn't regard it as the _____ [lovely] and _____ [awe-inspiring] river in the world.
5. But when the Mississippi floods, it is _____ [dangerous] than any other river in North America.

EXERCISE 29-1 (29b–d) The following sentences each contain at least one error in the use of articles. Correct these errors. Example:

EXERCISE 28-1 (28a–b)

1. As the play opens, Claudius has **brutally** murdered his brother the king, and seduced Gertrude, the queen.
2. Hamlet feels **unsure** about what to do to avenge his father's death.
3. Hamlet reacts **angrily** when he learns of his uncle's treachery; then he hesitates.
4. His indecision causes, **directly** or **indirectly**, the deaths of several other characters.
5. You will probably feel **bad** after reading this play.

EXERCISE 28-2 (28c–d)

1. In my opinion, **nowhere** is there a **prettier** river.
2. Last summer, I went with my family to the source of the Mississippi, Lake Itasca, in Minnesota; getting up **earlier** than the rest of the family, I walked to the shore at dawn.
3. The river is, of course, **less powerful** at the source than it is downstream, yet I thought it was **more impressive**.
4. **Everyone** who lives along the river's shores **regards** it as the **loveliest** and **most awe-inspiring** river in the world.
5. But when the Mississippi floods, it is **more dangerous** than any other river in North America.

EXERCISE 29-1 (29b–d)

1. On weekends, I hike in **the** Berkshire Mountains, which are not far away.
2. My camping gear is almost complete, but I still need **a** new tent.
3. **The only** sporting goods store in town is having **a** sale on camping equipment.
4. I also noticed that **the** iodine pills I take with me to purify my drinking water are almost gone.
5. As a **rule, hikers** need to stay in good shape and build their endurance.
6. Much has been written lately about **the** effect of acid rain on wilderness areas.
7. When hikers get caught in a sudden rainstorm, **the** legs are often the first part of the body to get cold.
8. In Massachusetts, **the** most beautiful time to hike in the woods is October.
9. Once while I was backpacking, I saw **a** peregrine falcon.
10. **The falcon** was circling overhead, hunting for food.

EXERCISE 31-1 (31a–b)

1. Why would anyone want to dress as a slice of pizza**?**
2. At first June's father declared, "Absolutely not**!**" Then she whined repeatedly, "Why**?** Why**?** Why**?**"

When I first came here, I lived in an apartment on the Smith Street.

1. On weekends, I hike in Berkshire Mountains, which are not far away.
2. My camping gear is almost complete, but I still need new tent.
3. Only sporting goods store in town is having sale on camping equipment.
4. I also noticed that iodine pills I take with me to purify my drinking water are almost gone.
5. As a rule, the hikers need to stay in good shape and build their endurance.
6. Much has been written lately about effect of acid rain on wilderness areas.
7. When hikers get caught in a sudden rainstorm, legs are often the first part of the body to get cold.
8. In Massachusetts, most beautiful time to hike in the woods is October.
9. Once while I was backpacking, I saw peregrine falcon.
10. Falcon was circling overhead, hunting for food.

EXERCISE 31-1 (31a–b) Correct the punctuation in the following sentences. Example:

June asked her father if she could dress as a slice of pizza for Halloween.̷

1. Why would anyone want to dress as a slice of pizza.
2. At first June's father declared, "Absolutely not!!!" Then she whined repeatedly, "Why. Why. Why?"
3. She questioned whether he remembered his youth at all?
4. Taking another approach, her father asked, "Don't you find the idea of dressing as a slice of pizza a little unusual."?
5. "Dad!" she politely pointed out, "we are discussing Halloween! aren't we"?

EXERCISE 32-1 (32a–b) Edit the following items to form grammatically correct sentences. Remember that a sentence must include a subject and a verb and must express a complete thought. Some items may already be complete sentences. Example:

Acclaimed by many critics as the greatest artist of all time, Michelangelo was born in Caprese, Tuscany, in 1474.

1. When he completed his famous statue of David, which now stands in the Galleria dell' Accademia in Florence. The artist was only thirty years old.
2. Painting the ceiling in the Vatican's Sistine Chapel. Occupied the artist for more than four years.
3. After 1520, Michelangelo focused on architecture as well as painting and sculpture. He designed several of the most famous Renaissance structures in Italy.
4. While this master produced works of architecture, painting, and sculpture. Other artists of his period did too.
5. Michelangelo's unique gift is evident. From his surviving masterpieces in all three major areas of visual art.

EXERCISE 32-2 (32a–c) Revise the following items to eliminate fragments, comma splices, and fused sentences. Example:

Thomas Lanier Williams, better known as Tennessee Williams. He wrote several of the most important American plays of the twentieth century, *H* he changed the way many people think of theater today.

1. *A Streetcar Named Desire* catapulted the playwright to prominence in 1948. When he was only thirty-seven years old.
2. Some of Williams's most popular plays were made into movies following an initial run on Broadway these films sometimes failed to live up to their dramatic sources.
3. The renowned director Elia Kazan guided both the stage and film versions of *Cat on a Hot Tin Roof* and *The Night of the Iguana,* he and Williams worked closely on several other projects as well.
4. Williams, always a versatile writer. Published essays, short stories, and poems. In addition to his dramatic works.
5. His contributions to literature and theater now captivate audiences throughout the world, for his books, films, and plays have been translated into numerous languages.

3. She questioned whether he remembered his youth at all.
4. Taking another approach, her father asked, "Don't you find the idea of dressing as a slice of pizza a little unusual?"
5. "Dad," she politely pointed out, "we are discussing Halloween, aren't we?"

EXERCISE 32-1 (32a–b)
Possible revisions:

1. When he completed his famous statue of David, which now stands in the Galleria dell' Accademia in Florence, **the** artist was only thirty years old.
2. Painting the ceiling in the Vatican's Sistine **Chapel occupied** the artist for more than four years.
3. (Correct as written.)
4. While this master produced works of architecture, painting, and sculpture, **other** artists of his period did too.
5. Michelangelo's unique gift is **evident from** his surviving masterpieces in all three major areas of visual art.

EXERCISE 32-2 (32a–c)
Possible revisions:

1. *A Streetcar Named Desire* catapulted the playwright to prominence in 1948, **when** he was only thirty-seven years old.

2. Some of Williams's most popular plays were made into movies following an initial run on Broadway, **though** these films sometimes failed to live up to their dramatic sources.
3. The renowned director Elia Kazan guided both the stage and film versions of *Cat on a Hot Tin Roof* and *The Night of the Iguana*. **He** and Williams worked closely on several other projects as well.
4. Williams, always a versatile writer, **published** essays, short stories, and poems, **in** addition to his dramatic works.
5. (Correct as written.)

EXERCISE 33-1 (33a)

Possible revisions:

1. The fateful story appeared in the December 1893 issue of *The Strand*, **and it** pitted Holmes against his archenemy, Professor Moriarty.
2. Holmes had encountered Moriarty in numerous battles over the years, **yet the** detective had always triumphed over the ingenious villain.
3. Doyle published Holmes's adventures nearly every month for a decade prior to the sleuth's demise, **so** Moriarty's triumph completely surprised most avid fans.
4. Ten years elapsed before the author resurrected his cerebral hero in 1903, **but** once Holmes

EXERCISE 33-1 (33a) Edit the following items to form single sentences, using coordinating conjunctions. Remember to insert a comma before the coordinating conjunction when joining two independent clauses. Example:

Followers of Sherlock Holmes reacted with dismay to the detective's death in "The Final Problem" by Arthur Conan Doyle. *and many* Many readers mailed letters of condolence to the author.

1. The fateful story appeared in the December 1893 issue of *The Strand*. It pitted Holmes against his archenemy, Professor Moriarty.
2. Holmes had encountered Moriarty in numerous battles over the years. The detective had always triumphed over the ingenious villain.
3. Doyle published Holmes's adventures nearly every month for a decade prior to the sleuth's demise. Moriarty's triumph completely surprised most avid fans.
4. Ten years elapsed before the author resurrected his cerebral hero in 1903. Once Holmes returned from the grave, the public quickly regained its enthusiasm for Doyle's intriguing character.
5. News of the detective's revival spread rapidly. Readers rushed to buy the thirteen new stories because they didn't want to miss a single adventure of their favorite crime fighter.

EXERCISE 33-2 (33b) Each of the following items contains three sentences. Use semicolons to form a single sentence out of the two that are most closely related. Example:

The *Aeneid* relates the voyages and adventures of the Trojan prince Aeneas. The poem covers the period from the defeat of Troy to the conquest of the Italian peninsula. The defeat and subsequent victory led to the founding of Rome.

1. Earlier, the Greek epics the *Iliad* and the *Odyssey* told the stories of the Trojan War and the return of the Greek hero

Odysseus to Ithaca when the war ended. The *Aeneid* combines the plots of the two Greek epics. It tells of the destruction of a nation in war and the return of a hero to his homeland.

2. Aeneas differs in several ways from Odysseus, the hero of the *Odyssey*. Aeneas struggles to suppress his personal wishes to the needs of his people. He epitomizes the Roman ideal of virtue.

3. The Roman poet Virgil composed the *Aeneid* to glorify the emperor. He traced Augustus's lineage to the ancient kings of Troy. Many poets later borrowed this ingratiating technique from Virgil.

4. The *Aeneid* promoted the view that Augustus was destined to lead the empire. It linked him to the glory of the Golden Age. Virgil depended on such propagandistic posturing to get the work published.

5. Virgil is considered one of the great masters of poetry from the classical period. His influence on other poets extends throughout the centuries. The fourteenth-century Italian poet Dante even portrayed Virgil as his guide through Hell and Purgatory in the *Divine Comedy*.

EXERCISE 33-3 (33c) Revise the following items so that each is a single sentence containing a conjunctive adverb or a transitional expression. Also correct any punctuation errors. Example:

Hurricanes strike with one of nature's most frightening displays of force, in fact, the destruction left in their wake rivals that of earthquakes and volcanic eruptions.

1. In the fall of 1969, a hurricane named Camille slammed into the Mississippi gulf coast. As a result, it dislocated thousands of families along the shore.

2. A massive tidal surge accompanied the storm consequently wind and water destroyed mile after mile of commercial and private property.

3. The storm wiped out most of the utilities and public facilities in the area. In addition Camille demolished nearly every commercial wharf and fishery in Biloxi.

4. One shrimp boat washed onto shore and came to rest far across the highway. Subsequently it was converted to a souvenir shop selling, among other items, canned wind from the hurricane.

returned from the grave, the public quickly regained its enthusiasm for Doyle's intriguing character.

5. News of the detective's revival spread rapidly**, and readers** rushed to buy the thirteen new stories because they didn't want to miss a single adventure of their favorite crime fighter.

EXERCISE 33-2 (33b)

1. The *Aeneid* combines the plots of the two Greek epics**; it** tells of the destruction of a nation in war and the return of a hero to his homeland.

2. Aeneas struggles to suppress his personal wishes to the needs of his people**; he** epitomizes the Roman ideal of virtue.

3. The Roman poet Virgil composed the *Aeneid* to glorify the emperor**; he** traced Augustus's lineage to the ancient kings of Troy.

4. The *Aeneid* promoted the view that Augustus was destined to lead the empire**; it** linked him to the glory of the Golden Age.

5. His influence on other poets extends throughout the centuries**; the** fourteenth-century Italian poet Dante even portrayed Virgil as his guide through Hell and Purgatory in the *Divine Comedy*.

Answers to Exercise 33-3 appear on page E-50.

EXERCISE 33-3 (33c)

1. In the fall of 1969, a hurricane named Camille slammed into the Mississippi gulf coast**; as** a result, it dislocated thousands of families along the shore.
2. A massive tidal surge accompanied the storm**; consequently,** wind and water destroyed mile after mile of commercial and private property.
3. The storm wiped out most of the utilities and public facilities in the area**; in** addition, Camille demolished nearly every commercial wharf and fishery in Biloxi.
4. One shrimp boat washed onto shore and came to rest far across the highway**; subsequently,** it was converted to a souvenir shop selling, among other items, canned wind from the hurricane. [The comma after subsequently is optional.]
5. Many anecdotes about this hurricane are darker stories**; for** instance, a number of people died while holding "hurricane parties" in their homes.

EXERCISE 34-1 (34a–b)

1. Over the years, people have left the cities in large numbers, draining the cities of much-needed tax money.
2. However, recent studies show that without a downtown area, parks, or a cultural base, suburbs cannot continue to attract

5. Many anecdotes about this hurricane are darker stories. For instance a number of people died while holding "hurricane parties" in their homes.

EXERCISE 34-1 (34a–b) Insert commas in the appropriate places in the following sentences. Example:

Usually thought to be havens for the rich ′ many suburbs now have the same problems as large cities.

1. Over the years people have left the cities in large numbers draining the cities of much-needed tax money.
2. However recent studies show that without a downtown area parks or a cultural base suburbs cannot continue to attract the middle- and upper-class residents they need to maintain their tax bases.
3. Typically families move into the suburbs stay a few years and then move on to "better" suburbs.
4. In some areas rents in the suburbs are lower than rents in the city itself but people would rather pay a higher rent than live in a declining suburb.
5. To solve the problem of suburban decay urban planners are rethinking the typical "city versus suburb" concept; they are trying to find ways to save both the city and the suburb.

EXERCISE 34-2 (34c–d) Correct any incorrect sentences by adding commas in the appropriate places. Some sentences may be correct as written. Example:

Until someone invents calorie-free ice cream ′ one of my fondest dreams ′ I will do aerobics for an hour every day.

1. Hikers who live in mountainous areas tend to keep in shape without arduous exercise classes.
2. However, this campus in the middle of a plain does not offer much in the way of strenuous hiking.
3. People who bicycle to school or work also keep in shape.

4. Members of the bicycle team who ride forty miles every day sweep past my house every morning while I leisurely eat my breakfast and exercise my mind by reading the newspaper.
5. Perhaps I should create a new exercise program "Mental Aerobics."

EXERCISE 34-3 (34e) Find the coordinate or cumulative adjectives in the following sentences and add commas where necessary. If an adjective group is correct as it stands, write "correct" above it. Example:

Carlo bought a sleek, rugged pickup.

1. Suddenly, he found that he had more "good" friends than he had had before he bought the shiny sporty truck.
2. They would gather around his truck in large excited crowds, talking about the amazing new features of the engine.
3. They were especially impressed by the computerized electrical system.
4. Poor beleaguered Carlo was immediately enlisted to help move Jim's huge record collection to his new off-campus apartment.
5. Carlo suspected that these intense quickly formed friendships would last just as long as his truck stayed in good working order.

EXERCISE 34-4 (34a–k) In the following passage, some commas are missing, and others are used incorrectly. Correct the passage. (*Note:* Every sentence has at least one error.)

On June 5 1993 I decided to take the train across the country from Philadelphia Pennsylvania to San Francisco California, and stop along the way to see old college friends. "All aboooaaarrrd" called the uniformed train conductor and we were off. The lush green eastern part of the country which is the most familiar to me seemed to take forever to pass by but that was nothing compared to the unending flat plains. Finally we reached the "Mile-High-City" Denver. There ahead of us, were the majestic, Rocky Mountains. Inching upward the train took over an hour to get to the pass above the city; then, we were suddenly swiftly and terrifyingly rushing through a four-mile tunnel. On the other side was the cool green Colorado River valley which marked the beginning of the

the middle- and upper-class residents they need to maintain their tax bases.
3. Typically, families move into the suburbs, stay a few years, and then move on to "better" suburbs.
4. In some areas, rents in the suburbs are lower than rents in the city itself, but people would rather pay a higher rent than live in a declining suburb.
5. To solve the problem of suburban decay, urban planners are rethinking the typical "city versus suburb" concept; they are trying to find ways to save both the city and the suburb.

EXERCISE 34-2 (34c–d)
1. (Correct as written.)
2. However, this campus, in the middle of a plain, does not offer much in the way of strenuous hiking.
3. (Correct as written.)
4. Members of the bicycling team, who ride forty miles every day, sweep past my house every morning while I leisurely eat my breakfast and exercise my mind by reading the newspaper.
5. Perhaps I should create a new exercise program, "Mental Aerobics."

EXERCISE 34-3 (34e)
1. Suddenly, he found that he had **more "good"** [correct] friends than he had had before he bought the **shiny, sporty** truck.

The answer to Exercise 34-4 appears on pages E-52 and E-53.

2. They would gather around his truck in **large, excited** crowds, talking about the **amazing new** [correct] features of the engine.
3. They were especially impressed by the **computerized electrical** [correct] system.
4. **Poor, beleaguered** Carlo was immediately enlisted to help move Jim's **huge record** [correct] collection to his **new off-campus** [correct] apartment.
5. Carlo suspected that these **intense, quickly formed** friendships would last just as long as his truck stayed in **good working** [correct] order.

EXERCISE 34-4 (34a–k)

On June 5, 1993, I decided to take the train across the country from Philadelphia, Pennsylvania, to San Francisco, **California, and** stop along the way to see old college friends. "All aboooaaarrrd," called the uniformed train conductor, and we were off. The lush, green eastern part of the country, which is the most familiar to me, seemed to take forever to pass by, but that was nothing compared to the unending, flat plains. Finally, we reached the "Mile-High City" of Denver. There ahead of **us were** the **majestic Rocky** Mountains. Inching upward, the train took over an hour to get to the pass above the city; **then we** were suddenly, swiftly, and terrifyingly rushing through a four-mile tunnel. On the

most spectacular, train ride I had ever taken. The Rockies are a part of the country worth seeing don't you think?

EXERCISE 35-1 (35a) Rewrite the following sentences to show possession properly. Example:

My familys time is spent in a variety of ways when late summer arrives on the farm.

1. Aunt Doris afternoons are filled with gardening as she tends her gladioli and dahlias.
2. The cantaloupes ends must be fragrant before the melons are ready to eat.
3. On my brother-in-laws days off, he mows the lawns or tinkers with car engines.
4. The energy of my mother is absorbed in canning green beans and pickles.
5. Many folks efforts are needed to put up the huge fields of baled hay.

EXERCISE 35-2 (35a–e) Edit the following paragraph to correct any errors in apostrophe use.

During the summer of 92, my friends and I spent much of our spare time swimming in the New River. Wed ride down those back roads around McCoy, Virginia, in the pickup truck of my sister-in-law, our whoops of excitement shattering the pastures quiet. Its a lot of fun to rent a big black float and glide slowly down the rivers green current's; your sure to cool off no matter how hot it is. We were all so tired of minding our p"s and q"s at work that some relaxation in the sun was just what we needed. The honeysuckles scent along the banks would improve anyones attitude. Riding over the rapid's reminded us of how much fun country summers can be. Who would'nt hate to see cold weather come?

EXERCISE 36-1 (36a) Revise the following sentences by adding quotation marks where appropriate. Example:

"When you reach the arboretum," the letter explained, "be sure to see that odd old magnolia near the front gate."

1. Writing further advice, Wiley suggested, If you take the path along the river in May, the wildflowers will amaze you.
2. Down by the railroad tracks, he continued, turn right toward the swamp; you might see a green heron or a wood duck.
3. The water's edge is thick with cattails, alders, and, unfortunately, litter, the next paragraph informed us.
4. Look out over the river, the old naturalist wrote, and imagine it before it became polluted.
5. Instructors in my department have been leading forestry students through this arboretum for twenty years, he declared proudly in the letter's last line.

EXERCISE 36-2 (36e–h) Correct the following sentences by inserting quotation marks where needed. Some sentences may be correct as written. Example:

William Faulkner's short story "A Rose for Emily" is certainly one

of the most disturbing pieces of literature ever written.

1. Miss Emily wasn't exactly the genteel lady she appeared to be.
2. The past, in the world of this eerie story, could be defined as anything that has maimed or still haunts.
3. Arsenic aided Miss Emily in arranging her horrific nuptials.
4. Dust and rose are two words that are repeated throughout the tale.
5. Dust is also a frequent image in another Faulkner short story, Dry September.

EXERCISE 36-3 (36a–j) Edit the following passage to correct problems with the use of quotation marks.

Which of your predecessors has influenced your present style? asked the interviewer.

The novelist sighed. Influence is such an overused word. However, Carson McCullers's A Rock, a Tree, a Cloud, David Leavitt's Territory, and Andrew Holleran's Ties are among my favorite works. Although these pieces are hardly "light" reading, their depictions of love are important to me.

And how would you define love? the interviewer inquired.

I don't know. Perhaps something so "passionate" is beyond anything as rational as a definition, the novelist suggested, reaching for a coffee cup.

other side was the cool**,** green Colorado River valley**,** which marked the beginning of the most **spectacular train** ride I had ever taken. The Rockies are a part of the country worth seeing, don't you think?

EXERCISE 35-1 (35a)
1. Aunt **Doris's** afternoons . . .
2. The **ends of the cantaloupes** must be fragrant . . .
3. On my **brother-in-law's** days off . . .
4. **My mother's energy** is . . .
5. Many **folks'** efforts . . .

EXERCISE 35-2 (35a–e)
Possible revisions:

During the summer of **'92,** my friends and I spent much of our spare time swimming in the New River. **We'd** ride down those back roads around McCoy, Virginia, in **my sister-in-law's** pickup truck, our **whoops** of excitement shattering the **pasture's** quiet. **It's** a lot of fun to rent a big black float and glide slowly down the **river's** green **currents; you're** sure to cool off no matter how hot it is. We were all so tired of minding our **p's** and **q's** at work that some relaxation in the sun was just what we needed. The **honeysuckle's** scent along the banks would improve **anyone's** attitude. Riding over the **rapids** reminded us of how much fun country summers can be. Who **wouldn't** hate to see cold weather come?

Answers to Exercises 36-1, 36-2, and 36-3 appear on pages E-54 and E-55.

EXERCISE 36-1 (36a)

1. Writing further advice, Wiley suggested, "If you take the path along the river in May, the wildflowers will amaze you."
2. "Down by the railroad tracks," he continued, "turn right toward the swamp; you might see a green heron or a wood duck."
3. "The water's edge is thick with cattails, alders, and, unfortunately, litter," the next paragraph informed us.
4. "Look out over the river," the old naturalist wrote, "and imagine it before it became polluted."
5. "Instructors in my department have been leading forestry students through this arboretum for twenty years," he declared proudly in the letter's last line.

EXERCISE 36-2 (36e–h)

Possible revisions:

1. (Correct as written, or could be revised:) Miss Emily wasn't exactly the genteel "lady" she appeared to be.
2. The past, in this eerie story's world, could be defined as "anything that has maimed or still haunts."
3. Arsenic aided Miss Emily in arranging her horrific "nuptials."
4. "Dust" and "rose" are two words that are repeated throughout the tale.
5. Dust is also a frequent image in another Faulkner short story, "Dry September."

EXERCISE 37-1 (37a–g) Revise the following paragraph by adding appropriate punctuation where needed and deleting or correcting incorrect punctuation.

Many Americans commemorate their dead during a religious holiday on November 2 called All Souls' Day. [This observance is obviously related to All Hallows' Eve . . . Halloween . . . with its emphasis on mystery and death.] Mexicans have their own version of this holiday; the Day of the Dead, when the souls of dead relatives are believed to return to earth. [This belief parallels that of the ancient Celts of Europe, who celebrated a similar holiday, Samhain (pronounced "sah-win"), when the gates to the afterlife were believed to swing open on the night of October 31.] Accompanying this Mexican holiday are many unique customs, such as: constructing altars and preparing special foods to honor the dead. *Pan de muerto* . . . "bread of the dead" . . . is a sweet bread decorated with bone-shaped dough. One of the most popular traditions is that of the *coronas:* which are artificial wreaths of flowers made to decorate graves.

EXERCISE 38-1 (38a–g) Correct the capitalization errors in the following passage.

in new orleans, louisiana, some african-american communities celebrate a person's death with a jazz funeral. in the american south, many funeral traditions from africa were preserved and are still practiced. the jazz funeral tradition came originally from the dahomey and yoruba peoples in west africa. most traditional african religions recognize one or more gods as the highest entities, but spirits exist between gods and humans in the hierarchy. when humans die, they enter the spirit world; a funeral must therefore be done properly. at a jazz funeral, a band leads a procession from the church to the grave playing dirges and solemn french military music. on the way back, however, the band plays lively jazz, and everyone dances.

EXERCISE 39-1 (39a–e) Edit the following paragraph to ensure correct use of abbreviations and acronyms.

Mr Hardy was the first person in the community to suspect foul play in the local man's disappearance. During the p.m. of Dec 7, Mr Turner, an employee of the I.R.S., was last seen walk-

ing his Vietnamese pot-bellied pig among the bare sycamores in chilly 30°f weather. Dr Gigi Divine et al., jogging through the dusk, glimpsed Mr Turner at exactly 10;32, feeding his pet a hot yam. By 1145 pm, when relatives came looking for him, Mr Turner was nowhere to be found. Only the pig was left, snuffling nervously.

EXERCISE 40-1 (40) Decide whether the numbers in brackets in the following sentences should be spelled out or not. If so, spell them out in the spaces provided; if not, write the numeral in the space. Example:

The most famous geyser is the ___*one*___ [1] in Yellowstone National Park: Old Faithful.

1. _____ [2] scientists have discovered that changes in the eruptions of geysers in California can predict the earthquakes.
2. They studied _____ [1] geyser for _____ [18] years, from _____ [1973] to _____ [1991].
3. They found that the geyser's regular eruptions became irregular _____ [1] to _____ [3] days before each of _____ [3] major earthquakes.
4. Before the _____ [1989] earthquake that hit San Francisco, the time between eruptions fluctuated from _____ [90] to _____ [150] minutes.
5. Unfortunately, all of the earthquakes happened at least _____ [155] miles from the geyser, so this _____ [1] geyser alone may not be reliable for earthquake prediction.

EXERCISE 41-1 (41a–e) Revise the following paragraph to correct the use of italics. (Underline to indicate words that should be set in italic type.)

"Au revoir" and "auf Wiedersehen," my family shouted as my ship, the Princess Santorini, edged away from the crowded and noisy docks. I had a week to while away as we crossed the Atlantic, but with a backpack full of books, I would not be bored. Literary is definitely the word that would describe my selections. As the ship cut through the gray-green water, I pored over Wuthering Heights by Emily Brontë, Walt Whitman's Leaves of Grass, and Robert

EXERCISE 36-3 (36a–j)

"Which of your predecessors has influenced your present style?" asked the interviewer.

The novelist sighed. "'Influence' is such an overused word. However, Carson McCullers's 'A Rock, a Tree, a Cloud,' David Leavitt's 'Territory,' and Andrew Holleran's 'Ties' are among my favorite works. Although these pieces are hardly **light** reading, their depictions of love are important to me."

"And how would you define 'love'?" the interviewer inquired.

"I don't know. Perhaps something so **passionate** is beyond anything as rational as a definition," the novelist suggested, reaching for a coffee cup.

EXERCISE 37-1 (37a–g)

Many Americans commemorate their dead during a religious holiday on November 2 called All Souls' Day. (This observance is obviously related to All Hallows' Eve—Halloween—with its emphasis on mystery and death.) Mexicans have their own version of this holiday: the Day of the Dead, when the souls of dead relatives are believed to return to earth. (This belief parallels that of the ancient Celts of Europe, who celebrated a similar holiday, Samhain [pronounced "sah-win"], when the gates to the afterlife were believed to swing open on the night of

Answers to Exercises 38-1, 39-1, 40-1, and 41-1 appear on page E-56.

October 31.) Accompanying this Mexican holiday are many unique customs, such **as constructing** altars and preparing special foods to honor the dead. *Pan de muerto*—"bread of the dead"—is a sweet bread decorated with bone-shaped dough. One of the most popular traditions is that of the *coronas*, which are artificial wreaths of flowers made to decorate graves.

EXERCISE 38-1 (38a–g)

In New Orleans, Louisiana, some African-American communities celebrate a person's death with a jazz funeral. In the American South, many funeral traditions from Africa were preserved and are still practiced. The jazz funeral tradition came originally from the Dahomey and Yoruba peoples in West Africa. Most traditional African religions recognize one or more gods as the highest entities, but spirits exist between gods and humans in the hierarchy. When humans die. . . At a jazz funeral, a band leads a procession from the church to the grave playing dirges and solemn French military music. On the way back, however, the band plays lively jazz, and everyone dances.

Bly's Iron John. For more casual reading, I examined the travel magazine Our World in preparation for my arrival in Europe.

EXERCISE 39-1 (39a–e)

Mr. Hardy was the first person in the community to suspect foul play in the local man's disappearance. During the **evening** of **Dec.** 7, **Mr.** Turner, an employee of the **IRS**, was last seen walking his Vietnamese pot-bellied pig among the bare sycamores in chilly **30°F** weather. **Dr.** Gigi Divine **and others,** jogging through the dusk, glimpsed **Mr.** Turner at exactly **10:32,** feeding his pet a hot yam. By **11:45 p.m.,** when relatives came looking for him, **Mr.** Turner was nowhere to be found. Only the pig was left, snuffling nervously.

EXERCISE 40-1 (40)

1. Two
2. one; eighteen; 1973; 1991
3. one; three; three
4. 1989; 90; 150
5. 155; one

EXERCISE 41-1 (41a–e)

"Au revoir" and *"auf Wiedersehen,"* my family shouted as my ship, the *Princess Santorini,* edged away from the crowded and noisy docks. . . . *Literary* is definitely the word that would describe my selections. As the ship cut through the gray-green water, I pored over *Wuthering Heights* by Emily Brontë, Walt Whitman's *Leaves of Grass,* and Robert Bly's *Iron John.* For more casual reading, I examined the travel magazine *Our World* in preparation for my arrival in Europe.

Credits

We thank the following authors and publishers for permission to quote from their works.

Academic Index. Excerpt from *Academic Index™*. Copyright © 1993 by Information Access Company. Reprinted by permission of Information Access Company.

The American Heritage Dictionary. Excerpt from *The American Heritage Dictionary of the English Language,* Third Edition. Copyright © 1992 by Houghton Mifflin Company. Reprinted by permission.

Maya Angelou. Excerpt from "Foreword" by Maya Angelou, in *African Canvas: The Art of West African Women* by Margaret Courtney-Clarke. Copyright © 1990 by Rizzoli International Publications. Reprinted by permission of Rizzoli International Publications.

Lucy Bunkley-Williams and Ernest H. Williams, Jr. Excerpt from "Global Assault on Coral Reefs" by Lucy Bunkley-Williams and Ernest H. Williams, Jr., in *Natural History,* April 1990. Copyright © 1990 by the American Museum of Natural History. Reprinted by permission of *Natural History*.

Joan Didion. Excerpt from "Insider Baseball" by Joan Didion. First published in *The New York Review of Books,* 1988.

Deborah Digges. "Milk" from *Vesper Sparrows* by Deborah Digges. Copyright © 1986 by Deborah Digges. Reprinted with permission of Atheneum Publishers, an imprint of Macmillan Publishing Company.

Robert Frost. Excerpt from "Stopping by Woods on a Snowy Evening" from *The Poetry of Robert Frost* by Robert Frost, edited by Edward Connery Lathem. Copyright © 1951 by Robert Frost. Copyright 1923, © 1969 by Henry Holt and Company, Inc. Reprinted by permission of Henry Holt and Company, Inc.

Langston Hughes. Excerpt from "Dream Variations" from *Selected Poems* by Langston Hughes. Copyright © 1926 by Alfred A. Knopf,

Index

This marginal index applies to the material in the annotations of this instructor's edition. Handbook topics are indexed in the student edition.

Information of Special Interest for ESL Writers

Problem areas that are among the most common for advanced ESL writers, according to research conducted for this book, are indicated with an asterisk (∗).

Contents

CLARITY

Well organized and easy to reference, *The HarperCollins Concise Handbook for Writers* is neither too elementary nor too advanced for today's students. The text presents writing issues in a clear and concise manner and supports them with numerous examples that help illustrate the concepts.

34c Commas with restrictive and nonrestrictive clauses, phrases, and appositives

Restrictive and Nonrestrictive Clauses

The following two sentences are both correct, but they describe different circumstances.

┌─── Restrictive ───┐
1. Carla's brother who lives in Alaska is getting married.

Carla must have two or more brothers; the clause *who lives in Alaska* serves to clarify which one of these brothers is getting married—the one who lives in Alaska (see 19k for a discussion of clauses).

┌─── Nonrestrictive ───┐
2. Jane's brother, who lives in Alaska, is getting married.

Jane has only one brother. The clause *who lives in Alaska* merely provides extra information about Jane's brother. It does not identify a particular brother because Jane has only one.

The clause in sentence 1 is called a restrictive clause because it restricts the word it is modifying—in this case *brother*—down from all of Carla's brothers to a particular one. In sentence 2, the same clause, *who lives in Alaska*, is *nonrestrictive* because it does not restrict the word *brother* to a particular one.

┌─── Restrictive ───┐
3. Americans who live in Alaska tend to be interested in nature.

In sentence 3, the clause *who live in Alaska* restricts the noun *Americans* from all Americans to only those who live in Alaska.

┌─────────── Nonrestrictive ───────────┐
4. Americans, who have one of the highest standards of living in
the world, do not eat the healthiest diet.

Here the clause *who have one of the highest standards of living in the world* does *not* restrict the noun *Americans* to a more limited subgroup. Sentence 4 does *not* say a subgroup of Americans—those with a high standard of living—do not eat the most healthful diet. It says that *all* Americans have one of the highest standards of living and

34c
^
,

The HarperCollins Concise Handbook for Writers

Peter Dow Adams
Essex Community College

with **Amy Tickle**, ESL specialist, Michigan State University

ISBN: 0-06-040168-0 hardbound (with exercises)
ISBN: 0-06-501994-6 paperbound

The HarperCollins Concise Handbook for Writers is the first text of its kind written specifically for the reality of today's classroom. It addresses the needs of a new student population that includes non-traditional students, non-native speakers, and students who need a basic introduction to college-level writing. Suitable for freshman composition, basic writing, and ESL sections of composition courses, this student-friendly handbook incorporates all the latest teaching techniques and theories as well as practical tips for composing on a computer.

Correction Symbols (Abbreviations)

abbr	Faulty abbreviation, 39
ad *or* adj/adv	Misuse of adjective or adverb, 28
agr	Agreement error, 21, 23
arg	Problem with your argument, 3c–3e
art	Article, 29
awk	Awkward
cap	Use capital letter, 38
case	Error in case, 24
coord	Coordination problem, 11a
cs	Comma splice, 32c
dm	Dangling modifier, 13c
-*ed*	Incorrect -*ed* ending, 25f
emph	Emphasis, 11b
exact	Inexact word, 18
frag	Sentence fragment, 32b
fs	Fused sentence (run-on sentence), 32c
gl/t	See the Glossary of Terms
gl/us	See the Glossary of Usage
gr	Grammar, 19, 20
hyph	Error in use of hyphen (-), 42
inc	Incomplete sentence, 15e
ital	Italics (underlining), 41
lc	Use lowercase letter, 38
logic	Logical fallacy, 3f
mixed	Mixed construction, 15a–d
mm	Misplaced modifier, 13a–e
ms	Problem with manuscript form, 43
num	Error in use of numbers, 40
p	Punctuation error, 31–37
. ? !	period, question mark, exclamation point, 31
⌃	comma, 33a, 33d, 34
no ⌃	no comma, 34k
;	semicolon, 33b, c
⌄	apostrophe, 35
" "	quotation marks, 36a–h, j
no " "	no quotation marks, 36i
:	colon, 37a
. . .	ellipses, 37b
( )	parentheses, 37c

[ ]	brackets, 37d
—	dash, 37e
/	slash, 37f
par, ¶	New paragraph, 7, 8, 10
¶ coh	Paragraph needs coherence, 8
¶ dev	Paragraph needs more development, 7d
¶ foc	Paragraph needs focus, 7a
¶ lgth	Paragraph is too long or short, 7c
¶ un	Paragraph needs unity, 7b
pass	Ineffective use of passive voice, 26g
prep	Incorrect preposition, 16b
ref	Error in pronoun reference, 22
rep	Unintended repetition, 16c
rev	Revise, 5
-*s*	Error in -*s* ending, 25e
shift	Paragraph or sentence includes a shift in tense, person, number, mood, or voice, 9
sp	Spelling error, 44
sub	Sentence has a subordination problem, 11b
t	Error in verb tense, 26a–f
trans	Transition is needed within or between paragraphs, 8a
und	Underline (italics), 41
usage	Mistake in usage, 16a
v	Voice, 26g
var	Sentences need more variety, 14
vb	Error in verb form, 25
verbal	Error in use of gerund, infinitive, or participle, 27
w	Wordy, 16d
wc	Awkward or inappropriate word choice, 16e
//	Faulty parallelism, 12
∧	Insert
⌣	Transpose
X	Obvious error
#	Add space
⌒	Close up space
⸜	Delete

Writing Menu

W9-AOE-071